Pearson Arab World Editions—Business & Economics

The Arab world's location between three continents ensures its place at the center of an increasingly integrated global economy, as distinctive as any business culture. We think learning should be as dynamic, relevant, and engaging as the business environment. Our new Arab World Editions for Business & Economics provide this uniquely Arab perspective for students in and of the Arab world.

Each Arab World Edition integrates cases, companies, research, people and discussions representing the diverse economic, political, and cultu situations across the nations that span the Arab world, whilst retainin the quality, research, and relevant global perspectives of the world's leading business thinkers.

We hope that you find this edition a valuable contribution to your teaching or business studies. We aim to set a new benchmark for contextualized learning with our adapted and new titles, and hope that they will prove a valuable contribution in the success of students and teachers along each step of their business program.

Supplementary support includes PowerPoint slides, instructor manuals, test bank generators and MyLab online tutorial and homework systems.

Titles span a range of subjects and disciplines, including:

- Management—Robbins & Coulter
- Principles of Marketing—Kotler & Armstrong
- Economics—Hubbard & O'Brien
- Statistics for Business—Benghezal
- Principles of Managerial Finance—Gitman
- Marketing Management—Kotler & Keller
- Organizational Behavior—Robbins, Judge & Hasham
- Human Resource Management—Dessler
- Strategic Management—David
- Introductory Mathematical Analysis for Business, Economics, and Life and Social Sciences—Haeussler
- Marketing Research—Malhotra
- Operations Management—Heizer
- Auditing and Assurance Services—Arens

To find out more, go to www.pearson.com/middleeast/awe

Organizational Behavior

Arab World Edition

STEPHEN P. ROBBINS
San Diego State University

TIMOTHY A. JUDGE
University of Florida

ELHAM S. HASHAM
Notre Dame University, Lebanon

Acquisitions Editor: Rasheed Roussan
Senior Development Editor: Sophie Bulbrook
Editor: Fay Gibbons
Copy-editor: Valerie Bingham
Proofreaders: Sylvia Worth, Peter Gill
Design Manager: Sarah Fach
Permissions Editor: Sarah Deakin
Picture Researchers: Alison Prior, Zo Naciri
Indexer: Indexing Specialists (UK) Ltd
Marketing Manager: Sue Mainey
Production Controller: Christopher Crow
Cover Designer: Sarah Fach
Typesetter: Graphicraft
Typeface: ITC New Baskerville Std 10.5pt/12pt
Printed in Malaysia (CTP-VVP)

Pearson Education Limited
Edinburgh Gate
Harlow
Essex CM20 2JE
England

and Associated Companies throughout the world

The rights of Stephen Robbins, Timothy Judge, and Elham Hasham to be identified as authors of this work have been asserted by them in accordance with the Copyright, Designs and Patents Act 1988.

Authorized adaptation from the United States edition, entitled Organizational Behavior, 13th Edition, ISBN: 0136007171 by Robbins, Stephen P.; Judge, Timothy A., published by Pearson Education, Inc, publishing as Prentice Hall, Copyright © 2009

Credits and acknowledgments for material borrowed from other sources and reproduced, with permission, in this textbook appear on the appropriate page within the text, in the endnotes, or on page 527.

20 19 18 17 16
IMP 10 9 8 7 6 5 4 3 2

ISBN: 978-1-4082-5965-8

To my mother, Juliet, my father, Said, and my brothers,
Francois and Anthony:
Thank you, and thank God.
—Elham S. Hasham

About the Authors

Stephen P. Robbins

Education

Ph.D. University of Arizona

Professional Experience

Academic Positions: Professor, San Diego State University, Southern Illinois University at Edwardsville, University of Baltimore, Concordia University in Montreal, and University of Nebraska at Omaha.

Research: Research interests have focused on conflict, power, and politics in organizations, behavioral decision making, and the development of effective interpersonal skills.

Books Published: World's best-selling author of textbooks in both management and organizational behavior. His books have sold more than six million copies, have been translated into 20 languages, and editions have been adapted for Canada, Australia, South Africa, and India. These include

- *Essentials of Organizational Behavior*, 10th ed. (Prentice Hall, 2010)
- *Management*, 11th ed., with Mary Coulter (Prentice Hall, 2011)
- *Human Resource Management*, 10th ed., with David DeCenzo (Wiley, 2010)
- *Prentice Hall's Self-Assessment Library 3.4* (Prentice Hall, 2010)
- *Fundamentals of Management*, 7th ed., with David DeCenzo and Mary Coulter (Prentice Hall, 2011)
- *Supervision Today!*, 6th ed., with David DeCenzo (Prentice Hall, 2010)
- *Training in Interpersonal Skills*, 6th ed., with Phillip Hunsaker (Prentice Hall, 2011)
- *Managing Today!*, 2nd ed. (Prentice Hall, 2000)
- *Organization Theory*, 3rd ed. (Prentice Hall, 1990)
- *The Truth About Managing People*, 2nd ed. (Financial Times/Prentice Hall, 2008)
- *Decide and Conquer: Make Winning Decisions and Take Control of Your Life* (Financial Times/Prentice Hall, 2004).

Other Interests

In his 'other life,' Dr. Robbins actively participates in masters' track competition. Since turning 50 in 1993, he has won 22 national championships and 14 world titles. He is the current world record holder at 100 meters (12.37 seconds) and 200 meters (25.20 seconds) for men 65 and over.

Timothy A. Judge

Education

Ph.D. University of Illinois at Urbana-Champaign

Professional Experience

Academic Positions: Matherly-McKethan Eminent Scholar in Management, Warrington College of Business Administration, University of Florida; Stanley M. Howe Professor in Leadership, Henry B. Tippie College of Business, University of Iowa; Associate Professor (with tenure), Department of Human Resource Studies, School of Industrial and Labor Relations, Cornell University; Lecturer, Charles University, Czech Republic, and Comenius University, Slovakia; Instructor, Industrial/Organizational Psychology, Department of Psychology, University of Illinois at Urbana-Champaign.

Research: Dr. Judge's primary research interests are in (1) personality, moods, and emotions, (2) job attitudes, (3) leadership and influence behaviors, and (4) careers (person-organization fit, career success). Dr. Judge has published more than 120 articles in these and other major topics in journals such as *Journal of Organizational Behavior, Personnel Psychology, Academy of Management Journal, Journal of Applied Psychology, European Journal of Personality, and European Journal of Work and Organizational Psychology.*

Fellowship: Dr. Judge is a fellow of the American Psychological Association, the Academy of Management, the Society for Industrial and Organizational Psychology, and the American Psychological Society.

Awards: In 1995, Dr. Judge received the Ernest J. McCormick Award for Distinguished Early Career Contributions from the Society for Industrial and Organizational Psychology, and in 2001, he received the Larry L. Cummings Award for mid-career contributions from the Organizational Behavior Division of the Academy of Management. In 2007, he received the Professional Practice Award from the Institute of Industrial and Labor Relations, University of Illinois.

Books Published: H. G. Heneman III, and T. A. Judge, *Staffing Organizations,* 6th ed. (Madison, WI: Mendota House/Irwin, 2009).

Other Interests

Although he cannot keep up (literally!) with Steve's accomplishments on the track, Dr. Judge enjoys golf, cooking and baking, literature (he's a particular fan of Thomas Hardy, and is a member of the Thomas Hardy Society), and keeping up with his three children, who range in age from 7 to 21.

Elham S. Hasham

Education

Ph.D. Educational Leadership, Management & Administration, University of Leicester, England

Professional Experience

Professional and Academic Positions: At Notre Dame University, Lebanon, Dr Hasham is currently an Associate Professor, Coordinator of undergraduate and graduate courses and Graduate Advisor. She previously held posts as Dean of Students (North Lebanon Campus), Director of Admissions and International Recruitment, and Acting Director of Tests and Measurements. Dr Elham is also CEO of Australian Consulting Engineers and Architects (ACEA), and Australian Lebanese Design Services (ALDS); and Coordinator of a Human Resource Management Program, Master of International Business, which is a joint venture between Notre Dame University, Lebanon and Bordeaux University, Paris.

Research: Dr. Hasham's research interests include Organizational Behavior, Business Ethics, Intercultural Communication and Management, Global Human Resource Management, Leadership and Quality Decision Making, Entrepreneurship, Strategic Management, Marketing and Business Policy Strategy. She has presented numerous papers at both regional and international conferences, resulting in publications in refereed journals and conference proceedings, and has written a variety of articles and case studies for a number of books published by Pearson Education.

Memberships: Dr. Hasham is a member of various prestigious associations and organizations such as the Lebanese League of Women in Business (LLWB); the Human Resource Association of Lebanon (HRAL); the Notre Dame University Education Society; the International Association of Universities (IAU); NAFSA: Association of International Educators; and the European Association of International Educators (EAIE).

Other Interests

Dr. Hasham is interested in all activities that can develop her intellectual, spiritual, physical, and social status. She is a people's person and has excellent interpersonal skills that have contributed to a worldwide network. She also enjoys reading, music, tennis, swimming, and nature in general.

Dr. Hasham is an advocate of participative management and believes that we need human capital, and must invest in people, to receive the performance and productivity that we seek as leaders.

Brief Contents

Contents

2   The Individual

2   *Foundations of Individual Behavior: Personality and Values* 37

3 *Attitudes and Job Satisfaction* 69

4 *Perception and Individual Decision Making* 89

5 *Motivation: Concepts and Applications* 113

6 *Emotions and Moods* 151

9 *Communication* 229

10 *Leadership* 257

11 *Power and Politics* 289

12 *Conflict and Negotiation* 315

4 The Organization System

14 *Organizational Culture* 365

5 Organization Dynamics

17   *Organizational Behavior in the Family Business* 447

6 Specifics in OB

18 Intercultural Management: The Significance to Organizational Behavior 471

19 *Female Entrepreneurs in the Arab World* 491

Appendix A Research in Organizational Behavior

Comprehensive Cases

Foreword

This book has been the world's No. 1 best-selling organizational behavior textbook for nearly three decades. It has sold in excess of three million copies, been translated into 10 different languages, and has adapted editions published for Europe, Canada, Australia, South Africa, and the Philippines. It is with great pride that we introduce this Arab World Edition.

I think you will find this book will provide the latest research in organizational behavior, written in an interesting and conversational style, with examples that make it relevant to Arab World students. Most importantly, this book will provide you with the relevant knowledge and skills needed for managing and working with people in diverse organizations.

Stephen P. Robbins, Ph.D. and Timothy A. Judge, Ph.D.

Preface

Welcome to the first Arab World Edition of *Organizational Behavior*! Pearson has pioneered this project with the aim of highlighting the practices of organizational behavior in organizations within the Arab world. This edition is addressed to both undergraduate and graduate students of the region, with the goal of making relevant research come alive for students. This textbook covers several themes and topics that are related to organizational behavior in general and in particular to organizational behavior in the Arab world. While maintaining many of the hallmark features, we have also introduced new features. These special features will enable you to understand certain issues much better, and also provide a smooth transition from one chapter to another. The writing style, level of English, and pedagogy have been carefully considered to meet the needs of students in the Arab world.

The most significant aspect of this edition is the introduction of many examples, cases, incidents, and illustrations talking about people, companies, and organizations that are well known in both the industry and services domain throughout the Arab world. Examples are taken from the Gulf Cooperation Council (GCC), the Levant, North Africa, Turkey, and Cyprus. This Arab World Edition reflects the attitudes and behavioral patterns of employers and employees in many of the prominent organizations across the Arab world, while examples from other countries provide a global context.

Organization

Part 1 introduces the concept of organizational behavior (OB). It looks at the skills that managers need to be successful and to get the job done. It also explains the various disciplines of OB as well as the challenges and opportunities it presents to both employers and employees.

Part 2 speaks about individuals and how they should behave within the organization by explaining the reasons why people behave in certain ways. This part looks at the personality, values, attitudes, emotions, and moods of individuals. Once we understand these, we can identify how to satisfy and motivate people for greater productivity.

Part 3 deals with group behavior by explaining the importance of working in teams. We must realize that leaders need excellent communication skills to interact with different types of people. The other organizational issues covered in this section are power, politics, conflict, and negotiation.

Part 4 covers the basics of organizational structure and corporate culture. In addition, it explains the HR policies and practices that are practiced in the Arab world.

Part 5 speaks about organizational dynamics by looking at the challenges of change and stress, and the nature of the family business which is common in the Arab world.

Finally, Part 6 looks at intercultural management and how it affects organizational behavior. It also addresses the role that women are starting to play in business and how they are contributing to organizational behavior.

Key Changes to the Arab World Edition

Arab World Cases and Trends

Each chapter has been carefully adapted to include regional case studies and examples, connecting the theory of organizational behaviour with real Arab companies and people that students will be able to relate to. These include:

Opening Vignettes
- The Strength of General Electric in the Arab World (Chapter 1)
- What Do Arabs Think About Arabs? (Chapter 4)
- Facebook Dominates in the Arab World (Chapter 9)
- Al-Wasta (Chapter 11)
- Aramex—Empowerment Through Organizational Structure (Chapter 13)
- The Culture at Arab World Companies (Chapter 14)
- Human Resource Policy at Azadea (Chapter 15)
- Family Business Success Stories from the Region: The Habtoor Empire (Chapter 17)
- A Sheikha and a Queen (Chapter 19)

Critical Analyses
- Equal opportunity at Crepaway (Chapter 1)
- Qatar: A Country with a Vision (Chapter 2)
- Job satisfaction in the UAE (Chapter 3)
- Team Effectiveness in Egypt (Chapter 8)
- Etisalat-Zain Deal Blocked (Chapter 12)
- Organizational Structure at Food & Co. (Chapter 13)
- So7i Wa Sari3 (Chapter 15)
- From London to Lebanon (Chapter 17)

Photo Cases
- Saudi Aramco (Chapter 1)
- Qatari Business Women's Forum (Chapter 2)
- Etihad Airways (Chapter 6)
- Mobinil (Chapter 9)
- SABIC (Chapter 9)
- Sheikh Zayad bin Sultan Al Nahayan (Chapter 10)
- Qatar International Islamic Bank (QIIB) (Chapter 12)
- Etisalat (Chapter 13)
- Ritz Carlton, Oman (Chapter 14)
- The Tharawat Family Business Forum (Chapter 17)

New Features
- Two new features—*What Do You Think?* and *Picture This*—allow students to get more involved in the process and interact in class.
- End-of-chapter features have been changed to *Discussion Exercise, Ethical Considerations, Critical Analysis* and *Research Exercise*. These hands-on, in-class exercises are included in each chapter, along with material in the Instructor's Manual that will make for unique and entertaining exercises to highlight a key chapter concept.
- *OB in the News, International OB* and *Point/CounterPoint* features have been adapted to include examples from the Arab region.
- The Arab World Edition benefits from the addition of an English–Arabic glossary for quick, easy reference, and to aid students' understanding of key terms throughout the book.

New Chapters

The Arab World Edition contains three brand new chapters on topics that are particularly relevant to this part of the world:

- Organizational Behavior in the Family Business (Chapter 17).
- Intercultural Management: The Significance to Organizational Behavior (Chapter 18).
- Female Entrepreneurs in the Arab World (Chapter 19).

MyManagementLab®

Teaching and Learning Support

Mymanagementlab (www.pearsonmiddleeastawe.com/robbinsjudge) is an easy-to-use online tool that personalizes course content and provides robust assessment and reporting to measure student and class performance. All the resources you need for course success are in one place—flexible and easily adapted for your course experience. Resources include a Pearson eText (an eBook version of all chapters), quizzes, personalized study plans, video clips, and PowerPoint presentations, all of which engage students while helping them to study independently.

In particular, mymanagementlab supports more active learning styles, involving students as they study management and prepare for tests and quizzes. Mymanagementlab also contains key video, testing, and other support resources that offer instructors many ways to enliven their classroom and save time—all in one convenient place.

Instructor's Resource Center

At www.pearsonmiddleeastawe.com/robbinsjudge, instructors can access a variety of print, digital, and presentation resources available with this text in downloadable format. Registration is simple and gives you immediate access to new titles and new editions. As a registered faculty member, you can download resource files and receive immediate access and instructions for installing course management content on your campus server.

If you need assistance, our dedicated technical support team is ready to help with the media supplements that accompany this text. Visit http://247pearsoned.custhelp.com for answers to frequently asked questions, and toll-free user support phone numbers, and live chat support.

The following fully adapted supplements are available to adopting instructors:

- **Instructor's Manual**—Provides ideas and resources in the classroom
- **Test Item File**—Revised and updated from previous editions to include Arab examples, the test item file contains over 2,500 questions that require students to apply what they have read in the text. Questions are also tagged to reflect the AACSB Learning Standards.
- **TestGen Test Generating Software**—Test management software containing all the material from the Test Item File. This software is completely user friendly and allows instructors to view, edit, and add test questions with just a few mouse clicks.
- **PowerPoint Slides**—Ready-to-use PowerPoint presentations designed for classroom presentation. Use them as they are, or edit content to fit your individual classroom needs.

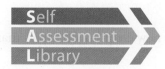

Self-Assessment Library (S.A.L.)

A hallmark of the Robbins series, S.A.L. is a unique learning tool that allows you to assess your knowledge, beliefs, feelings, and actions in regard to a wide range of personal skills, abilities, and interests. Self-assessments have been integrated into each chapter, including a self-assessment at the beginning of each chapter. S.A.L. helps students better understand their interpersonal and behavioral skills as they relate to the theoretical concepts presented in each chapter.

Highlights

- **67 research-based self-assessments**—Our entire collection of 67 instruments are from sources such as *Journal of Social Behavior and Personality, Harvard Business Review, Organizational Behavior: Experiences and Cases, Journal of Experimental Education, Journal of Applied Measurement,* and others.
- **Work–life and career focused**—All self-assessments are focused to help individuals better manage their work lives or careers. Organized in four parts, these instruments offer you one source from which to learn more about yourself.
- **Online**—The Self-Assessment Library is available online via MyManagementLab.
- **Save feature**—Students can take the self-assessments an unlimited number of times, and save and print their scores for class discussion.
- **Scoring key**—The key to the self-assessments has been edited by Steve Robbins to allow students to quickly make sense of the results of their score.
- **Instructor's manual**—An *Instructor's Manual* guides instructors in interpreting self-assessments and helps facilitate better classroom discussion.

Acknowledgments

Getting this book into your hands was a team effort. It took faculty reviewers and a talented group of designers and production specialists, editorial personnel, and marketing and sales staff.

Foremost, I want to thank Stephen P. Robbins and Timothy A. Judge for giving the framework of this pioneer project. I want to salute the genuine contributions, support and cooperation received from the Pearson team: Sophie Bulbrook, Senior Development Editor, and Rasheed Roussan, Acquisitions Editor. Sincere gratitude goes to Fay Gibbons, Editor, for her patience. I would also like to thank Francois S. Hasham and Nafez H. Shahin, for their continuous moral support.

Instructors from the Arab world reviewed all chapters in this edition and their comments, compliments, and suggestions have significantly improved the final product. I'd like to extend my sincerest thanks to the following:

Mohammed A. Al-Waqfi, United Arab Emirates University

Dr. Tamer A. Awad, University College of Bahrain

Eman Azmi, King Saud University

Dr. Shaju George, Royal University for Women, Bahrain

Dr. Adnan Iqbal, Prince Sultan University

James T. Kunnanatt, United Arab Emirates University

Dr. Penny MacDonald, American University of Kuwait

Muhammad A. Malallah, University of Jordan

Samer Nakhle, University of Fribourg

Adel Rayan, Assiut University, Egypt

Nihad Shaker Sakallah, Prince Mohammad Bin Fahd University

Additional appreciation goes to all those who contributed material and allowed me to feature cases about them or their companies in this book:

Rev. Father Ziad Antoun, Notre Dame University, Lebanon

Charbel Aoun, Attorney

Nadine Fayad Comair, FOCUS Magazine

Kamal Comair, INDEVCO

Eric Davoine, University of Fribourg

Musa Freiji, Tanmia

Bchara Ghawi, So7i Wa Sari3

Amal Harb, Rotana

Walid Harb, Tannourine Hospital

Anthony S. Hasham, Australian Lebanese Design Services

Reine Jabre, So7i Wa Sari3

Olga Kampaxi, Rotana

Marwan Kanaan, Zaatar w Zeit

Carol-Ann Goff Kfouri, Notre Dame University

Claire Kfouri, Engineer

The Menhem Family, Damco

Joseph Mghames, Azadea

Farid Muna, MEIRC

Gisele Nacouzi, INDEVCO

Samer Nahkle, University of Fribourg

Maroun Nassar, Rotana

Fay Niewiadomski, ICTN

Bassem Sleiman, London Taxi

Nelly Sleiman, London Taxi

Khaled Tayyara, Zaatar w Zeit

Hani Tuffaha, Aramex

Monique Bassila Zaarour, So7i Wa Sari3

Finally, this text would not have been possible without the many contributions of reviewers, consultant board members, and accuracy checkers in previous editions. I'd like to thank them all for their valuable insight and suggestions.

Elham Hasham

Part 1 Introduction

LEARNING OBJECTIVES

This chapter will enable you to:

1 Understand the importance of interpersonal skills in the workplace.

2 Realize the significance of a manager's functions, roles, and skills.

3 Define *organizational behavior (OB)*.

4 Show the value to OB of systematic study.

5 Identify the major behavioral science disciplines that contribute to OB.

6 Demonstrate why there are few absolutes in OB.

7 Identify the challenges and opportunities managers have in applying OB concepts.

8 Consider the three levels of analysis and characteristics of the OB model in general.

What Is Organizational Behavior?

It is far more productive to study human behavior—why people do the things they do—and to seek benefit from the learning, than it is to try to fight it. —Jim Murray

The Strength of General Electric in the Arab World

With over 1,700 employees, General Electric (GE) has a strong presence in Bahrain, Jordan, Kuwait, Lebanon, Oman, Qatar, the Kingdom of Saudi Arabia (KSA), the United Arab Emirates (UAE), Egypt and Algeria. The executive officer in the region is Nabil Habayeb, President and Chief Executive of GE Middle East and Africa. With regional activity since the 1930s, GE has built up a productive distribution across the region via strategic partnerships and investments.

In the Middle East, GE's employees organize and participate in volunteer activities and charitable initiatives, through GE Volunteers, to involve the local community. The major objective is to create a positive atmosphere to enhance productivity and quality. In addition, the Women's Network has been successful in encouraging gender diversity within GE's leadership team, and incorporating an increasing number of women into senior management positions in GE's organization worldwide.

GE now plans to strengthen its commitment to the Saudi Arabian economy with an investment that will support Saudi Arabia's "Vision 2020" national development plan. Having opened the GE Energy Manufacturing Technology Center in Dammam in June 2011, GE intends to focus on advancing the three goals of the Vision 2020 plan, which are (1) to create new jobs for Saudi nationals; (2) to strengthen the manufacturing and export sectors; and (3) to encourage the private sector to contribute to Saudi Arabia's socio-economic prosperity.

The GE Manufacturing Technology Center will provide more than 2,000 jobs at GE, which will support many Saudi families. GE also signed a memorandum of understanding with Saudi Arabia's Technical and Vocational Training Corporation (TVTC) to enhance the GE joint technical program (GE JTP). This program has allowed the company the opportunity to increase training, and place employees according to their areas of expertise. As a result, organizational performance will be more effective.

The launching of the Center was a major event that attracted over 400 people representing local communities, government and GE's key customers. Among the major customers represented were the Saudi Basic Industries Corporation (SABIC), the Saudi Electricity Company (SEC), and oil company Saudi Aramco. The presence of such a center in the region is significant as it encourages the affiliations of nations and people, with the intention of improving working conditions and facilities that will secure higher productivity.

Source: Based on "GE Energy Manufacturing Technology Center: Another Milestone in an 80 Year Relationship", June 2011, http://middleeast.geblogs.com/en/ge-energy-manufacturing-technology-center-another-milestone-in-an-80-year-relationship/.

The opening case about General Electric and its presence in the Arab world clearly demonstrates how GE has encouraged both individuals and organizations to interact in ways that create positive benefits for all concerned. As we see, managing people is all about respect and understanding. Without a doubt, GE highlights diversity, innovation, and the community as a means of improving the behavior of people from the various Arab countries as they collaborate with GE. GE appreciates people and respects their cultural differences: as a result, it has been successful in the Arab world. The case illustrates why organizational behavior is so important and why managers at all levels must understand the wide range of issues that affect the behavior of people.

To see how much you know about organizational behavior, try the following from the Self-Assessment Library before we continue.

Self Assessment Library

HOW MUCH DO I KNOW ABOUT ORGANIZATIONAL BEHAVIOR?

In the Self-Assessment Library (available online), take assessment IV.G.1 (How Much Do I Know About Organizational Behavior?) and answer the following questions:

1. *How did you score? Are you surprised by your score?*
2. *How much of effective management do you think is common sense? Did your score on the test change your answer to this question?*

In this chapter will discuss all the concepts that managers need to know to treat employees well so as to encourage them to be more productive and to show loyalty to the organization. We will also see the skills that both employers and employees must possess to create a healthy work environment. In addition, we will learn exactly what every chapter in this book will include.

The Importance of Interpersonal Skills

1 Understand the importance of interpersonal skills in the workplace.

Managers must understand the importance of interpersonal skills for managerial effectiveness. Business schools realize the importance that an understanding of human behavior plays in determining a manager's effectiveness, and courses on people skills are a requirement of many curricula. As the director of leadership at Massachusetts Institute of Technology (MIT) Sloan School of Management explains, "MBA students may get by on their technical and quantitative skills the first couple of years out of school. But soon, leadership and communication skills come to the front in distinguishing the managers whose careers really take off."[1] In other words, if we were to ask any director, chairperson or dean of a business faculty for feedback, we would definitely receive a similar response to that mentioned above.

The importance of developing managers' interpersonal skills is related to the need for organizations to get and keep high-performing employees. Regardless of labor market conditions, outstanding employees are always in short supply.[2] Companies with reputations as good places to work—such as Aramex, Etisalat, Picasso Billboards, American Express, Aramco, HSBC, Microsoft, and Marriott— have great advantage. Far more important is the quality of the employee's job and the supportiveness of the work environment.[3] So having managers with good interpersonal skills is likely to make the workplace more pleasant, which, in turn, makes it easier to hire and keep qualified people.

In addition, creating a pleasant workplace appears to make good economic sense. For instance, companies with reputations as good places to work definitely attract individuals. Such companies are those included among the *100 Best Companies to Work for in America* and the *Forbes 40 Middle East Companies*, and these have been found to generate superior financial performance.[4]

Technical skills are necessary but they are not enough to succeed in management. In today's competitive and demanding workplace, managers can't succeed on their technical skills alone. They must also have good people skills. The basis of this book is to help both managers and potential managers develop those people skills and realize how important they are to their success.

What Managers Do

2 Realize the significance of a manager's functions, roles, and skills.

Let's begin by briefly defining the terms **manager** and **organization**—the place where managers work. Then let's look at the manager's job; specifically, what do managers do?

Managers make sure that everyday activities are done by supervising other people. They make decisions, allocate resources, and direct others to attain goals. Managers work in an organization, which is a social unit composed of two or more people, that should coordinate functions on a continuous basis to achieve a common goal or set of goals. On the basis of this definition, manufacturing and service firms are organizations, and so are schools, hospitals, churches, military units, retail stores, police departments, factories, universities, and government agencies. Thus, the people who oversee the activities of others and who are responsible for attaining goals in these organizations are managers; however, they may sometimes be called *administrators*, especially in not-for-profit organizations such as hospitals and charity associations that are humanitarian-oriented.

Manager

An individual who achieves goals through other people.

Organization

A consciously coordinated social unit, composed of two or more people, that functions on a relatively continuous basis to achieve a common goal or set of goals.

Management Functions

In the early part of the twentieth century, Henri Fayol, a French industrialist, found that all managers perform five management functions: planning, organizing, commanding, coordinating, and controlling.[5] Today, these have been reduced to four: planning, organizing, leading, and controlling.

As you saw earlier, organizations exist to achieve goals, but within an organization someone is needed to define these goals and the means for achieving them. Who is the person who performs that role? It is, of course, the manager, who we described above. Managers have different levels, however—lower, mid, upper—(this will be elaborated in Chapter 13 when we talk about organizational structure and channels of communication)—but, collectively, they are known as management. Management has the job of dealing with each of the four management functions. Let's have a closer look at each of these functions.

The **planning** function includes defining an organization's goals, establishing an overall strategy for achieving those goals, and developing a comprehensive set of plans to integrate and coordinate activities.

Managers are also responsible for designing an organization's structure. We call this function **organizing**. It includes determining what tasks are to be done, who is to do them, how the tasks are to be grouped, who reports to whom, and where decisions are to be made.

Next, every organization contains people, and it is management's job to direct and coordinate those people. This is called **leading**. When managers motivate employees, direct the activities of others, select the most effective communication

Planning

A process that includes defining goals, establishing strategy, and developing plans to coordinate activities.

Organizing

Determining what tasks are to be done, who is to do them, how the tasks are to be grouped, who reports to whom, and where decisions are to be made.

Leading

A function that includes motivating employees, directing others, selecting the most effective communication channels, and resolving conflicts.

Controlling

Monitoring activities to ensure that they are being accomplished as planned and correcting any significant deviations.

channels, make correct decisions or resolve conflicts among members, they are engaging in leading and accordingly practicing leadership.

The final of the four functions managers perform is **controlling**. To ensure that things are going as they should, management must monitor the organization's performance. Actual performance is then compared with previous goals. If there are any significant differences, it is management's job to get the organization back on track. This monitoring, comparing, and potential correcting is what is meant by the controlling function.

To conclude, the functional approach answers the question 'What do managers do?' The answer is that they plan, organize, lead, and control. These functions will be explained in more detail in coming chapters.

Management Roles

In the late 1960s, Henry Mintzberg, a graduate student at Massachusetts Institute of Technology (MIT)—a well-known university in the US—undertook a careful study of five executives to determine what those managers did in their jobs. After long observations, Mintzberg concluded that managers perform ten different, highly interrelated roles—or sets of behaviors—relevant to their jobs.[6] Table 1-1 shows these ten roles divided into three groups: (1) interpersonal, (2) informational, and (3) decisional, and we shall learn more about them in the next sections.

TABLE 1-1   Mintzberg's Managerial Roles

Role	Description
Interpersonal	
Figurehead	Symbolic head; required to perform a number of routine duties of a legal or social nature
Leader	Responsible for the motivation and direction of employees
Liaison	Maintains a network of outside contacts who provide favors and information
Informational	
Monitor	Receives a wide variety of information; serves as nerve center of internal and external information of the organization
Disseminator	Transmits information received from outsiders or from other employees to members of the organization
Spokesperson	Transmits information to outsiders on organization's plans, policies, actions, and results; serves as expert on organization's industry
Decisional	
Entrepreneur	Searches organization and its environment for opportunities and initiates projects to bring about change
Disturbance handler	Responsible for corrective action when organization faces important, unexpected disturbances
Resource allocator	Makes or approves significant organizational decisions
Negotiator	Responsible for representing the organization at major negotiations

Source: Adapted from H. Mintzberg, The Nature of Managerial Work, 1st edn. (New Jersey: Prentice Hall, 1997), © 1973. Reprinted and electronically reproduced by permission of Pearson Education, Inc., Upper Saddle River, New Jersey.

Interpersonal Roles   All managers are required to perform duties that are required of them as part of their duties and responsibilities. For instance, when the president of a college hands out diplomas at commencement or a factory supervisor gives a group of high school students a tour of the plant, this is known as the *figurehead* role. All managers also have a *leadership* role that includes hiring, training, motivating, and disciplining employees. The third role within the interpersonal grouping is the *liaison* role. Mintzberg described this activity as contacting outsiders who provide the manager with information. These may be individuals or groups inside or outside the organization. For instance, Jeffery Immelt, CEO of General Electric, has established effective contacts with prominent Arab business leaders. Accordingly, he has built networks and signed agreements. One such partnership is with Mubadala Development Company, represented by its CEO and Managing Director (MD), Khaldoon Al Mubarak.

On July 22, 2008, Immelt, of General Electric, and Al Mubarak, of Mubadala Development Company, announced an agreement on a global partnership.[7] They intended to build on their existing strong relationship and shared views about opportunities for growth in the Arab and global markets. The agreement committed both organizations to developing new joint ventures and investments. In May 2009, the executives of the two companies made significant progress in both areas: signing a commercial finance joint-venture agreement and establishing a regional training center for next-generation business leaders. These developments would have been unlikely to succeed if the two CEOs had not been able to fill the roles of figurehead, leadership and liaison at relevant times within their own companies.

Informational Roles   Mintzberg also identified the *monitor* role which allows managers to collect information from outside the organization and institution. This information can be obtained by reading magazines and talking with other people to learn of changes in the public's tastes and what competitors may be planning. Managers also act as a channel to transmit the information they receive from outside sources to organizational members and this is the *disseminator* role. That is, they gather information from outside sources and share it with people inside the organization. In addition, managers perform a *spokesperson* role when they represent the organization and present information to people outside the organization.

Decisional Roles   Mintzberg identified four roles that are related to making choices. In the *entrepreneur* role, managers initiate and oversee new projects that will improve their organization's performance. As *disturbance handlers*, managers take corrective action in response to unforeseen problems. As *resource allocators*, managers are responsible for allocating human, physical, and monetary resources. Finally, managers perform a *negotiator* role, in which they discuss issues and bargain with other units to gain advantages for their own unit.

What Do You Think?

Is there any particular management role that you feel describes your competencies?

Management Skills

Think about your abilities as a student. That is, what do you consider to be things that you can do very well? We can also call these abilities skills or competencies, but whatever the name, they are used to help us reach our goals at any level, either personal or professional.

At a professional level, Robert Katz has identified three essential management skills: (1) technical, (2) human, and (3) conceptual.[8]

Technical Skills   These include the ability to apply specialized knowledge or expertise. When you think of the skills of professionals such as civil engineers or dentists, you typically focus on their **technical skills**. Through extensive formal education, they have learned the special knowledge and practices of their field. All jobs require some specialized expertise, and these technical skills are usually developed on the job.

Human Skills   **Human skills** include the ability to work with, understand, and motivate other people, both individually and in groups. They are the interpersonal skills we discussed at the beginning of this chapter. Many people may have the technical skills but not the interpersonal skills because they might be poor listeners, unable to understand the needs of others, or have difficulty managing conflicts. Since managers get things done through other people, as we discussed earlier, they must have good human skills to communicate, motivate, and delegate.

Conceptual Skills   **Conceptual skills** include the mental ability to analyze and understand difficult situations. Decision making, for instance, requires managers to identify problems, develop alternative solutions to correct those problems, evaluate those alternative solutions, and select the best one. Thus, managers may have the technical and interpersonal competencies yet still fail because of an inability to process and interpret information and that makes all the difference.

Effective Versus Successful Managerial Activities

Fred Luthans and his associates looked at the issue of what managers do from a somewhat different perspective.[9] They asked the question "Do managers who move up the ladder quickly in an organization do the same activities and with the same emphasis as managers who do the best job?" Logically, you would think that managers who are the most effective in their jobs would also be the ones who are promoted the fastest. But that's not always the case.

Luthans and his partners studied more than 450 managers. What they found was that these managers all engaged in four managerial activities:

1. **Traditional management.** Decision making, planning, and controlling
2. **Communication.** Exchanging routine information and processing paperwork
3. **Human resource management.** Motivating, disciplining, managing conflict, staffing, and training
4. **Networking.** Socializing and interacting with outsiders.

According to the above-mentioned study, the 'average' manager in the study spent 32 percent of his or her time in traditional management activities, 29 percent communicating, 20 percent in human resource management activities, and 19 percent networking. However, the amount of time and effort that different managers spent on those four activities varied a great deal. Specifically, as shown in Figure 1-1, managers who were *successful* (defined

Technical skills

The ability to apply specialized knowledge or expertise.

Human skills

The ability to work with, understand, and motivate other people, both individually and in groups.

Conceptual skills

The mental ability to analyze and diagnose complex situations.

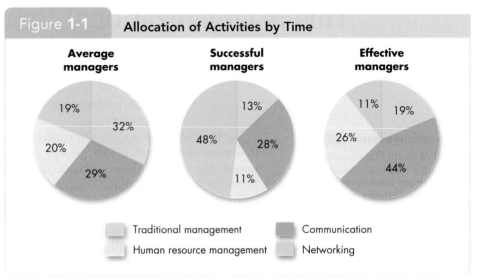

Figure **1-1**   **Allocation of Activities by Time**

Source: Based on F. Luthans, R. M. Hodgetts, and S. A. Rosenkrantz, *Real Managers* (Cambridge, MA: Ballinger, 1988).

in terms of the speed of promotion within their organization) had a very different emphasis than managers who were *effective* (defined in terms of the quantity and quality of their performance and the satisfaction and commitment of their employees).

Among successful managers, networking made the largest relative contribution to success, and human resource management activities made the least contribution. Among effective managers, communication made the largest relative contribution and networking the least. More recent studies, conducted in a variety of countries (Australia, Italy, Japan, and the United States), further confirm the link between networking and success within an organization.[10] For example, one study found that Australian managers who actively networked received more promotions and enjoyed other rewards associated with career success. A study on employee motivation conducted by Bayt.com (2009) on the countries of the Gulf Cooperation Council (GCC), Levant, and North Africa found that 58 percent of the respondents (population 13,376) agreed that managers "communicated what was going on in the organization," and this led to more effective relations.[11]

What Do You Think?

Let's stop here and consider the definitions of 'success' and 'effective,' and whether they are culturally oriented. Do you think these mean different things in different cultures?

A Review of the Manager's Job

The functions, roles, skills, activities, and approaches to management all have a common thread. Each recognizes the great importance of managing people. Regardless of whether it is called 'the leading function,' 'interpersonal roles,' 'human skills,' or 'human resource management, communication, and networking activities,' it is clear that managers need to develop their people skills if they are going to be effective and successful; that is, they must be a 'people person.'

This Is Organizational Behavior

 Define organizational behavior (OB).

Organizational behavior (OB)

A field of study that investigates the impact that individuals, groups, and structure have on behavior within organizations, for the purpose of applying such knowledge toward improving an organization's effectiveness.

Organizational behavior (OB) is a field of study that investigates how individuals and groups behave within organizations, and the importance of organizational structure. Applying this information should lead to improving an organization's effectiveness.

So in general what does OB study? It studies three determinants of behavior in organizations: individuals, groups, and structure. In addition, OB applies the knowledge gained about individuals, groups, and the effect of structure on behavior in order to make organizations work more effectively. In sum, OB is concerned with the study of what people do in an organization and how their behavior—work, absenteeism, employment turnover, productivity, human performance, and management—affects the organization's overall performance; this is something that Microsoft—a prominent name in the Arab world—is very much aware of.

Consequently, OB includes the basic topics of motivation, leader behavior and power, interpersonal communication, group structure and processes, learning, attitude development and perception, change processes, conflict, work design, and work stress.[12]

Complementing Intuition with Systematic Study

4 *Show* the value to OB of systematic study.

We are creatures of habit. As young children, we watched the actions and behaviors of others and we tried to understand and then copy what we saw. It is part of human nature to watch people and attempt to 'read' their actions. That is, we

Microsoft understands how organizational behavior affects organizational performance. The company encourages good employee relations by providing a great work environment, generous benefits, and challenging jobs. The wall-painting you see in the picture (displayed for the employees' enjoyment) is only one of many benefits that employees can enjoy. In addition, the company offers employees dry-cleaning and laundry service, valet parking, and take-home meals, and this allows them to focus fully on their work. As a result, employee loyalty and productivity are high at Microsoft.

observe what others do and try to explain to ourselves why they have behaved in a certain way. In addition, we ask ourselves how we might have responded to the same situation, or what they might have done, under different conditions. With all these considerations in mind, it is common to make wrong judgments. So we then start asking for methods of improving predictions; do we use a systematic approach or will intuition do the job?

The systematic approach proposes that behavior does not happen by chance. There are basic consistencies underlying the behavior of all individuals that can be identified and then modified to reflect individual differences. Thus, **systematic study** means looking at relationships, attempting to attribute causes and effects, and basing our conclusions on scientific evidence.

An approach that complements systematic study is evidence-based management. **Evidence-based management (EBM)** involves basing managerial decisions on the best available scientific evidence. We'd want doctors to make decisions about patient care based on the latest available evidence, and EBM argues that we want managers to do the same. That means managers must become more scientific in how they think about management problems. For example, a manager might pose a managerial question, search for the best available evidence, and apply the relevant information to the question or case at hand. (See Appendix A for a basic review of research methods used in studies of organizational behavior.)

People usually create preconceived ideas because they don't have enough information. Very often, this can be harmful. We will talk about this issue in several of the coming chapters, and in particular in Chapter 4 when we speak about perceptions and their effects.

For example, you are on an introductory course in organizational behavior. On the first day of class, your instructor asks you to answer the following question: 'What's the most effective way to motivate employees at work?' You might feel you need some time to think, but you probably won't have any problem coming up with suggestions on motivation.

That's one of the main challenges of teaching, or taking, a course in OB. You enter an OB course with a lot of *preconceived notions* or ideas that you accept as *facts*. You think you already know a lot about human behavior.[13] That's not true in finance, accounting, or even marketing. So, in contrast to many other disciplines, OB not only introduces you to a comprehensive set of concepts and theories; but it also has to deal with a lot of commonly accepted 'facts' about human behavior and organizations that you've learned over the years. Some examples might include: 'You can't teach an old dog new tricks,' 'Leaders are born, not made,' and 'Two heads are better than one.' But these 'facts' aren't always true. Thus, one of the objectives of organizational behavior is to *replace* certain ideas that we accept without question, with science-based conclusions.

How do you want your doctor to make a decision about a medical problem you have? Based on the latest relevant research and evidence? Definitely. This is what EBM is all about and it stresses that professionals and managers, no matter what country they work in, should do the same.

Systematic study

Looking at relationships, attempting to attribute causes and effects, and drawing conclusions based on scientific evidence.

Evidence-based management (EBM)

Basing managerial decisions on the best available scientific evidence.

What Do You Think?

Do people rely on facts or intuition based on their culture and beliefs? Do you believe culture influences the way people think and make decisions?

Intuition

A gut feeling not necessarily supported by research.

Systematic study and EBM add to **intuition**, or that 'gut feeling,' because it comes from inside the person. Many times it works and we find that the best decision has been made, but if we make all decisions with intuition or gut instinct, we're likely to be making decisions with incomplete information.

Our objective is to encourage you to enhance your intuitive views of behavior with a systematic analysis, in the belief that such analysis will improve your accuracy in explaining and predicting behavior. That does not mean that you should stop depending on your intuition, nor are we arguing that research is always right. However, we are advising you to use as much evidence as possible to guide your intuition and experience.

Disciplines That Contribute to OB

5 *Identify the major behavioral science disciplines that contribute to OB.*

Organizational behavior is an applied behavioral science that depends on the contributions of other behavioral disciplines, such as psychology, social psychology, sociology, and anthropology. Figure 1-2 shows that psychology explains contributions at the individual or micro-level of analysis, while the other disciplines have contributed to our understanding of macro-concepts, such as group processes and organization.

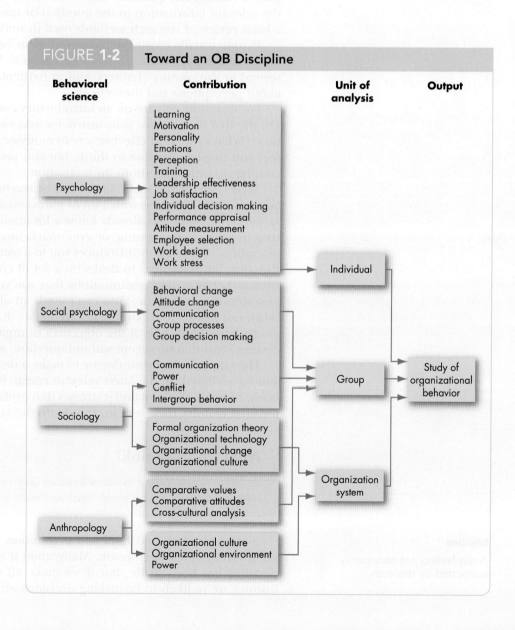

FIGURE **1-2**   **Toward an OB Discipline**

Behavioral science	Contribution	Unit of analysis	Output
Psychology	Learning Motivation Personality Emotions Perception Training Leadership effectiveness Job satisfaction Individual decision making Performance appraisal Attitude measurement Employee selection Work design Work stress	Individual	
Social psychology	Behavioral change Attitude change Communication Group processes Group decision making		
Sociology	Communication Power Conflict Intergroup behavior	Group	Study of organizational behavior
	Formal organization theory Organizational technology Organizational change Organizational culture		
Anthropology	Comparative values Comparative attitudes Cross-cultural analysis	Organization system	
	Organizational culture Organizational environment Power		

Psychology

Psychology

The science that seeks to measure, explain, and sometimes change the behavior of humans and other animals.

Psychology is the science that seeks to measure, explain, and sometimes change the behavior of humans and other animals. Psychologists concern themselves with studying and attempting to understand individual behavior. Industrial and organizational psychologists concern themselves with the problems of fatigue, boredom, and other factors relevant to working conditions that could negatively affect efficient work performance. Other factors that have been investigated are learning, perception, personality, emotions, training, leadership effectiveness, needs and motivational forces, job satisfaction, decision-making processes, performance appraisal, attitude measurement, employee-selection techniques, work design, and job stress.

Social Psychology

Social psychology

An area of psychology that blends concepts from psychology and sociology and that focuses on the influence of people on one another.

Social psychology focuses on peoples' influence on one another, and has made important contributions to the study of group behavior, power, and conflict. One major area of concern to social psychologists has been *change*—how to implement it and how to reduce resistance. In addition, social psychologists have made significant contributions in the areas of measuring, understanding, and changing attitudes; communication patterns; and building trust.

OB in the News

Other Disciplines Make Use of OB Concepts

It may surprise you to learn that, increasingly, other business disciplines are employing OB concepts.

Of the business disciplines, marketing has the closest overlap with OB. One of the primary areas of marketing is consumer research, and trying to predict consumer behavior is not that different from trying to predict employee behavior. Both require an understanding of the dynamics and underlying causes of human behavior, and there's a lot of correspondence between the disciplines.

What's perhaps more surprising is the degree to which the so-called hard disciplines are making use of soft OB concepts. Behavioral finance, behavioral accounting, and behavioral economics (also called *economic psychology*) all have grown in importance and interest in the past several years.

On reflection, this shouldn't be so surprising. Your common sense will tell you that humans are not perfectly rational creatures, and in many cases our actions don't conform to a rational model of behavior. Although some elements of irrationality are incorporated into economic thought, increasingly finance, accounting, and economics researchers find it useful to draw from OB concepts.

For example, investors have a tendency to place more weight on private information (information that only they, or a limited group of people, know) than on public information, even when there is reason to believe that the public information is more accurate. To understand this phenomenon, finance researchers use OB concepts. In addition, behavioral accounting research might study

how feedback influences auditors' behavior, or the functional and dysfunctional implications of earnings warnings on investor behavior.

The point is that while you take separate courses in various business disciplines, the lines between them are increasingly being blurred as researchers draw from common disciplines to explain behavior. We think that's a good thing because it more accurately matches the way managers actually work, think, and behave.

Sources: Based on W. Chuang and B. Lee, "An Empirical Evaluation of the Overconfidence Hypothesis," *Journal of Banking and Finance*, September 2006, pp. 2489–2515; and A. R. Drake, J. Wong, and S. B. Salter, "Empowerment, Motivation, and Performance: Examining the Impact of Feedback and Incentives on Nonmanagement Employees," *Behavioral Research in Accounting* 19, 2007, pp. 71–89.

Sociology

The study of people in relation to their social environment or culture.

Sociology

While psychology focuses on the individual, **sociology** studies people in relation to their social environment or culture. Sociologists have contributed to OB through their study of group behavior in organizations through research on organizational culture, formal organization theory and structure, organizational technology, communications, power, and conflict.

Anthropology

Anthropology

The study of societies to learn about human beings and their activities.

Anthropology is the study of societies to learn about human beings and their activities. Such research has helped us to understand the differences in values, attitudes, and behavior between people in different countries and within different organizations. Much of our current understanding of organizational culture, organizational environments, and differences between national cultures, is a result of the work of anthropologists or those using their methods.

There Are Few Absolutes in OB

6 *Demonstrate why there are few absolutes in OB.*

We are not saying that organizational behavior is simple. You may remember that earlier we discussed human behavior and how people understand things in different ways. Well, that is because human beings are complex. Because we are not alike, our ability to make simple and accurate observations is limited. Two people often act very differently in the same situation, and the same person's behavior changes in different situations. For instance, not everyone is motivated by money, no matter how strange that may seem to certain people.

That doesn't mean, of course, that we can't offer reasonably accurate explanations of human behavior or make valid predictions. However, it does mean that OB concepts must reflect situational, or contingency, conditions. We can say that x leads to y, but only under conditions specified in z—the **contingency variables**. The science of OB was developed by applying general concepts to a particular situation, person, or group. For example, OB scholars would avoid stating that everyone likes complex and challenging work (the general concept). Why? Because not everyone wants a challenging job. Some people prefer routine over the varied, or the simple over the complex. In other words, a job that is appealing to one person may not be to another, so the appeal of the job is contingent or dependent on the person who holds it.

Contingency variables

Situational factors: variables that moderate the relationship between two or more other variables.

The rest of this book will outline many research-based theories about how people behave in organizations. However, don't expect to find a lot of straightforward cause-and-effect relationships. There aren't many! Organizational behavior reflects the subjects it deals with. People are complex and complicated and so are the theories developed to explain their actions. Let's now have a closer look at the challenges and opportunities that organizational behavior offers.

Challenges and Opportunities for OB

7 *Identify the challenges and opportunities managers have in applying OB concepts.*

It is so important for managers to understand the behavior patterns of individuals in organizations because it is this understanding that will enable managers to deal with sudden changes in the behavior of employees. Shifts in behavior are due to so many reasons; but, whatever the reason, an effective manager is one who is able to address the issue and find a solution. Employees are aging; more and more women are in the workplace; corporate downsizing and temporary workers are affecting the bonds of loyalty that historically tied many employees to their employers; and global competition is requiring employees to become more flexible and to learn to cope with rapid change. In short, there are a lot of challenges and opportunities today for managers to use OB concepts. In this section, we will review some of the most critical issues confronting managers.

One of the challenges mentioned above is the aging workforce. For instance, the average age of Bahrain's workforce is currently 29.4 years. A report by UK-based think tank Global Futures and Foresight, entitled "The Future of Travel and Tourism in the Middle East—A Vision to 2020,"[14] predicts this to increase by about a third in the next 40 years: 33.6 by 2020, and 40.9 in 2050. The report also predicts that this trend is likely to occur across the whole Arab world. For example, it is predicted that the average age of workers in Oman will nearly double, from 19 today to 37.2 in 2050. However, the aging workforce problem is not unique to the Middle East, as it is predicted that a fifth of the population of Europe will be aged 65 or over in 2020.[15]

The Significance of Globalization

Organizations are no longer constrained by national borders. Burger King is owned by a British firm, and McDonald's sells hamburgers in Moscow, the UAE, the US, Lebanon, and Saudi Arabia. ExxonMobil, a so-called American company, receives almost 75 percent of its revenues from sales outside the US. Accordingly, the issue of foreign labor has become very crucial. The Gulf Cooperation Council (GCC) has over 12 million foreign workers. In the UAE, 90 percent of the workforce was foreign in 2006, with 42.5 percent specifically Indian in 2008.[16]

Moreover, new employees at the Finland-based phone-maker Nokia are increasingly being recruited from India, China, and other developing countries—with non-Finns now outnumbering Finns at Nokia's renowned research center in Helsinki. And all major automobile manufacturers now build cars outside their borders. For instance, Honda builds cars in Ohio, Ford in Brazil, Volkswagen in Mexico, Mercedes in South Africa, and BMW in Egypt.

Leading payment solution provider, Visa, aims to increase the financial literacy of 20 million people worldwide by May 2013. In 2010 it launched the MyMoneySkills website (www.mymoneyskills.me), a financial initiative specially tailored for the Middle East region. The initiative focuses on helping people in the region strengthen their knowledge of personal finance and learn valuable skills such as how to plan a budget and use a credit card wisely. As part of the scheme, Visa introduced a free, FIFA World Cup branded game called 'Financial Football,' which is aimed at engaging and educating younger people on financial management.

Source: "Visa Launches New Financial Literacy Initiative in Middle East" www.ameinfo.com/226951.html

Visa has also responded to globalization by launching a financial initiative especially for the Middle East Region.

These examples illustrate that the world has become a global village. In the process, the manager's job is changing.

Increased Foreign Assignments   If you're a manager sent to another country—an expatriate—you will find yourself having to manage a workforce that is likely to be very different in needs, aspirations, and attitudes from those you are used to back home. You need to be ready to accept these differences and understand how to deal with them.

Working with People from Different Cultures   Even in your own country, you're going to find yourself working with people who were born and raised in different cultures. What motivates you may not motivate them. Your style of communication may be straightforward and open, but they may find this approach uncomfortable and threatening. To work effectively with people from different cultures, you need to understand how their culture, geography, and religion have shaped them and how to adapt your management style to their differences.

And, in particular, when discussing issues pertinent to the Arab world, we must be aware that every Arab country also has its specific values and style of interaction.

Managing Workforce Diversity

One of the most significant challenges facing organizations is adapting to people who are different and this is known as *workforce diversity*. Globalization focuses on differences between people *from* different countries, while workforce diversity addresses differences among people *within* given countries as we just mentioned above.

Workforce diversity means that organizations are becoming a more varied mix of people in terms of gender, age, race, and ethnicity (see Box 1-1). Managing this diversity has become a global concern not just in the Arab world, but also in the US, Canada, Australia, South Africa, Japan, and Europe. For instance, managers in Canada, Australia and the UAE are finding it necessary to adjust to large influxes of Asian workers. Between 2001 and 2007, more than US$200bn was sent out of the GCC by foreign workers. Expatriates as a percentage of total population in GCC states are: UAE—80 percent; Qatar—80 percent; Kuwait—60 percent; Bahrain—40 percent; Saudi Arabia—33 percent; Oman—25 percent.[17]

> **Workforce diversity**
> The concept that organizations are becoming more diverse in terms of gender, age, race, ethnicity, sexual orientation, and inclusion of other groups.

What Do You Think?

Have you ever been treated differently at work just because of your gender or age?

Embracing Diversity   It used to be considered that people who were different would somehow want to 'fit' in the organization. But things are different these days: we now recognize that employees don't leave their cultural values, lifestyle preferences, and differences at home when they come to work. Therefore, the challenge is to become more accommodating to diverse groups of people by accepting their different lifestyles, family needs, and work styles. The melting-pot assumption—the presence of people from different backgrounds—is being replaced by one that recognizes and values differences.[18]

Changing Demographics   The most significant change in the US labor force during the last half of the twentieth century was the rapid increase in the number of female workers.[19] In 1950, for instance, only 29.6 percent of the workforce was women, but by 2003 it reached 46.7 percent.

BOX 1-1
Major Workforce Diversity Categories

Gender

Women are a growing percentage of the workforce in most countries throughout the world. However, Kapiszewski's report on employment in the GCC described varying degrees to which women are allowed to enter the workforce in the MENA region, largely as a result of cultural and religious issues. For example, in Saudi Arabia, only 10 percent of the workforce are women, but in the UAE there are a number of women ministers in government.

National Origin

The population in the GCC states has grown significantly in the last 50 years; from 4 million in 1950 to 40 million in 2006. However, these figures are not due to natural growth but to the continuous influx of foreign workers. The labour laws in most of the GCC countries now require that employment should be offered firstly to the national citizens. Only if there is no suitable candidate should the job be offered to citizens of other GCC states, then to non-Gulf Arabs and only finally to other expatriates.

Age

The average age of Bahrain's workforce is expected to rise from its current level of 29.4 years to 40.9 years by 2050. The number of pensioners is also expected to rise rapidly. The twin trends of population growth and aging are likely to have a major impact on travel and tourism, and also to affect wealth distribution and the health of people.

Countries like Bahrain need to assess how the existence of an aging workforce will affect their crucial oil and gas sector. For example, is it likely to increase the existing shortage of skilled petroleum engineers and geologists in the region?

Race, Disability and Religion

In many countries, there is legislation to ensure fairness in relation to factors such as race, disability and religion. Organizations need to ensure that jobs and workplaces are accessible to the mentally and physically challenged. They also need to be sensitive to the customs, rituals, holidays, and dress of individuals and ensure that these will have no negative impact on the way people are treated within the organization.

Sources: Based on data from Andrzej Kapiszewski "Arab Versus Asian Migrant Workers in the GCC Countries," United Nations Expert Group Meeting on International Migration and Development in the Arab Region, Beirut, May 15/16, 2006, www.un.org/esa/population/meetings/EGM_Ittmig_Arab/P02_Kapiszewski.pdf; and Geoffrey Bew, "Ageing workforce on the rise," *Gulf Daily News: The Voice of Bahrain,* June 9, 2007, www.gulf-daily-news.com/NewsDetails.aspx?storyid=184783.

The report about global employment trends submitted by the International Labor Office offered specifics about the female workforce in the Middle East. It found that: "Another persistent labour market issue in the region is the considerable gap between the sexes in terms of labour force participation and access to decent and productive employment opportunities. Although labour force participation among women has been increasing over the years, the female participation rate is only around a third of the male rate. Estimated at 25.4 percent in 2009, the Middle East's female participation rate is the lowest among all regions."[20]

Implications   The solution is surprisingly simple. Managers need to change and stop treating everyone alike; they need to recognize differences and respond to them in ways that ensure employee retention and greater productivity.

Abdallah S. Jum'ah, former president and CEO of Saudi Aramco, describes the need for leaders to understand cultural issues. He emphasizes the importance of and benefits of diversity, commenting that diversity in the workplace relates to men and women, people of different nations, and to people of different faiths.

Source: Stephen L. Brundage, "Jum'ah Shares Attributes of Leadership at Alkhobar Toastmasters Conference," *Arab News*, April 3, 2010, http://arabnews.com/saudiarabia/article38382.ece.

For instance, workforce diversity training can increase creativity and innovation in organizations, and diversity in the workplace can improve decision making by providing different perspectives on problems.[21] When diversity is not managed properly, there is a potential for higher turnover, more difficult communication, and more interpersonal conflicts.

Improving Quality and Productivity

In the 1990s, organizations around the world added capacity in response to increased demand. Companies built new facilities, expanded services, and added staff. The result? Today, almost every industry suffers from excess supply. The retail world suffers from too many malls and shopping centers. Automobile factories can build more cars than consumers can afford. The telecoms industry is drowning in debt from building capacity that might take 50 years to absorb, and most cities and towns now have far more restaurants than their communities can support. Does this sound familiar?

Excess capacity translates into increased competition. And increased competition is forcing managers to reduce costs and, at the same time, improve their organizations' productivity and the quality of the products and services they offer. Management guru Tom Peters says, "Almost all quality improvement comes via simplification of design, manufacturing, layout, processes, and procedures." To achieve these objectives, managers are implementing programs such as quality management and process reengineering—programs that require extensive employee involvement.

Managers need to realize that the more they involve their employees, the more they ensure success by improving quality and productivity. The importance of talents or skills is that it contributes to customer satisfaction. A qualified workforce is a major resource for business growth. The lack of employees with potential can be damaging for business, so they must find those competent people. Then the challenge is to keep them and get the greatest quality performance and productivity from them.[22]

These employees will not only be a major force in carrying out changes but increasingly will actively participate in planning those changes. This is the essence of organizational behavior.

Improving Customer Service

American Express recently turned Jameela Wardan's worst nightmare into a nonevent. It was 10:00 P.M. Jameela was home in Beirut, packing for a week-long trip, when she suddenly realized she had left her AmEx Gold Card at a restaurant in Tripoli earlier in the evening. The restaurant was over 60 kilometers away. She had a flight to catch at 7:30 the next morning, and she wanted her card for the trip. She called American Express. The phone was quickly answered by a friendly and helpful AmEx customer service representative. He told Jameela not to worry. He asked her a few questions and told her that help was on the way. Jameela was speechless when her doorbell rang at 11:45 P.M.— less than two hours after she had called AmEx. At her door was a courier with a new card. The experience made her a customer for life.

The majority of employees in developed countries work as fast-food counter workers, sales clerks, waiters or waitresses, nurses, automobile repair technicians, consultants, financial planners, and flight attendants—that is, in service jobs. In 2008, services accounted for 43.3 percent of the world's employment, 58.4 percent in the Middle East and 80 percent in the US. Consequently, it is no surprise that the Middle East is becoming more aware of the concept of service, and the opportunities presented by service-based businesses. His Highness Shaikh Mohammad Bin Rashid Al Maktoum, vice-president and prime minister of the UAE and and ruler of Dubai, said, "The services sector has been the key driver of economic growth with an annual growth rate of 21 percent since 2000, constituting US$27.6 billion or 74 percent of Dubai's GDP in 2005, making it a very competitive economy".[23]

The common characteristic of these jobs is that they require interaction with customers. And because an organization can't exist without customers, management needs to ensure that employees do whatever it takes to please customers.[24]

Customer service is the store manager's most important general responsibility: "Instill in your employees the meaning and importance of customer service as outlined in the retail philosophy, 'our store is a place where the word "no" does not exist'; empower staff to 'use their best judgment' in all customer service matters.'"[25] OB can help managers achieve this goal and, more generally, can contribute to improving an organization's performance by showing managers how employee attitudes and behavior are associated with customer satisfaction.

Management needs to create a customer-responsive culture. Hussein Hachem, CEO of the MEA region for Aramex, says, "Through day-to-day interactions, customers actively shape Aramex; we develop effective solutions and deliver excellent services based on their needs."[26] OB can provide considerable guidance in helping managers create such cultures—cultures in which employees are friendly and courteous, accessible, knowledgeable, prompt in responding to customer needs, and willing to do what's necessary to please the customer.[27]

Improving People Skills

We opened this chapter by demonstrating how important people skills are to managerial effectiveness. We said that this book has been written "to help both managers and potential managers develop those people skills."

As you proceed through the chapters, we'll present relevant concepts and theories that can help you explain and predict the behavior of people at work.

Aramex aims to meet the needs of its customers and considers this to be the foundation of its success. In an effort to enhance interaction and develop an effective network, Aramex decided to use Facebook and Twitter, as these sites reach a large audience. As founder and CEO of Aramex, Fadi Ghandour, pictured here, has over 2,200 followers on his Twitter page alone. Hussein Hachem, CEO, Middle East and Africa, says that the web has allowed Aramex to maintain close and constant channels of communication with both employees and customers, and that the connection is rewarding.

Source: "Aramex MEA: The Middle East's Biggest Courier Firm," www.bme.eu.com/article/aramex-middle-easts-biggest-courier-firm.

In addition, you'll gain insights into what enhances specific people skills such as motivating jobs, techniques for improving your listening skills, and how to create more effective teams.

Stimulating Innovation and Change

Today's successful organizations must adopt innovation and master the art of change. Victory goes to organizations that maintain their flexibility, continually improve their quality, and beat their competition to the marketplace with innovative products and services. An organization's employees can either be the building block for innovation and change, or they can be a major stumbling block. The challenge for managers is to stimulate their employees' creativity and tolerance for change. The field of OB provides various ideas and techniques to help achieve these goals.

With change, it is imperative that organizations be fast and flexible if they are to survive. The result is that most managers and employees today work in a climate best characterized as 'temporary.'

Jobs are continually being redesigned; tasks are increasingly being done by flexible teams rather than individuals; companies are relying more on temporary workers; jobs are being subcontracted out to other firms; and pensions are being redesigned to move with people as they change jobs.

Workers need to continually update their knowledge and skills to perform new job requirements. Today's managers and employees must learn to cope with temporariness. They have to learn to live with flexibility, and uncertainty. The study of OB can provide important insights into helping you better understand a work world of continuous change, how to overcome resistance to change, and how best to create an organizational culture that depends on change.

Helping Employees Balance Work–Life Conflicts

The typical employee in the 1960s or 1970s showed up at the workplace every week, and the workplace and hours were clearly specified. That's no longer true for a large segment of today's workforce. Employees are increasingly complaining that the line between work and nonwork time has become confusing, creating personal conflicts and stress.[28] However, today's workplace presents opportunities for workers to create and structure their work roles so as to reach a balance between work life and personal life.

One study of employee motivation stressed the importance of work–life balance for the employees of 13 Arab world countries. The study received 13,376 responses and 91 percent of the overall population claimed that work–life balance is very important and motivates them.[29]

Employees recognize that work can interfere with their personal lives, and they're not happy about it. A number of factors are responsible for this negative impact. First, the creation of global organizations means their world never sleeps; that is, many employees of global firms are 'on call' 24 hours a day. Second, communications technology enables employees to do their work at home, in their cars, or on the beach in Hawaii. This allows many people in technical and professional jobs to do their work any time and from any place. Third, organizations are asking employees to put in longer hours. Finally, fewer families have only a single breadwinner. Today's married employee is typically part of a dual-career couple. This makes it increasingly difficult for married employees to find the time to fulfill commitments to home, spouse, children, parents, and friends.

Employees want jobs that help them manage work–life conflicts. In fact, evidence indicates that balancing work and life demands now surpasses job security as an employee priority.[30] A majority of college and university students say that attaining a balance between personal life and work is a primary career goal. They want 'a life' as well as a job. Organizations that don't help their people achieve a work–life balance will find it difficult to attract and retain the most capable and motivated employees.

In later chapters, we will see how OB offers a number of suggestions to guide managers in designing workplaces and jobs that can help employees deal with work–life conflicts. Emotional intelligence will be explained in Chapter 16.

Creating a Positive Work Environment

Although competitive pressures on most organizations are stronger than ever, we've noticed an interesting shift in both OB research and management practice, at least in some organizations. Instead of responding to competition by increasing pressures, some organizations are trying to realize a competitive advantage by encouraging and supporting a positive work environment. For example, Jeff Immelt, CEO of GE, whom we mentioned earlier in this chapter, and Jim McNerney are both followers of Jack Welch (former CEO of GE), who is considered to have been one of the best CEOs in the world. All of these CEOs have tried to maintain high-performance expectations (a characteristic of GE's culture) while also supporting a positive work environment in their organizations (GE and Boeing). "In this time of turmoil and cynicism about business, you need to be passionate, positive leaders," Mr. Immelt recently told his top managers.

Positive organizational scholarship

An area of OB research that concerns how organizations develop human strength, foster vitality and resilience, and unlock potential.

At the same time, a real growth-area in OB research has been **positive organizational scholarship** (also called *positive organizational behavior*), which is concerned with how organizations develop human strengths, encourage energy and resilience, and unlock potential.

It is helpful for employers to know their own strengths and weaknesses, as well as those of their employees, and this will enable organizations to think about how to utilize their employees' strengths rather than focus on their limitations.

So many organizations in the Arab world have become more aware of the importance of offering working mothers the facilities and flexibility they need for childcare. Accordingly, we find increasing numbers of workplaces nurseries, such as the one pictured here, and because the mother knows that she can see her child during her break, she is able to focus more on her work and becomes more efficient. Maternity leave is another means of motivation for working mothers.

For example, positive organizational scholars have studied a concept called 'reflected best-self'—asking employees to think about situations in which they were at their 'personal best' in order to understand how to exploit their strengths. These researchers argue that we all have things at which we are unusually good, yet too often we focus on addressing our limitations and too rarely think about how to exploit our strengths.[31]

Although positive organizational scholarship does not deny the presence (or even the value) of the negative (such as critical feedback), it does challenge researchers to look at OB through a new lens. It also challenges organizations to think about how to use their employees' strengths rather than focus on their limitations.

Improving Ethical Behavior

In an organizational world characterized by cutbacks, expectations of increasing worker productivity, and tough competition in the marketplace, it's not surprising that many employees feel pressured to cut corners, break rules, and engage in other forms of questionable practices.

Members of organizations are increasingly finding themselves facing **ethical dilemmas**, that is, situations in which they are required to define right and wrong conduct. So many questions remain a problem for these organizational members. Should I 'blow the whistle'? Should I follow orders that I don't personally agree with? Do I give an inflated performance evaluation to an ordinary employee knowing that such an evaluation could save that employee's job? Do I allow myself to 'play politics' in the organization if it will help my career advancement?

What constitutes good ethical behavior has never been clearly defined; employees see people all around them engaging in unethical practices such as espionage or bribery. When caught, these people give excuses such as 'everyone does it' or 'you have to take every opportunity nowadays.' Is it any wonder that employees are expressing decreased confidence and trust in management and that they're increasingly uncertain about what constitutes appropriate ethical behavior in their organizations?[32]

Ethical dilemmas

Situations in which individuals are required to define right and wrong conduct.

Managers and their organizations are responding to this problem from a number of directions.[33] They're writing and distributing codes of ethics to guide employees through ethical dilemmas. They're offering seminars, workshops, and other training programs to try to improve ethical behaviors. They're providing in-house advisors who can be contacted, in many cases anonymously, for assistance in dealing with ethical issues, and they're creating protection mechanisms for employees who reveal internal unethical practices.

Today's managers need to create an ethically healthy climate for their employees, where they can do their work productively and confront a minimal degree of ambiguity regarding what constitutes right and wrong behaviors. In upcoming chapters, we'll discuss the kinds of actions managers can take to create an ethically healthy climate and help employees sort through ethically ambiguous situations. We'll also present ethical-dilemma exercises at the end of each chapter that will allow you to think through ethical issues and assess how you would handle them.

Developing an OB Model

8 *Consider the three levels of analysis and characteristics of the OB model in general.*

Let's now present a general model that defines the field of OB, determines the framework, and identifies its dependent and independent variables. The end result will be a number of issues that will become the topics of many of the sections of coming chapters in the remainder of this book. First, let's clarify one thing. Such an OB model is a guideline for organizations in whatever geographical location or culture. Thus, it can be a model for any organization in whatever country, and, in particular, it can be a feasible OB model for the Arab world. In other words, the OB model is common in structure across all organizations owing to national culture, but differs in implementation because of organizational culture.

Accordingly, an OB model includes the specific characteristics that define it as an example to follow. So when we talk about productivity, absenteeism, turnover, effectiveness, efficiency, job satisfaction, and work behavior, we really cannot say that the essence of these issues differs from one country to another. However, what does differ is the way in which we deal with them. In the following sections, we will discuss these OB characteristics and identify how they are dealt with in the Arab world.

What Do You Think?

Does a person's nationality affect their behavior?

An Overview

A model is a simplified representation of some real-world idea. A mannequin in a boutique is a model. Similarly, the accountant's formula Assets + Liabilities = Owners' Equity is a model. Figure 1-3 presents the skeleton on which we will construct our OB model, made of three levels: individual, group, and the organization systems. The three basic levels that will be elaborated in a coming section in this chapter are interdependent and allow us to arrive at a better understanding of organizational behavior.

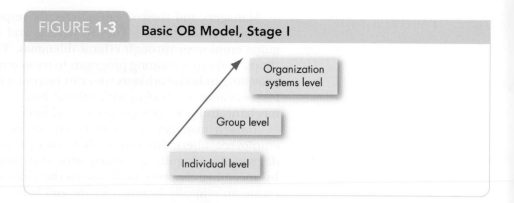

FIGURE **1-3**   Basic OB Model, Stage I

Organization systems level

Group level

Individual level

The Dependent Variables

Dependent variable

A response that is affected by an independent variable.

A **dependent variable** is the key factor that you want to explain or predict and that is affected by some other factor. What are the primary dependent variables in OB? Scholars have historically tended to emphasize productivity, absenteeism, turnover, deviant workplace behavior, organizational citizenship behavior and job satisfaction. Each of these dependent variables will be briefly discussed below.

Productivity

A performance measure that includes effectiveness and efficiency.

Effectiveness

Achievement of goals.

Efficiency

The ratio of effective output to the input required to achieve it.

Productivity   An organization is productive if it achieves its goals and does so by transferring inputs to outputs at the lowest cost. Thus, **productivity** implies a concern for both **effectiveness** and **efficiency**.

A hospital, for example, is *effective* when it successfully meets the needs of its clientele. It is *efficient* when it can do so at a low cost. If a hospital manages to achieve higher output from its present staff by reducing the average number of days a patient is confined to a bed, or by increasing the number of staff–patient contacts per day, we say that the hospital has gained productive efficiency. A business firm is effective when it attains its sales or market share goals, but its productivity also depends on achieving those goals efficiently. Popular measures of organizational efficiency include return on investment, profit per dollar of sales, and output per hour of labor.

To illustrate, the mission statement and philosophy of Notre Dame University, Lebanon, stresses achieving quality learning outcomes through efficient and effective methodology. In summary, one of OB's major concerns is productivity. We want to know what factors will influence the effectiveness and efficiency of individuals, of groups, and of the overall organization.

Absenteeism

The failure to report to work.

Absenteeism   Absenteeism is defined as the failure to report to work. Absenteeism is a huge cost and disruption to employers and includes lost productivity or the additional costs for overtime pay or hiring temporary employees. Because of the instability in the Arab world, many organizations may take advantage of their employees: they know that employees will not leave because there are few other opportunities available to them. As a result, employees may express their frustration by not coming to work.

It's obviously difficult for an organization to operate smoothly and to attain its objectives if employees fail to show up to their jobs. The work flow is disrupted, and often important decisions must be delayed. In organizations that rely heavily on assembly-line production, absenteeism can be considerably more than a disruption: it can result in a drastic reduction in the quality of output, and, in some cases, it can bring about a complete shutdown of the production facility. Of course, this does not contribute to effectiveness and efficiency.

The Director of Administration at Notre Dame University (NDU) in Lebanon, Reverend Father Ziad Antoun emphasized the importance of providing a safe, healthy and comfortable work environment for employees. NDU is one of the many institutions where employees have different facilities to enhance their performance. Access to a gym and other sports facilities allows faculty and staff the opportunity to take advantage of breaks to improve their physical and mental wellbeing. After all, the healthier and more energetic people are, the more productive and satisfied they become and thus absenteeism is reduced.

Although most absences have a negative impact on the organization, there are situations where the organization may benefit by an employee's voluntarily choosing not to come to work. For instance, in jobs in which an employee needs to be alert—consider surgeons and airline pilots, for example—it may be better for the organization if an ill or fatigued employee does *not* report to work. The cost of an accident in such jobs could be disastrous. But these examples are clearly atypical. For the most part, we can assume that organizations benefit when employee absenteeism is low.

Turnover

Voluntary and involuntary permanent withdrawal from an organization.

Turnover   **Turnover** is the voluntary and involuntary permanent withdrawal from an organization; that is, when employees decide to leave the organization for whatever reason. We must realize that a high turnover rate results in increased recruiting, selection, and training costs in organizations worldwide; the Arab world is no exception. Zed Ayesh, Managing Director, Flagship Consultancy says, "Mobility of skilled professionals remains a challenge to UAE businesses. This is costing businesses a substantial deal of wasted resources and weakening their competitive positions against those which are having a stable workforce with lesser turnover rates."[34] In addition, it can disrupt the efficient running of an organization when knowledgeable and experienced personnel leave and replacements must be found and prepared to assume positions of responsibility.

On the other hand, turnover can actually be positive because it can create an opportunity to replace an underperforming individual with someone who has higher skills or motivation, allow opportunities for promotions, and add new and fresh ideas to the organization.[35]

However, turnover often involves the loss of people the organization doesn't want to lose. For instance, one study covering 900 employees who had resigned from their jobs found that 92 percent earned performance ratings of 'satisfactory' or better from their superiors.[36] So when turnover is high, or when it involves valuable performers, it can be a disruptive factor that affects the organization's effectiveness.

International OB

Organizational Citizenship at Byblos Bank

Byblos Bank was founded in 1950 and now operates in 11 countries in the Middle East, Europe, and Africa. One of the largest banks in Lebanon, it has total assets of about US$20.5bn and 1,800 employees.

Lebanon has always experienced uncertainty, owing to the unfortunate circumstances that have created ambiguity and instability in the country. Byblos Bank was one of the many operations that faced several difficulties during these periods,

for example having to ensure that employees could reach the Bank's locations, and that clients were kept satisfied. The risks involved were clear; however, management was aware that they could not afford to lose either qualified employees or clients.

Primarily, Byblos Bank was concerned for the bodily safety of employees and since many were unable to get to their designated workplaces, management reassigned them to locations closer to home. This genuine

empathy encouraged employees to remain committed to their jobs and they ultimately contributed more than their usual duties, to maintain the credibility of the Bank.

Moreover, the Bank stayed in contact with as many clients as possible to keep them afloat during such hard times. This initiative was welcomed and appreciated, and translated itself into greater loyalty.

Source: "Cash flow in a conflict," *Executive Magazine*, April 2010, Issue No. 129, pp. 46–50.

Deviant workplace behavior

Voluntary behavior that violates significant organizational norms and, in so doing, threatens the wellbeing of the organization or its members. Also called antisocial behavior or workplace incivility.

Deviant Workplace Behavior   Given the cost of absenteeism and turnover to employers, more and more OB researchers are studying these behaviors as indicators or markers of deviant behavior. Deviance can range from someone playing his music too loudly to violence. Managers need to understand this wide range of behaviors to address any form of employee dissatisfaction. If managers don't understand *why* an employee is acting up, the problem will never be solved.

We can define **deviant workplace behavior** (also called *antisocial behavior* or *workplace incivility*) as voluntary behavior that violates significant organizational values and thus threatens the wellbeing of the organization or its members. What are organizational values or norms in this context? They can be company policies that prohibit certain behaviors such as stealing. They also can be unspoken rules that are widely shared, such as not playing loud music in one's workspace. But deviant workplace behaviors can be much more serious than an employee's playing loud music. For example, an employee may insult a colleague, steal, gossip excessively, or engage in sabotage—destroying company property, all of which can cause chaos in an organization.

Deviant workplace behavior is an important concept because it's a response to dissatisfaction, and employees express this dissatisfaction in many ways. Controlling one behavior may be ineffective unless one gets to the root of the cause. The sophisticated manager will deal with root causes of problems that may result in deviance rather than solve one surface problem (excessive absence), only to see another one appear (increased theft or sabotage). Consequently, managers must address any radical changes in employee behavior and try to know the reasons for such behavior to avoid any repetition.

Organizational citizenship behavior (OCB)

Discretionary behavior that is not part of an employee's formal job requirements but that nevertheless promotes the effective functioning of the organization.

Organizational Citizenship Behavior   Organizational citizenship behavior (OCB) is careful behavior that is not part of an employee's formal job requirements but that nevertheless promotes the effective functioning of the organization.[37]

Successful organizations need employees who will do more than just their usual job duties—who will provide performance that is *beyond* expectations, as Byblos Bank demonstrates (see the 'International OB' box opposite). In today's dynamic workplace, where tasks are increasingly done in teams and where flexibility is critical, organizations need employees who will engage in 'good citizenship' behaviors, such as helping others on their team, volunteering for extra work, avoiding unnecessary conflicts, respecting the spirit as well as the letter of rules and regulations, and gracefully tolerating occasional work-related impositions and nuisances.

Job satisfaction

A positive feeling about one's job resulting from an evaluation of its characteristics.

Job Satisfaction   The final dependent variable we will look at is **job satisfaction**, which is a positive feeling about one's job resulting from an evaluation of its characteristics. Unlike the previous variables, job satisfaction represents an attitude rather than a behavior. It is very important because it demonstrates relationship to performance and many OB experts consider it to be the issue that adds value to the organization.

The belief that satisfied employees are more productive than dissatisfied employees has been a basic issue among managers for years, though only now has research begun to support this theory after decades of questions about the satisfaction–performance relationship.[38] Researchers with strong humanistic values argue that satisfaction is a legitimate objective of an organization. Not only is satisfaction negatively related to absenteeism and turnover, but also, they argue, organizations have a responsibility to provide employees with jobs that are challenging and intrinsically rewarding. More details will be given in Chapter 3 about employee satisfaction in the Arab world. It can be agreed, however, that all employees have a similar understanding of what makes for job satisfaction: good work conditions, incentives, appreciation, acknowledgment, rewards, and respect.

What Do You Think?

As an employee, what do you consider to be a key dependent variable for you as an individual?

The Independent Variables

In the previous section, we discussed the dependent variables, productivity, absenteeism, turnover, deviant workplace behavior, OCB, and job satisfaction. In the next section, we will investigate the major determinants that will bring us to the independent variables. An **independent variable** is the presumed cause of some change in a dependent variable.

We now discuss the three basic levels of an organization as we identified in Figure 1-3 on page 24.

Independent variable

The presumed cause of some change in a dependent variable.

Individual Level Variables   When individuals enter an organization, each is different. Moreover, people enter organizations with certain characteristics that will influence their behavior at work. The most obvious of these are personal or biographical characteristics such as age, gender, and marital status; personality characteristics; an inherent emotional framework; values and attitudes; and basic ability levels. These characteristics are essentially in place when an individual enters the workforce, and there is little management can do to change them. Yet they have a very real impact on employee behavior. Therefore, each of these factors will be discussed as independent variables in Chapters 2, 3 and 4.

There are four other individual-level variables that have been shown to affect employee behavior: perception, individual decision making, learning, and motivation. These topics will be introduced and discussed in detail in Chapters 2, 5, 6, and 7.

Group Level Variables   The complexity of the OB model described earlier in this chapter is increased when we acknowledge that individuals behave differently when they are in groups. Therefore, the next step is the study of group behavior to enable us to really understand OB.

Chapter 7 lays the foundation for an understanding of the dynamics of group behavior. That chapter will show how individuals in groups are influenced by the patterns of behavior they are expected to show, what the group considers to be acceptable standards of behavior, and the degree to which group members are attracted to each other. Chapter 8 translates our understanding of groups to the design of effective work teams. Chapters 9, 10, 11 and 12 will demonstrate how communication patterns, leadership, power and politics, and levels of conflict affect group behavior.

Organization System Level Variables   Organizational behavior reaches its highest level of sophistication when we add formal structure to our previous knowledge of individual and group behavior. The design of the formal organization; the organization's internal culture; and the organization's human resource policies and practices—selection processes, training and development programs, performance evaluation methods—all have an impact on the dependent variables. These are discussed in detail in Chapters 13, 14 and 15.

Toward a Contingency OB Model

Our final model, Figure 1-4, shows the six key dependent variables and a large number of independent variables, organized by level of analysis. Throughout this book we will introduce important contingency variables that will improve the explanation of the connection between the independent and dependent variables in our OB model.

Note that we have included the concepts of change and stress in Figure 1-4, acknowledging the dynamics of behavior and the fact that work stress is an individual, group, and organizational issue. Specifically, in Chapter 16, we will discuss the change process, ways to manage organizational change, key change issues currently facing managers, consequences of work stress, and techniques for managing stress.

Also note that Figure 1-4 highlights the links between the three levels of analysis. For instance, organizational structure is linked to leadership. This link is meant to convey that authority and leadership are related; that is, management exerts its influence on group behavior through leadership. Similarly, communication—discussed in Chapter 9—is the means by which individuals transmit information; thus, it is the link between individual and group behavior.

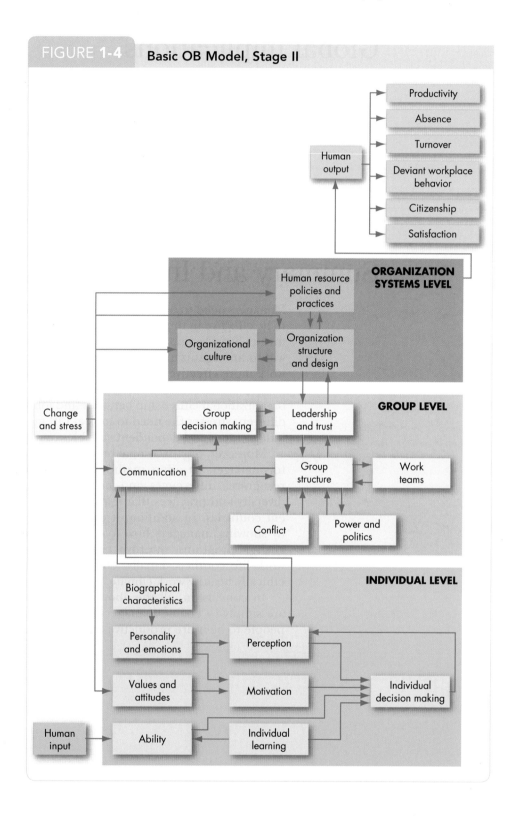

FIGURE 1-4   Basic OB Model, Stage II

Global Implications

In this introductory chapter we have discussed many issues relating to organizational behavior and, in particular, we have considered how globalization presents challenges and opportunities for OB. This end-of-chapter section, 'Global Implications,' will also appear in all the following chapters and will review how the topics about OB presented in each chapter are affected by cultural differences within and between countries. It will all revolve around the question, 'How does what we know about OB vary based on culture?' We will find that some OB principles don't vary much across cultures, but others vary a great deal from culture to culture.

Summary and Implications for Managers

Managers need to develop their interpersonal, or people, skills if they are going to be effective in their jobs. Organizational behavior (OB) is a field of study that investigates the impact that individuals, groups, and structure have on behavior within an organization, and it applies that information to make organizations work more effectively. Specifically, OB focuses on how to improve productivity; reduce absenteeism, turnover, and deviant workplace behavior; and increase organizational citizenship behavior and job satisfaction. The fact that people are different stresses the need to look at OB in a contingency framework, using the independent and dependent variables to explain cause-and-effect relationships.

Moreover, organizational behavior offers both challenges and opportunities for managers. It offers methods to improve a manager's people skills. It also recognizes differences and helps managers to see the value of workforce diversity and practices that may need to be changed when managing in different countries. In addition, it can improve quality and employee productivity by showing managers how to empower their people, design and implement change programs, improve customer service, and help employees balance work–life conflicts. Finally, OB can offer managers guidance in creating an ethically healthy work climate.

In conclusion, all the above recommendations, suggestions and warnings are simply to enable managers to perform better and, as a result, encourage people to be more productive and achieve organizational goals.

Point >> << Counterpoint

IN SEARCH OF THE QUICK FIX

Walk into your nearest major bookstore and you'll find a large section of books devoted to management and managing human behavior. A close look at the titles will reveal that there is certainly no shortage of popular books on topics related to organizational behavior. Many bookstores contain books about management, managing human behavior, and organizational behavior. Publishers offer hundreds of titles that promise information on leadership in addition to quick solutions to problems.

Organizations are always looking for leaders; and managers and manager-wannabes are continually looking for ways to hone their leadership skills. Publishers respond to this demand by offering hundreds of titles that promise insights into the subject of leadership. Books like these can provide people with the secrets to leadership that others know about.

On the other hand, even though popular books on organizational behavior may have cute titles and be fun to read, they can be dangerous. They make the job of managing people seem much simpler than it really is. Also, they are often based on the author's opinions rather than actual experiences.

Organizational behavior is a complex subject. Few, if any, simple statements about human behavior are applicable to all people in all situations. Beware of the quick fix! We all want to find quick and simple solutions to our complex problems. But here's the bad news: For problems related to organizational behavior, quick and simple solutions are often wrong because they fail to consider the diversity among organizations, situations, and individuals.

Questions for Review

1 What are the importance of interpersonal skills?

2 What do managers do in terms of functions, roles, and skills?

3 What is organizational behavior (OB)?

4 Why is it important to complement intuition with systematic study?

5 What are the major behavioral science disciplines that contribute to OB?

6 Why are there few absolutes in OB?

7 What are the challenges and opportunities for managers in using OB concepts?

8 What are the three levels of analysis, and the characteristics of the OB model in general?

Discussion Exercise

A DAY IN THE LIFE OF HUSSAM

Hussam is the general and marketing manager of a small subsidiary of the German company Electro, in Dubai, which was founded two years ago. Hussam is the first Arab manager in the company, an achievement that he attributes to the fact that he graduated from Germany's best engineering university and is proficient in English, Arabic, and German. Today, Hussam arrives at the office early to review his schedule for the day.

9.00: Meeting with all employees to communicate the revised business goals for 2010. Hussam has scheduled 30 minutes to revise his presentation: this subsidiary has 45 employees from 15 different cultures, and misunderstandings occur frequently. The company is experiencing financial difficulties, and Hussam needs to be an inspirational leader.

10.30: Meeting with the IT and sales managers. These two managers have been in constant conflict for the past two months. Hussam has already met with them individually. Today, he will try to get them to resolve their differences. The conflict is related to the implementation of a new IT system for the sales department.

11.30: Call the two best advertising agencies in the country. Hussam has to decide which agency to work with for next season's campaign. One agency has a better reputation, but Hussam is developing a friendship with the manager of the other one. Hussam has to make sure he makes the right choice for the company.

2.30: Meeting with Petra, his personal assistant. Hussam has noticed that her performance has declined recently and that on some occasions she did not treat irritated clients properly. Hussam wants to understand what is happening with her, to clarify her job objectives, and to remotivate her. He wants every employee to respect the key organizational values: 'Clients are kings' and 'Excellence in everything we do.'

4.00: Call Holger, the international human resources manager in Berlin, to discuss the 'German expat problem.' Of the German expatriates sent to Dubai, 20 percent returned to Germany before the end of their assignment. Moreover, the expatriates that stayed in Dubai never performed up to their supervisors' expectations. Hussam needs some advice from Holger.

Discuss the relationship of the above to organizational behavior and what we studied in this chapter.

Ethical Considerations

Do you think it's ever okay to lie? If you were negotiating for the release of hostages, most people would probably agree that if lying would lead to the hostages' safety, it's okay. What about in business, where the stakes are rarely life or death? Business executives such as Martha Stewart have gone to jail for lying (submitting a false statement to federal investigators). Is misrepresentation or omitting factors okay as long as there is no outright lie?

Consider the negotiation process. A good negotiator never shows all his cards, right? And so omitting certain information is just part of the process. Well, it may surprise you to learn that the law will hold you liable for omitting information if partial disclosure is misleading or if one side has superior information not accessible to the other.

In one case (*Jordan v. Duff and Phelps*), a company (Duff and Phelps) withheld information from an employee—Jordan—about the impending sale of the company. The problem: Jordan was leaving the organization and therefore sold his shares in the company. Ten days later, when the sale of the company became public, those shares became worth much more. Jordan sued his former

employer on the grounds that it should have disclosed this information to him. Duff and Phelps countered that it had never lied to Jordan. The Court of Appeals argued that in such situations, one party cannot take 'opportunistic advantage' of the other. In the eyes of the law, sometimes omitting relevant facts can be as bad as lying.

Questions

1. In a business context, is it ever okay to lie? If yes, what are those situations? Why is it okay to lie in these situations?

2. A recent survey revealed that 24 percent of managers said they have fired someone for lying. Do you think it's fair to fire an employee who lies, no matter what the nature of the lie? Explain.

3. In business, is withholding information for your own advantage the same as lying? Why or why not?

4. In a business context, if someone has something to gain by lying, what percentage of people, do you think, would lie?

Sources: Based on "Lying at Work Could Get You Fired," *UPI*, March 5, 2006; "Brain Scans Detect More Activity in Those Who Lie," Reuters, November 29, 2004; www.msnbc.msn.com/id/6609019; and P. Ekman and E. L. Rosenberg, *What the Fact Reveals: Basic and Applied Studies of Spontaneous Expression Using the Facial Action Coding System (CAPS)*, 2nd ed. (New York: Oxford University Press, 2004).

Critical Analysis

EQUAL OPPORTUNITY AT CREPAWAY

Crepaway was founded in 1985 by two brothers, Charles and Claude Thoumy. It is a Lebanese diner chain, set up as a limited liability company in 2003. There are nine outlets located in different areas of Lebanon, and franchises have been established in parts of the Middle East, including Egypt, Qatar, and Saudi Arabia. Crepaway understand that employees are the elements that keep the operation alive.

All local and regional outlets have the same organizational structure, which is directly related to the company's strategy. Crepaway believes in equal employment opportunity. Job application forms contain the following statement: "We employ on the basis of equal opportunities for all and we do not and will not discriminate on the basis of race, religion, national origin, sex, age or handicap." Consequently, management plans for the workforce to be formed with an equal percentage presence of males/females and Christians/Muslims, and so on.

Once recruited, employees undergo training in Lebanon and then join the location in the country in which they will be working. In addition, to enhance productivity and motivate employees, Crepaway offers both financial and non-financial incentives such as bonuses and 'employee of the month' awards. Moreover, employee safety is of great importance to the management of Crepaway and, thus, employees must be trained in first aid and the safety of the environment, such as fire fighting. Why? This tells employees that management cares about their wellbeing, which is a motivational factor.

Questions

1. One activity that managers engage in is human resource (HR) management. How would you analyze the HR activities that Crepaway carries out?

2. From the information you have read, what kind of organizational behavior exists?

3. How does Crepaway manage workforce diversity?

4. How does the concern for wellbeing motivate employees?

Source: Information obtained from *Crepaway* stand at Job Fair at Notre Dame University, Lebanon, May 2010.

Research Exercise

Do your own research and find a case or incident that is relevant to one of the concepts we have discussed in this chapter. It should be about the Arab world and show the similarities and/or differences to the West.

Part 2 The Individual

LEARNING OBJECTIVES

This chapter will enable you to:

1 Contrast the two types of ability: intellectual and physical.

2 Identify the key biographical characteristics and describe how they are relevant to OB.

3 Define *learning* and outline the principles of the three major theories of learning.

4 Define *shaping* and show how it can be used in OB.

5 Define *personality*, describe how it is measured, and explain the factors that determine an individual's personality.

6 Describe the Myers-Briggs Type Indicator personality framework and assess its strengths and weaknesses.

7 Identify the key traits in the Big Five personality model and demonstrate how the Big Five traits predict behavior at work.

8 Identify other personality traits relevant to OB.

9 Define *values*, demonstrate the importance of values, and contrast terminal and instrumental values.

10 Show the relationship between individual personality and the workplace.

11 Identify Hofstede's five value dimensions of national culture.

Foundations of Individual Behavior: Personality and Values

2

Without mission, there's no purpose. Without vision, there's no destination. Without values, there are no guiding principles.

—Paul B. Thornton

Nabela's Story

Nabela is 28 and Jordanian. Her grade average was not enough to allow her to enroll at university. She tried to find work but remained unemployed for eight years. "I was depressed and tired. I kept thinking of the future and of what was going to happen to me. I had nothing to do and was dependent on my family. They had seen me through high school, and to end up the way I was, for me, was a waste," explains Nabela.

"I then started to take courses in hairdressing at a vocational training center. I even trained at a beauty salon," she says. She then decided that she must do something with her life, so she took out a loan and set up her own hair salon. "I wanted to ensure my future, especially as I am an unmarried female. I took out a loan from a local institution that was targeting youth to start their own projects. I now feel productive. I have an identity, a place of my own, a future," Nabela says.

She continues, "I have peace of mind. I no longer fear the future." She works on her own in order to pay back the loan through the money she earns. After she repays her loan, Nabela wants to expand her salon and employ people.

Source: Jordan Human Development Report, "Business and Youth in the Arab World," *International Business Leaders Forum*, 2006.

Nabela's story is all about individual behavior. She experienced bad times because she couldn't find a job and she thought that she had no abilities. After she took a positive attitude and showed more confidence, Nabela was able to decide what she wanted to do with her life.

In this chapter we look at how individual differences in the form of ability (which includes intelligence) and biographical characteristics (such as age) affect employee performance and satisfaction. Then we will learn more about personality and values, and how people learn behaviors, and what management can do to shape those behaviors.

But before we move on to the next section, consider the following Self-Assessment Library, where you can assess what your attitude is toward achievement.

WHAT'S MY ATTITUDE TOWARD ACHIEVEMENT?

In the Self-Assessment Library (available online), take assessment I.C.7 (What's My Attitude Toward Achievement?) and answer the following questions:

1. *Are you surprised by your results?*

2. *How do your results compare with those of others?*

Ability

1 *Contrast the two types of ability: intellectual and physical.*

Ability
An individual's capacity to perform the various tasks in a job.

Intellectual abilities
The capacity to do mental activities—thinking, reasoning, and problem solving.

Let's start this chapter by talking about ability because we will then understand more about individual behavior. So, then, what is ability? **Ability** refers to an individual's *capacity* to perform the various tasks in a job. Other synonyms— words that mean the same—for ability are *skill* and *competence*. These expressions will be used often throughout this textbook since OB is all about the ability, skill, competence, or capacity to complete certain tasks. An individual's overall abilities are essentially made up of two sets of factors: intellectual and physical.

The fact is that people, no matter how motivated they are, have both strengths and weaknesses in terms of ability that make them either superior or inferior to others in performing certain tasks or activities. To illustrate, it is difficult to imagine that everyone can act as well as Ilham Shahine or Farid Showki, play basketball as well as Michael Jordan, or even sing as well as Nancy Ajram or Hani Shaker.

In short, the issue is not whether people differ in terms of their abilities. Clearly, we do. The issue is knowing *how* people differ in abilities and using that knowledge to help employees perform their jobs better.

Intellectual Abilities

Intellectual abilities are needed to perform mental activities—for thinking, reasoning, and problem solving. People in most societies place a high value on intelligence, and for good reason. Compared with others, smart people generally earn more money and attain higher levels of education. Smart people are also more likely to emerge as leaders of groups. Intelligence quotient (IQ) tests, for example, are designed to determine a person's general intellectual abilities. So, too, are popular college admission tests, which are familiar to the Arab

TABLE 2-1	Dimensions of Intellectual Ability	
Dimension	**Description**	**Job Example**
Number aptitude	Ability to do speedy and accurate arithmetic	Accountant: Computing the sales tax on a set of items
Verbal comprehension	Ability to understand what is read or heard, and the relationship of words to each other	Plant manager: Following corporate policies on hiring
Perceptual speed	Ability to identify visual similarities and differences quickly and accurately	Fire investigator: Identifying clues to support a charge of arson
Inductive reasoning	Ability to identify a logical sequence in a problem and then solve the problem	Market researcher: Forecasting demand for a product in the next time period
Deductive reasoning	Ability to use logic and assess the implications of an argument	Supervisor: Choosing between two different suggestions offered by employees
Spatial visualization	Ability to imagine how an object would look if its position in space were changed	Interior decorator: Redecorating an office
Memory	Ability to retain and recall past experiences	Salesperson: Remembering the names of customers

student, such as the SAT and graduate admission tests in business (GMAT). The seven most frequently cited dimensions making up intellectual abilities are: number aptitude, verbal comprehension, perceptual speed, inductive reasoning, deductive reasoning, spatial visualization, and memory.[1] Table 2-1 describes these dimensions.

As we saw in Table 2-1, jobs differ in the demands they place on individuals in various job descriptions to use their intellectual abilities. The more complicated a job is in terms of information-processing demands, the more general intelligence and verbal abilities will be necessary to perform the job successfully.[2] Of course, a high IQ is not a requirement for all jobs.

What Do You Think?

Is intelligence a major requirement for dealing with people?

Interestingly, while intelligence is a big help in performing a job well, it doesn't make people happier or more satisfied with their jobs. The relationship between intelligence and job satisfaction is about zero. Why? Research suggests that although intelligent people perform better and tend to have more interesting jobs, they are also more critical in evaluating their job conditions. Thus, smart people have it better, but they also expect more.[3]

Physical Abilities

Although the changing nature of work suggests that intellectual abilities are becoming increasingly important for many jobs, **physical abilities** have been, and will remain, important for successfully doing certain jobs. Research on the requirements needed in hundreds of jobs has identified nine basic abilities involved in the performance of physical tasks.[4] These are described in Table 2-2 and divided into strength, flexibility, and other factors. Individuals differ in the extent to which they have each of these abilities. Not surprisingly, there is also little relationship among them.

Physical abilities

The capacity to do tasks that demand stamina, dexterity, strength, and similar characteristics.

International OB

Cultural Intelligence Is Necessary

A 'people person' can establish relationships with others easily, whether the other person is from their own country or from another country with very different values and traditions. To understand and respect others you need to have 'cultural intelligence' and show 'cultural awareness.' These two attributes are essential if you are to communicate effectively, whether at a personal or a business level. In short, you need to be "culture smart" to succeed.

Cultural intelligence is important because when conducting business with people from different cultures, misunderstandings can often occur, and, as a result, cooperation and productivity may suffer. When it comes to business, organizations must be aware of these cultural differences because the needs and preferences of people change from one society to another.

MasterCard Worldwide realizes that they need to satisfy the needs of their customers from all over the world. To do this, they aim to apply good intercultural management. In 2010 MasterCard appointed a new head of regional business development for Asia/Pacific, the Middle East, and Africa and a new general manager in the Middle East and Africa. They hoped that these two administrators would bring broad experience and knowledge of cultural differences, enabling the company to maximize both market share and customer loyalty.

Cultural intelligence can be seen as one aspect of overall intelligence, rather like emotional intelligence. It can also be thought of as being one aspect of cognitive ability. What is clear, however, is that being able to interact well with individuals from different cultures is a key asset in today's global business environment.

Source: "Company Bulletin," *Executive Magazine*, Issue No. 129, April, 2010, p. 24.

TABLE 2-2   Nine Basic Physical Abilities

Strength Factors

1. Dynamic strength	Ability to exert muscular force repeatedly or continuously over time
2. Trunk strength	Ability to exert muscular strength using the trunk (particularly abdominal) muscles
3. Static strength	Ability to exert force against external objects
4. Explosive strength	Ability to expend a maximum of energy in one or a series of explosive acts

Flexibility Factors

5. Extent flexibility	Ability to move the trunk and back muscles as far as possible
6. Dynamic flexibility	Ability to make rapid, repeated flexing movements

Other Factors

7. Body coordination	Ability to coordinate the simultaneous actions of different parts of the body
8. Balance	Ability to maintain equilibrium despite forces pulling off balance
9. Stamina	Ability to continue maximum effort requiring prolonged effort over time

Picture This

Your best friend has just changed jobs and is moving into a new office and has asked you to help him to move the furniture and boxes with him. Which of the physical abilities mentioned in Table 2-2 would you need to depend on?

Biographical Characteristics

Biographical characteristics
Personal characteristics—such as age, gender, race, and length of tenure—that are objective and easily obtained from personnel records.

As we discussed in Chapter 1, this textbook is essentially concerned with finding and analyzing the variables that have an impact on employee productivity, absence, turnover, deviance, citizenship, and satisfaction. The list of those variables—as shown in Figure 1-4—is long and contains some complicated concepts. For instance, motivation is difficult to assess and thus we need to look at factors that are easily definable and readily available. Such information is usually available in an employee's personnel file. These are known as **biographical characteristics** such as age, gender, race, and tenure.

Age

What is the relationship between age and job performance? There is a widespread belief that job performance declines with increasing age. Evidence indicates that employers think about older workers differently.[5] They see a number of positive qualities that older workers bring to their jobs, such as experience, judgment, a strong work ethic, and commitment to quality. But older workers are also perceived as lacking flexibility and as being resistant to new technology. And in a time when organizations are looking for individuals who are adaptable and open to change, the negatives associated with age clearly affect the hiring of older workers. What effect does age actually have on turnover, absenteeism, productivity, and satisfaction?

The older you get, the less likely you are to quit your job. That conclusion is based on studies of the age–turnover relationship.[6] Of course, this shouldn't be too surprising. As workers get older, they have fewer alternative job opportunities. In addition, older workers are less likely to resign than are younger workers because their long tenure tends to provide them with higher wage rates, longer paid vacations, and more attractive pension benefits.

Home Depot values the work ethic of older employees such as assistant manager Ellen Van Valen shown here, who is in her late 60s. Home Depot is one of a growing number of firms that are recruiting older workers because, compared with younger workers, they have lower turnover rates and training costs and, in many cases, better work performance. Van Valen believes that age has little to do with the desire to work but says that "older folks seem to catch on a lot quicker."

Source: Douglas Healey/ *New York Times*.

What Do You Think?

Does age affect the way people behave? Should age dictate the things people choose to do?

It's tempting to assume that age is inversely related to absenteeism. The age–absence relationship is a function of whether the absence is avoidable or unavoidable.[7] In general, older employees have lower rates of avoidable absence, such as a shopping trip, than do younger employees. However, they have higher rates of unavoidable absence, such as health problems, due to the poorer health associated with aging and the longer recovery period that older workers need when injured.

How does age affect productivity? There is a widespread belief that productivity declines with age. It is often assumed that an individual's skills—particularly speed, agility, strength, and coordination—decrease over time, and that job boredom and lack of intellectual stimulation contribute to reduced productivity. Some reviews find that age and job performance are unrelated.[8] This finding seems to be true for almost all types of jobs—both professional and nonprofessional. In sum, any decline in physical skills due to age has no impact on productivity; if there is some decline due to age, it is often replaced by gains due to experience.[9]

Our final concern is with the relationship between age and job satisfaction. Most studies indicate a positive association between age and satisfaction, at least up to age 60.[10] Other studies, however, have found a U-shaped relationship.[11] In general, satisfaction tends to increase among professionals as they age, whereas it falls among nonprofessionals during middle age and then rises again in the later years, and the most feasible explanation is that these studies are mixing both professional and non-professional employees.

Gender

The importance of the gender issue in the Arab world is shown in the 'OB in the News' box on page 44. However, we must recognize that very few important differences exist between men and women that will actually affect their job performance. There are, for instance, no consistent male–female differences in problem-solving ability, analytical skills, competitive drive, motivation, sociability, or learning ability.[12] However, psychological studies have found that women are more willing to conform to authority, and that men are more aggressive and more likely than women to have expectations of success; but those differences are minor in many work situations. One issue that does seem to differ between genders is preference for work schedules.[13] Working mothers are more likely to prefer part-time work, flexible work schedules, and telecommuting (working from home) in order to accommodate their family responsibilities.

What about absence and turnover rates? Are women less stable employees than men? First, with respect to turnover, the evidence shows no significant differences.[14] The research on absence, however, consistently indicates that women have higher rates of absenteeism than men do.[15] The most logical explanation for this finding is that the research found that cultural aspects have historically placed home and family responsibilities on the woman. This is definitely applicable to so many cultures around the world, including the Arab culture. Despite this, and because of economic difficulties, roles have changed or even reversed. In addition to caring for the home and the children, women have also become secondary breadwinners. Moreover, most men are involving themselves 'at home' and assisting women with their domestic responsibilities.

The woman's role in the workplace is now being recognized in the Arab world. For example, the Qatari Business Women's Forum (QBWF) was set up to raise awareness of the role that women play in business in Qatar. The organization holds meetings and seminars and arranges training with the aim of increasing the skills and knowledge of Qatari businesswomen—in this photo, members of the QBWF are shown together in the closing ceremony of the 2011 forum. The QBWF also aims to raise awareness of the role played by women in Qatari business and investment, and is a founding member of Middle East and North Africa Businesswomen Network, which has members from 11 countries.

Picture This

Men, you are newly married and establishing a home and family. Would you allow your wife to work or do you want her to be just a housewife? Ladies, would you marry someone who was not willing to allow you to work?

Race

What is race? It is the biological heritage people use to identify themselves according to their roots—the country they originally come from.

Race has been stressed in OB because of its relationship to employment outcomes such as personnel selection decisions, performance evaluations, pay, and workplace discrimination. The major dilemma faced by employers who use mental ability tests for selection, promotion, training, and similar personnel decisions is concern that they may have a negative impact on racial and ethnic groups.[16] The challenge, then, is to ensure that all people are treated equally and in accordance with their competencies and qualifications.

Tenure

Extensive reviews have been conducted on the seniority–productivity relationship.[17] If we define *seniority* as time on a particular job, then tenure—the number of years an individual has been with the organization, expressed as work experience—appears to be a good predictor of employee productivity. The research relating tenure to absence, turnover, and job satisfaction is quite straightforward. Studies consistently demonstrate seniority to be negatively related to absenteeism.[18]

What Do You Think?

Have your biographical characteristics been important in a job you have had? Have you ever paid close attention to any one characteristic in particular when dealing with others in a work situation?

OB in the News

Whatever Men Can Do, Women Can Do Also

"The rise of women in Arab countries goes beyond redressing historical injustices against them and ensuring their equitable treatment—notwithstanding that both are obligations for Arab societies. Indeed, the advancement of women is a prerequisite for a comprehensive Arab renaissance."

Women's welfare in the workplace in the Arab world has some way to go before reaching a level that is truly equitable and accommodating, and which incorporates a more feminine viewpoint, taking into account the special set of needs and priorities that a female workforce can bring to the table. "The opinions of Jordan's female employees towards their work and their treatment in the workplace are hugely authoritative tools for revealing the true nature of the business environment from a woman's perspective in the region today," Rabea Ataya, CEO of Bayt.com, said.

The results of a survey conducted by Bayt.com indicate that even though women still believe that men have a gender-based advantage, they do not see themselves as helpless victims of the system. The results showed that 60 percent of working women in the Middle East think they are treated equally with men, and

another 7 percent feel that they are treated even better than their male counterparts. This is largely due to what seems to be a sense of empowerment, ownership, and control over their workplace destinies and careers—a sense of ownership that comes with professional maturity, and with confidence in the system and in their own abilities and aptitudes for growth, learning, flexibility, and change.

One question asked whether women believed that their opportunities in the workplace have improved significantly. For those that answered 'yes', the results were: Bahrain (31 percent); Egypt (24 percent); Jordan (34 percent); Kuwait (27 percent); Tunisia (24 percent); UAE (28 percent); Algeria (25 percent); Lebanon (19 percent); Oman (48 percent); Qatar (28 percent); KSA (27 percent); Syria (24 percent). These results indicate that the Arab female still feels that she is unable to prove herself in the workplace.

Another point of research was about women in senior positions in organizations in the Arab world. The specific question asked to what extent women are in top management positions in the workplace. There was almost a general agreement in response across the region: 22 percent said 'yes to a large

extent;' 28 percent answered 'yes to a fair extent;' 27 percent said 'to a small extent;' 20 percent said 'no;' and 5 percent responded with 'don't know/can't say.'

A final relevant piece of information was about compensation packages. In particular, it asked women how their compensation compares with those of male colleagues in a similar position. The results were quite surprising. In Bahrain, 24 percent believe they are paid less and 52 percent say that pay is equal: Kuwait (58 percent less & 28 percent equal); KSA (52 percent less & 29 percent equal); UAE (49 percent less & 36 percent equal); Lebanon (39 percent less & 46 percent equal); Jordan (38 percent less & 44 percent equal) and Qatar (48 percent less & 31 percent equal). We see that there is a discrepancy in responses, and females still have smaller paychecks than males in the Arab world. It seems that gender differences continue to exist in the region.

Sources: Statistics and quotes taken from UNDP Saudi Arabia website, www.undp.org.sa/sa/index.php?option=com_content&view=article&id=23&Itemid=48&lang=ar Arab Human Development Report 2010; Women Rise Up the Ranks in Middle East Workplace, Latest Bayt.com and YouGovSiraj Study Shows," Bayt.com press release, August 2008; and "Women in the Middle East Workplace" survey, July 2008, Bayt.com.

Learning

> **3** *Define* learning *and outline the principles of the three major theories of learning.*

Whether we want to admit it or not, the biographical traits and the types of ability we saw in the previous sections do have an impact on the learning process. In this section, we define *learning*, present three popular learning theories, and describe how managers can facilitate employee learning.

Learning
A relatively permanent change in behavior that occurs as a result of experience.

A Definition of *Learning*

What is **learning**? *Learning* occurs all the time. Therefore, a generally accepted definition of learning is "any relatively permanent change in behavior that occurs as a result of experience."[19] Ironically, we can say that changes in behavior indicate that learning has taken place and that learning is a change in behavior.

The previous definition suggests that we can see changes taking place, but we can't see the learning itself. The concept is theoretical and, hence, not directly observable:[20]

> You have seen people in the process of learning, you have seen people who behave in a particular way as a result of learning and some of you (in fact, I guess the majority of you) have "learned" at some time in your life. In other words, we infer that learning has taken place if an individual behaves, reacts, responds as a result of experience in a manner different from the way he formerly behaved.

Our definition has several components that deserve clarification. First, learning involves change. Change may be good or bad from an organizational point of view. People can learn unfavorable as well as favorable behaviors. Second, the change must be obvious because some changes may be only reflexive or a result of fatigue (or a sudden burst of energy) and thus may not represent learning. Third, some form of experience is necessary for learning. Experience may be acquired directly through observation or practice, or it may be acquired indirectly, as through reading. The crucial test still remains: Does this experience result in a relatively permanent change in behavior? If the answer is 'yes,' we can say that learning has taken place.

In the Arab world, learning is also required to enhance and develop competencies. To illustrate, The Arab Leadership Academy (ALA), a Kuwaiti company, has joined forces with Linkage Inc. of Burlington, Massachusetts, USA, to offer Arab leaders a leadership development program that focuses on on-the-job learning, peer learning and competency-based learning.[21]

Theories of Learning

Three theories have been offered to explain the process by which we acquire patterns of behavior. These are classical conditioning, operant conditioning, and social learning.

Classical conditioning

A type of conditioning in which an individual responds to some stimulus that would not ordinarily produce such a response.

Classical Conditioning   Classical conditioning came out of experiments to teach dogs to salivate in response to the ringing of a bell even if no food was offered, conducted in the early 1900s by Russian physiologist Ivan Pavlov.[22]

In an organizational setting, classical conditioning is very practical. For example, at one manufacturing plant, every time the top executives from the head office were scheduled to make a visit, the plant management would clean up the administrative offices and wash the windows. This went on for years. Eventually, employees would turn on their best behavior and look good whenever the windows were cleaned—even when the cleaning was not due to a visit from top management. People had learned to associate the cleaning of the windows with a visit from the head office.

Therefore, classical conditioning is passive. Something happens, and we react in a specific way. It is encouraged in response to a specific, identifiable event and becomes a simple reflexive behavior. But most behavior—particularly the complex behavior of individuals in organizations—is voluntary rather than reflexive.

Operant conditioning

A type of conditioning in which desired voluntary behavior leads to a reward or prevents a punishment.

Operant Conditioning   Operant conditioning argues that behavior is a function of its consequences. That is, people learn to behave to get something they want or to avoid something they don't want. Operant behavior means voluntary or learned behavior in contrast to reflexive or unlearned behavior. The tendency to repeat such behavior is influenced by the reinforcement (types of support)

Toyota Motor Corporation applies social learning theory in teaching employees skills they need to meet the company's high standards of quality and efficiency. At its Global Production Center training facility in Toyota City, Japan, employees from factories around the world learn production techniques through observation and direct experience. Trainees first watch computerized 'visual manuals' to learn basic skills. Then, under the tutelage of an experienced production master, they practice the skills. In this photo, a trainer (left) models a spray-painting technique while a trainee practices the skill.

or lack of reinforcement brought about by the consequences of the behavior. Therefore, reinforcement strengthens a behavior and increases the likelihood that it will be repeated.

To illustrate, a professor places a mark by a student's name each time that student makes a contribution to class discussions. Operant conditioning would argue that this practice is motivating because it conditions students to expect a reward (earning class credit) each time they show a specific behavior (speaking up in class). The concept of operant conditioning was part of a broader concept of **behaviorism**, which argues that behavior follows stimuli in a relatively unthinking manner.

Behaviorism

A theory that argues that behavior follows stimuli in a relatively unthinking manner.

Picture This

Your boss tells you that if you work overtime during this busy season, you will be compensated for it at your next performance appraisal. However, when performance-appraisal time comes, you find that you are given no positive reinforcement (acknowledgment) for your overtime work. The next time your boss asks you to work overtime, what will you do? Your behavior can be explained by operant conditioning: If a behavior fails to be positively reinforced, the probability that the behavior will be repeated declines.

Social Learning   Social learning is an extension of operant conditioning— discussed in the previous section—that assumes that behavior is a function of consequences. Social learning also acknowledges the existence of observational learning and the importance of perception in learning. People respond to how they perceive and define consequences, not to the objective consequences themselves.

Individuals can learn by observing what happens to other people and by just being told about something as well as through direct experiences. For example, much of what we have learned comes from watching models such as parents,

Social-learning theory

The view that people can learn through observation and direct experience.

teachers, peers, television performers, bosses, and so forth. This view that we can learn through both observation and direct experience is called **social-learning theory.**[23]

The influence of models is central to the social-learning viewpoint. Four processes have been found to determine the influence that a model will have on an individual:

1. **Attentional processes.** People learn by paying attention to a model's critical features.
2. **Retention processes.** People learn by remembering the model's action.
3. **Motor reproduction processes.** People learn not just by watching the model but by actually doing.
4. **Reinforcement processes**. People learn to exhibit the model's behavior when they know that positive incentives or rewards are provided.

Shaping: A Managerial Tool

4 Define shaping *and show how it can be used in OB.*

Managers are always concerned with how they can teach employees to behave in ways that most benefit the organization. Managers want employees to be effective and efficient. When we attempt to mold individuals by guiding their learning step-by-step, we are **shaping behavior**.

Shaping behavior

Systematically reinforcing each successive step that moves an individual closer to the desired response.

Consider a situation in which an employee's behavior is different from that required by management. If management rewarded the individual only when he showed desirable responses, there might be very little reinforcement taking place. In such a case, shaping offers a logical approach toward achieving the desired behavior.

For this reason, we *shape* behavior by systematically reinforcing each step that moves the individual closer to the desired response. If an employee who has always been a half-hour late for work comes in only 20 minutes late, we can reinforce that improvement.

Methods of Shaping Behavior   There are four ways to shape behavior through positive reinforcement, negative reinforcement, punishment, and extinction.

Following a response with something pleasant is called *positive reinforcement.* This would describe, for instance, a boss who praises an employee for a job well done. Following a response by the termination or withdrawal of something unpleasant is called *negative reinforcement.* For example, if your college instructor asks a question and you don't know the answer, looking through your lecture notes is less likely to make the instructor call on you because you are avoiding eye contact. This is a negative reinforcement because you have learned that looking busily through your notes prevents the instructor from calling on you.

Punishment is causing an unpleasant condition in an attempt to eliminate an undesirable behavior such as giving an employee a 2-day suspension from work without pay for stealing from the office. Furthermore, eliminating any reinforcement that is maintaining a behavior is called *extinction*. That is, an effective way for instructors to discourage students from asking questions in class is to ignore them when they raise their hands to ask questions. Hence, students stop raising hands since it is met with an absence of reinforcement.

Both positive and negative reinforcement result in learning. However, both punishment and extinction weaken behavior and tend to decrease its subsequent frequency. In shaping behavior, a critical issue is the timing of reinforcements. This is an issue we'll consider now.

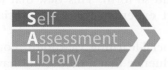

HOW GOOD AM I AT DISCIPLINING OTHERS?

In the Self-Assessment Library (available online), take assessment II.B.5 (How Good Am I at Disciplining Others?).

Continuous reinforcement

Reinforcing a desired behavior each time it is demonstrated.

Intermittent reinforcement

Reinforcing a desired behavior often enough to make the behavior worth repeating, but not every time it is demonstrated.

Fixed-interval schedule

Spacing rewards at uniform time intervals.

Variable-interval schedule

Distributing rewards in time so that reinforcements are unpredictable.

Fixed-ratio schedule

Initiating rewards after a fixed or constant number of responses.

Variable-ratio schedule

Varying the reward relative to the behavior of the individual.

OB Mod (organizational behavior modification)

The application of reinforcement concepts to individuals in the work setting.

Schedules of Reinforcement   The two major types of reinforcement schedules are *continuous* and *intermittent*. First, a **continuous reinforcement** schedule reinforces the desired behavior each and every time it is demonstrated. Take, for example, the case of someone who never arrives at work on time. Every time he or she is not late, their manager might compliment them on their desirable behavior. Second, with **intermittent reinforcement**, on the other hand, not every instance of the desirable behavior is reinforced, but reinforcement is given often enough to make the behavior worth repeating.

An intermittent reinforcement can be of a ratio or interval type. *Ratio schedules* depend on how many responses the subject makes, whereas *interval schedules* depend on how much time has passed since the previous reinforcement.

When rewards are spaced at uniform time intervals, the reinforcement schedule is a **fixed-interval schedule**. The critical variable is time, which is held constant. This is the predominant schedule for most salaried workers in the Arab world. When you get your paycheck on a weekly, semimonthly, monthly, or other predetermined time basis, you're rewarded on a fixed-interval reinforcement schedule.

If rewards are distributed in time so that reinforcements are unpredictable, the schedule is a **variable-interval schedule**. When an instructor advises her class that pop quizzes will be given during the term (the exact number of which is unknown to the students) and the quizzes will account for 20 percent of the term grade, she is using a variable-interval schedule. Similarly, a series of randomly timed unannounced visits to a company office by the corporate audit staff is an example of a variable-interval schedule.

In a **fixed-ratio schedule**, after a fixed or constant number of responses are given, a reward is initiated. For example, a piece-rate incentive plan is a fixed-ratio schedule; the employee receives a reward based on the number of work pieces generated. If the piece rate for a zipper installer in a dressmaking factory is US$5 per dozen, the reinforcement (money in this case) is fixed to the number of zippers sewn into garments. After every dozen is sewn in, the installer has earned another US$5.

When the reward varies relative to the behavior of the individual, he or she is said to be reinforced on a **variable-ratio schedule**. Salespeople on commission are examples of individuals on such a reinforcement schedule. On some occasions, they may make a sale after only 2 calls on a potential customer. On other occasions, they might need to make 20 or more calls to secure a sale. The reward, then, is variable in relation to the number of successful calls the salesperson makes.

Table 2-3 summarizes the schedules of reinforcement by describing in detail the type of reinforcement, the effects the reinforcement has on behavior, and by presenting an example for each reinforcement schedule.

Behavior Modification   To conclude this section on learning, we must mention the concept of behavior modification, also known as **OB Mod (organizational behavior modification)**, which represents the application of reinforcement concepts to individuals in the workplace. The typical OB Mod program follows a five-step problem-solving model: (1) identify critical behaviors; (2) develop baseline data; (3) identify behavioral consequences; (4) develop and implement an intervention strategy; and (5) evaluate performance improvement.[24]

TABLE 2-3   Schedules of Reinforcement

Reinforcement Schedule	Nature of Reinforcement	Effect on Behavior	Example
Continuous	Reward given after each desired behavior	Fast learning of new behavior but rapid extinction	Compliments
Fixed-interval	Reward given at fixed time intervals	Average and irregular performance with rapid extinction	Weekly paychecks
Variable-interval	Reward given at variable time intervals	Moderately high and stable performance with slow extinction	Pop quizzes
Fixed ratio	Reward given at fixed amounts of output	High and stable performance attained quickly but also with rapid extinction	Piece-rate pay
Variable-ratio	Reward given at variable amounts of output	Very high performance with slow extinction	Commissioned sales

Everything an employee does on the job is not equally important in terms of performance outcomes. The first step in OB Mod, therefore, is to identify the critical behaviors that make a significant impact on the employee's job performance. The second step requires the manager to develop some baseline performance data. This is obtained by determining the number of times the identified behavior is occurring under present conditions. The third step is to perform a functional analysis to identify the behavioral contingencies or consequences of performance. This tells the manager the reasons why we stop the behavior and the consequences that are currently maintaining it.

Once the functional analysis is complete, the manager is ready to develop and implement an intervention strategy to strengthen desirable performance behaviors and weaken undesirable behaviors. The appropriate plan of action will include changing some elements of the performance–reward linkage—structure, processes, technology, groups, or the task—with the goal of making high-level performance more rewarding. The final step in OB Mod is to evaluate performance improvement to determine if the modifications that were made have been effective and rewarding to both the employee and the organization.

On the whole, organizations will use OB Mod to improve employee productivity; to reduce errors, absenteeism, tardiness, and accident rates; and to improve friendliness toward customers.[25]

Problems with OB Mod and Reinforcement Theory   As we all know, everything in life has both its advantages and disadvantages. Organizational behavior issues are no exception. Accordingly, we need to highlight the problems with the reinforcement theory and OB modification.

Picture This

You receive praise from a supervisor. Specifically, your course instructor compliments you for asking a good question. A behaviorist would argue that this shapes your behavior because you find the stimulus (the compliment) pleasant and therefore respond by attempting to ask other questions that will generate the same reward. However, imagine, for example, that you had to weigh the pleasant feelings produced by your professor's praise against the negative comments from jealous classmates. Your choice of what to do would likely be dictated by weighing the value of these stimuli, which may be a rather complex mental process involving thinking and feeling. This will be discussed later in this chapter.

To identify critical behaviors and improve employee performance, Hussein Wehbe, country manager of Aramex Bahrain, initiated managerial involvement. More than 20 members of management from the Bahrain office joined the couriers in delivering shipments. The aim was for managers to gain a feel for what their staff experience every day and to appreciate their hard work. Accompanying the couriers helped managers to study one aspect of OB Mod, identifying behaviors that might cause problems or that were particularly desirable.

Source: Aramex Bahrain Management Spend a Day in Life of a Courier," *Aramex.com*, May 2010

Personality

<table>
<tr><td>**5**</td><td>*Define* personality, *describe how it is measured, and explain the factors that determine an individual's personality.*</td></tr>
</table>

In the previous sections, we learned about ability and learning and other specific characteristics that may affect them. Now we turn our attention to personality. Why are some people quiet and passive, while others are loud and aggressive? Are certain personality types better adapted than others for certain job types? These and other questions are critical to help us understand the essence of organizational behavior, but first we need to address a more basic question: What is personality?

What Is Personality?

When psychologists talk of personality, they mean a dynamic concept describing the growth and development of a person's whole psychological system and the stress here is on the word *whole*. That is, we shouldn't focus on parts of the person, but rather on the aggregate whole that is greater than the sum of the parts.

Defining *Personality*   The most common definition of *personality* was produced by Gordon Allport nearly 70 years ago. He said personality is "the dynamic organization within the individual of those psychophysical systems that determine his unique adjustments to his environment."[26] For our purposes, let's think of **personality** as the sum total of ways in which an individual reacts to and interacts with others.

Personality
The sum total of ways in which an individual reacts to and interacts with others.

Measuring Personality

The most important reason managers need to know how to measure personality is that research has shown that personality tests are useful in hiring decisions. In other words, it allows managers to place the right person in the right place. Scores on personality tests help managers forecast who is the best candidate for a job.[27] And some managers want to know how people score on personality tests to better understand and more effectively manage the people who work for them. Far and away the most common means of measuring personality is through self-report surveys, through which employees can paint a clear picture of themselves for managers. Nonetheless, there are weaknesses to this method. One example is that the respondent might lie or practice impression management—that is, the person could falsely create a good impression. Another problem is accuracy. In other words, a perfectly good candidate could have just been in a bad mood when the survey was taken.

Personality Determinants   An early debate in personality research was concerned with whether an individual's personality was the result of heredity or of the environment. Was the personality predetermined at birth, or was it the result of the individual's interaction with his or her surroundings? Clearly, there's no simple black-and-white answer. Personality appears to be a result of both hereditary and environmental factors.

Heredity refers to factors determined at conception. Physical stature, facial attractiveness, gender, temperament, muscle composition and reflexes, energy level, and biological rhythms are generally considered to be either completely or substantially influenced by our parents.

Studies of young children lend strong support to the power of heredity.[28] Evidence demonstrates that traits such as shyness, fear, and aggression can be traced to inherited genetic characteristics. This finding suggests that some personality traits may be built into the same genetic code that affects factors such as height and hair color.

To illustrate, the study of many twins suggests that the parental environment doesn't add much to personality development. In other words, the personalities of identical twins raised in different households are more similar to each other than to the personalities of the siblings that were actually raised in the same household.

Definitely, this does not suggest that personality never changes. Over periods of time, people's personalities do change. An analogy to intelligence may make this clearer. Children become smarter as they age so that nearly everyone is smarter at age 20 than they were at age 10. Still, if Ahmad at age 10 is smarter than Tarek at age 10, he will probably also be so when they are both aged 20. The same holds true with personality: If you are more dependable than your sibling now, then that is likely to be true in 20 years, even though you both should become more dependable over time.

Early work on the structure of personality tried to identify and label enduring characteristics that describe an individual's behavior. Popular characteristics include being shy, aggressive, submissive, lazy, ambitious, loyal, and timid. When someone exhibits these characteristics in a large number of situations, we call them **personality traits**.[29] The more consistent the characteristic and the more frequently a trait occurs in diverse situations, the more important that trait is in describing the individual (see Figure 2-1).

Over the past 20 years, two approaches—the Myers-Briggs Type Indicator and the Big Five Model—have become the dominant frameworks for identifying and classifying traits.

Heredity

Factors determined at conception, one's biological, physiological, and inherent psychological makeup.

Personality traits

Enduring characteristics that describe an individual's behavior.

Figure **2-1**

Source: PEANUTS. Reprinted with permission of United Features Syndicate, Inc.

The Myers-Briggs Type Indicator

6 Describe the Myers-Briggs Type Indicator personality framework and assess its strengths and weaknesses.

The Myers-Briggs Type Indicator (MBTI) is the most widely used personality-assessment instrument in the world.[30] It's a 100-question personality test that asks people how they usually feel or act in particular situations. On the basis of their answers, individuals are classified as extraverted or introverted (E or I), sensing or intuitive (S or N), thinking or feeling (T or F), and judging or perceiving (J or P). These terms are defined as follows:

Myers-Briggs Type Indicator (MBTI)

A personality test that taps four characteristics and classifies people into 1 of 16 personality types.

- *Extraverted versus introverted.* Extraverted individuals are outgoing, sociable, and assertive. Introverts are quiet and shy.
- *Sensing versus intuitive.* Sensing types are practical and prefer routine and order. They focus on details. Intuitives rely on unconscious processes and look at the 'big picture.'
- *Thinking versus feeling.* Thinking types use reason and logic to handle problems. Feeling types rely on their personal values and emotions.
- *Judging versus perceiving.* Judging types want control and prefer their world to be ordered and structured. Perceiving types are flexible and spontaneous.

These classifications together describe 16 personality types. To illustrate, let's take several examples. INTJs are visionaries. They usually have original minds and great drive for their own ideas and purposes. They are skeptical, critical, independent, determined, and often stubborn. ESTJs are organizers. They are realistic, logical, analytical, and decisive, and have a natural head for business or mechanics. They like to organize and run activities. The ENTP type is a conceptualizer. He or she is innovative, individualistic, versatile, and attracted to entrepreneurial ideas. This person tends to be resourceful in solving challenging problems, but may neglect routine assignments.

The MBTI is widely used in practice by organizations including Apple Computer and General Electric. In spite of its popularity, the evidence is mixed as to whether the MBTI is a valid measure of personality—with most of the evidence suggesting that it isn't.[31] One problem is that it forces a person into either one type or another (that is, you're either introverted or extraverted). There is no in-between, though people can be both extraverted and introverted to some degree. The best we can say is that the MBTI can be a valuable tool for increasing self-awareness and providing career guidance. But because results tend to be unrelated to job performance, managers probably shouldn't use it as a selection test for job candidates.

The Big Five Personality Model

Identify the key traits in the Big Five personality model and demonstrate how the Big Five traits predict behavior at work.

The MBTI may lack strong supporting evidence, but the same can't be said about the five-factor model of personality called the **Big Five Model**, or the 'Big Five.' An impressive body of research supports its thesis that five basic dimensions underlie all others and encompass most of the significant variation in human personality.[32]

The Big Five factors are:

Big Five model

A personality assessment model that taps five basic dimensions.

Extraversion

A personality dimension describing someone who is sociable, gregarious, and assertive.

Agreeableness

A personality dimension that describes someone who is good natured, cooperative, and trusting.

Conscientiousness

A personality dimension that describes someone who is responsible, dependable, persistent, and organized.

Emotional stability

A personality dimension that characterizes someone as calm, self-confident, secure (positive) versus nervous, depressed, and insecure (negative).

Openness to experience

A personality dimension that characterizes someone in terms of imagination, sensitivity, and curiosity.

- **Extraversion**: Extraverts tend to be hyperactive, assertive, and sociable. Introverts tend to be reserved, shy, and quiet.
- **Agreeableness**: Highly agreeable people are cooperative, warm, and trusting. People who score low on agreeableness are cold and disagreeable.
- **Conscientiousness**: A highly conscientious person is responsible, organized, dependable, and persistent. Those who score low on this dimension are easily distracted, disorganized, and unreliable.
- **Emotional stability**: People with positive emotional stability tend to be calm, self-confident, and secure. Those with high negative scores tend to be nervous, anxious, depressed, and insecure.
- **Openness to experience**: Extremely open people are creative, curious, and artistically sensitive. Those at the other end of the openness category are conventional and find comfort in the familiar.

How Do the Big Five Traits Predict Behavior at Work?   Research on the Big Five has found relationships between these personality dimensions and job performance.[33] As the authors of the most-cited review put it: "The preponderance of evidence shows that individuals who are dependable, reliable, careful, thorough, able to plan, organized, hardworking, persistent, and achievement-oriented tend to have higher job performance in most if not all occupations."[34]

One particular study about the Five-Factor Model (FFM) personality traits and Organizational Citizenship Behavior (OCB) in the United Arab Emirates found interesting results.[35] In general, the results appear to support FFM as a predictor of OCB. For example, employees who scored highly for conscientiousness, openness to experience, or agreeableness tended to have high scores for interpersonal performance. In other words, it seems that good FFM traits make people more effective, enhancing their communication and interpersonal skills as well as their team performance.

Although conscientiousness is the Big Five trait most consistently related to job performance, the other traits are related to aspects of performance in some situations. All five traits also have other implications for work and for life. Figure 2-2 looks at the implications of each of these traits.

Picture This

You are recruited as a receptionist in the emergency section of a hospital. What are the personality traits you need to cope with this job?

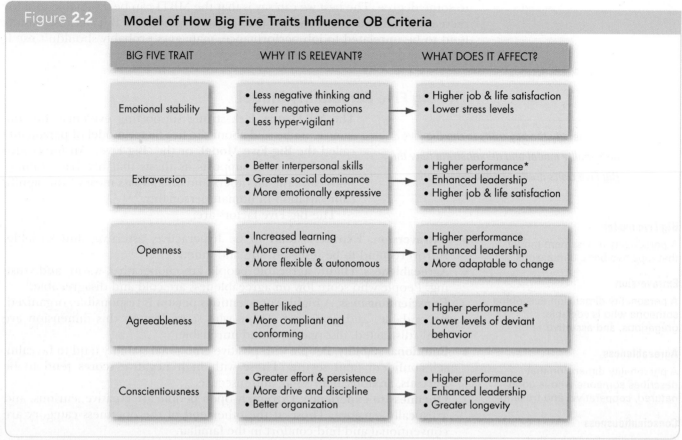

Figure 2-2   Model of How Big Five Traits Influence OB Criteria

BIG FIVE TRAIT	WHY IT IS RELEVANT?	WHAT DOES IT AFFECT?
Emotional stability	• Less negative thinking and fewer negative emotions • Less hyper-vigilant	• Higher job & life satisfaction • Lower stress levels
Extraversion	• Better interpersonal skills • Greater social dominance • More emotionally expressive	• Higher performance* • Enhanced leadership • Higher job & life satisfaction
Openness	• Increased learning • More creative • More flexible & autonomous	• Higher performance • Enhanced leadership • More adaptable to change
Agreeableness	• Better liked • More compliant and conforming	• Higher performance* • Lower levels of deviant behavior
Conscientiousness	• Greater effort & persistence • More drive and discipline • Better organization	• Higher performance • Enhanced leadership • Greater longevity

*In jobs requiring significant teamwork or frequent interpersonal interactions.

Other Personality Traits Relevant to OB

8 *Identify other personality traits relevant to OB.*

Although the Big Five traits have proven to be highly relevant to OB, they don't use all the traits we can use to describe someone's personality. Now we'll look at other, more specific, personality attributes that have been found to be powerful predictors of behavior in organizations. In particular, we will address one's core self-evaluation, Machiavellianism, narcissism, self-monitoring, propensity for risk taking, and the Type A, Type B, and proactive personalities.

Core self-evaluation
The degree to which an individual likes or dislikes himself or herself, whether the person sees himself or herself as capable and effective, and whether the person feels in control of his or her environment or powerless over the environment.

Core Self-Evaluation   People who have positive **core self-evaluations** like themselves and see themselves as effective, capable, and in control of their environment. This self-perspective is the concept of core self-evaluation. Those with negative core self-evaluations tend to dislike themselves, question their capabilities, and view themselves as powerless over their environment.[36] In Chapter 3, we will see that core self-evaluations relate to job satisfaction because people with positive core self-evaluations see more challenge in their job and actually attain more complex jobs.

Moreover, people with positive core self-evaluations perform better than others because they set more ambitious goals, are more committed to their goals, and persist longer at attempting to reach these goals. Meanwhile, you might wonder whether someone can be *too* positive. In other words, what happens when someone thinks he or she is capable, but is actually incompetent? One study of Fortune 500 CEOs, for example, showed that many are overconfident, and their perceived infallibility often causes them to make bad decisions.[37]

Nabil Habayeb, President and CEO of General Electric Middle East, considers the region's environmental problems to be huge, and thinks that they can only be resolved through developing a shared approach. Habayeb believes that what is needed is an understanding of problems by the leadership, a commitment to resolve problems, and a partnership with all stakeholders. Habayeb's positive core self-evaluation is reflected in these ambitious goals, and his commitment to achieving them.

Machiavellianism

The degree to which an individual is pragmatic, maintains emotional distance, and believes that ends can justify means.

Machiavellianism   The personality characteristic of **Machiavellianism** (often abbreviated Mach) is named after Niccolo Machiavelli, who wrote in the sixteenth century on how to gain and use power. An individual high in Machiavellianism is realistic, maintains emotional distance, and believes that ends can justify means. The phrase 'If it works, use it' is consistent with a high-Mach perspective. A considerable amount of research has been directed toward relating high- and low-Mach personalities to certain behavioral outcomes.[38] High Machs manipulate more, win more, are persuaded less, and persuade others more than do low Machs.[39] It has also been found that high Machs flourish (1) when they interact face-to-face with others rather than indirectly; (2) when the situation has a minimal number of rules and regulations, thus allowing latitude for improvisation; and (3) when emotional involvement with details irrelevant to winning distracts low Machs.[40] Thus, whether high Machs make good employees depends on the type of job. In jobs that require bargaining skills (such as labor negotiation) or that offer substantial rewards for winning (such as commissioned sales), high Machs will be productive.

Narcissism

The tendency to be arrogant, have a grandiose sense of self-importance, require excessive admiration, and have a sense of entitlement.

Narcissism   In psychology, **narcissism** describes a person who has a very high sense of self-importance, requires excessive admiration, has a sense of entitlement, and is arrogant. To illustrate, Anwar likes to be the center of attention. He likes to look at himself in the mirror a lot. He has extravagant dreams and seems to consider himself a person of many talents. Anwar is a narcissist. The term is from the Greek myth of Narcissus, the story of a man so vain and proud that he fell in love with his own image in the mirror.

Because narcissists often want to gain the admiration of others and receive affirmation of their superiority, they tend to 'talk down' to those who threaten them, treating others as if they were inferior. Narcissists also tend to be selfish and exploitive, and they often carry the attitude that others exist for their benefit.[41] Studies indicate that narcissists are rated by their bosses as less effective at their jobs than others, particularly when it comes to helping other people.[42]

Self-monitoring

A personality trait that measures an individual's ability to adjust his or her behavior to external, situational factors.

Self-Monitoring   **Self-monitoring** refers to an individual's ability to adjust his or her behavior to external, situational factors.[43] Individuals high in self-monitoring show considerable adaptability in adjusting their behavior to external situational factors. They are highly sensitive to external cues and can behave differently in different situations. High self-monitors are capable of presenting striking contradictions between their public persona and their private self. Low self-monitors can't hide themselves. The evidence indicates that high self-monitors tend to pay closer attention to the behavior of others and are more capable of conforming than are low self-monitors.[44] They also receive better performance ratings, are more likely to emerge as leaders, and show less commitment to their organizations.[45] In addition, high self-monitoring managers tend to be more mobile in their careers, receive more promotions (both internal and cross-organizational), and are more likely to occupy central positions in an organization.[46]

Risk Taking   Donald Trump stands out for his willingness to take risks. He started with almost nothing in the 1960s. By the mid-1980s, he had made a fortune by betting on a New York City real estate market. Then, trying to capitalize on his previous successes, Trump overextended himself. By 1994, he had a *negative* net worth of US$850 million. Never fearful of taking chances, 'The Donald' leveraged the few assets he had left on several New York, New Jersey, and Caribbean real estate ventures. He hit it big again. In 2007, *Forbes* estimated his net worth at US$2.9 billion.

People differ in their willingness to take chances. This propensity to assume or avoid risk has been shown to have an impact on how long it takes managers to make a decision, and how much information they require before making a choice. For instance, 79 managers worked on simulated personnel exercises that required them to make hiring decisions.[47] High-risk-taking managers made more rapid decisions and used less information in making their choices than did the low-risk-taking managers. Interestingly, decision accuracy was the same for both groups.

For instance, a high-risk-taking propensity may lead to more effective performance for a stock trader in a brokerage firm because that type of job demands rapid decision making. On the other hand, a willingness to take risks might prove a major obstacle to an accountant who performs auditing activities. The latter job might be better filled by someone with a low-risk-taking propensity.

Type A personality

Aggressive involvement in a chronic, incessant struggle to achieve more and more in less and less time and, if necessary, against the opposing efforts of other things or other people.

Type A and B Personalities   Do you know people who are very competitive and always seem to be experiencing a sense of time urgency? People who want things done immediately? If you do, it's a good bet those people have a **Type A personality**. A person with a Type A personality is "aggressively involved in a chronic, incessant struggle to achieve more and more in less and less time, and, if required to do so, against the opposing efforts of other things or other persons."[48] People with Type A personality:

1. Are always moving, walking, and eating rapidly
2. Feel impatient with the rate at which most events take place
3. Strive to think or do two or more things at once
4. Cannot cope with leisure time
5. Are obsessed with numbers, measuring their success in terms of how many or how much of everything they acquire.

Type B personality

Rarely harried by the desire to obtain a wildly increasing number of things or participate in an endless growing series of events in an ever decreasing amount of time.

In contrast to the Type A personality is the **Type B personality**, who is exactly opposite. Type Bs are "rarely harried by the desire to obtain a wildly increasing number of things or participate in an endless growing series of events in an ever-decreasing amount of time."[49] Type Bs never suffer from a sense of time urgency with its accompanying impatience, can relax without guilt, and so on.

So as a result of all these 'quick' characteristics, do Type As differ from Type Bs in their ability to get hired? The answer appears to be 'yes.'[50] Type As do

Real estate developer Donald Trump is willing to take chances. His risk-taking personality enables him to thrive in situations that others find perilous and stressful. Undeterred by financial setbacks, Trump continues to build his net worth by developing new projects such as the Trump International Hotel and Tower in Chicago (shown here), co-producing and starring in *The Apprentice*, marketing lines of clothing and furniture, and authoring best-selling books.

better than Type Bs in job interviews because they are more likely to be judged as having desirable traits such as high drive, competence, aggressiveness, and success motivation.

What Do You Think?

Do you have a Type A or Type B personality?

Proactive Personality   Did you ever notice that some people actively take the initiative to improve their current situation or create new ones, while others sit by passively reacting to situations? The former individuals have been described as having **proactive personalities**.[51] Proactives identify opportunities, show initiative, take action, and persevere until meaningful change occurs. They create positive change in their environment, regardless of, or even in spite of, constraints or obstacles.[52] Not surprisingly, proactives have many desirable behaviors that organizations look for. If an organization requires people with entrepreneurial initiative, proactives make good candidates; however, these are people who are also more likely to leave an organization to start their own businesses.[53] As individuals, proactives are more likely than others to achieve career success.[54] They select, create, and influence work situations in their favor. Proactives are more likely than others to seek out job and organizational information, develop contacts in high places, engage in career planning, and demonstrate persistence in the face of career obstacles.

In this section, we discussed personality traits—the enduring characteristics that describe a person's behavior—we now will take a closer look at values. Although personality and values are related, they're not the same. Values are often very specific and describe belief systems rather than behavioral tendencies. Some beliefs or values don't say much about a person's personality, and we don't always act in ways that are consistent with our values.

Proactive personality

People who identify opportunities, show initiative, take action, and persevere until meaningful change occurs.

Values

Define values, demonstrate the importance of values, and contrast terminal and instrumental values.

Values
Basic convictions that a specific mode of conduct or end-state of existence is personally or socially preferable to an opposite or converse mode of conduct or end-state of existence.

Value system
A hierarchy based on a ranking of an individual's values in terms of their intensity.

Is execution right or wrong? If a person likes power, is that good or bad? The answers to these questions are related to a person's values. Some might say that execution is right because it is an appropriate penalty for crimes such as murder; as the saying goes, 'an eye for an eye' or, as we say in the Arab world, 'a tooth for a tooth.' However, others might argue, just as strongly, that no government has the right to take anyone's life.

Values represent basic beliefs that guide the actions of an individual, but many times the way the individual behaves may be very different to the way in which all other people behave. In other words, values show an individual's judgment as to what is right, good, or desirable. A person's **value system** is identified by the importance we give to values such as freedom, pleasure, self-respect, honesty, obedience, and equality.

Initially, values are established in our early years—from parents, teachers, friends, and others. As children, we are told that certain behavior is *always* desirable or *always* undesirable. For instance, our parents taught us that if you are in a place where there is an old person standing while you are sitting, the right thing to do is to stand and give your seat to the old person.

What Do You Think?

Our parents taught us that it is wrong to lie. However, many people tell what they call a 'white lie'. Is that right? The answer will partly explain some of the values you have.

The Importance of Values

Values are important to the study of organizational behavior because they lay the foundation for our understanding of people's attitudes and motivation and because they influence our perceptions. Values also generally influence attitudes and behavior.[55]

Picture This

You understand that paying employees on the basis of their performance is right, while paying on the basis of seniority is wrong. Thus, how do you feel when you find out that the organization you've just joined rewards seniority and not performance? You're likely to be disappointed—and this can lead to job dissatisfaction and a decision not to show a high level of effort because 'it's probably not going to lead to more money anyway.'

Terminal values
Desirable end-states of existence; the goals a person would like to achieve during his or her lifetime.

Instrumental values
Preferable modes of behavior or means of achieving one's terminal values.

Terminal versus Instrumental Values   Milton Rokeach created the Rokeach Value Survey (RVS).[56] It consists of two sets of values. One he called **terminal values**—the goals persons would like to achieve during their lifetime such as a comfortable life, equality, and social recognition. The other set he called **instrumental values**—the type of behavior that will allow you to achieve the terminal values such as ambition, broad-mindedness, and helpfulness.

Several studies confirm that RVS values differ among groups.[57] People in the same occupations or categories (for example, corporate managers, union members, parents, students) tend to hold similar values. For instance, one study compared corporate executives, members of the steelworkers' union, and members of a community activist group. Although there was a good deal of

TABLE 2-4 Mean Value Ranking of Executives, Union Members, and Activists (Top Five Only)					
Executives		**Union Members**		**Activists**	
Terminal	**Instrumental**	**Terminal**	**Instrumental**	**Terminal**	**Instrumental**
1. Self-respect	1. Honest	1. Family security	1. Responsible	1. Equality	1. Honest
2. Family security	2. Responsible	2. Freedom	2. Honest	2. A world of peace	2. Helpful
3. Freedom	3. Capable	3. Happiness	3. Courageous	3. Family security	3. Courageous
4. A sense of accomplishment	4. Ambitious	4. Self-respect	4. Independent	4. Self-respect	4. Responsible
5. Happiness	5. Independent	5. Mature love	5. Capable	5. Freedom	5. Capable

Source: Based on W.C. Frederick and J. Weber, "The Values of Corporate Managers and Their Critics: An Empirical Description and Normative Implications," in W.C. Frederick and L.E. Preston (eds.), *Business Ethics: Research Issues and Empirical Studies* (Greenwich, CT: JAI Press, 1990), pp. 123–144.

overlap among the three groups,[58] there were also some very significant differences, as shown in Table 2-4. For example, the activists had value preferences that were quite different from those of the other two groups. They ranked 'equality' as their most important terminal value; executives and union members ranked this value 12 and 13, respectively.

The Relationship Between an Individual's Personality and the Workplace

10 Show the relationship between individual personality and the workplace.

Times have changed; people have changed; values have changed. Organizations used to only be concerned with personality because their primary objective was to match individuals to specific jobs. Although that concern still exists, today organizations have a different approach. Consequently, organizations are interested in how well the individual's personality *and* values match the personality and values of the *organization*. Why? Managers today are more interested in an applicant's *flexibility* to meet changing situations and to show commitment to the organization.

In the coming sections, we will discuss person–job fit and person–organization fit in more detail.

Person–Job Fit

Personality–job fit theory

A theory that identifies six personality types and proposes that the fit between personality type and occupational environment determines satisfaction and turnover.

The effort to match job requirements with personality characteristics is best explained in John Holland's **personality–job fit theory**.[59] Holland presents six personality types and proposes that satisfaction and the propensity to leave a position depend on the degree to which individuals successfully match their personalities to a job. Each one of the six personality types has a matching occupation. Table 2-5 describes the six types and their personality characteristics and gives examples of congruent occupations.

How do we interpret the information in Table 2-5? At first glance, it is saying that satisfaction is highest and turnover is lowest when personality and occupation—person–job fit—are in agreement. In brief, the overall reasons are (1) there do appear to be differences in personality among individuals, (2) there are different

TABLE 2-5   Holland's Typology of Personality and Congruent Occupations

Type	Personality Characteristics	Congruent Occupations
Realistic: Prefers physical activities that require skill, strength, and coordination	Shy, genuine, persistent, stable, conforming, practical	Mechanic, drill press operator, assembly-line worker, farmer
Investigative: Prefers activities that involve thinking, organizing, and understanding	Analytical, original, curious, independent	Biologist, economist, mathematician, news reporter
Social: Prefers activities that involve helping and developing others	Sociable, friendly, cooperative, understanding	Social worker, teacher, counselor, clinical psychologist
Conventional: Prefers rule-regulated, orderly, and unambiguous activities	Conforming, efficient, practical, unimaginative, inflexible	Accountant, corporate manager, bank teller, file clerk
Enterprising: Prefers verbal activities in which there are opportunities to influence others and attain power	Self-confident, ambitious, energetic, domineering	Lawyer, real estate agent, public relations specialist, small business manager
Artistic: Prefers ambiguous and unsystematic activities that allow creative expression	Imaginative, disorderly, idealistic, emotional, impractical	Painter, musician, writer, interior decorator

types of jobs, and (3) people in jobs that match their personalities should be more satisfied and less likely to resign than people in jobs that have nothing in common with their personality.

Person–Organization Fit

We just saw in the previous section that it is important to match people to their jobs. Moreover, it is equally essential to match people to the *organizations*—person–organization fit. So, how can people match the organization? What we are talking about here is the culture inside the organization, that is, 'how we do things here.' People must be able to adjust to this style; so thus, there is a fit between employees' personalities and the overall organization's culture.

The person–organization fit essentially argues that people are attracted to and selected by organizations that match their values, and they leave organizations that are not compatible with their personalities.[60] If we go back to the Big Five model discussed earlier in this chapter, we could expect that extraverts fit well with aggressive and team-oriented cultures, that people who are agreeable match up better with a supportive organizational climate than one that focuses on aggressiveness, and that open and flexible people go into organizations that emphasize innovation rather than standardization.[61]

Managers who follow these guidelines at the time of hiring should be able to select new employees who fit better with the organization's culture, and this, in turn, should result in higher employee satisfaction and reduced turnover. In summary, the fit of employees' values with the culture of their organization predicts job satisfaction, commitment to the organization, and low turnover.[62]

Linking Cultures and Behavior

11   *Identify Hofstede's five value dimensions of national culture.*

Now is the time to think about the issue of how culture affects behavior. Let's consider these questions: How do we evaluate cultures? How do we know how to deal with the differences and accept them? Many frameworks have been developed but the two most widely used approaches for analyzing the differences among cultures are Geert Hofstede's framework[63] and the Global Leadership and Organizational Behavior Effectiveness (GLOBE) program.[64]

Hofstede's Framework for Assessing Cultures

In the 1970s, Geert Hofstede studied the work-related values and found that managers and employees vary on five value dimensions of national culture:

- *Power Distance* **Power distance** describes the degree to which people in a country accept that power in institutions and organizations is distributed unequally. A high rating on power distance means that large inequalities of power and wealth exist and are tolerated in the culture, whereas a low power distance rating characterizes societies that stress equality and opportunity.
- *Indiviualism versus Collectivism* **Individualism** is the degree to which people prefer to act as individuals rather than as members of groups and believe in individual rights. On the other hand, **collectivism** emphasizes a tight social framework in which people expect others in groups of which they are a part to look after them and protect them.
- *Masculinity versus Femininity* Hofstede's construct of **masculinity** is the degree to which the culture favors traditional masculine roles such as achievement, power, and control, as opposed to viewing men and women as equals. A high masculinity rating indicates the culture has separate roles for men and women, with men dominating the society. A high **femininity** rating means the culture sees little differentiation between male and female roles and treats women as the equals of men in all respects.
- *Uncertainty avoidance* In cultures that score high on uncertainty avoidance, people have an increased level of anxiety about uncertainty and ambiguity and use laws and controls to reduce uncertainty. Cultures low on **uncertainty avoidance** are more accepting of ambiguity and are less rule oriented, take more risks, and more readily accept change.
- *Long-term versus short-term orientation* People in a culture with **long-term orientation** look to the future and value thrift, persistence, and tradition. In a culture with **short-term orientation**, people value the here and now, accept change more readily and don't see commitments as impediments to change.

So how do different countries compare with respect to Hofstede's dimensions? A study of about 40 countries showed that Malaysia ranks 1, the highest with respect to power distance. That is, there are large inequalities of power and wealth in Malaysia. The Arab countries rank 7, and that is also high. The United States ranks 1 in individualism. In other words, contrary to what people may think, individuals in the US focus on their own rights rather than on being part of a group. In fact, the US is the most individualistic nation of all, closely followed by Australia and Great Britain; the Arab countries rank 26.

The United States also tends to be short term in orientation and acceptance of change. Moreover, the US is low in power distance; that is, people in the US accept class differences among people, whereas the Arab countries have large inequalities of power. The US and the Arab countries are both relatively low on uncertainty avoidance, meaning that most adults are relatively tolerant of uncertainty and ambiguity. The US scores relatively high on masculinity but the Arab countries also show little equality between men and women. In other words, these people emphasize traditional gender roles, at least relative to countries such as Denmark, Finland, Norway, and Sweden.

Hofstede's culture dimensions have been enormously influential on OB researchers and managers even though there has been much criticism because some results are unexpected. For example, Japan, which is often considered a

---

Power distance

A national culture attribute that describes the extent to which a society accepts that power in institutions and organizations is distributed unequally.

Individualism

A national culture attribute that describes the degree to which people prefer to act as individuals rather than as members of groups.

Collectivism

A national culture attribute that describes a tight social framework in which people expect others in groups of which they are a part to look after them and protect them.

Masculinity

A national culture attribute that describes the extent to which the culture favours traditional masculine work roles of achievement, power, and control. Societal values are characterized by assertiveness and materialism.

Femininity

A national culture attribute that has little differentiation between male and female roles, where women are treated as the equals of men in all aspects of the society.

Uncertainty avoidance

A national culture attribute that describes the extent to which a society feels threatened by uncertain and ambiguous situations and tries to avoid them.

Long-term orientation

A national culture attribute that emphasizes the future, thrift, and persistence.

Short-term orientation

A national culture attribute that emphasizes the past and present, respect for tradition, and fulfillment of social obligations.

highly collectivist nation, is considered only average on collectivism under Hofstede's dimensions.[65] Nevertheless, Hofstede has been one of the most widely cited social scientists ever, and his framework has left a lasting mark on OB.

The GLOBE Framework for Assessing Cultures

Another approach begun in 1993 and that has contributed to the ongoing cross-cultural investigation of leadership and national culture is Global Leadership and Organizational Behavior Effectiveness (GLOBE). Using data from 825 organizations in 62 countries, the GLOBE team identified nine dimensions on which national cultures differ.[66] Some of these—such as power distance, individualism/collectivism, uncertainty avoidance, gender differentiation (similar to masculinity versus femininity), and future orientation (similar to long-term versus short-term orientation)—are similar to the Hofstede dimensions. The main difference in the GLOBE framework is that it added dimensions, such as humane orientation (the degree to which a society rewards individuals for being altruistic, generous, and kind to others) and performance orientation (the degree to which a society encourages and rewards group members for performance improvement and excellence.)

Which framework is better? That's hard to say, and each has its specifics. We give more emphasis to Hofstede's dimensions here because they have stood the test of time and the GLOBE study confirmed them. However, researchers continue to debate the differences between these frameworks, and future studies may, in time, favor the perspective of the GLOBE study.[67]

Global Implications

As you will see, there may be no global or cross-cultural research on some of the topics we discuss in a chapter, and this chapter is no exception. We therefore confine our comments here to areas where there has been the most cross-cultural research: (1) How does research on intellectual abilities generalize across cultures? (2) Do biographical characteristics such as gender and age operate similarly across cultures? (3) Do the principles of learning work in different cultures? (4) Do personality frameworks, such as the Big Five model, transfer across cultures? and (5) Because values differ across cultures, how can an understanding of these differences be helpful in explaining and predicting behavior of employees from different countries?

Let's answer these questions based on what we have discussed in the relevant sections of this chapter.

Intellectual Abilities

Evidence strongly supports the ideas that the structures and measures of intellectual abilities generalize across cultures. Thus, someone in Venezuela or Sudan does not have a different set of mental abilities from a US or Czech worker. There is some evidence that IQ scores vary to some degree across cultures, but those differences are much smaller when we consider educational and economic differences.[68]

Biographical Characteristics

Obviously, some biographical characteristics vary across cultures. Some cultures are more homogeneous than others, and the average age of citizens varies across countries as was explained in the corresponding section at the beginning of this chapter. That doesn't mean, however, that the relationships we've described between age and performance, or between gender and turnover, are different across cultures. Honestly, we don't have much good scientific evidence on whether, for example, gender or age affects absenteeism similarly across cultures. Thus, we really don't know the degree to which gender (or other biographical factors) varies in importance in predicting OB outcomes in different countries.

OB researchers don't always answer the questions we want them to answer. For example, AACSB International, the largest accreditation association for business schools, frequently faults business schools for not producing research that's relevant to managers. Even though we think OB research has a lot to offer, it's not perfect and we must remember this.

Learning

There is little research on how theories of learning generalize to organizations and employees in different cultures. This is due to the fact that much of the research on learning theories is fairly old, conducted before there was a lot of cross-cultural research.

Personality

The five personality factors identified in the Big Five model appear in almost all cross-cultural studies.[69] The Big Five model was discussed in depth earlier in this chapter but, for instance, differences tend to be in the emphasis on dimensions and whether countries are predominantly individualistic or collectivistic. For example, Chinese managers use the category of conscientiousness more often and the category of agreeableness less often than do US managers. And the Big Five appear to predict a bit better in individualistic rather than collectivist cultures.[70]

Values

The two common measures of culture assessment are Hofstede's cultural dimensions and the GLOBE framework, which were discussed in the previous section. Both highlight the proportions on which national cultures differ. As we explained, there are great differences among countries and they help us to realize that employee behavior will depend on these values.

Summary and Implications for Managers

This chapter looked at ability, biographical characteristics, learning, personality, and values and the relationship between all these variables and their contribution to the workplace. Let's now try to summarize what we found and consider their importance for a manager who is trying to understand organizational behavior.

Ability Ability directly influences an employee's level of performance. Given management's desire to get high-performing employees, what can be done?

First, an effective selection process will improve the fit. Applicants can then be tested, interviewed, and evaluated on the degree to which they possess the necessary abilities. Second, promotion and transfer decisions affecting individuals already in the organization's employ should reflect the abilities of candidates. Third, the fit can be improved by fine-tuning the job to better match an incumbent's abilities. Examples would be changing some of the equipment used or reorganizing tasks within a group of employees.

Biographical Characteristics Biographical characteristics are readily observable to managers. However, just because they're observable doesn't mean they should be openly used in management decisions. We also need to be aware of other biases we or other managers may have.

Learning Any observable change in behavior is *prima facie* evidence that learning has taken place. Positive reinforcement is a powerful tool for modifying behavior. By identifying and rewarding performance-enhancing behaviors, management increases the likelihood that those behaviors will be repeated. Our knowledge about learning further suggests that reinforcement is a more effective tool than punishment. Although punishment eliminates undesired behavior more quickly than negative reinforcement does, punished behavior tends to be only temporarily suppressed rather than permanently changed. Managers, therefore, are advised to use reinforcement rather than punishment.

Personality What value, if any, does the Big Five model provide to managers? "The outcome of those 80-plus years of research was that personality and job performance were not meaningfully related across traits or situations."[71] However, the past 20 years have been more promising, largely due to the findings surrounding the Big Five. Each of the Big Five traits has numerous implications for important OB criteria. Of course, managers still need to take situational factors into consideration.[72] Factors such as job demands, the degree of required interaction with others, and the organization's culture are examples of situational variables that moderate the personality–job performance relationship. You need to evaluate the job, the work group, and the organization to determine the optimal personality fit. Other traits, such as core self-evaluation or narcissism, may be relevant in certain situations, too.

Values Why is it important to know an individual's values? Values often underlie and explain attitudes, behaviors, and perceptions. So knowledge of an individual's value system can provide insight into what 'makes the person tick.' Employees' performance and satisfaction are likely to be higher if their values fit well with the organization. Managers are more likely to appreciate, evaluate positively, and allocate rewards to employees who 'fit in,' and employees are more likely to be satisfied if they perceive that they do fit in. This argues for management to strive during the selection of new employees to find job candidates who have not only the ability, experience, and motivation to perform, but also a value system that is compatible with the organization's

Point >> << Counterpoint

ALL HUMAN BEHAVIOR IS LEARNED[73]

*H*uman beings are essentially blank sheets that are shaped by their environment. B.F. Skinner, in fact, summarized his belief in the power of the environment to shape behavior when he said, "Give me a child at birth and I can make him into anything you want."

The factors of society that contribute to the power of learned behavior are the role of parents, the importance of education, job training, and the use of rewards.

*O*n the other hand, even though people can learn and can be influenced by their environment, little attention has been paid to the role that evolution has played in shaping human behavior. Human beings are basically shaped at birth.

All living creatures are 'designed' by specific combinations of genes and many of the characteristics that have helped are emotions, risk avoidance, stereotyping, and competition.

As a result, we find that people in organizational settings often behave in ways that don't appear to be beneficial to themselves or their employers.

Questions for Review

1 Define ability and the two types—intellectual and cognitive ability. How are they relevant to OB?

2 What are the key biographical characteristics, and why are they relevant to OB?

3 What is learning, and what are the major theories of learning?

4 What is shaping, and how can it be used as a management tool?

5 How does culture affect our understanding of intellectual abilities, biographical characteristics, and learning?

6 What is personality? How do we typically measure it? What factors determine personality?

7 What is the Myers-Briggs Type Indicator (MBTI), and what does it measure?

8 What are the Big Five personality traits, and how do they predict work behavior?

9 What are values, why are they important and do they differ across cultures?

10 What is the difference between terminal and instrumental values?

Discussion Exercise

Some people believe that older workers become slower at producing and may have more difficulty solving problems or learning new skills. Do you agree or disagree? Does age affect the ability to learn and to adapt to change?

Do some more research about age in the workplace in your country and prepare to discuss it in class.

Ethical Considerations

The global financial crisis of 2008 definitely affected the businesses in the Gulf. The changes in the situation of so many prominent companies was welcomed by business journalists since they looked for opportunities to write about details that would shock readers. This aim can conflict with the ethical code that encourages the media to focus on disclosing correct information. Just as the crisis began to become more threatening to the economy, many governments of Arab countries and the GCC issued laws to limit the reactions of the media and to preserve the values

that the media should practice. For example, the government of the United Arab Emirates introduced a strict draft law. It listed the consequences that the media would have to face if they went beyond their boundaries by giving damaging or misleading information. Among the many penalties was a high fine that they would have to pay. Since many journalists were unable to afford the fine, the media stopped doing its job. What is your reaction from an ethical standpoint? Why can the media be damaging, and how can (or should) it be controlled?

Source: Paul Cochrane, "The Bubble's Jagged Edge," *Executive Magazine*, Issue No. 125, December, 2009, p. 40.

Critical Analysis

QATAR: A COUNTRY WITH A VISION

Significant changes in recent years have occurred in Qatar. HE Al-Sheikh Hamad Bin Khalifeh II has made significant contributions to the development of the country. In addition, women have become able to use their vision, experiences and professional abilities in the roles of wife, mother, and manager.

A key player at the moment is the wife of the Prince, Al-Sheikha Moza, who has shown herself to be an individual with values. Al-Sheikha Moza works hard to preserve her identity as a wife and mother while she participates in social, cultural and educational activities, and encourages the female population of Qatar to do the same. Al-Shiekha Moza's major concern is quality—quality in everything one does—and she stresses this for both males and females.

Qatari women have also demonstrated their abilities in many professions such as engineering, construction, interior design, pharmacy, medicine, and nutrition. Fifty percent of the investors and dealers of the Doha Stock Exchange are women, and 346 companies in Qatar are owned by businesswomen.

Finally, if we refer to the statistics from the survey given in the earlier 'OB in the News' box, we see that 28 percent of Qatar's female population believes that conditions and opportunities have improved for them. In addition, 31 percent feel that they have equal compensation to their male coworkers. Given that the overall impression is that the Arab female is not given the opportunity to shine and expose her abilities, these numbers are quite interesting for an Arab country.

Questions

1. How does Qatar deal with the issue of gender despite the fact that it is an Arab country?

2. How can we relate what's happening in Qatar to the learning process?

3. Describe Sheikha Moza'a personality according to the Big Five Personality Model.

4. What risks do you think Al-Sheikha Moza took to implement what she has achieved in Qatar?

Source: "Al-Sheikha Moza: Caused Quality Changes," *Al-Iktissad Wal-Aamal, Arab Business Magazine*, Special Issue, May 2010/Year 32, pp. 10–12.

Research Exercise

Do your own research and find a case or incident that is relevant to the concepts we have discussed in this chapter. However, it should not be from the Arab world, so that you can show similarities and differences with other regions of the world.

LEARNING OBJECTIVES

This chapter will enable you to:

1 Contrast the three components of an attitude.

2 Summarize the relationship between attitudes and behavior.

3 Compare and contrast the major job attitudes

4 Define *job satisfaction* and show how it can be measured.

5 Summarize the main causes of job satisfaction.

6 Identify four employee responses to dissatisfaction.

7 Show whether job satisfaction is a relevant concept in all cultures.

Attitudes and Job Satisfaction

3

Ability is what you are capable of doing. Motivation determines what you do. Attitude determines how well you do it. —Lou Holtz

Google: Is This a Great Place to Work or What?

Sergey Brin and Larry Page were simply two students who had a university course project. Today, they are known as the creators of the number one search engine in the world—Google. Google is very popular in the Arab world, where students and individuals from all countries and sectors use it as a major source of information.

Because of its reputation and concern for its employees, Google is one of the workplaces where many would like to work at because it spares no expense to keep its workers happy. For example, large amounts of chef-prepared food are available all day; in addition there is a huge gym with state-of-the-art equipment, including a climbing wall, a volleyball court, and two lap pools. There is a masseuse too. There are on-site car washes, oil changes, haircuts, dry cleaning, and free medical checkups, and dental work. Childcare next door and a backup childcare service in case the employee is running late are also made available.

Free transportation is the latest benefit because the location of Google's main operations, Silicon Valley, has some of the worst traffic in the United States. So now Google provides its employees with free high-tech shuttle buses, equipped with comfortable leather seats, bicycle racks, and wireless internet access, and powered by biodiesel engines. Although its free shuttle and other benefits programs have attracted the most attention, Google offers a many other great benefits.

Among them are:

- Automatic life insurance at two times annual salary
- For employees with six or more years of seniority, 25 vacation days per year
- For new parents, parental leave at 75 percent pay for six weeks, and reimbursement for up to US$500 for take-away meals during the first four weeks at home with the new baby
- Tuition reimbursement of US$8,000 per calendar year
- A US$2,000 bonus for referral of employees who are hired and stay at least 60 days
- A gift-matching program for employee contributions of up to US$3,000 per year to nonprofit organizations
- Reimbursement of up to US$5,000 to use towards adoption expenses.

A recent survey suggested that of all the factors that might increase job satisfaction, employees believe benefits are the most important. Google seems to get that.

Sources: M. Helft, "Google's Buses Help Its Workers Beat the Rush," *New York Times*, March 10, 2007, pp. A1, B9; E. Esen, SHRM Job Satisfaction Series: 2005 Job Satisfaction (Alexandria, VA: Society for Human Resource Management, 2005); and "Benefits," Google.com, www.google.com/support/jobs/bin/static.py?page=benefits.html&benefits=us.

As we just read in the opening case, Google, like many organizations, is very concerned with the attitudes of its employees. Google offers a comfortable workplace and facilities that can contribute to creativity and productivity. By keeping its employees satisfied, Google understands that performance and output will increase, as will commitment to the organization. In this chapter, we look at attitudes, their link to behavior, and how employees' satisfaction or dissatisfaction with their jobs affects the workplace.

What are your attitudes toward your job? Use the following Self-Assessment Library to determine your level of satisfaction with your current or past jobs.

Self **A**ssessment **L**ibrary

HOW SATISFIED AM I WITH MY JOB?

In the Self-Assessment Library (available online), take assessment I.B.3 (How Satisfied Am I with My Job?) and then answer the following questions. If you currently do not have a job, answer the questions for your most recent job.

1. *How does your job satisfaction compare to that of others in your class who have taken the assessment?*

2. *Why do you think your satisfaction is higher or lower than average?*

Attitudes

1 Contrast the three components of an attitude.

Attitudes are revealed in statements that evaluate situations, objects, people, or events; they can be either positive or negative. They reflect how we feel about something. Attitudes are complex, so in order to fully understand attitudes, we need to consider what they are made up of.

What Are the Main Components of Attitudes?

Attitudes
Evaluative statements or judgments concerning objects, people, or events.

Cognitive component
The opinion or belief segment of an attitude.

Affective component
The emotional or feeling segment of an attitude.

Behavioral component
An intention to behave in a certain way toward someone or something.

Researchers have assumed that attitudes have three components or parts: cognition, affect, and behavior.[1] Let's look at each.

The **cognitive component** of an attitude is the aspect of an attitude that is a description of, or a belief in, the way things are. For instance, 'My salary is so low; I deserve more' describes how an employee feels. It follows that the **affective component** is the emotional or feeling segment of an attitude and is reflected in a statement like 'I am so angry over how little I'm paid for the amount of work I do.' Finally, and we'll discuss this issue more later in this section, affect can lead to behavioral outcomes. The **behavioral component** of an attitude refers to an intention to behave in a certain way toward someone or something. That is, the employee is so frustrated that they decide to do something about it, and thus says 'I'm going to look for another job that pays better and appreciates my hard work.'

Figure 3-1 illustrates how the three components of an attitude are related. In this particular example, an employee didn't get a promotion he thought he deserved; a coworker got it instead. The employee's attitude toward his supervisor is illustrated as follows: the employee thought he deserved the promotion (cognition), the employee strongly dislikes his supervisor (affect), and the employee is looking for another job (behavior).

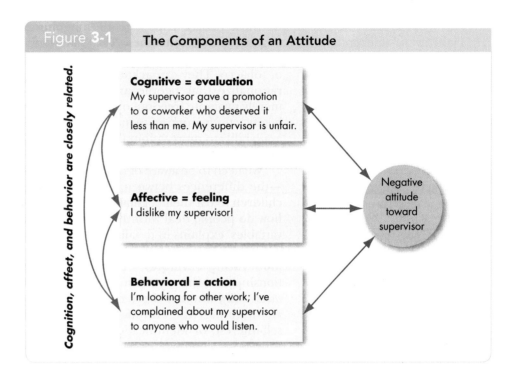

Figure 3-1   **The Components of an Attitude**

Cognition, affect, and behavior are closely related.

Cognitive = evaluation
My supervisor gave a promotion to a coworker who deserved it less than me. My supervisor is unfair.

Affective = feeling
I dislike my supervisor!

Behavioral = action
I'm looking for other work; I've complained about my supervisor to anyone who would listen.

Negative attitude toward supervisor

Picture This

Cherine is committed to her work. She gladly puts in overtime although she is never paid for it. But when Nadia came and started to get paid for extra work she did, Cherine was very unhappy. She felt her supervisor was being unfair and she became complacent, coming into to work late. Identify the three components of attitudes in this situation.

Is There a Relationship Between Behavior and Attitudes?

2 Summarize the relationship between attitudes and behavior.

Early research on attitudes assumed that they were causally related to behavior; that is, the attitudes people hold determine what they do. Common sense, too, suggests a relationship. Isn't it logical that people watch television programs they like, or that employees try to avoid assignments they are not interested in?

One researcher—Leon Festinger—argued that attitudes *follow* behavior. Did you ever notice how people change what they say so it doesn't contradict what they do? In other words, they do something, and then say something that fits with that action. Festinger argued that these cases of attitude following behavior illustrate the effects of **cognitive dissonance**.[2] *Cognitive dissonance* refers to any incompatibility an individual might perceive between two or more attitudes or between behavior and attitudes. For example, you might not like American cars and you always tell your friends that you will never buy any American model. However, for your birthday, your parents buy you a new Chevrolet; all of a sudden, American cars are good.

Research has generally concluded that people seek consistency among their attitudes and between their attitudes and their behavior.[3] They do this by altering the attitudes or the behavior or by developing a rationalization for the discrepancy. Tobacco executives provide an example.[4] How, you might wonder,

Cognitive dissonance

Any incompatibility between two or more attitudes or between behavior and attitudes.

do these people cope with the ongoing data linking cigarette smoking and negative health outcomes? They can deny any relation between smoking and cancer, for instance. They can brainwash themselves by talking about the benefits of tobacco. They can acknowledge the negative consequences of smoking but rationalize that people are going to smoke and that tobacco companies merely promote freedom of choice. They can accept the research evidence and begin actively working to make less dangerous cigarettes or at least reduce their availability to more vulnerable groups, such as teenagers. Or they can quit their job because the dissonance or pressure is too great.

We need to be aware of the fact that it is almost impossible to avoid dissonance —the differences between attitude and behavior. For example, you tell your children to eat their vegetables because they are good for you, but *you* don't. So how do people deal with these gaps? The following section about 'moderating variables' explains in detail.

Moderating Variables   The most powerful moderators of the attitudes relationship are the *importance* of the attitude, its *correspondence to behavior*, its *accessibility*, whether there exist *social pressures*, and whether a person has *direct experience* with the attitude.[5] Important attitudes reflect fundamental values, self-interest, or identification with individuals or groups that a person values. Attitudes that individuals consider important tend to show a strong relationship to behavior.

The more closely the attitude and the behavior are matched or correspond, the stronger the relationship. Specific attitudes tend to predict specific behaviors, whereas general attitudes tend to best predict general behaviors. For instance, asking someone specifically about her intention to stay with an organization for the next six months is likely to better predict turnover for that person than if you asked her how satisfied she was with her job overall. On the other hand, overall job satisfaction would better predict a general behavior such as whether the individual was engaged in her work or motivated to contribute to her organization.[6]

Attitudes we remember easily are more likely to predict our behavior. Interestingly, you're more likely to remember attitudes you frequently express.

Marriott Hotels, a common name in the Arab world, strives for consistency between attitudes and behavior through its motto 'Spirit To Serve.' CEO Bill Marriott (pictured here with some employees) follows the motto by visiting hotel employees throughout the year. "I want our associates to know that there really is a guy named Marriott who cares about them," he says. Marriott honors employees with job excellence awards for behavior that exemplifies the attitude of service.

"Giving back to the communities in which we live and work" is an important value for Deloitte & Touche, which has offices all over the world. The company encourages its employees to further promote this attitude through its annual Impact Day when, for one day, employees are allowed to leave their regular work in order to participate in an act of community service and experience 'giving back to the community.' Here, Deloitte volunteers support students on Middle East Impact Day, by painting the walls for their school playground.

So the more you talk about your attitude on a subject, the more you're likely to remember it, and the more likely it is to shape your behavior.

Finally, the attitude–behavior relationship is likely to be much stronger if an attitude refers to something with which the individual has direct personal experience.

Picture This

You, a university student with no significant work experience, are asked about your reaction to an authoritarian supervisor. How would you respond? What if the same situation was asked of an employee who has actually worked and experienced such attitudes and behavior? Whose response is more likely to predict actual behavior?

What Are the Major Job Attitudes?

3   Compare and contrast the major job attitudes.

People possess numerous attitudes, but OB focuses on work-related attitudes.

Most of the research in OB has looked at three work-related attitudes: job satisfaction, job involvement, and organizational commitment to be discussed below. A few other attitudes attracting attention from researchers include perceived organizational support and employee engagement, and we'll also briefly discuss these.

What Do You Think?

Do you show the same attitudes towards work as you do towards other aspects of your life?

International OB

Organizational Commitment at Aramex

Aramex was founded in 1982 with two offices, in Amman and New York. Under the leadership of CEO Fadi Ghandour, it has grown into a global brand and was the first Arab-based international company represented on the NASDAQ stock exchange. In 2005, the company, under the name Arab International Logistics (Aramex), went public on the Dubai Financial Market.

Aramex's strengths are based on a quality management system that aims to provide enhanced services, and its investment in developing its employees to become 'knowledge workers'. Aramex staff are trained extensively, and empowered to act creatively to find solutions to any problems that occur.

The company also prides itself on its approaches to innovation. Employees are encouraged to listen to customers and so identify ways in which their service can be improved in the future. The focus throughout is on serving customers with efficiency and care, for example by devising better ways of communicating with customers or faster ways to track their shipments.

Aramex also encourages its staff to become involved in the community in which the business operates. The aim is to contribute to the progress of those communities through supporting education, sport, entrepreneurship and literacy, encouraging and rewarding innovation and achievement.

Aramex's performance is recognized in awards such as the highest level Transported Asset Protection Association (TAPA) certifications for its facilities in Bahrain, Riyadh, Dammam, Beirut, Amman, and Jebel Ali Free Zone in Dubai. A key factor in this award is the way in which Aramex's customized technology has enabled it to put in place advanced security standards to protect its customers' shipments.

Sources: Based on "About Aramex," www.aramex.org/public/english.aspx?page_id=10; and "Aramex Facilities Receive Top TAPA Rating," Aramex Press Release, October 22, 2008, www.ameinfo.com/172579.html.

Job satisfaction

A positive feeling about one's job resulting from an evaluation of its characteristics.

Job involvement

The degree to which a person identifies with a job, actively participates in it, and considers performance important to self-worth.

Psychological empowerment

Employees' belief in the degree to which they affect their work environment, their competence, the meaningfulness of their job, and their perceived autonomy in their work.

Organizational commitment

The degree to which an employee identifies with a particular organization and its goals and wishes to maintain membership in the organization.

Job Satisfaction   The term **job satisfaction** describes a positive feeling about a job, resulting from an evaluation of its characteristics. That is, a person with a high level of job satisfaction holds positive feelings about his or her job, while a dissatisfied person holds negative feelings. Because of its high importance in OB, we'll review this attitude in detail later in this chapter.

Job Involvement   **Job involvement** measures the degree to which people identify psychologically with their job and consider their performance level important to self-worth.[7] Employees with a high level of job involvement strongly identify with and really care about the kind of work they do. Another closely related concept is **psychological empowerment**, which is employees' beliefs in the degree to which they influence their work environment, their competence, the meaningfulness of their job, and the perceived autonomy in their work.[8]

High levels of both job involvement and psychological empowerment are positively related to organizational commitment and job performance.[9] In addition, high job involvement has been found to be related to a reduced number of absences and lower resignation rates.[10]

Organizational Commitment   The third job attitude we'll discuss is **organizational commitment**, a state in which an employee identifies with a particular organization and its goals and wishes to remain a member in the organization.[11] So, high job involvement means identifying with your specific job, while high organizational commitment means identifying with the overall environment of your organization.

There are three separate dimensions to organizational commitment:[12]

Affective commitment

An emotional attachment to an organization and a belief in its values.

Continuance commitment

The perceived economic value of remaining with an organization compared with leaving it.

Normative commitment

An obligation to remain with an organization for moral or ethical reasons.

Perceived organizational support

The degree to which employees believe an organization values their contribution and cares about their wellbeing.

Employee engagement

An individual's involvement with, satisfaction with, and enthusiasm for the work he or she does.

1. **Affective commitment.** An **affective commitment** is an emotional attachment to the organization and a belief in its values. For example, INDEVCO or SABIC employees may be affectively committed to their company because of its concern for the environment, a cause that they support as environmentalists.
2. **Continuance commitment.** A **continuance commitment** is the economic value of remaining with an organization compared with leaving it. Employees may be committed to an employer not because they are satisfied but because they are paid well and it would hurt their family to quit.
3. **Normative commitment.** A **normative commitment** is an obligation to remain with the organization for moral or ethical reasons. For example, you have initiated a new training program at work and you remain because you feel a strong responsibility to your employer.

In sum, whatever the type of commitment, as we saw in the previous section, employees determine their connection to the workplace and this, in turn, determines their level of performance.

Perceived Organizational Support (POS)   **Perceived Organizational Support (POS)** is the degree to which employees believe that the organization appreciates and values their contribution and cares about their wellbeing. For example, employees believe the organization would help them if they had any family emergency or that it would forgive an honest mistake. Research shows that people perceive their organization as supportive when rewards are deemed fair, when employees have a voice in decisions, and when their supervisors are seen as supportive.[13] Employees with strong POS perceptions are more likely to have higher levels of organizational citizenship behaviors and job performance.[14]

Employee Engagement   The concept of **employee engagement** describes employees' involvement with, satisfaction with, and enthusiasm for the work they do. Highly engaged employees have a passion for their work and feel a deep connection to their company; disengaged employees have essentially become indifferent—putting time but not energy or attention into their work. This is best explained by McGregor's Theory X and Y that will be discussed in Chapter 5.

Multinational company, Philips, offer a wide range of healthcare, lighting and consumer lifestyle products. To encourage employee engagement, Phillips launched an innovation program, in partnership with the Mohammed Bin Rashid Al Maktoum Foundation, which focuses on recognizing and acknowledging employee contributions and aims to promote innovation and entrepreneurship in 22 Arab League states.

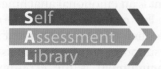

AM I ENGAGED?

In the Self-Assessment Library (available online), take assessment IV.B.1 (Am I Engaged?). (Note: If you do not currently have a job, answer the questions for your most recent job.)

Are These Job Attitudes Really All That Distinct?   You might wonder whether these job attitudes are really distinct. If people feel deeply involved in their job (high job involvement), shouldn't they like it (high job satisfaction)? Similarly, shouldn't people who think their organization is supportive (high perceived organizational support) also feel committed to it (strong organizational commitment)? Evidence suggests that these attitudes are highly related, perhaps to a troubling degree. For example, the correlation between perceived organizational support and affective commitment is very strong.[15] The problem is that a strong correlation means the variables may be redundant (so, for example, if you know someone's affective commitment, you basically know the perceived organizational support).

What Do You Think?

How do you show your commitment to a person, work, course or situation?

OB in the News

Job Satisfaction: Does It Differ Across Cultures?

Evidence shows that job satisfaction levels in the United States are dropping. The Conference Board, which surveys large numbers of workers every year, reports the following percentages of individuals reporting that they are at least moderately satisfied with their jobs: 61 percent in 1987; 59 percent in 1995; 51 percent in 2000; 52 percent in 2005; and 45 percent in 2009.

What are the strongest areas of dissatisfaction? Only one in five employees is satisfied with their company's promotions and bonus plans. Surprisingly, satisfaction has dropped the most among those making the highest incomes, although they still have somewhat higher satisfaction than those with relatively low earnings.

Even though US workers remain relatively satisfied with their jobs, especially compared with employees in other countries, this doesn't explain why job satisfaction levels are dropping. One reason may be that in their drive to increase productivity, many companies continue to downsize, leaving the remaining workers overburdened.

Downsizing also lowers the morale of layoff survivors.

On the other hand, evidence shows that employees in the Arab world have higher percentages of job satisfaction. A study conducted in the countries of the GCC (UAE, KSA, Kuwait, Oman, Qatar, Bahrain), Levant (Lebanon, Syria, Jordan), and North Africa (Egypt, Morocco, Algeria, Tunisia) resulted in 13,376 respondents. Although there was overall satisfaction with authority and responsibilities at work as well as the work environment, about two in five of the respondents are not satisfied with the level of job security and compensation and benefits. However, satisfaction with physical work conditions and working space in most of the countries is good.

Let's look at some of the most important statistics. Overall, between 75 and 85 percent of people in each country said that were 'very satisfied' or 'satisfied' with the responsibilities at work. The results to the question about being satisfied with flexibility of work schedules were also quite consistent across all the countries, ranging between

41 and 48 percent. Interpersonal relations with fellow workers gave high outcomes on the scale of very satisfied and satisfied, with Oman with the highest at 84 percent.

The results for the other countries about interpersonal relations with colleagues were: UAE, 75 percent; Syria, 72 percent; KSA, 74 percent; Qatar, 75 percent; Lebanon, 79 percent; Kuwait, 72 percent; Jordan, 77 percent; Egypt, 75 percent; and Bahrain, 80 percent. In other words, results show that employees in the Arab world are generally satisfied with work conditions and have strong relationships with their peers.

Sources: Based on K. Gurchiek, "Show Workers Their Value, Study Says," *HR Magazine*, October 2006, p. 40; "US Job Satisfaction Declines," *USA Today*, April 9, 2007, p. 1B; S. Moore, L. Grunberg, and E. Greenberg, "The Effects of Similar and Dissimilar Layoff Experiences on Work and Well-Being Outcomes," *Journal of Occupational Health Psychology*, July 2004, pp. 247–257. Statistics taken from "Employee Motivation in the Middle East Study" September, 2009, Bayt.com.

Job Satisfaction

4 *Define* job satisfaction *and show how it can be measured.*

We introduced job satisfaction briefly earlier in this chapter, but now let's look at the concept more closely. Which questions do you ask when you consider job satisfaction? How do we measure job satisfaction? How satisfied are employees in their jobs? What causes an employee to have a high level of job satisfaction? How do dissatisfied and satisfied employees affect an organization?

> ## What Do You Think?
>
> *What do you think would satisfy you as an employee?*

Measuring Job Satisfaction

We previously defined job satisfaction as a positive feeling about a job resulting from an evaluation of the characteristics of the job. First, let's address a major question: What is a job made up of? Well, a person's job is not only writing programs, waiting on customers, or driving a truck, it also requires interacting with coworkers and bosses, following organizational rules and policies, meeting performance standards, and living with working conditions that are often not perfect. This brings us to the second important question: How do we measure job satisfaction?

The two most widely used approaches are a single global rating and a summation score made up of a number of job facets. The single global rating method is nothing more than a response to one question, such as 'All things considered, how satisfied are you with your job?' Respondents circle a number between 1 and 5 that corresponds to answers from 'highly satisfied' to 'highly dissatisfied.'[16] The other approach—a summation of job facets—is more sophisticated. It identifies key elements in a job and asks for the employee's feelings about each. Typical elements here are the nature of the work, supervision, present pay, promotion opportunities, and relations with coworkers.[17] Respondents rate them on a standardized scale, and researchers add the ratings to create an overall job satisfaction score.

Is one of these approaches superior to the other? Intuitively, summing up responses to a number of job factors seems likely to achieve a more accurate evaluation of job satisfaction. The research, however, doesn't support the intuition.[18] This is one of those rare instances in which simplicity seems to work as well as complexity, and comparisons of the two methods indicate that one is essentially as valid as the other. The best explanation for this outcome is that the concept of job satisfaction is so broad that the single question captures its essence. Another explanation may be that some important aspects are left out of the summation of job facets. Both methods are helpful. For example, the single global rating method isn't very time-consuming, which frees managers to address other workplace issues and problems. And the summation of job facets helps managers focus on where problems exist, making it easier to deal with unhappy employees and solve problems faster and more accurately.

How Satisfied Are People in Their Jobs?

Are most people satisfied with their jobs? The 'OB in the News' feature, opposite, suggests that most people in the Arab world are. Figure 3-2 shows the average levels of motivation at work across selected Arab countries. However, job

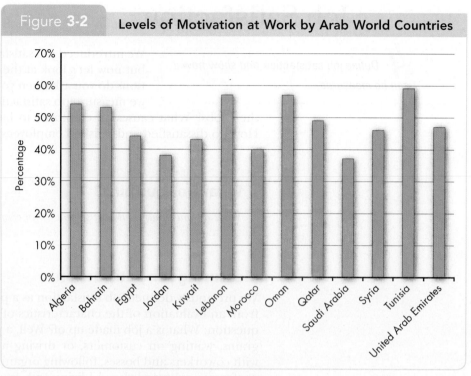

| Figure **3-2** | **Levels of Motivation at Work by Arab World Countries** |

Source: Data collected from "Employee Motivation Study," September 2009, Bayt.com.

satisfaction levels in general are dropping, and satisfaction levels differ according to the aspect of job satisfaction we are referring to, as seen in Figure 3-3. You will notice that people are usually less satisfied with their pay and promotion possibilities more than other aspects of their jobs.[19]

What Causes Job Satisfaction?

> 5 *Summarize the main causes of job satisfaction.*

Think about the best job or responsibility you have ever had. What made it so satisfying for you? Chances are you probably liked the work you did. In fact, of the major job-satisfaction facets (work itself, pay, advancement opportunities, supervision, coworkers), enjoying the work is almost always the one most strongly correlated with high levels of overall job satisfaction. Interesting jobs that provide training, variety, independence, and control satisfy most employees.[20] In other words, most people prefer work that is challenging and stimulating over work that is predictable and routine.

You've probably noticed that pay comes up often when people discuss job satisfaction. There is an interesting relationship between salary and job satisfaction. For people who are poor (for example, living below the poverty line) or who live in poor countries, pay does correlate with job satisfaction and with overall happiness. But, once an individual reaches a level of comfortable living, the relationship virtually disappears. In other words, people who earn US$80,000 are, on average, no happier with their jobs than those who earn close to US$40,000. Take a look at Figure 3-4. It shows to what extent employees in the Arab world are satisfied with their pay and compensation. Of course, there are individuals who are satisfied with their compensation and those who are not. It is, however, interesting to see that the percentage of those who are dissatisfied is equal to those who are satisfied.

Money does motivate people, as we will discover in Chapter 5; however, we will also learn that what motivates us is not necessarily the same as what makes

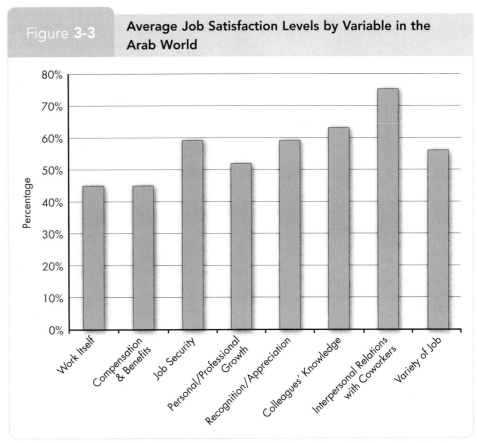

Figure **3-3**   **Average Job Satisfaction Levels by Variable in the Arab World**

Source: Data collected from "Employee Motivation Study," September 2009, Bayt.com.

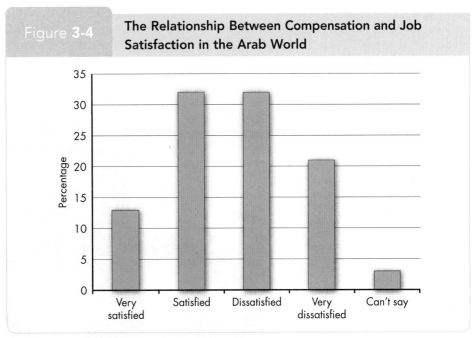

Figure **3-4**   **The Relationship Between Compensation and Job Satisfaction in the Arab World**

Source: Data collected from "Employee Motivation Study," September 2009, Bayt.com.

us happy. Maybe your goal isn't to be happy. But if it is, money's probably not going to do much to get you there.[21] In fact, job satisfaction is not just about job conditions. Personality also plays a role. People who are less positive about themselves are less likely to like their jobs. Research has shown that people who have positive core self-evaluations, that is, those who believe in themselves and have high self-confidence are more satisfied with their jobs than those with negative core self-evaluations.

The Impact of Satisfied and Dissatisfied Employees on the Workplace

6 *Identify four employee responses to dissatisfaction.*

There are consequences when employees like their jobs and when they dislike their jobs. One theoretical model—the exit–voice–loyalty–neglect framework—is helpful in understanding the consequences of job dissatisfaction. The four responses differ from one another along two dimensions: constructive/destructive and active/passive, and can be defined as follows:[22]

Exit
Dissatisfaction expressed through behavior directed toward leaving the organization.

Voice
Dissatisfaction expressed through active and constructive attempts to improve conditions.

Loyalty
Dissatisfaction expressed by passively waiting for conditions to improve.

Neglect
Dissatisfaction expressed through allowing conditions to worsen.

- *Exit.* The **exit** (active-destructive) response involves directing behavior toward leaving the organization, including looking for a new position as well as resigning.
- *Voice.* The **voice** (active-constructive) response involves actively and constructively attempting to improve conditions, including suggesting improvements, discussing problems with superiors, and undertaking some forms of union activity.
- *Loyalty.* The **loyalty** (passive-constructive) response involves passively but optimistically waiting for conditions to improve, including speaking up for the organization in the face of external criticism and trusting the organization and its management to 'do the right thing.'
- *Neglect.* The **neglect** (passive-destructive) response involves passively allowing conditions to worsen, including chronic absenteeism or lateness, reduced effort, and increased error rate.

A major focus of Nissan Motor Company's Diversity Development Office in Japan is helping female employees develop their careers. Nissan provides women, such as assembly-line workers, with one-on-one counseling services of career advisors, and training programs to develop applicable skills. Women can also visit Nissan's corporate intranet to read interviews with 'role models,' women who have made substantial contributions to the company. Nissan believes that hiring more women and supporting their careers will contribute to the company's competitive edge.

Exit and neglect behaviors encompass our performance variables—productivity, absenteeism, and turnover. But this model expands employee response to include voice and loyalty—constructive behaviors that allow individuals to tolerate unpleasant situations or to revive satisfactory working conditions.

As helpful as this framework is in presenting the possible consequences of job dissatisfaction, it's quite general. We now discuss more specific outcomes of job satisfaction and dissatisfaction in the workplace.

What Do You Think?

What response do you think you would display if you disliked your job?

Now we have looked at ways in which satisfaction and dissatisfaction may affect the performance of employees, we will see in more detail in the following sections the relationship between levels of satisfaction and other variables.

Job Satisfaction and Job Performance   Many researchers used to believe that the relationship between job satisfaction and job performance was an issue that could never be proven; however, a review of 300 studies suggested that the correlation is pretty strong.[23] As we move from the individual level to that of the organization, we also find support for the satisfaction–performance relationship.[24] When satisfaction and productivity data are gathered for the organization as a whole, we find that organizations with more satisfied employees tend to be more effective than organizations with fewer satisfied employees.

Job Satisfaction and OCB   It seems logical to assume that job satisfaction should be a major determinant of an employee's organizational citizenship behavior (OCB).[25] Satisfied employees would seem more likely to talk positively about the organization, help others, and go beyond the normal expectations in their job.

Why do those satisfied with their jobs contribute more OCBs? When employees find that the organization is fair, trust develops and, consequently, they are more willing to voluntarily engage in behaviors that go beyond the usual job requirements. In other words, organizational commitment increases.

Job Satisfaction and Absenteeism   We find a consistent negative relationship between satisfaction and absenteeism, but the correlation is moderate to weak.[26] While it certainly makes sense that dissatisfied employees are more likely to miss work, other factors have an impact on the relationship and reduce the correlation coefficient. For example, organizations that allow employees sick leave benefits are encouraging all their employees—including those who are highly satisfied—to take days off.

Job Satisfaction and Turnover   Satisfaction is also negatively related to turnover, but the correlation is stronger than what we found for absenteeism.[27]

Evidence indicates that an important moderator of the satisfaction–turnover relationship is the employee's level of performance.[28] In particular, the level of satisfaction is less important in predicting turnover for superior performers because the organization makes considerable efforts to keep these people. For instance, they get pay raises, praise, recognition, and increased promotional opportunities. However, the opposite tends to apply to poor performers because the organization makes few attempts to retain them. On the contrary, there may even be pressures to encourage them to quit. Therefore, we would expect that

Service organizations know that whether customers are satisfied and loyal depends on how frontline employees deal with customers. Singapore Airlines has earned a reputation among world travellers for outstanding customer service. The airline's 'putting people first' philosophy applies to both its employees and customers. In recruiting flight attendants, the airline selects people who are warm, hospitable, and happy to serve others. Through extensive training, Singapore molds recruits into attendants focused on complete customer satisfaction.

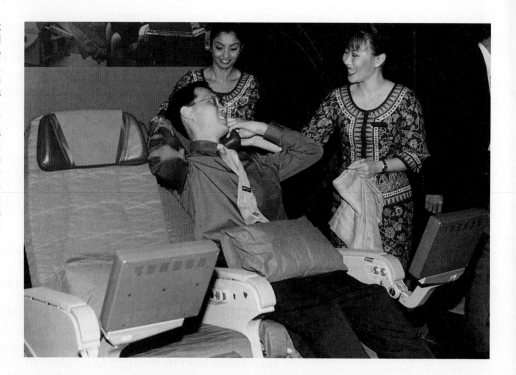

job satisfaction is more important in influencing poor performers to stay than in influencing superior performers to stay. Regardless of level of satisfaction, the poor performers are more likely to remain with the organization because the receipt of recognition, praise, and other rewards gives them more reasons to do so.

Job Satisfaction and Customer Satisfaction   The evidence indicates that satisfied employees increase customer satisfaction and loyalty.[29] Why? The answer is obvious: satisfied employees are more likely to be friendly and responsive, and this is something that customers definitely appreciate. Moreover, because satisfied employees remain in the organization and thus turnover decreases, customers enjoy seeing familiar faces and receiving experienced service. As a result, customer satisfaction and loyalty is established. Nevertheless, there also seems to be a negative relationship. Dissatisfied customers can increase an employee's job dissatisfaction. That is, employees who interact with rude and thoughtless customers usually experience job dissatisfaction.[30]

Managers Often 'Don't Get It'   With all the evidence we just reviewed above, it should come as no surprise that job satisfaction can affect lower-level employees. So, we ask ourselves, 'Why do managers still not understand what is happening in the workplace?' Unfortunately, despite these results, many managers don't care if their employees are satisfied or not. One study of 262 large employers found that 86 percent of senior managers believed their organization treated its employees well, but only 55 percent of the employees agreed. Another study found 55 percent of managers thought morale was good in their organization, compared with only 38 percent of employees.[31] Managers first need to care about job satisfaction, and then they need to measure it rather than just assume that everything is going well. These are all the issues related to employee motivation and performance enhancement that will be dealt with in Chapter 5.

Global Implications

Is Job Satisfaction Specific to Cultures?

7 Show whether job satisfaction is a relevant concept in different cultures.

Although most of the research on job satisfaction has been conducted in the United States, we cannot presume that job satisfaction is exclusively a US concept. The evidence strongly suggests that this is *not* the case; people in other cultures can and do form judgments of job satisfaction. Moreover, it appears that similar factors cause, and result from, job satisfaction across cultures. To illustrate, we noted earlier that pay is positively, but relatively weakly, related to job satisfaction.

Are Employees in Western Cultures More Satisfied with Their Jobs than Those in the East?

Although job satisfaction appears to be a relevant concept across cultures, that doesn't mean there are no cultural differences in job satisfaction. Evidence suggests that employees in Western cultures have higher levels of job satisfaction than those in Eastern cultures.[32] Figure 3-5 provides the results of a global study of the job satisfaction levels of workers in 15 countries. (This study included 23 countries, but for presentation purposes, we report the results for only the largest.) As the figure shows, the highest levels of job satisfaction appear to be in the United States and Western Europe. Is the reason for this that employees in Western cultures have better jobs? Or are individuals in Western cultures simply more positive (and less self-critical)? Although both factors are probably at play, evidence suggests that individuals in Eastern cultures value negative emotions more than do individuals in Western cultures, whereas those in Western cultures tend to emphasize positive emotions and individual happiness.[33] That may be why employees in Western cultures such as the US and Scandinavia are more likely to have higher levels of satisfaction.

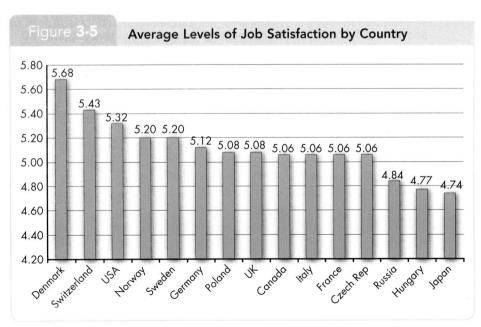

Figure 3-5   Average Levels of Job Satisfaction by Country

Source: M. Benz and B. S. Frey, "The Value of Autonomy: Evidence from the Self-Employed in 23 Countries," working paper 173, Institute for Empirical Research in Economics, University of Zurich, November 2003 (http://ssrn.com/abstract=475140).

Note: Scores represent average job-satisfaction levels in each country as rated on a 1 = very dissatisfied to 10 = very satisfied scale.

Summary and Implications for Managers

The sections of this chapter have presented information that should help managers to become more interested in their employees' attitudes because attitudes may predict problems and because they influence behavior. In addition, satisfied and committed employees have lower rates of turnover, absenteeism, and negative behaviors, and ultimately they perform better on the job. As one review put it, "A sound measurement of overall job attitude is one of the most useful pieces of information an organization can have about its employees."[34]

The most important thing managers can do to raise employee satisfaction is focus on the intrinsic parts of the job, such as making the work challenging and interesting. Although paying employees poorly will likely not attract high-quality employees to the organization, or keep high performers, managers should realize that high pay alone is unlikely to create a satisfying work environment. Furthermore, creating a satisfied workforce is hardly a guarantee of successful organizational performance; but evidence strongly suggests that whatever managers can do to improve employee attitudes will lead to organizational effectiveness.

Point ≫ ≪ Counterpoint

MANAGERS CAN CREATE SATISFIED EMPLOYEES

A review of the evidence has identified four factors that contribute to high levels of employee job satisfaction: mentally challenging work, equitable rewards, supportive working conditions, and supportive colleagues.[35] The general understanding is that management is able to control each of the above-mentioned factors.

To explain, people prefer jobs that allow them opportunities to expose their skills and abilities. In addition, employees want pay systems that are just and within their expectations. Moreover, employees want work environments that are safe and comfortable to facilitate their work. Furthermore, most employees fulfill a need for social interaction from their workplace.

There is evidence that challenges the idea that managers control the factors that influence employee job satisfaction. It fits nicely with the view that managers directly influence organizational processes and outcomes. The most recent findings indicate that it is largely genetically determined.[36] Whether a person is happy or not is essentially determined by gene structure. Approximately 50 to 80 percent of people's differences in happiness, or subjective wellbeing, has been found to be attributable to their genes. Identical twins, for example, tend to have very similar careers, report similar levels of job satisfaction, and change jobs at similar rates.

The only place managers will have any significant influence is in the selection process. If managers want satisfied workers, they need to screen out negative people who get little satisfaction from their jobs no matter what the work conditions are.

Questions for Review

1 What are the main components of attitudes? Are these components related or unrelated?

2 Does behavior always follow from attitudes? Why or why not? Compare and contrast the relationship between the two.

3 What are the major job attitudes? In what ways are these attitudes alike? What is unique about each?

4 How do we measure job satisfaction?

5 What causes job satisfaction? For most people, is pay or the work itself more important?

6 What outcomes does job satisfaction influence? What does this mean to management?

7 Is job satisfaction influenced by culture?

Discussion Exercise

The following factors are considered important to achieve satisfaction within the workplace:

Autonomy and independence	Management recognition of employee job performance
Benefits	Meaningfulness of job
Career advancement and development opportunities	Networking
Communication between employees and management	Opportunities to use skills/abilities
Compensation and pay	Organization's commitment to professional development
Contribution of work to organization's business goals	Overall corporate culture
Feeling safe in the work environment	Relationship with coworker
Flexibility to balance life and work issues	Relationship with immediate supervisor
Job security	The work itself
Job-specific training	The variety of work

Which are your top five for job satisfaction? Discuss. Do most people seem to value the same job factors? Why or why not?

Ethical Considerations

'One man's misfortune is another's good fortune.' What is your reaction to this saying? Individuals just look out for personal gain regardless of how it might influence others. What's the best word to describe this? Could it be greed? After all, selfishness is an attitude and part of human nature and often it dictates how individuals perform in organizations. For instance, they may have a 'personal agenda' and not be aiming to achieve organizational goals. Discuss the ethical implications. To what extent do you think that job satisfaction may be linked to a person's greed and need for personal gain?

For more ideas on this topic, see Michael Young, "The need for greed," *Executive Magazine*, Issue No. 117, April, 2009, p. 128.

Critical Analysis

JOB SATISFACTION IN THE UAE

The United Arab Emirates (UAE) is a federation of seven emirates in the Arabian Peninsula. The UAE has a population of six million, of which approximately 80 percent are non-nationals (expatriates) from more than 200 countries.

In a survey conducted by job site www.Bayt.com and research company YouGovSiraj.com, only 27 percent of the 9,760 respondents expressed high satisfaction with their work. Those who expressed the most satisfaction with their jobs were Lebanese and Moroccan nationals. The lowest ratings were given by Gulf nationals. Dissatisfaction appeared to be due largely to poor work organization; this resulted in low motivation levels (65 percent of UAE workers said they felt motivated in their work). If employees feel undervalued, they could become dissatisfied and leave. Such behavior results in a financial loss for the employer as it costs more to recruit new than to retain existing staff.

As a follow-up, readers of the *Gulf News* were asked "How satisfied are you with your job?" In readers' comments, posted online, job dissatisfaction was most often about salary, either late salary payments, low salaries, or failure to increase salaries. For one UAE receptionist, promises by her employer of an increase in pay did not materialize, and that led to her dissatisfaction with the job. It was also determined that the UAE government needed to legislate on salaries and that apartment rents were too high for the salaries offered.

Readers also gave suggestions about how to become satisfied with jobs and suggested working for an employer who promotes equal opportunity, and finding a job that matches one's qualifications and skills. A proposal was made that experience in other departments would enable employees to be more committed and would improve job competencies. *Gulf News* readers also said that staff needed training to improve their attitude about their jobs, to increase interest, and to offer a career path. In the online postings, concern was expressed that the system of three-year work visas caused employees and employers to have only short-term working relationships. As some multinational companies may be located in the UAE for only a short while, this may also contribute negatively to commitment and job satisfaction. Some managers consider that commitment to an organization is influenced by a 'fit' between the person, the job, and the organization.

Questions

1. What are three things that employers could do to increase the job satisfaction of their staff?
2. How can employers increase employee commitment?

Sources: "Expat Numbers Rise Rapidly as UAE Population Touches 6m," *UAE Interact*, October 2009, http://uaeinteract.com/docs/Expat_numbers_rise_rapidly_as_UAE_population_touches_6M/37883.htm"; and C. Maceda, "UAE's Job Satisfaction Rating Very Low," *gulfnews.com*, April 2008, http://gulfnews.com/business/general/uae-s-job-satisfaction-rating-very-low-1.99982.

Research Exercise

Do your own research and find a case or incident that is relevant to the concepts we have discussed in this chapter. It should be about a local organization and show how business practices in the the Arab world are both similar and different to other regions in the world.

LEARNING OBJECTIVES

This chapter will enable you to:

1 Define *perception* and explain the factors that influence it.

2 Explain attribution theory and list the three determinants of attribution.

3 Identify the shortcuts individuals use in making judgments about others.

4 Explain the link between perception and decision making.

5 Apply the rational model of decision making and contrast it with bounded rationality and intuition.

6 List and explain the common decision biases or errors.

7 Explain how individual differences and organizational constraints affect decision making.

8 Contrast the three ethical decision criteria.

9 Define *creativity* and discuss the three-component model of creativity.

Perception and Individual Decision Making

4

Great business decisions in corporate history often come from intuition rather than 'data.' Data is important, but should not replace intuition.

—Kamran Siddiqi, CEO of GM Visa International, Middle East

What Do Arabs Think About Arabs?

Unfortunately, stereotyping exists in all cultures and it keeps people from making their own judgments and evaluation of either a situation or an individual. As a result, many tend to develop preconceived ideas without understanding the actual events.

Arab–Arab stereotypes also exist and that is why it is important to allow Arabs the opportunity to learn more about each other. Only when we understand culture and values can we be more equipped to handle specific situations. This was very clear when fighting broke out before and after two international association football matches between Egypt and Algeria in November, 2009.

To erase these negative perceptions, a Jordanian NGO founded Safar in 2005. The objective is to offer young Arabs between the ages of 15 and 35 travel grants so they can experience first-hand how people in their own region live and interact with one another. Safar's program manager, Mais Irqsusi, explains that it also gives participants the space and opportunities to follow their own learning.

One of Safar's founders, Rasha Najdi, explains that Arabs are in the habit of developing generalized conceptions. She illustrates this by talking about how individuals have changed their outlook toward certain football players, political standpoints, and even the face veil once they became more aware of the circumstances and the people themselves. Najdi strongly encourages Arab youth to live with one another, and interact on a daily basis, because this is the most effective way to eliminate negative stereotypes.

"I believe it is a healthy process through which an Arab individual can have a good experience in exploring other's attitudes and cultures, instead of formulating misconceptions about the other," Najdi stresses.

Source: Ethar Shalaby, "NGO Tackles Arab–Arab Stereotypes," *Hiwar Magazine*, April 29, 2010, http://hiwar.dedi.org.eg/index.php/en/top-news/380-ngo-tackles-arab-arab-stereotypes.

The chapter opening considers perceptions. What we perceive can be very far from the reality. Many times, we judge one person based on our experience with someone else from the same town, background, or even from the same belief system. We should never generalize; this is not just. We must not 'judge a book by its cover' but read it carefully and understand it before we make a final decision. This chapter focuses on the issues and factors that contribute to and affect perception, and how they contribute to decision making.

The following Self-Assessment Library considers perceptions of older people.

Self Assessment Library »»

WHAT'S MY ATTITUDE TOWARDS OLDER PEOPLE?

In the Self-Assessment Library (available online), take assessment IV.C.1 (What's My Attitude Toward Older People?) and answer the following questions:

1. *Were you surprised by your score? Why or why not?*
2. *Do you think a problem with measures like this is that people aren't honest in responding?*
3. *Do you think your perceptions would change if you were rating your older family members or tutors, rather than strangers?*

What Is Perception?

1 Define perception *and explain the factors that influence it.*

Perception

A process by which individuals organize and interpret their sensory impressions in order to give meaning to their environment.

Perception is a process by which individuals organize and interpret their sensory impressions in order to give meaning to their environment. However, what we perceive can be very different from reality. For example, all employees in a firm may view it as a great place to work—favorable working conditions, interesting job assignments, good pay, excellent benefits, understanding and responsible management—but, as most of us know, it's very unusual to find such agreement.

Why is perception important in the study of OB? Simply because people's behavior is based on their perception of what reality is, not on reality itself. *The world as it is perceived is the world that is behaviorally important.*

Factors That Influence Perception

How do we explain the fact that individuals may look at the same thing yet perceive it differently? A number of factors help us to shape and sometimes interfere with perception. These factors are found in the *perceiver*, in the object, or *target*, being perceived; or in the context of the *situation* in which the perception is made. Figure 4-1 explains in detail the factors that influence perception.

When an individual looks at a target and attempts to interpret what he or she sees, that interpretation is heavily influenced by the individual characteristics of the perceiver. Personal characteristics such as attitudes, personality, motives, interests, past experiences, and expectations can affect the way we see and understand things. We all can establish an idea of how certain people should behave, and this may have nothing to do with their personality. For instance, if you expect police officers to be authoritative and young people to be lazy, then you may perceive them as such, regardless of their actual traits.

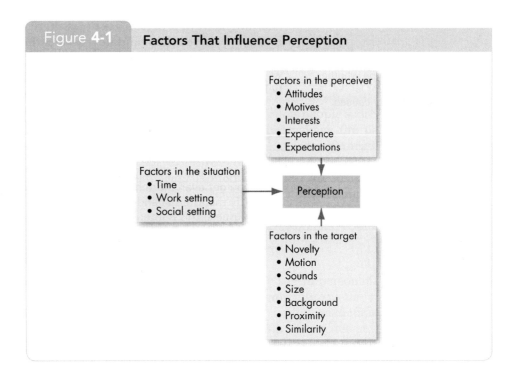

Figure 4-1   Factors That Influence Perception

Moreover, we tend to notice loud people and attractive people more than quiet and unattractive people in a group. We don't look at people one by one but, rather, we look at them and how they appear in a group because we have a tendency to group close things and similar things together.

To explain this further, the context within which we see objects or events is important. The time at which we see an object or event can influence attention, as can location, light, heat, or any number of situational factors.

Picture This

On Saturday evening at a wedding reception you may not notice someone who is all dressed up. But imagine that same person dressed in the same way for your Monday morning management class. Does that same person catch your attention? Neither the perceiver, nor the target changed between Saturday night and Monday morning, but the situation is different.

Person Perception: Making Judgments About Others

2 Explain attribution theory and list the three determinants of attribution.

Now that we have introduced the idea of perception, let's move to see how these perception concepts can be applied to OB. This is more specifically the issue of *person perception*, or the perceptions people form about each other.

Attribution Theory

Nonliving objects such as desks, machines, and buildings have no beliefs, motives, or intentions; however, people do. That's why, when we observe people, we try to understand why they behave in certain ways. Our perception

Attribution theory

An attempt to determine whether an individual's behavior is internally or externally caused.

and judgment of a person's actions, therefore, will be significantly influenced by the way we see them and how we feel they usually behave.

This brings us to **attribution theory**, which tries to explain the ways in which we judge people differently, depending on the meaning we attribute to a given behavior.[1]

Picture This

You have a job interview and you attribute your nervousness to the interview. That is, you know exactly how important the interview is for you to get the job, but you get even more nervous when you are late because of traffic. We need to identify the internal and external causes. For instance, you could control your nervousness; this is internal. On the other hand, you have no control over traffic; this is an external cause.

The determination of whether the causes are internal or external depends on three factors: (1) distinctiveness, (2) consensus, and (3) consistency.

Distinctiveness refers to whether an individual displays different behaviors in different situations. Are you always nervous or just because of the interview? What we want to know is whether this behavior is unusual. If it is, we are likely to give it an external attribution. If it's not unusual, we will probably judge the behavior to be internal. Do you think that everyone usually gets nervous at an interview? If everyone who faces a similar situation responds in the same way, we can say the behavior shows *consensus*. From an attribution perspective, if consensus is high, you would probably give an external attribution to the employee's nervousness, whereas if other employees are nervous, you would attribute this to an internal cause.

Finally, an observer looks for *consistency* in a person's actions. Does the person respond the same way over time? Will you be nervous every time you go for an interview or is it only this time? The more consistent the behavior, the more we are inclined to attribute it to internal causes.

Figure 4-2 summarizes the key elements in attribution theory. It tells us, for instance, that if an employee, Ahmad Ramzi, generally performs at about the same level on other related tasks as he does on his current task (low distinctive-

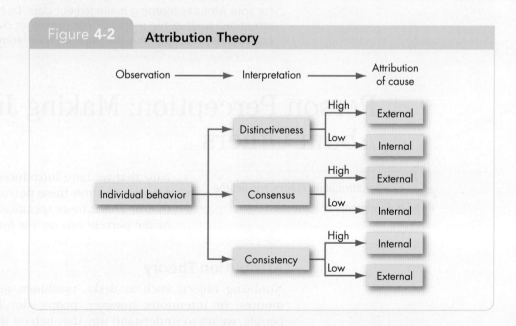

Figure **4-2**   **Attribution Theory**

ness), if other employees frequently perform differently—better or worse—than Ahmad does on that current task (low consensus), and if Ahmad's performance on this current task is consistent over time (high consistency), you or anyone else judging Ahmad's work will be likely to hold him responsible for his task performance (internal attribution).

Evidence suggests that when we make judgments about the behavior of other people, we tend to underestimate the influence of external factors and overestimate the influence of internal or personal factors.[2] This is described as **fundamental attribution error** and explains why a sales manager is encouraged to attribute the poor performance of sales agents to laziness rather than to the difficult product line introduced by a competitor. Individuals and organizations also tend to attribute their own successes to internal factors such as ability or effort, while putting the blame for failure on external factors such as bad luck or unproductive coworkers. This is known as the **self-serving bias**.[3] It is only part of human nature that we blame others for our failures. For example, when the famous and former (and now deceased) Enron CEO Ken Lay was tried for fraud, he blamed former Chief Financial Officer Andrew Fastow, saying, "I think the primary reason for Enron's collapse was Andy Fastow and his little group of people and what they did."

Fundamental attribution error

The tendency to underestimate the influence of external factors and overestimate the influence of internal factors when making judgments about the behavior of others.

Self-serving bias

The tendency for individuals to attribute their own successes to internal factors and put the blame for failures on external factors.

Frequently Used Shortcuts in Judging Others

3 Identify the shortcuts individuals use in making judgments about others.

We use a number of shortcuts when we judge others. These techniques are frequently valuable: They allow us to make accurate perceptions rapidly and provide valid data for making predictions. However, they do present many problems. They can and do get us into trouble. Understanding these shortcuts can help you recognize when they can result in significant distortions.

Selective Perception   Any characteristic that makes a person, an object, or an event stand out will increase the probability that we will perceive it. Why? Because it is impossible for us to assimilate everything we see; we can take in only certain stimuli. This tendency explains why you're more likely to notice cars like your own or why a boss may reprimand some people and not others who are doing the same thing. Because we can't observe everything going on about us, we engage in **selective perception**.

To illustrate, a study was conducted in which 23 business executives read a comprehensive case describing the organization and activities of a steel company.[4] Six were in sales, five in production, four in accounting, and eight in other functions. Each manager was asked to identify the most important problem in the case. Eighty-three percent of the sales executives rated sales important; only 29 percent of the others did so. The researchers concluded that participants perceived as important the aspects of a situation specifically related to their own unit's activities and goals. A group's perception of organizational activities is selectively altered to align with the interests they represent.

Because we cannot assimilate all that we observe, we take in bits and pieces. But we don't choose them randomly; rather, we select them according to our interests, background, experience, and attitudes. Selective perception allows us to 'speed-read' others, but not without the risk of drawing an inaccurate picture.

Selective perception

The tendency to selectively interpret what one sees on the basis of one's interests, background, experience, and attitudes.

Halo effect

The tendency to draw a general impression about an individual on the basis of a single characteristic.

Halo Effect   When we draw a general impression about an individual on the basis of a single characteristic, such as intelligence, sociability, or appearance, a **halo effect** is operating.[5]

In 2009 Sheikh Mohammed Bin Rashid Al Maktoum expressed the view that some Western media had stereotypical views of Arabs, the UAE and the emirate of Dubai. In an internet forum with journalists, the ruler of Dubai and vice-president of the UAE, said, "It seems that the success of the Arab, whether individual or state, city or a company, is seen as unacceptable. It seems that seeing distinct images of successful Arabs and Arab countries disturbs some people. They would rather stick with the distorted images of Arab stereotypes in their minds."

Source: N. Gangal, "Sheikh Mohammed Slams Stereotyped Perceptions of Arabs," *ArabianBusiness.com*, ITP Publishing Group, April 2009.

Contrast effects

Evaluation of a person's characteristics that is affected by comparisons with other people recently encountered who rank higher or lower on the same characteristics.

Stereotyping

Judging someone on the basis of one's perception of the group to which that person belongs.

Profiling

A form of stereotyping in which a group of individuals is singled out—typically on the basis of race or ethnicity—for intensive inquiry, scrutiny, or investigation.

The reality of the halo effect was confirmed in a classic study in which subjects were given a list of traits, such as intelligent, skillful, practical, hard working, determined, and friendly, and asked to evaluate the person to whom those traits applied.[6] It was concluded that the person was wise, funny, popular, and imaginative. However, when the same list was changed, and unfriendly replaced friendly, a completely different picture appeared. In sum, they allowed one single trait to influence their overall impression of the person they were judging.

What Do You Think?

Have you ever been misjudged as a result of the halo effect? Have you ever judged someone else on the basis of a single characteristic?

Contrast Effects   We usually evaluate people as we compare them to others we have met and this example demonstrates how **contrast effects** can interfere with perceptions.

To illustrate, a job applicant may receive a good evaluation if preceded by non-competent applicants and a less positive evaluation if preceded by strong applicants.

Stereotyping   When we judge someone on the basis of our perception of the group to which he or she belongs, we are using the shortcut called **stereotyping**.[7] We discussed the problems of stereotyping in the Arab world in the opening case of this chapter.

One specific type of stereotypes is **profiling**—a form of stereotyping in which a group of individuals is singled out, typically on the basis of race or ethnicity, for intensive inquiry, scrutiny, or investigation. One of the problems of stereotypes is that they *are* widespread and often use generalizations, despite the fact that they may not contain any truth when applied to a particular person or situation. So we constantly have to check ourselves to make sure we're not unfairly or inaccurately applying a stereotype in our evaluations and decisions. Stereotypes are an example of the warning, 'The more useful, the more danger from misuse.'

Specific Applications of Shortcuts in Organizations

People in organizations are always judging each other. Managers must appraise or evaluate their employees' performances. We evaluate how much effort our coworkers are putting into their jobs. When a new person joins a work team, the other members immediately make a judgment based on what they see from the outside. In many cases, our judgments have important consequences for the organization. Let's briefly look at a few of the most obvious applications.

Employment Interview   A major input into who is hired and who is rejected in an organization is the employment interview. It's fair to say that few people are hired without an interview. But evidence indicates that interviewers make perceptual judgments that are often inaccurate.[8] They generally draw early impressions that very quickly become stuck in their heads. Research shows that we form impressions of others within a tenth of a second, based on our first glance at them.[9] As a result, information received early in the interview carries greater weight than does information that comes later, and a 'good applicant' is probably characterized more by the absence of bad characteristics rather than by the presence of good characteristics. For instance, an interviewer immediately notices that Yusra is poorly dressed but does not focus on the good language skills she has. Thus, the good characteristic is overshadowed by the negative one of her dress code.

Performance Expectations   People attempt to validate their perceptions of reality, even when those perceptions are faulty.[10] This characteristic is particularly relevant when we consider performance expectations on the job. The terms **self-fulfilling prophecy** and *Pygmalion effect* have evolved to characterize the fact that an individual's behavior is determined by other people's expectations. In other words, if managers expect big things from their people, they're not likely to disappoint them. Similarly, if managers expect people to perform minimally, they'll tend to behave so as to meet those low expectations. The expectations become reality. The self-fulfilling prophecy has been found to affect the performance of students in school, soldiers in combat, and even accountants.[11]

Performance Evaluation   Performance evaluations are very much dependent on the perceptual process.[12] An employee's future is closely tied to the appraisal, pay raises, and continuation of employment. Although the appraisal can be objective (for example, a salesperson is appraised on how many dinars of sales are generated), many jobs are evaluated in subjective terms. Subjective evaluations of performance, though often necessary, are problematic because all the errors we've discussed thus far—selective perception, contrast effects, halo effects, and so on—affect them. Ironically, sometimes performance ratings say as much about the evaluator as they do about the employee! We'll discuss performance evaluations more fully in Chapter 15.

Self-fulfilling prophecy

A situation in which a person inaccurately perceives a second person, and the resulting expectations cause the second person to behave in ways consistent with the original perception.

The Link Between Perception and Individual Decision Making

4 Explain the link between perception and decision making.

Individuals in organizations make **decisions**. That is, they make choices from among two or more alternatives. Top managers, for instance, determine their organization's goals, what products or services to offer, how best to finance operations, or where to locate a new manufacturing plant. Middle- and lower-level managers determine production schedules, select new employees, and decide how pay raises are to be allocated. Of course, making decisions is not the only job responsibility of managers. Nonmanagerial employees also make decisions that affect their jobs and the organizations for which they work.

They decide whether to come to work on any given day, how much effort to put in at work, and whether to comply with a request made by the boss. In recent years, organizations have been empowering their nonmanagerial employees with job-related decision-making authority that was historically reserved for managers alone. Individual decision making, therefore, is an important part of organizational behavior. But how individuals in organizations make decisions and the quality of their final choices are largely influenced by their perceptions.

Decision making occurs as a reaction to a **problem**.[13] That is, a gap exists between the actual state of affairs and some desired state, requiring us to consider alternative courses of action. Unfortunately, not all problems come neatly packaged and labeled 'problem.' One person's *problem* is another person's *satisfactory state of affairs.* To explain, one manager may view her division's 2 percent decline in quarterly sales to be a serious problem requiring immediate action on her part. In contrast, her counterpart in another division of the same company, who also had a 2 percent sales decrease, might consider that percentage

Decisions

Choices made from among two or more alternatives.

Problem

A discrepancy between the current state of affairs and some desired state.

quite acceptable. So the awareness that a problem exists and whether a decision needs to be made is a perceptual issue.

What Do You Think?

'One person's problem is another person's satisfactory state of affairs.' Can you think of the Arabic version of this expression? Do you agree with this expression?

Moreover, every decision requires us to interpret and evaluate information. We typically receive data from multiple sources and need to screen, process, and interpret it to determine which data are relevant to the decision and which are not. The perceptions of the decision maker will answer that question. We also need to develop alternatives and evaluate the strengths and weaknesses of each. Again, because alternatives don't come with their strengths and weaknesses clearly marked, an individual decision maker's perceptual process will have a large influence on the final outcome. Finally, the way we make decisions depends on individuals: do they want all the information before they can decide or do they depend on their own feelings? These are the issues that will be discussed in the next section.

Decision Making in Organizations

5 Apply the rational model of decision making and contrast it with bounded rationality and intuition.

Business schools generally train students to follow rational decision-making models. While these models have considerable merit, they don't always describe how people actually make decisions. This is where we need to consider OB. If we are to improve how we make decisions in organizations, we need to understand the decision-making errors that people commit (in addition to the perception errors just discussed). In the next sections, we will give a brief overview of the rational decision-making model, bounded rationality and intuition.

Rational
Characterized by making consistent, value-maximizing choices within specified constraints.

Rational decision-making model
A decision-making model that describes how individuals should behave in order to maximize some outcome.

The Rational Model, Bounded Rationality, and Intuition

Rational Decision Making   We often think the best decision maker is **rational**, that is, makes sense and makes consistent, value-maximizing choices within specified constraints.[14] These decisions follow a six-step **rational decision-making model**.[15] The six steps are listed in Box 4-1 below.

BOX 4-1
Steps in the Rational Decision-Making Model

1. Define the problem.
2. Identify the decision criteria.
3. Allocate weights to the criteria.
4. Develop the alternatives.
5. Evaluate the alternatives.
6. Select the best alternative.

The rational decision-making model relies on a number of assumptions, including that the decision maker has complete information, is able to identify all the relevant options in an unbiased manner, and chooses the option with the highest utility.[16] As you might imagine, most decisions in the real world don't follow the rational model. For instance, people are usually content to find an acceptable or reasonable solution to a problem rather than an optimal one. Choices tend to be limited to the neighborhood of the problem and of the current alternative. As one expert in decision making put it, "Most significant decisions are made by judgment, rather than by a defined prescriptive model."[17]

Bounded Rationality   Most people respond to a complex problem by reducing it to a level that simplifies it and allows them to understand it. The limited information-processing capability of human beings makes it impossible to assimilate and understand all the information necessary to optimize.[18] So people *satisfice;* that is, they seek solutions that are satisfactory and sufficient.

Kamran Siddiqi is General manager of Visa International Middle East. For Siddiqi, *intuition* is one of the three great leadership 'truths'. He believes that "Intuition is finely honed experience and observation, the greatest asset of a leader. Great business decisions in corporate history often came from intuition rather than data. Data is important, but should not replace intuition."

Source: "My First CEO: Kamran Siddiqi," *ArabianBusiness.com*, ITP Publishing Group, April 1, 2007.

Bounded rationality

A process of making decisions by constructing simplified models that extract the essential features from problems without capturing all their complexity.

Intuitive decision making

An unconscious process created out of distilled experience.

> ### Picture This
> When you considered which college to attend, did you look at every alternative? Did you carefully identify all the criteria that were important in your decision? Probably not. Well, don't feel bad. Few people made their college choice this way. Many people just went to the same place their friends chose, thus that end our search. Therefore, take the satisficing choice—the first acceptable one—rather than an optimal one.

Because the human mind cannot formulate and solve complex problems with full rationality, we operate within the confines of **bounded rationality**. That is, we construct simplified models that extract the essential features from problems without capturing all their complexity.[19]

Intuition   Perhaps the least rational way of making decisions is to rely on intuition. **Intuitive decision making** is a nonconscious process created from distilled experience.[20] Its defining qualities are that it occurs outside conscious thought; it relies on holistic associations, or links between disparate pieces of information; it's fast; and it's affectively charged, meaning that it usually engages the emotions.[21]

Intuition is not rational, but that doesn't necessarily make it wrong and there are many great leaders who depend on it. And intuition doesn't necessarily operate in opposition to rational analysis; rather, the two can complement each other. And intuition can be a powerful force in decision making.

For most of the twentieth century, experts believed that decision makers' use of intuition was irrational or ineffective. That's no longer the case.[22] There is growing recognition that rational analysis has been overemphasized and that, in certain instances, relying on intuition can improve decision making.[23] But while intuition can be invaluable in making good decisions, we can't rely on it too much. Because it can't be measured, it's hard to know when our feelings are right or wrong. The key is not to either abandon it or rely solely on intuition but to supplement it with evidence and good judgment.

Common Biases and Errors in Decision Making

6 *List and explain the common decision biases or errors.*

Decision makers engage in bounded rationality, but an accumulating body of research tells us that decision makers also allow systematic biases and errors to enter into their judgments.[24] These come from attempts to shortcut the

International OB

How Culture Influences Decision Making

Very few people take time to consider how their decisions are made. Consequently, we may find the ways in which people from different cultures make decisions to be unusual. However, it is these very cultural differences that dictate how individuals think and behave and we must be aware of the diversity. The following are guidelines to how different cultures make decisions.

Identifying Problems

Logically, the first step in decision making is to admit that there is a problem and identify the details. For example, you are managing a large construction project but your major supplier will be late in delivering material. What do you do? If you are from the US,

Canada or Western Europe, you may contact another supplier. Someone from Thailand, Indonesia, or Malaysia may just say it's fate and delay the project.

Making Predecisions

This depends on whether people are from an individualistic or collectivistic culture. Americans have highly individualistic orientations and thus make decisions alone. On the other hand, a Japanese person would never make a decision without consulting with colleagues first.

Generating and Evaluating Alternatives

In India, structure is very formal and people expect decisions to be made by others according to their rank;

empowerment is not an option. In contrast, employees in Sweden expect to be involved in every decision that involves them.

Making Choices

Managers in the US and some other countries will be respected for their 'decisiveness' if they make decisions quickly. However, in the Arab world, it is considered essential to take yout time and think carefully before making a decision. The more important the issue, the more time an Egyptian, say, is expected to take.

Source: K. Roth, "Implementing International Strategy at the Business Unit Level: The Role of Managerial Decision-Making Characteristics," *Journal of Management* 18 (1992), pp. 769–789.

decision process. To minimize effort and avoid difficult trade-offs, people tend to rely too heavily on experience, impulses, gut feelings, and convenient rules of thumb. In many instances, these shortcuts are helpful. However, they can lead to severe distortions of rationality. Following are the most common biases in decision making.

Overconfidence Bias   It's been said that "no problem in judgment and decision making is more dangerous than overconfidence."[25]

From an organizational standpoint, one of the most interesting findings related to overconfidence is that those individuals whose intellectual and interpersonal abilities are *weakest* are most likely to overestimate their performance and ability.[26] So as managers and employees become more knowledgeable about an issue, they become less likely to display overconfidence.[27] And overconfidence is most likely to appear when organizational members are considering issues or problems that are outside their area of expertise.[28] In other words, self-confidence is great, but do not overdo it to the point of arrogance.

Anchoring bias

A tendency to fixate on initial information, from which one then fails to adequately adjust for subsequent information.

Anchoring Bias   The **Anchoring bias** is a tendency to fixate on initial information and fail to adequately adjust for subsequent information[29]. The anchoring bias occurs because our mind appears to give a disproportionate amount of emphasis to the first information it receives.[30] Anchors are widely used by people in professions where persuasion skills are important—such as advertising, management, politics, real estate, and law.

Consider the role of anchoring in negotiations. Any time a negotiation takes place, so does anchoring. As soon as someone states a number, your ability to ignore that number has been compromised. For instance, when a prospective employer asks how much you were making in your prior job, your answer typically anchors the employer's offer. You may want to keep this in mind when you negotiate your salary, but remember to set the anchor only as high as you realistically can.

Confirmation Bias   The rational decision-making process assumes that we objectively gather information. But we don't. We *selectively* gather it. The **confirmation bias** represents a specific case of selective perception that we discussed earlier. We seek out information that reaffirms our past choices, and we discount information that contradicts them.[31]

Availability Bias   Many more people fear flying than fear driving in a car. But if flying on a commercial airline were as dangerous as driving, the equivalent of two 747s filled to capacity would have to crash every week, killing all aboard, to match the risk of being killed in a car accident. Yet the media gives much more attention to air accidents, so we tend to overstate the risk of flying and understate the risk of driving.

This illustrates the **availability bias**, which is the tendency for people to base their judgments on information that is readily available to them.[32] In fact, availability bias can also explain why managers, when doing annual performance appraisals, tend to give more weight to recent employee behaviors than to their behaviors of six or nine months ago.

Escalation of Commitment   Another distortion that creeps into decisions in practice is a tendency to escalate commitment when making a series of decisions.[33] **Escalation of commitment** refers to staying with a decision even when there is clear evidence that it's wrong. For example, consider a friend who has been with his fiancé for several years. Although he admits to you that things aren't going too well in the relationship, he says he is still going to marry her. His justification: "I have a lot invested in the relationship!"

It has been well documented that individuals escalate commitment to a failing course of action when they view themselves as responsible for the failure.[34] Escalation of commitment has obvious implications for managerial decisions. Many an organization has suffered large losses because a manager was determined to prove his original decision was right by continuing to commit resources to what was a lost cause from the beginning.

What Do You Think?

Would you stay in a job just because you have been there for a number of years, even though you are not satisfied in that job?

Randomness Error   Human beings have a lot of difficulty dealing with chance. Most of us like to believe we have some control over our world and our destiny. Although we undoubtedly can control a good part of our future through rational decision making, the truth is that the world will always contain random events. Our tendency to believe we can predict the outcome of random events is the **randomness error**. In the Arab culture, many people depend heavily on God and place their problems in His hands. You will often hear the expressions 'Inshallah,' 'God Willing,' or 'As God wills.'

Hindsight Bias   The **hindsight bias** is the tendency to believe falsely, after the outcome of an event is actually known, that we'd have accurately predicted

---

Confirmation bias

The tendency to seek out information that reaffirms past choices and to discount information that contradicts past judgments.

Availability bias

The tendency for people to base their judgments on information that is readily available to them.

Escalation of commitment

An increased commitment to a previous decision in spite of negative information.

Randomness error

The tendency of individuals to believe that they can predict the outcome of random events.

Hindsight bias

The tendency to believe falsely, after an outcome of an event is actually known, that one would have accurately predicted that outcome.

that outcome.[35] When something happens and we have accurate feedback on the outcome, we seem to be pretty good at concluding that the outcome was relatively obvious, and we usually say, "I was expecting that to happen."

The hindsight bias reduces our ability to learn from the past. It permits us to think that we're better at making predictions than we really are, and can result in our being more confident about the accuracy of future decisions than we have a right to be.

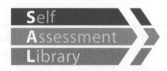

AM I A DELIBERATE DECISION MAKER?

In the Self-Assessment Library (available online), take assessment IV.A.2 (Am I a Deliberate Decision Maker?). Would it be better to be a more deliberate decision maker? Why or why not?

Influences on Decision Making: Individual Differences and Organizational Constraints

7 *Explain how individual differences and organizational constraints affect decision making.*

In the previous section, we examined the rational decision-making model, bounded rationality, and some of the most common biases and errors in decision making. We now turn to a discussion of factors that influence how people make decisions and the degree to which they are at risk of errors and biases. Let's discuss the individual differences and organizational constraints.

Individual Differences

Decision making in practice is characterized by bounded rationality, common biases and errors, and the use of intuition. In addition, individual differences create deviations from the rational model. In this section, we look at two differences: personality and gender, which were both discussed in detail in Chapter 2.

Personality There hasn't been much research on personality and decision making. One possible reason is that most researchers who conduct decision-making research aren't trained to investigate personality. However, the studies that have been conducted suggest that personality does influence decision making. Research has considered conscientiousness and self-esteem, discussed in Chapter 2. Let's look at each in the context of decision making.

Some research has shown that specific facets of conscientiousness—rather than the broad trait itself—affect escalation of commitment that was discussed earlier in this chapter.[36] Interestingly, one study revealed that two facets of conscientiousness—achievement striving and dutifulness—actually had opposite effects on escalation of commitment. For example, achievement-striving people were more likely to escalate their commitment, whereas dutiful people were less likely. Why might this be the case? Generally, achievement-oriented people hate to fail, so they escalate their commitment, hoping to overcome failure. Dutiful people, however, are more inclined to do what they see as best for the organization.

OB in the News

inJAz Bahrain's Business Ethics program

InJAz Bahrain is preparing for the launch and implementation of the new Business Ethics Programme in partnership with Tamkeen (Labour Fund) and Aluminum Bahrain (Alba) for February 2009.

The Business Ethics Programme intends to meet the Private Sector requirements in fostering ethical decision-making in young people as they prepare to enter the workforce. In this program, students will learn to recognize, analyse and apply basic terminology and theories common to the study of ethics. Overall, students will explore their own ethical values and philosophy and learn to evaluate the decision-making process.

Sheikha Hessa Bint Khalifa AlKhalifa, Executive Director of inJAz Bahrain, expressed her pleasure by saying: "inJAz Bahrain was established with the aim to bring individuals and corporates in the Kingdom together to work for the development of our youth. inJAz Bahrain's success, development and sustainability is greatly attributed to the support it receives from all parties. We are very grateful to Tamkeen and Aluminum Bahrain for sponsoring the program. In addition, our appreciation is extended to all inJAz Bahrain board members for their continuous support in providing direction, funding and volunteers to help inJAz Bahrain achieve its objectives."

As co-sponsor and advocate of developing Bahrain's youth, Alba's Chairman Mr. Mahmood Hashim Al Kooheji commented: "At Alba, we contribute to initiatives that empower Bahraini youth to achieve leading positions in the region and beyond. We are firmly committed to playing a vital role in programmes that match our role in supporting the national economy. We are honoured to be partnering with inJAz Bahrain, an active participant to the Kingdom's development. Youth empowerment is one of the most important channels that we can focus on now, and Business Ethics is a topic that needs to be addressed early on. We look forward to making this programme the first of many successes to come."

A multitude of local businesses and individuals are attracted to the subject matter of Business Ethics and have expressed willingness to help, offering expertise on a number of levels, such as training, orientation, coordination and actually delivering the program at the 29 assigned secondary schools next semester.

Commenting on this support, Badria Naqi, inJAz Bahrain Development Director, said: "We are very pleased and excited to see the outpouring of volunteers offer their time and expertise for Business Ethics. This programme exceedingly reflects the true meaning of partnership."

With this latest programme from inJAz Bahrain, the non-profit organization works towards fulfilling its mission of inspiring and preparing young Bahrainis to succeed in a global economy.

Source: Adapted from a press release, Bahrain, "inJAz Bahrain Partnership Drives Business Ethics Program," January 2009, www.ameinfo.com/180846.html.

Second, achievement-striving individuals appear to be more supportive to the hindsight bias, perhaps because they have a greater need to justify the appropriateness of their actions.[37]

Finally, people with high self-esteem appear to be especially susceptible to the self-serving bias. Why? Because they are strongly motivated to maintain their self-esteem, so they use the self-serving bias to preserve it. That is, they blame others for their failures while taking credit for successes.[38]

Gender Recent research on rumination offers insights into gender differences in decision making.[39] Overall, the evidence indicates that women analyze decisions more than men do.

Rumination refers to reflecting at length. In terms of decision making, it means overthinking problems. Women, in general, are more likely than men to engage in rumination. Twenty years of study have found that women spend much more time than men analyzing the past, present, and future. They're more likely to overanalyze problems before making a decision and to reevaluate a decision once it has been made. On the positive side, this is likely to lead to more careful consideration of problems and choices.

Why women ruminate more than men is not clear. One view is that parents encourage and reinforce the expression of sadness and anxiety more in girls than in boys. Another theory is that women, more than men, base their self-esteem and wellbeing on what others think of them. A third theory is that women are more empathetic and more affected by events in others' lives, so they have more to ruminate about.

Organizational Constraints

Organizations can constrain decision makers, creating deviations from the rational model. For instance, managers shape their decisions to reflect the organization's performance evaluation and reward system, to comply with the organization's formal regulations, and to meet organizationally imposed time constraints. Previous organizational decisions also act as precedents to constrain current decisions.

Performance Evaluation Managers are strongly influenced in their decision making by the criteria on which they are evaluated. If a division manager believes the manufacturing plants under his responsibility are operating best when he hears nothing negative, we shouldn't be surprised to find his plant managers spending a good part of their time ensuring that negative information doesn't reach him.

Reward Systems The organization's reward system influences decision makers by suggesting to them what choices are preferable in terms of personal payoff. For example, if the organization rewards risk aversion, managers are more likely to make conservative decisions. To illustrate, from the 1930s through the

At McDonald's restaurants throughout the world, formal regulations shape employee decisions by standardizing the behavior of restaurant crew members such as those pictured here. McDonald's requires that employees follow rules and regulations for food preparation and service to meet the company's standards of food quality and safety, and its reliable and friendly service. For example, McDonald's requires 72 safety protocols to be conducted every day in each restaurant as part of a daily monitoring routine for restaurant managers.

mid-1980s, General Motors consistently gave out promotions and bonuses to managers who kept a low profile and avoided conflict. The result was that GM managers became very good at avoiding tough issues and passing controversial decisions on to committees.

Formal Regulations   Managers at any McDonalds restaurant will say that rules and regulations cover almost all their decisions and that they have little freedom of choice. All but the smallest of organizations create rules and policies to program decisions, which are intended to get individuals to act in the intended manner. And of course, in so doing, they limit the decision maker's choices.

System-Imposed Time Constraints   Organizations impose deadlines on decisions. For instance, a report on new-product development may have to be ready for the executive committee to review by the first of the month. Almost all important decisions come with explicit deadlines. These conditions create time pressures on decision makers and often make it difficult, if not impossible, to gather all the information they might like to have before making a final choice.

Historical Precedents   Decisions aren't made in a vacuum. They have a context. In fact, individual decisions are accurately characterized as points in a stream of decisions. Decisions made in the past are ghosts that continually haunt current choices—that is, commitments that have already been made constrain current options. It's common knowledge that the largest determinant of the size of any given year's budget is last year's budget.[40]

Choices made today, therefore, are largely a result of choices made over the years.

What About Ethics in Decision Making?

8 Contrast the three ethical decision criteria.

Ethical considerations should be extremely important in organizational decision making in all countries and cultures. This is certainly more true today than at any time in the recent past, given that businesses are always under observation and must behave in an ethical and socially responsible way. The ongoing dilemma of how to behave according to values, morals, and principles does not differ from one country to another. What does differ is the decision made by individuals regarding which path to take. In the following section, we present three ways in which to frame decisions ethically.

Three Ethical Decision Criteria

An individual can use three different criteria in making ethical choices.[41] The first is the *utilitarian* criterion, in which decisions are made solely on the basis of their outcomes or consequences. The goal of **utilitarianism** is to provide the greatest good for the greatest number. This view tends to dominate business decision making. It is consistent with goals such as efficiency, productivity, and high profits. By maximizing profits, for instance, a business executive can argue that he is securing the greatest good for the greatest number—as he lays off 15 percent of his employees.

Another ethical criterion is to focus on *rights*. This calls on individuals to make decisions consistent with fundamental liberties and privileges, as set forth in official documents. An emphasis on rights in decision making means respecting and protecting the basic rights of individuals, such as the right to privacy,

Utilitarianism

A system in which decisions are made to provide the greatest good for the greatest number.

Whistle-blowers
Individuals who report unethical practices by their employer to outsiders.

to free speech, and to due process. For instance, this criterion protects **whistle-blowers** when they reveal unethical practices by their organization to the press or government agencies, on the grounds of their right to free speech.

A third criterion is to focus on *justice*. This requires individuals to impose and enforce rules fairly and impartially so that there is an equitable distribution of benefits and costs. Union members support this view. It justifies paying people the same wage for a given job, regardless of performance differences, and using seniority as the primary determination in making layoff decisions.

Each of these criteria has advantages and liabilities. A focus on utilitarianism promotes efficiency and productivity, but it can result in ignoring the rights of some individuals, particularly those with minority representation in the organization. The use of rights as a criterion protects individuals from injury and is consistent with freedom and privacy, but it can create a formal work environment that hinders productivity and efficiency. Moreover, a focus on justice protects the interests of the underrepresented and less powerful, but it can encourage a sense of entitlement that reduces risk taking, innovation, and productivity.

Improving Creativity in Decision Making

9 Define creativity *and discuss the three-component model of creativity.*

Although following the steps of the rational decision-making model that we discussed in the previous section will often improve decisions, a rational decision maker also needs **creativity**, that is, the ability to produce novel (new) and useful ideas.[42] These are ideas that are different from what's been done before but that are appropriate to the problem or opportunity presented.

Why is creativity important to decision making? It allows the decision maker to more fully evaluate and understand the problem, including seeing problems others can't see.

Creativity
The ability to produce novel and useful ideas.

Creative Potential   Most people have creative potential they can use when faced with a decision-making problem. But to use that potential to the maximum, they have to get out of the psychological routine many of us fall into and

Saudi Aramco aims to create an environment that encourages and enables creativity. It set up the Saudi Innovation Exhibition, 'Towards a Creative Society, Ibtikar 2010' to give recognition to inventions and innovators. Omar Bazuhair, Saudi Aramco's chief engineer, explained that the inventions serve as examples of how the success of the company is based firmly on the creativity of its workforce.

learn how to think about a problem in many ways. In other words, we must get into the habit of thinking 'out of the box'—that is, creatively.

A study of the lifetime creativity of 461 men and women found that fewer than 1 percent were exceptionally creative.[43] But 10 percent were highly creative, and about 60 percent were somewhat creative. This suggests that most of us have creative potential; we just need to learn to discover and use it.

Three-Component Model of Creativity What can individuals and organizations do to stimulate employee creativity? The **three-component model of creativity** is the best answer to this question.[44] This model proposes that individual creativity essentially requires expertise, creative-thinking skills, and intrinsic task motivation, and these are shown in Figure 4-3. Studies confirm that the higher the level of each of these three components, the higher the creativity.

Expertise is the foundation for all creative work and is enhanced when individuals have abilities, knowledge, proficiencies, and similar expertise in their specific field of work. For example, you wouldn't expect someone with a minimal knowledge of programming to be very creative as a software engineer.

The second component is *creative-thinking skills* and this includes personality characteristics associated with creativity, the ability to use analogies, and the talent to see the familiar in a different light.

For instance, in the opening case of Chapter 3 about Google, we read how the company provides all it can to keep employees happy because Google understands that satisfied employees will be more creative.

The final component in the three-component model of creativity is *intrinsic task motivation*. This is the desire to work on something because it's interesting, involving, exciting, satisfying, or personally challenging. This motivational component is what turns creativity *potential* into *actual* creative ideas. Factors that encourage creativity include: a culture that encourages the flow of ideas; fair and constructive judgment of ideas; rewards and recognition for creative work; sufficient financial, material, and information resources; freedom to decide what work is to be done and how to do it; a supervisor who communicates effectively, shows confidence in others, and supports the work group; and work group members who support and trust each other.[45]

Three-component model of creativity

The proposition that individual creativity requires expertise, creative-thinking skills, and intrinsic task motivation.

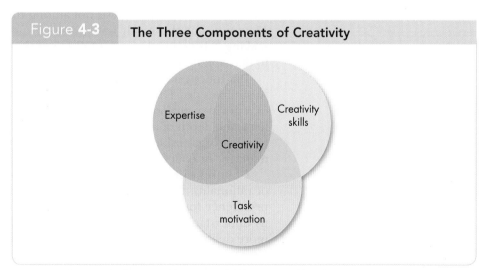

| Figure **4-3** | **The Three Components of Creativity** |

Source: Copyright © 1997, by The Regents of the University of California. Reprinted from *The California Management Review* 40, no. 1. By permission of the University of California Press.

What Do You Think

What helps you to be more creative?

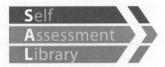

HOW CREATIVE AM I?

In the Self-Assessment Library (available online), take assessment I.A.5 (How Creative Am I?).

Global Implications

Let's stop and think about the global differences in all the concepts we have discussed in this chapter. The three areas that have attracted the most research, as we saw, are (1) attributions, (2) decision making, and (3) ethics.

Attributions Although research on cultural differences in perception is just starting to accumulate, there has been some research on cultural differences in attributions. The evidence is mixed, but most of it suggests that there *are* cultural differences across cultures in the attributions people make.[46] For instance, a study of Korean managers found that, contrary to the self-serving bias, they tended to accept responsibility for group failure "because I was not a capable leader" instead of attributing failure to group members.[47] On the other hand, it has been found that the Arab countries experience individualistic behavior and usually managers do not take responsibility for personal actions or even for groups that they are in charge of.

Decision Making The rational model makes no acknowledgment of cultural differences, nor does the bulk of OB research literature on decision making. A 2007 review of cross-cultural OB research covered 25 areas, but cultural influence on decision making was not among them. Another 2007 review identified 15 topics, but the result was the same: no research on culture and decision making.[48] It seems that most OB research assumes that culture doesn't matter to decision making.

But Indonesians, for instance, don't necessarily make decisions the same way Australians do. Therefore, we need to recognize that the cultural background of a decision maker can have a significant influence on the selection of problems, the depth of analysis, the importance placed on logic and rationality, and whether organizational decisions should be made autocratically by an individual manager or collectively in groups.[49]

Cultures differ, for example, in terms of time orientation, the importance of rationality, their belief in the ability of people to solve problems, and their preference for collective decision making. Differences in time orientation help us understand why managers in Egypt make decisions at a much slower and more deliberate pace than their US counterparts. While rationality is valued in North America, that's not true elsewhere in the world. A North American manager might make an important decision intuitively but know it's important to appear to proceed in a rational fashion because rationality is highly valued in the West. In countries such as Iran, where rationality is not as paramount as other factors, efforts to appear rational are not necessary.

In short, we have reason to believe there are important cultural differences in decision making. Unfortunately, though, there is not yet much research to support these beliefs. OB is a research-based discipline, but research does not always respond quickly to important practical concerns.

Ethics   What is seen as an ethical decision in Qatar may not be seen as such in Canada. The reason is that there are no global ethical standards.[50] To illustrate, because bribery is commonplace in many Arab countries, a Canadian working in these countries might face a dilemma with questions such as 'Should I pay a bribe to secure business if it is an accepted part of that country's culture?' For instance, a manager of a large US company operating in China caught an employee stealing. Following company policy, the employee was fired and turned over to the local authorities. Later, the manager was horrified to learn that the employee had been summarily executed.[51]

In sum, although ethical standards may seem ambiguous in the West, criteria defining right and wrong are actually much clearer in the West than in most Arab countries. Few issues are black and white there; most are gray.

Summary and Implications for Managers

Perception   Individuals base their behavior not on the way their external environment actually is but rather on what they see or believe it to be. Whether a manager successfully plans and organizes the work of employees and actually helps them to structure their work more efficiently and effectively is far less important than how employees perceive the manager's efforts. Similarly, employees judge issues such as fair pay for work performed, the validity of performance appraisals, and the adequacy of working conditions in very individual ways; we cannot be assured that they will interpret conditions about their jobs in a positive light. Therefore, to influence productivity, it's necessary to assess how workers perceive their jobs.

Absenteeism, turnover, and job satisfaction are also reactions to an individual's perceptions. Dissatisfaction with working conditions and the belief that an organization lacks promotion opportunities are judgments based on attempts to create meaning out of the job. The employee's conclusion that a job is good or bad is an interpretation. Managers must spend time understanding how each individual interprets reality, and when there is a significant difference between what someone sees and what exists, try to eliminate the distortions.

Individual Decision Making   Individuals think and reason before they act. This is why an understanding of how people make decisions can be helpful for explaining and predicting their behavior.

In some decision situations, people follow the rational decision-making model. But few important decisions are simple or unambiguous enough for the rational model's assumptions to apply. So we find individuals looking for solutions that satisfy rather than optimize, injecting biases and prejudices into the decision process, and relying on intuition.

Given the evidence we've described throughout this chapter on how decisions are actually made in organizations, what can managers do to improve their decision making? We offer four suggestions.

First, analyze the situation. Adjust your decision-making approach to the national culture you're operating in and to the criteria your organization evaluates and rewards. For instance, if you're in a country that doesn't value rationality, don't feel obliged to follow the rational decision-making model or even to try to make your decisions appear rational. Adjust your decision approach to ensure that it's compatible with the organization's culture.

Second, be aware of biases. Then try to minimize their impact. Box 4-2 below offers some suggestions.

Third, combine rational analysis with intuition. These are not conflicting approaches to decision making. By using both, you can actually improve your decision-making effectiveness.

Finally, try to enhance your creativity. Actively look for innovative solutions to problems, attempt to see problems in new ways, and use analogies. In addition, try to remove work and organizational barriers that might become barriers to your creativity.

BOX 4-2
Reducing Biases and Errors

Focus on Goals. Without goals, you can't be rational, you don't know what information you need, you don't know which information is relevant and which is irrelevant, you'll find it difficult to choose between alternatives, and you're far more likely to experience regret over the choices you make. Clear goals make decision making easier and help you eliminate options that are inconsistent with your interests.

Look for Information that Disagrees with Your Beliefs. One of the most effective means for counteracting overconfidence and the confirmation and hindsight biases is to actively look for information that contradicts your beliefs and assumptions. When we overtly consider various ways we could be wrong, we challenge our tendencies to think we're smarter than we actually are.

Don't Try to Create Meaning out of Random Events. The educated mind has been trained to look for cause-and-effect relationships. When something happens, we ask why. And when we can't find reasons, we often invent them. You have to accept that there are events in life that are outside your control. Ask yourself if patterns can be meaningfully explained or whether they are merely coincidence. Don't attempt to create meaning out of coincidence.

Increase Your Options. No matter how many options you've identified, your final choice can be no better than the best of the option set you've selected. This argues for increasing your decision alternatives and for using creativity in developing a wide range of diverse choices. The more alternatives you can generate, and the more diverse those alternatives, the greater your chance of finding an outstanding one.

Source: S. P. Robbins, *Decide & Conquer: Making Winning Decisions and Taking Control of Your Life* (Upper Saddle River, NJ: Financial Times/Prentice Hall, 2004), pp. 164–168.

Point >< Counterpoint

WHEN IN DOUBT, DO!

*L*ife is full of decisions and choices. The real question is not 'To be, or not to be' but rather 'To do, or not to do?' For example, should I confront my professor about my midterm grade? Should I buy a new car? Should I accept a new job? Should I choose this major? Very often, we are unsure of our decision. In such cases, it is almost always better to choose action over inaction. In life, people more often regret inaction than action. In brief, when in doubt, just do!

*O*n the other hand, if we say when in doubt you should always act, people may make mistakes following such simple advice. For example, you're out of work, but you still decide to purchase your dream car—a BMW, fully loaded. Not the smartest idea. So why is the motto 'just do it' dangerous? Because there are different degrees of regrets. So the bottom line is that we can't apply simple rules such as 'just do it' to important decisions.[52]

Questions for Review

1 What is perception, and what factors influence our perception?

2 What is attribution theory? What are the three determinants of attribution and its implications for explaining organizational behavior?

3 What shortcuts do people frequently use in making judgments about others?

4 What is the link between perception and decision making? How does one affect the other?

5 What is the rational model of decision making? How is it different from bounded rationality and intuition?

6 What are some of the common decision biases or errors that people make?

7 What are the influences of individual differences, organizational constraints, and culture on decision making?

8 Are unethical decisions more a function of an individual decision maker or the decision maker's work environment? Explain.

9 What is creativity, and explain the three-component model of creativity?

Discussion Exercise

Corporate whistle-blowers—individuals who report company wrongdoings—are often punished for their courage and integrity. The decision is not easy because individuals think about the consequences on both a personal and professional level. Discuss the issue of 'whistle-blowing' in the Arab world.

Ethical Considerations

How would you respond to each of the following situations?

1. You are a middle manager in a company with about 1,000 employees. You're negotiating a contract with a very large potential customer whose representative has suggested that you could almost certainly get his business if you gave him and his wife an all-expenses-paid cruise to Cyprus. You know the representative's employer wouldn't approve of such a 'deal,' but you have the authority to make such an expense. What would you do?

2. Your company's policy on reimbursement for meals while traveling on business is that you will be repaid for your out-of-pocket costs, not to exceed US$80 per day. You don't need receipts for these expenses—the company will take your word. When traveling, you tend to eat at fast-food places and rarely spend in excess of US$20 a day. Most of your colleagues put in reimbursement requests in the range of US$55 to US$60 per day, regardless of what their actual expenses are. Why don't you start requesting more also?

3. Assume that you're the manager at a gaming company, and you're responsible for hiring a group to outsource the production of a highly anticipated new game. Because your company is a giant in the industry, numerous companies are trying to get the bid. One of them offers you some advantages if you give that firm the bid; but ultimately, it is up to your bosses to decide on the company. You don't mention the incentive, but you push upper management to give the bid to the company that offered you the compensation. Is withholding the truth as bad as lying? Why or why not?

Effective managers must be good decision makers. How can decisions be made if information is missing? What role does integrity play in making decisions?

Critical Analysis

DECISION MAKING PROCESSES AT STEEL INC.

John Pieterson and Jack Gack are both employees of Steel Incorporated. The company counts more than 5,000 employees and has a presence in almost all European countries. Steel Inc. transforms bulk steel into smaller components, ready to be used in consumer products. Products range from toy parts to food cans. Like most steel companies, Steel Inc. is a traditional company characterized by a low level of flexibility and high levels of bureaucracy. The company has several branches and subsidiaries located all over Europe in order to stay close to its customers.

The decision-making processes at Steel Inc. are crucial to the company's operations. Once a customer (new or existing) approaches the firm, decision making has to happen at a quick pace. Obviously, decisions with regard to level of customization, speed of manufacturing, and prices determine which of the competing companies gets the order. When making a proposal, a huge number of factors must be considered. Not only does all internal information have to be considered, but external information such as competitors' proposals also must be taken into account. If Steel Inc. takes too long to deliver a clear proposal, cannot deliver the demanded products fast enough, or bids too high, competitors will seal the deal.

Although Steel Inc. has gone through some changes, the bureaucratic structure still has a big impact on the jobs of both Pieterson and Gack. John Pieterson is a manager at a subsidiary in The Netherlands. In formulating a proposal or bid for a customer's order, he can be characterized as a very rational person. Although he takes somewhat longer than his colleagues to do similar work, he has always secured a lot of customer orders and is therefore considered a very successful manager within the company. However, Steel Inc.'s success in recent years has affected his decision making. He now drafts a proposal faster, but he also considers less information. In some cases, he even takes competitor prices as a starting point and simply adapts those a little. Still, the change doesn't seem to harm his performance, and orders keep coming in.

Jack Gack, located at a branch in Finland, performs the same job as Pieterson. However, Gack has been very unsuccessful lately. Of course he makes rational decisions, but he also includes a fair share of intuition. Although often criticized, Gack is not willing to let go of his intuition. He truly believes that external factors contributed to his bad performance. Subordinates have also started to talk about Gack's possible incompetence. Top management has looked at Pieterson's success and now wonders whether to impose that style on Jack.

Questions

1. Which biases in decision making can be identified in the performances of both Pieterson and Gack?

2. How can the identified biases be overcome?

3. Is rational decision making better than intuitive decision making? If so, when?

4. Should top management change Gack's decisionmaking style?

Source: Based on Doug Caverly, "Google Goes to the Middle East," *WebProNews*, December 4, 2006, www.webpronews.com/google-goes-to-the-middle-east-2006-12

Research Exercise

Do your own research at an organization of your choice in your own city and find a case or incident that is relevant to any of the concepts we have discussed in this chapter. Find out how business in the Arab world compares with that in other regions of the world.

LEARNING OBJECTIVES

This chapter will enable you to:

1 Describe the key elements of motivation.

2 Identify four early theories of motivation and evaluate their applicability today.

3 Compare contemporary theories of motivation.

4 Identify the motivational theories of equity and expectancy.

5 Describe the job characteristics model and evaluate the way it motivates by changing the work environment.

6 Compare and contrast the main ways jobs can be redesigned.

7 Identify alternative work arrangements and employee involvement measures and show how they might motivate employees.

8 Demonstrate how the different types of variable-pay programs can increase employee motivation.

9 Show how flexible benefits turn benefits into motivators.

10 Identify the motivational benefits of intrinsic rewards.

Motivation: Concepts and Applications

5

Motivation is everything ... you have to inspire the next guy down the line and get him to inspire his people.

—Lee Iacocca

Four Motivating Incentives at ICTN

The International Consulting and Training Network (ICTN) was founded in 1993 and offers management consulting training services. Founder and CEO Fay Niewiadomski has three decades' experience in management, consulting, research, academia, and training. ICTN's publicity material states: "ICTN is committed to recognizing that human potential is an organization's greatest source of wealth; establishing a culture of continuous learning; training effective leaders; and building trust through the power of communication."

ICTN has locations in Beirut, Lebanon; Amman, Jordan; and Dubai, United Arab Emirates, but it is extremely active across the MENA (Middle East and North Africa) region. In addition, the company has familiarized itself with the culture and needs of Ghana, Pakistan, Morocco, Tunisia, Algeria, the Kingdom of Saudi Arabia, Kuwait, Egypt, Qatar, Oman, and all other countries in the MENA region.

Niewiadomski believes that employees are motivated through participative management and aims to practice what she preaches. When consulting, she starts by observing behavior and performance, aiming to gain as much information as possible. She then questions and coaches employees to encourage individual expression. Niewiadomski can appear to be a humble person who underestimates herself, but in fact she shows a genuine insight into her subordinates, peers and clients. She stresses that anything changeable is solvable and hates to be surrounded by negative people. Her approach is to use subtle influencing techniques and she is really pleased when people adopt her ideas.

The philosophy of ICTN is that people will be motivated if they are involved in all processes and gain a sense of belonging to the company. Within ICTN, employees receive extra motivation by being given the opportunity to become either a partner or a franchisee, on condition that they bring added value.

ICTN's core values are summarized as IMPACT (Integrity—Mastery—Professionalism—Accountability—Commitment—Teamwork), and employees of ICTN must exhibit seven core competencies: (1) customer focus; (2) communication; (3) continuous learning; (4) planning and organizing; (5) a sense of urgency; (6) creativity; and (7) attention to detail.

Niewiadomski has introduced four incentive projects to motivate all ICTN's members. First, employees are given 10 percent of their annual salary to cover the expenses of any program they feel will increase their competencies. Second, anyone who puts in overtime can store the time in the time bank for personal use later. Third, all employees are invited to act as consultants or give training sessions. Finally, once a month an employee volunteers to provide training to coworkers, with the aim of increasing synergy, interaction and respect.

In summary, Niewiadomski's approach is based on the saying 'real talent is hard to find, hard to shape, once found a treasure to keep.'

Source: Based on an interview with, and information provided by, Fay Niewiadomski, CEO.

W hat motivates people like Fay Niewiadomski to excel? Is there anything organizations can do to encourage that sort of motivation in their employees? Before we answer that question through the many issues we will discuss in this chapter, let's try a self-assessment of your confidence in your ability to succeed.

Self Assessment Library »»

HOW CONFIDENT AM I IN MY ABILITIES TO SUCCEED?

In the Self-Assessment Library (available online), take assessment IV.A.3 (How Confident Am I in My Abilities to Succeed?) and answer the following questions:

1. *How did you score relative to other class members? Does that surprise you?*

2. *Do you think self-confidence is critical to success? Can a person be too confident?*

Motivation is one of the most frequently researched topics in OB.[1] One reason for its popularity is shown in a recent poll that found that about 55 percent of employees in the United States have no enthusiasm for their work.[2] Moreover, another study showed that workers admitted to wasting about two hours per day, not counting lunch and scheduled breaks (the biggest time-wasters were internet surfing and talking with coworkers).[3]

Clearly, motivation seems to be an issue. The good news is that all this research provides us with considerable insights into how to improve motivation.

In this chapter, we'll review the basics of motivation, assess a number of motivation theories, and provide an integrative model that shows how the best of these theories fit together. We'll then look at applying motivation concepts and link these theories to practices such as employee involvement and skill-based pay. These links highlight how, as a manager, you can use motivation theories to get the best out of your employees.

Defining *Motivation*

1 Describe the key elements of motivation.

What is motivation? It's the result of the interaction between an individual and a situation. Certainly, some individuals, such as Fay Niewiadomski, understand how to get their employees to succeed. Their energy comes from the absolute conviction that the people around them are the essence of success. They believe that if employees are given incentives and involved in the overall processes, they are bound to demonstrate commitment to the organization and behave accordingly. Similarly, students who find it difficult to concentrate on a textbook for more than 20 minutes may read a complete book by Gibran Khalil Gibran in one day. For such individuals, the difference in motivation is driven by the situation. So as we analyze the concept of motivation, keep in mind that the level of motivation varies both between individuals and within individuals, at different times.

Motivation accounts for an individual's intensity, direction, and persistence of effort toward attaining a goal.[4] While general motivation is concerned with effort toward *any* goal, we'll narrow the focus to *organizational* goals in order to reflect our singular interest in work-related behavior.

The three key elements in our definition are intensity, direction, and persistence. *Intensity* is concerned with how hard a person tries. This is the element most of us focus on when we talk about motivation. The effort is channeled in a *direction* that benefits the organization. Finally, motivation has a *persistence*

Motivation
The processes that account for an individual's intensity, direction, and persistence of effort toward attaining a goal.

dimension, a measure of how long a person can maintain effort. Motivated individuals stay with a task long enough to achieve their goal.

> ### Picture This
>
> Your mother asks you to help your little sister with her math homework. You can't be bothered but mum says that if you don't, you cannot watch the final game tonight. You just remember that your favorite team, Al-Ahli, will be playing. Are you motivated?

This definition of motivation is applicable to all cultures and individuals, no matter what background they come from. Ultimately, intensity, direction, and persistence are the three triggers for anyone, anywhere. The Arab world is no exception.

Early Theories of Motivation

> **2** *Identify four early theories of motivation and evaluate their applicability today.*

The 1950s were a rich period in the development of motivation concepts. Four specific theories were formulated during this period, and we'll discuss these in detail in the following sections of this chapter. Although we have developed more valid explanations of motivation, as you'll see later in the chapter, these theories represent a foundation from which contemporary theories have developed, and managers still use them and their terminology in explaining employee motivation.

Hierarchy of Needs Theory

Hierarchy of needs theory

A hierarchy of five needs—physiological, safety, social, esteem, and self-actualization—in which, as each need is substantially satisfied, the next need becomes dominant.

Probably the most well-known theory of motivation is Abraham Maslow's **hierarchy of needs**.[5]

Maslow suggested that within every human being there exists a hierarchy of five needs:

1. **Physiological.** Includes hunger, thirst, shelter, and other bodily needs
2. **Safety.** Security and protection from physical and emotional harm
3. **Social.** Affection, belongingness, acceptance, and friendship
4. **Esteem.** Internal factors such as self-respect, autonomy, and achievement, and external factors such as status, recognition, and attention
5. **Self-actualization.** Drive to become what one is capable of becoming; includes growth, achieving one's potential, and self-fulfillment.

As each of these needs is satisfied, the next need becomes dominant. Figure 5-1 shows the individual moving up the steps of the hierarchy. From the standpoint of motivation, the theory would say that, although no need is ever fully satisfied, a partially satisfied need no longer motivates. So if you want to motivate someone, according to Maslow, you need to understand what level of the hierarchy that person is currently on and focus on satisfying the needs at or above that level.

Lower-order needs

Needs that are satisfied externally, such as physiological and safety needs.

Self-actualization

The drive to become what a person is capable of becoming.

Higher-order needs

Needs that are satisfied internally, such as social, esteem, and self-actualization needs.

Maslow describes the physiological and safety needs as **lower-order needs** that are satisfied externally or by extrinsic rewards such as pay, union contracts, and tenure. Social, esteem, and **self-actualization** are described as the **higher-order needs** that are satisfied internally or by intrinsic rewards from within the person. Both extrinsic and intrinsic rewards will be discussed further, later in the chapter.

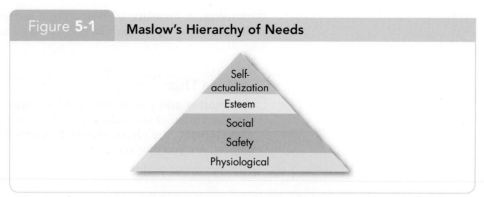

Figure **5-1**   **Maslow's Hierarchy of Needs**

Self-actualization

Esteem

Social

Safety

Physiological

Source: Adapted from A. H. Maslow, *Motivation and Personality*, 3rd ed., R. D. Frager and J. Fadiman (eds). © 1997. Reprinted and electronically reproduced by permission of Pearson Education, Inc., Upper Saddle River, New Jersey.

Maslow's needs theory has received wide recognition, particularly among practicing managers. This can be attributed to the theory's intuitive logic and ease of understanding. Unfortunately, however, research does not validate the theory. Maslow provided no empirical substantiation, and several studies that sought to validate the theory found no support for it.[6]

One well-known thinker from the Arab world, Ibn Khaldoun, left us with food for thought on what motivates a person to work. Khaldoun's ideas match those of Maslow: at times keeping workers motivated becomes a problem in the organization but the need to earn a living begins with the need to provide for one's own survival. Khaldoun went on to say that the needs then progressively grow until individuals start to gain more influence.

Clayton Alderfer attempted to rework Maslow's need hierarchy to align it more closely with empirical research. His revised need hierarchy is labeled **ERG theory**.[7] Alderfer argued that there are three groups of core needs—*existence* (similar to Maslow's physiological and safety needs), *relatedness* (similar to Maslow's social and status needs), and *growth* (similar to Maslow's esteem needs and self-actualization). Unlike Maslow, Alderfer didn't assume that these needs existed in a rigid hierarchy. An individual could be focusing on all three need categories simultaneously. Despite these differences, empirical research hasn't been any more supportive of ERG theory than of the need hierarchy.[8]

Old theories, especially ones that are intuitively logical, apparently die hard. Although the need hierarchy theory and its terminology have remained popular with practicing managers, there is little evidence that need structures are organized along the dimensions proposed by Maslow or Alderfer, that unsatisfied needs motivate, or that a satisfied need activates movement to a new need level.[9]

Theory X and Theory Y

Douglas McGregor proposed two distinct views of human beings: one basically negative, labeled **Theory X**, and the other basically positive, labeled **Theory Y**.[10] After viewing the way in which managers dealt with employees, McGregor concluded that managers' views of the nature of human beings are based on a certain grouping of assumptions, and that managers tend to mold their behavior toward employees according to these assumptions.

Under Theory X, managers believe that employees dislike work and must be coerced into performing it. In contrast to these negative views about the nature of human beings, under Theory Y, managers assume that employees can view work as being as natural as rest or play, and therefore the average person can learn to accept, and even seek, responsibility.

ERG theory

A theory that posits three groups of core needs: existence, relatedness, and growth.

Theory X

The assumption that employees dislike work, are lazy, dislike responsibility, and must be coerced to perform.

Theory Y

The assumption that employees like work, are creative, seek responsibility, and can exercise self-direction.

To understand Theory X and Theory Y more fully, think in terms of Maslow's hierarchy. Theory Y assumes that higher-order needs dominate individuals. McGregor himself held to the belief that Theory Y assumptions were more valid than Theory X. Therefore, he proposed such ideas as participative decision making, responsible and challenging jobs, and good group relations as approaches that would maximize an employee's job motivation.

Unfortunately, there is no evidence to confirm that either set of assumptions is valid or that accepting Theory Y assumptions and altering one's actions accordingly will lead to more motivated workers. OB theories need to have empirical support before we can accept them.

Two-Factor Theory

Two-factor theory

A theory that relates intrinsic factors to job satisfaction and associates extrinsic factors with dissatisfaction. Also called motivation-hygiene theory.

Another prominent psychologist, Frederick Herzberg proposed the **two-factor theory**—also called *motivation-hygiene theory*.[11] Herzberg investigated the question 'What do people want from their jobs?' He asked people to describe, in detail, situations in which they felt exceptionally *good* or *bad* about their jobs.

From the responses, Herzberg concluded that the replies people gave when they felt good about their jobs were significantly different from the replies given when they felt bad. It was shown that certain characteristics tend to be consistently related to job satisfaction and others to job dissatisfaction. Intrinsic factors such as advancement, recognition, responsibility, and achievement seem to be related to job satisfaction. Respondents who felt good about their work tended to relate these factors to themselves. On the other hand, dissatisfied respondents tended to cite extrinsic factors, such as supervision, pay, company policies, and working conditions.

Hygiene factors

Factors—such as company policy and administration, supervision, and salary—that, when adequate in a job, placate workers. When these factors are adequate, people will not be dissatisfied.

According to Herzberg, the factors that lead to job satisfaction are separate and distinct from those that lead to job dissatisfaction. As a result, Herzberg characterized conditions surrounding the job such as quality of supervision, pay, company policies, physical working conditions, relations with others, and job security as **hygiene factors**. When they're adequate, people will not be dissatisfied; neither will they be satisfied. If we want to motivate people on their jobs, Herzberg suggested emphasizing factors associated with the work itself or with outcomes directly derived from it, such as promotional opportunities, opportunities for personal growth, recognition, responsibility, and achievement. These are the characteristics that people find intrinsically rewarding.

The two-factor theory has not been well-supported by research and has received criticisms such as the following:

1. The procedure that Herzberg used is limited by its methodology. When things are going well, people tend to take credit themselves. They blame failure on external factors.
2. The reliability of Herzberg's methodology is questioned. There have been various interpretations and this implies that what motivates one person may not necessarily motivate another.
3. No overall measure of satisfaction was utilized. A person may dislike part of a job yet still think the job is acceptable overall.
4. Herzberg assumed a relationship between satisfaction and productivity, but the research methodology he used looked only at satisfaction and not at productivity.

What Do You Think?

Does satisfaction lead to higher productivity?

Riad Salameh, Governor of the Central Bank of Lebanon, has proven himself a high achiever. In 2009 his clear-cut vision won him recognition by *The Banker* magazine as 'Central Banker of the Year.' His achievements were also recognized when, in the same year, he became the first Arab central bank governor to ring the opening bell at the New York Stock Exchange on Wall Street.

McClelland's theory of needs

A theory which states that achievement, power, and affiliation are three important needs that help explain motivation.

Need for achievement (nAch)

The drive to excel, to achieve in relation to a set of standards, and to strive to succeed.

Need for power (nPow)

The need to make others behave in a way in which they would not have behaved otherwise.

Need for affiliation (nAff)

The desire for friendly and close interpersonal relationships.

McClelland's Theory of Needs

Consider this: You have one ball, and there are five targets set up in front of you. Each one is at a bigger distance and more difficult to hit. Target A is easy. If you hit it, you get US$2. Target B is a bit farther out, but about 80 percent of the people who try can hit it. It pays US$4. Target C pays US$8, and about half the people who try can hit it. Very few people can hit Target D, but the payoff is US$16 for those who do. Finally, Target E pays US$32, but it's almost impossible to achieve. Which target would you try for? If you selected C, you're likely to be a high achiever. Why? To explain this, we now go on to McClelland's theory of needs.

McClelland's theory of needs was developed by David McClelland and his associates.[12]

The theory focuses on three needs, defined as follows:

- **Need for achievement (nAch)** is the drive to excel, to achieve in relation to a set of standards, to strive to succeed.
- **Need for power (nPow)** is the need to make others behave in a way in which they would not have behaved otherwise.
- **Need for affiliation (nAff)** is the desire for friendly and close interpersonal relationships.

Of the three needs, McClelland and other researchers focused most of their attention on nAch. High achievers like Riad Salameh perform best when they perceive their probability of success as at least 0.5—that is, when they estimate that they have a 50–50 chance of success. They also like to set goals that require stretching themselves a little.

Relying on an extensive amount of research, we can make some reasonably well-supported predictions of the relationship between achievement need and job performance. Although less research has been done on power and affiliation needs, there are consistent findings there, too. First, when jobs have a high degree of personal responsibility and feedback and an intermediate degree of risk, high achievers are strongly motivated. High achievers, for example, are successful in entrepreneurial activities such as running their own businesses and managing self-contained units within large organizations.[13]

Second, a high need to achieve does not necessarily make someone a good manager, especially in large organizations. People with a high achievement need are interested in how well they do personally and not in influencing others to do well. Third, the needs for affiliation and power tend to be closely related to managerial success. The best managers are high in their need for power and low in their need for affiliation.[14] In fact, a high power motive may be a requirement for managerial effectiveness.[15]

Although McClelland's theory has the best research support, it has less practical effect than the others because the three needs are subconscious and are therefore difficult and costly to measure.

Contemporary Theories of Motivation

3 *Compare contemporary theories of motivation.*

Although well-known, the previous theories of motivation have not held up well under close examination. However, there are a number of contemporary theories that represent the current state of thinking in explaining employee motivation, each of which has a reasonable degree of valid supporting research.

Cognitive Evaluation Theory

"It's strange," said Maryam. "I started work at the Red Crescent as a volunteer. I put in 15 hours a week helping people and I loved coming to work. Then, three months ago, they hired me full-time at $11 an hour. I'm doing the same work I did before. But I'm not finding it nearly as much fun."

Cognitive evaluation theory

A theory that states that allocating extrinsic rewards for behavior that had been previously intrinsically rewarding tends to decrease the overall level of motivation.

There's an explanation for Maryam's reaction. It's called **cognitive evaluation theory**, which proposes that the introduction of extrinsic rewards such as pay, for work effort that was previously intrinsically rewarding due to the pleasure associated with the content of the work itself, tends to decrease overall motivation.[16]

Cognitive evaluation theory suggests that when extrinsic rewards are used by organizations as payoffs for superior performance, the intrinsic rewards that come from individuals doing what they like are reduced. In other words, when extrinsic rewards are given to someone for performing an interesting task, it causes intrinsic interest in the task itself to decline; this explains what happened to Maryam.

What Do You Think?

What satisfies you more, the intrinsic or extrinsic reward?

We noted earlier that cognitive evaluation theory has been supported by research. Yet, it has also been under attack. So, where does it stand today? Can we say that when organizations use extrinsic motivators such as pay and promotions and verbal rewards to stimulate workers' performance, they do so at the expense of reducing intrinsic interest and motivation in the work being done? The answer is not a simple 'yes' or a simple 'no.' Figure 5-2 may support this.

Figure **5-2**

THE WALL STREET JOURNAL

"What do you *mean* money isn't everything? This is a bank!"

Source: From the *Wall Street Journal*, February 8, 1995. Reprinted with permission of Cartoon Features Syndicate.

International OB

Motivation and Culture: What's the Relationship?

Culture is the behavior, beliefs, and thoughts of a certain group of people. A recent study found interesting differences in managers' perceptions of employee motivation. The study examined managers from three distinct cultural regions: North America, Asia, and Latin America. The results of the study revealed that North American managers perceive their employees as being motivated more by extrinsic factors (for example, pay) than intrinsic factors (for example, doing meaningful work). Asian managers perceive their employees as being motivated by both extrinsic and intrinsic factors, while Latin American managers perceive their employees as being motivated by intrinsic factors.

In the Arab world, managers tend to use a 'top-down' approach. Due to the culture and the normal direction in which managers interact with their employees, motivating employees in the Arab world may be more challenging because managers exert more control over their employees, offer less participation, value opinions less, believe employees have less job readiness, share less information, and believe employees have less psychological readiness.

However, there is a risk in giving to much importance to generalizations like those. In August 2009, Bayt.com, a regional job portal, interviewed about 13,400 professionals in the MENA region and Pakistan. The survey aimed to shed light on employee motivation. The overall results revealed that: 21 percent of workers in the MENA region are highly motivated; 24 percent are motivated; 18 percent are slightly motivated; 19 percent are not so motivated; and 15 percent are not motivated at all. The survey showed that the top motivating factors for employees are long-term growth opportunities, company reputation, and personal motivation from the line manager.

Comparing motivation across the MENA region, it was found that 28 percent of Lebanese respondents said they were 'highly' motivated at work. This compares with 24 percent of Qataris, 21 percent of Egyptians, 20 percent of Moroccans and Kuwaitis, 19 percent of Emiratis and 17 percent of Jordanians and Saudis. Considering the political and economical instability in the country, Lebanon displayed surprisingly high levels of satisfaction. Lebanese respondents are satisfied with the recognition and appreciation they receive at work: 66 percent are satisfied with their job security, 57 percent are satisfied with their personal and professional growth, while 43 percent are satisfied with the compensation and benefits they receive.

Sources: S. E. DeVoe and S. S. Iyengar, "Managers' Theories of Subordinates: A Cross-Cultural Examination of Manager Perceptions of Motivation and Appraisal of Performance," *Organizational Behavior and Human Decision Processes*, January 2004, pp. 47–61; "Lebanon Has Highest Level of Employee Motivation in the region," *Lebanon This Week*, Issue No. 133, September 2009, p. 4; and "Employee Motivation in the Middle East Study" *Bayt.com*, September 2009, www.bayt.com/en/research-report-5601.

Extrinsic rewards that are verbal (such as receiving praise from a supervisor or coworker) or tangible (such as money) can actually have different effects on individuals' intrinsic motivation. That is, verbal rewards increase intrinsic motivation, whereas tangible rewards weaken it. When people are told they will receive a tangible reward, they come to count on it and focus more on the reward than on the task.[17]

Verbal rewards, however, seem to keep people focused on the task and encourage them to do it better. The 'International OB' box, above, presents this issue.

What does all of this mean? It means choose your job carefully. Make sure you're choosing to do something for reasons other than extrinsic rewards. For organizations, managers need to provide intrinsic rewards in addition to extrinsic incentives. In other words, managers need to make the work interesting, provide recognition, and support employee growth and development. Employees who feel that what they do is within their control and a result of free choice are likely to be more motivated and committed.[18]

Goal-Setting Theory

The coach of many sports teams is likely to give his players last words similar to these before a big game: 'Each one of you is physically ready. Now, get out there and do your best. No one can ever ask more of you than that.'

Goal-setting theory

A theory that says that specific and difficult goals, with feedback, lead to higher performance.

You've heard the sentiment a number of times yourself: 'Just do your best. That's all anyone can ask for.' But what does 'do your best' mean? Do we ever know if we've achieved that uncertain goal? The research on **goal-setting theory** addresses these issues, and the findings, as you'll see, are impressive in terms of the effect that goal specificity, challenge, and feedback have on performance. That is, when the goal is clear and all factors are presented, then feedback can be determined better. So instead of saying, 'do your best,' the coach could have said, 'Because I know you are ready, you can at least try to beat your own previous record of 3/0. Let's do it!'

If factors such as acceptance of the goals are held constant, we can also state that the more difficult the goal, the higher the level of performance. Of course, it's logical to assume that easier goals are more likely to be accepted. But once a hard task is accepted, the employee can be expected to exert a high level of effort to try to achieve it.

But why are people motivated by difficult goals?[19] First, challenging goals get our attention and thus tend to help us focus. Second, difficult goals energize us because we have to work harder to attain them. For example, think of your study habits. Do you study as hard for an easy exam as you do for a difficult one? Probably not. Third, when goals are difficult, people continue trying to reach them. Finally, difficult goals lead us to discover strategies that help us perform the job or task more effectively. If we have to struggle for a way to solve a difficult problem, we often think of a better way to go about it.

People do better when they get feedback on how well they are progressing toward their goals because feedback helps to identify differences between what they have done and what they want to do; that is, feedback acts to guide behavior. But all feedback is not equally powerful. Self-generated feedback—for which employees are able to monitor their own progress—has been shown to be a more powerful motivator than externally generated feedback.[20]

In addition to feedback, three other factors have been found to influence the goals–performance relationship: goal commitment, task characteristics, and national culture.

First, goal-setting theory presupposes that an individual is committed to the goal; that is, an individual is determined not to lower or give up the goal. This means that individuals believe they can achieve the goal and want to achieve it.[21] Second, with respect to task characteristics, goals seem to have a more realistic effect on performance when tasks are simple rather than difficult, familiar rather than new, and independent rather than interdependent.[22]

Finally, goal-setting theory is culture bound. It's well adapted to countries such as the United States and Canada because its key components align reasonably well with North American cultures. Geert Hofstede's analysis compares cultures, but does not show figures directly related to goal setting. However, differences can be seen in the following Hofstede results. Countries in the Arab world show high Power Distance (PDI) (typically around 80) and Uncertainty Avoidance (UAI) (68) scores. The Masculinity index (MAS) is the third highest Hofstede Dimension for the region, though, at 52 it only slightly higher than the 50.2 average for countries around the world. The lowest-scoring dimension for the Arab world is Individualism (IDV), scoring 38, well below the world average of 64.[23]

Our overall conclusion is that difficult and specific goals are a strong motivating force. The motivating power of goal-setting theory has been demonstrated

Most companies in the Kingdom of Saudi Arabia (KSA) set specific targets and goals—indeed it is this approach that may have helped them to emerge from the major global financial crisis in 2008. In 2010, in order to learn more about strategic goal-setting and how this can be beneficial to organizations, Dr. Robert Kaplan was invited to present his Balanced Scorecard strategy to various organizations at the second Balanced Scorecard Forum in KSA.

on so many tasks, by numerous participants, in many different kinds of industries. Basically, it was found that setting specific, challenging goals for employees is the best thing managers can do to improve performance.

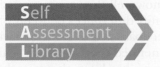

WHAT ARE MY COURSE PERFORMANCE GOALS?

In the Self-Assessment Library (available online), take assessment I.C.5 (What Are My Course Performance Goals?).

Implementing Goal-Setting How do managers make goal-setting theory operational? That's often left up to the individual manager or leader. Some managers determine aggressive performance targets that General Electric called 'stretch goals.' For example, some CEOs, such as General Electric's Jack Welch and Procter & Gamble's A. G. Laffey, are known for the demanding performance goals they set, and Nissan's Carlos Ghosn became a reference for goal-setting in the world of organizational behavior and employee interaction. However, the problem with leaving it up to the individual manager is that, in many cases, managers don't set goals.

A more systematic way to utilize goal setting is with a management by objectives program. **Management by objectives (MBO)** supports employees participating with managers to set goals that can be confirmed and that are tangible, verifiable, and measurable. In other words, employee involvement can be the incentive that people need to become more motivated and committed. The organization's overall objectives are translated into specific objectives for each succeeding level, (that is, divisional, departmental, individual). But because lower-unit managers jointly participate in setting their own goals, MBO works from the 'bottom up' as well as from the 'top down' (these channels of communication will be discussed in detail in Chapter 9). The result is a hierarchy that links objectives at one level to those at the next level. And for the individual employee, MBO provides specific personal performance objectives.

Management by objectives (MBO)

A program that encompasses specific goals, participatively set, for an explicit time period, with feedback on goal progress.

Although the flow of communication will be explained in Chapter 9, we must emphasize here that the most common style of communication in the Arab world is top-downwards. As a result, participation is often limited and thus the concept of MBO may not be a common or popular leadership style. However, there are always exceptions to the rule. Note the ideas of Ibn Khaldoun (the Arab guru who we introduced earlier in this chapter) from six hundred years ago. He spoke about involvement in a very inspiring fashion and said, "If the ruler continues to keep a forceful grip on his subjects, group feeling will be destroyed. If the ruler is mild and overlooks the bad sides of his subjects, they will trust him and take refuge with him . . ." In other words, Ibn Khaldoun is stressing that employee involvement through open communication channels will lead to more confidence, trust and higher performance.

Four ingredients are common to MBO programs: goal specificity, participation in decision making (including participation in the setting of goals or objectives), an explicit time period, and performance feedback.[24]

Many of the elements in MBO programs match propositions of goal-setting theory. For example, having an explicit time period to accomplish objectives matches goal-setting theory's emphasis on goal specificity. Similarly, we noted earlier that feedback about goal progress is a critical element of goal-setting theory. The only area of possible disagreement between MBO and goal-setting theory relates to the issue of participation: MBO strongly advocates it, whereas goal-setting theory demonstrates that managers assigning goals is usually just as effective.

Nevertheless, MBO's popularity should not be taken to mean that it always works. There are a number of documented cases in which MBO has been implemented but failed to meet management's expectations.[25]

When MBO doesn't work, the reasons tend to be factors such as unrealistic expectations regarding results, lack of commitment by top management, and an inability or unwillingness of management to allocate rewards based on goal accomplishment. Failures can also arise out of cultural incompatibilities. For instance, Fujitsu recently stopped its MBO-type program because management found it didn't fit well with the Japanese culture's emphasis on minimizing risk and emphasizing long-term goals.

Self-Efficacy Theory

In relation to Maslow's hierarchy of needs, which we discussed at the beginning of this chapter, the satisfying of self-esteem leads to greater self-confidence. **Self-efficacy** (also known as *social cognitive theory* or *social learning theory*) refers to an individual's belief that he or she is capable of performing a task.[26] The higher your self-efficacy, the more confidence you have in your ability to succeed in a task.

So, in difficult situations, people with low self-efficacy are more likely to lessen their effort or give up altogether, while those with high self-efficacy will try harder to master the challenge.[27]

In addition, individuals high in self-efficacy seem to respond to negative feedback with increased effort and motivation, while those low in self-efficacy are likely to lessen their effort when given negative feedback.[28]

How can managers help their employees achieve high levels of self-efficacy? It can be reached by bringing together goal-setting theory and self-efficacy theory.

Goal-setting theory and self-efficacy theory don't compete with one another; rather, they complement each other. As Figure 5-3 shows, when a manager sets difficult goals for employees, this leads employees to have a higher level of self-efficacy and also leads them to set higher goals for their own performance. Why is this the case? Research has shown that setting difficult goals for people communicates confidence.

Self-efficacy

An individual's belief that he or she is capable of performing a task.

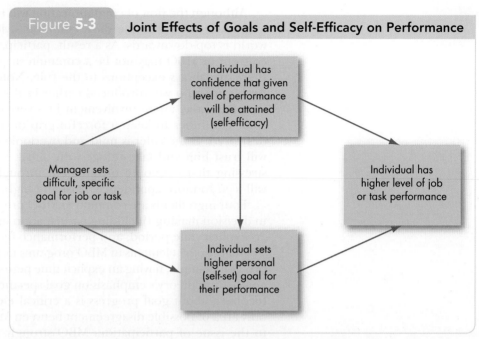

Figure **5-3**   **Joint Effects of Goals and Self-Efficacy on Performance**

Source: Based on E. A. Locke and G. P. Latham, "Building a Practically Useful Theory of Goal Setting and Task Motivation: A 35-Year Odyssey," *American Psychologist*, September 2002, pp. 705–717.

Picture This

Imagine your boss sets a high goal for you, and you learn that it is higher than the goals set for your coworkers. How would you interpret this?

The researcher who developed self-efficacy theory, Albert Bandura, argues that there are four ways self-efficacy can be increased.[29]

1. **Enactive mastery** allows employees to gain experience with the task or on job that will increase confidence in doing it in the future.
2. **Vicarious modeling** allows confidence to increase because your confidence grows when you see someone else doing the task.
3. **Verbal persuasion** allows employees to acquire more confidence because people tell you that you do have the potential and skills—'you can do it.'
4. **Arousal** energizes people; that is, by using psychology, they are encouraged to perform better.

Reinforcement Theory

Reinforcement theory

A theory that says that behavior is a function of its consequences.

A counterpoint to goal-setting theory is **reinforcement theory**. The former is a cognitive approach, proposing that an individual's purposes direct his or her action. However, reinforcement theory takes a behavioristic approach, arguing that reinforcement leads behavior.

Reinforcement theory ignores the inner state of the individual and concentrates only on what happens to people when they take action. Because it does not concern itself with what initiates behavior, it is not a theory of motivation. But it does provide a powerful means of analysis of what controls behavior, and for this reason it is typically considered in discussions of motivation.[30]

Although it's clear that so-called reinforcers such as pay can motivate people, it's just as clear that for people the process is much more complicated than stimulus–response. In its pure form, reinforcement theory ignores feelings, attitudes, expectations, and other cognitive variables that are known to affect behavior. For instance, if you consistently are told off for producing more than your colleagues, you'll likely reduce your productivity. But your lower productivity may also be explained in terms of goals, inequity, or expectancies.

Equity Theory

4 Identify the motivational theories of equity and expectancy.

Ibtisam graduated last year from the Arab Open University with a degree in accounting. After interviews with a number of organizations on campus, she accepted a position with a top public accounting firm and was assigned to the firm's Kuwaiti office. Ibtisam was very pleased with the offer she received: challenging work with a prestigious firm, an excellent opportunity to gain valuable experience, and the highest salary any accounting major was offered last year— US$4,550 per month. But Ibtisam was the top student in her class; she was articulate and mature, and she fully expected to receive a commensurate salary.

Twelve months have passed since Ibtisam joined her employer. The work has proved to be as challenging and satisfying as she had hoped. Her employer is extremely pleased with her performance; in fact, Ibtasim recently received a US$200-per-month raise. However, Ibtisam's motivational level has dropped dramatically in the past few weeks. Why? Her employer has just hired a fresh college graduate, who lacks the one-year experience Ibtisam has gained, for US$4,800 per month—US$50 more than Ibtisam now makes! Ibtisam is furious. She is even talking about looking for another job.

Ibtisam's situation illustrates the role that equity plays in motivation. Employees make comparisons of their job inputs (for example, effort, experience, education, competence) and outcomes (for example, salary levels, raises, recognition) relative to those of others. We perceive what we get from a job situation (outcomes) in relation to what we put into it (inputs), and then we compare our outcome–input ratio with the outcome–input ratios of relevant others. If we perceive our ratio to be equal to that of the relevant others with whom we compare ourselves, a state of equity is said to exist; we perceive our situation as fair and that justice prevails. When we see the ratio as unequal, we experience equity tension. When we see ourselves as underrewarded, the tension creates anger; when we see ourselves as overrewarded, the tension creates guilt.

Employees might compare themselves to friends, neighbors, coworkers, or colleagues in other organizations, or compare their present job with past jobs they themselves have had. Whoever an employee chooses will be influenced by the information the employee holds about them as well as by the attractiveness of the individual. This has led to focusing on four moderating variables: gender, length of tenure, level in the organization, and amount of education or professionalism.[31]

There are four criteria for comparisons that an employee can use:

1. *Self–inside.* An employee's experiences in a different position inside the employee's current organization
2. *Self–outside.* An employee's experiences in a situation or position outside the employee's current organization
3. *Other–inside.* Another individual or group of individuals inside the employee's organization
4. *Other–outside.* Another individual or group of individuals outside the employee's organization.

Equity theory

A theory that says that individuals compare their job inputs and outcomes with those of others and then respond to eliminate any inequities.

Moreover, based on the **equity theory**, when employees perceive inequity, they can be predicted to make one of six choices:[32]

OB in the News

What Motivates Employees?

PAC Engineering, a building construction contractor established in the early 1990s, has its headquarters in Lebanon. In 2010, the number of employees was over 10,000 and the company had multi-million dollar projects to its name. PAC Engineering operates in many areas of the region such as Qatar, the United Arab Emirates, Saudi Arabia, Kuwait, Egypt, Sudan, and Libya.

At the beginning, the company had no trouble motivating and retaining competent engineers, but later it faced great difficulty because construction reached a standstill.

Even though the company was flourishing, top management at PAC witnessed a high turnover as its engineers were finding more attractive offers in the region. The CEO was quite aware of the problem and its consequences and thus hired a human resources consulting firm to pinpoint the cause of problem.

The problem was quickly identified and PAC Engineering's motivation strategy focused on finding work opportunities for the engineers in Lebanon so that they would stay with their families and save the extra expenses of working

abroad. However, when engineers were sent to handle projects in Dubai, they started comparing their salaries with those of engineers working for companies in Dubai. The implications of the equity theory now was a challenge for PAC.

Once again, the consulting firm was called upon. There was a close investigation of the company's financial packages, which were redesigned to offer more incentives and enhance motivation. For the first time in Lebanon, PAC Engineering introduced a 'partnership scheme' for its high-level executives and engineers.

1. Change their inputs (for example, exert less effort).
2. Change their outcomes (for example, individuals paid on a piece-rate basis can increase their pay by producing a higher quantity of units of lower quality).
3. Misinterpret perceptions of self (for example, 'I used to think I worked at a moderate pace, but now I realize that I work a lot harder than everyone else.').
4. Misinterpret perceptions of others (for example, 'Mazen's job isn't as desirable as I previously thought it was.').
5. Choose a different referent (for example, 'I may not make as much as my brother-in-law, but I'm doing a lot better than my dad did when he was my age.').
6. Leave the field (for example, quit the job).

Furthermore, the equity theory establishes the following propositions relating to inequitable pay:

A. Given payment by time, overrewarded employees will produce more than will equitably paid employees.
B. Given payment by quantity of production, overrewarded employees will produce fewer, but higher-quality, units than will equitably paid employees.
C. Given payment by time, underrewarded employees will produce less or a poorer quality of output.
D. Given payment by quantity of production, underrewarded employees will produce a large number of low-quality units in comparison with equitably paid employees.

Some of these propositions have been supported, but others haven't.[33] First, inequities created by overpayment do not seem to have a very significant impact on behavior in most work situations. Apparently, people have a great deal more tolerance of overpayment inequities than of underpayment inequities or are better able to rationalize them. Second, not all people are equity sensitive.[34]

For example, there is a small part of the working population who actually prefer that their outcome–input ratios be less than the referent comparison's.

Distributive justice

Perceived fairness of the amount and allocation of rewards among individuals.

Organizational justice

An overall perception of what is fair in the workplace, composed of distributive, procedural, and interactional justice.

Procedural justice

The perceived fairness of the process used to determine the distribution of rewards.

Interactional justice

The perceived degree to which an individual is treated with dignity, concern, and respect.

Unfortunately, the Arab culture opens the door for inequities due to nepotism or 'wasta.' This is a cause of much frustration in the workplace.

Finally, recent research has been directed at expanding what is meant by equity, or fairness,[35] by focusing on **distributive justice**, which is the employee's perceived fairness of the amount and allocation of rewards among individuals. It is also considered as **organizational justice**, which we define as an overall perception of what is fair in the workplace; it is described in Figure 5-4. Employees perceive their organizations as just when they believe the outcomes they have received and the way in which the outcomes were awarded are fair. Moreover, **procedural justice** is the perceived fairness of the *process* used to determine the distribution of rewards. Two key elements of procedural justice are *process control* and *explanations*. Process control is the opportunity to present one's point of view about desired outcomes to decision makers. Explanations are clear reasons for the outcome that management gives to a person. Thus, for employees to see a process as fair, they need to feel that they have some control over the outcome and that they were given an adequate explanation about why the outcome occurred.

A recent addition to research on organizational justice is **interactional justice**, which is an individual's perception of the degree to which he or she is treated with dignity, concern, and respect. In other words, when people are treated in an unjust manner (at least in their own eyes), they respond by retaliating (for example, badmouthing a supervisor).[36] Because interactional justice or injustice is related to the sender of the information (usually one's supervisor), whereas procedural injustice often results from impersonal policies, we would expect perceptions of injustice to be more closely related to one's supervisor.

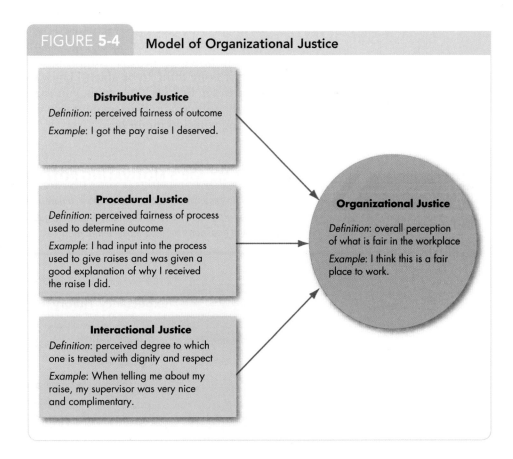

FIGURE **5-4**   **Model of Organizational Justice**

Distributive Justice

Definition: perceived fairness of outcome

Example: I got the pay raise I deserved.

Procedural Justice

Definition: perceived fairness of process used to determine outcome

Example: I had input into the process used to give raises and was given a good explanation of why I received the raise I did.

Interactional Justice

Definition: perceived degree to which one is treated with dignity and respect

Example: When telling me about my raise, my supervisor was very nice and complimentary.

Organizational Justice

Definition: overall perception of what is fair in the workplace

Example: I think this is a fair place to work.

Expectancy Theory

Expectancy theory

A theory that says that the strength of a tendency to act in a certain way depends on the strength of an expectation that the act will be followed by a given outcome and on the attractiveness of that outcome to the individual.

Currently, one of the most widely accepted explanations of motivation is Victor Vroom's **expectancy theory**,[37] Although it has its critics, most of the evidence supports the theory.[38]

Expectancy theory argues that the strength of a tendency to act in a certain way depends on the strength of an expectation that the act will be followed by a given outcome and on the attractiveness of that outcome to the individual. For instance, Jamila was motivated to stay long hours in the office when she first started because she expected to be paid overtime; imagine her disappointment when she wasn't. The theory, therefore, focuses on three relationships, as explained in Figure 5-5:

1. Effort–performance relationship: The probability perceived by the individual that exerting a given amount of effort will lead to performance.
2. Performance–reward relationship: The degree to which the individual believes that performing at a particular level will lead to the attainment of a desired outcome.
3. Rewards–personal goals relationship: The degree to which organizational rewards satisfy an individual's personal goals or needs and the attractiveness of those potential rewards for the individual.[39]

In short, expectancy theory helps explain why a lot of workers aren't motivated on their jobs and do only the minimum necessary to get by. This is evident when we look at the theory's three relationships in a little more detail. Let's consider the following questions employees need to answer in the affirmative if their motivation is to be maximized. First, if I make a maximum effort, will it be recognized in my performance appraisal? Second, if I get a good performance appraisal, will it lead to organizational rewards? Third, if I'm rewarded, are the rewards ones that I find personally attractive?

In the previous sections, we focused on motivation theories; in the following sections, we will focus on applying motivation concepts. We link motivation theories to practices such as employee involvement and skill-based pay. Why? Because it's one thing to be able to know specific motivation theories; it's quite another to see how, as a manager, you can use them. Before we continue, let's look at the following self-assessment that will provide some information on how motivating your job might be.

WHAT'S MY JOB'S MOTIVATING POTENTIAL?

In the Self-Assessment Library (available online), take assessment I.C.9 (What's My Job's Motivating Potential?) and answer the following questions. If you currently do not have a job, answer the questions for your most recent job.

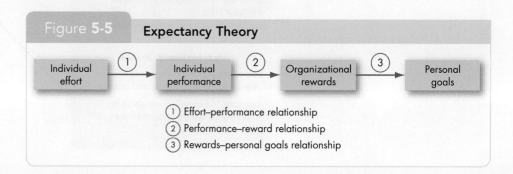

Figure 5-5   **Expectancy Theory**

Individual effort → (1) → Individual performance → (2) → Organizational rewards → (3) → Personal goals

(1) Effort–performance relationship
(2) Performance–reward relationship
(3) Rewards–personal goals relationship

Motivating by Job Design: The Job Characteristics Model

5 *Describe the job characteristics model and evaluate the way it motivates by changing the work environment.*

Increasingly, research on motivation is focused on approaches that link motivational concepts to changes in the way work is structured. In this section, we will look at how the job itself can contribute to motivation.

Research in **job design** provides stronger evidence that the way the elements in a job are organized can act to increase or decrease effort and to allow employees to develop their skills. This research also offers detailed insights into what those elements are. We'll first review the job characteristics model and then discuss some ways jobs can be redesigned. Finally, we'll explore some alternative work arrangements.

Job design

The way the elements in a job are organized.

The Job Characteristics Model

Developed by J. Richard Hackman and Greg Oldham, the **job characteristics model (JCM)** proposes that any job can be described in terms of five core job dimensions.[40]

Job characteristics model (JCM)

A model that proposes that any job can be described in terms of five core job dimensions: skill variety, task identity, task significance, autonomy, and feedback.

1. **Skill variety** is the degree to which a job requires a variety of different activities so the worker can use a number of different skills and talents. For instance, an example of a job scoring high on skill variety would be the job of an owner–operator of a garage who does electrical repairs, rebuilds engines, does body work, and interacts with customers. A job scoring low on this dimension would be the job of a body shop worker who only sprays paint 8 hours a day.

2. **Task identity** is the degree to which a job requires completion of a whole and identifiable piece of work. An example of a job scoring high on identity would be the job of a cabinetmaker who designs a piece of furniture, selects the wood, builds the object, and finishes it to perfection. A job scoring low

Skill variety

The degree to which a job requires a variety of different activities.

Task identity

The degree to which a job requires completion of a whole and identifiable piece of work.

Employee development through job design is an issue that all organizations should seriously consider. Various training organizations such as Meirc Training & Consulting, employees of which are pictured here, offer courses in how best to use job design to develop employees' skills and motivation. Meirc is one of the most established firms of this kind in the Arab world, providing its services to more than 1,500 firms across the region.

Task significance

The degree to which a job has a substantial impact on the lives or work of other people.

Autonomy

The degree to which a job provides substantial freedom, independence, and discretion to the individual in scheduling the work and in determining the procedures to be used in carrying it out.

Feedback

The degree to which carrying out the work activities required by a job results in the individual obtaining direct and clear information about the effectiveness of his or her performance.

on this dimension would be the job of a worker in a furniture factory who only makes table legs.

3. **Task significance** is the degree to which a job has a significant impact on the lives or work of other people. An example of a job scoring high on significance would be the job of a nurse handling the diverse needs of patients in a hospital intensive care unit. A job scoring low on this dimension would be the job of a janitor sweeping floors in a hospital.

4. **Autonomy** is the degree to which a job provides substantial freedom, independence, and discretion to the individual in scheduling the work and in determining the procedures to be used in carrying it out. An example of a job scoring high on autonomy is the job of a salesperson who schedules his or her own work each day and decides on the most effective sales approach for each customer without supervision. A job scoring low on this dimension would be the job of a salesperson who is given a set of leads each day and is required to follow a standardized sales script with each potential customer.

5. **Feedback** is the degree to which carrying out the work activities required by a job results in the individual obtaining direct and clear information about the effectiveness of his or her performance. An example of a job with high feedback is the job of a factory worker who assembles iPods and tests them to see if they operate properly. A job scoring low on feedback would be the job of a factory worker who, after assembling an iPod, is required to route it to a quality-control inspector who tests it for proper operation and makes needed adjustments.

Figure 5-6 presents the job characteristics model. Note how the first three dimensions—skill variety, task identity, and task significance—combine to create meaningful work. That is, if these three characteristics exist in a job, the model predicts that the job will be seen as important, valuable, and worthwhile. Note, too, that jobs with high autonomy give a feeling of personal responsibility for the results and that, if a job provides feedback, employees will know how effectively they are performing.

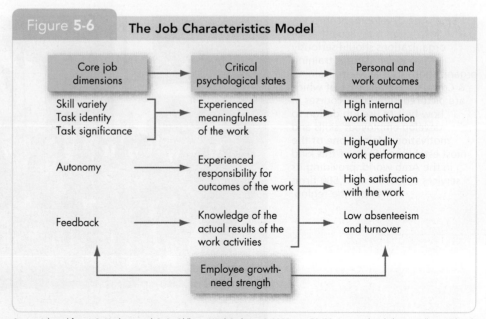

Figure 5-6   The Job Characteristics Model

Source: Adapted from J. R. Hackman and G. R. Oldham, *Work Redesign* © 1980; pp. 78–80. Reprinted and electronically reproduced by permission of Pearson Education, Inc., Upper Saddle River, New Jersey.

From a motivational standpoint, the JCM says that individuals obtain internal rewards when they learn (knowledge of results) that they personally (experienced responsibility) have performed well on a task that they care about (experienced meaningfulness).[41]

The more these three psychological states are present, the greater will be employees' motivation, performance, and satisfaction, and the lower their absenteeism and likelihood of leaving the organization.

The core dimensions can be combined into a single predictive index, called the **motivating potential score (MPS)**, which is calculated as follows:

Motivating potential score (MPS)

A predictive index that suggests the motivating potential in a job.

$$\text{MPS} = \frac{\text{Skill variety} + \text{Task identity} + \text{Task significance}}{3} \times \text{Autonomy} \times \text{Feedback}$$

Jobs that are high on motivating potential must be high on at least one of the three factors that lead to experienced meaningfulness, and they must be high on both autonomy and feedback. If jobs score highly on motivating potential, the model predicts that motivation, performance, and satisfaction will be positively affected and that the likelihood of absence and turnover will be reduced.

The JCM has been well researched. And most of the evidence supports the general framework of the theory—that is, there is a set of job characteristics, and these characteristics affect behavioral outcomes.[42]

But it appears that the MPS model doesn't work—that is, we can better derive motivating potential by adding the characteristics rather than using the complex MPS formula.[43]

Overall, though, it appears that jobs that have the intrinsic elements of variety, identity, significance, autonomy, and feedback are more satisfying and generate higher performance from people than jobs that lack these characteristics.

Picture This

Take some time to think about your job or a job you have done in the past. Do you have the opportunity to work on different tasks, or is your day pretty routine? Are you able to work independently, or do you constantly have a supervisor or coworker looking over your shoulder? What do you think your answers to these questions say about your job's motivating potential? Revisit your answers to the self-assessment at the beginning of this section and then calculate your MPS from the job characteristics model.

How Can Jobs Be Redesigned?

6 Compare and contrast the main ways jobs can be redesigned.

"Every day was the same thing," Fareed Ghalib said. "Stand on that assembly line. Wait for an instrument panel to be moved into place. Unlock the mechanism and drop the panel into the jeep as it moved by on the line. Then I plugged in the wires. I repeated that for eight hours a day. I don't care that they were paying me US$24 an hour. I was going crazy. I did it for almost a year and a half. Finally, I just said to my wife that this isn't going to be the way I'm going to spend the rest of my life. My brain was no longer functioning on that jeep assembly line. So I quit. Now I work in a print shop and I make less than US$15 an hour. But let me tell you, the work I do is really interesting. The job changes all the time, I'm continually learning new things, and the work really challenges me! I look forward every morning to going to work again."

Fareed Ghalib's job at the jeep plant involved repetitive tasks that provided him with little variety, autonomy, or motivation. In contrast, his job in the print shop is challenging and stimulating. Let's look at some of the ways to put JCM

Audi Bank is a great advocate of job rotation—also known as 'cross-training.' In order to widen the range of opportunities available, not only are employees rotated within their usual branch, but they are also sent on assignments between different branches. As a result, not only are Audi's employees less likely to become bored and demotivated, but they are also able to develop their skills and abilities, increasing their usefulness to the organization.

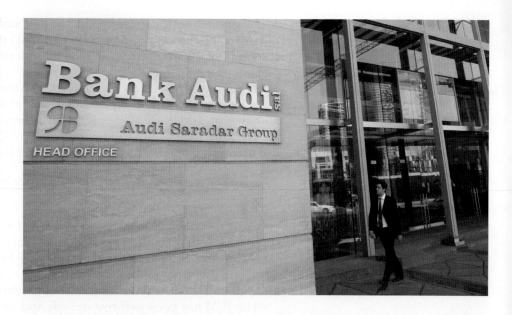

into practice to make jobs more motivating, such as job rotation, job enlargement, and job enrichment.

Job Rotation If employees suffer from too much routine in their work, one alternative is to use **job rotation** (or what many now call *cross-training*.) We define this practice as the periodic shifting of an employee from one task to another. When an activity is no longer challenging, the employee is rotated to another job, usually at the same level, that has similar skill requirements.

Singapore Airlines, one of the best-rated airlines in the world, uses job rotation extensively. For example, a ticket agent may take on the duties of a baggage handler. Job rotation is one of the reasons Singapore Airlines is rated as a highly desirable place to work. Many manufacturing firms have adopted job rotation as a means of increasing flexibility and avoiding layoffs.[44]

For instance, banks in the Arab world practice this for the sake of familiarizing employees with all aspects of their workplace and, in addition, to keep them motivated through giving them challenging and non-routine tasks.

The strengths of job rotation are that it reduces boredom, increases motivation through diversifying the employee's activities, and helps employees better understand how their work contributes to the organization. Job rotation also has indirect benefits for the organization because when employees have a wider range of skills to give, management has more flexibility in scheduling work, adapting to changes, and filling vacancies.[45] However, job rotation is not without drawbacks. Training costs are increased, and productivity is reduced by moving a worker into a new position. Job rotation also creates disruptions. Members of the work group have to adjust to the new employee. And supervisors may also have to spend more time answering questions and monitoring the work of recently rotated employees.

Job Enlargement More than 35 years ago, the idea of expanding jobs horizontally, or what we call **job enlargement**, grew in popularity. Increasing the number and variety of tasks that an individual performed resulted in jobs with more diversity. Instead of only sorting the incoming mail by department, for instance, a mail sorter's job could be enlarged to include physically delivering the mail to the various departments or mailing outgoing letters. The difference between job rotation and job enlargement may seem subtle. However, in job

Job rotation

The periodic shifting of an employee from one task to another.

Job enlargement

Increasing the number and variety of tasks that an individual performs. Job enlargement results in jobs with more diversity.

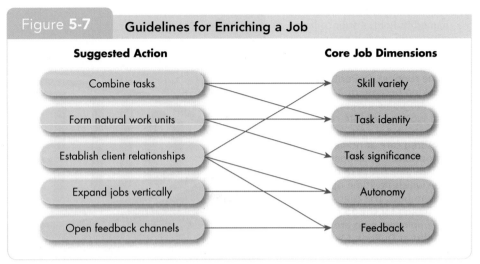

Figure 5-7 Guidelines for Enriching a Job

Suggested Action

- Combine tasks
- Form natural work units
- Establish client relationships
- Expand jobs vertically
- Open feedback channels

Core Job Dimensions

- Skill variety
- Task identity
- Task significance
- Autonomy
- Feedback

Source: J. R. Hackman and J. L. Suttle (eds.), *Improving Life at Work* (Glenview, IL: Scott Foresman, 1977), p. 138. Reprinted by permission of Richard Hackman and J. Lloyd Suttle.

rotation, jobs are not redesigned. Employees simply move from one job to another, but the nature of the work does not change. Job enlargement, however, involves actually changing the job.

Job enrichment

The vertical expansion of jobs, which increases the degree to which the worker controls the planning, execution, and evaluation of the work.

Job Enrichment   **Job enrichment** refers to the vertical expansion of jobs. It increases the degree to which the worker controls the planning, execution, and evaluation of the work. An enriched job organizes tasks so as to allow the worker to do a complete activity, increases the employee's freedom and independence, increases responsibility, and provides feedback so individuals will be able to assess and correct their own performance.[46]

How does management enrich an employee's job? Figure 5-7 offers suggested guidelines based on the job characteristics model. *Combining tasks* takes existing and fractionalized tasks and puts them back together to form a new and larger module of work. *Forming natural work units* means that the tasks an employee does create an identifiable and meaningful whole. *Establishing client relationships* increases the direct relationships between workers and their clients (these may be an internal customer as well as someone outside the organization). *Expanding jobs vertically* gives employees responsibilities and control that were formerly reserved for management. *Opening feedback channels* lets employees know how well they are performing their jobs and whether their performance is improving, deteriorating, or remaining at a constant level.

We just saw the various ways in which we can make jobs more motivating. These practices are becoming more common in the Arab world. In the next subsection, we are going to identify certain alternative work arrangements that are also being implemented in organizations in the Arab world.

Alternative Work Arrangements

7 Identify alternative work arrangements and employee involvement measures and show how they might motivate employees.

Beyond redesigning the nature of the work itself and involving employees in decisions, another approach to making the work environment more motivating is to alter work arrangements. We'll discuss three alternative work arrangements: flextime, job sharing, and telecommuting. With the increasing advances in technology, all these alternative work arrangements have become more popular.

In 2011, *Working Mother* magazine named DuPont, a science-based products and services company, as one of the top 100 best places to work for working mothers for the 23rd time running. DuPont received this ranking because of its mother-friendly programs such as flexitime, remote working, on-site child care, discounts at day-care centres and sponsored care at home. With so many options, the company works with employees to help them decide which flexitime option will suit them best. This is an excellent advantage for the 15 percent of employees who are working mothers at DuPont, Middle East.

Flextime

Flexible work hours.

Flextime Aisha is the classic 'morning person.' She rises each day at 5 A.M., sharp and full of energy. However, as she puts it, "I'm usually ready for bed right after the 7 P.M. news."

Aisha's work schedule as an auditor at The Abd Financial Services Group is an example of **flextime**, short for 'flexible work time.' It allows her some degree of freedom as to when she comes to work and when she leaves. Her office opens at 6 A.M. and closes at 7 P.M. It's up to her how she schedules her 8-hour day within this 13-hour period. Because Aisha is a morning person and also has a 7-year-old son who gets out of school at 3 P.M. every day, she opts to work from 6 A.M. to 3 P.M. 'My work hours are perfect. I'm at the job when I'm mentally most alert, and I can be home to take care of my son after he gets out of school.'

Flexibility of work timings is a means of motivation that truly applies to all workplaces no matter where located. Research findings (Bayt.com) show that countries in the MENA region do implement flextime, although owing to cultural issues, it may be unorthodox. In the UAE, 68 percent are satisfied with work-time flexibility. Relevant statistics are as follows: Syria, 68 percent; KSA, 69 percent; Oman, 74 percent; Lebanon, 69 percent; Jordan, 68 percent; Egypt, 70 percent. These figures show a certain consistency across the Arab world.[47]

The benefits of flextime are reduced absenteeism, increased productivity, reduced overtime expenses, reduced hostility toward management, reduced traffic congestion around work sites, elimination of tardiness, and increased autonomy and responsibility for employees that may increase employee job satisfaction.[48]

On the other hand, flextime's major drawback is that it's not applicable to every job.

Job sharing

An arrangement that allows two or more individuals to split a traditional 40-hour-a-week job.

Job Sharing Another common arrangement is **job sharing**. It allows two or more individuals to split a traditional 40-hour-a-week job. So, for example, one person might perform the job from 8 A.M. to noon, while another performs the same job from 1 P.M. to 5 P.M.; or the two could work full days but alternate the days.

Job sharing, although not yet popular in the Arab world, allows an organization to draw on the talents of more than one individual in a given job. A bank manager who oversees two job sharers describes it as an opportunity to get two heads but 'pay for one.'[49]

It also opens up the opportunity to acquire skilled workers—for instance, women with young children and retirees—who might not be available on a full-time basis.[50]

From the employee's perspective, job sharing increases flexibility to increase motivation and satisfaction for those to whom a 40-hour-a-week job is just not practical. But the major drawback from management's perspective is finding compatible pairs of employees who can successfully coordinate the complications of one job.[51]

Telecommuting   It might be close to the ideal job for many people. No commuting, flexible hours, freedom to dress as you please, and few or no interruptions from colleagues. It's called **telecommuting**, and it refers to employees who do their work at home at least two days a week on a computer that is linked to their office.[52] (A closely related term—*the virtual office*—is increasingly being used to describe employees who work out of their home on a relatively permanent basis.)

What kinds of jobs lend themselves to telecommuting? Three categories have been identified as most appropriate: routine information-handling tasks, mobile activities, and professional and other knowledge-related tasks.[53]

Writers, attorneys, analysts, and employees who spend the majority of their time on computers or the telephone are natural candidates for telecommuting. For instance, telemarketers, customer-service representatives, reservation agents, and product-support specialists spend most of their time on the phone. As telecommuters, they can access information on their computers at home as easily as in the company's office.

A study conducted in the Middle East found that almost three quarters of the region's professionals—72 percent—believe that telecommuting is a good idea for both the employer and employee, according to a poll carried out by job site Bayt.com. It also showed that 87 percent of job seekers said

Telecommuting
Working from home at least two days a week on a computer that is linked to the employee's office.

Telecommuting is appropriate for the knowledge-based work of employees at KPMG, a global network of professional firms that provides audit, tax, and advisory services. Kelvin Brown, a senior manager in KPMG's research and development tax concession section, works on his laptop at his beef cattle farm near Harden, Australia, a four-hour drive away from the company's office in Sydney. For Brown, working from home increases his productivity and allows him more time to spend with his family.

that telecommuting was beneficial, with only 12 percent saying that it was not a good idea.[54]

The potential pluses of telecommuting for management include a larger labor pool from which to select, higher productivity, less turnover, improved morale, and reduced office-space costs. The major downside for management is less direct supervision of employees. In addition, in today's team-focused workplace, telecommuting may make it more difficult for management to coordinate teamwork.[55]

Alternative work arrangements can lead to enhanced employee performance by increasing motivation. However, when you attempt to assess why an employee is not performing to the level at which you believe he or she is capable of performing, take a look at the work environment to see if it's supportive. Does the employee have adequate tools, equipment, materials, and supplies? Does the employee have favorable working conditions, helpful coworkers, supportive work rules and procedures, sufficient information to make job-related decisions, adequate time to do a good job, and the like? If not, performance will suffer.

Employee Involvement

Employee involvement

A participative process that uses the input of employees and is intended to increase employee commitment to an organization's success.

What specifically do we mean by **employee involvement**? We define it as a participative process that uses the input of employees to increase their commitment to the organization's success. The underlying logic is that if we involve workers in the decisions that affect them and increase their autonomy and control over their work lives, employees will become more motivated, more committed to the organization, more productive, and more satisfied with their jobs.[56]

Examples of Employee Involvement Programs

Let's look at the three major forms of employee involvement—participative management, representative participation, and quality circles—in more detail.

Participative management

A process in which subordinates share a significant degree of decision-making power with their immediate superiors.

Participative Management The distinct characteristic common to all **participative management** programs is the use of joint decision making. That is, subordinates actually share a significant degree of decision-making power with their immediate superiors. Participative management has, at times, been promoted as a solution for poor morale and low productivity. But for it to work, the issues in which employees get involved in must be relevant to their interests, employees must have the competence and knowledge to make a useful contribution, and there must be trust and confidence between all parties involved.[57]

Employee involvement is undoubtedly one such incentive that cannot be overlooked. Very few leaders in the MENA region appear to be advocates of participative management. In the past the most typical approach was an autocratic style of leadership, but this approach may be changing.

Representative participation

A system in which workers participate in organizational decision making through a small group of representative employees.

Representative Participation Companies practice **representative participation** when, rather than participating directly in decisions, workers are represented by a small group of employees who actually participate. Representative participation has been called "the most widely legislated form of employee involvement around the world."[58]

The goal of representative participation is to redistribute power within an organization, putting labor on a more equal footing with the interests of management and stockholders.

Dr. Walid Harb, pictured here, is the CEO of Tannourine Government Hospital. Harb has created an employee-friendly culture that motivates employees. Every department head is delegated authority with open channels of communication that make employees feel involved. Accordingly, employees trust in the decisions of the CEO. Employees are satisfied, motivated and feel they are involved in the decision-making process. The sense of belonging increases and, consequently, they are more committed to the organization and performance and productivity are greater.

The two most common forms representative participation takes are works councils and board representatives.[59] Works councils are groups of nominated or elected employees who must be consulted when management makes decisions involving personnel. Board representatives are employees who sit on a company's board of directors and represent the interests of the firm's employees.

Quality Circles   Companies such as Hewlett-Packard, General Electric, Xerox, Procter & Gamble, IBM, and Motorola use quality circles. A **quality circle** is defined as a work group of 8 to 10 employees and supervisors who have a shared area of responsibility and who meet once a week, on company time and on company premises—to discuss their quality problems, investigate causes of the problems, recommend solutions, and take corrective actions. The companies mentioned above are located in several countries of the Arab world and employ locals who are exposed to quality circles as a means of employee involvement.

Linking Employee Involvement Programs and Motivation Theories

Employee involvement draws on a number of the motivation theories we discussed at the beginning of this chapter. For instance, McGregor's Theory Y is consistent with participative management, and Theory X aligns with the more traditional autocratic style of managing people. In terms of Herzberg's two-factor theory, employee involvement programs could provide employees with intrinsic motivation by increasing opportunities for growth, responsibility, and involvement in the work itself. Similarly, the opportunity to make and implement decisions—and then seeing them work out—can help satisfy an employee's need for responsibility, achievement, recognition, growth, and enhanced self-esteem. So employee involvement is compatible with ERG theory and efforts to stimulate the achievement need. And extensive employee involvement programs clearly have the potential to increase employee intrinsic motivation in work tasks.

Using Rewards to Motivate Employees

Quality circle

A work group of 8–10 employees and supervisors who have a shared area of responsibility and who meet once a week to discuss quality problems.

Pay is not a primary factor driving job satisfaction. However, it does motivate people, and companies often underestimate the importance of pay in retaining talent. A 2006 study found that whereas only 45 percent of employers thought that pay was a key factor in losing top talent, 71 percent of top performers indicated that it was a top reason.[60]

Probably the most important aspect of organizational satisfaction is monetary compensation. Unfortunately, many employees in the Arab world are not completely satisfied by their level of pay. For example, in a 2011 study of employees in the Middle East, only 3 percent said they were highly satisfied with their rate of pay, and 45 percent indicated a low level of satisfaction.[61] Let's now look at the ways in which pay structures can be established.

Given that pay is so important, we need to understand what to pay employees and how to pay them. To do that, management must make some strategic decisions. In this section, we consider four major strategic rewards decisions that need to be made: (1) what to pay employees by establishing a pay structure; (2) how to pay individual employees through variable pay plans and skill-based pay plans; (3) what benefits to offer, such as flexible benefits; and (4) how to construct employee recognition programs.

What to Pay: Establishing a Pay Structure

8 Demonstrate how the different types of variable-pay programs can increase employee motivation.

There are many ways to pay employees. The process of initially setting pay levels can be rather complex and entails balancing *internal equity*—the worth of the job to the organization through job evaluation—and *external equity*—the external competitiveness of an organization's pay relative to pay elsewhere in its industry through pay surveys. Obviously, the best pay system pays the job what it is worth (internal equity) while also paying competitively relative to the labor market.

Pay more, and you may get better-qualified, more highly motivated employees who will stay with the organization longer. But pay is often the highest single operating cost for an organization, which means that paying too much can make the organization's products or services too expensive.

How to Pay: Rewarding Individual Employees through Variable-Pay Programs

Variable-pay program

A pay plan that bases a portion of an employee's pay on some individual and/or organizational measure of performance.

A number of organizations are moving away from paying people based only on credentials or length of service and toward using variable-pay programs that act as incentives for employees. Piece-rate plans, merit-based pay, bonuses, profit-sharing, gainsharing, and employee stock ownership plans are all forms of **variable-pay programs**. Instead of paying a person only for time on the job or seniority, a variable-pay program bases a part of an employee's pay on some individual and/or organizational measure of performance. Earnings therefore move up and down with the measure of performance.[62]

It is exactly the fluctuation in variable pay that has made these programs attractive to management. It turns part of an organization's fixed labor costs into a variable cost, thus reducing expenses when performance declines. In addition, when pay is tied to performance, the employee's earnings recognize contribution rather than being a form of entitlement. Thus, low performers find, over time, that their pay decreases, while high performers enjoy pay increases with their contributions.

Let's now examine the different types of variable-pay programs in more detail.

Piece-rate pay plan

A pay plan in which workers are paid a fixed sum for each unit of production completed.

Piece-Rate Pay   Piece-rate wages have been popular for more than a century as a means of compensating productive workers. In **piece-rate pay plans**, workers are paid a fixed sum for each unit of production completed. When employees get no base salary and are paid only for what they produce, this is a pure piece-rate plan. For instance, people who work in circuses selling popcorn and soda are paid this way. If they sell only 40 bags of popcorn, they make US$40. The harder they work and the more popcorn they sell, the more they earn. However, the limitation of these plans is that they are not feasible for many jobs.

Merit-based pay plan

A pay plan based on performance appraisal ratings.

Merit-Based Pay   Merit-based pay plans pay for individual performance. However, unlike piece-rate plans, which pay based on objective output, **merit-based pay plans** are based on performance appraisals. A main advantage of merit pay plans is that they allow employers to differentiate pay based on performance so that those people thought to be high performers are given bigger raises. The plans can be motivating because, if they are designed correctly, individuals perceive a strong relationship between their performance and the rewards they receive.

In an effort to motivate and retain top performers, more companies are increasing the differential between top and bottom performers to encourage employees and ensure them that their efforts are recognized and appreciated. Otherwise, if all employees are rewarded regardless of their productivity, this will open the door to ill feelings among coworkers, and thus lead to negative interaction within the organization. To be more specific, the Equity theory that was discussed earlier in this chapter will then be non-existent.

Despite the attraction of pay for performance, merit pay plans have several limitations. One of them is that, typically, such plans are based on an annual performance appraisal. Thus, the merit pay is as valid or invalid as the performance ratings on which it is based. Another limitation of merit pay is that sometimes the pay raise pool fluctuates based on economic conditions or other factors that have little to do with an individual employee's performance.

Bonuses   For many jobs, annual bonuses are a significant component of the total compensation. In some organizations, the bonus can exceed the base salary. Increasingly, bonus plans are casting a larger net within organizations to include lower-ranking employees. Many companies now routinely reward production employees with bonuses in the thousands of dollars when company profits improve. One advantage of bonuses over merit pay is that a **bonus** rewards employees for recent performance rather than historical performance. So many organizations around the world follow the bonus scheme. The Arab world is no exception at all.

Skill-Based Pay   **Skill-based pay** is an alternative to job-based pay. Rather than having an individual's job title define his or her pay category, skill-based pay, also called competency-based or knowledge-based pay, sets pay levels on the basis of how many skills employees have or how many jobs they can do.[63]

For instance, employees can improve their annual salaries by learning new skills such as leadership, workforce development, and functional excellence. For employers, the attraction of skill-based pay plans is that they increase the flexibility of the workforce. Skill-based pay also facilitates communication across the organization because people gain a better understanding of each others' jobs.

What about the downside of skill-based pay? People can learn all the skills the program calls them to learn, but this can frustrate employees after they've become challenged by an environment of learning, growth, and continual pay raises. There is also a problem created by paying people for acquiring skills for which there may be no immediate need. This happened at IDS Financial Services.[64]

The company found itself paying people more money even though there was little immediate use for their new skills. IDS eventually dropped its skill-based pay plan and replaced it with one that equally balances individual contribution and gains in work-team productivity. Finally, skill-based plans don't address the level of performance. They deal only with whether someone can perform the skill.

Profit-Sharing Plans   **Profit-sharing plans** are organization-wide programs that distribute compensation based on some established formula designed around a company's profitability. These can be direct cash outlays or, particularly in the case of top managers, allocations of stock options. In fact, not all profit-sharing plans need be great in scale. For example, Jihad Ltufi started his own car-wash business at the age of 13. As demand grew, Jihad employed his brother, Imad, and friend, Maher Musa and pays them each 25 percent of the profits he makes on each car.

Bonus

A pay plan that rewards employees for recent performance rather than historical performance.

Skill-based pay

A pay plan that sets pay levels on the basis of how many skills employees have or how many jobs they can do.

Profit-sharing plan

An organization-wide program that distributes compensation based on some established formula designed around a company's profitability.

Gainsharing

A formula-based group incentive plan.

Gainsharing   Another variable-pay program that has received a great deal of attention in recent years is **gainsharing**.[65] This is a formula-based group incentive plan. Improvements in group productivity from one period to another determine the total amount of money that is to be allocated. Gainsharing's popularity seems to be narrowly focused among large companies. Gainsharing is different from profit-sharing in that rewards are related to productivity gains rather than on profits. On a positive note, employees in a gainsharing plan can receive incentive awards even when the organization isn't profitable.

Employee stock ownership plan (ESOP)

A company-established benefits plan in which employees acquire stock, often at below-market prices, as part of their benefits.

Employee Stock Ownership Plans   Employee stock ownership plans (ESOPs) are company-established benefit plans in which employees acquire stock, often at below-market prices, as part of their benefits.

The research on ESOPs indicates that they increase employee satisfaction.[66] But their impact on performance is less clear. ESOPs have the potential to increase employee job satisfaction and work motivation. But for this potential to be realized, employees need to psychologically experience ownership.[67] That is, in addition to merely having a financial stake in the company, employees need to be kept regularly informed of the status of the business and also have the opportunity to exercise influence over it. The evidence consistently indicates that it takes ownership and a participative style of management to achieve significant improvements in an organization's performance.[68] In the Gulf region ESOP is extremely rare, largely because so many organizations are family-owned. However, as the demand for talented and experienced employees increases, the awareness of ESOPs as a source of motivation is growing, and many companies across other parts of the Arab world have adopted the ESOP as a means of motivation.

Evaluation of Variable Pay   Do variable-pay programs increase motivation and productivity? The answer is a qualified 'yes.' For example, studies generally support the idea that organizations with profit-sharing plans have higher levels of profitability than those without them.[69]

Similarly, gainsharing has been found to improve productivity in a majority of cases and often has a positive impact on employee attitudes.[70]

Another study found that whereas piece-rate pay-for-performance plans stimulated higher levels of productivity, this positive affect was not observed for risk-averse employees. Despite all these studies, not everyone responds positively to variable-pay plans.[71]

Flexible Benefits: Developing a Benefits Package

9 *Show how flexible benefits turn benefits into motivators.*

Ahmad Abdo and Ibtisam Nohra both work for Etisalat, a well-established company in the Arab world, but they have very different needs in terms of employee benefits. Ahmad is married and has three young children and a wife who is at home full time. Ibtisam, too, is married, but her husband has a high-paying job with the government, and they have no children. Ahmad is concerned about having a good medical plan and enough life insurance to support his family in case it's needed. In contrast, Ibtisam's husband already has her medical needs covered on his plan, and life insurance is a low priority for both Ibtisam and her husband. In contrast, Ibtisam is more interested in extra vacation time and long-term financial benefits such as a tax-deferred savings plan.

A standardized benefits package for all employees at Etisalat would be unlikely to satisfactorily meet the needs of both Ahmad and Ibtisam. Etisalat could, however, cover both sets of needs if it offered flexible benefits. So, what are flexible benefits?

Flexible benefits allow employees to put together a benefits package individually tailored to their own needs and situation. It replaces the traditional "one-benefit-plan-fits-all" programs that used to dominate organizations.[72] Consistent with expectancy theory's thesis that organizational rewards should be linked to each individual employee's goals, flexible benefits individualize rewards by allowing each employee to choose the compensation package that best satisfies his or her current needs.

The average organization provides fringe benefits worth approximately 40 percent of an employee's salary. Traditional programs don't meet diverse needs, but flexible benefits do. They can be uniquely tailored to accommodate differences in employee needs based on age, marital status, spouses' benefit status, number and age of dependents, and the like. The three most popular types of benefits plans are modular plans, core-plus options, and flexible spending accounts.[73]

Employees of software developer Oracle Corporation, shown here in the company's cafeteria, receive a basic benefits package and may also choose coverage levels and additional benefits that meet their individual needs and those of their dependents. Such flexible benefits are consistent with the expectancy theory thesis that links rewards to the individual employee goals. The OracleFlex plan gives employees flex credits they can use to purchase benefits so they can control the amount they spend for each benefit option. Employees with remaining credits may direct them toward taxable income or to their 401(k) savings, health care reimbursement, or dependent care reimbursement accounts.

> ### What Do You Think?
>
> *How can flexible benefits turn benefits into motivators?*

First, *modular plans* are predesigned packages of benefits, with each module put together to meet the needs of a specific group of employees. So a module can be designed for single employees with no dependents and another for parents who need additional life insurance, disability insurance, and expanded health coverage. Second, *core-plus plans* consist of basic essential benefits and a menu-like selection of other benefit options from which employees can select and add to the core. Typically, each employee is given 'benefit credits,' which allow the 'purchase' of additional benefits that uniquely meet his or her needs. The third, *flexible spending plans* allow employees to set aside up to the dollar amount offered in the plan to pay for particular services. It's a convenient way for employees to pay for health care and dental premiums. Flexible spending accounts can increase employee take-home pay because employees don't have to pay taxes on the dollars they spend out of these accounts.

Intrinsic Rewards: Employee Recognition Programs

10 Identify the motivational benefits of intrinsic rewards.

Lama makes only US$8.50 per hour working at her fast-food job in Doha, Qatar, and the job isn't very challenging or interesting. Yet Lama talks enthusiastically about her job, her boss, and the company that employs her. "What I like is the fact that Ghassan (her supervisor) appreciates the effort I make. He compliments me regularly in front of the other people on my shift, and I've been chosen Employee of the Month twice in the past six months. Did you see my picture on that plaque on the wall?"

Organizations are increasingly recognizing what Lama knows: important work rewards can be both intrinsic and extrinsic. Rewards are intrinsic in the form of employee recognition programs (as shown in Figure 5-8) and extrinsic in the form of compensation systems. In this section, we deal with ways in which managers can reward and motivate employee performance.

Flexible benefits

A benefits plan that allows each employee to put together a benefits package individually tailored to his or her own needs and situation.

Figure **5-8**

THE WALL STREET JOURNAL

EMPLOYEE OF THE MONTH

Source: From the *Wall Street Journal*, October 21, 1997. Reprinted by permission of Cartoon Features Syndicate.

Employee recognition programs range from a private 'thank you' up to widely publicized formal programs in which specific types of behavior are encouraged and the procedures for attaining recognition are clearly identified. Some research has suggested that whereas financial incentives may be more motivating in the short term, in the long run, nonfinancial incentives are more motivating.[74]

This kind of recognition has become popular in many organizations and businesses in the Arab world. Managers realize the importance of appreciation to improve morale and enhance performance and commitment. This is being implemented at fast-food franchises such as McDonalds, Pizza Hut, and Kentucky Fried Chicken as well as several others. One particular example is seen at Antoine Saliba's, a well-known jewelry shop in Lebanon that has a picture of the 'Employee of the Month' displayed for all coworkers and customers to see. In addition, employees receive bonuses on sales they make.

In retailers like Saliba there are many benefits to being employee of the month, for example:

- having priority when approaching customers;
- being the first to choose days off;
- gaining recognition in the showroom;
- increasing the chances of having a rise in salary;
- getting a bonus on salary.

The Saliba management decide who will be awarded Employee of the Month by using a monthly evaluation form that assesses staff members according to various criteria: performance at work, neatness, interoffice behavior, managerial response, smiley face/hostessing, team order, credits, e-mail, best report, not having received any warnings, and days off. Points are removed for negative behavior or performance, and if an employee falls below 50 points, a warning will be issued.

In contrast, other managers use a far more informal approach. Julia Stewart, president of Applebee's restaurants, frequently leaves sealed notes on the chairs of employees after everyone has gone home.[75] These notes explain how critical

Stewart thinks the person's work is or how much she appreciates the completion of a recent project. Stewart also relies heavily on voicemail messages left after office hours to tell employees how appreciative she is for a job well done. Applebee's is a food franchise located in many Arab world countries such as Bahrain, Jordan, Kuwait, Lebanon, Qatar, KSA, and UAE and their managers are also becoming more aware of the importance of employee recognition as a motivator.

A few years ago, 1,500 employees were surveyed in a variety of work settings to find out what they considered to be the most powerful workplace motivator. Their response was, "Recognition, recognition, and more recognition."[76]

As illustrated in Figure 5-9, Phoenix Inn, a West Coast chain of small hotels in the US, encourages employees to smile by letting customers identify this desirable behavior and then recognize employees who are identified smiling most often by giving them rewards and publicity. Similarly, the majority of hotels in the Arab world, whether international chains or regional chains, such as The Royale, The Four Seasons, and Crowne Plaza, ask for guest feedback on employee performance and behavior.

An obvious advantage of recognition programs is that they are inexpensive (praise, of course, is free!).[77] It shouldn't be surprising, therefore, to find that employee recognition programs have grown in popularity. A 2002 survey of 391 companies in the US found that 84 percent had some program to recognize worker achievements and that four in ten said they were doing more to support employee recognition than they had been doing just a year earlier.[78]

A similar 2009 survey of 13,376 respondents from the Arab world acknowledged the importance of recognition and appreciation for good work as a means for satisfaction and motivation. Employees were asked about the degree to which their work was recognized and appreciated by their supervisors.

Figure **5-9**

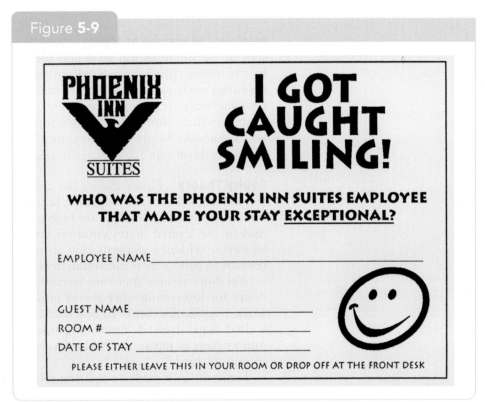

Source: Phoenix Inn Suites.

The results were relatively similar, with between 54 and 61 percent of respondents in each country being satisfied or very satisfied with the degree of recognition and appreciation they receive, between 1 and 5 percent saying they don't know / can't say, and the remainder being dissatisfied or very dissatisfied.[79] We can see from this that, generally across the region, many employees feel their work is not sufficiently recognized and appreciated. The Arab world corporate culture needs to be enhanced and supervisors educated on the significance of the importance of showing employees that we see them and acknowledge their contributions to the organization.

Despite the increased popularity of employee recognition programs, critics argue that these programs are highly susceptible to political manipulation by management.[80] When applied to jobs where performance factors are relatively objective, such as sales, recognition programs are likely to be perceived by employees as fair. However, in most jobs, the criteria for good performance aren't self-evident, which allows managers to manipulate the system and recognize their favorite employees. As a result, abuse of such a system can undermine the value of recognition programs and lead to the demoralization and demotivation of employees.

Global Implications

Our discussions of the goal-setting theories stressed that care needs to be taken in applying these theories because they assume cultural characteristics that are not universal. This is true for many of the theories presented in this chapter. We need to consider the cross-cultural transferability of all motivation theories. In addition, do the motivational approaches discussed in this chapter vary by culture? First, let's take a look at the cross-cultural transferability of several motivation theories.

Maslow's Hierarchy of Needs   Maslow's needs hierarchy argues that people start at the physiological level and then move progressively up the hierarchy in this order: physiological, safety, social, esteem, and self-actualization. In countries such as Japan, Greece, and Mexico, where uncertainty–avoidance characteristics are strong, security needs would be on top of the need hierarchy. Countries that score high on nurturing characteristics—such as Arab countries and Denmark, Sweden, Norway, the Netherlands, and Finland—would have social needs on top.[81]

Equity Theory   Equity theory has gained a relatively strong following in the United States. That's not surprising because US-style reward systems are based on the assumption that workers are highly sensitive to equity in reward allocations. And in the United States equity is meant to closely tie pay to performance. However, evidence suggests that in many Arab cultures, employees expect rewards to reflect their individual needs as well as their performance.[82]

But don't assume there are *no* cross-cultural consistencies. For instance, the desire for interesting work seems important to almost all workers, regardless of their national culture. In one study, employees in Belgium, Britain, and the United States ranked 'interesting work' number one among 11 work goals. And workers in Japan, the Netherlands, and Germany ranked this factor either second or third.[83]

Similarly, in a study comparing job-preference outcomes among graduate students in the United States, Canada, Australia, and Singapore, growth, achievement, and responsibility were rated the top three and had identical rankings.[84]

Both of these studies suggest some universality to the importance of intrinsic factors in the two-factor theory.

Because we have discussed some very different approaches in this chapter, let's break down our analysis by approach. Not every approach has been studied by cross-cultural researchers, so we don't discuss every motivational approach. However, we consider cross-cultural differences in many of the approaches that have been discussed in this chapter, such as job characteristics and job enrichment, telecommuting, variable pay, flexible benefits, and employee involvement.

Job Characteristics and Job Enrichment   As the authors note, because the job characteristics model is relatively individualistic (considering the relationship between the employee and his or her work), this suggests that job enrichment strategies may not have the same effects in more collectivistic cultures that they do in individualistic cultures.

Telecommuting   Does the degree to which employees telecommute vary by country? Does its effectiveness depend on culture? First, one study suggests that telecommuting is more common in the United States than in all the European Union (EU) countries except the Netherlands. What about the rest of the world? Unfortunately, there is very little data comparing telecommuting rates in other parts of the world. Regardless of country, interest is higher among employees than among employers.[85]

Variable Pay   You'd probably think that individual pay systems (such as merit pay or pay-for-performance) would work better in individualistic cultures like the United States than in collectivistic cultures like the Arab countries or China. Similarly, you'd probably hypothesize that group-based rewards such as gainsharing or profit-sharing would work better in collectivistic cultures than in individualistic cultures. Unfortunately, there isn't much research on the issue, though it is critical that wherever the plan is implemented, it be communicated clearly and administered fairly.[86]

Flexible Benefits   Today, almost all major corporations in the United States offer flexible benefits. And they're becoming the norm in other countries, too. For instance, a recent survey of 136 Canadian organizations found that 93 percent have adopted or will adopt flexible benefits in the near term.[87]

There are few statistics about the Arab world but we do notice more awareness as to the positive outcomes of flexible benefits in a salary survey conducted by Bayt.com in 2011.

Employee Involvement   Employee involvement programs differ among countries.[88]

For instance, a study comparing the acceptance of employee involvement programs in four countries, including the United States and India, confirmed the importance of modifying practices to reflect national culture.[89]

Studies in the Arab world are limited but one study does shed some light.[90] The research, at Notre Dame University, investigated, first, the level of employee satisfaction within the workplace, and second, how satisfaction affected productivity and performance. The respondents generally agreed that their 'bosses' did not communicate with them and, most importantly, did not involve them in decision making or problem solving. Overall, they were not encouraged to participate, offer suggestions or make recommendations. The employees emphasized that if they had been given these opportunities, they would have had greater commitment, and would have felt that they were being treated as individuals with constructive ideas.

Summary and Implications for Managers

The theories we've discussed in this chapter address different outcome variables. Some, for instance, are directed at explaining turnover, while others emphasize productivity. The theories also differ in their predictive strength. Overall, we've presented a number of motivation theories and applications—Need Theories, Goal-Setting Theory, Reinforcement Theory, Equity Theory/Organizational Justice, and Expectancy Theory—in addition to the alternative work arrangements, flexible benefits, variable-pay programs, and rewards. Although it's always dangerous to synthesize a large number of complex ideas into a few simple guidelines, the following suggestions summarize the essence of what we know about motivating employees in organizations.

Employees should have firm, specific goals, and they should get feedback on how well they are faring in pursuit of those goals. As a result, employees can contribute to a number of decisions that affect them: setting work goals, choosing their own benefits packages, solving productivity and quality problems, and the like. This can increase employee productivity, commitment to work goals, motivation, and job satisfaction.

Moreover, rewards should be contingent on performance. Importantly, employees must perceive a clear relationship between performance and rewards. Regardless of how closely rewards are actually correlated to performance criteria, if individuals perceive this relationship to be low, the results will be low performance, a decrease in job satisfaction, and an increase in turnover and absenteeism.

Furthermore, employees should perceive rewards as equating with the inputs they bring to the job. At a simplistic level, this should mean that experience, skills, abilities, effort, and other obvious inputs should explain differences in performance and, hence, pay, job assignments, and other obvious rewards.

In conclusion, managers should be sensitive to individual differences. For example, employees from Asian cultures prefer not to be singled out as special because it makes them uncomfortable, whereas employees from the Arab world ask for special attention. Remember, employees have different needs. Don't treat them all alike. Moreover, spend the time necessary to understand what's important to each employee. This allows you to individualize goals, level of involvement, and rewards to align with individual needs. Also, design jobs to align with individual needs and therefore maximize the motivation potential in jobs.

Point >> << Counterpoint

PRAISE MOTIVATES

Some of the most memorable, and meaningful, words we've ever heard have probably been words of praise. Genuine compliments mean a lot to people—and can go a long way toward inspiring the best performance. Too often we assume that simple words of praise mean little, but most of us enjoy genuine praise from people who are in a position to evaluate us. Of course, praise is not everything, but it is a very important and often an underutilized motivator. And best of all, it's free.

Praise is highly overrated. There is no doubt that it's nice to receive compliments, but in practice, praise has some real pitfalls.

First, a lot of praise is not genuine. Falsely praising people can be negative. That is, if we are told we're wonderful time after time, we start to believe it, even when we aren't.

Second, the more praise we give, the less meaningful it becomes. If we go around telling everyone they're special, soon it means nothing to those who do achieve something terrific.

Third, some of the most motivating people are those who are difficult to please. They are known for being difficult to please, which means most people will work harder to meet their expectations. Praise may seem like it's free, but at the same time it may encourage employees to think that mediocrity is okay.

Questions for Review

1 Define *motivation*. What are the key elements of motivation?

2 What are the early theories of motivation?

3 What are the contemporary theories of motivation? How do these complement one another?

4 What are the key points of both the equity and expectancy theories?

5 What is the job characteristics model? How does it motivate employees?

6 What are the three major ways that jobs can be redesigned? In your view, in what situations would one of the methods be favored over the others?

7 What are the three alternative work arrangements of flextime, job sharing, and telecommuting? What are the advantages and disadvantages of each?

8 What are employee involvement programs? How might they increase employee motivation?

9 How can flexible benefits motivate employees?

10 What are the motivational benefits of intrinsic rewards?

Discussion Exercise

'Women Are More Motivated to Get Along, Men Are More Motivated to Get Ahead'

Research indicates that men are more likely to be described active, decisive, and competitive. Women are more likely to be described as caring, emotional, and considerate.

It seems that compared with women, men are relatively more motivated to excel at tasks and jobs. Compared with men, women are more motivated to maintain relationships. Do you agree with this? Discuss.

Ethical Considerations

Jameela has been Omar's personal assistant for five years. She really enjoys her job and also appreciates the fact that Omar allows her to get involved in the day-to-day activities of the office. In addition, Jameela is consulted and gives feedback on the advertising campaigns that Omar prepares. At this point, CREATE ADS has landed one of its largest accounts. However, Omar felt that his creativity was lacking and he was having great difficulty coming up with a unique campaign for his clients.

As usual, he asked Jameela for her input. In fact, she offered a very original idea that enabled Omar to complete the project. Jameela was satisfied with her contribution and she was sure that Omar would acknowledge her efforts and generously reward her.

Imagine her disappointment when, during the presentation to his clients, Omar told them that it was his idea. The clients loved it. Jameela was shocked!

Was Omar right to behave that way? Explain. If you were Jameela, how would you react? What affect would this have on your motivation?

Critical Analysis

REDUCING TRAVEL COSTS AT APPLEBEE'S

Applebee's International, whose headquarters are in Kansas City, in the US, is a large restaurant chain with roughly 2,000 restaurants in the US and 16 other countries. Among these are the Arab countries Bahrain, Jordan, Kuwait, Lebanon, Qatar, Saudi Arabia, and the United Arab Emirates. The company owns and operates 25 per cent of the restaurants but the remainder are franchised. Applebee's has been growing and developing over time, opening roughly 100 new restaurants per year, and is now an international franchise. Consequently, the chain has found that its travel expenses have grown as well.

The Applebee strategy has challenged the regular style of 'doing things.' Instead of building large restaurants, Applebee's has focused on smaller spaces that are cheaper and faster to build—their philosophy: Faster is Better. Enter the market before the competition does and always offer customers an unforgettable adventure.

There is no doubt that many expenses are incurred to achieve such great success. For Applebee's, much of that was spending on travel and even though it was money well spent, the firm was interested in finding ways to contain the costs. Andrew Face, Applebee's senior manager of human resources, was asked by his boss, the senior vice-president of HR, to redesign Applebee's travel system.

Face's job was to eliminate non-essential travel costs at the same time that he increased corporate travel benefits.

Face's first idea was to outsource—to look to an off-site call center, through which he would be able to negotiate group discounts for travel costs. But Face's boss thought outsourcing to a vendor wouldn't offer the type of support Applebee's needed for its employee travelers. For example, managers' plans would often change, and they needed flexibility in the travel system to accommodate that.

However, Face eventually decided on QualityAgent, a web-based system that offered employee support. Because Applebee's was concerned about removing users off the old system (using travel agents), participation was voluntary. But Face got an e-mail every time an employee used QualityAgent to make an airline reservation that didn't fall within the Applebee's travel policy, so he could send an e-mail before the employee purchased the ticket to remind the person of the policy. He also got weekly reports on travel usage to control costs and usage patterns better and to avoid abuse.

Although these elements saved Applebee's money, Face wasn't finished. He decided to provide employees with more incentives for using the system. To employees who followed travel policy and took six or more trips per year, Face promised a pair of domestic airline tickets if the company saved US$100,000 in costs that first year. Eventually he got usage up to 55 to 60 percent of employee travel.

Questions

1. Consider the variable-pay programs discussed in this chapter. Of which type of program is Applebee's program an example? Explain.

2. If you were asked to revise Applebee's program to include more individual incentives, how might you do that?

3. How would you react to such a program? Explain your reactions.

4. Are these sorts of incentives applicable to the Arab world?

Source: Adapted from L. Thornburg, "Applebee's International Cuts Travel Costs," *SHRM Online*, February 2007, www.shrm.org.

Research Exercise

If there is an Applebee's in your home country, do some research about their motivational techniques. If there is no Applebee's in your home country, do some research about another chain of restaurants in your country. Share your findings in class and discuss taking into consideration the cultural issues also.

LEARNING OBJECTIVES

This chapter will enable you to:

1 Differentiate emotions from moods and list the basic emotions and moods.

2 Discuss whether emotions are rational and what functions they serve.

3 Identify the sources of emotions and moods.

4 Show the impact emotional labor has on employees.

5 Describe affective events theory and identify its applications.

6 Contrast the evidence for and against the existence of emotional intelligence.

7 Apply concepts about emotions and moods to specific OB issues.

8 Contrast the experience, interpretation, and expression of emotions across cultures.

Emotions and Moods

You don't want people to get caught up in the emotion because change isn't emotion. It's real work and organization and strategy . . . that's just the truth of it. —Michelle Obama

Stabbed in the Back

'Do unto others as you would have them do unto you.' This famous saying has been translated into so many languages and is applicable to so many situations. It is sound advice: we should really think before we act and consider what the consequences of our actions will be. Most importantly, we should not allow personal feelings and emotions to interfere with work processes. We should always look at things objectivity, to ensure fairness.

Bassam had been with Abdul-Fattah Constructions in Kuwait for ten years. The owner, Othman Abdul-Fattah, was extremely satisfied with Bassam's work as project manager. In addition, his outstanding inter-personal skills had allowed him to establish excellent rapport with employees, clients, and colleagues.

Because he had all these qualities, Othman asked Bassam to train Najeeb, who would be managing their upcoming project in Qatar. Othman wanted an evaluation after three months. The problem was that Bassam immediately had a negative feeling about Najeeb. Nonetheless, as a professional, he was determined to give Najeeb the opportunity to prove himself. However, his negative feelings intensified when he discovered that Najeeb had already made a contact in Qatar and was working on his own 'agenda.' Needless to say, Bassam now watched over Najeeb like a hawk and, despite his good nature, Bassam allowed his emotions to dominate him.

Although Najeeb was competent, Bassam just did not like him. His evaluation of Najeeb was negative and he did not recommend him for the position. Actually, Othman was surprised because Najeeb came to the company highly recommended from his former employer. He discussed the appraisal with Bassam, but he was aware that Bassam had strong feelings against Najeeb.

As the opening case shows, emotions can lead us to action. However, we must be careful not to be unfair. Before we go further into emotions and moods, get an assessment of your mood state right now. Take the following self-assessment to find out what sort of mood you're in.

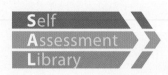

HOW ARE YOU FEELING RIGHT NOW?

In the Self-Assessment Library (available online), take assessment IV.D.1 (How Are You Feeling Right Now?) and answer the following questions:

1. *What was higher, your positive mood score or negative mood score? How do these scores compare with those of your classmates?*
2. *Did your score surprise you? Why or why not?*
3. *What sorts of things influence your positive moods, your negative moods?*

Given the obvious role that emotions play in our work and everyday lives, it might surprise you to learn that, until recently, the field of OB has given the topic of emotions little or no attention.[1] How could this be? We can offer two possible explanations.

The first is the *myth of rationality*.[2] The protocol of the work world has always been in control of emotions. A well-run organization didn't allow employees to express frustration, fear, anger, love, hate, joy, grief, and similar feelings. The prevailing thought was that such emotions were not reasonable. Even though researchers and managers knew that emotions were an inseparable part of everyday life, they tried to create organizations that were emotion free. That, of course, wasn't possible.

The second explanation is that many believed that emotions of any kind are disruptive.[3] When researchers considered emotions, they looked at strong negative emotions—especially anger—that interfered with an employee's ability to work effectively. They rarely viewed emotions as constructive or contributing to enhanced performance.

Certainly some emotions, particularly when shown at the wrong time, can interrupt employee performance. But this doesn't change the fact that employees bring their emotional sides with them to work every day and that no study of OB would be comprehensive without considering the role of emotions in workplace behavior.

What Do You Think?

From the opening case, do you think that Bassam treated Najeeb fairly?

What Are Emotions and Moods?

1 Differentiate emotions from moods and list the basic emotions and moods.

Before we can proceed with our analysis, we need to clarify three terms that are closely interrelated: *affect*, *emotions*, and *moods*.

Affect is a term that covers a broad range of feelings that people experience. It's an umbrella concept that includes both emotions and moods.[4] **Emotions** are deep feelings that are directed at someone or something and tend to be fairly short term.[5] **Moods**

Affect

A broad range of feelings that people experience.

Emotions

Intense feelings that are directed at someone or something.

Moods

Feelings that tend to be less intense than emotions and that lack a contextual stimulus.

are feelings that tend to be less intense than emotions, last longer and do not always have a stimulus.[6]

For example, if someone is rude to you, you'll feel angry. That intense feeling of anger probably comes and goes fairly quickly, maybe even in a matter of seconds. When you're in a bad mood, though, you can feel bad for several hours.

Emotions are reactions to a person or an event; for instance, seeing a friend at work may make you feel glad, while dealing with a rude client may make you feel angry. You show your emotions when you're "happy about something, angry at someone, afraid of something."[7] Moods, in contrast, aren't usually directed at a person or an event. But emotions can turn into moods when you lose focus on the event or object that started the feeling. Similarly, good or bad moods can make you more emotional in response to an event. So when a colleague criticizes how you spoke to a client, you might become angry at him. That is, you show emotion (anger) toward a specific object (your colleague). But as the specific emotion dissipates, you might just feel generally depressed. You can't attribute this feeling to any single event; you're just not your normal self. You might then overreact to other events. This affect state describes a mood. Figure 6-1 shows the relationships among affect, emotions, and mood more clearly.

First, as Figure 6-1 shows, affect is a broad term that encompasses emotions and moods. Second, there are differences between emotions and moods. Some of these differences—that emotions are more likely to be caused by a specific event, and emotions are more fleeting than moods—we just discussed above. Other differences are more indirect. For example, unlike moods, emotions tend to be more clearly revealed with facial expressions such as anger or disgust. Also, some researchers speculate that emotions may be more action-oriented—they may lead us to some immediate action—while moods may be more cognitive, meaning they may cause us to think for a while.[8]

Finally, the figure also shows that emotions and moods can mutually influence each other. For example, an emotion, if it's strong and deep enough, can turn into a mood: getting your dream job may generate the emotion of joy, but it also can put you in a good mood for several days. Similarly, if you're in a good or bad mood, it might make you experience a more intense positive or negative emotion than would otherwise be the case. For example, if you're in a bad

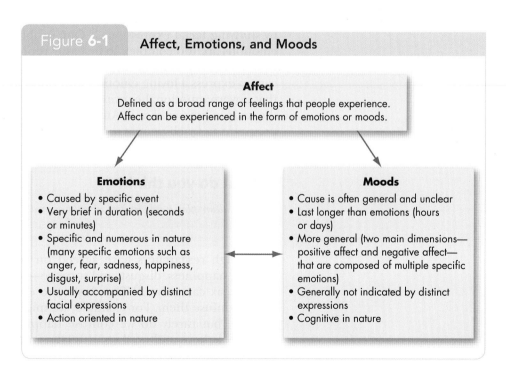

Figure 6-1   Affect, Emotions, and Moods

Affect

Defined as a broad range of feelings that people experience. Affect can be experienced in the form of emotions or moods.

Emotions

- Caused by specific event
- Very brief in duration (seconds or minutes)
- Specific and numerous in nature (many specific emotions such as anger, fear, sadness, happiness, disgust, surprise)
- Usually accompanied by distinct facial expressions
- Action oriented in nature

Moods

- Cause is often general and unclear
- Last longer than emotions (hours or days)
- More general (two main dimensions—positive affect and negative affect—that are composed of multiple specific emotions)
- Generally not indicated by distinct expressions
- Cognitive in nature

mood, you might 'blow up' in response to a coworker's comment when normally it would have just generated a mild reaction. Because emotions and moods can mutually influence each other, there will be many points throughout the chapter where emotions and moods will be closely connected.

Although affect, emotions, and moods are separable in theory, in practice the distinction isn't always crystal clear. In fact, in some areas, researchers have studied mostly moods, and in other areas, mainly emotions. So, when we review the OB topics on emotions and moods, you may see more information on emotions in one area and moods in another.

What Do You Think?

How do your emotions and moods usually affect your personal and professional behavior?

We have given many examples to enable you to clearly differentiate among these terms so that as we progress through this chapter, you will be able to see the relationships among topics and how they are applicable to OB.

The Basic Emotions

How many emotions are there? In what ways do they differ? There are dozens of emotions, including anger, contempt, enthusiasm, envy, fear, frustration, disappointment, embarrassment, disgust, happiness, hate, hope, jealousy, joy, love, pride, surprise, and sadness. There have been numerous research efforts to limit and define the dozens of emotions into a fundamental or basic set of emotions.[9] But some researchers argue that it makes no sense to think of basic emotions because even emotions we rarely experience, such as shock, can have a powerful effect on us.[10] René Descartes, often called the founder of modern philosophy, identified six "simple and primitive passions"—wonder, love, hatred, desire, joy, and sadness—and argued that "all the others are composed of some of these six or are species of them."[11]

In contemporary research, psychologists have tried to identify basic emotions by studying facial expressions.[12] One problem with this approach is that some emotions are too complex to be easily represented on our faces. Take love, for example. Many think of love as the most universal of all emotions,[13] yet it's not easy to express a loving emotion with one's face only. Also, cultures have norms that govern emotional expression, so how we *experience* an emotion isn't always the same as how we *show* it. And many companies today offer anger-management programs to teach people to contain or even hide their inner feelings.[14]

What do you think?

Does culture play a role in how we express or do not express our emotions and feelings?

Enough researchers have agreed on six universal emotions—anger, fear, sadness, happiness, disgust, and surprise—with most other emotions under one of these six categories.[15] The closer two emotions are, the more likely people are to confuse them. For example, we might sometimes mistake happiness for surprise, but rarely do we confuse happiness and disgust. Culture definitely plays a role here and we'll see this later in this chapter.

The Basic Moods: Positive and Negative Affect

One way to classify emotions is by whether they are positive or negative.[16] Positive emotions—such as joy and gratitude—express a favorable evaluation or feeling. Negative emotions—such as anger or guilt—express the opposite (see Figure 6-2). Keep in mind that emotions can't be neutral. Being neutral is being nonemotional.[17]

When we group emotions into positive and negative categories, they become mood states because we are now looking at them more generally instead of isolating one particular emotion. In Figure 6-2, excitement is a specific emotion that is a pure marker of high positive affect, while boredom is a pure marker of low positive affect. Some emotions—such as contentment (a mixture of high positive affect and low negative affect) and sadness (a mixture of low positive affect and high negative affect)—are in between.

So, we can think of **positive affect** as a mood dimension consisting of positive emotions such as excitement, self-assurance, and cheerfulness at the high end and boredom, sluggishness, and tiredness at the low end. In contrast, **negative affect** is a mood dimension consisting of nervousness, stress, and anxiety at the high end and relaxation, tranquility, and poise at the low end. Positive and negative affect play out at work and beyond in that they color our perceptions, and these perceptions can become their own reality.

For example, one flight attendant posted an anonymous blog on the web that said: "I work in a pressurized aluminum tube and the environment outside my 'office' cannot sustain human life. That being said, the human life inside is not worth sustaining sometimes . . . in fact, the passengers can be jerks, and idiots. I am often treated with no respect, nobody listens to me . . . until I threaten to kick them off the plane."[18] Clearly, if flight attendants are in a bad mood, it's going to influence their perceptions of passengers, which will, in turn, influence their behavior.

Importantly, negative emotions are likely to translate into negative moods. People think about events that created strong negative emotions five times as long as they do about events that created strong positive ones.[19] So, we should expect people to recall negative experiences more readily than positive ones. Perhaps one of the reasons is that, for most of us, they're also more unusual. Indeed, research shows that there is a **positivity offset**, meaning that at zero input (when nothing in particular is going on), most individuals experience a mildly positive mood.[20] So, for most people, positive moods are somewhat more common than

Positive affect

A mood dimension that consists of specific positive emotions such as excitement, self-assurance, and cheerfulness at the high end, and boredom, sluggishness, and tiredness at the low end.

Negative affect

A mood dimension that consists of emotions such as nervousness, stress, and anxiety at the high end, and relaxation, tranquility, and poise at the low end.

Positivity offset

The tendency of most individuals to experience a mildly positive mood at zero input (when nothing in particular is going on).

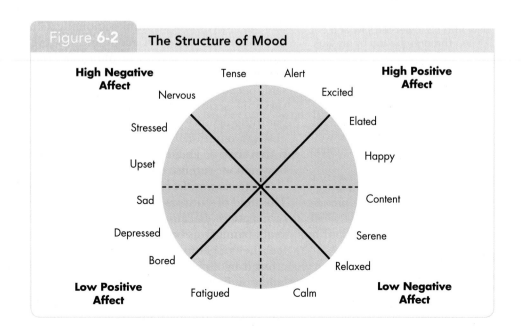

Figure 6-2 **The Structure of Mood**

negative moods. The positivity offset also appears to operate at work. A particular study showed that the mood of employees at the start of their day will determine the course of the whole day.[21] Performance will correspond to how they feel at the start of that day. We usually instruct people to keep their emotions at home; do not bring your problems to work. However, this is often difficult because if "someone wakes up on the wrong side of the bed" on a certain day, then their negative mood will dictate the rest of their day and how they interact with others in the workplace. The opposite is also true: if employees are in a good mood, then their performance is usually strong and they are effective during the day.

The Function of Emotions

2 *Discuss whether emotions are rational and what functions they serve.*

Do Emotions Make Us Irrational?   How often have you heard someone say, "Oh, you're just being emotional"? This suggests that the demonstration or even experience of emotions is likely to make us seem weak, brittle, or irrational. However, the research disagrees and is increasingly showing that emotions are actually critical to rational thinking. In fact, there has been evidence of such a link for a long time.

We must have the ability to experience emotions to be rational. Why? Because our emotions provide important information about how we understand the world around us. Although we might think of a computer as intellectually superior, a human so void of emotion would be unable to function. The key to good decision making is the ability to employ both thinking *and* feeling in one's decision.

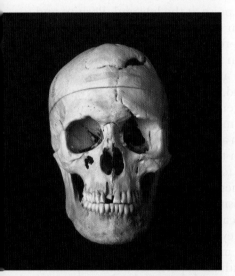

This skull belonged to Phineas Gage. While working on a railroad in Vermont in 1848, an iron bar flew into his lower-left jaw and out through the top of his skull. Remarkably, Gage survived his injury and was still able to read and speak and perform well on cognitive ability tests. However, he had lost his ability to experience emotion. He was emotionless at even the saddest misfortunes or the happiest occasions. The researchers found that losing the ability to emote led to the loss of the ability to reason. From this discovery, researchers learned that our emotions provide us with valuable information that helps our thinking process.

Evolutionary psychology

An area of inquiry which argues that we must experience the emotions we do because they serve a purpose.

> ### Picture This
>
> Think about a manager making a decision to fire an employee. Would you really want the manager to make the decision without regarding either his or the employee's emotions?

What Functions Do Emotions Serve?   Why do we have emotions? What role do they serve? We have just discussed one function in the previous section—that we need them to think rationally. Charles Darwin, the person who tried to explain the theory of evolution, however, took a broader approach. In *The Expression of the Emotions in Man and Animals*, Darwin argued that emotions developed over time to help humans solve problems. Emotions are useful, he said, because they motivate people to engage in actions that are important for survival—actions such as looking for food, seeking shelter, choosing mates, guarding against enemies, and predicting others' behaviors. For example, disgust (an emotion) motivates us to avoid dangerous or harmful things (such as rotten foods). Excitement (also an emotion) motivates us to take on situations in which we require energy and initiative (for example, facing a new career).

Following on Darwin are researchers who focus on **evolutionary psychology**. This field of study says we must experience emotions—whether they are positive or negative—because they serve a purpose.[22] For example, although we tend to think of anger as being 'bad,' it actually can help us protect our rights when we feel they're being violated. For example, a person showing anger when double-crossed by a colleague is serving a warning for others not to repeat the same behavior. Positive emotions also serve a purpose. For example, a service employee who feels empathy for a customer may provide better customer service than an seemingly unfeeling employee.

Sources of Emotions and Moods

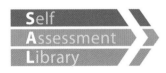
3 Identify the sources of emotions and moods.

Have you ever said, "I got up on the wrong side of the bed today."? What does this imply? Basically that you are not feeling well or 'you are in a bad mood.' Have you ever shouted at a coworker or family member for no particular reason? If you have, it probably makes you wonder where emotions and moods come from. Here we discuss some of the primary influences on moods and emotions and most of them are by-products of culture.

Personality   Moods and emotions have a trait component—most people have built-in tendencies to experience certain moods and emotions more frequently than others do. Moreover, people naturally differ in how intensely they experience the same emotions. For example, one manager may be easily moved to anger, while another may be distant and unemotional and this is due to **affect intensity**, or how strongly they experience their emotions.[23] In other words, affectively intense people experience both positive and negative emotions more deeply—when they're sad, they're really sad, and when they're happy, they're really happy.

Affect intensity
Individual differences in the strength with which individuals experience their emotions.

WHAT'S MY AFFECT INTENSITY?

In the Self-Assessment Library (available online), take assessment IV.D.2 (What's My Affect Intensity?).

Day of the Week and Time of the Day   Are people in their best moods on the weekends? Well, sort of. People tend to be in their worst moods (highest negative affect and lowest positive affect) early in the week and in their best moods (highest positive affect and lowest negative affect) late in the week.[24]

What about time of the day? We often think that people differ, depending on whether they are 'morning' or 'evening' people. However, the vast majority of us follow the same pattern. Regardless of what time people go to bed at night or get up in the morning, levels of positive affect tend to peak around the halfway point between waking and sleeping. Negative affect, however, shows little fluctuation throughout the day. This basic pattern seems to hold whether people describe themselves as morning people or evening people.

What does this mean for organizational behavior? Monday morning is probably not the best time to ask someone for a favor or give bad news. Our workplace interactions will probably be more positive from midmorning onward and also later in the week.

Weather   When do you think you would be in a better mood—when it's 70 degrees and sunny or when it's a gloomy, cold, rainy day? Many people believe their mood is tied to the weather. However, evidence suggests that weather has little effect on mood. One expert concluded, "Contrary to the prevailing cultural view, these data indicate that people do not report a better mood on bright and sunny days (or, conversely, a worse mood on dark and rainy days.)"[25] *Illusory correlation* explains why people tend to *think* that nice weather improves their mood. Illusory correlation occurs when people associate two events but in reality there is no connection.

Stress   As you might imagine, stress affects emotions and moods. For example, students have higher levels of fear before an exam, but their fear disappears once the exam is over.[26] At work, stressful daily events such as a nasty e-mail, a deadline, the loss of a big sale, or being reprimanded by your boss negatively affect employees' moods. Also, the effects of stress build over time. As the authors of one study note, "a constant diet of even low-level stressful events has the potential to cause workers to experience gradually increasing levels of strain over time."[27] Such increasing levels of stress and strain at work can worsen our moods, and we experience more negative emotions.

Social Activities   Do you tend to be happiest when you are out with friends? For most people, social activities increase positive mood and have little effect on negative mood. But do people in a positive mood seek out social interactions, or do social interactions cause people to be in a good mood? It seems that both are true.[28] And does the *type* of social activity matter? Indeed it does. Research suggests that physical (skiing or hiking with friends), informal (going to a party), or epicurean (eating with others) activities are more strongly associated with increases in positive mood than formal (attending a meeting) or sedentary (watching TV with friends) events.[29]

Sleep   Adults in America report that they sleep less as they grow older.[30] Does this lack of sleep make people grumpier? Sleep quality does affect mood. Undergraduates and adult workers who are sleep deprived report greater feelings of fatigue, anger, and hostility.[31] One of the reasons less sleep, or poor sleep quality, puts people in a bad mood is that it affects decision making and makes it difficult to control emotions.[32]

Exercise   You often hear it said that people should exercise to improve their mood. But does 'sweat therapy' really work? It appears so. Research consistently shows that exercise enhances people's positive mood.[33] It appears that the therapeutic effects of exercise are strongest for those who are depressed. Although

People in the Arab world are becoming more and more aware of the importance of exercise, not only for physical wellbeing, but also for mental alertness. As a result, we are witnessing commitment to 'working out' as a stress releaser. It's the goal of every business to keep employees motivated by creating a positive working atmosphere that nurtures creative energy and rewards success. Companies including Johnson & Johnson and Procter & Gamble hope to achieve positive returns on the investments they make in their employees' health and wellness. The hope is that exercise will put people in a positive mood, creating healthier, happier, more productive employees.

the effects of exercise on moods are consistent, they are not terribly strong. So, exercise may help put you in a better mood, but don't expect miracles.

Age   Do you think that young people experience more extreme, positive emotions (so-called 'youthful exuberance') than older people do? If you answered 'yes,' you were wrong. One study of people aged 18 to 94 years revealed that negative emotions seem to occur less as people get older. Periods of highly positive moods lasted longer for older individuals, and bad moods faded for them more quickly than for younger people.[34] The study implies that emotional experience tends to improve with age, so that as we get older, we experience fewer negative emotions.

Gender   The common belief is that women are more emotional than men. Is there any truth to this? The evidence does confirm that women are more emotionally expressive than are men;[35] they experience emotions more intensely, they tend to 'hold onto' emotions longer than men, and they display more frequent expressions of both positive and negative emotions, except anger.[36] Although there may be innate differences between the genders, research suggests that emotional differences also are due to the different ways men and women have been socialized.[37] Men are taught to be tough and brave. Showing emotion is inconsistent with this image. Women, in contrast, are socialized to be nurturing. For instance, women are expected to express more positive emotions on the job (shown by smiling) than men, and they do.[38] Consequently, we can say that emotions and moods are culture oriented.

International OB

Emotional Recognition: Universal or Culture Specific?

Early researchers studying how we understand emotions based on others' expressions believed that all individuals, regardless of their culture, could recognize the same emotion and behave or perform accordingly. So, for example, a frown would be recognized as indicating the emotion sadness, no matter where one was from. However, more recent research suggests that this universal approach to the study of emotions is incorrect because there are subtle differences in the degree to which we can tell what emotions people from different cultures are feeling, based on their facial expressions.

One study examined how quickly and accurately we can read the facial expressions of people of different cultural backgrounds.

Although individuals were at first faster at recognizing the emotional expression of others from their own culture, when living in a different culture, the speed and accuracy at which they recognized others' emotions increased as they became more familiar with the culture. For example, as Chinese residing in the United States adapted to their surroundings, they were able to recognize the emotions of people native to the US more quickly. In fact, foreigners are sometimes better at recognizing emotions among the citizens in their non-native country than are those citizens themselves.

Interestingly, these effects begin to occur relatively quickly. For example, Chinese students living in the United States for an average of 2.4 years were better at recognizing

the facial expressions of US citizens than they were at reading the facial expressions of Chinese citizens. Why is this the case? According to the authors of the study, it could be that because they are limited in speaking the language, they rely more on nonverbal communication. What is the upshot for OB? When conducting business in a foreign country, the ability to correctly recognize others' emotions can facilitate interactions and lead to less miscommunication. Otherwise, a slight smile that is intended to communicate disinterest may be mistaken for happiness.

Source: Based on H. A. Elfenbein and N. Ambady, "When Familiarity Breeds Accuracy: Cultural Exposure and Facial Emotion Recognition," *Journal of Personality and Social Psychology*, August 2003, pp. 276–290.

Emotional Labor

4 *Show the impact emotional labor has on employees.*

If you've ever had a job working in retail sales or waiting on tables in a restaurant, you know the importance of being friendly and smiling. Even though there were days when you didn't feel cheerful, you knew management expected you to be enthusiastic when dealing with customers. So you pretended to be interested and concerned about your customer, and in so doing, you expressed emotional labor.

Every employee shows physical and mental labor when they put their bodies and minds into their job. But jobs also require **emotional labor**. Emotional labor is an employee's expression of organizationally desired emotions during interpersonal transactions at work.[39] In other words, although employees may not be feeling well or in a good mood, they still show a smile and are friendly and patient with customers.

The concept of emotional labor started with studies of service jobs. Airlines expect their flight attendants, for instance, to be cheerful; we expect funeral directors to be sad; and we expect doctors to be emotionally neutral. But really, emotional labor is relevant to almost every job. Your managers expect you, for example, to be courteous, not hostile, in interactions with coworkers. The true challenge arises when employees have to project one emotion while simultaneously feeling another.[40] This difference in attitude is **emotional dissonance**, and it can take have a heavy effect on employees. Bottled-up feelings of frustration, anger, and resentment can eventually lead to emotional exhaustion and burnout.[41] It's from the increasing importance of emotional labor as a key factor of effective job performance that an understanding of emotion has gained importance within the field of OB.

Emotional labor creates dilemmas for employees. There are people with whom you have to work that you just don't like. Maybe you consider them to be rude. Maybe you know they've said negative things about you behind your back. Regardless, your job requires you to interact with these people on a regular basis. So you're forced to pretend to be friendly.

It can help you, on the job especially, if you separate emotions into felt and displayed emotions.[42] **Felt emotions** are an individual's actual emotions. In contrast, **displayed emotions** are those that the organization requires workers to show and considers appropriate in a given job. They're not innate; they're learned.

Effective managers have learned to be serious when giving an employee a negative performance evaluation and to hide their anger when they've been passed over for promotion. And a salesperson who hasn't learned to smile and appears friendly, regardless of his or her true feelings at the moment, isn't typically going to last long on most sales jobs. That is, how we *experience* an emotion isn't always the same as how we *show* it.[43]

Another point is that displaying false emotions requires us to hide the emotions we really feel. In other words, individuals have to 'act' to keep their jobs. **Surface acting** is hiding one's inner feelings and forgoing emotional expressions in response to display rules. For example, when a worker smiles at a customer even when he doesn't feel like it, he is surface acting. **Deep acting** is trying to modify one's true inner feelings based on display rules. For example, a health care provider trying to genuinely feel more emotions for her patients is deep acting.[44]

Interestingly, as important as managing emotions is to many jobs, it seems that the market does not necessarily reward emotional labor. A recent study found that emotional demands matter in setting compensation levels, but only when jobs are already cognitively demanding—such as jobs in law and nursing. But, for instance, child-care workers and waiters—holders of jobs with high emotional demands but relatively low cognitive demands—receive little compen-

Emotional labor

A situation in which an employee expresses organizationally desired emotions during interpersonal transactions at work.

Emotional dissonance

Inconsistencies between the emotions people feel and the emotions they project.

Felt emotions

An individual's actual emotions.

Displayed emotions

Emotions that are organizationally required and considered appropriate in a given job.

Surface acting

Hiding one's inner feelings and forgoing emotional expressions in response to display rules.

Deep acting

Trying to modify one's true inner feelings based on display rules.

For organizations such as Etihad Airways, pictured here, the use of positive displayed emotions by airline staff is essential in order to promote customer satisfaction; it is standard practice for the pilot and flight attendants to stand and greet airline passengers with a warm reception and smiling faces as they enter the plane.

sation for the emotional demands of their work.[45] Why should emotional demands only be rewarded in cognitively complex jobs? One explanation may be that it's hard to find qualified people who are willing and able to work in such jobs.

Affective Events Theory

5 *Describe affective events theory and identify its applications.*

Affective events theory (AET)

A model that suggests that workplace events cause emotional reactions on the part of employees, which then influence workplace attitudes and behaviors.

As we have seen throughout the previous sections, emotions and moods are an important part of our lives, especially our work lives. But how do our emotions and moods influence our job performance and satisfaction? A model called **affective events theory (AET)** has increased our understanding of the links.[46] AET demonstrates that employees react emotionally to things that happen to them at work and that this reaction influences their job performance and satisfaction.

Figure 6-3 summarizes AET. The theory begins by recognizing that emotions are a response to an event in the work environment. The work environment includes everything surrounding the job—the variety of tasks and degree of autonomy, job demands, and requirements for expressing emotional labor. This environment creates work events that can be problems, good events, or both. Examples of problems are colleagues who refuse to carry their share of work, conflicting directions from different managers, and time pressures. Examples of encouraging events include meeting a goal, getting support from a colleague, and receiving recognition for an accomplishment.[47]

These work events lead to positive or negative emotional reactions. But employees' personalities and moods direct them to respond with greater or lesser intensity to the event. For instance, people who score low on emotional stability are more likely to react strongly to negative events. And their mood introduces the reality that their general affect cycle creates fluctuations. So a person's emotional response to a given event can change, depending on mood. Finally, emotions influence a number of performance and satisfaction variables, such as organizational citizenship behavior, organizational commitment, level of effort, intentions to quit, and workplace deviance.

In addition, tests of the theory suggest that an emotional reaction is actually a set of emotional experiences started by a single event. It contains elements of

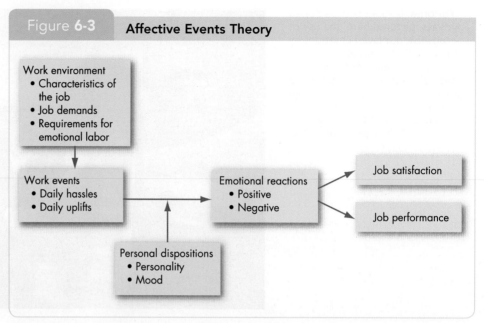

Figure **6-3** **Affective Events Theory**

Source: Based on N. M. Ashkanasy and C. S. Daus, "Emotion in the Workplace: The New Challenge for Managers," *Academy of Management Executive,* February 2002, p. 77.

both emotions and mood cycles. Current emotions influence job satisfaction at any given time, along with the history of emotions surrounding the event. In addition, because moods and emotions change over time, their effect on performance also fluctuates. Moreover, emotion-driven behaviors are typically short in duration and of high variability. Furthermore, because emotions, even positive ones, tend to be different to behaviors required to do a job, they typically have a negative influence on job performance.[48]

Picture This

You are an aeronautical engineer for Boeing. Because of the downturn in the demand for commercial jets, you've just learned that the company is considering laying off 10,000 employees. This layoff could include you. This event is likely to make you feel negative emotions and especially fear that you might lose your job and primary source of income. Your boss assures you that your job is safe but you hear rumors. These events, in turn, create emotional ups and downs. One day, you're feeling upbeat and positive that you'll survive the cuts. The next day, you might be depressed and anxious. These emotional swings take your attention away from your work and lower your job performance and satisfaction.[49]

In summary, AET offers two important messages.[50] First, emotions provide valuable awareness of understanding employee behavior. Second, employees and managers shouldn't ignore emotions and the events that cause them, even when they appear to be minor, because they accumulate.

Emotional Intelligence

6 *Contrast the evidence for and against the existence of emotional intelligence.*

After looking at emotional labor and the affective events theory, let's consider emotional intelligence and its contributions to the understanding of employees' behavior in response to certain organizational events. We should mention that emotional intelligence will also be discussed in Chapter 16 when we talk about organizational change and how we can deal with it.

> ### Picture This
>
> Dalal is a store manager. She has a very strange character. She is often grumpy and sometimes when employees make mistakes she overreacts and becomes extremely angry. The strange thing is that she doesn't understand why her employees dislike her. How would you describe Dalal's attitude?

Emotional intelligence (EI)

The ability to detect and to manage emotional cues and information.

We can say that Dalal has low emotional intelligence. **Emotional intelligence (EI)** is a person's ability to (1) be self-aware (to recognize own emotions as they are experienced), (2) detect emotions in others, and (3) manage emotional cues and information. That is, people who know their own emotions and are good at reading emotion signals—for instance, knowing why they're angry and how to express themselves without violating norms—are most likely to be effective.[51]

In 2009, Six Seconds, in partnership with Dubai Knowledge Village (DKV) studied the relationship between emotional intelligence and performance. The particular objective was to determine the extent to which the 'soft skills' of emotional intelligence matter in the working environment of the Arab world. Four hundred and eighteen leaders were studied and a strong correlation was found between EI skills and performance outcomes. The professional and personal success factors that were assessed included effectiveness, influence, decision making, health, quality of life, relationships and career status. The researchers concluded that over 58 percent of the variation in the leaders' performance could be explained by 'emotional intelligence' factors.[52]

What are the implications? The study suggests that, to advance in the Arab world, it is necessary to understand and develop emotional intelligence. Emotional intelligence is crucial for professional success and especially for those who want to pursue entrepreneurship.

Several other studies suggest that EI plays an important role in job performance. It is EI not IQ that characterizes high performers. One interesting study looked at the successes and failures of 11 American presidents—from Franklin Roosevelt to Bill Clinton. They were evaluated on six qualities—communication, organization, political skill, vision, cognitive style, and emotional intelligence. It was found that the key quality that differentiated the successful (such as Roosevelt, Kennedy, and Reagan) from the unsuccessful (such as Johnson, Carter, and Nixon) was emotional intelligence.[53] Research about EI in the Arab world is very recent but it has become a significant topic and we can expect more studies in the future.

EI has been a controversial concept in OB. It has supporters and critics. In the following sections, we will review the arguments for and against the significance of EI in OB.

The Case for EI

The arguments in favor of EI include its intuitive appeal, the fact that EI predicts criteria that matter, and the idea that EI is biologically based.

Intuitive Appeal   There's a lot of intuitive attraction to the EI concept. Almost everyone would agree that it is good to possess street smarts and social intelligence. People who can detect emotions in others, control their own emotions, and handle social interactions well will have a powerful position in the business world.

Ebay is an auction site that has become familiar to people in the Arab world. Meg Whitman, former CEO of eBay, is a leader with high emotional intelligence. She is a successful performer in a job that demands interacting socially with employees, customers, and political leaders throughout the world. Whitman is described as self-confident, yet humble, trustworthy, culturally sensitive, and expert at building teams and leading change. Shown here, Whitman welcomed Gloria Arroyo, president of the Philippine Islands, where eBay has an auction site, to eBay headquarters.

EI Predicts Criteria That Matter   More and more evidence is suggesting that a high level of EI means a person will perform well on the job. One study found that EI predicted the performance of employees in a cigarette factory in China.[54] Another study found that being able to recognize emotions in others' facial expressions and to emotionally 'eavesdrop' (that is, pick up signals about peoples' emotions) predicted feedback of how valuable those people were to their organization.[55] Finally, a review of 59 studies indicated that, overall, EI correlated moderately with job performance.[56]

EI Is Biologically Based   One study has shown that people with damage to the part of the brain that governs emotional processing score significantly lower than others on EI tests. Even though these brain-damaged people scored no lower on standard measures of intelligence than people without the same brain damage, they were still unable to contribute to normal decision making.

The Case Against EI

Even though there are many supporters, EI has just as many critics. Its critics say that EI is unclear and impossible to measure, and they question its validity.

EI Is Too Vague a Concept   To many researchers, it's not clear what EI is. Is it a form of intelligence? Most of us wouldn't think that being self-aware or self-motivated or having empathy is a matter of intellect. Moreover, many times different researchers focus on different skills, making it difficult to get a definition of EI. One researcher may study self-discipline. Another may study empathy. Another may look at self-awareness.

EI Can't Be Measured   Many critics have raised questions about measuring EI. Because EI is a form of intelligence, for instance, there must be right and wrong answers about it on tests, they argue. Some tests do have right and wrong answers, although the validity of some of the questions on these measures is questionable.

For example, one measure asks you to associate particular feelings with specific colors, as if purple always makes us feel cool and not warm. Other measures are self-reported, meaning there is no right or wrong answer. For example, an EI test question might ask you to respond to the statement, 'I'm good at reading other people.' In general, the measures of EI are diverse, and researchers have not subjected them to as much study as they have measures of personality and general intelligence.[57]

The Validity of EI Is Suspect   Some critics argue that because EI is so closely related to intelligence and personality, once you control these factors, EI has nothing unique to offer. There is some foundation to this argument. EI appears to be highly correlated with measures of personality, especially emotional stability.[58] But there hasn't been enough research on whether EI adds insight beyond measures of personality and general intelligence in predicting job performance.

Weighing the arguments for and against EI, it's still too early to tell whether the concept is useful. It *is* clear, though, that the concept is here to stay. Try it for yourself and look at the following self-assessment exercise.

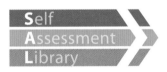

WHAT'S MY EMOTIONAL INTELLIGENCE SCORE?

In the Self-Assessment Library (available online), take assessment I.E.1 (What's My Emotional Intelligence Score?).

OB Applications of Emotions and Moods

Apply concepts about emotions and moods to specific OB issues.

In this section, we assess how an understanding of emotions and moods can improve our ability to explain and predict the selection process in organizations, decision making, creativity, motivation, leadership, interpersonal conflict, negotiation, customer service, job attitudes, and deviant workplace behaviors. We also look at how managers can influence our moods.

Selection

One implication from the evidence to date on EI is that employers should consider it a factor in hiring employees, especially in jobs that demand a high degree of social interaction. In fact, more and more employers are starting to use EI measures to hire people. For example, at L'Oreal, salespersons selected on EI scores did much better than those hired using the company's old selection procedure. On an annual basis, salespeople selected on the basis of emotional competence sold US$91,370 more than other salespeople did, for a net revenue increase of US$2,558,360.[59]

Decision Making

As we saw in Chapter 4, traditional approaches to the study of decision making in organizations have emphasized rationality. More and more OB researchers, though, are finding that moods and emotions have important effects on decision making.

Positive moods and emotions seem to help decision making. People in a good mood or those experiencing positive emotions are more likely than others to use rules that everyone is familiar with[60] to help make good decisions quickly. Positive emotions also enhance problem-solving skills so that positive people find better solutions to problems.[61]

OB researchers continue to debate the role of negative emotions and moods in decision making. Although one often-cited study suggested that depressed people reach more accurate judgments,[62] more recent evidence has suggested that people who are depressed make poorer decisions. Why? Because depressed people are slower at processing information and tend to weigh all possible options rather than the most likely ones.[63] Although it would seem that weighing all possible options is a good thing, the problem is that depressed people search for the perfect solution when rarely is any solution perfect.

Creativity

People who are in a good mood tend to be more creative than people in a bad mood.[64] They produce more ideas, others think their ideas are original, and they tend to identify more creative options to problems.[65] It seems that people who are experiencing a positive mood or emotion are more flexible and open in their thinking, which may explain why they're more creative.[66] Supervisors should actively try to keep employees happy because doing so creates more good moods (employees like their leaders to encourage them and provide positive feedback on a job well done), which in turn leads people to be more creative.[67]

A study reported in 2010 by Tareq N. Hashem investigated the impact of managers' emotional intelligence on marketing creativity in Jordan's commercial banks.[68] Statistical analysis showed that the components of emotional intelligence (such as self-awareness, emotions control, motivation, social skills, and empathy) significantly affect marketing creativity.

Some researchers, however, do not believe that a positive mood makes people more creative. They argue that when people are in a positive mood, they may relax and not engage in the critical thinking necessary for some forms of creativity.[69] However, this view is controversial.[70] Until there are more studies on the subject, we can safely conclude that for many tasks, positive moods increase our creativity.

Motivation

Two studies have highlighted the importance of moods and emotions on motivation. The first study had two groups of people solve a number of word puzzles. One group saw a funny video clip, which was intended to put the group in a good mood before having to solve the puzzles. The other group was not shown the clip and just started working on solving the word puzzles right away. The results? The positive-mood group reported higher expectations of being able to solve the puzzles, worked harder at them, and solved more puzzles as a result.[71]

The second study found that giving people feedback—whether real or fake—about their performance influenced their mood, which then influenced their motivation.[72] So a cycle can exist in which positive moods cause people to be more creative, which leads to positive feedback from those observing their work. This positive feedback then further reinforces their positive mood, which may then make them perform even better, and so on.

Both of these studies highlight the effects of mood and emotions on motivation and suggest that organizations that promote positive moods at work are likely to have more motivated workers. Will leaders become more effective if they understand and accept these concepts?

Known as an enthusiastic cheerleader for Microsoft, CEO Steve Ballmer travels the world, delivering passion-filled speeches to inspire employees and business partners. Through his emotionally charged speeches, Ballmer presents a road map for employees and partners of Microsoft's competitive focus and company vision. "I want everyone to share my passion for our products and services," he says. "I want people to understand the amazing positive way our software can make leisure time more enjoyable and work and businesses more successful."

Leadership

Effective leaders rely on emotional appeals to help convey their messages.[73] In fact, the expression of emotions in speeches is often the critical element that makes us accept or reject a leader's message. "When leaders feel excited, enthusiastic, and active, they may be more likely to energize their subordinates and convey a sense of efficacy, competence, optimism, and enjoyment."[74]

Corporate executives know that emotional content is critical if employees are to buy into their vision of their company's future and accept change. When higher-ups offer new visions, especially when the visions contain distant or vague goals, it is often difficult for employees to accept those visions and the changes they'll bring. By arousing emotions and linking them to an appealing vision, leaders increase the likelihood that managers and employees alike will accept change.[75]

What Do You Think?

Do you feel that emotions and moods of employees can result in creativity, motivation and effective leadership?

Negotiation

Negotiation is also an emotional process; however, we often say that skilled negotiators have a 'poker face;' that is, they are able to keep their emotions and reactions hidden to others. Several studies have shown that negotiators who fake anger have an advantage over the opponent. Why? Because when negotiators show anger, the opponent concludes that they have shown all they can, so the opponent gives in.[76]

Customer Service

A worker's emotional state influences customer service, which influences levels of repeat business and levels of customer satisfaction.[77] Providing quality customer service makes demands on employees because it often puts them in a state of emotional dissonance, which we explained earlier in this chapter. Over time, this state can lead to job burnout, declines in job performance, and lower job satisfaction.[78]

In addition, employees' emotions may transfer to the customer. Studies indicate a matching effect between employee and customer emotions, an effect that is called **emotional contagion**—the 'catching' of emotions from others.[79] How does emotional contagion work? The primary explanation is that when someone experiences positive emotions and laughs and smiles at you, you begin to copy that person's behavior. So when employees express positive emotions, customers tend to respond positively. Emotional contagion is important because when customers catch the positive moods or emotions of employees they shop longer. But what about negative emotions and moods? Are they contagious, too? Absolutely. When an employee feels unfairly treated by a customer, for example, it's harder to display the positive emotions the organization expects.[80]

Emotional contagion

The process by which people's emotions are caused by the emotions of others.

Job Attitudes

Ever hear the advice, "Never take your work home with you," meaning that people should forget about their work once they go home? A it turns out, that's easier said than done. Several studies have shown that people who had a good day at work tend to be in a better mood at home that evening. And people who had a bad day tend to be in a bad mood once they're at home.[81] Evidence also suggests that people who have a stressful day at work have trouble relaxing after they get off work.[82]

Even though people do emotionally take their work home with them, by the next day, the effect is usually gone.[83] So, although it may be difficult or even unnatural to "never take your work home with you," it doesn't appear that, for most people, a negative mood resulting from a bad day at work carries over to the next day.

Deviant Workplace Behaviors

Negative emotions can lead to a number of deviant workplace behaviors.

Anyone who has spent much time in an organization realizes that people often behave in ways that violate established norms and that threaten the organization, its members, or both. As we saw in Chapter 1, these actions are called *workplace deviant behaviors*.[84] Many of these different behaviors can be traced to negative emotions.

For instance, envy is an emotion that occurs when you resent someone for having something that you don't have but that you strongly desire—such as a better work assignment, larger office, or higher salary.[85] It can lead to spiteful deviant behaviors. An envious employee, for example, could then act hostilely by backstabbing another employee, negatively distorting others' successes, and positively distorting his own accomplishments.[86] Evidence suggests that people who feel negative emotions, particularly those who feel angry or hostile, are more likely than people who don't feel negative emotions to engage in deviant behavior at work.[87]

How Managers Can Influence Moods

In general, you can improve peoples' moods by showing them a funny video clip, giving them a small bag of candy, or even having them taste a pleasant

Crying at Work Gains Acceptance

As we have noted, many employers discourage the expression of emotions at work, especially when those emotions are negative. Recently, though, there are signs that the situation is starting to change.

One day, only four months into her first job, Hannac Shamsa, now 24, was called into the big boss's office and told that her immediate supervisor was not happy with her work. She started crying on the spot. "I was just fired," she said. "I had been working so hard."

Kathryn Brady, 34, is a finance manager for a large corporation in Atlanta. Occasionally she has had bosses who have driven her to tears. Brady argues that when she has cried, it has been out of frustration, not weakness. "The misinterpretation that I'm weak is just not fair," she says.

People from many cultures believe that these emotional displays are signs of weakness. The Arab world has a reputation for not encouraging signs of emotions, especially if it shows a person's weak spots. In particular, fathers usually tell their sons that "a man never cries; it's a sign of weakness."

On the reality show *The Apprentice*, Martha Stewart warned one of the contestants not to cry.

"Cry, and you're out of here," she said. "Women in business don't cry, my dear."

Although that 'old school' wisdom still holds true in many places, it is changing in others. George Merkle, CEO of a San Antonio credit company, does not mind if his employees cry. If someone cries, he says, "No apology needed. I know it's upsetting, and we can work our way through it."

_____

Sources: P. Kitchen, "Experts: Crying at Work on the Rise," *Newsday*, June 10, 2007; and S. Shellenbarger, "Read This and Weep," *Wall Street Journal*, April 26, 2007, p. D1.

beverage.[88] But what can companies do to improve their employees' moods? Managers can use humor and give their employees small tokens of appreciation for work well done. Also, research indicates that when leaders are in a good mood, group members are more positive and, as a result, the members cooperate more.[89]

Finally, selecting positive team members can have a contagion effect as positive moods transmit from team member to team member. It makes sense, then, for managers to select team members who are predisposed to experience positive moods.

Global Implications

8 *Contrast the experience, interpretation, and expression of emotions across cultures.*

Does the degree to which people *experience* emotions vary across cultures? Do peoples' *interpretations* of emotions vary across cultures? Finally, do the norms for the *expression* of emotions differ across cultures? Let's tackle each of these questions.

Does the Degree to Which People Experience Emotions Vary Across Cultures?

Yes. In China, for example, people report experiencing fewer positive and negative emotions than people in other cultures, and the emotions they experience are less intense than what other cultures report. Compared with Mainland Chinese, Taiwanese are more like US workers in their experience of emotions:

on average, Taiwanese report more positive and fewer negative emotions than their Chinese counterparts.[90] In general, people in most cultures appear to experience certain positive and negative emotions, but the frequency of their experience and their intensity varies to some degree.[91]

Do Peoples' Interpretations of Emotions Vary Across Cultures?

In general, people from all over the world interpret negative and positive emotions the same way. We all view negative emotions, such as hate, terror, and rage, as dangerous and destructive. Similarly, we all desire positive emotions such as joy, love, and happiness. However, some cultures value certain emotions more than others. For example, US culture values enthusiasm, while the Chinese consider negative emotions to be more useful and constructive than do people in the United States. In general, pride is seen as a positive emotion in the highly individualistic Arab world, but Eastern cultures tend to view pride as undesirable.[92]

Do the Norms for the Expression of Emotions Differ Across Cultures?

Research has shown that in collectivist countries people are more likely to believe the emotional displays of another and that this has something to do with their own relationship with the person expressing the emotion, while people in individualistic cultures don't think that another's emotional expressions are directed at them. Evidence that is given from everyday situations and experiences indicates that in Arab countries there's a bias against expressing emotions, especially intense negative emotions.

In general, and not surprisingly, it's easier for people to accurately recognize emotions within their own culture than it is in other cultures. For example, an Arab businessperson is more likely to accurately label the emotions underlying the facial expressions of a fellow Arab colleague than those of a US colleague.[93]

What's acceptable in one culture may seem extremely unusual or even dysfunctional in another. Managers need to know the emotional norms in each culture they do business in, or with, so they don't send unintended signals or misread the reactions of others. For example, a US manager in Japan should know that while US culture tends to view smiling positively, the Japanese attribute frequent smiling to a lack of intelligence.[94]

Summary and Implications for Managers

On the whole, emotions and moods are similar in that both are affective in nature. But they're also different—moods are more general and less contextual than emotions. And events do matter. The time of day and day of the week, stressful events, social activities, and sleep patterns are some of the factors that influence emotions and moods.

Moreover, emotions and moods have proven themselves to be relevant for virtually every OB topic we study. Increasingly, organizations are selecting employees they believe have high levels of emotional intelligence. Emotions, especially positive moods, appear to facilitate effective decision making and creativity. Although the research is relatively recent, research suggests that mood is linked to motivation, especially through feedback, and that leaders rely on emotions to increase their effectiveness. The display of emotions is important to negotiation and customer service, and the experience of emotions is closely linked to job attitudes and behaviors that follow from attitudes, such as deviant behavior in the workplace.

Can managers control their colleagues' and employees' emotions and moods? Certainly there are limits, practical and ethical. Emotions and moods are a natural part of an individual's makeup. Where managers make mistakes is in ignoring their coworkers' and employees' emotions and assessing others' behavior as if it were completely rational. As one consultant put it, "You can't divorce emotions from the workplace because you can't divorce emotions from people."[95] Managers who understand the role of emotions and moods will significantly improve their ability to explain and predict their coworkers' and employees' behavior.

Point   Counterpoint

THE COSTS AND BENEFITS OF ORGANIZATIONAL DISPLAY RULES

Organizations today realize that good customer service means good business. After all, who wants to end a shopping trip at the grocery store with an unfriendly face? Research clearly shows that organizations that provide good customer service have higher profits than those with poor customer service.[96] An integral part of customer-service training is to set rules to teach employees to interact with customers in a friendly, helpful, professional way—and evidence indicates that such rules work: having rules increases the odds that employees will display the emotions expected of them.[97]

Reiner Braun is director for sales and marketing, BMW Middle East. When sales improved significantly in the region he stated that this was partly a result of investing in customer service.[98]

Asking employees to act friendly is good for them, too. Research shows that employees of organizations that require them to display positive emotions actually feel better as a result.[99] And, if someone feels that being asked to smile is bad for him, he doesn't belong in the service industry in the first place.

Organizations should not try to regulate the emotions of employees. Companies should not be 'the thought police' and force employees to feel and act in ways that serve only organizational needs. Service employees should be professional and courteous, yes, but many companies expect them to take abuse and refrain from defending themselves. That's wrong. As the philosopher Jean Paul Sartre wrote, we have a responsibility to be authentic—true to ourselves—and within reasonable limits organizations have no right to ask us to be otherwise.

Employees shouldn't be openly nasty or hostile, of course, but who appreciates a fake smile? Think about trying on an outfit in a store and the clerk automatically says it looks "absolutely wonderful" when you know it doesn't and you sense the clerk is lying. Most customers would rather talk with a 'real' person than someone obliged to an organization's display rules.

It's unnatural to expect someone to smile all the time or to passively take abuse from customers, clients, or fellow employees. Organizations can improve their employees' psychological health by encouraging them to be themselves, within reasonable limits.

Questions for Review

1 What are the similarities and differences between emotions and moods? What are the basic emotions and the basic mood dimensions?

2 Are emotions and moods rational? What functions do emotions and moods serve?

3 What are the primary sources of emotions and moods?

4 What is emotional labor, and why is it important to understanding OB?

5 What is affective events theory? Why is it important to understanding emotions?

6 What is emotional intelligence, and what are the arguments for and against its importance?

7 What effect do emotions and moods have on different OB issues? As a manager, what steps would you take to improve your employees' moods?

8 Does the degree to which people experience emotions vary across cultures? Do people's interpretations of emotions vary across cultures, and do different norms across cultures govern the expression of emotions?

Discussion Exercise

In this chapter, we discussed how people determine emotions from facial expressions. There has been research on whether people can tell whether someone is lying based on their facial expression. Discuss whether facial expressions can show or hide when someone is lying, and what other signs you might look for.

Ethical Considerations

It shouldn't happen within organizations—but Fares, the boss, had a favorite employee, Reem, and Reem knew it. So, whenever Reem was upset or not happy with her coworkers, she would start crying and run to the boss. Reem was very effective at playing on Fares' emotions. What was even worse was that Fares would never investigate the complaints he heard from Reem; he would just do whatever would make her happy. It got to a point where everyone was gossiping and saying that Reem was taking advantage of Fares and they were very angry about the situation. Do you think Fares was behaving fairly as a boss? What are the ethical implications involved in this situation?

Critical Analysis

HAPPINESS: JUST AN EMOTION!

Jessica Pryce-Jones is author of the book *Happiness at Work: Maximizing Your Psychological Capital For Success*. Adrian Furnham is an organizational and applied psychologist.

They both believe in the effects of happiness in the workplace, considering that the best employee is that person who is motivated, resilient, accepts a challenge, and is willing to learn and do more to succeed. In fact, optimism is difficult to fake. You are either positive or negative; you either see the glass half empty or half full. It is true that bosses are best avoided when they are in a bad mood, particularly for annual appraisals. Good moods result in encouraging, forgiving, and more tolerant individuals. On the other hand, negative moods are related to blaming and attacking others. That is, negative people make bad colleagues and team members.

Pryce-Jones determines that several questions can allow employers to identify how employees can manage the 5Cs of happiness at work—Contribution, Conviction, Culture, Commitment and Confidence. Samples of those questions are:

1. What do they do to check that their personal and team or organizational goals are aligned?
2. What are their personal values which are particularly aligned with your organization?
3. What do they do when they don't know what to do?
4. What do they find really worthwhile at work?
5. When do they take a risk and why?
6. When they hesitate to do things, why or what lies behind that hesitation?
7. What kind of feedback and recognition do they like best?
8. Ask them on a scale of total pessimist to total optimist where they fall? What do they think that means in terms of their work?

Pryce-Jones sees a gradual shift in the situation. "We're still waiting for a change in the recruitment process. But once people understand the effects that a happier employee has in terms of productivity and performance, I'm sure that will happen. That's because happier employees are literally twice as productive as their least happy colleagues. The happiest employees focus 80 percent of their time at work on what they are there to do; the least happy only 40 percent of their time. In all, that amounts to a staggering two days a week in terms of output, so you definitely don't want unhappy workers in your team."

Questions

1. Elaborate upon Pryce-Jones' 5Cs of happiness. Which C(s) best describes people from the Arab world?
2. Are you an optimist or pessimist? How does this affect your everyday life and your interaction with others?
3. What do you think a company can do to change its emotional climate and increase productivity?

Source: Based on J. Pryce-Jones, *Happiness at Work: Maximising Your Psychological Capital For Success* (Chichester: John Wiley & Sons, 2010); and S. K. Thekkepat, "Profiting from happiness", *GulfNews.com*, October 8, 2010.

Research Exercise

In 2010, the Emirates Palace Hotel in Abu Dhabi displayed a 13-meter Christmas tree decorated with US$11 million worth of jewels. The hotel considered that that this was a way of celebrating occasions important to guests while they are away from their home countries and families.

Conduct some research into the techniques that businesses in the Arab world use to affect their customer's moods. Which do you think are more successful, and why?

Part 3 The Group

LEARNING OBJECTIVES

This chapter will enable you to:

1 Define *group* and differentiate between different types of groups.

2 Identify the five stages of group development.

3 Show how role requirements change in different situations.

4 Demonstrate how norms and status exert influence on an individual's behavior.

5 Show how group size affects group performance.

6 Contrast the benefits and disadvantages of cohesive groups.

7 Contrast the strengths and weaknesses of group decision making.

8 Compare the effectiveness of interacting, brainstorming, nominal, and electronic meeting groups.

9 Evaluate evidence for cultural differences in group status and social loafing as well as the effects of diversity in groups.

Foundations of Group Behavior

7

The greater the loyalty of a group toward the group, the greater is the motivation among the members to achieve, the greater the probability that the group will achieve its goals. —Rensis Likert

The Significance of Group Dynamics

A 2010 study of projects conducted in Europe, the Middle East and Africa (EMEA) found that productivity can be 20 percent less expensive and 30 percent faster if teams work together effectively and focus on organizational goals.

Positive interactions within the group encourage innovative thinking; they may lead to creative, practical solutions; and they may result in deep levels of learning. On the other hand, ineffective group dynamics can prevent communication, and create a poor organization culture, low morale, high turnover of staff and increased costs.

Training organizations like SKOPOS Consulting, a leading provider of customized organizational development (OD) solutions to companies in the Middle East and Africa, typically claim to "enhance group chemistry" in organizations. They hope to do this by focusing on areas such as leadership development, change management and culture transformation. They often encourage the use of cross-functional teams, and emphasize the importance of having clear organizational vision, mission, and values.

Organizations that offer this type of training stress that group dynamics are important to the success of projects in all countries and regions. SKOPOS is currently focusing on the development of advanced techniques to enhance group dynamics and enable EMEA companies to enhance productivity, efficiency and profitability.

SKOPOS seeks the most appropriate procedures that will result in effective end results for any specific situation no matter what the obstacles may be. Similarly, SKOPOS is concerned for the welfare of companies and wants to emphasize that output can be maximized through strong group interaction. Accordingly, it allows companies to create cultures of high performance, leadership, innovation, efficiency, and organizational flexibility, in addition to professional and personal growth.

"The EMEA study shows just how important group dynamics is to expediting work and raising the bottom line. We are aligning our OD solutions to ensure that they foster positive group dynamics and complement the unique needs of EMEA businesses," said Dr. Hussein El Kazzaz, Managing Director, SKOPOS Consulting.

Among the advantages of active groups are enhanced channels of communication, comfortable corporate culture, high morale, low turnover and reduction of expenses. SKOPOS enhances group chemistry in organizations by implementing programs covering: leadership development, change management, culture transformation, strategy execution through cross-functional teams, organizational design, and organizational vision, mission, and values.

SKOPOS Consulting moved its headquarters from the US to the Middle East in 2002 to deliver world-class organizational development techniques to the Arab business community. The consultancy assists enterprises in defining, developing, and sustaining a corporate culture of growth and business excellence.

SKOPOS maintains operations in Dubai, Cairo, and Bahrain. It recently launched a new company called RightScope that focuses on specific developmental areas at the organizational, team and individual levels.

Sources: "Effective Group Dynamics Cut EMEA Project Costs by 20 Percent," *Business Intelligence Middle East*, January 2011, www.bi-me.com/main.php?id=50528&t=1; and "SKOPOS Focuses on Group Development Solutions," *Albawaba*, January 20, 2011, www.albawaba.com/skopos-focuses-group-development-solutions (© 2000–2012 Al Bawaba).

From what you have just read in the opening case, you can see that groups in any industry are beneficial in reaching productive outcomes and that group dynamics are significant to the success of projects. Before we launch into a discussion of the benefits and pitfalls of groups, first examine your own attitude towards working in groups. Take the following self-assessment and answer the accompanying questions.

Self Assessment Library >>

WHAT'S MY ATTITUDE TOWARD WORKING IN GROUPS?

In the Self-Assessment Library (available online), take assessment IV.E.1 (What's My Attitude Toward Working in Groups?) and answer the following questions:

1. *Are you surprised by your results? If yes, why? If not, why not?*
2. *Do you think it is important to always have a positive attitude toward working in groups? Why or why not?*

The objectives of this chapter and Chapter 8 are to introduce you to basic group concepts, provide you with a foundation for understanding how groups work, and show you how to create effective teams. Let's begin by defining the *group* and explaining why people join groups.

Defining and Classifying Groups

1 *Define* group *and differentiate between different types of groups.*

Group

Two or more individuals, interacting and interdependent, who have come together to achieve particular objectives.

Formal group

A designated work group defined by an organization's structure.

A **group** is defined as two or more individuals, interacting and interdependent, who have come together to achieve particular objectives. Groups can be either formal or informal. By **formal groups**, we mean those defined by the organization's structure, with designated work assignments establishing tasks. In formal groups, the behaviors that team members should engage in are directed toward organizational goals. The six members making up an airline flight crew are an example of a formal group. In contrast, **informal groups** are alliances that are neither formally structured, nor organizationally determined. These groups are natural formations in the work environment that appear in response to the need for social contact. Three employees from different departments who regularly eat lunch or have coffee together are an example of an informal group. These types of interactions among individuals, even though informal, deeply affect their behavior and performance.

It's possible to further subclassify groups as command, task, interest, or friendship groups.[1] Command and task groups are dictated by formal organization, whereas interest and friendship groups are informal alliances.

Informal group

A group that is neither formally structured nor organizationally determined; such a group appears in response to the need for social contact.

Command group

A group composed of the individuals who report directly to a given manager.

Task group

People working together to complete a job task.

Interest group

People working together to attain a specific objective with which each is concerned.

Friendship group

People brought together because they share one or more common characteristics.

A **command group** is determined by the organization chart. It is composed of the individuals who report directly to a given manager. The teachers reporting to the principal of an elementary school form a command group.

Task groups represent individuals working together to complete a job task. However, a task group's boundaries are not limited to its immediate superior. For instance, if a college student is accused of a campus crime, dealing with the problem might require communication and coordination among the dean of academic affairs, the dean of students, the registrar, the director of security, and the student's advisor. Such a formation would constitute a task group. It should be noted that all command groups are also task groups, but because task groups can cut across the organization, the opposite need not be true.

People who may or may not be aligned into common command or task groups may affiliate to attain a specific objective with which each is concerned. This is an **interest group**. Employees who come together to have their vacation schedules changed, to support a colleague who has been fired, or to seek improved working conditions represent the formation of a united body to support their common interest.

Groups often develop because the individual members have one or more common characteristics. We call these formations **friendship groups**. Social alliances, which frequently extend outside the work situation, can be based on similar age or ethnic heritage, support for the same football team, interest in the same alternative rock band, or the holding of similar political views, to name just a few such characteristics.

There is no single reason why individuals join groups. Because most people belong to a number of groups, it's obvious that different groups provide different benefits to their members. Box 7-1 summarizes the most popular reasons people have for joining groups.

BOX 7-1
Why Do People Join Groups?

Security. By joining a group, individuals can reduce the insecurity of 'standing alone.' People feel stronger, have fewer self-doubts, and are more resistant to threats when they are part of a group.

Status. Inclusion in a group that is viewed as important by others provides recognition and status for its members.

Self-esteem. Groups can provide people with feelings of self-worth. That is, in addition to conveying status to those outside the group, membership can also give increased feelings of worth to the group members themselves.

Affiliation. Groups can fulfill social needs. People enjoy the regular interaction that comes with group membership. For many people, these on-the-job interactions are their primary source for fulfilling their needs for affiliation.

Power. What cannot be achieved individually often becomes possible through group action. There is power in numbers.

Goal achievement. There are times when it takes more than one person to accomplish a particular task—there is a need to pool talents, knowledge, or power in order to complete a job. In such instances, management will rely on the use of a formal group.

What Do You Think?

Which one of the reasons mentioned in Box 7-1 applies to your decision to join a particular group?

Stages of Group Development

Groups generally pass through a standardized sequence in their evolution. We call this sequence the five-stage model of group development. Although research indicates that not all groups follow this pattern,[2] it is a useful framework for understanding group development. In this section, we describe the five-stage general model and an alternative model for temporary groups with deadlines.

The Five-Stage Model

Five-stage group-development model

The five distinct stages groups go through: forming, storming, norming, performing, and adjourning.

As shown in Figure 7-1, the **five-stage group-development model** characterizes groups as proceeding through five distinct stages: forming, storming, norming, performing, and adjourning.[3]

Forming stage

The first stage in group development, characterized by much uncertainty.

The **forming stage**, is characterized by a great deal of uncertainty about the group's purpose, structure, and leadership. Members 'test the waters' to determine what types of behaviors are acceptable. This stage is complete when members have begun to think of themselves as part of a group.

Storming stage

The second stage in group development, characterized by intragroup conflict.

The **storming stage** is one of intragroup conflict. Members accept the existence of the group, but there is resistance to the constraints that the group imposes on individuality. Furthermore, there is conflict over who will control the group. When this stage is complete, there will be a relatively clear hierarchy of leadership within the group.

Norming stage

The third stage in group development, characterized by close relationships and cohesiveness.

The third stage is one in which close relationships develop and the group demonstrates cohesiveness. There is now a strong sense of group identity and teamspirit. This **norming stage** is complete when the group structure solidifies and the group has determined a common set of expectations of what defines correct member behavior.

Performing stage

The fourth stage in group development, during which the group is fully functional.

The fourth stage is the **performing stage**. The structure at this point is fully functional and accepted. Group energy has moved from getting to know and understanding each other, to performing the task at hand. For example, a leading Middle Eastern public relations consultancy group ASDA'A Bursson-Marsteller received the International Business Awards title of 'PR Campaign of the Year' in 2010. This reflects their effective group coordination, an essential element in their five-year campaign to launch the 828-meter-high Burj Khalifa.

For permanent work groups, performing is the last stage in the group development. However, for temporary committees, teams, task forces, and similar groups that have a limited task to perform, there is an **adjourning stage**. In this

Adjourning stage

The final stage in group development for temporary groups, characterized by concern with wrapping up activities rather than task performance.

stage, the group prepares to break up. High task performance is no longer the group's top priority. Instead, attention is directed toward wrapping up activities.

Many interpreters of the five-stage model have assumed that a group becomes more effective as it progresses through the first four stages. Although this assumption may be generally true, what makes a group effective is more complex than this model acknowledges.[4] Under some conditions, high levels of

Figure 7-1   Stages of Group Development

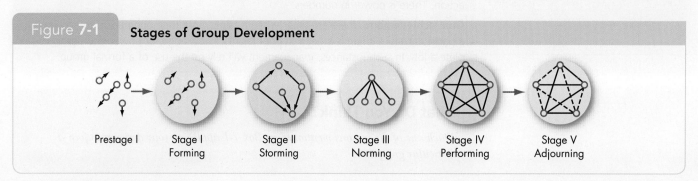

| Prestage I | Stage I Forming | Stage II Storming | Stage III Norming | Stage IV Performing | Stage V Adjourning |

for industry and construction

Damco is a company that specializes in the production and distribution of ready-mix concrete and employs numerous professional and qualified workers, technicians and scientists in order to fulfill the needs of its clients and meet their strict requirements. "At Damco, we view ourselves as one group and encourage teamspirit," says Ramy Menhem, Partner at Damco. "We value collective cooperation among coworkers, while stressing on unity to accomplish the same objectives. Accordingly, we strongly encourage our employees to rely on the existing corporate structure for the benefit of all. Structure enhances collaboration and communication so that everyone knows exactly what is expected."

Punctuated-equilibrium model

A set of phases that temporary groups go through that involves transitions between inertia and activity.

conflict may be conducive to high group performance. So we might expect to find situations in which groups in Stage II outperform those in Stage III or IV. Similarly, groups do not always proceed clearly from one stage to the next. Sometimes, in fact, several stages go on simultaneously, as when groups are storming and performing at the same time.

Another problem with the five-stage model, in terms of understanding work-related behavior, is that it ignores organizational context.[5] For instance, a study of a cockpit crew in an airliner found that within 10 minutes, three strangers assigned to fly together for the first time had become a high-performing group. What allowed for this speedy group development was the strong organizational context surrounding the tasks of the cockpit crew. This context provided the rules, task definitions, information, and resources needed for the group to perform. They didn't need to develop plans, assign roles, determine and allocate resources, resolve conflicts, and set norms the way the five-stage model predicts.

An Alternative Model for Temporary Groups with Deadlines

Temporary groups with deadlines don't seem to follow the usual five-stage model. Studies indicate that they have their own special set of actions or inaction. First, the meeting sets the group's direction and this first phase of group activity is one of no activity. Next, a transition takes place at the end of this first phase, which occurs exactly when the group has used up half its given time. Then, a transition initiates major changes that lead to a second phase of passiveness. Finally, the group's last meeting is characterized by accelerated activity.[6] This pattern, is called the **punctuated-equilibrium model**.

In other words, the punctuated-equilibrium model characterizes groups as showing long periods of inactivity mixed with brief changes triggered by their members' awareness of time and deadlines. Keep in mind, however, that this model doesn't apply to all groups. It's essentially limited to temporary task groups who are working under a time-constrained completion deadline.[7]

After focusing on what groups are and how they function, the next section deals with the overall properties of groups and how they determine the behavior of group members.

Group Properties: Roles, Norms, Status, Size, and Cohesiveness

Role

A set of expected behavior patterns attributed to someone occupying a given position in a social unit.

Work groups are not unorganized crowds of people. Work groups have properties that shape the behavior of members and make it possible to explain and predict a large portion of individual behavior within the group as well as the performance of the group itself. Some of these properties are roles, norms, status, group size, and the degree of group cohesiveness.

Group Property 1: Roles

3 Show how role requirements change in different situations.

Shakespeare once said, "All the world's a stage, and all the men and women merely players." Using the same metaphor, all group members are actors, each playing a **role**. That is, there is a set of expected behavior patterns attributed to someone occupying a given position in a social unit. The understanding of role behavior would be simplified if each of us chose one role and 'played it out' regularly and consistently. Unfortunately, we are required to play a number of diverse roles, both on and off our jobs. As we'll see, one of the

His Excellency Sheikh Sultan Bin Tahnoon Al Nahyan plays a number of diverse roles. He is a member of Abu Dhabi's Executive Council, and Chairman of Abu Dhabi's National Exhibition Company and the Abu Dhabi Authority for Culture and Heritage. He is also a board member of the Abu Dhabi Economic Council and the Abu Dhabi Environment Agency, a patron of the Middle East Council of the Urban Land Institute, and Chairman of Abu Dhabi Tourism Authority. Each of these positions imposes different role requirements on Sheikh Sultan.

tasks in understanding behavior is grasping the role that a person is currently playing.

For example, Basheer is a plant manager with OCC Industries, a large electrical equipment manufacturer in Cairo. He has a number of roles that he fulfills on that job—for instance, OCC employee, member of middle management, electrical engineer, and primary company spokesperson in the community. Off the job, Basheer finds himself in still more roles: husband, father, tennis player, member of the Elite Country Club, and president of his homeowners' association. Many of these roles are compatible; however, some create conflicts. A conflict could arise for example if an offer of promotion required Basheer to relocate, but his family wanted to stay in Egypt.

What Do You Think?

Can the demands of Basheer's job be coordinated with the demands of his roles as husband and father?

Like Basheer, we are all required to play a number of roles, and our behavior varies with the role we are playing. Basheer's behavior when he attends a Rotary meeting is different from his behavior on the golf course later that same day. Thus, different groups impose different role requirements on individuals.

Role Identity   Certain attitudes and actual behaviors are consistent with a role, and they create the **role identity**. People have the ability to shift roles rapidly when they recognize that a situation and its demands clearly require major changes.

Role Perception   Our view of how we're supposed to act in a given situation is a **role perception**. Based on an interpretation of how we believe we are supposed to behave, we engage in certain types of behavior. Where do we get these perceptions? We get them from stimuli all around us such as friends, books, and television.

Role identity

Certain attitudes and behaviors consistent with a role.

Role perception

An individual's view of how he or she is supposed to act in a given situation.

Role expectations

How others believe a person should act in a given situation.

Psychological contract

An unwritten agreement that sets out what management expects from an employee and vice versa.

Role conflict

A situation in which an individual is confronted by divergent role expectations.

Role Expectations   The way others believe you should act in a given situation is defined as **role expectations**. How you behave is determined to a large extent by the role defined in the context in which you are acting.

In the workplace, it can be helpful to look at the topic of role expectations through the perspective of the **psychological contract**—an unwritten agreement that exists between employees and their employer. This psychological contract sets out mutual expectations—what management expects from workers and vice versa.[8] In effect, this contract defines the behavioral expectations that go with every role. For instance, management is expected to treat employees justly, provide acceptable working conditions, clearly communicate what is a fair day's work, and give feedback on how well an employee is doing. Accordingly, employees are expected to respond by demonstrating a good attitude, following directions, and showing loyalty to the organization.

What happens when role expectations as implied in the psychological contract are not met? When management fails to live up to expectations, we can expect negative effects on employee performance and satisfaction. When employees fail to live up to expectations, the result is usually some form of disciplinary action up to and including firing.

Role Conflict   When an individual is confronted by divergent role expectations, the result is **role conflict**. It exists when an individual finds that compliance with one role requirement may make it difficult to comply with another.[9] At the extreme, it would include situations in which two or more role expectations are mutually contradictory.

Our previous discussion of the many roles Basheer had to deal with included several role conflicts—for instance, Basheer's attempt to reconcile the expectations placed on him as a husband and father with those placed on him as an executive with OCC Industries. The former, as you will remember, emphasizes stability and concern for the desire of his wife and children to remain in Cairo. OCC, on the other hand, expects its employees to be responsive to the needs and requirements of the company. Although it might be in Basheer's financial and career interests to accept a relocation, the conflict comes down to choosing between family and career role expectations.

> ## What Do You Think?
>
> *How many roles do you play in your everyday life?*

An Experiment: Zimbardo's Prison Experiment   One of the most illuminating role experiments was done a number of years ago by psychologist Philip Zimbardo, and his associates, of Stanford University in the US.[10] They created a 'prison' in the basement of the Stanford psychology building, hired at US$15 a day two dozen emotionally stable, physically healthy, law-abiding students who scored 'normal average' on extensive personality tests, randomly assigned them the role of either 'guard' or 'prisoner,' and established some basic rules.

To get the experiment off to a 'realistic' start, Zimbardo got the cooperation of the local police department. The police went, unannounced, to each future prisoner's home, arrested and handcuffed them, put them in a squad car in front of friends and neighbors, and took them to police headquarters, where they were booked and fingerprinted. From there, they were taken to the Stanford prison.

At the start of the planned two-week experiment, there were no measurable differences between the individuals assigned to be guards and those chosen to be prisoners. In addition, the guards received no special training but were told to maintain law and order in the prison and not to take any nonsense from the prisoners. Physical violence was forbidden. Furthermore, the prisoners were allowed visits from relatives and friends but were allowed out only for meals, exercise, toilet privileges, head-count lineups, and work details.

It took the 'prisoners' little time to accept the authority positions of the guards or the mock guards to adjust to their new authority roles. The prisoners actually began to believe and act as if they were, as the guards constantly reminded them, inferior and powerless. And every guard, at some time during the simulation, engaged in abusive, authoritative behavior. For example, one guard said, "I was surprised at myself . . . I made them call each other names and clean the toilets out with their bare hands. I practically considered the prisoners cattle, and I kept thinking: 'I have to watch out for them in case they try something.'" Another guard added, "I was tired of seeing the prisoners in their rags and smelling the strong odors of their bodies that filled the cells. I watched them tear at each other on orders given by us. They didn't see it as an experiment. It was real and they were fighting to keep their identity. But we were always there to show them who was boss." Surprisingly, during the entire experiment—even after days of abuse—not one prisoner said, "Stop this. I'm a student like you. This is just an experiment!"

The simulation actually proved *too successful* in demonstrating how quickly individuals learn new roles. The researchers had to stop it after only six days because of the participants' pathological reactions. And remember, these were individuals chosen precisely for their normalcy and emotional stability.

What can we conclude from this prison simulation? The participants in this experiment had, like the rest of us, learned stereotyped conceptions of guard and prisoner roles from the mass media and their own personal experiences in power and powerlessness relationships gained at home (parent–child), in school (teacher–student), and in other situations. This, then, allowed them easily and rapidly to assume roles that were very different from their inherent personalities. In this case, we saw that people with no prior personality pathology or training in their roles could execute extreme forms of behavior consistent with the roles they were playing.

The above discussion covered the various functions of roles and their effects on employee behavior. Now, before we move on to the properties of groups, an exercise on trust may give us more insight into how people behave with one another.

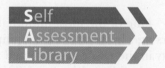

DO I TRUST OTHERS?

In the Self Assessment Library (available online), take assessment II.B.3 (Do I Trust Others?). You can also check out assessment II.B.4 (Do Others See Me as Trusting?).

4 *Demonstrate how norms and status exert influence on an individual's behavior.*

Group Properties 2 and 3: Norms and Status

Did you ever notice that employees don't criticize their bosses in public? Why? The answer is norms.

All groups have established **norms**—that is, acceptable standards of behavior that are shared by the group's members. Norms tell members what they should and should not do under certain circumstances. From an individual's standpoint, they tell what is expected of you in certain situations.

Norms

Acceptable standards of behavior within a group that are shared by the group's members.

When agreed to and accepted by the group, norms act as a means of influencing the behavior of group members with a minimum of external controls. Different groups, communities, and societies have different norms, but they all have them.[11]

Norms can cover virtually any aspect of group behavior.[12] Probably the most common group norm is a *performance norm*. Work groups typically provide their members with clear guidelines on how hard they should work, how to get the job done, what their level of output should be, and the like. These norms are extremely powerful in affecting an individual employee's performance—they are capable of significantly modifying a performance prediction that was based on the employee's ability and level of personal motivation, although, arguably, the most important performance norms are not the only kind. Other types include *appearance norms* (for example, dress codes, unspoken rules about when to look busy), *social arrangement norms* (for example, with whom group members eat lunch, whether to form friendships on and off the job), and *resource allocation norms* (for example, assignment of difficult jobs, distribution of resources like pay or equipment).

The Hawthorne Studies A series of studies were carried out at Western Electric Company's Hawthorne Works in Chicago, in the US, between 1924 and 1932. Known as the Hawthorne Studies, these demonstrated the importance of norms in influencing worker behavior.

The Hawthorne researchers began by examining the relationship between the physical environment and productivity. Lighting and other working conditions were selected to represent this physical environment. The researchers' initial findings contradicted their anticipated results.

They began with illumination experiments with various groups of workers. The researchers played with the intensity of lighting upward and downward, while at the same time noting changes in group output. Results varied, but one thing was clear: In no case was the increase or decrease in output related to the increase or decrease in illumination. So the researchers introduced a control group. An experimental group was presented with low and high levels of illumination, while the controlled unit worked under a constant illumination intensity. Again, the results were surprising to the Hawthorne researchers. As the light level was increased in the experimental unit, output rose for both the control group and the experimental group. But to the surprise of the researchers, as the light level was dropped in the experimental group, productivity continued to increase in both groups.

In fact, a productivity decrease was observed in the experimental group only when the light intensity had been reduced to that of moonlight. The Hawthorne researchers concluded that illumination intensity was only a minor influence among the many influences that affected an employee's productivity. The Hawthorne studies concluded that group influences were significant in affecting individual behavior and that group standards were highly effective in establishing individual worker output.

The Hawthorne studies made an important contribution to our understanding of group behavior—particularly the significant place that norms have in determining individual work behavior.

Conformity As a member of a group, you desire acceptance by the group. Because of your desire for acceptance, you are ready to accept the group's norms. There is considerable evidence that groups can place strong pressures on individual members to change their attitudes and behaviors to conform to the group's standard.[13]

From the Hawthorne studies, observers gained valuable insights into how individual behavior is influenced by group norms. The group of workers determined the level of fair output and established norms for individual work rates that conformed to the output. To enforce the group norms, workers used sarcasm, ridicule, and even physical force to influence individual behaviors that were not acceptable to the group.

Reference groups

Important groups to which individuals belong or hope to belong and with whose norms individuals are likely to conform.

Conformity

The adjustment of one's behavior to align with the norms of the group.

Do individuals conform to the pressures of all the groups to which they belong? Obviously not; people belong to many groups and their norms change. In some cases, they may even have contradictory norms. So what do people do? They conform to the important groups to which they belong or hope to belong. The important groups have been called **reference groups**, and they're characterized as ones in which a person is aware of other members, defines himself or herself as a member or someone who would like to be a member, and feels that the group members are significant to him or her.[14] The implication, then, is that all groups do not impose equal conformity pressures on their members.

The impact that group pressures for **conformity** can have on an individual member's judgment and attitudes was demonstrated in the now-classic studies by Solomon Asch.[15] Asch made up groups of seven or eight people, who sat around a table and were asked to compare two cards held by the experimenter. One card had one line, and the other had three lines of different length. The object was to announce aloud which of the three lines matched the single line. But what happens if the members in the group begin to give incorrect answers? Will the pressures to conform result in an unsuspecting subject (USS) altering an answer to align with the others? That was what Asch wanted to know.

The results obtained by Asch demonstrated that over many experiments and many trials 75 percent of the subjects gave at least one answer that conformed— that is, that they knew was wrong but that was consistent with the replies of other group members—and the average for conformers was 37 percent. What meaning can we draw from these results? They suggest that there are group norms that press us toward conformity, known as 'peer pressure.' That is, we desire to be one of the group and avoid being visibly different.

The preceding conclusions are based on research that was conducted 50 years ago. Has time changed their validity? And should we consider these findings generalizable across cultures? The evidence indicates that there have been changes in the level of conformity over time; and Asch's findings are culture bound.[16] Specifically, levels of conformity have steadily declined since Asch's studies in the early 1950s. In addition, conformity to social norms is higher in collectivist cultures than in individualistic cultures. Nevertheless, even in individualistic countries, you should consider conformity to norms to still be a powerful force in groups.

Deviant Workplace Behavior   Talal is frustrated by a coworker who always spreads rumors about him. Duha is tired of a member of her work team who, when confronted with a problem, takes out her frustration by yelling and screaming at other work team members. And Rima recently quit her job as a dental hygienist after being sexually harassed by her employer.

What do these three episodes have in common? They represent employees being exposed to acts of deviant workplace behavior.[17] **Deviant workplace behavior**—(also known as *antisocial behavior* or *workplace incivility*), is voluntary behavior that violates significant organizational norms and, in doing so, threatens the wellbeing of the organization or its members. Table 7-1 provides a typology of deviant workplace behaviors, with examples of each.

Few organizations will admit to creating or supporting conditions that encourage and maintain deviant norms. Yet they exist. Employees report, for example, an increase in rudeness and disregard toward others by bosses and coworkers in recent years. And nearly half of employees who have suffered this incivility report that it has led them to think about changing jobs, with 12 percent actually quitting because of it.[18]

As with norms in general, individual employees' antisocial actions are shaped by the group context within which they work. Evidence demonstrates that the antisocial behavior exhibited by a work group is a significant predictor of an individual's antisocial behavior at work.[19] In other words, deviant workplace behavior is likely to increase where it's supported by group norms. What this means for managers is that when deviant workplace norms are practiced, employee cooperation, commitment, and motivation are likely to suffer. This, in turn, can lead to reduced employee productivity and job satisfaction and increased turnover.

Deviant workplace behavior
Voluntary behavior that violates significant organizational norms and, in so doing, threatens the wellbeing of the organization or its members. Also called antisocial behavior or workplace incivility.

TABLE 7-1 Typology of Deviant Workplace Behavior	
Category	**Examples**
Production	Leaving early
	Intentionally working slowly
	Wasting resources
Property	Sabotage
	Lying about hours worked
	Stealing from the organization
Political	Showing favoritism
	Gossiping and spreading rumors
	Blaming coworkers
Personal aggression	Sexual harassment
	Verbal abuse
	Stealing from coworkers

Source: Adapted from S. L. Robinson and R. J. Bennett, "A Typology of Deviant Workplace Behaviors: A Multidimensional Scaling Study," *Academy of Management Journal,* April 1995, p. 565.

Otsuka Yuriko has high status at the Canon manufacturing plant in Ami, Japan. As an employee in a cell-manufacturing unit, she wears a badge on the sleeve of her work uniform labeled Eiji Meister. Yuriko earned the badge by completing an apprenticeship program and becoming proficient in all the tasks required to assemble a machine. Because she has mastered all the tasks, Yuriko can train other employees in her work unit, and her contributions are critical to her group's success.

Status

A socially defined position or rank given to groups or group members by others.

Status characteristics theory

A theory that states that differences in status characteristics create status hierarchies within groups.

Status   Status is a socially defined position or rank given to groups or group members by people in society. Even the smallest group will develop roles, rights, and rituals to differentiate its members. Status is an important factor in understanding human behavior because it is a significant motivator and has major behavioral consequences when individuals understand the differences between what they believe their status to be and what others perceive it to be.

What Determines Status?   According to **status characteristics theory**, status tends to be derived from one of three sources:[20]

1. **The power a person has over others**:   Because they likely control the group's resources, people who control the outcomes of a group through their power tend to be perceived as high status.
2. **A person's ability to contribute to a group's goals**:   People whose contributions are critical to the group's success tend to have high status.
3. **An individual's personal characteristics**:   Someone whose personal characteristics such as good looks, intelligence, money, or a friendly personality are positively valued by the group typically has higher status than someone who has fewer valued attributes.

Status and Norms   Status has been shown to have some interesting effects on the power of norms and pressures to submit. For instance, high-status members of groups are often given more freedom to deviate from norms than are other group members.[21] High-status people are also better able to resist conformity pressures than their lower-status peers. An individual who is highly valued by a group but who doesn't much need or care about the social rewards the group provides is particularly able to pay minimal attention to conformity norms.[22]

Status and Group Interaction   Interaction among members of groups is influenced by status. We find, for instance, that high-status people tend to be more assertive.[23] They speak out more often, criticize more, state more commands, and interrupt others more often. But status differences actually prevent diversity of ideas and creativity in groups because lower-status members tend to be less active participants in group discussions. In situations in which lower-status members possess expertise and insights that could aid the group, their expertise and insights are not likely to be fully utilized, thus reducing the group's overall performance.

Status Inequity   It is important for group members to believe that the status hierarchy is equitable. Perceived inequity creates disequilibrium, which results in various types of corrective behavior.[24]

The concept of equity presented in Chapter 5 applies to status. People expect rewards to be proportionate to costs incurred. If Elham and Amal are the two finalists for the head nurse position in a hospital, and it is clear that Elham has more seniority and better preparation for assuming the promotion, Amal will view the selection of Elham to be equitable. However, if Amal is chosen because she is the daughter-in-law of the hospital director (a process known as 'wasta' in the Arab world), Elham will believe an injustice has been committed.

Groups generally agree within themselves on status criteria and, hence, there is usually high concurrence in group rankings of individuals. However, individuals can find themselves in a conflict situation when they move between groups whose status criteria are different or when they join groups whose members have come from many backgrounds. As we'll see in Chapter 8, this can be a particular problem when management creates teams made up of employees from across varied functions within the organization.

Group Property 4: Size

5 Show how group size affects group performance.

Does the size of a group affect the group's overall behavior? The answer to this question is a definite 'yes,' but the effect depends on what dependent variables you look at.[25] The evidence indicates, for instance, that smaller groups are faster at completing tasks than are larger ones and that individuals perform better in smaller groups than in larger ones.[26] Large groups—those with a dozen or more members—are good for gaining diverse input. So if the goal of the group is fact-finding, larger groups should be more effective. On the other hand, smaller groups are better at doing something productive with that input. Groups of approximately seven members tend to be more effective for taking action.

One of the most important findings related to the size of a group has been labeled **social loafing**. Social loafing is the tendency for individuals to expend less effort when working collectively than when working individually.[27] It directly challenges the logic that the productivity of the group as a whole should at least equal the sum of the productivity of the individuals in that group.

What causes this social loafing effect? It may be due to a belief that others in the group are not carrying their fair share. If you see others as lazy, you can reestablish equity by reducing your effort. Another explanation is the dispersion of responsibility. Because the results of the group cannot be attributed to any single person, the relationship between an individual's input and the group's output is clouded. In such situations, individuals may be tempted to become 'free riders' and coast on the group's efforts. In other words, there will be a reduction in efficiency when individuals think that their contribution cannot be measured.

The implications for OB of this effect on work groups are significant. When managers use collective work situations to enhance morale and teamwork, they must also provide means by which they can identify individual efforts. If this

Social loafing

The tendency for individuals to expend less effort when working collectively than when working individually.

Studies indicate that these employees in Miles, China, collecting harvest grapes for the production of red wine, perform better in a group than when working alone. In collectivist societies such as China, employees show less propensity to engage in social loafing. Unlike individualistic cultures, such as the United States, where people are dominated by self-interest, the Chinese are motivated by in-group goals.

isn't done, management must weigh the potential losses in productivity from using groups against any possible gains in worker satisfaction.[28]

There are several ways to prevent social loafing: (1) Set group goals so that the group has a common purpose to move toward; (2) increase intergroup competition, which again focuses the group on the shared outcome; (3) engage in peer evaluation so that each person's contribution to the group is evaluated by each group member; and (4) if possible, distribute group rewards based, in part, on each member's unique contributions.[29] Although none of these actions is a guarantee that will prevent social loafing in all cases, they should help minimize its effect.

Group Property 5: Cohesiveness

6 *Contrast the benefits and disadvantages of cohesive groups.*

Cohesiveness

The degree to which group members are attracted to each other and are motivated to stay in the group.

Groups differ in their **cohesiveness**—the degree to which members are attracted to each other and are motivated to stay in the group.[30] For instance, some work groups are cohesive because the members have spent a great deal of time together, or the group's small size facilitates high interaction, or the group has experienced external threats that have brought members close together. Cohesiveness is important because it has been found to be related to group productivity.[31]

Studies consistently show that the relationship between cohesiveness and productivity depends on the performance-related norms established by the group.[32] If performance-related norms are high (for example, high output, quality work, cooperation with individuals outside the group), a cohesive group will be more productive than will a less cohesive group. But if cohesiveness is high and performance norms are low, productivity will be low. If cohesiveness is low and performance norms are high, productivity increases, but it increases less than in the high-cohesiveness/high-norms situation. When cohesiveness and performance-related norms are both low, productivity tends to fall into the low-to-moderate range. These conclusions are summarized in Figure 7-2.

What can you do to encourage group cohesiveness? You might try one or more of the following suggestions: (1) make the group smaller, (2) encourage

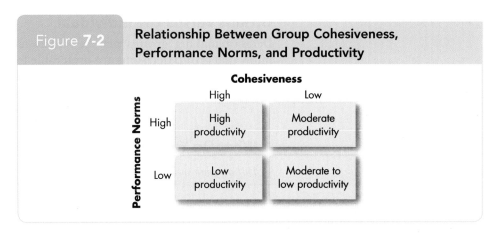

Figure **7-2**   **Relationship Between Group Cohesiveness, Performance Norms, and Productivity**

agreement with group goals, (3) increase the time members spend together, (4) increase the status of the group and the perceived difficulty of attaining membership in the group, (5) stimulate competition with other groups, (6) give rewards to the group rather than to individual members, and (7) physically isolate the group.[33]

Group Decision Making

Contrast the strengths and weaknesses of group decision making.

The belief that two heads are better than one has long been accepted. This belief has expanded to the point that, today, many decisions in organizations are made by groups, teams, or committees.[34] In this section, we discuss group decision making.

International OB

Group Cohesiveness Across Cultures

A recent study attempted to determine whether motivating work groups by giving them more complex tasks and greater autonomy results in increased group cohesiveness. Researchers studied bank teams in the United States, an individualist culture, and in Hong Kong, a collectivist culture. Both teams were composed of individuals from each respective country. The results showed that, regardless of what culture the teams were from, giving teams difficult tasks, and more freedom to accomplish those tasks, created a more tight-knit group. Consequently, team performance was enhanced.

However, the teams differed in the extent to which increases in task complexity and autonomy resulted in greater group cohesiveness. Teams in individualist cultures responded more strongly than did teams in collectivist cultures, became more united and committed, and, as a result, received higher performance ratings from their supervisors than teams from collectivist cultures. Why do these cultural differences exist? One explanation is that collectivist teams already have a strong predisposition to work together as a group, so there's less need for increased teamwork.

This has implications for managers in the Arab world, as the Arab culture is also a collectivist culture. However, managers in individualist cultures may need to work harder to increase team cohesiveness. One way to do this is to give teams more challenging assignments and provide them with more independence.

Source: Based on D. Man and S. S. K. Lam, "The Effects of Job Complexity and Autonomy on Cohesiveness in Collectivist and Individualistic Work Groups: A Cross-Cultural Analysis," *Journal of Organizational Behavior*, December 2003, pp. 979–1001.

Groups versus the Individual

Decision-making groups may be widely used in organizations, but does that imply that group decisions are preferable to those made by an individual alone? The answer to this question depends on a number of factors. Let's begin by looking at the strengths and weaknesses of group decision making.[35]

What Do You Think?

Do you work well in a group or do you perform better by yourself?

Strengths of Group Decision Making   Groups generate *more complete information and knowledge*. By aggregating the resources of several individuals, groups bring more input into the decision process. In addition to more input, groups can bring heterogeneity to the decision-making process. They offer *increased diversity of views*. This opens up the opportunity for more approaches and alternatives to be considered. Finally, groups lead to increased *acceptance of a solution*. Many decisions fail after the final choice is made because people don't accept the solution. Group members who participated in making a decision are likely to support the decision and encourage others to accept it.

Weaknesses of Group Decision Making   In spite of the pluses noted, group decisions have their drawbacks. They're time-consuming because groups typically take more time to reach a solution than would be the case if an individual were making the decision. There are *conformity pressures in groups*. The desire by group members to be accepted and considered an asset to the group can result in squashing any overt disagreement. Group discussion can be *dominated by one or a few members*. Finally, group decisions suffer from *ambiguous responsibility*. In an individual decision, it's clear who is accountable for the final outcome. In a group decision, the responsibility of any single member is decreased.

Effectiveness and Efficiency   Whether groups are more effective than individuals depends on the criteria you use to define effectiveness. In terms of *accuracy*, group decisions are generally more accurate than the decisions of the average individual in a group, but they are less accurate than the judgments of the most accurate group member.[36] If decision effectiveness is defined in terms of *speed*, individuals are superior. If *creativity* is important, groups tend to be more effective than individuals. And if effectiveness means the degree of *acceptance* the final solution achieves, then the group should be given credit.[37]

But effectiveness cannot be considered without also assessing efficiency. With few exceptions, group decision making needs more work hours than if an individual were to tackle the same problem alone. The exceptions tend to be the instances in which, to achieve comparable quantities of diverse input, the single decision maker must spend a great deal of time reviewing files and talking to people. Because groups can include members from diverse areas, the time spent searching for information can be reduced. However, as we noted, these advantages in efficiency tend to be the exception. Groups are generally less efficient than individuals. In deciding whether to use groups, then, consideration should be given to assessing whether increases in effectiveness are more than enough to offset the reductions in efficiency.

Summary   In summary, groups offer an excellent vehicle for performing many of the steps in the decision-making process. They are a source of both breadth and depth of input for information gathering. If the group is composed of individuals with diverse backgrounds, the alternatives generated should be more extensive and the analysis more critical. When the final solution is agreed on, there are more people in a group decision to support and implement it. These pluses, however, can be more than offset by the time consumed by group decisions, the internal conflicts they create, and the pressures they generate toward conformity. Therefore, in some cases, individuals can be expected to make better decisions than groups.

Groupthink and Groupshift

Two by-products of group decision making have received a considerable amount of attention from researchers in OB. As we'll show, these two phenomena have the potential to affect a group's ability to appraise alternatives objectively and to arrive at quality decision solutions.

The first phenomenon, called **groupthink**, is related to norms. It describes situations in which group pressures for conformity deter the group from critically appraising unusual, minority, or unpopular views. Groupthink is a disease that attacks many groups and can dramatically affect their performance. The second phenomenon is called **groupshift**. It indicates that, in discussing a given set of alternatives and arriving at a solution, group members tend to exaggerate the initial positions they hold. In some situations, caution dominates, and there is a conservative shift. More often, however, the evidence indicates that groups tend toward a risky shift. Let's look at each of these phenomena in more detail.

Groupthink

A phenomenon in which the norm for consensus overrides the realistic appraisal of alternative courses of action.

Groupshift

A change in decision risk between a group's decision and an individual decision that a member within the group would make; the shift can be toward either conservatism or greater risk.

Groupthink   Have you ever felt like speaking up in a meeting, a classroom, or an informal group but decided against it? One reason may have been shyness. On the other hand, you may have been a victim of groupthink, a phenomenon that occurs when group members are so overly concerned about conforming to the norm that this overrides the realistic appraisal of other options. It describes a deterioration in an individual's mental efficiency, reality testing, and moral judgment as a result of group pressures.[38]

We have all seen the symptoms of the groupthink phenomenon:

1. Group members rationalize any resistance to the assumptions they have made. No matter how strongly the evidence may contradict their basic assumptions, members behave so as to reinforce those assumptions continually.
2. Members apply direct pressures on those who momentarily express doubts about any of the group's shared views or who question the validity of arguments supporting the alternative favored by the majority.
3. Members who have doubts or hold differing points of view seek to avoid moving away from what appears to be group consensus by keeping silent about misgivings and even minimizing to themselves the importance of their doubts.
4. There appears to be an illusion of unanimity. If someone doesn't speak, it's assumed that he or she is in full accord. In other words, abstention (not voting) becomes viewed as a 'yes' vote.[39]

Groupthink appears to be closely aligned with conformity. Individuals who hold a position that is different from that of the dominant majority are under pressure to withhold, or modify their true feelings and beliefs. As members of a group, we find it more pleasant to be in agreement—to be a positive part of the group—than to be a disruptive force, even if disruption is necessary to improve the effectiveness of the group's decisions.

OB in the News

Groupthink for an Enron Jury?

Although most of us view Enron as the very symbol of corporate corruption, not every Enron employee behaved unethically. Twenty former Enron employees—most notably Ken Lay, Jeff Skilling, and Andrew Fastow—were either convicted of, or pleaded guilty to, fraudulent behavior. The conviction of another Enron executive you've probably never heard of—former broadband finance chief Kevin Howard—provides a fascinating, and disturbing, glimpse into how juries use group pressure to reach decisions.

Howard's first trial ended in a hung jury. In the second trial, he was found guilty of conspiracy, fraud, and falsifying records. However, shortly after his conviction, two jurors and two alternate jurors said they were pressured by other jurors to reach a unanimous decision even though they believed Howard was innocent. Juror Ann Marie Campbell said, in a sworn statement, "There was just so much pressure to change my vote that I felt like we had to compromise and give in to the majority because I felt like there was no other choice." Campbell said at one point a male juror tried to "grab her by the shoulders" to convince her, and another "banged his fist on the table during deliberations." Another jury member said, "There was an atmosphere of 'let's fry them.'"

On appeal, a judge threw out Howard's conviction, based, in part, on the earlier judge's instruction to the convicting jury, which had pressured them to reach a unanimous decision. The Kevin Howard case shows how strong groupthink pressures can be and the degree to which individuals can be pressured to give in to the majority.

Source: K. Hays, "Judge Dismisses Enron Convictions," *Houston (Texas) Chronicle*, February 1, 2007.

Does groupthink attack all groups? No. It seems to occur most often when there is a clear group identity, when members hold a positive image of their group that they want to protect, and when the group perceives a collective threat to this positive image.[40]

What can managers do to minimize groupthink?[41] First, they can monitor group size. People grow more intimidated and hesitant as group size increases, and, although there is no magic number that will eliminate groupthink, individuals are likely to feel less personal responsibility when groups get larger than about ten. Managers should also encourage group leaders to play an impartial role. Leaders should actively seek input from all members and avoid expressing their own opinions, especially in the early stages of deliberation. In addition, managers should appoint one group member to defend the situation; this member's role is to openly challenge the majority position and offer different perspectives. Still another suggestion is to use exercises that stimulate active discussion of diverse alternatives without threatening the group and intensifying identity protection.

Groupshift In comparing group decisions with the individual decisions of members within the group, evidence suggests that there are differences.[42] In some cases, group decisions are more conservative than individual decisions. More often, the shift is toward greater risk.[43]

What appears to happen in groups is that the discussion leads to a significant shift in the positions of members toward a more extreme position in the direction in which they were already leaning before the discussion. So conservative types become more cautious, and more aggressive types take on more risk. The group discussion tends to exaggerate the initial position of the group.

Groupshift can be viewed as actually a special case of groupthink. The decision of the group reflects the dominant decision-making norm that develops during the group's discussion. Whether the shift in the group's decision is toward greater caution or more risk depends on the dominant prediscussion norm.

The most likely explanation for the shift toward risk is that the group diffuses responsibility. Group decisions free any single member from accountability for the group's final choice. Greater risk can be taken because even if the decision fails, no one member can be held wholly responsible.

So how should we use the findings on groupshift? We should recognize that group decisions exaggerate the initial position of the individual members, that the shift has been shown more often to be toward greater risk, and that whether a group will shift toward greater risk or caution is a function of the members' prediscussion inclinations.

Having discussed group decision making and its pros and cons, we now turn to the techniques by which groups make decisions. These techniques reduce some of the dysfunctional aspects of group decision making.

Group Decision Making Techniques

8 *Compare the effectiveness of interacting, brainstorming, nominal, and electronic meeting groups.*

The most common form of group decision making takes place in **interacting groups**. In these groups, members meet face-to-face and rely on both verbal and nonverbal interaction to communicate with each other. But as our discussion of groupthink demonstrated, interacting groups often monitor themselves and pressure individual members toward conformity of opinion. Brainstorming, the nominal group technique, and electronic meetings have been proposed as ways to reduce many of the problems found in the traditional interacting group.

Brainstorming is meant to overcome pressures for conformity in an interacting group that retard the development of creative alternatives.[44] It does this by utilizing an idea-generation process that specifically encourages any and all alternatives while withholding any criticism of those alternatives.

Interacting groups

Typical groups in which members interact with each other face-to-face.

Brainstorming

An idea-generation process that specifically encourages any and all alternatives while withholding any criticism of those alternatives.

> ## What Do You Think?
>
> *Are two heads better than one? When a group generates many ideas to be considered, is that a good thing or not?*

In a typical brainstorming session, a half-dozen to a dozen people sit around a table. The group leader states the problem in a clear manner so that it is understood by all participants. Members then identify as many alternatives as they can in a given length of time. No criticism is allowed, and all the alternatives are recorded for later discussion and analysis. One idea stimulates others, and judgments of even the most bizarre suggestions are withheld until later to encourage group members to 'think the unusual' (see Figure 7-3).

Brainstorming may indeed generate ideas—but not in a very efficient manner. Research consistently shows that individuals working alone generate more ideas than a group in a brainstorming session. Why? One of the primary reasons is because of 'production blocking.' In other words, when people are generating ideas in a group, there are many people talking at once, which blocks the thought process and eventually impedes the sharing of ideas.[45] The following two techniques go further than brainstorming by offering methods that help groups arrive at a preferred solution.[46]

The **nominal group technique** restricts discussion or interpersonal communication during the decision-making process. Group members are all physically

Nominal group technique

A group decision-making method in which individual members meet face-to-face to pool their judgments in a systematic but independent fashion.

Figure **7-3**

Source: S. Adams, *Build a Better Life by Stealing Office Supplies* (Kansas City, MO: Andrews & McMeal, 1991), p. 31.
© Scott Adams/Dis. by United Media.

present, as in a traditional committee meeting, but members operate independently. Specifically, a problem is presented and then the group takes the following steps:

1. Members meet as a group, but before any discussion takes place, each member independently writes down ideas on the problem.
2. After this silent period, each member presents one idea to the group. Each member takes a turn, presenting a single idea, until all ideas have been presented and recorded. No discussion takes place until all ideas have been recorded.
3. The group discusses the ideas for clarity and evaluates them.
4. Each group member silently and independently rank-orders the ideas. The idea with the highest aggregate ranking determines the final decision.

The chief advantage of the nominal group technique is that it permits a group to meet formally but does not restrict independent thinking, as does an interacting group.

The most recent approach to group decision making blends the nominal group technique with sophisticated computer technology.[47] It's called a computer-assisted group, or an **electronic meeting**. Once the required technology is in place, the concept is simple. Up to 50 people sit around a horseshoe-shaped table, empty except for a series of computer terminals. Issues are presented to participants, who type their responses into their computers. Individual comments, as well as aggregate votes, are displayed on a projection screen. The proposed advantages of electronic meetings are anonymity, honesty, and speed.

In sum, each of the four group decision techniques—interacting, brainstorming, nominal, electronic—has its own set of strengths and weaknesses. The choice of one technique over another depends on what criteria you want to emphasize and the cost–benefit trade-off. For instance, as Table 7-2 indicates, an interacting group is good for achieving commitment to a solution, brainstorming develops group cohesiveness, the nominal group technique is an inexpensive means for generating a large number of ideas, and electronic meetings minimize social pressures and conflicts.

Electronic meeting

A meeting in which members interact on computers, allowing for anonymity of comments and aggregation of votes.

TABLE 7-2 Evaluating Group Effectiveness	Type of Group			
Effectiveness Criteria	**Interacting**	**Brainstorming**	**Nominal**	**Electronic**
Number and quality of ideas	Low	Moderate	High	High
Social pressure	High	Low	Moderate	Low
Money costs	Low	Low	Low	High
Speed	Moderate	Moderate	Moderate	Moderate
Task orientation	Low	High	High	High
Potential for interpersonal conflict	High	Low	Moderate	Low
Commitment to solution	High	Not applicable	Moderate	Moderate
Development of group cohesiveness	High	High	Moderate	Low

Global Implications

9 Evaluate evidence for cultural differences in group status and social loafing as well as the effects of diversity in groups.

As in most other areas of OB, most of the research on groups has been conducted in the United States, but that situation is changing quickly where research on groups in being conducted in all countries around the world. In particular, there are three areas (status and culture, social loafing, group diversity) where cross-cultural issues are important and they should always be considered.

Status and Culture Do cultural differences affect status? The answer is a resounding 'yes.'[48]

The importance of status does vary between cultures. Arabs and the French, for example, are highly status conscious. Countries also differ on the criteria that create status. For instance, status for Latin Americans and Asians tends to be derived from family position and formal roles held in organizations. In contrast, although status is still important in countries such as the United States and Australia, it is often bestowed more for accomplishments than on the basis of titles and family trees.[49]

The message here is to make sure you understand who and what holds status when interacting with people from a culture different from your own. For instance, a US manager may not understand that physical office size means nothing to a Japanese executive. In addition, the same manager may fail to realize the importance the British place on family origin and social class. As a result, due to the lack of awareness, this same manager may unintentionally offend managers in foreign countries and, in so doing, negatively affect interpersonal effectiveness.

Social Loafing Social loafing appears to have a Western bias. It's consistent with individualistic cultures, such as the United States and Canada, that are dominated by self-interest. It is *not* consistent with collective societies, in which individuals are motivated by in-group goals. For instance, in studies comparing employees from the US with employees from the People's Republic of China, the Chinese showed no readiness to engage in social loafing. In fact, the Chinese actually performed better in a group than when working alone. As Arab society is also collectivist, we would expect Arab employees to work better in groups as well.

Group Diversity   More and more research is being done on how diversity influences group performance. Some of this research looks at cultural diversity, and some of it considers diversity on other characteristics such as race or gender. Collectively, the research points to both benefits and disadvantages of group diversity.

In terms of costs, diversity appears to lead to increased group conflict, especially in the early stages of a group's foundation. This conflict often results in lower group morale and group members leaving. One study of groups that were either culturally diverse (composed of people from different countries) or homogeneous (composed of people from the same country) found that, on a survival exercise, the diverse and homogenous groups performed equally well, but the diverse groups were less satisfied with their groups, were less cohesive, and had more conflict.[50]

In terms of the benefits to diversity, more evidence is accumulating that, over time, culturally and demographically diverse groups may perform better, if they can get over their initial conflicts. Why might this be the case?

Research shows that diversity such as national origin, race, and gender actually reminds people of possible differences that exist in attitudes, values, and opinions. Although those differences of opinion can often lead to conflict, they also provide an opportunity to solve problems in unique ways.

In sum, the impact of cultural diversity on groups is a mixed bag. It is difficult to be in a diverse group in the short term. Nonetheless, if the group members can accept their differences, over time, diversity may help them be more open-minded and creative, thus allowing them to do better in the long run. We should realize, however, that even when there are positive effects of diversity on group performance, they are unlikely to be especially strong.

Summary and Implications for Managers

Group behavior can be explained in terms of performance and satisfaction.

Performance   A number of group properties show a relationship with performance. Among the most prominent are role perception, norms, status differences, size of the group, and cohesiveness.

There is a positive relationship between role perception and an employee's performance evaluation.[51] The degree of relationship that exists between an employee and the boss in the perception of the employee's job influences the degree to which the boss will judge that employee as an effective performer. In other words, the more employees fulfill their roles as expected by their bosses, the higher the performance evaluation for employees.

In addition, norms control group member behavior by establishing standards of right and wrong. The norms of a given group can help to explain the behaviors of its members for managers. When norms support high output, managers can expect individual performance to be higher than when group norms aim to limit output. Similarly, norms that support antisocial behavior increase the likelihood that individuals will engage in other workplace activities.

Status differences also create frustration and can negatively influence productivity and the willingness to remain with an organization. Among individuals who are equity sensitive, inequality is likely to lead to reduced motivation and an increased search for ways to bring about fairness, such as looking for another job. In addition, because lower-status people tend to participate less in group discussions, groups characterized by high status differences among members are likely to inhibit input from the lower-status members and to underperform their potential.

The impact of size on a group's performance depends on the type of task in which the group is engaged. Larger groups are more effective at fact-finding activities. Smaller groups are more effective at action-taking tasks. Our knowledge of social loafing suggests that, if management uses larger groups, efforts should be made to provide measures of individual performance within the group.

Likewise, cohesiveness can play an important function in influencing a group's level of productivity, depending on the group's performance-related norms.

Satisfaction   As with the role perception–performance relationship, high agreement between a boss and an employee as to the perception of the employee's job shows a significant association with high employee satisfaction.[52] Similarly, role conflict is associated with job-related tension and job dissatisfaction.[53]

Most people prefer to communicate with others at their own status level, or a higher one, rather than with those below them.[54] As a result, we should expect satisfaction to be greater among employees whose job minimizes interaction with individuals who are lower in status than themselves.

Furthermore, the group size–satisfaction relationship is what one would intuitively expect: larger groups are associated with lower satisfaction.[55] As size increases, opportunities for participation and social interaction decrease, as does the ability of members to identify with the group's accomplishments. At the same time, having more members also results in conflict, and the formation of subgroups, which act to make the group affiliation less attractive.

Point >< Counterpoint

ARE GROUPS THE BEST DESIGN?

Groups, not individuals, are the ideal building blocks for an organization. There are several reasons for designing all jobs around groups.

First, in general, groups make better decisions than the average individual acting alone.

Second, with the growth in technology, society is becoming more intertwined. Look at the growth of social networking sites such as MySpace, Facebook, and YouTube. People are connected anyway, so why not design work in the same way?

Third, small groups are good for people. They can satisfy social needs and provide support for employees in times of stress and crisis. Evidence indicates that social support—both when they provide it and when they receive it—makes people happier and even allows them to live longer.

Fourth, groups are very effective tools for implementation for decisions. Groups gain commitment from their members so that group decisions are likely to be willingly and more successfully carried out.

Fifth, groups can control and discipline individual members in ways that are often extremely difficult through impersonal quasi-legal disciplinary systems. Group norms are powerful control devices.

Sixth, groups are a means by which large organizations can fend off many of the negative effects of increased size. Groups help prevent communication lines from growing too long, the hierarchy from growing too steep, and individuals from getting lost in the crowd.

The rapid growth of team-based organizations in recent years suggests that we may well be on our way toward a day when almost all jobs are designed around groups.

Countries such as the United States, Canada, Australia, and the United Kingdom value the individual. Designing jobs around groups is inconsistent with the values of these countries. Moreover, as entrepreneurship has spread throughout Eastern Europe, Asia, the Arab world, and other more collective societies, we should expect to see *less* emphasis on groups and *more* on the individual in workplaces throughout the world.

Western culture strongly values individual achievement and encourages competition. Even in team sports, people want to identify individuals for recognition. Adults enjoy being part of a group only when they can maintain a strong individual identity. When they are assigned to groups, all sorts of bad things happen, including conflict, groupthink, social loafing, and deviant behavior.

Western workers want to be hired, evaluated, and rewarded on their individual achievements. They are not likely to accept a group's decision on such issues as their job assignments and wage increases, nor are they comfortable in a system in which the sole basis for their promotion or termination is the performance of their group.

Though teams have grown in popularity as a device for employers to organize people and tasks, we should expect resistance to any effort to treat individuals solely as members of a group—especially among workers raised in individualistic societies.

Questions for Review

1 Define *group*? What are the different types of groups?

2 What are the five stages of group development?

3 Do role requirements change in different situations? If so, how?

4 How do group norms and status influence an individual's behavior?

5 How does group size affect group performance?

6 What are the advantages and limitations of cohesive groups?

7 What are the strengths and weaknesses of group (versus individual) decision making?

8 How effective are interacting, brainstorming, nominal, and electronic meeting groups?

9 What is the evidence for the effect of culture on group status and social loafing? How does diversity affect groups and their effectiveness over time?

Discussion Exercise

Sometimes, the desire to maintain group harmony overrides the importance of making sound decisions. When that occurs, team members are said to engage in 'groupthink'. Discuss factors that could lead to groupthink, and what groups can do to prevent groupthink from occurring.

Ethical Considerations

You are always asked to take part in a group project as part of each course requirement.

If group members end up 'working around' shirkers (members who do not contribute to the group work) do you think this information should be communicated to the instructor so that the individual's contribution to the project is judged more fairly? If so, does the group have a responsibility to communicate this to the shirking group member? If not, isn't the shirking group member unfairly reaping the rewards of getting the reward without effort? Discuss.

Critical Analysis

IF TWO HEADS ARE BETTER THAN ONE, ARE FOUR EVEN BETTER?

Yusra Radwan, 26, is a marketing manager for Ka'Wah, a small chain of coffee shops in Bahrain. Recently, Yusra's wealthy uncle passed away and left US$100,000 to Yusra, his only niece. Yusra considers her current salary to be adequate to meet her current living expenses, so she'd like to invest the money so that when she buys a house she'll have comfortable savings set aside.

One of Yusra's neighbors, Badr, is a financial advisor. Badr told Yusra there are several investment options to consider. She asked him to present her with two of the best options, and this is what he came up with:

1. **A very low-risk AAA municipal bond fund.** With this option, and based on the information Badr provided, Yusra estimates that after five years she stands virtually zero chance of losing money, with an expected gain of approximately US$7,000.

2. **A moderate-risk mutual fund.** Based on the information Badr provided her, Yusra estimates that with this option she stands a 50 percent chance of making US$40,000, but also a 50 percent chance of losing US$20,000.

Yusra prides herself on being rational and objective in her thinking. However, she's unsure of what to do in this case. Badr refuses to help her, telling her that she's already limited herself by asking for only two options. While driving to her parents' house for the weekend, Yusra finds herself comparing the two options. Her older brother Ziad is also visiting the family this weekend, so Yusra decides to gather her family around the table after dinner, lay out the two options, and go with their decision. "You know the old saying—two heads are better than one," she says to herself, "so four heads should be even better."

Questions

1. Has Yusra made a good decision about the way she is going to make the final judgment?
2. Which investment would you choose? Why?
3. Which investment do you think most people would choose?
4. Based on what you have learned about groupshift, which investment do you think Yusra's family will choose?

Research Exercise

What aspects of group behavior discussed in this chapter were the most interesting to you? Carry out some research into how group properties could explain group behaviour in the Arab world. Share your findings with the class.

LEARNING OBJECTIVES

This chapter will enable you to:

1 Analyze the growing popularity of using teams in organizations.

2 Contrast groups and teams.

3 Compare and contrast four types of teams.

4 Identify the characteristics of effective teams.

5 Show how organizations can create team players.

6 Decide when to use individuals instead of teams.

7 Show how the understanding of teams differs in a global context.

Understanding Work Teams

Talent wins games, but teamwork and intelligence win championships. —Michael Jordan

Toyota's Team Culture

Many companies proudly promote their team culture. At Toyota, the promotion seems sincere. Teamwork is one of Toyota's core values, along with trust, continuous improvement, long-term thinking, standardization, innovation, and problem solving. The firm's value statement says the following: "To ensure the success of our company, each team member has the responsibility to work together, and communicate honestly, share ideas, and ensure team member understanding."

So how does Toyota's culture reflect its emphasis on teamwork? First, although individualism is a prominent value in Western culture, it is deemphasized at Toyota. In its place is an emphasis on systems, in which people and products are seen as intertwined value streams and people are trained to be problem solvers so as to make the product system leaner and better. Second, before hiring, Toyota tests candidates to ensure they are not only competent and technically skilled but also oriented toward teamwork—able to trust their team, be comfortable solving problems

collaboratively, and motivated to achieve collective outcomes.

Third, and not surprisingly, Toyota structures its work around teams. Every Toyota employee knows the saying "All of us are smarter than any of us." Teams are used not only in the production process but also at every level and in every function: in sales and marketing, in finance, in engineering, in design, and at the executive level. Fourth, Toyota considers the team to be the power center of the organization.

The leader serves the team, not the other way around. When asked whether he would feature himself in advertisements the way other automakers had (most famously, 'Dr. Z,' Daimler's CEO Dieter Zetsche), Toyota's CEO in the US, Yuki Funo, said, "No. We want to show everybody in the company. The heroes. Not one single person."

Sources: J. K. Liker and M. Hoseus, *Toyota Culture: The Heart and Soul of the Toyota Way* (New York: McGraw-Hill, 2008); and D. Kiley, "The Toyota Way to No. 1," *Business Week*, April 26, 2007, www.businessweek.com.

Teams are increasingly becoming the primary means for organizing work in contemporary business firms. In fact, this trend is so widespread that many prominent companies are no longer hiring individuals but whole teams. The opening case shows us how Toyota has succeeded because of its team-oriented culture and, accordingly, how its staff are comfortable working in Toyota's organizational culture. What do you think of your skills in leading and building a team? Before we continue, take the following self-assessment to find out.

Self Assessment Library

HOW GOOD AM I AT BUILDING AND LEADING A TEAM?

In the Self-Assessment Library (available online), take assessment II.B.6 (How Good Am I at Building and Leading a Team?) and answer the following questions:

1. *Did you score as high as you thought you would? Why or why not?*

2. *Do you think you can improve your score? If so, how? If not, why not?*

3. *Do you think there is such a thing as team players? If yes, what are their behaviors?*

Why Have Teams Become So Popular?

1 *Analyze the growing popularity of using teams in organizations.*

Decades ago, when companies such as Volvo introduced teams into their production processes, it made news because no one else was doing it. Today, it's just the opposite. It's the organization that *doesn't* use teams that has become newsworthy. Teams are everywhere.

How do we explain the current popularity of teams? As organizations have restructured themselves to compete more effectively and efficiently, they have turned to teams as a better way to use employee talents. Management has found that teams are more flexible and responsive to changing events than are traditional departments or other forms of permanent groupings. Teams have the capability to quickly come together, implement, refocus, and break up. But don't overlook the motivational properties of teams. Consistent with our discussion in Chapter 5 of the role of employee involvement as a motivator, teams facilitate employee participation in operating decisions. So another explanation for the popularity of teams is that they are an effective means for management to democratize their organizations and increase employee motivation; the more employee involvement, the more they will be motivated and engaged, and this will in turn translate into enhanced productivity.

What Do You Think?

Are you a team player?

The fact that organizations have turned to teams doesn't necessarily mean they're always effective. So how effective are teams? What conditions affect their potential? How do teams work together? These are some of the questions we'll answer in this chapter.

Meirc Training & Consulting is an independent multinational company with over 54 years of experience. Their effective work teams have welcomed more than 250,000 participants from around 1,800 organizations, among which are prominent firms from all over the Arab world. The key to the team's success is synergy, which enhances collaboration and motivates individuals to perform better.

Differences between Groups and Teams

Contrast groups and teams.

Work group

A group that interacts primarily to share information and to make decisions to help each group member perform within his or her area of responsibility.

Work team

A group whose individual efforts result in performance that is greater than the sum of the individual inputs.

Groups and teams are not the same thing. In this section, we define and clarify the difference between work groups and work teams.[1]

In Chapter 7, we defined a *group* as two or more individuals, interacting and interdependent, who have come together to achieve particular objectives. A **work group** is a group that interacts primarily to share information and to make decisions to help each member perform within his or her area of responsibility.

Work groups have no need or opportunity to engage in collective work that requires joint effort. So their performance is simply the combination of each group member's individual contribution. There is no positive synergy or combined energy that would create an overall level of performance that is greater than the sum of the inputs.

On the other hand, a **work team** generates positive synergy through coordinated effort. The individual efforts result in a level of performance that is greater than the sum of those individual inputs. Figure 8-1 highlights the differences between work groups and work teams.

These definitions help clarify why so many organizations have recently restructured work processes around teams. Management is looking for positive synergy that will allow the organizations to increase performance. The extensive use of teams creates the *potential* for an organization to generate greater outputs with no increase in inputs. Notice, however, that we said *potential*. There is nothing magical in the creation of teams that ensures the achievement of positive synergy. The name has nothing to do with it, calling a *group* a *team* doesn't automatically increase its performance. As we show later in this chapter, effective teams have certain common characteristics. If management hopes to gain increases in organizational performance through the use of teams, it needs to ensure that its teams possess these characteristics.

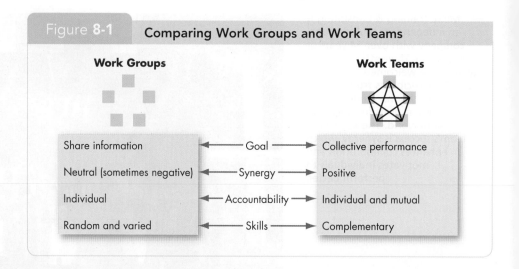

Figure 8-1   **Comparing Work Groups and Work Teams**

Work Groups		Work Teams
Share information	← Goal →	Collective performance
Neutral (sometimes negative)	← Synergy →	Positive
Individual	← Accountability →	Individual and mutual
Random and varied	← Skills →	Complementary

Types of Teams

3   *Compare and contrast four types of teams.*

Teams can do a variety of things. They can make products, provide services, negotiate deals, coordinate projects, offer advice, and make decisions.[2] In this section, we'll describe the four most common types of teams you're likely to find in an organization: *problem-solving teams, self-managed work teams, cross-functional teams,* and *virtual teams,* as shown in Figure 8-2.

Problem-solving teams

Groups of 5 to 12 employees from the same department who meet for a few hours each week to discuss ways of improving quality, efficiency, and the work environment.

Problem-Solving Teams

Twenty years ago or so, teams were just beginning to grow in popularity, and most of those teams took similar form. They were typically composed of 5 to 12 employees from the same department who met for a few hours each week to discuss ways of improving quality, efficiency, and the work environment.[3] We call these **problem-solving teams**.

At Tanmia, the UAE's National Human Resource Development and Employment Authority, employees work in problem-solving teams, with each team focusing on one product at a time. Team members are encouraged to suggest improvements in manufacturing work methods and processes, as well as commenting on product quality.

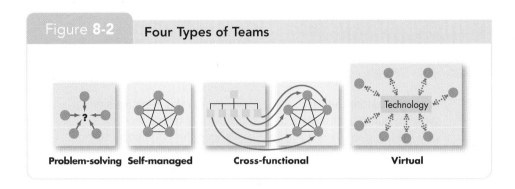

Figure **8-2**   **Four Types of Teams**

Problem-solving   Self-managed   Cross-functional   Virtual

In problem-solving teams, members share ideas or offer suggestions on how work processes and methods can be improved, but they rarely have the authority to implement any of their suggested actions.

Self-Managed Work Teams

Although problem-solving teams involve employees in decisions, they 'only' make recommendations. Some organizations have gone further and created teams that can not only solve problems but also implement solutions and take responsibility for outcomes.

Self-managed work teams

Groups of 10 to 15 people who take on responsibilities of their former supervisors.

Self-managed work teams are groups of employees (typically 10 to 15 in number) who perform highly related or interdependent jobs and take on many of the responsibilities of their former supervisors.[4] Typically, these tasks are involved in planning and scheduling work, assigning tasks to members, making operating decisions, taking action on problems, and working with suppliers and customers. Fully self-managed work teams even select their own members and have the members evaluate each other's performance. As a result, supervisory positions take on decreased importance and may even be eliminated.

But we must be careful: the overall research on the effectiveness of self-managed work teams has not been positive.[5] Moreover, although individuals on these teams do tend to report higher levels of job satisfaction compared with other individuals, they also sometimes have higher absenteeism and turnover rates. Thus, inconsistency in findings suggests that the effectiveness of self-managed teams depends on the strength and make-up of team norms, the type of tasks the team undertakes, and the reward structure the team operates under—each of which can significantly influence how well the team performs.

Cross-Functional Teams

The Boeing Company created a team made up of employees from production, planning, quality, tooling, design engineering, and information systems to automate the company's C-17 program. The team's suggestions resulted in drastically reduced cycle time and cost as well as improved quality on the C-17 program.[6]

Cross-functional teams

Employees from about the same hierarchical level, but from different work areas, who come together to accomplish a task.

This Boeing example illustrates the use of **cross-functional teams**. These are teams made up of employees from about the same hierarchical level but from different work areas, who come together to accomplish a task.

Today, cross-functional teams are so widely used that it is hard to imagine a major organizational initiative without one. For instance, all the major automobile manufacturers—including Toyota, Honda, Nissan, BMW, GM, Ford, and Chrysler—currently use this form of team to coordinate complex projects. And Harley-Davidson relies on specific cross-functional teams to manage each line of its motorcycles. These teams include Harley employees from design, manufacturing, and purchasing, as well as representatives from key outside suppliers.[7]

International OB

Global Virtual Teams

Years ago, before the vast working public ever dreamed of e-mail, instant messaging, or live videoconferencing, work teams used to be in the same locations, with possibly one or two members a train or plane ride away. Today, however, the reach of corporations spans many countries, so the need for teams to work together across international lines has increased. To deal with this challenge, multinationals use global virtual teams to gain a competitive advantage.

Global virtual teams have advantages and disadvantages. On the positive side, because team members come from different countries with different knowledge and points of view, they may develop creative ideas and solutions to problems that work for multiple cultures. On the negative side, global virtual teams face more challenges than traditional teams that meet face-to-face. For one thing, miscommunication can lead to misunderstandings, which can create stress and conflict among team members. Also, members who do not accept individuals from different cultures may hesitate to share information openly, which can create problems of trust.

To create and implement effective global virtual teams, managers must carefully select employees whom they believe will thrive in such an environment. Employees must be comfortable with communicating electronically with others, and they must be open to different ideas. When dealing with team members in other countries, speaking multiple languages may also be necessary. Team members also must realize that the values they hold may be vastly different from their teammates' values. For instance, an individual from a country that values relationships and sensitivity, such as Sweden, might face a challenge when interacting with someone from Spain, which values assertiveness and competitiveness.

Although global virtual teams face many challenges, companies that implement them effectively can realize tremendous rewards through the diverse knowledge they gain.

Source: Based on N. Zakaria, A. Amelinckx, and D. Wilemon, "Working Together Apart? Building a Knowledge-Sharing Culture for Global Virtual Teams," *Creativity and Innovation Management*, March 2004, pp. 15–29.

Cross-functional teams are an effective means for allowing people from diverse areas within an organization (or even between organizations) to exchange information, develop new ideas and solve problems, and coordinate complex projects. Of course, cross-functional teams are no picnic to manage. Their early stages of development are often very time-consuming, as members learn to work with diversity and complexity. It takes time to build trust and teamwork, especially among people from different backgrounds with different experiences and perspectives.

Virtual Teams

Virtual teams

Teams that use computer technology to tie together physically dispersed members in order to achieve a common goal.

The previously described types of teams do their work face to face. **Virtual teams** use computer technology to tie together physically separated members in order to achieve a common goal.[8] They allow people to collaborate online—using communication links such as wide-area networks, videoconferencing, or e-mail—whether they're only a room away or continents apart. Virtual teams are so common, and technology has advanced so far, that it's probably not necessary to call these teams 'virtual.' Nearly all teams today do at least some of their work remotely.

Nevertheless, virtual teams do face special challenges, some of which are discussed in the 'International OB' feature above. They may suffer because there is less social rapport and less direct interaction among members. They aren't able to duplicate the normal give-and-take of face-to-face discussion. Especially when members haven't personally met, virtual teams tend to be more task oriented and exchange less social–emotional information than face-to-face teams. Not surprisingly, virtual team members report less satisfaction with the group interaction process than do face-to-face teams. For virtual teams to be effective, management should ensure that (1) trust is established among team members; (2) team progress is monitored closely; and (3) the efforts and products of the virtual team are publicized throughout the organization.[9]

Creating Effective Teams

> **4** *Identify the characteristics of effective teams.*

Many have tried to identify factors related to team effectiveness.[10] However, recent studies have organized what was once a 'list of characteristics'[11] into a relatively focused model.[12] Figure 8-3 summarizes what we currently know about what makes teams effective. As you'll see, it builds on many of the group concepts introduced in Chapter 7.

The following discussion is based on the model in Figure 8-3. Keep in mind two issues before we proceed. First, teams differ in form and structure. Because the model we present attempts to generalize across all varieties of teams, you need to be careful not to rigidly apply the model's predictions to all teams.[13] You should use the model as a guide. Second, the model assumes that it's already been determined that teamwork is preferable to individual work. Creating 'effective' teams in situations in which individuals can do the job better is equivalent to solving the wrong problem perfectly.

The key components of effective teams can be divided into four general categories. First are the resources and other *contextual* influences that make teams effective. The second relates to the team's *composition*. The third category is *work design*. Finally, *process* variables reflect those things that go on in the team that influence effectiveness. What does *team effectiveness* mean in this model? Typically, it has included objective measures of the team's productivity, managers' ratings of the team's performance, and aggregate measures of member satisfaction.

Context: What Factors Determine whether Teams Are Successful

The four contextual factors that appear to be most significantly related to team performance are the presence of adequate resources, effective leadership, a climate of trust, and a performance evaluation and reward system that reflects team contributions.

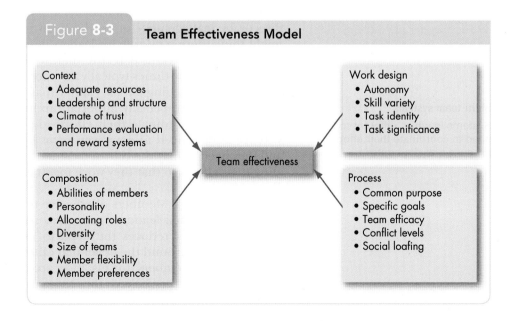

Figure 8-3   **Team Effectiveness Model**

Context
- Adequate resources
- Leadership and structure
- Climate of trust
- Performance evaluation and reward systems

Work design
- Autonomy
- Skill variety
- Task identity
- Task significance

Team effectiveness

Composition
- Abilities of members
- Personality
- Allocating roles
- Diversity
- Size of teams
- Member flexibility
- Member preferences

Process
- Common purpose
- Specific goals
- Team efficacy
- Conflict levels
- Social loafing

At the International Consulting and Training Network (ICTN), CEO Fay Niewiadomski encourages her staff, shown in this photo, to be team players. She conducts regular team-building workshops and her approach is based on the principle that employees become more effective when they have the support of top management.

Adequate Resources Teams are part of a larger organization system. As such, every work team relies on resources outside the group to support it. A scarcity of resources directly reduces the ability of a team to perform its job effectively. As one set of researchers concluded, after looking at 13 factors potentially related to group performance, "perhaps one of the most important characteristics of an effective work group is the support the group receives from the organization."[14] This support includes timely information, proper equipment, adequate staffing, encouragement, and administrative assistance. Teams must receive the necessary support from management and the larger organization if they are to succeed in achieving their goals.

Leadership and Structure Teams can't function if they can't agree on who is to do what and ensure that all members contribute equally in sharing the work load. Agreeing on the specifics of work and how they fit together to integrate individual skills requires team leadership and structure. This can be provided directly by management or by the team members themselves. Although you might think there is no role for leaders in self-managed teams, that couldn't be further from the truth. It is true that, in self-managed teams, team members absorb many of the duties typically assumed by managers. However, a manager's job becomes managing *outside* (rather than inside) the team.

Leadership is especially important in **multi-team systems**—where different teams need to coordinate their efforts to produce a desired outcome. In such systems, leaders need to empower teams by delegating responsibility to them, and they need to play the role of facilitator, making sure the teams are coordinating their efforts so that they work together rather than against one another.[15]

Multi-team systems

Systems in which different teams need to coordinate their efforts to produce a desired outcome.

Climate of Trust Members of effective teams trust each other. And they also exhibit trust in their leaders.[16] Interpersonal trust among team members facilitates cooperation, reduces the need to monitor each other's behavior, and bonds members around the belief that others on the team won't take advantage of them. Team members, for instance, are more likely to take risks and expose weaknesses when they believe they can trust others on their team. Similarly, as discussed in Chapter 10, trust is the foundation of leadership. Trust in leadership is important in that it allows a team to be willing to accept and commit to its leader's goals and decisions.

Performance Evaluation and Reward Systems   The traditional, individually oriented evaluation and reward system must be modified to reflect team performance.[17] Individual performance evaluations and incentives may interfere with the development of high-performance teams. So in addition to evaluating and rewarding employees for their individual contributions, management should consider group-based appraisals, profit-sharing, gainsharing, small-group incentives, and other system modifications that reinforce team effort and commitment.

What Do You Think?

How do you get team members to be both individually and jointly accountable?

Team Composition

The team composition category includes variables that relate to how teams should be staffed. In this section, we address the ability and personality of team members, allocation of roles, diversity of members, size of the team, and members' preference for teamwork.

Abilities of Members   Part of a team's performance depends on the knowledge, skills, and abilities of its individual members.[18] We occasionally read about an athletic team composed of average players who, because of excellent coaching, determination, and precision teamwork, beats a far more talented group of players; but such cases are unusual. However, a team's performance is not merely the summation of its individual members' abilities. These abilities simply set limits for what members can do and how effectively they will perform on a team.

OB in the News

Surgical Teams Lack Teamwork

Surgery is almost always performed by a team, but in many cases, it's a team in name only. So says a new study of more than 2,100 surgeons, anesthesiologists, and nurses. When the researchers surveyed these surgery team members, they asked them to "describe the quality of communication and collaboration you have experienced" with other members of the surgical unit. Perhaps not surprisingly, surgeons were given the lowest ratings for teamwork and nurses the highest

ratings. "The study is somewhat humbling to me," said Martin Makary, the lead author on the study and a surgeon at Johns Hopkins. "There's a lot of pride in the surgical community. We need to balance out the captain-of-the-ship doctrine." The researchers attribute many operating room errors, such as sponges left in patients and operations performed on the wrong part of the body, to poor teamwork. But improving the system is easier said than done. One recent study in Pennsylvania, US, found that over

an 18-month period, there were 174 cases of surgeons operating on the wrong limb or body part. For its part, Johns Hopkins is modeling surgical team training after airline crew training. "Teamwork is an important component of patient safety," says Makary.

Sources: E. Nagourney, "Surgical Teams Found Lacking, in Teamwork," *New York Times*, May 9, 2006, p. D6; and "Nurses Give Surgeons Poor Grades on Teamwork in OR," *Forbes*, May 5, 2006.

Senior product scientists Syed Abbas and Albert Post and technology team manager Laurie Coyle functioned as a high-ability team in developing Unilever's new Dove Nutrium soap bar. In solving the complex problems involved in product innovation, the intelligent members of Unilever's research and development teams have advanced science degrees, the ability to think creatively, and the interpersonal skills needed to perform effectively with other team members.

Source: Ruth Fremson/ *New York Times*.

To perform effectively, a team requires three different types of skills. First, it needs people who have *technical expertise*. Second, it needs people who have the *problem-solving and decision-making skills* to be able to identify problems, generate alternatives, evaluate those alternatives, and make competent choices. Finally, teams need people who have good listening, feedback, conflict resolution, and other *interpersonal skills*.[19] No team can achieve its performance potential without developing all three types of skills. The right mix is crucial. Too much of one at the expense of others will result in lower team performance. But teams don't need to have all the complementary skills in place at their beginning. It's not uncommon for one or more members to take responsibility for learning the skills in which the group is deficient, thereby allowing the team to reach its full potential.

Research on the abilities of team members has revealed some interesting insights into team composition and performance. First, when the task needs considerable thought, like solving a complex problem such as reengineering an assembly line, high-ability teams composed of mainly intelligent members do better than lower-ability teams, especially when the work load is distributed evenly. This is so because team performance does not depend on the weakest link. High-ability teams are also more adaptable to changing situations in that they can more effectively adapt prior knowledge to suit a set of new problems.

Second, although high-ability teams generally have an advantage over lower-ability teams, this is not always the case. When tasks are simple (for example, tasks that individual team members might be able to solve on their own), high-ability teams do not perform as well, perhaps because, in such tasks, high-ability teams become bored and turn their attention to other activities that are more stimulating, whereas low-ability teams stay on task.

Finally, the ability of the team's leader also matters. Research shows that smart team leaders help less intelligent team members when they struggle with a task. But a less intelligent leader can neutralize the effect of a high-ability team.[20]

Personality of Members We demonstrated in Chapter 2 that personality has a significant influence on individual employee behavior. This can also be extended to team behavior. Many of the dimensions identified in the Big Five personality model have been shown to be relevant to team effectiveness. A recent review of the literature suggested that three of the Big Five traits were especially important for team performance.[21] Specifically, teams that rate higher on mean levels of conscientiousness and openness to experience tend to perform better. Moreover, the minimum level of team member agreeableness also matters: Teams did worse when they had one or more highly disagreeable members. Perhaps one bad apple *can* spoil the whole bunch!

Research has also provided us with a good idea about why these personality traits are important to teams. Conscientious people are valuable in teams because they're good at backing up other team members, and they're also good at sensing when that support is truly needed. Open team members communicate better with one another and throw out more ideas, which leads teams composed of open people to be more creative and innovative.[22]

Even if an organization does a really good job of selecting individuals for team roles, most likely they'll find there aren't enough conscientious people to do the jobs.

Picture This

Suppose an organization needs to create 20 teams of four people each and has 40 highly conscientious people and 40 who score low on conscientiousness. Would the organization be better off (A) putting all the conscientious people together (forming 10 teams with the highly conscientious people and 10 teams of members low on conscientiousness) or (B) including in each team two people who scored high and two who scored low on conscientiousness?

Perhaps surprisingly, the evidence tends to suggest that option A is the best choice; performance across the teams will be higher if the organization forms 10 highly conscientious teams and 10 teams low in conscientiousness. "This may be because, in such teams, members who are highly conscientious not only must perform their own tasks but also must perform or re-do the tasks of low-conscientious members. It may also be because such diversity leads to feelings of contribution inequity."[23]

Allocation of Roles Teams have different needs, and people should be selected for a team to ensure that all the various roles are filled.

We can identify nine potential team roles as shown in Figure 8-4. Successful work teams have people to fill all these roles and have selected people to play these roles based on their skills and preferences.[24] On many teams, individuals will play multiple roles. Managers need to understand the individual strengths that each person can bring to a team, select members with their strengths in mind, and allocate work assignments that fit with members' preferred styles. By matching individual preferences with team-role demands, managers increase the likelihood that the team members will work well together.

Diversity of Members In Chapter 7, we discussed research on the effect of diversity on groups. How does *team* diversity affect *team* performance?

Many of us hold the optimistic view that diversity should be a good thing—diverse teams should benefit from differing perspectives and do better. Unfortunately, the evidence appears to favor the pessimists. One review concluded, "Studies on diversity in teams from the last 50 years have shown that surface-level social-category differences such as race/ethnicity, gender, and age tend to . . . have negative effects" on the performance of teams.[25]

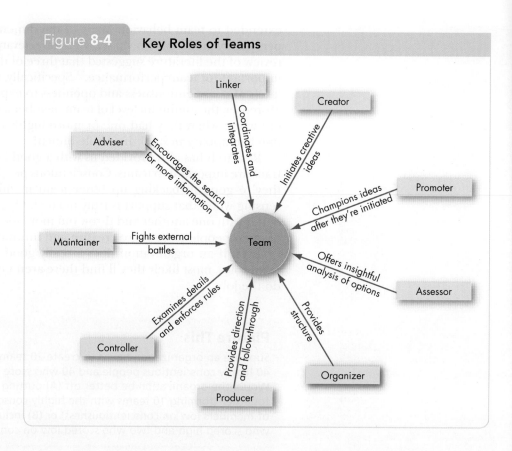

Figure 8-4   Key Roles of Teams

Linker — Coordinates and integrates

Creator — Initiates creative ideas

Adviser — Encourages the search for more information

Promoter — Champions ideas after they're initiated

Maintainer — Fights external battles

Team

Assessor — Offers insightful analysis of options

Controller — Examines details and enforces rules

Producer — Provides direction and follow-through

Organizer — Provides structure

One of the problems with teams is that while diversity may have real potential benefits, a team is deeply focused on commonly held information. But if diverse teams are to realize their creative potential, they need to focus not on their similarities but on their differences. There is some evidence, for example, that when team members believe others have more expertise, they will work to support those members, leading to higher levels of effectiveness.[26] The key is for diverse teams to communicate what they uniquely know and also what they don't know.

The degree to which members of a work unit (group, team, or department) share a common demographic attribute, such as age, sex, race, educational level, or length of service in the organization, and the impact of that attribute on turnover is a variable known as **organizational demography**. Organizational demography suggests that attributes such as age or the date that someone joins a specific work team or organization should help us to predict turnover. Essentially, the logic goes like this: turnover will be greater among those with dissimilar experiences because communication is more difficult. Conflict and power struggles are more likely, and they are more severe when they occur. The increased conflict makes unit membership less attractive, so employees are more likely to quit. Similarly, the losers in a power struggle are more likely to leave voluntarily or to be forced out.[27]

Organizational demography

The degree to which members of a work unit share a common demographic attribute, such as age, sex, race, educational level, or length of service in an organization, and the impact of this attribute on turnover.

What Do You Think?

How does team diversity affect team performance?

At hospitality company, Rotana, there is great diversity among employees, which they consider plays a big part in their success. Their qualified teams are trained to offer excellence and so ensure guest satisfaction. Embracing their differences and sharing their diverse attributes enables better communication among team members, low staff turnover, and fewer power struggles.

Size of Teams   Think small. Generally speaking, the most effective teams have five to nine members. And experts suggest using the smallest number of people who can do the task. Unfortunately, there is a tendency for managers to mistakenly make teams too large. While a minimum of four or five may be necessary to develop diversity of views and skills, managers seem to seriously underestimate how coordination problems can increase as team members are added.

When teams have excess members, cohesiveness and mutual accountability decline, social loafing increases, and more and more people do less talking relative to others. Moreover, large teams have trouble coordinating with one another, especially when under time pressure. So in designing effective teams, managers should try to keep them at nine or fewer members. If a natural working unit is larger and you want a team effort, consider breaking the group into subteams.[28]

Member Preferences   Not every employee is a team player. Given the option, many employees will select themselves *out* of team participation. When people who would prefer to work alone are required to team up, there is a direct threat to the team's morale and to individual member satisfaction.[29] This suggests that, when selecting team members, individual preferences should be considered, along with abilities, personalities, and skills. High-performing teams are likely to be composed of people who prefer working as part of a group.

Work Design

Effective teams need to work together and take collective responsibility for completing significant tasks. An effective team must be more than a 'team in name only.'[30] Based on terminology introduced in Chapter 5, the work-design category includes variables such as freedom and autonomy, the opportunity to use different skills and talents (skill variety), and the ability to complete a whole and identifiable task or product (task identity), and to work on a task or project that has a substantial impact on others (task significance). The evidence indicates that these characteristics enhance member motivation and increase team effectiveness.[31] These work-design characteristics motivate because they increase members' sense of responsibility and ownership of the work and because they make the work more interesting to perform.[32]

Team Processes

The final category related to team effectiveness is process variables. These include member commitment to a common purpose, establishment of specific team goals, team efficacy, a managed level of conflict, and minimization of social loafing.

Why are processes important to team effectiveness? One way to answer this question is to return to the topic of social loafing. We found that 1 + 1 + 1 doesn't necessarily add up to 3. In team tasks for which each member's contribution is not clearly visible, there is a tendency for individuals to decrease their effort. Social loafing in other words illustrates a process loss as a result of using teams. But team processes should produce positive results. That is, teams should create outputs greater than the sum of their inputs. The development of creative alternatives by a diverse group would be one such instance. Figure 8-5 illustrates how group processes can have an impact on a group's actual effectiveness.[33] Research teams are often used in research laboratories because they can draw on the diverse skills of various individuals to produce more meaningful research as a team than could be generated by all the researchers working independently. That is, they produce positive synergy. Their process gains exceed their process losses.

Figure 8-5   Effects of Group Processes

$$\boxed{\text{Potential group effectiveness}} \; + \; \boxed{\text{Process gains}} \; - \; \boxed{\text{Process losses}} \; = \; \boxed{\text{Actual group effectiveness}}$$

Common Plan and Purpose   An effective team has a common plan and purpose that provides direction, momentum, and commitment for members.[34] This purpose is a vision, or master plan. It's wider than specific goals.

Members of successful teams put a tremendous amount of time and effort into discussing, shaping, and agreeing on a purpose that belongs to them both collectively and individually. It provides direction and guidance under any and all conditions. Like a ship following the wrong course, teams that don't have good planning skills are doomed; perfectly executing the wrong plan is a lost cause.[35] Effective teams also show **reflexivity**, meaning that they reflect on and adjust their master plan when necessary. A team has to have a good plan, but it also has to be willing and able to adapt when condition call for it.[36]

Specific Goals   Successful teams translate their common purpose into specific, measurable, and realistic performance goals. Just as we demonstrated in Chapter 5 how goals lead individuals to higher performance, goals also energize teams. Specific goals facilitate clear communication. They also help teams maintain their focus on getting results.

Also, consistent with the research on individual goals, team goals should be challenging. Difficult goals have been found to raise team performance on those criteria for which they're set. So, for instance, goals for quantity tend to raise quantity, goals for speed tend to raise speed, goals for accuracy raise accuracy, and so on.[37]

Team Efficacy   Effective teams have confidence in themselves. They believe they can succeed. We call this *team efficacy*.[38] Success leads to success. Teams that

Reflexivity
A team characteristic of reflecting on and adjusting the master plan when necessary.

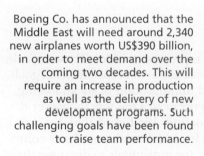

Boeing Co. has announced that the Middle East will need around 2,340 new airplanes worth US$390 billion, in order to meet demand over the coming two decades. This will require an increase in production as well as the delivery of new development programs. Such challenging goals have been found to raise team performance.

have been successful raise their beliefs about future success, which, in turn, motivates them to work harder. What, if anything, can management do to increase team efficacy? Two possible options are helping the team to achieve small successes and providing skill training. Small successes build team confidence. As a team develops an increasingly stronger performance record, it also increases the collective belief that future efforts will lead to success. In addition, managers should consider providing training to improve members' technical and interpersonal skills. The greater the abilities of team members, the greater the likelihood that the team will develop confidence and the capability to deliver on that confidence.

Mental models

Team members' knowledge and beliefs about how the work gets done.

Mental Models   Effective teams have accurate and common **mental models**— knowledge and beliefs (a 'psychological map') about how the work gets done. If team members have the wrong mental models, which is particularly likely to happen with teams under acute stress, their performance suffers.[39] The similarity of team members' mental models matters, too. If team members have different ideas about how to do things, the teams will fight over how to do things rather than focus on what needs to be done.[40]

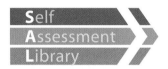

WHAT IS MY TEAM EFFICACY?

In the Self-Assessment Library (available online), take assessment IV.E.2 (What Is My Team Efficacy?).

Conflict Levels   Conflict on a team isn't necessarily bad. As will be discussed in depth in Chapter 12, teams that are completely empty of conflict are likely to become indifferent. So conflict can actually improve team effectiveness.[41] But not all types of conflict. Relationship conflicts—those based on interpersonal incompatibilities, tension, and anger toward others—are almost always dysfunctional. However, on teams performing nonroutine activities, disagreements among members about task content (called *task conflicts*) are not harmful. In fact, it is often beneficial because it reduces the likelihood of groupthink. Task conflicts stimulate discussion, promote critical assessment of problems and options, and can lead to better team decisions. Thus, effective teams can be characterized as having an appropriate level of conflict.

Social Loafing   In Chapter 7, we talked about the fact that individuals can hide inside a group. They can engage in social loafing and coast on the group's effort because their individual contributions can't be identified. Effective teams undermine this tendency by holding themselves accountable at both the individual and team levels. Successful teams make members individually and jointly accountable for the team's purpose, goals, and approach.[42] Therefore, members should be clear on what they are individually responsible for and what they are jointly responsible for.

Turning Individuals into Team Players

5   *Show how organizations can create team players.*

So far, we've made a strong case for the value and growing popularity of teams. But many people are not natural team players. There are also many organizations that have historically nurtured individual accomplishments. Finally, countries differ in terms of how they rate on individualism and collectivism. Teams fit well with countries that score high on collectivism, as Arab countries do. But what if an organization wants to introduce teams into a work population that is made up largely of individuals born and raised in an individualistic society, such as that of the US or UK? A veteran employee of a large company, who had done well working in an individualistic company in an individualist country, described the experience of joining a team: "I'm learning my lesson. I just had my first negative performance appraisal in 20 years."[43]

What Do You Think?

What can organizations do to enhance team effectiveness—to turn individual contributors into team members?

The following are the primary options managers have for trying to turn individuals into team players.

Selection: Hiring Team Players   Some people already possess the interpersonal skills to be effective team players. When hiring team members, in addition to the technical skills required to fill the job, care should be taken to ensure that candidates can fulfill their team roles as well as technical requirements.[44]

Many job candidates don't have team skills. This is especially true for those socialized around individual contributions. When faced with such candidates, managers basically have three options. The candidates can undergo training to 'make them into team players.' If this isn't possible or doesn't work, the other two options are to transfer the individual to another unit within the organization that does not have teams (if this possibility exists) or not to hire the candidate. In established organizations that decide to redesign jobs around teams, it should be expected that some employees will resist being team players and may be untrainable.

Training: Creating Team Players   A large proportion of people raised on the importance of individual accomplishments can be trained to become team players. Training specialists conduct exercises that allow employees to experience the satisfaction that teamwork can provide. They typically offer workshops to help employees improve their problem-solving, communication, negotiation, conflict-management, and coaching skills. Employees also learn the five-stage group development model described in Chapter 7.

Outside consultants can also be brought in to give workers practical skills for working in teams and to encourage employees to become enthusiastic and accept the value of teamwork. For example, HigherPro, a Jordanian company, gave a training workshop about teamwork aimed at corporate managers, business people, and HR/organizational behavior specialists. Participants were trained in three particular aspects of team work: working together effectively, being a valuable team player, and filling the role of team leader. Basel Saliba, HigherPro's Chief Executive Officer and Master Trainer describes the typical HigherPro workshop as "an experience and not a class. We understand that trainees come from different environments and backgrounds, and have their own challenges and questions. Each trainee needs to be cared for in their own way. We do not hold mere workshops, we raise leaders in both work and life."[45]

Rewarding: Providing Incentives to Be a Good Team Player   An organization's reward system needs to be reworked to encourage cooperative efforts rather than competitive ones.[46] For instance, Hallmark Cards, Inc., added to its basic individual-incentive system an annual bonus based on achievement of team goals. In the Arab world, INDEVCO implements this system also.

Promotions, pay raises, and other forms of recognition should be given to individuals who work effectively as collaborative team members. This doesn't mean individual contributions should be ignored; rather, they should be balanced with selfless contributions to the team. Examples of behaviors that should be rewarded include training new colleagues, sharing information with teammates, helping to resolve team conflicts, and mastering new skills that the team needs but in which it is deficient.

Finally, don't forget the intrinsic rewards that employees can receive from teamwork. Teams provide camaraderie or team spirit. It's exciting and satisfying to be an integral part of a successful team. The opportunity to engage in personal development and to help teammates grow can be a very satisfying and rewarding experience for employees.

Beware! Teams Aren't Always the Answer

> *6 Decide when to use individuals instead of teams.*

Teamwork takes more time and often more resources than individual work. For instance, teams have increased communication demands, conflicts to be managed, and meetings to be run. So the benefits of using teams have to exceed the costs. And that's not always the case.[47] In the excitement to enjoy the benefits of teams, some managers have introduced them into situations in which the work is better done by individuals. So before you rush to implement teams, you should carefully evaluate whether the work requires or will benefit from a collective effort.

How do you know if the work of your group would be better done in teams? It's been suggested that three tests be applied to see if a team fits the situation.[48] First, can the work be done better by more than one person? A good indicator is the difficulty of the work and the need for different points of view. Simple tasks that don't require diverse input are probably better left to individuals. Second, does the work create a common purpose or set of goals for the people in the group that is more than the aggregate of individual goals? For instance, many new-car dealer service departments have introduced teams that link customer-service personnel, mechanics, parts specialists, and sales representatives. Such teams can better manage collective responsibility for ensuring that customer needs are properly met.

The final test to assess whether teams fit the situation is to determine whether the members of the group are interdependent. Using teams makes sense when there is interdependence between tasks—when the success of the whole depends on the success of each one *and* the success of each one depends on the success of the others. Football, for instance, is an obvious *team* sport. Success requires a great deal of coordination between interdependent players. On the other hand, swim teams are not really teams. They're groups of individuals, performing individually and whose total performance is simply the total summation of their individual performances.

Global Implications

7 Show how the understanding of teams differs in a global context.

Although research on global considerations in the use of teams is just beginning, three areas are particularly worth mentioning: the extent of teamwork, self-managed teams, and team cultural diversity.

Extent of Teamwork   Although the use of work teams is common in the United States, some evidence suggests that the extent of teamwork—the degree to which US teams deeply affect the way work is done—is not as significant in the United States as in other countries. One study comparing US workers with Canadian and Asian workers revealed that 51 percent of workers in Asia-Pacific and 48 percent of Canadian employees report high levels of teamwork. But only about one-third (32 percent) of US employees say their organization has a high level of teamwork.[49] Thus, although teamwork is widely used in the United States, this evidence suggests that there still is a heavy role for individual contributions. Given that US culture is highly individualistic, that may continue to be true for quite some time.

What Do You Think?

Given that Arab societies are collectivist, what do you think this implies about levels of teamwork across organizations in the region?

Self-Managed Teams   Although self-managed teams have not proven to be the solution many thought they would be, special care needs to be taken when introducing self-managed teams globally. For instance, evidence suggests that these types of teams have not succeeded in Mexico, largely due to that culture's low tolerance of ambiguity and uncertainty, and employees' strong respect for hierarchical authority.[50] Thus, in countries that are relatively high in power distance—meaning that roles of leaders and followers are clearly delineated—a team may need to be structured so that leadership roles are spelled out and power relationships are identified. Countries in the Arab world are high in power distance, which suggests that this will also be the case in most countries in the region.

Team Cultural Diversity and Team Performance   Earlier, we discussed research on team diversity in terms of factors such as race or gender. But what about diversity created by national differences? Like the earlier research, evidence indicates that these elements of diversity interfere with team processes, at least in the short term.[51] Cultural diversity does seem to be an asset for tasks that call for a variety of viewpoints. But culturally heterogeneous teams have more difficulty learning to work with each other and solving problems. The good news is that these difficulties seem to disappear with time. Although newly formed culturally diverse teams underperform newly formed culturally homogeneous teams, the differences disappear after about 3 months.[52] The reason is that it takes culturally diverse teams a while to learn how to work through disagreements and different approaches to solving problems.

Summary and Implications for Managers

Few trends have influenced jobs as much as the massive movement to introduce teams into the workplace. The shift from working alone to working on teams requires employees to cooperate with others, share information, confront differences, and give up personal interests for the greater good of the team.

Effective teams have common characteristics. They have adequate resources, effective leadership, a climate of trust, and a performance evaluation and reward system that reflects team contributions. These teams have individuals with technical expertise as well as problem-solving, decision-making, and interpersonal skills, and the right traits, especially conscientiousness and openness.

Effective teams also tend to be small—with fewer than ten people, preferably of diverse backgrounds. They have members that fill role demands and who prefer to be part of a group. And the work that members do provides freedom and autonomy, the opportunity to use different skills and talents, the ability to complete a whole and identifiable task or product, and work that has a substantial impact on others. Finally, effective teams have members who believe in the team's capabilities and are committed to a common plan and purpose, an accurate shared mental model of what is to be accomplished, specific team goals, a manageable level of conflict, and a minimal degree of social loafing.

Finally, because individualistic organizations and societies attract and reward individual accomplishments, it can be difficult to create team players in these environments. To make the conversion, management should try to select individuals who have the interpersonal skills to be effective team players, provide training to develop teamwork skills, and reward individuals for cooperative efforts.

Point >< Counterpoint

SPORTS TEAMS ARE GOOD MODELS FOR WORKPLACE TEAMS

Studies from sports teams such as football and basketball have found a number of elements of successful sports teams that can be transferred to successful work teams.

Successful teams integrate cooperation and competition. Sports teams with the best win–loss record had coaches who promote a strong spirit of cooperation and a high level of healthy competition among their players.

Successful teams score early wins. Early successes build teammates' faith in themselves and their capacity as a team. Teams that are winning at the end of the first half often go on to win. So managers should provide teams with early tasks that are simple and provide "easy wins."

Successful teams avoid losing. A couple of failures can lead to a downward spiral if a team becomes demoralized. Managers need to instill confidence in team members that they can turn things around when they encounter setbacks.

Practice makes perfect. Successful sport teams execute on game day but learn from their mistakes in practice. Practice should be used to try new things and fail. A wise manager encourages work teams to experiment and learn.

Successful teams use half-time breaks. The best coaches in basketball and football use half-time during a game to reassess what is working and what isn't. Managers of work teams should similarly build in assessments at the approximate halfway point in a team project to evaluate what it can do to improve.

Winning teams have stable membership. Stability improves performance. Studies of professional basketball teams have found that when teammates have more time together they are more able to anticipate one another's moves, and they are clearer about one another's roles.

Successful teams evaluate after failures and successes. The best sports teams study the game video. Similarly, work teams should routinely assess their successes and failures and should learn from them.

Sports metaphors are useful. For example, a recent *Harvard Business Review* article argues that winners in business play hardball, which means they pick their shots, seek out competitive encounters, set the pace of innovation, and test the edges of the possible. Like sports teams, in business you have to play hardball, which means playing to win. That is what the sports model can teach us.

There are flaws in using sports as a model for developing effective work teams. Here are just four.

All sports teams aren't alike. In tennis, for instance, there is little interaction among teammates when they play doubles. The performance of the team is largely the sum of the performance of its individual players. In contrast, football has much more interdependence among players. Geographic distribution is dense. Usually all players are involved in every play, team members have to be able to switch from offense to defense at a moment's notice, and there is continuous movement by all, not just the player who has the ball. The performance of the team is more than the sum of its individual players. So when using sports teams as a model for work teams, you have to make sure you're using the correct comparison.

Work teams are more varied and complex than sports teams. In an athletic league, the design of the task, the design of the team, and the team's context vary relatively little from team to team. But these variables can vary tremendously between work teams. As a result, coaching plays a much more significant part of a sports team's performance than in that of a work team. Performance of work teams is a function of getting the team's structural and design variables right. So, in contrast to sports, managers of work teams should focus more on getting the team set up for success than on coaching.

A lot of employees can't relate to sports metaphors. Not everyone on work teams can relate to sports. Some people aren't as interested in sports and aren't as knowledgeable about sports terminology. And team members from different cultures may not know the sports metaphors you're using. Most Americans, for instance, are unfamiliar with the rules and terminology of Australian Rules football.

Work team outcomes aren't easily defined in terms of wins and losses. Sports teams typically measure success in terms of wins and losses. Such measures of success are rarely as clear for work teams. When managers try to define success in wins and losses, it tends to infer that the workplace is ethically no more complex than the playing field, which is rarely true.

Sources: See N. Katz, "Sports Teams as a Model for Workplace Teams: Lessons and Liabilities," *Academy of Management Executive*, August 2001, pp. 56–67; "Talent Inc.," *The New Yorker* online, July 22, 2002, www.newyorker.com/online; and D. Batstone, "HBR Goes CG?," *Worthwhile* magazine, April 14, 2004, www.worthwhilemag.com.

Questions for Review

1 How do you explain the growing popularity of teams in organizations?

2 What is the difference between a group and a team?

3 What are the four types of teams?

4 What conditions or context factors determine whether teams are effective?

5 How can organizations create team players?

6 When is work performed by individuals preferred over work performed by teams?

7 What are three ways in which our understanding of teams differs in a global context?

Discussion Exercise

We have seen that effective work teams are sometimes compared to sports teams. Can we say the same about warfare? There are nine basic principles of war: the objective; the offensive; unity of command; mass; economy of force; maneuver; surprise; security; and simplicity. Discuss these with your classmates and identify how they affect the way team members should interact with one another.

Sources: Department of Military Science, Worcester Polytechnic Institute, "Nine Principles of War," December 30, 2008; Lt. Cmdr. C.E. van Avery, "12 New Principles of War," *Armed Forces Journal*, July 2007.

Ethical Considerations

"Okay, I admit it. I'm not a team player. I work best when I work alone and am left alone," says Zaki, who works at a furniture factory in Morocco.

Zaki's design department has been broken up into three design teams. Maysa has been assigned as team leader, and has explained to Zaki that, when they work together, the strengths of the team will be increased and the weaknesses limited.

Although Zaki respects Maysa, he's not convinced. "I've worked here for four years. I'm very good at what I do. And my performance reviews confirm that. I've been rated in the highest performance category every year I've been here. But now everything is changing. My evaluations

and pay raises are going to depend on how well the team does. And, get this, 50 percent of my evaluation will depend on how well the team does—and this isn't a great team. I'm really frustrated and demoralized. They hired me for my design skills. They knew I wasn't a social type. Now they're forcing me to be a team player. This doesn't play to my strengths at all."

Is it unethical for Zaki's employer to force him to be a team leader? Does this employer have any responsibility to provide Zaki with an alternative that would allow him to continue to work independently? If you were Zaki, how would you respond?

Critical Analysis

TEAM EFFECTIVENESS IN EGYPT

Research by El-Kot and Leat explored a number of top organizations in Egypt and their support of teams from within. They noted that a range of types of team are found in Egyptian organizations. They affect organizational performance and influence team-work effectiveness, and tend to be given a high level of autonomy.

The existence of such a strong culture of teams should not be surprising if you remember Hofstede's[53] findings that the Arab culture is a collectivistic society, with long-term commitment to the family, extended family, or extended relationships.

According to the El-Kot and Leat research, Egyptian managers recommend several factors that appear to increase team effectiveness in organizations:

- having an organizational culture that provides a suitable environment for team work;
- using rewards to create team members' satisfaction;
- setting clear goals so that the team members can aim for specific targets;
- giving the teams more responsibility for making decisions.

By adopting the ideas of team working, Egypt appears to be practicing Western practices. This can perhaps be explained by the fact that Egyptian managers have been exposed to contact with Western organizations for many years.

The question now is why Egyptian companies have integrated teamwork, team autonomy, and suitable rewards systems. Might it be that these changes have only taken place because of foreign investment in Egypt?

Questions

1. What are some advantages and disadvantages of giving teams a lot of autonomy to make decisions?

2. Discuss the contextual factors—adequate resources, leadership and structure, climate of trust, and performance evaluation and reward systems—and how they influence team performance in the Egyptian companies discussed above

3. What kind of team-building activities do you think these companies in Egypt might have their employees engage in?

Source: Ghada El-Kot and Mike Leat (2005), "Investigating Team Work in the Egyptian Context," *Personnel Review*, Vol. 34, No. 2, pp. 246–261.

Research Exercise

Read the questions below, consider the options, and do some relevant research that will allow you to complete the following Teamwork Quiz. There is only one answer to each question. Provide evidence from your research to back up your answers and discuss your responses in class.

1. **When it comes to conflict, the highest-performing teams should:**
   (a) Discourage it
   (b) Encourage conflict about attitudes; discourage conflict about behaviors
   (c) Encourage conflict about tasks; discourage conflict about personalities

2. **When it comes to making decisions, teams are:**
   (a) superior to individuals
   (b) inferior to individuals
   (c) better than the average of its members, but not necessarily as good as the best performer.

3. **When it comes to creativity, teams are:**
   (a) less creative than individuals
   (b) more creative than individuals
   (c) about equally creative.

4. **The most commonly cited problem with teamwork is:**
   (a) trusting one another
   (b) listening to one another
   (c) sustaining motivation.

5. **The most important skills (competencies) that team members need to have are:**
   (a) task and people skills
   (b) speaking and listening skills
   (c) rationality and intuition skills.

Source: L. Thompson, "Leading High Impact Teams," *Kellogg School of Management, Northwestern University*, 2007, www.kellogg.northwestern.edu/execed/Programs/TEAM.aspx. Reprinted by permission of Professor Leigh L. Thompson.

facebook

يساعدك فيس بوك على التواصل والتشارك مع كل الأشخاص في حياتك.

LEARNING OBJECTIVES

This chapter will enable you to:

1 Identify the main functions of communication.

2 Describe the communication process and distinguish between formal and informal communication.

3 Contrast downward, upward, and lateral communication and provide examples of each.

4 Contrast oral, written, and nonverbal communication.

5 Contrast formal communication networks and the grapevine.

6 Analyze the advantages and challenges of electronic communication.

7 Show how channel richness underlies the choice of communication channel.

8 Identify common barriers to effective communication.

9 Show how to overcome the potential problems in cross-cultural communication.

Communication

9

The art of communication is the language of leadership.
—James Humes

Facebook Dominates in the Arab World

Facebook has become a major means of communication in the Middle East and North Africa (MENA) region, with more users than there are people reading newspapers; the total number of Arabic, English, and French newspaper readers is about 14 million, whereas there are more than 15 million registered Facebook users. The overall impression is that newspapers are becoming less interesting. With the exception of the *Daily Star* (Lebanon) and *The National* (Dubai), which are geared towards expats, people are satisfied with the internet for offering interesting lively interaction.

Since the introduction of the Arabic interface for Facebook in March 2009, 3.5 million users have signed up for the service in the region, with Egypt and Saudi Arabia showing the strongest growth. More than 3.4 million Egyptians have Facebook accounts, as well as 2.3 million Saudis and 1.8 million Moroccans. Along with Tunisia and the UAE, these five countries account for 70 percent of Facebook users in the Arab world. The GCC has 5 million Facebook users, with 45 percent from Saudi Arabia and 31 percent from the UAE. North Africa has 7.7 million Facebook users, with Egypt accounting for 44 percent of North African users; Egypt has the largest Facebook community in MENA.

"Arab youth's interest in Facebook is primarily motivated by the website's potential for communication, which far exceeds the capabilities of classical Internet applications such as messenger applications, e-mail groups, and on-line forums. Even when at their best, utilizing webcams and video-conferencing, these services do not adequately satisfy user's appetites for communication and interaction," says Wessam Fauad, an expert in the Field of Social Informatics.

Facebook has changed the lives of many people in the region. It has offered them the channel for open communication and exchange of knowledge, and facilitated interaction. In brief, electronic communication networks such as Facebook have reached a large portion of any society and that has allowed people from all ends of the earth to connect. Establishing rapport is very important to most people, but particularly so to people of the Arab world because social interaction is part of the culture; any way that this can be facilitated is always welcome.

Sources: Based on N. Ungerleider, "Facebook in the Arab world: More popular than newspapers," *trueslant.com*, May 2010, http://trueslant.com/nealungerleider/2010/05/25/facebook-in-the-arab-world-more-popular-than-newspapers/; W. Fauad, "Facebook and the Arab Youth: Social Activism or Cultural Liberation?", *Arab Insight*, March 2009, www.arabinsight.org/aiarticles/220.pdf; Malin Carrington, "Facebook Reach Beats Newspapers in Middle East & North Africa," *Spot On Public Relations*, May 2010, www.pitchengine.com/spotonpr/facebook-reach-beats-newspapers-in-middle-east--north-africa/65841/.

The opening case illustrates the profound effects of electronic communication and social networking. Facebook has become a popular communication channel worldwide, the Arab world being no exception. In this chapter, we'll analyze the power of communication, consider several methods of communication, and look at ways in which it can be made more effective. Consider the following self-assessment to see what your face-to-face communication style is.

Self Assessment Library

WHAT'S MY FACE-TO-FACE COMMUNICATION STYLE?

In the Self-Assessment Library (available online), take assessment II.A.1 (What' My Face-to-Face Communication Style?) and answer the following questions:

1. *How did you score relative to your classmates?*

2. *Do you think your communication style changes depending on the mode of communication (face-to-face, telephone, email, etc.)?*

There are many communication issues. Research indicates that poor communication is probably the most frequently cited source of interpersonal conflict.[1] Because individuals spend nearly 70 percent of their waking hours communicating—writing, reading, speaking, listening—it seems logical to conclude that one of the most challenging forces to successful group performance is a lack of effective communication. In addition, good communication skills are very important to your career success. A 2007 study of recruiters found that they rated communication skills as *the* most important characteristic of an ideal job candidate.[2]

No individual, group, or organization can exist without communication: the transfer of meaning among its members. It is only through transmitting meaning from one person to another that information and ideas can be passed on. It must also be understood. In a group in which one member speaks only German and the others do not know German, the individual speaking German will not be fully understood. Therefore, **communication** must include both the *transfer and the understanding of meaning.*

An idea, no matter how great, is useless until it is transmitted and understood by others. Perfect communication, if there were such a thing, would exist when a thought or an idea was transmitted so that the mental picture perceived by the receiver was exactly the same as that envisioned by the sender. Although elementary in theory, perfect communication is never achieved in practice, for reasons we shall expand on later in the chapter.

Before making too many generalizations concerning communication and problems in communicating effectively, we need to review briefly the functions that communication performs and describe the communication process.

Communication
The transfer and understanding of meaning through verbal and nonverbal messages.

Functions of Communication

1 Identify the main functions of communication.

Communication serves four major functions within a group or organization: control, motivation, emotional expression, and information.[3]

Communication acts to *control* member behavior in several ways. Organizations have authority hierarchies and formal guidelines that employees are required to follow. For instance, when employees are required to communicate any job-related grievance to their immediate boss, to follow their job description, or to follow company policies, communication is performing a control function. But informal communication also controls behavior. When work groups make fun of an employee who produces too much (and makes the rest of the group look bad), they are informally communicating with, and controlling, the member's behavior.

Communication supports *motivation* by clarifying to employees what is to be done, how well they are doing, and what can be done to improve performance. We saw this operating in our review of goal-setting and reinforcement theories in Chapter 5. The formation of specific goals, feedback on progress toward the goals, and reinforcement of desired behavior all stimulate motivation and require communication.

For many employees, their work group is a primary source for social interaction. The communication that takes place within the group is a fundamental mechanism by which members show their frustrations and feelings of satisfaction. Communication, therefore, provides a release for the *emotional expression* of feelings and for fulfillment of social needs.

The final function that communication performs relates to its role in facilitating decision making. It provides the *information* that individuals and groups need to make decisions by transmitting the data to identify and evaluate alternative choices.

No one of these four functions should be seen as being more important than the others. For groups to perform effectively, they need to maintain some form of control over members, stimulate members to perform, provide a means for emotional expression, and make decision choices. You can assume that almost every communication interaction that takes place in a group or an organization performs one or more of these four functions.

Zain Bahrain, part of the global telecom giant Vodafone and formerly known as MTC-Vodafone, aims to be considered a number one choice for employees in Bahrain. The company encourages open channels of communication to strengthen employee development and motivation.

The Communication Process

2 *Describe the communication process and distinguish between formal and informal communication.*

Communication process

The steps between a source and a receiver that result in the transfer and understanding of meaning.

Formal channels

Communication channels established by an organization to transmit messages related to the professional activities of members.

Informal channels

Communication channels that are created spontaneously and that emerge as responses to individual choices.

Before communication can take place, a purpose, expressed as a message to be conveyed, is needed. It passes between a sender and a receiver. The message is encoded (converted to a symbolic form) and passed by way of some medium (channel) to the receiver, who retranslates (decodes) the message initiated by the sender. The result is transfer of meaning from one person to another.[4]

Figure 9-1 shows this **communication process**. The key parts of this model are: (1) the sender, (2) encoding, (3) the message, (4) the channel, (5) decoding, (6) the receiver, (7) noise, and (8) feedback.

The *sender* starts a message by encoding a thought. The *message* is the actual physical product from the sender's *encoding*. When we speak, the speech is the message. When we write, the writing is the message. When we gesture, the movements of our arms and the expressions on our faces are the message.

The *channel* is the medium through which the message travels. It is selected by the sender, who must determine whether to use a formal or informal channel. **Formal channels** are established by the organization and transmit messages that are related to the professional activities of members. They traditionally follow the authority chain within the organization. Other forms of messages, such as personal or social, follow **informal channels** in the organization. These informal channels are spontaneous and emerge as a response to individual choices.[5]

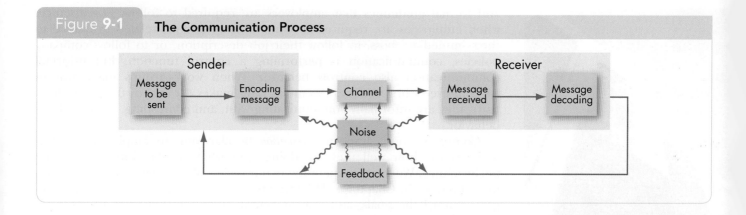

Figure 9-1   The Communication Process

The *receiver* is the object to whom the message is directed. But before the message can be received, the symbols in it must be translated into a form that can be understood by the receiver. This step is the *decoding* of the message. *Noise* represents communication barriers that distort the clarity of the message. Examples of possible noise sources include perceptual problems, information overload, or cultural differences. The final link in the communication process is a feedback loop. *Feedback* is the check on how successful we have been in transferring our messages as originally intended. It determines whether understanding has been achieved.

> **Picture This**
>
> You are the head of the R&D department and one of your researchers has given out confidential information. How do you deal with this situation, and through which communication channel?

Direction of Communication

3 *Contrast downward, upward, and lateral communication and provide examples of each.*

Communication can flow vertically or laterally. The vertical dimension can be further divided into downward and upward directions.[6]

Downward Communication

Communication that flows from one level of a group or organization to a lower level is downward communication. When we think of managers communicating with employees, the downward pattern is the one we are usually thinking of. It's used by group leaders and managers to assign goals, provide job instructions, inform employees of policies and procedures, point out problems that need attention, and offer feedback about performance. But downward communication doesn't have to be oral or face-to-face contact. When management sends letters to employees' homes to advise them of the organization's new sick leave policy, it's using downward communication. Another example of downward communication is an e-mail from a team leader to the members of the team, reminding them of an upcoming deadline.

Downward communication does, however, have problems. First, managers must explain the reasons *why* a decision was made. One study found that employees were twice as likely to be committed to changes when the reasons behind them were fully explained. Although this may seem like common sense, many managers feel they are too busy to explain things, or that explanations will cause conflicts. Evidence clearly indicates, though, that explanations increase employee commitment and support of decisions.[7]

Another problem in downward communication is its one-way nature; generally, managers inform employees but rarely ask for their advice or opinions; they do not listen to their employees. A 2006 study revealed that nearly two-thirds of employees say their boss rarely or never asks their advice. The author of the study noted, "Organizations are always striving for higher employee engagement, but evidence indicates they unnecessarily create fundamental mistakes." People need to be respected and listened to.

What Do You Think?

Do you agree that listening is one of those things that is easy to talk about but difficult to do?

The best communicators are those who explain the reasons behind their downward communications, but also solicit upward communication from the employees they supervise. That leads us to the next direction: Upward communication.

Upward Communication

Upward communication flows to a higher level in the group or organization. It's used to provide feedback to higher-ups, inform them of progress toward goals, and relay current problems. Upward communication keeps managers aware of how employees feel about their jobs, coworkers, and the organization in general. Managers also rely on upward communication for ideas on how things can be improved.

To engage in effective upward communication, try to reduce distractions (meet in a conference room if you can, rather than your boss's office), communicate in headlines not paragraphs (your job is to get your boss's attention, not to engage in discussion), support your headlines with actionable items (what you believe should happen), and prepare an agenda to make sure you use your boss's attention well.[8]

Lateral Communication

When communication takes place among members of the same work group, among members of work groups at the same level, among managers at the same level, or among any other horizontally equivalent personnel, we describe it as lateral communication.

Why would there be a need for horizontal communications if a group or an organization's vertical communications are effective? The answer is that horizontal communication is often necessary to save time and facilitate coordination. Lateral communications can, from management's viewpoint, be good or bad. Because strict adherence to the formal vertical structure for all communications

Mobinil emphasizes the importance of upward and downward communication in its Code of Conduct. This states that "All employees need to communicate honestly, accurately, and regularly to ensure information flow between all departments. Upward and downward communication creates a culture of open communication. Employees are encouraged to express their concerns, ideas, and suggestions in order to have a say in shaping management's decisions [. . .] In reinforcing a transparent culture, management is also committed to announcing any necessary policy/procedure updates and amendments to all employees through appropriate internal communication channels."

Source: Mobinil Code of Conduct (www.mobinil.com/aboutmobinil/ CodeOfConduct.pdf).

can affect the efficient and accurate transfer of information, lateral communications can be beneficial. In such cases, they occur with the knowledge and support of superiors. But they can create dysfunctional conflicts when the formal vertical channels are broken, when members go above or around their superiors to get things done, or when bosses find out that actions have been taken or decisions have been made without their knowledge.

Interpersonal Communication

> **4** *Contrast oral, written, and nonverbal communication.*

How do group members transfer meaning between and among each other? There are three basic methods. People essentially rely on oral, written, and nonverbal communication.

Oral Communication

The main means of sending messages is oral communication. Speeches, formal one-on-one and group discussions, and the informal rumors, or grapevine, are popular forms of oral communication.

The advantages of oral communication are speed and feedback. A verbal message can be conveyed and a response received in very short amounts of time. If the receiver is unsure of the message, rapid feedback allows for early detection by the sender and, hence, allows for early correction. As one professional put it, "Face-to-face communication on a consistent basis is still the best way to get information to and from employees."[9]

The major disadvantage of oral communication surfaces whenever a message has to be passed through a number of people. The more people a message must pass through, the greater the potential problems because each person interprets the message in his or her own way. The message's content, when it reaches its destination, is often very different from that of the original. In an organization, where decisions and other means of communication are verbally passed up and down the authority hierarchy, there are considerable opportunities for messages to become misinterpreted.

International OB

Cultural Differences in Oral Communication

A study by R.S. Zaharna into the cultural differences in communication identified that the Arab and the North American cultures have two distinct perspectives for viewing language and, thus, two differing preferences for structuring persuasive and appealing messages.

A particular distinction has been made between Arabic and American cultures in terms of direct versus indirect communication styles. When comparing communication patterns the two cultures show variations relating to directness versus indirectness, and clarity versus ambiguity. The American cultural preference is for clear and direct communication as evidenced by the common expressions: 'Say what you mean,' 'Don't beat around the bush,' and 'Get to the point'.

Another dominant communication divide relates to value orientations. Americans focus on the 'doing' culture, whereas the Arabs stress a 'being' culture. For example, where an American might emphasize the importance of achievement and its measurement, an Arab would focus on 'what he *is*' rather than 'what he *does*'.

In general, the Arabs prefer indirect, vague, or ambiguous statements, in other words they tend to use language to promote social harmony. Any direct question or answer is risky, since it could expose the other person to a public loss of credibility. In contrast, Americans see such ambiguity as frustrating and confusing: they prefer direct and open communication, which they associate with honesty. Finally, an American tends to give the specifics and details, describing the whole in terms of its parts. In contrast, an Arab speaker would simply describe the whole, without feeling the need to explain the details.

Source: Based on R. S. Zaharna, "Bridging Cultural Differences: American Public Relations Practices & Arab Communication Patterns," *Public Relations Review*, 21 (1995), 241–255. Adapted with permission of Elsevier.

Written Communication

Written communications include memos, letters, fax transmissions, e-mail, instant messaging, organizational periodicals, notices placed on bulletin boards, and any other device that is transmitted via written words or symbols.

Why would a sender choose to use written communications? They're often tangible and verifiable. When they're printed, both the sender and receiver have a record of the communication; and the message can be stored for an indefinite period. If there are questions concerning the content of the message, it is physically available for later reference. This feature is particularly important for complex and lengthy communications. The marketing plan for a new product, for instance, is likely to contain a number of tasks spread out over several months. By putting it in writing, those who have to initiate the plan can readily refer to it over the life of the plan. A final benefit of all written communication comes from the process itself. People are usually more careful with the written word than with the oral word. They're forced to think more thoroughly about what they want to convey in a written message than in a spoken one. Thus, written communications are more likely to be well thought out, logical, and clear.

Of course, written messages have drawbacks. They're time-consuming. You could convey far more information to a college instructor in a one-hour oral exam than in a one-hour written exam. In fact, you could probably say the same thing in 10 to 15 minutes that it would take you an hour to write. So, although writing may be more precise, it also consumes a great deal of time. The other major disadvantage is feedback, or lack of it. Oral communication allows the receiver to respond rapidly. Written communication, however, does not have a built-in feedback mechanism. The result is that the mailing of a memo is no assurance that it has been received, and, if received, there is no guarantee the recipient will interpret it as the sender intended. An accurate summary presents feedback evidence that the message has been received and understood.

Nonverbal Communication

Every time we verbally give a message to someone, we also impart a nonverbal message. In some instances, the nonverbal component may stand alone. No discussion of communication would be complete without consideration of *nonverbal communication*—which includes body movements, tone of voice or emphasis we give to words, facial expressions, and the physical distance between the sender and receiver.

It can be argued that every *body movement* has a meaning, and no movement is accidental. For example, through body language, we say, "Help me, I'm lonely;" or "Leave me alone, I'm depressed." Rarely do we send our messages consciously. We act out our state of being with nonverbal body language. We lift one eyebrow for disbelief. We rub our noses for puzzlement. We clasp our arms to isolate ourselves or to protect ourselves. We shrug our shoulders for indifference, wink one eye for intimacy, tap our fingers for impatience, slap our forehead for forgetfulness.[10]

The two most important messages that body language conveys are (1) the extent to which an individual likes another and is interested in his or her views and (2) the relative perceived status between a sender and receiver.[11] For instance, we're more likely to position ourselves closer to people we like and touch them more often. Similarly, if you feel that you're of higher status than another, you're more likely to display body movements—such as crossed legs or a slouched seated position—that reflect a casual and relaxed manner.[12]

Body language adds to, and often complicates, verbal communication. A body position or movement does not by itself have a precise or universal meaning, but when it is linked with spoken language, it gives fuller meaning to a sender's message.

If you read the minutes of a meeting, you wouldn't grasp the impact of what was said in the same way you would if you had been there or if you saw the meeting on video. Why? There is no record of nonverbal communication. The emphasis given to words or phrases is missing. Table 9-1 illustrates how *intonations* can change the meaning of a message. *Facial expressions* also convey meaning. A sad face says something different from a smile. Facial expressions, along with voice tones, can show arrogance, aggressiveness, fear, shyness, and other characteristics that would never be communicated if you read a transcript of what had been said.

The way individuals space themselves in terms of *physical distance* also has meaning. What is considered proper spacing is largely dependent on cultural norms. For example, what is considered a businesslike distance in some European countries would be viewed as intimate in many parts of North America. If someone stands closer to you than is considered appropriate, it may indicate aggressiveness or sexual interest; if farther away than usual, it may mean disinterest or displeasure with what is being said. In the Arab culture, people tend to use a closer physical proximity when communicating.

It's important for the receiver to be alert to these nonverbal aspects of communication. You should look for nonverbal cues as well as listen to the literal meaning of a sender's words. You should particularly be aware of contradictions between the messages. Your boss may say I am free to talk to you about an urgent budget problem, but you may see nonverbal signals suggesting that this is not the time to discuss the subject. Regardless of what is being said, an individual who frequently looks at a wristwatch is giving the message that the

TABLE 9-1   Intonations: It's the Way You Say It!

Change your tone and you change your meaning:

Placement of the emphasis	What it means
Why don't I take *you* to dinner tonight?	I was going to take someone else.
Why don't *I* take you to dinner tonight?	Instead of the guy you were going with.
Why ***don't*** I take you to dinner tonight?	I'm trying to find a reason why I **shouldn't** take you.
Why don't I take you to dinner tonight?	Do you have a problem with me?
Why don't I *take* you to dinner tonight?	Instead of going on your own.
Why don't I take you to *dinner* tonight?	Instead of lunch tomorrow.
Why don't I take you to dinner *tonight*?	Not tomorrow night.

Source: Based on M. Kiely, "When 'No' Means 'Yes,'" *Marketing*, October 1993, pp. 7–9. Reproduced in A. Huczynski and D. Buchanan, *Organizational Behavior*, 4th ed. (Essex, UK: Pearson Education, 2001), p. 194.

conversation should be finished. We misinform others when we express one message verbally, such as trust, but nonverbally communicate a contradictory message that reads, "I don't have confidence in you."

Organizational Communication

> 5 *Contrast formal communication networks and the grapevine.*

In this section, we move from interpersonal communication to organizational communication. Our first focus will be to describe and distinguish formal networks and the grapevine. In the following section we discuss technological innovations in communication.

Formal Small-Group Networks

Formal organizational networks can be very complicated. They can, for instance, include hundreds of people and a half-dozen or more hierarchical levels. To simplify our discussion, we've divided these networks into three common small groups of five people each (see Figure 9-2). These three networks are the chain,

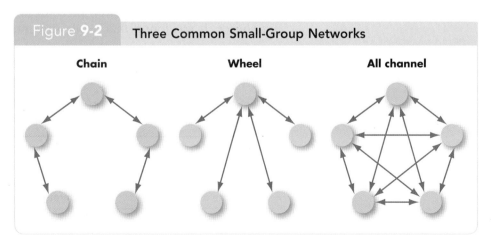

Figure 9-2   Three Common Small-Group Networks

Chain   Wheel   All channel

wheel, and all channel. Although these three networks have been extremely simplified, they allow us to describe the unique qualities of each.

The *chain* rigidly follows the formal chain of command. This network shows the communication channels you might find in a rigid three-level organization. The *wheel* relies on a central figure to act as the passage for all of the group's communication. It simulates the communication network you would find on a team with a strong leader. The *all-channel* network permits all group members to actively communicate with each other. The all-channel network is most often characterized in practice by self-managed teams, in which all group members are free to contribute and no one person takes on a leadership role.

As Table 9-2 demonstrates, the effectiveness of each network depends on the dependent variable you're concerned about. For instance, the structure of the wheel facilitates the emergence of a leader; the all-channel network is best if you are concerned with having high member satisfaction; and the chain is best if accuracy is most important. That is, Table 9-2 leads us to the conclusion that no single network will be best for all occasions; it depends on the situation and the tasks involved.

The Grapevine

Grapevine
An organization's informal communication network.

The formal system is not the only communication network in a group or organization. There is also an informal one called the **grapevine**.[13] Although the grapevine may be informal, it's still an important source of information. For instance, a survey found that 75 percent of employees hear about matters first through rumors on the grapevine.[14]

> ### What Do You Think?
>
> *What kind of internal environment can the 'grapevine' create?*

The grapevine has three main characteristics.[15] First, it is not controlled by management. Second, it is seen by most employees as being more believable and reliable than formal information issued by top management. Finally, it is largely used to serve the self-interests of the people within it.

One of the most famous studies of the grapevine investigated the communication pattern among 67 managerial personnel in a small manufacturing firm.[16] The basic approach used was to learn from each communication recipient how he or she first received a given piece of information and then trace it back to its source. It was found that, while the grapevine was an important source of

TABLE 9-2 Small-Group Networks and Effective Criteria			
Criteria	Chain	Wheel	All Channel
Speed	Moderate	Fast	Fast
Accuracy	High	High	Moderate
Emergence of a leader	Moderate	High	None
Member satisfaction	Moderate	Low	High

information, only 10 percent of the executives acted as liaison individuals (that is, passed the information on to more than one other person). For example, when one executive decided to resign to enter the insurance business, 81 percent of the executives knew about it, but only 11 percent transmitted this information to others.

Is the information that flows along the grapevine accurate? The evidence indicates that about 75 percent of what is carried is accurate.[17] But what conditions foster an active grapevine? What gets the rumor wheel rolling?

It's often assumed that rumors start because they make interesting gossip. This is rarely the case. Rumors emerge as a response to situations that are *important* to us, when there is *ambiguity*, and under conditions that cause *anxiety*.[18] The fact that work situations frequently contain these three elements explains why rumors flourish in organizations. The secrecy and competition that typically prevail in large organizations—around issues such as the appointment of new bosses, the relocation of offices, downsizing decisions, and the realignment of work assignments—create conditions that encourage and sustain rumors on the grapevine. A rumor will persist either until the wants and expectations creating the uncertainty underlying the rumor are fulfilled or until the anxiety is reduced.

What can we conclude from the preceding discussion? Certainly the grapevine is an important part of any group or organization communication network and is well worth understanding. It gives managers a feel for the morale of their organization, identifies issues that employees consider important, and helps understand employee anxieties. The grapevine also serves employees' needs: small talk serves to create a sense of closeness and friendship among those who share information, although research suggests that it often does so at the expense of those in the 'out' group.[19]

Can management entirely eliminate rumors? No. What management should do, however, is minimize the negative consequences of rumors by limiting their range and impact. Box 9-1 offers a few suggestions for minimizing those negative consequences.

Electronic Communications

6 Analyze the advantages and challenges of electronic communication.

An indispensable medium of communication in today's organizations is electronic. Electronic communications include e-mail, instant messaging and text messaging, networking software, internet or web logs (blogs), and video-conferencing. Let's discuss each.

BOX 9-1
Suggestions for Reducing the Negative Consequences of Rumors

1. Announce timetables for making important decisions.

2. Explain decisions and behaviors that may appear inconsistent or secretive.

3. Emphasize the downside, as well as the upside, of current decisions and future plans.

4. Openly discuss worst-case possibilities—it is almost never as anxiety provoking as the unspoken fantasy.

Source: Adapted from L. Hirschhorn, "Managing Rumors," in L. Hirschhorn (ed.), *Cutting Back* (San Francisco: Jossey-Bass, 1983), pp. 54–56. Used with permission.

E-mail E-mail uses the internet to transmit and receive computer-generated text and documents. Its growth has been spectacular, and its use is now so dominating that it's hard to imagine life without it.

When Bill Gates goes to work, he has three screens synchronized, two of which are for e-mail (the other is Internet Explorer). As a communication tool, e-mail has a long list of benefits. E-mail messages can be quickly written, edited, and stored. They can be distributed to one person or thousands with a click of a mouse. They can be read at the convenience of the recipient. In addition, the cost of sending formal e-mail messages to employees is a fraction of the cost of printing, duplicating, and distributing a comparable letter or brochure.[20]

However, e-mail, of course, is not without drawbacks. The following are some of the most significant limitations of e-mail and recommendations as to what organizations should do to reduce or eliminate these problems:

- *Misinterpreting the message.* It's true that we often misinterpret verbal messages, but the potential for misinterpretation with e-mail is even greater. If you're sending an important message, make sure you reread it for clarity. And if you're upset about the presumed tone of someone else's message, keep in mind that you may be misinterpreting it.[21]

- *Communicating negative messages.* When companies have negative information to communicate, managers need to think carefully. E-mail may not be the best way to communicate the message. Employees need to be careful communicating negative messages via e-mail, too. For example, if an employee wrote an e-mail critical of some strategic decisions made by his or her employer, it could have damaging effects for both the company and the employee.

- *Overuse of e-mail.* An estimated 6 trillion e-mails are sent every year, and someone has to answer all those messages! As people become established in their careers and their responsibilities expand, so do their inboxes. A survey of Canadian managers revealed that 58 percent spent two to four hours per day reading and responding to e-mails.

- *E-mail emotions.* We tend to think of e-mail as a sort of faceless form of communication. But that doesn't mean it's unemotional. As you no doubt know, e-mails are often highly emotional. E-mail tends to have an effect on people; senders write things they'd never be comfortable saying in person. Facial expressions tend to temper our emotional expressions, but in e-mail, there is no other face to look at, and so many of us fire away. An increasingly common way of communicating emotions in e-mail is with emoticons. For example, Yahoo!'s e-mail software allows the user to pick from 32 emoticons. Although emoticons used to be considered for personal use only, increasingly adults are using them in business e-mails. Still, some see them as too informal for business use.

  In brief, when others send negative messages, remain calm and try not to respond similarly.

- *Privacy concerns.* There are two privacy issues with e-mail. First, you need to be aware that your e-mails may be, and often are, monitored. Also, you can't always trust that the recipient of your e-mail will keep it confidential. For these reasons, you shouldn't write anything you wouldn't want made public. Second, you need to exercise caution in forwarding e-mail from your company's e-mail account to a personal, or "public," (for example, Gmail, Yahoo!, MSN) e-mail account. These accounts often aren't as secure as corporate accounts, so when you forward a company e-mail to them, you may be violating your organization's policy or unintentionally disclosing confidential data. Many employers hire vendors that sift through e-mails, using software to catch not only the obvious ('insider trading') but the vague ('that thing we talked about') or guilt ridden ('regret'). Another survey revealed that nearly 40 percent of companies have employees whose only job is to read other employees' e-mail. Remember, you are being watched—so be careful what you e-mail![22] This is also very true of companies in the Arab world.

Instant Messaging and Text Messaging   Like e-mail, instant messaging (IM) and text messaging (TM) use electronic messages. Unlike e-mail, though, IM and TM are either in 'real' time (IM) or use portable communication devices (TM). In just a few years, IM/TM is everywhere. As you no doubt know from experience, IM is usually sent via desktop or laptop computer, whereas TM is transmitted via cellphones or handheld devices such as Blackberrys.

What Do You Think?

Text messaging or SMSs are a common means of communication today. Do you believe that they really give the correct message or do they open the door for misinterpretations?

Despite their advantages, IM and TM aren't going to replace e-mail. E-mail is still probably a better device for conveying long messages that need to be saved. IM is preferable for one- or two-line messages that would take up space in an e-mail inbox. On the downside, some IM/TM users find the technology distracting. Their continual presence can make it hard for employees to concentrate and stay focused.

One other point: It's important not to let the informality of text messaging ("omg! r u serious? brb") spill over into business e-mails. Many prefer to keep

Malaysia's airline AirAsia is taking advantage of the flexibility of text messaging to make it more convenient for travelers to book flights. AirAsia flight attendants are shown here with a mobile phone billboard during the launch of the world's first airline booking through a short messaging service (SMS). The SMS makes it easier for travelers to book their seats by text messaging from the convenience of their mobile phone wherever they are.

business communication relatively formal. A survey of employers revealed that 58 percent rate grammar, spelling, and punctuation as 'very important' in e-mail messages.[23] By making sure your professional communications are, well, professional, you'll show yourself to be mature and serious. That doesn't mean, of course, that you have to give up TM or IM; you just need to maintain the boundaries between how you communicate with your friends and how you communicate professionally.

Networking Software   Nowhere has communication been transformed more than in the area of networking. You are without a doubt familiar with and perhaps a user of social networking platforms such as Facebook, MySpace, and Twitter. In the past year there has been a massive increase in Facebook and Twitter use in the Arab world.

Rather than being one huge site, Facebook, which has over 500 million active users, is actually composed of separate networks based on schools, companies, or regions. It might surprise you to learn that individuals over 25 are the fastest-growing users of Facebook.

To get the most out of social networks, while avoiding irritating your contacts, use them 'for high-value items only'—not as an everyday or even every-week tool. Also, remember that a prospective employer might check your MySpace or Facebook entry. In fact, some entrepreneurs have developed software that mines such websites for companies (or individuals) that want to check up on a job applicant (or potential date). So keep in mind that what you post may be read by people other than your intended contacts.[24]

Web Logs (Blogs)   Web logs (blogs) are websites that give comments or criticism about a single person or company, and they are usually updated daily.

Thousands of Microsoft employees have blogs. Google, General Motors, Nike, IBM, and many other large organizations also have corporate blogs. In February 2011, Business to Community identified the ten most successful blogs in the world. One of them was the blog of Caterpillar (one of leading names in

Web log (blog)

A website where entries are written, generally displayed in reverse chronological order, about news, events, and personal diary entries.

Facebook founder and CEO Mark Zuckerberg continues to transform communication. He announced a new platform strategy that allows third parties to develop services on the Facebook site, offering communication opportunities for business entrepreneurs. For Zuckerberg, Facebook is more than a social networking site. He describes it as a communication tool that facilitates the flow of information between users and their friends, family members, and professional connections.

Source: "Facebook Expands Into MySpace's Territory", *The New York Times*, May 2007.

construction in the Arab world.) The objective of Caterpillar is to engage both customers and the community in problem solving.

So what's the downside? Although some companies have policies in place governing the content of blogs, many don't, and 39 percent of individual bloggers say they have posted comments that could be considered as harmful to their company's reputation. Many bloggers think their personal blogs are outside their employer's reach, but if someone else in the company happens to read a blog entry, there is nothing to keep him or her from sharing that information with others, and the employee could be dismissed as a result.

Video-Conferencing   *Video-conferencing* permits employees in an organization to have meetings with people at different locations. Live audio and video images of members allow them to see, hear, and talk with each other. Video-conferencing technology, in effect, allows employees to conduct interactive meetings without the necessity of all being physically in the same location.

To illustrate, Notre Dame University in Lebanon conducts video-conferences across its campuses within Lebanon. These can be for faculty meetings or for actual classroom interaction between instructors and students. Moreover, cameras and microphones are being attached to individual computers so that people can participate in video conferences without even leaving their desks. As the cost of this technology drops, video-conferencing is likely to be increasingly seen as an alternative to expensive and time-consuming travel.

Knowledge Management

Knowledge management (KM)

The process of organizing and distributing an organization's collective wisdom so the right information gets to the right people at the right time.

Our final topic under organizational communication is **knowledge management (KM)**. This is a process of organizing and distributing an organization's collective wisdom so the right information gets to the right people at the right time. When done properly, KM provides an organization with both a competitive edge and improved organizational performance because it makes its employees smarter. It can also help control leaks of important company information so that an organization's competitive advantage is preserved for as long as possible.

Effective KM begins by identifying what knowledge matters to the organization.[25] Management needs to review processes to identify those that provide the most value. Then it can develop computer networks and databases that can make that information readily available to the people who need it the most. But KM won't work unless the culture supports sharing of information.[26] As we'll show in Chapter 11, information that is important and scarce can be a source of power. And people who hold that power are often reluctant to share it with others. So KM requires an organizational culture that promotes, values, and rewards sharing knowledge. Finally, KM must provide the mechanisms and the motivation for employees to share knowledge that they find useful on the job and that enables them to achieve better performance.[27] *More* knowledge isn't necessarily *better* knowledge. Information overload needs to be avoided by designing the system to capture only relevant information and then organizing it so it can be quickly accessed by the people whom it can help.

Finally, security is a huge concern with any KM system. In response to the risk of company information being leaked, most companies actively monitor employee internet use and e-mail records, and some even use video surveillance and record phone conversations. Necessary though they may be, such surveillance and monitoring practices may seem an invasion of employees' privacy. An organization can address employee concerns by involving them in the creation of information-security policies, and giving them some control over how their personal information is used.[28]

OB in the News

Communication in the Arab World

Without a doubt, effective communication processes and strategies are critical to enhanced organizational performance. This is applicable to organizations all over the world regardless of culture. However, in the Arab world, individuals believe that open communication is not practiced in our organizations. What do you think? Organizations can only experience a comfortable corporate culture if internal communication is effective. Accordingly, if employees are happy with the internal environment, then they are probably going to be more productive.

It is fair to say that there are both advantages and disadvantages to internal communication. The positive consequences focus on enhancing the sense of belongingness to the organization. Whereas the negative consequences can affect the organization's image and may damage the external communication efforts.

Organizations in general, and Arab organizations in particular, must ensure that a well-established communication strategy is implemented. Two major communication channels that organizations can benefit from are the intranet and the newsletter. These demonstrate managerial support of transparency and offer the opportunity for employees to share knowledge, opinions, and suggestions. Such a policy should definitely be promoted by the inspiration and participative behavior of leaders.

Moreover, when organizations encourage employees to engage in social activities, reward them for their contributions, and help their development by conducting workshops and training sessions. Employees will feel more loyal to the organization, their self-esteem, sense of security, and morale are boosted and, thus, their commitment to the organization's vision, mission, and goals increase.

Organizations should have better comprehension of their communication strategies and how they affect performance and profitability. If we get too concerned with external communication, we lose direction and this, in turn, weakens internal communication channels. We must never forget that satisfied and secure employees are the building blocks of successful organizations.

Source: Mark Helou and Ramsay G. Najjar, "Internal Communication and Corporate Inner Peace," *Executive* magazine, Issue 114, January, 2009.

Saudi Basic Industries Corporation (SABIC) is one of the world's leading manufacturers of chemicals, fertilizers, plastics, and metals. It has created a global network, supplying these materials to producers of many of the world's most popular products. To ensure that there is effective flow of information between SABIC and its customers, they aim to identify and exploit new channels for networking and knowledge sharing.

Choice of Communication Channel

7 Show how channel richness underlies the choice of communication channel.

Channel richness

The amount of information that can be transmitted during a communication episode.

Why do people choose one channel of communication over another—for instance, a phone call instead of a face-to-face talk? Is there any general insight we might be able to provide regarding choice of communication channel? The answer to this question is a qualified 'yes.' A model of media richness has been developed to explain channel selection among managers.[29]

Research has found that channels differ in their capacity to convey information. Some are rich in that they have the ability to (1) handle multiple cues simultaneously, (2) facilitate rapid feedback, and (3) be very personal. Others are narrow in that they score low on these three factors. As Figure 9-3 illustrates, face-to-face conversation scores highest in terms of **channel richness** because it provides for the maximum amount of information to be transmitted during a communication episode. That is, it offers multiple information cues (words, postures, facial expressions, gestures, and intonations), immediate feedback (verbal and nonverbal), and the personal touch of 'being there.' Impersonal written media such as formal reports and bulletins rate lowest in richness.

The choice of one channel over another depends on whether the message is routine or nonroutine. The former types of messages tend to be straightforward and have a minimum of ambiguity. The latter are likely to be complicated and have the potential for misunderstanding. Managers can communicate routine messages efficiently through channels that are lower in richness. However, they can communicate nonroutine messages effectively only by selecting rich channels.

Evidence indicates that high-performing managers tend to be more media sensitive than low-performing managers.[30] That is, they're better able to match appropriate media richness with the ambiguity involved in the communication.

The media richness model is consistent with organizational trends and practices of the past decade. It is not just coincidence that more and more senior managers have been using meetings to facilitate communication and regularly leaving the isolated safety of their executive offices to manage by walking around. These executives are relying on richer channels of communication to transmit the more ambiguous messages they need to convey. The past decade

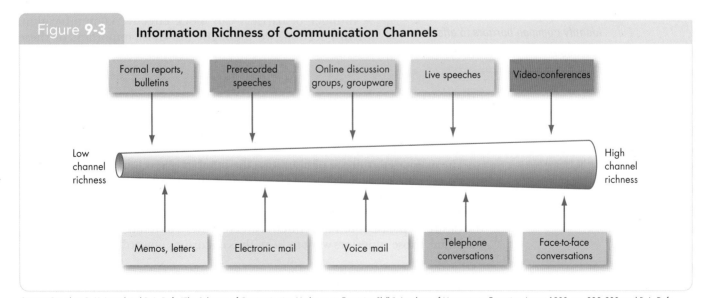

Figure **9-3** **Information Richness of Communication Channels**

Sources: Based on R. H. Lengel and R. L. Daft, "The Selection of Communication Media as an Executive Skill," *Academy of Management Executive*, August 1988, pp. 225–232; and R. L. Daft and R. H. Lengel, "Organizational Information Requirements, Media Richness, and Structural Design," *Managerial Science*, May 1996, pp. 554–572. Reproduced from R. L. Daft and R. A. Noe, *Organizational Behavior* (Fort Worth, TX: Harcourt, 2001), p. 311.

Yahoo! Middle East is a result of the acquisition of Maktoob.com by Yahoo! in 2009. The objective was to have the site as a destination of choice for users in the Middle East, offering them opportunities for interaction and effective exchange of information. The partnership added to Yahoo!'s existing services by delivering Arabic-language content and services. In March, 2010, Anas Abbar was appointed Head of Product and Product Marketing Management to cover global and regional products in the region. Abbar offered 18 years' related experience, having been involved in enabling the use of the Arabic language on the Microsoft platform of communication.

Source: "Yahoo! Middle East announces new appointment," March, 2010, www.zawya.com.

has been characterized by organizations closing facilities, imposing large lay-offs, restructuring, merging, consolidating, and introducing new products and services at an accelerated pace—all nonroutine messages high in ambiguity and requiring the use of channels that can convey a large amount of information. It is not surprising, therefore, to see the most effective managers expanding their use of rich channels.

Barriers to Effective Communication

8 *Identify common barriers to effective communication.*

A number of barriers can block effective communication. In this section, we highlight the most important of these barriers.

Filtering

Filtering

A sender's manipulation of information so that it will be seen more favorably by the receiver.

Filtering refers to a sender's information that will be seen as positive by the receiver. For example, when a manager tells his boss what he feels his boss wants to hear, he is filtering information.

The major determinant of filtering is the number of levels in an organization's structure. The more vertical levels in the organization's hierarchy, the more opportunities there are for filtering. But you can expect some filtering to occur wherever there are status differences. Factors such as fear of giving bad news and the desire to please one's boss often lead employees to tell their superiors what they think those superiors want to hear, thus distorting upward communications.

Selective Perception

Selective perception is when the receivers in the communication process selectively see and hear based on their needs, motivations, experience, background, and other personal characteristics. Receivers also project their interests and expectations into communications as they decode them. An employment interviewer who expects one female job applicant to put her family ahead of her career is likely to see that in all female applicants, regardless of whether the applicants actually feel that way. As we said in Chapter 4, we don't see reality; we interpret what we see and call it reality.

Information Overload

Information overload

A condition in which information inflow exceeds an individual's processing capacity.

Individuals have a finite capacity for processing data. When the information we have to work with exceeds our processing capacity, the result is **information overload**. And with e-mails, IM, phone calls, faxes, meetings, and the need to keep current in one's field, the potential for today's managers and professionals to suffer from information overload is high.

What happens when individuals have more information than they can sort out and use? They tend to select, ignore, pass over, or forget information. Or they may put off further processing until the overload situation is over. In general, the result is lost information and less effective communication.

Emotions

How the receiver feels at the time of receipt of a communication influences how he or she interprets it. The same message received when you're angry is often interpreted differently than it is when you're happy. Extreme emotions such as extreme happiness or depression are most likely to interfere with effective communication. In such instances, we are most ready to disregard our rational and objective thinking processes and substitute emotional judgments.

Language

Even when we're communicating in the same language, words mean different things to different people. Age and context are two of the biggest factors that influence the language a person uses and the definitions he or she gives to words. In particular, jargon—language that is only common to those in the same profession—must be avoided.

Although we probably speak a common language—English or Arabic—our use of that language is far from uniform. If we knew how each of us modified the language, communication difficulties would be minimized. The problem is that members in an organization usually don't know how those with whom they interact have modified the language. Senders tend to assume that the words and terms they use mean the same to the receiver as they do to them. This is especially important in the Arab world, as although most people's first language will be Arabic, a lot of business is carried out in English.

Communication Apprehension

Communication apprehension

Undue tension and anxiety about oral communication, written communication, or both.

Another major barrier to effective communication is that some people—an estimated 5 to 20 percent of the population[31]—suffer from debilitating **communication apprehension**, or anxiety. Lots of people are afraid of speaking in front of a group, but communication apprehension is a more serious problem because it affects a whole category of communication techniques. People who suffer from it experience tension and anxiety in oral communication, written communication, or both.[32] For example, oral apprehensives may find it extremely difficult to talk with others face-to-face or may become extremely anxious when they have to use the telephone. As a result, they may rely on memos or faxes to convey messages when a phone call would be not only faster but also more appropriate.

Gender Differences

Gender differences are sometimes a barrier to effective communication. Deborah Tannen's research shows that men tend to use talk to emphasize status, whereas women tend to use it to create connections. These tendencies, of course, don't apply to *every* man and *every* woman. As Tannen puts it, her generalization means "a larger percentage of women or men *as a group* talk in a particular way, or individual women and men *are more likely* to talk one way or the other."[33] She has found that women speak and hear a language of connection and intimacy; men speak and hear a language of status, power, and independence. So, for many men, conversations are primarily a means to preserve independence and maintain status in a hierarchical social order. For many women, conversations are negotiations for closeness in which people try to seek and give confirmation and support.

For example, men complain that women talk on and on about their problems. Women criticize men for not listening. What's happening is that when men hear a problem, they frequently assert their desire for independence and control by offering solutions. Many women, on the other hand, view telling a problem as a means to promote closeness. The women present the problem to gain support and connection and this contributes to distancing men and women in their efforts to communicate.

'Politically Correct' Communication

A final barrier to effective communication is politically correct communication, communication so concerned with being inoffensive that meaning and simplicity are lost or free expression is hindered.

There are plenty of words and phrases we can use that do not offend others. But there are also situations in which our desire to avoid offense blocks communication by keeping us from saying what's really on our mind or changes our communication in such a way as to make it unclear.

Certain words can and do stereotype, intimidate, and insult individuals. In an increasingly diverse workforce, we must be sensitive to how words might offend others. For example, CNN fined its broadcasters for using the word *foreign* instead of *international*. But there's a downside to political correctness: it can complicate our vocabulary, making it more difficult for people to communicate. To illustrate, you probably know what these three terms mean: *garbage, quotas,* and *women*. But each of these words also has been found to offend one or more groups. They've been replaced with terms such as *postconsumer waste materials, educational equity,* and *people of gender*. The problem is that this latter group of terms is much less likely to convey a uniform message than the words they replaced. By removing certain words from our vocabulary, we make it harder to communicate accurately. When we further replace these words with new terms whose meanings are less well understood, we reduce the likelihood that our messages will be received as we intended them.

In sum, we must be sensitive to how our choice of words might offend others. But we also have to be careful not to sanitize our language to the point at which it limits clarity of communication. There is no simple solution to this dilemma. However, you should be aware of the trade-offs and the need to find a proper balance.

Global Implications

9 *Show how to overcome the potential problems in cross-cultural communication.*

Effective communication is difficult under the best of conditions. Cross-cultural factors clearly create the potential for increased communication problems. This is illustrated in Figure 9-4. A gesture that is well understood and acceptable in one culture can be meaningless in another. Unfortunately, as business has become more global, companies' communication approaches have not stayed aware of this.

Cultural Barriers

One author has identified four specific problems related to language difficulties in cross-cultural communications.[34]

First, there are *barriers caused by semantics.* As we've noted previously, words mean different things to different people. This is particularly true for people from different national cultures. Some words, for instance, don't translate between cultures. Understanding the word *sisu* will help you in communicating with people from Finland, but this word is untranslatable into English. It means something similar to having "guts" or "to be persistent."

Second, there are *barriers caused by word connotations.* Words imply different things in different languages. Negotiations between Western and Japanese

Figure 9-4	Hand Gestures Mean Different Things in Different Countries

The A-OK Sign

In the United States, this is just a friendly sign for 'All right!' or 'Good going.' In Australia and Islamic countries, it is equivalent to what generations of high school students know as 'flipping the bird.'

The 'Hook'em Horns' Sign

This sign encourages University of Texas athletes, and it's a good luck gesture in Brazil and Venezuela. In parts of Africa, it is a curse. In Italy, it is signaling to another that 'your spouse is being unfaithful.'

'V' for Victory Sign

In many parts of the world, this means 'victory' or 'peace.' In England, if the palm and fingers face inward, it means 'Up yours!' especially if executed with an upward jerk of the fingers.

Finger-Beckoning Sign

This sign means 'come here' in the United States. In Malaysia, it is used only for calling animals. In Indonesia and Australia, it is used for beckoning 'ladies of the night.'

Source: "What's A-O-K in the USA Is Lewd and Worthless Beyond," *New York Times*, August 18, 1996, p. E7. From Roger E. Axtell, *Gestures: The Do's and Taboos of Body Language Around the World.* Copyright © 1991. Reproduced with permission of John Wiley & Sons, Inc.

International OB

Lost in Translation?

In global commerce, language can be a barrier to conducting business effectively. Many US companies have overseas parents, including DaimlerChrysler AG, Bertelsmann, Diageo PLC, and Anglo-Dutch Unilever PLC. Similarly, many companies have an overseas presence; for example, Ford has manufacturing plants in Belgium, Germany, Spain, Sweden, Turkey, and the United Kingdom, and BMW has assembly plants in Indonesia, Egypt, Malaysia, Thailand, and India. To make matters more complicated, as a result of mergers and acquisitions, companies are often owned by multiple overseas parents, creating an even greater strain on communication. Although English is the dominant language at many multinational companies, failing to speak a host country's language can make it tougher for

managers to do their jobs well, especially if they are misinterpreted or if they misinterpret what others are saying. Such communication problems make it tougher to conduct business effectively and efficiently and may result in lost business opportunities.

To avoid communication problems, many companies require their managers to learn the local language. For example, German-based Siemens requires its managers to learn the language of their host country. Ernst Behrens, the head of Siemens's China operations, learned to speak Mandarin fluently. Robert Kimmett, a former Siemens board member, believes that learning a host country's language gives managers "a better grasp of what is going on inside a company . . . not just the facts and figures but also texture and nuance."

However, learning a foreign language can be difficult for managers. The challenge for Western managers is often deepened when the language is very different, for example Mandarin or Arabic. To compensate, Western managers sometimes rely solely on body language and facial expressions to communicate. The problem? Cultural differences in these nonverbal forms of communication may result in serious misunderstandings. To avoid this pitfall, managers should to familiarize themselves with their host country's culture.

Source: Based on K. Kanhold, D. Bilefsky, M. Karnitschnig, and G. Parker, "Lost in Translation? Managers at Multinationals May Miss the Job's Nuances If They Speak Only English," *Wall Street Journal*, May 18, 2004, p. B.1.

executives, for instance, can be difficult because the Japanese word *hai* translates as 'yes,' but its connotation is 'yes, I'm listening' rather than 'yes, I agree.'

Third are *barriers caused by tone differences*. In some cultures, language is formal, and in others, it's informal. In some cultures, the tone changes, depending on the context: People speak differently at home, in social situations, and at work. Using a personal, informal style in a situation in which a more formal style is expected can be embarrassing and off-putting.

Fourth, there are *barriers caused by differences among perceptions*. People who speak different languages actually view the world in different ways. Eskimos perceive snow differently because they have many words for it. People from Thailand perceive 'no' differently than do other nationalities because the former have no such word in their vocabulary.

Cultural Context

A better understanding of the cultural barriers just discussed and their implications for communicating across cultures can be achieved by considering the concepts of high- and low-context cultures.[35]

Cultures tend to differ in the importance to which context influences the meaning that individuals take from what is actually said or written in light of who the other person is. Countries such as China, Korea, Japan, Vietnam, and Arab countries are **high-context cultures** (see Figure 9.5). They rely heavily on nonverbal and subtle situational cues in communicating with others. That is,

High-context cultures

Cultures that rely heavily on nonverbal and subtle situational cues in communication.

Figure 9-5   High- Versus Low-Context Cultures

High context

Chinese
Korean
Japanese
Vietnamese
Arab
Greek
Spanish
Italian
English
North American
Scandinavian
Swiss
German

Low context

Low-context cultures

Cultures that rely heavily on words to convey meaning in communication.

what is *not* said may be more significant than what *is* said, and a person's official status, place in society, and reputation carry considerable weight in communications. In contrast, people from Europe and North America reflect their **low-context cultures**. They rely essentially on words to convey meaning. Body language and formal titles are secondary to spoken and written words.

What do these contextual differences mean in terms of communication? Actually, quite a lot. Communication in high-context cultures implies considerably more trust by both parties. What may appear, to an outsider, as casual and insignificant conversation is important because it reflects the desire to build a relationship and create trust. Oral agreements imply strong commitments in high-context cultures. And who you are—your age, seniority, rank in the organization—is highly valued and heavily influences your credibility. But in low-context cultures, enforceable contracts tend to be in writing, precisely worded, and highly legalistic. Similarly, low-context cultures value directness. Managers are expected to be explicit and precise in conveying intended meaning. It's quite different in high-context cultures, in which managers tend to "make suggestions" rather than give orders.

A Cultural Guide

When communicating with people from a different culture, what can you do to reduce misperceptions, misinterpretations, and misevaluations? You can begin by trying to assess the cultural context and listening to others, and the coming self-assessment exercise can be helpful. You're likely to have fewer difficulties if people come from a similar cultural context to you. In addition, the following four rules can be helpful:[36]

1. *Assume differences until similarity is proven.* Most of us assume that others are more similar to us than they actually are. But people from different countries are often very different from us. You are therefore far less likely to make an error if you assume that others are different from you rather than assume similarity until difference is proven.
2. *Emphasize description rather than interpretation or evaluation.* Interpreting or evaluating what someone has said or done, in contrast to description, is based more on the observer's culture and background than on the observed situation. As a result, delay judgment until you've had sufficient time to observe and interpret the situation from the differing perspectives of all the cultures involved.

3. *Practice empathy.* Before sending a message, put yourself in the recipient's shoes. What are his or her values, experiences, and frames of reference? What do you know about his or her education, upbringing, and background that can give you added insight? Try to see the other person as he or she really is.
4. *Treat your interpretations as a working hypothesis.* Once you've developed an explanation for a new situation or think you empathize with someone from a foreign culture, treat your interpretation as a hypothesis that needs further testing rather than as a certainty. Carefully assess the feedback provided by recipients to see if it confirms your hypothesis.

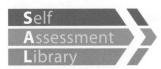

HOW GOOD ARE MY LISTENING SKILLS?

In the Self-Assessment Library (available online), take assessment II.A.2 (How Good Are My Listening Skills?).

Summary and Implications for Managers

A careful review of this chapter shows a common theme regarding the relationship between communication and employee satisfaction: The less the uncertainty, the greater the satisfaction. Distortions, ambiguities, and inconsistencies in communications all increase uncertainty and, hence, they have a negative impact on satisfaction.[37]

The less distortion that occurs in communication, the more goals, feedback, and other management messages to employees will be received as they were intended.[38] This, in turn, should reduce ambiguities and clarify the group's task. Extensive use of vertical, lateral, and informal channels will increase communication flow, reduce uncertainty, and improve group performance and satisfaction.

Findings in the chapter further suggest that the goal of perfect communication is unattainable. Yet there is evidence that demonstrates a positive relationship between effective communication (which includes factors such as perceived trust, perceived accuracy, desire for interaction, top-management receptiveness, and upward information requirements), and worker productivity.[39] Choosing the correct channel, being an effective listener and using feedback may, therefore, make for more effective communication. But the human factor generates distortions that can never be fully eliminated. The communication process represents an exchange of messages, but the outcome is meanings that may or may not approximate those that the sender intended. Whatever the sender's expectations, the decoded message in the mind of the receiver represents his or her reality. And it is this 'reality' that will determine performance, along with the individual's level of motivation and degree of satisfaction.

Paying close attention to communication effectiveness is all the more important given the ways in which communication technology has transformed the workplace. Despite the great advantages of electronic communication formats, the pitfalls are numerous. Because we gather so much meaning from how a message is communicated—voice tone, facial expressions, body language—the potential for misunderstandings in electronic communication is great. E-mail, IM and TM, and networking software are vital aspects of organizational communication, but we need to use these tools wisely, or we'll not be as effective as managers as we might be.

Finally, there are a lot of barriers to effective communication, such as gender and culture. By keeping these barriers in mind, we can overcome them and increase our communication effectiveness.

Point >< Counterpoint

KEEP IT A SECRET

We're better off keeping more things to ourselves.[40] Workplace gossip is out of control, and very often, we can't trust people with secrets. Tell a friend never, ever to tell something to someone else, and you've increased their desire to share the 'juicy news' with others. A good rule of thumb is that if you're sure a confidante has told no one else, that probably means he or she has told only three other people. You might think this is a negative reaction, but research suggests that so-called confidantes rarely keep secrets, even when they swear they will.

Organizational secrets are all the more important to keep quiet. Organizations are rumor mills, and we can permanently damage our careers and the organizations for which we work by disclosing confidential information. Improper disclosure of organizational information is a huge cost and concern for organizations.

The problem with keeping secrets is that they are expensive to maintain.

One social psychologist found that when people are instructed not to disclose certain information, it becomes more distracting and difficult for them to do so. In fact, the more people are instructed to keep something to themselves, the more they see the secret in everything they do. "We don't realize that in keeping it secret we've created an obsession in a jar," he says. So keeping things hidden takes a toll on our psyche—it (usually unnecessarily) adds to the mental burdens we carry with us.

Questions For Review

1 What are the primary functions of the communication process in organizations?

2 What are the key parts of the communication process, and how do you distinguish formal and informal communication?

3 What are the differences among downward, upward, and lateral communication?

4 What are the unique challenges to oral, written, and nonverbal communication?

5 How are formal communication networks and the grapevine similar and different?

6 What are the main forms of electronic communication? What are their unique benefits and challenges?

7 Why is channel richness fundamental to the choice of communication channels?

8 What are some common barriers to effective communication?

9 What unique problems underlie cross-cultural communication?

Discussion Exercise

Select a topic from the following list:

1. Employee turnover in an organization can be functional.

2. Some conflict in an organization is good.

3. An employer has a responsibility to provide every employee with an interesting and challenging job.

4. Individuals who have majored in business or economics make better employees than those who have majored in history or English.

5. The place where you get your college degree is more important in determining your career success than what you learn while you're there.

Debate the subject in class and then evaluate by answering the following questions.

(a) How effective was communication during these debates?

(b) What barriers to communication existed?

(c) What purposes does nonverbal communication serve?

Ethical Considerations

You work for a company that has no specific policies regarding non-work-related uses of computers and the internet. It also has no electronic monitoring devices to determine what employees are doing on their computers. Are any of the following actions unethical? Explain your position on each.

1. Using the company's e-mail system for personal reasons during the workday

2. Playing computer games during the workday

3. Using your office computer for personal use (to check ESPN.com, shop online) during the workday

4. Using your employer's portable communication device (Blackberry) for personal use

5. Conducting any of the above activities at work but before or after normal work hours

6. For telecommuters working from home, using a computer and internet access line paid for by your employer to visit online shopping sites during normal working hours

Critical Analysis

THE LIMITATIONS OF ELECTRONIC COMMUNICATION

In 2005, Dianna Abdala was a recent graduate of Suffolk University's law school (in Boston, US) and she passed the bar exam. She was then interviewed and offered a job at a law firm, started by William Korman, a former US state prosecutor.

The following is a summary of their e-mail communications:

- - - - -Original Message- - - - -
From: Dianna Abdala
Sent: Friday, February 03, 2006 9:23 p.m.
To: William A. Korman
Subject: Thank you

Dear Attorney Korman,

At this time, I am writing to inform you that I will not be accepting your offer. After careful consideration, I have come to the conclusion that the pay you are offering would neither fulfill me nor support the lifestyle I am living in

light of the work I would be doing for you. I have decided instead to work for myself, and reap 100% of the benefits that I sew [sic].

Thank you for the interviews.

Dianna L. Abdala, Esq.

    Original Message
From: William A. Korman
To: Dianna Abdala
Sent: Monday, February 06, 2006 12:15 p.m.
Subject: RE: Thank you

Dianna- -

Given that you had two interviews, were offered and accepted the job (indeed, you had a definite start date), I am surprised that you chose an e-mail and a 9:30 p.m. voicemail message to convey this information to me. It smacks of immaturity and is quite unprofessional. Indeed, I did rely upon your acceptance by ordering stationary [sic] and business cards with your name, reformatting a computer and setting up both internal and external e-mails for you here at the office. While I do not quarrel with your reasoning, I am extremely disappointed in the way this played out. I sincerely wish you the best of luck in your future endeavors.

Will Korman

- - - - -Original Message- - - - -
From: Dianna Abdala
Sent: Monday, February 06, 2006 4:01 p.m.
To: William A. Korman
Subject: Re: Thank you

A real lawyer would have put the contract into writing and not exercised any such reliance until he did so.

Again, thank you.

- - - - -Original Message- - - - -
From: William A. Korman
To: Dianna Abdala
Sent: Monday, February 06, 2006 4:18 p.m.
Subject: RE: Thank you

Thank you for the refresher course on contracts. This is not a bar exam question. You need to realize that this is a very small legal community, especially the criminal defense bar. Do you really want to [offend] more experienced lawyers at this early stage of your career?

- - - - -Original Message- - - - -
From: Dianna Abdala
To: William A. Korman
Sent: Monday, February 06, 2006 4:28 p.m.
Subject: Re: Thank you

bla bla bla

After this e-mail exchange, Korman forwarded the correspondence to several colleagues, and it quickly spread.

Questions

1. With whom do you agree here—Abdala or Korman?
2. What mistakes do you think each party made?
3. Do you think this exchange will damage Abdala's career? Korman's firm?
4. What does this exchange tell you about the limitations of e-mail?

Sources: Dianna Abdala, Wikipedia, http://en.wikipedia.org/wiki/Dianna_Abdala; and J. Sandberg, "Infamous Email Writers Aren't Always Killing Their Careers After All," *Wall Street Journal*, February 21, 2006, p. B1.

Research Exercise

Speech coaching is a growing business. Although electronic forms of communication clearly have grown significantly, that doesn't mean that oral communication no longer matters.

So what do these speech coaches do? Do your own research and find out what speech coaches do and discuss this in class with your colleagues. Is speech coaching used in the Arab world?

LEARNING OBJECTIVES

This chapter will enable you to:

1 Define *leadership* and contrast leadership and management.

2 Summarize the conclusions of trait theories.

3 Identify behavioural theories and their main limitations.

4 Assess contingency theories of leadership by their level of support.

5 Understand the significance of leader–follower participation.

6 Define *charismatic leadership* and show how it influences followers.

7 Contrast transformational leadership and transactional leadership and discuss how transformational leadership works.

8 Define *authentic leadership* and show why ethics and trust are vital to effective leadership.

9 Demonstrate the importance of mentoring, self-leadership, and virtual leadership to our understanding of leadership.

10 Determine the challenges that leaders face.

11 Explain how to find and create effective leaders.

12 Assess whether charismatic and transformational leadership generalize across cultures.

Leadership

10

Great leaders always focus on others, not on themselves. They hire the right people, train them, trust them, respect them, listen to them, and make sure to be there for them. As a result, they get committed people who work hard and give their best because they feel involved, appreciated, and proud of what they do. —Lee Cockerell

Visionary Leaders at Meirc Training & Consulting

Founded in Lebanon in 1958 by the late Simon Siksek, Meirc Training & Consulting is one of the leading providers of management training and consulting to organizations throughout the Arab world.

The original Middle East Industrial Relations Counselors (Meirc) was sponsored by what were then the four major oil companies in the GCC countries: Saudi Aramco, Bahrain Petroleum Company, Qatar Petroleum Company, and Kuwait Oil Company. Meirc's *raison d'être* was to provide up-to-date advice on industrial relations, which later became known as human resources. Gradually, Meirc started serving all types of organizations in all types of industries, in the Middle East and beyond.

Values
Under the effective leadership of the late Mr. Siksek, the company's culture emphasized specific work ethics and values, including commitment to excellence, and quality of products and services. Siksek also stressed integrity, innovation, teamwork, and the concept of a 'Meirc family.' Each of the five chairmen and managing directors who succeeded him embraced the same set of values and company culture.

The current chairman, Dr. Farid A. Muna, continues the legacy and demonstrates extreme competencies that allow him to be successful. Muna appreciates the importance of the people who work with him and respects their qualifications. More significantly, he gives individuals the opportunity to prove their potential and allows them to grow with and for the organization.

Vision
Mr. Siksek's original mission was, "To serve the human resources of our region." This visionary statement evolved over the years and is currently described by these simple, yet powerful, words: "Cultivating professional competence and providing effective business and human capital solutions." In order to accomplish this vision, Meirc had to work hard, continuously and patiently, to maintain and sustain unique competitive advantages that are difficult for their competitors to copy. Meirc still works relentlessly on several strategic fronts such as people, research, and succession planning.

People

Farid Muna stresses that Meirc takes seriously the saying that "people are our greatest asset," and that it can take Meirc a long time (sometimes years) before the right talent is hired. Consultants normally have significant managerial experience—it is much more effective to teach management skills if one has the hands-on experience of a manager. Additionally, most of Meirc's consultants are multicultural by education or work experience: they have studied or worked in the West, and thus know what works well in the Middle East and what does not. Finally, Meirc strongly believes in the saying that "learning takes place from the cradle to the grave," and demonstrates it by continually investing in the development of its employees.

Research

Inspired by the words and actions of Meirc's founder, Farid Muna continues to promote the practice of conducting field research and the subsequent publication of its findings. Muna understands that to remain effective as a leader, one must stay abreast of the latest theories and practices to enhance the employer–employee relationship. Among the several books sponsored by Meirc are *Manpower and Oil in Arab Countries* (1960); *The Arab Executive* (1980); and *Developing Multicultural Leaders: The Journey to Leadership Success* (2011).

Succession Planning

Critical to the success of Meirc was the well-planned succession of its own managing directors. Under Farid Muna's consultative style of leadership, the top executives at Meirc established an effective process for succession planning, which should serve the firm for years to come.

Source: Case contributed by Dr. Farid A. Muna, Chairman, Meirc Training & Consulting.

As we read in the opening case, Siksek and Muna both demonstrated effective leadership through their display of respect and professionalism. In addition, they believed in their vision and were single-minded in their determination to ensure that Meirc Training & Consulting became the leading provider of management training and consulting to organizations throughout the Arab world. This chapter will discuss all the issues that contribute to effective leadership.

To assess yourself on another set of qualities that we'll discuss shortly, take the following self-assessment.

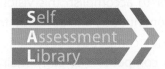

WHAT'S MY LEADERSHIP STYLE?

In the Self-Assessment Library (available online) take assessment II.B.1 (What's My Leadership Style?) and answer the following questions:

1. *How did you score on the two scales?*

2. *Do you think a leader can be both task-oriented and people-oriented? Do you think there are situations in which a leader has to make a choice between the two styles?*

3. *Do you think your leadership style will change over time? Why or why not?*

In this chapter, we'll look at the basic approaches to determining what makes an effective leader and what differentiates leaders from nonleaders. First, we'll present trait theories, which dominated the study of leadership up to the late 1940s. Then we'll discuss behavioral theories, which were popular until the late 1960s. Next, we'll introduce contingency theories and interactive theories. Thereafter, we will move on to the issues in leadership such as styles and characteristics in general, and in the Arab world in particular. But before we review any of these, let's first clarify what we mean by the term *leadership*.

What Is Leadership?

1 Define leadership *and contrast* leadership *and management.*

Leadership

The ability to influence a group toward the achievement of a vision or set of goals.

Leadership and *management* are two terms that are often confused. What's the difference between them?

John Kotter of the Harvard Business School argues that management is about coping with complexity.[1] Good management brings about order and consistency by presenting formal plans, designing organization structures, and monitoring results against the plans. Leadership, in contrast, is about coping with change. Leaders establish direction by developing a vision of the future; then they align people by communicating this vision and inspiring them to overcome obstacles. Management consists of implementing the vision and strategy provided by leaders, coordinating and staffing the organization, and handling day-to-day problems.

We define **leadership** as the ability to influence a group toward the achievement of a vision or set of goals. The source of this influence may be formal, such as that provided by the possession of managerial rank in an organization. Because management positions come with some degree of formally designated authority, individuals may assume a leadership role because of the position held in the organization. However, not all leaders are managers, nor are all managers leaders. However, leaders can emerge from within a group, as well as by formal appointment, to lead a group.

Carlos Ghosn is multi-cultural and multi-lingual, and has made a great impact as a leader at Michelin Tyres, Renault, and Nissan. In addition to his vision, he has impressive leadership traits, which include respect, diversity tolerance, transparency, and charisma. He is able to establish rapport with employees from all levels of the hierarchy. He considers that the key to success in any career is understanding, and choosing, what you love to do.

In brief, organizations need strong leadership *and* strong management for optimal effectiveness. In today's dynamic world, we need leaders to challenge the status quo, to create visions of the future, and to inspire organizational members to want to achieve the visions, just as Simon Siksek did in the opening case. We also need managers to formulate detailed plans, create efficient organizational structures, and oversee day-to-day operations.

Trait Theories

2 *Summarize the conclusions of trait theories.*

Trait theories of leadership

Theories that consider personal qualities and characteristics that differentiate leaders from nonleaders.

Throughout history, strong leaders such as Napoleon, Gamal Abdel Nasser, and Winston Churchill have been described in terms of their traits with adjectives like confident, strong-willed, determined, charismatic, and decisive.

Trait theories of leadership differentiate leaders from nonleaders by focusing on personal qualities and characteristics. Individuals are recognized as leaders and described in terms such as *charismatic, enthusiastic,* and *courageous.* The search for personality, social, physical, or intellectual attributes that would describe leaders and differentiate them from nonleaders goes back to the earliest stages of leadership research.

Researchers began organizing traits around the Big Five personality framework that was discussed in Chapter 2.[2] It then became clear that most of the dozens of traits emerging in various leadership reviews could be found under one of the Big Five and this approach resulted in consistent and strong support for traits as predictors of leadership. For instance, ambition and energy—two common traits of leaders—are part of extraversion. Rather than focus on these two specific traits, it is better to think of them in terms of the more general trait of extraversion.

Conscientiousness and openness to experience also showed strong and consistent relationships to leadership, though not quite as strong as extraversion. The traits of agreeableness and emotional stability weren't as strongly correlated with leadership. Overall, it does appear that the trait approach does have something to offer. In other words, leaders who are extraverted (individuals who like being around people and are able to assert themselves), conscientious (individuals who are disciplined and keep commitments they make), and open (individuals who are creative and flexible) do seem to have an advantage when it comes to leadership, suggesting that good leaders do have key traits in common.

What Do You Think?

Do you have the characteristics and traits of a good leader? Do you feel you have had them from birth or did you learn them?

Moreover, recent studies are indicating that another trait that may indicate effective leadership is emotional intelligence (EI), which we discussed in Chapter 6. Supporters of EI argue that without it, a person can have outstanding training, a highly analytical mind, a compelling vision, and an endless supply of terrific ideas, but still not make a great leader. But why is EI so critical to effective leadership? A core component of EI is empathy. Empathetic or sensitive leaders can understand others' needs, listen to what followers say (and don't say), and are able to read the reactions of others. As one leader noted, "The caring part of empathy, especially for the people with whom you work, is what inspires people to stay with a leader when the going gets rough. The mere fact that someone cares is more often than not rewarded with loyalty."[3]

OB in the News

Riding the Waves Requires Leadership Skill!

The extraordinary competence, vision, and leadership skills of the Governor of the Central Bank of Lebanon, Mr. Riad Salameh, enabled Lebanon to be less affected by the 2008 global financial crisis. It managed to stay abreast of the emergency and, thus, was not negatively influenced by the monetary turbulence. Salameh's keen observations and awareness of the local, regional, and international economy allowed him to lead the banking sector through those threatening times:

As of November 26, 2008, Central Bank Governor Riad Salameh announced that the combined assets of Lebanese banks totaled over US$100 billion—four times the country's GDP. Lebanese bankers agree that the central bank takes pride in shying away from complex investments and structured products that it does not understand.

Despite the severe challenges of the economic downturn worldwide, the Lebanese banking sector has demonstrated resiliency and dynamism, apparently weathering the storm. Whilst international markets were

struggling with the credit crunch and the high interbank interest rates of October 2008, Lebanese banks acted proactively in lending their ample liquidity to foreign financial institutions, and gaining high returns

As a result of Salameh's leadership and his ability to guide the banking sector to safe shores, his position as Central Bank Governor was once again renewed in 2011.

Sources: M. Mikhael, "Lebanon Basks in the Calm Eye of the Financial Storm," *Executive Magazine*, Issue No. 114 (2009); "Lebanon—Banked for the Storm," *Executive Magazine*, Issue No. 115 (2009).

Consequently, we offer two conclusions. First, traits can predict leadership and the Big Five seems to have supported that. Second, traits do a better job at predicting the emergence of leaders and the appearance of leadership than in actually distinguishing between *effective* and *ineffective* leaders.[4]

Behavioral Theories

> ③ *Identify behavioral theories and their main limitations.*

Behavioral theories of leadership
Theories proposing that specific behaviors differentiate leaders from nonleaders.

The discrepancies of early trait studies led researchers to start looking at the behaviors exhibited by specific leaders. They wondered if there was something different in the way that effective leaders behave. Many leaders have been very successful in leading their companies through difficult times.[5] And they have relied on a common leadership style that is tough-talking, intense, and autocratic. Does this suggest that autocratic behavior is a preferred style for all leaders? In this section, we look at three different **behavioral theories of leadership** to answer that question. First, however, let's consider the practical implications of the behavioral approach.

If the behavioral approach to leadership were successful, it would have implications quite different from those of the trait approach. Trait research provides a basis for *selecting* the 'right' persons to assume formal positions in groups and organizations requiring leadership. In contrast, if behavioral studies were to turn up critical behavioral determinants of leadership, we could *train* people to be leaders. The difference between trait and behavioral theories, in terms of application, lies in their underlying assumptions. Trait theories assume that leaders are born rather than made. However, if there were specific behaviors that identified leaders, then we could teach leadership; we could design programs that implanted these behavioral patterns in individuals who desired to be effective leaders.

Ohio State Studies

The most comprehensive of the behavioral theories resulted from research that began at Ohio State University, in the US, in the late 1940s.[6] Researchers wanted to identify independent dimensions of leader behavior and narrowed the list to two categories that were responsible for most of the leadership behavior described by employees. They called these two dimensions *initiating structure* and *consideration*.

Initiating structure refers to the extent to which leaders define and structure their role and those of employees in the search for goal attainment. It includes behavior that attempts to organize work, work relationships, and goals. A leader characterized as high in initiating structure could be described as someone who 'assigns group members to particular tasks, expects workers to maintain definite standards of performance, and emphasizes the meeting of deadlines.'

Consideration is described as the extent to which individuals are likely to have job relationships that are characterized by mutual trust, respect for employees' ideas, and regard for their feelings. We could describe a leader high in consideration as one who helps employees with personal problems, is friendly and approachable, treats all employees as equals, and expresses appreciation and support.

University of Michigan Studies

Leadership studies undertaken in the US at the University of Michigan's Survey Research Center at about the same time as those being done at Ohio State had similar research objectives: to locate behavioral characteristics of leaders that appeared to be related to measures of performance effectiveness.

The Michigan group also came up with two dimensions of leadership behavior that they labeled *employee oriented* and *production oriented*.[7] The **employee-oriented leaders** were described as emphasizing interpersonal relations; they took a personal interest in the needs of their employees and accepted individual differences among members. The **production-oriented leaders**, in contrast, tended to emphasize the technical or task aspects of the job; their main concern was in accomplishing their group's tasks, and the group members were a means to that end.

The conclusions the Michigan researchers arrived at strongly supported the leaders who were employee-oriented in their behavior. Employee-oriented leaders were associated with higher group productivity and greater job satisfaction. Production-oriented leaders tended to be associated with low group productivity and lower job satisfaction.

Referring to both the Ohio State and Michigan studies, Robert R. Blake and Jane S. Mouton designed a **managerial grid** (sometimes called the *leadership grid*) based on the styles of *concern for people* and *concern for production*, which essentially represent the Ohio State dimensions of consideration and initiating structure or the Michigan dimensions of employee oriented and production oriented.[8]

The grid, shown in Figure 10-1, has 9 possible positions along each axis, creating 81 different positions in which the leader's style may fall. The grid does not show results produced; rather, it shows the dominating factors in a leader's thinking in regard to getting results. Based on the findings of Blake and Mouton, managers were found to perform best under a 9,9 style, as contrasted, for example, with a 9,1 (authority type) or 1,9 (laissez-faire or flexible type) style.[9]

Summary of Trait Theories and Behavioral Theories

Judging from the evidence, the behavioral theories, like the trait theories, add to our understanding of leadership effectiveness. Leaders who have certain

---

Initiating structure

The extent to which a leader is likely to define and structure his or her role and those of subordinates in the search for goal attainment.

Consideration

The extent to which a leader is likely to have job relationships characterized by mutual trust, respect for subordinates' ideas, and regard for their feelings.

Employee-oriented leader

A leader who emphasizes interpersonal relations, takes a personal interest in the needs of employees, and accepts individual differences among members.

Production-oriented leader

A leader who emphasizes technical or task aspects of the job.

Managerial grid

A nine-by-nine matrix outlining 81 different leadership styles.

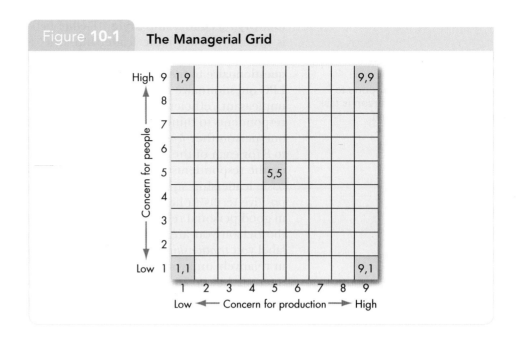

Figure 10-1   The Managerial Grid

Concern for people (vertical axis, Low 1 to High 9)

1,9 ... 9,9

5,5

1,1 ... 9,1

Low ← Concern for production → High (1 to 9)

traits and who display consideration and structuring behaviors, do appear to be more effective. We should remember, however, that as important as trait theories and behavioral theories are in determining effective versus ineffective leaders, they do not guarantee a leader's success. The context matters too.

Contingency Theories: Fiedler Model and Situational Leadership Theory

Assess contingency theories of leadership by their level of support.

Predicting leadership success is more complex than isolating a few traits or preferable behaviors. In the mid-twentieth century, many researchers were unable to obtain consistent results on traits and behaviors as predictors for leadership success, and this led to a focus on situational influences. The relationship between leadership style and effectiveness suggested that under condition *a*, style *x* would be appropriate, whereas style *y* would be more suitable for condition *b*, and style *z* would be more suitable for condition *c*. But what were the conditions *a,b,c* and so forth? It was one thing to say that leadership effectiveness was dependent on the situation and another to be able to isolate those situational conditions. Several approaches to isolating key situational variables have proven more successful than others and, as a result, have gained wider recognition. We shall consider three of these: the Fiedler model, Hersey and Blanchard's situational theory, and the path-goal theory.

Fiedler contingency model

The theory that effective groups depend on a proper match between a leader's style of interacting with subordinates and the degree to which the situation gives control and influence to the leader.

Fiedler Model

The first comprehensive contingency model for leadership was developed by Fred Fiedler.[10] The **Fiedler contingency model** proposes that effective group performance depends on the proper match between the leader's style and the degree to which the situation gives control to the leader.

Least preferred coworker (LPC) questionnaire

An instrument that purports to measure whether a person is task or relationship oriented.

Identifying Leadership Style   Fiedler believes a key factor in leadership success is the individual's basic leadership style. So he begins by trying to find out what that basic style is. Fiedler created the **least preferred coworker (LPC) questionnaire** to measure whether a person is task-or relationship-oriented. The LPC questionnaire contains sets of 16 contrasting adjectives (such as pleasant–unpleasant, efficient–inefficient, open–guarded, supportive–hostile). It asks respondents to think of all the coworkers they have ever had and to describe the one person they *least enjoyed* working with by rating that person on a scale of 1 to 8 for each of the 16 sets of contrasting adjectives. Fiedler believes that based on the respondents' answers to this LPC questionnaire, he can determine their basic leadership style. If the least preferred coworker is described in relatively positive terms (a high LPC score), then the respondent is primarily interested in good personal relations with this coworker. That is, if you essentially describe the person you are least able to work with in favorable terms, Fiedler would label you *relationship oriented*. In contrast, if the least preferred coworker is seen in relatively unfavorable terms (a low LPC score), the respondent is primarily interested in productivity and thus would be labeled *task oriented*.

To understand Fiedler's model, take the following self-assessment exercise before we move on.

WHAT IS MY LPC SCORE?

In the Self-Assessment Library (available online) take assessment IV.E.5 (What is My LPC Score?).

Leader–member relations

The degree of confidence, trust, and respect subordinates have in their leader.

Task structure

The degree to which job assignments are procedurized.

Position power

Influence derived from one's formal structural position in the organization; includes power to hire, fire, discipline, promote, and give salary increases.

Defining the Situation   After an individual's basic leadership style has been assessed through the LPC questionnaire, it is necessary to match the leader with the situation. Fiedler has identified three dimensions that define the key situational factors that determine leadership effectiveness:

1. **Leader–member relations** is the degree of confidence, trust, and respect members have in their leader.
2. **Task structure** is the degree to which the job assignments are procedurized (that is, structured or unstructured).
3. **Position power** is the degree of influence a leader has over power variables such as hiring, firing, discipline, promotions, and salary increases.

The next step in the Fiedler model is to evaluate the situation in terms of these three contingency variables. Leader–member relations are either good or poor, task structure is either high or low, and position power is either strong or weak.

Matching Leaders and Situations   How would you apply Fiedler's findings? You would seek to match leaders and situations. Individuals' LPC scores would determine the type of situation for which they are best suited. That 'situation' would be defined by evaluating the three contingency factors of leader–member relations, task structure, and position power. But remember that Fiedler views an individual's leadership style as being fixed. Therefore, there are really only two ways in which to improve leader effectiveness.

First, you can change the leader to fit the situation; for example, a group's performance could be improved by replacing that manager with one who is task oriented. The second alternative would be to change the situation to fit the leader. That could be done by restructuring tasks or increasing or decreasing the power that the leader has to control factors such as salary increases, promotions, and disciplinary actions.

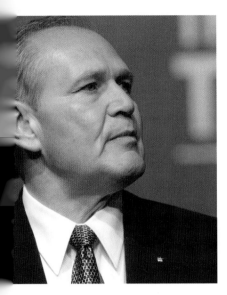

When Home Depot hired Robert Nardelli as CEO, the company believed he was 'the right guy' to improve the company's performance. Under his leadership, Home Depot's profits, sales, and number of stores doubled. But shareholders criticized his leadership because he failed to improve the company's stock price relative to his huge pay package. After leaving Home Depot, Nardelli was hired as 'the right guy' to revitalize Chrysler based on his turnaround expertise. Predicting the effectiveness of Nardelli's leadership as CEO of Home Depot and Chrysler illustrates the premise of contingency theories that leadership effectiveness is dependent on situational influences.

Cognitive resource theory

A theory of leadership that states that stress unfavorably affects a situation and that intelligence and experience can reduce the influence of stress on the leader.

Situational leadership theory (SLT)

A contingency theory that focuses on followers' readiness.

Path-goal theory

A theory that states that it is the leader's job to assist followers in attaining their goals and to provide the necessary direction and/or support to ensure that their goals are compatible with the overall objectives of the group or organization.

Evaluation   As a whole, reviews of the major studies that have tested the overall validity of the Fiedler model lead to a generally positive conclusion. That is, there is considerable evidence to support only three categories rather than the original eight. But there are problems with the LPC questionnaire and the logic underlying the LPC questionnaire is not well understood. Also, the contingency variables are complex and difficult for practitioners to assess.

Cognitive Resource Theory   More recently, Fiedler has reconsidered his original theory.[11] In this refinement, called **cognitive resource theory**, he focuses on the role of stress as a form of situational unfavorableness and how a leader's intelligence and experience influence his or her reaction to stress. The basis of the new theory is that stress is the enemy of rationality. It's difficult for leaders (or anyone else, for that matter) to think logically and analytically when they're under stress.

Hersey and Blanchard's Situational Theory

Paul Hersey and Ken Blanchard have developed a leadership model that has gained a strong following among management development specialists.[12] This model—called **situational leadership theory (SLT)**—has been incorporated into leadership training programs at more than 400 of the Fortune 500 companies; and more than 1 million managers per year from a wide variety of organizations are being taught its basic elements.[13]

Situational leadership is a contingency theory that focuses on the followers. Successful leadership is achieved by selecting the right leadership style, which Hersey and Blanchard argue is contingent on the level of the followers' readiness. Before we proceed, we should clarify two points: Why focus on the followers? And what do they mean by the term *readiness*?

The emphasis on the followers in leadership effectiveness reflects the reality that it is the followers who accept or reject the leader. Regardless of what the leader does, effectiveness depends on the actions of the followers. The term *readiness*, as defined by Hersey and Blanchard, refers to the extent to which people have the ability and willingness to accomplish a specific task.

SLT says that if followers are *unable* and *unwilling* to do a task, the leader needs to give clear and specific directions; if followers are *unable* and *willing*, the leader needs to display high task orientation to compensate for the followers' lack of ability and high relationship orientation to get the followers to "buy into" the leader's desires; if followers are *able* and *unwilling*, the leader needs to use a supportive and participative style; and if the employees are both *able* and *willing*, the leader doesn't need to do much. Research efforts to support this theory have generally been disappointing, so despite its intuitive appeal, approval of this theory must be cautioned against.

Path-Goal Theory

Developed by Robert House, path-goal theory extracts elements from the Ohio State leadership research on initiating structure and consideration and the expectancy theory of motivation.[14]

The Theory   The essence of **path-goal theory** is that it is the leader's job to provide followers with the information, support, or other resources necessary for them to achieve their goals. The term *path-goal* is derived from the belief that effective leaders clarify the path to help their followers get from where they are to the achievement of their work goals and to make the journey along the path easier by reducing roadblocks.

Leader Behaviors House identified four leadership behaviors. The *directive leader* lets followers know what is expected of them, schedules work to be done, and gives specific guidance as to how to accomplish tasks. The *supportive leader* is friendly and shows concern for the needs of followers. The *participative leader* consults with followers and uses their suggestions before making a decision. The *achievement-oriented leader* sets challenging goals and expects followers to perform at their highest level. In contrast to Fiedler, House assumes leaders are flexible and that the same leader can display any or all of these behaviors, depending on the situation.

What Do You Think?

Can leaders show different behaviors or are they identified by one specific behavior?

Path-Goal Variables and Predictions

As Figure 10-2 illustrates, path-goal theory proposes two classes of contingency variables that direct the leadership behavior–outcome relationship: those in the environment that are outside the control of the employee (task structure, the formal authority system, and the work group) and those that are part of the personal characteristics of the employee (locus of control, experience, and perceived ability). For example, the following are illustrations of predictions based on path-goal theory:

- Directive leadership leads to greater satisfaction when tasks are ambiguous or stressful than when they are highly structured and well laid out.
- Supportive leadership results in high employee performance and satisfaction when employees are performing structured tasks.
- Directive leadership is likely to be perceived as redundant among employees with high perceived ability or considerable experience.
- Employees with an internal locus of control will be more satisfied with a participative style.

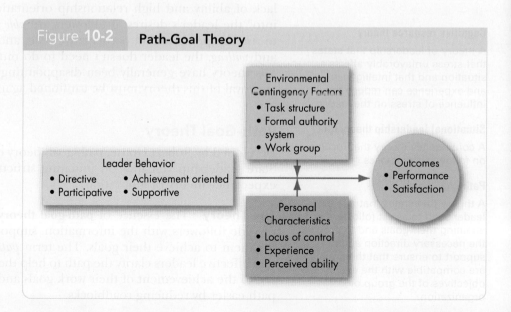

Figure 10-2   Path-Goal Theory

- Achievement-oriented leadership will increase employees' expectancies that effort will lead to high performance when tasks are ambiguously structured.

Summary of Contingency Theories

It is fair to say that none of the contingency theories has been as successful as their developers had hoped. In particular, results for situational leadership theory and path-goal theory have been disappointing.

One limitation of many of the theories we've covered so far is that they ignore the followers. Yet, as one leadership scholar noted, "leaders do not exist in a vacuum;" leadership is a symbolic relationship between leaders and followers.[15] But the leadership theories we've covered to this point have largely assumed that leaders treat all their followers in the same manner. That is, they assume that leaders use a fairly homogeneous style with all the people in their work unit. Next we look at a theory that considers differences in the relationships leaders form with different followers.

Leader–Member Exchange (LMX) Theory

Leader–member exchange (LMX) theory

A theory that supports leaders' creation of in-groups and out-groups; subordinates with in-group status will have higher performance ratings, less turnover, and greater job satisfaction.

Think of a leader you know. Did this leader tend to have favorites who made up his or her 'in-group'? If you answered 'yes,' you're acknowledging the foundation of leader–member exchange theory.[16] The **leader–member exchange (LMX) theory** argues that, because of time pressures, leaders establish a special relationship with a small group of their followers. These individuals make up the in-group—they are trusted, have the leader's attention, and are more likely to receive special privileges. Other followers fall into the out-group. They get less of the leader's time, get fewer of the preferred rewards that the leader controls, and have leader–follower relations based on formal authority interactions. This is a familiar concept in the Arab world, where many leaders develop their 'own circle' of followers and usually only have ears for them.

Just precisely how the leader chooses who falls into each category is unclear, but there is evidence that leaders tend to choose in-group members because they have demographic, attitude, and personality characteristics that are similar to the leader's or a higher level of competence than out-group members[17] (see Figure 10-3).

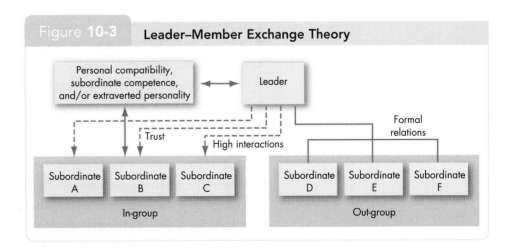

Figure 10-3   **Leader–Member Exchange Theory**

Decision Theory: Vroom and Yetton's Leader-Participation Model

5 *Understand the significance of leader–follower participation.*

Leader-participation model

A leadership theory that provides a set of rules to determine the form and amount of participative decision making in different situations.

The final theory we'll cover argues that the *way* leaders make decisions is as important as *what* they decide. Victor Vroom and Phillip Yetton developed a **leader-participation model** that relates leadership behavior and participation in decision making.[18] Recognizing that task structures have varying demands for routine and nonroutine activities, these researchers argued that leader behavior must adjust to reflect the task structure. Vroom and Yetton's model provides a sequential set of rules that should be followed in determining the form and amount of participation in decision making, as determined by different types of situations. The model is a decision tree incorporating seven contingencies (whose relevance can be identified by making 'yes' or 'no' choices) and five alternative leadership styles. The 12 contingency variables are listed in Box 10-1.

Inspirational Approaches to Leadership

Framing

A way of using language to manage meaning.

Traditional approaches to leadership—those we considered earlier in this chapter—ignore the importance of the leader as a communicator. **Framing** is a way of communicating to shape meaning. It's a way for leaders to influence how others see and understand events. Framing is especially important to an aspect of leadership ignored in the traditional theories: the ability of the leader to inspire others to act beyond their immediate self-interests.

In this section, we present two contemporary leadership theories with a common theme. They view leaders as individuals who inspire followers through their words, ideas, and behaviors. These theories are charismatic leadership and transformational leadership.

BOX 10-1
Contingency Variables in the Revised Leader-Participation Model

1. Importance of the decision
2. Importance of obtaining follower commitment to the decision
3. Whether the leader has sufficient information to make a good decision
4. How well structured the problem is
5. Whether an autocratic decision would receive follower commitment
6. Whether followers 'buy into' the organization's goals
7. Whether there is likely to be conflict among followers over solution alternatives
8. Whether followers have the necessary information to make a good decision
9. Time constraints on the leader that may limit follower involvement
10. Whether costs to bring geographically dispersed members together is justified
11. Importance to the leader of minimizing the time it takes to make the decision
12. Importance of using participation as a tool for developing follower decision skills

Amr Moussa is a charismatic leader. A native of Egypt, he is a former foreign minister and, until recently, was chief of the Arab League. Mussa's visionary insights resulted in his position as head of the Arab League for two terms. His persistence in following his vision of peace in the Arab world has won him the respect of prominent international figures. Although 75, he has been suggested for a possible major role in a future Egyptian government.

Charismatic Leadership

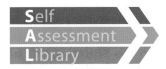

6 *Define* charismatic leadership *and show how it influences followers.*

John F. Kennedy, Amr Mussa, and Martin Luther King Jr. are often identified as being charismatic leaders. So what do they have in common?

What Is Charismatic Leadership?   Max Weber, a sociologist, was the first scholar to discuss charismatic leadership. More than a century ago, he defined *charisma* (from the Greek for 'gift') as "a certain quality of an individual personality, by virtue of which he or she is set apart from ordinary people and treated as endowed with supernatural, superhuman, or at least specifically exceptional powers or qualities."

Take the following self-assessment to see how you score on charismatic leadership.

Self Assessment Library

HOW CHARISMATIC AM I?

In the Self-Assessment Library (available online), take assessment II.B.2 (How Charismatic Am I?).

Charismatic leadership theory

A leadership theory that states that followers make attributions of heroic or extraordinary leadership abilities when they observe certain behaviors.

The first researcher to consider charismatic leadership in terms of OB was Robert House. According to House's **charismatic leadership theory**, followers make attributions of heroic or extraordinary leadership abilities when they observe certain behaviors.[19] There have been a number of studies that have attempted to identify the characteristics of the charismatic leader. One of the best reviews of the literature has documented four—vision, willingness to take personal risks to achieve that vision, sensitivity to follower needs, and behaviors that are out of the ordinary.[20] These characteristics are described in Box 10-2.

BOX 10-2
Key Characteristics of Charismatic Leaders

1. *Vision and articulation*. Has a vision—expressed as an idealized goal—that proposes a future better than the status quo; and is able to clarify the importance of the vision in terms that are understandable to others.

2. *Personal risk*. Willing to take on high personal risk, incur high costs, and engage in self-sacrifice to achieve the vision.

3. *Sensitivity to follower needs*. Perceptive of others' abilities and responsive to their needs and feelings.

4. *Unconventional behavior*. Engages in behaviors that are perceived as novel and counter to norms.

Source: Based on J. A. Conger and R. N. Kanungo, *Charismatic Leadership in Organizations* (Thousand Oaks, CA: Sage, 1998), p. 94.

Are Charismatic Leaders Born or Made?   Are charismatic leaders born with their qualities? Or can people actually learn how to be charismatic leaders? The answer to both questions is yes.

Although a small minority thinks that charisma is inherited and therefore cannot be learned, most experts believe that individuals also can be trained to exhibit charismatic behaviors and can thus enjoy the benefits that accompany being labeled 'a charismatic leader.'[21] One set of authors proposes that a person can learn to become charismatic by following a three-step process.[22] First, an individual needs to develop an aura of charisma by maintaining an optimistic view; using passion as a catalyst for generating enthusiasm; and communicating with the whole body, not just with words. Second, an individual draws others in by creating a bond that inspires others to follow. Third, the individual brings out the potential in followers by tapping into their emotions.

How Charismatic Leaders Influence Followers   How do charismatic leaders actually influence followers? It begins by the leader articulating an appealing **vision**. A vision is a long-term strategy for how to attain a goal or goals. The vision provides a sense of continuity for followers by linking the present with a better future for the organization, and this is what the former CEO of Apple, Steve Jobs, showed. A vision is incomplete unless it has an accompanying vision statement. A **vision statement** is a formal articulation of an organization's vision or mission. Once a vision and vision statement are established, the leader then communicates high performance expectations and expresses confidence that followers can attain them. This enhances follower self-esteem and self-confidence.

Vision

A long-term strategy for attaining a goal or goals.

Vision statement

A formal articulation of an organization's vision or mission.

Does Effective Charismatic Leadership Depend on the Situation?   There is an increasing body of research that shows impressive correlations between charismatic leadership and high performance and satisfaction among followers.[23] People working for charismatic leaders are motivated to exert extra work effort and, because they like and respect their leader, express greater satisfaction, as Sony's CEO demonstrates. It also appears that organizations with charismatic CEOs are more profitable. And charismatic college professors enjoy higher course evaluations.[24]

However, there is a growing body of evidence indicating that charisma may not always be generalizable; that is, its effectiveness may depend on the situation. That is, charismatic leadership may affect some followers more than others. Research suggests, for example, that people are especially receptive to charismatic leadership when they sense a crisis, when they are under stress, or when they

Sony Corporation, which recently celebrated 40 years of presence in the Middle East, chose a charismatic leader to inspire the company to return to its innovative roots. As Sony's first CEO and chairman from outside Japan, Howard Stringer, is reorganizing the company to lead the change in making the Sony brand more relevant to digital age consumers. Stringer's strong sense of humor, optimism, boundless energy, and confidence are motivating employees worldwide, from engineers to executives. One top manager says, "Howard's personality and his character and the way he communicates have been good for the company." In this photo, the fun-loving Stringer jokes with Sony top executives about the color of their ties during a press conference announcing his job as CEO.

fear for their lives. If an individual lacks self-esteem and questions his self-worth, he is more likely to absorb a leader's direction rather than establish his own way of leading or thinking.

The Dark Side of Charismatic Leadership   Many companies want a charismatic CEO. And to attract these people, boards of directors give them autonomy and resources. One study showed that charismatic CEOs were able to use their charisma to secure higher salaries even when their performance was average.[25]

Unfortunately, charismatic leaders who are too ambitious don't necessarily act in the best interests of their organizations.[26] Many of these leaders used their power to remake their companies in their own image. These leaders often completely blurred the boundary separating their personal interests from their organization's interests.

There are, on the other hand, strong leaders inside firms who could direct the company to greater heights. These individuals have been called **level-5 leaders** because they have four basic leadership qualities—individual capability, team skills, managerial competence, and the ability to stimulate others to high performance—plus a fifth dimension: a blend of personal humility and professional will. Level-5 leaders channel their ego needs away from themselves and into the goal of building a great company.

We don't mean to suggest that charismatic leadership isn't effective. Overall, its effectiveness is well supported. The point is that a charismatic leader isn't always the answer. Yes, an organization with a charismatic leader is more likely to be successful, but that success depends, to some extent, on the situation and on the leader's vision. Let's now look at the transformational leader.

Level-5 leaders

Leaders who are fiercely ambitious and driven but whose ambition is directed toward their company rather than themselves.

Transactional leaders

Leaders who guide or motivate their followers in the direction of established goals by clarifying role and task requirements.

Transformational Leadership

Contrast transformational leadership and transactional leadership and discuss how transformational leadership works.

A lot of research has focused on differentiating transformational leaders from transactional leaders.[27] Most of the leadership theories presented in the first part of this chapter—for instance, the Ohio State studies, Fiedler's model, and path-goal theory—have concerned **transactional leaders**. These kinds

Transformational leaders

Leaders who inspire followers to transcend their own self-interests and who are capable of having a profound and extraordinary effect on followers.

of leaders guide or motivate their followers in the direction of established goals by clarifying role and task requirements. **Transformational leaders** inspire followers to give up their own self-interests for the good of the organization and are capable of having a significant and extraordinary effect on their followers.

Transformational leaders pay attention to the concerns and developmental needs of individual followers; they change followers' awareness of issues by helping them to look at old problems in new ways; and they are able to excite and inspire followers to put out extra effort to achieve group goals. Box 10-3 briefly identifies and defines the characteristics that differentiate these two types of leaders.

Transactional and transformational leadership shouldn't be viewed as opposing approaches to getting things done.[28] Transformational and transactional leadership complement each other, but that doesn't mean they're equally important. Transformational leadership builds *on top of* transactional leadership and produces levels of follower effort and performance that go beyond what would occur with a transactional approach alone. But the reverse isn't true. So if you are a good transactional leader but do not have transformational qualities, you'll likely only be an ordinary leader. That is, the best leaders are transactional *and* transformational as we'll see in the following sections.

Full Range of Leadership Model   Figure 10-4 shows the full range of leadership model. Laissez-faire is the most passive and therefore the least effective of the leader behaviors. Leaders using this style are rarely viewed as effective. Leaders who practice management by exception leadership tend to be available only when there is a problem, which is often too late. Contingent reward leadership can be an effective style of leadership. However, leaders will not get their employees to go above and beyond the call of duty when practicing this style of leadership. Only with the four remaining leadership styles—which are all aspects of transformational leadership—are leaders able to motivate followers to perform above expectations and give up their own self-interest for the sake of the organization. Individualized consideration, intellectual stimulation, inspirational motivation, and

---

BOX 10-3
Characteristics of Transactional and Transformational Leaders

Transactional Leader

Contingent Reward: Contracts exchange of rewards for effort, promises rewards for good performance, recognizes accomplishments.

Management by Exception (active): Watches and searches for deviations from rules and standards, takes correct action.

Management by Exception (passive): Intervenes only if standards are not met.

Laissez-Faire: Abdicates responsibilities, avoids making decisions.

Transformational Leader

Idealized Influence: Provides vision and sense of mission, instills pride, gains respect and trust.

Inspirational Motivation: Communicates high expectations, uses symbols to focus efforts, expresses important purposes in simple ways.

Intellectual Stimulation: Promotes intelligence, rationality, and careful problem solving.

Individualized Consideration: Gives personal attention, treats each employee individually, coaches, advises.

Source: B. M. Bass, "From Transactional to Transformational Leadership: Learning to Share the Vision," *Organizational Dynamics*, Winter 1990, p. 22. Reprinted by permission of the publisher, Elsevier.

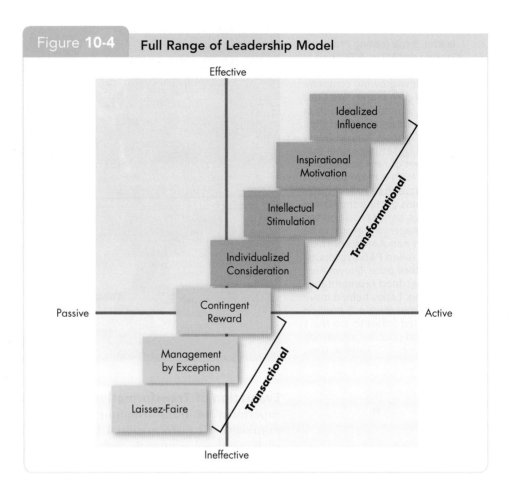

Figure 10-4   Full Range of Leadership Model

idealized influence all result in extra effort from workers, higher productivity, higher morale and satisfaction, higher organizational effectiveness, lower turnover, lower absenteeism, and greater organizational adaptability. Based on the model in Figure 10-4, leaders are generally most effective when they regularly use each of the four transformational behaviors.

How Transformational Leadership Works   In the past few years, a great deal of research has been conducted to explain how transformational leadership works. Transformational leaders encourage their followers to be more innovative and creative.[29] Transformational leaders are more effective because they themselves are more creative, but they're also more effective because they encourage those who follow them to be creative, too. In addition, followers of transformational leaders are more likely to pursue ambitious goals.

Just as research has shown that vision is important in explaining how charismatic leadership works, research has also shown that vision explains part of the effect of transformational leadership. Indeed, one study found that vision was even more important than a charismatic communication style in explaining the success of entrepreneurial firms.[30] Finally, transformational leadership also encourages commitment on the part of followers and instills in them a greater sense of trust in the leader.[31]

What Do You Think?

Transformation involves change; why is change a challenge for leaders?

A. G. Lafley is a transformational leader. Since joining Procter & Gamble as CEO in 2000, he has brought flexibility and creativity to a slow-growing company. He expanded core brands like Crest toothpaste to innovations such as teeth whiteners and toothbrushes. He shifted P&G's focus from in-house innovation by setting a goal that 50 percent of new products be developed with outside partners. With more than half of P&G's business outside the United States, Lafley recast his top management group to be 50 percent non-American. These changes have raised P&G's revenues, profits, and stock price. Shown here with Iams pet-food representative Euka, the dog, Lafley helped move the brand from the No. 5 position in the United States to the No. 1 spot, and doubled worldwide sales of Iams.

Evaluation of Transformational Leadership   The evidence supporting the superiority of transformational leadership over transactional leadership is impressive. Transformational leadership has been supported in occupations such as school principals and teachers, marine commanders, ministers, presidents of MBA associations, and sales reps, at various job levels. A review of 87 studies testing transformational leadership found that it was related to the motivation and satisfaction of followers and to the higher performance and perceived effectiveness of leaders.[32]

Transformational Leadership versus Charismatic Leadership   There is some debate about whether transformational leadership and charismatic leadership are the same. Although many researchers believe that transformational leadership is broader than charismatic leadership, studies show that in reality a leader who scores high on transformational leadership is also likely to score high on charisma. Therefore, in practice, measures of charisma and transformational leadership may be roughly equivalent.

Authentic Leadership: Ethics and Trust Are the Foundation of Leadership

8   *Define* authentic leadership *and show why ethics and trust are vital to effective leadership.*

Although charismatic leadership theories and transformational leadership theories as previously discussed have added greatly to our understanding of effective leadership, they do not explicitly deal with the role of ethics and trust. Some scholars have argued that a consideration of ethics and trust is essential to complete the picture of effective leadership. Here we consider these two concepts under the title of authentic leadership.[33]

What Is Authentic Leadership?

Authentic leaders

Leaders who know who they are, know what they believe in and value, and act on those values and beliefs openly and candidly. Their followers would consider them to be ethical people.

Authentic leaders know who they are, know what they believe in and value, and act on those values and beliefs openly and honestly. Their followers would consider them to be ethical people. The primary quality, therefore, produced by authentic leadership is trust. How does authentic leadership build trust? Authentic leaders share information, encourage open communication, and stick to their ideals. As a result, people come to have faith in authentic leaders.

Find out if you have the qualities of an ethical leader. Do the self-assessment test below.

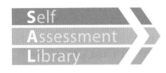

AM I AN ETHICAL LEADER?

In the Self-Assessment Library (available online), take assessment IV.E.4 (Am I an Ethical Leader?).

Ethics in Leadership and Corporate Social Responsibility

Only recently have ethicists and leadership researchers begun to consider the ethical implications in leadership.[34] Why now? One reason may be the growing general interest in ethics throughout the field of management. Another reason may be the discovery that many past leaders faced ethical problems. There are always ethical weaknesses of business leaders in the headlines.

Ethics covers leadership from a number of angles. Transformational leaders, for instance, have been described by one authority as supporting moral virtue when they try to change the attitudes and behaviors of followers.[35] Charisma, too, has an ethical component. Unethical leaders are more likely to use their charisma to enhance *power over* followers, directed toward self-serving ends. Ethical leaders are considered to use their charisma in a socially constructive way to serve others.[36]

Leaders should gain the trust of their followers and they can do that by leading by example and showing followers how to give back to the community with high integrity. One way in which leaders can show constructive contribution is by demonstrating Corporate Social Responsibility (CSR). A common definition of CSR given by The World Bank stresses the commitment of businesses to managing and improving their economic, environmental and social status at the firm, local, regional and global levels. Thus, in so doing, leaders give back to the community with financial donations or by volunteering their time to help people who need any kind of humanitarian assistance. There is also the issue of abuse of power by leaders, for example when they give themselves large salaries, bonuses, and stock options while, at the same time, they seek to cut costs by laying off long-time employees.

Socialized charismatic leadership

A leadership concept that states that leaders convey values that are other-centered versus self-centered and who role model ethical conduct.

Leadership effectiveness needs to address the *means* a leader uses in trying to achieve goals, as well as the content of those goals. Recently, scholars have tried to integrate ethical and charismatic leadership by advancing the idea of **socialized charismatic leadership**—leadership that highlights values that are other-centered versus self-centered by leaders who model ethical conduct.[37]

Now let's examine the issue of trust and its role in shaping strong leaders.

What Is Trust?

Trust, or lack of trust, is an increasingly important leadership issue in today's organizations.[38] In this section, we define *trust* and provide you with some guidelines for helping build credibility and trust.

Trust

A positive expectation that another will not act opportunistically.

Trust is a positive expectation that another will not—through words, actions, or decisions—act opportunistically.[39] The two most important elements of our definition are that it implies familiarity and risk.

The phrase *positive expectation* in our definition assumes knowledge and familiarity about the other party. Trust takes time to form and build. Most of us find it hard, if not impossible, to trust someone immediately if we don't know anything about them. But as we get to know someone and the relationship matures, we gain confidence in our ability to form a positive expectation.

The term *opportunistic* refers to the existing risk in any trusting relationship. By its very nature, trust provides the opportunity for disappointment or to be taken advantage of.[40] But trust is not actually taking risk; rather, it is a *willingness* to take risk.[41] So when I trust someone, I expect that they will not take advantage of me. This willingness to take risks is common to all trust situations.[42]

What are the key dimensions that underlie the concept of trust? Evidence has identified five: integrity, competence, consistency, loyalty, and openness[43] (see Figure 10-5).

Integrity refers to honesty and truthfulness. *Competence* is an individual's technical and interpersonal knowledge and skills. *Consistency* relates to an individual's reliability, predictability, and good judgment in handling situations. *Loyalty* is the willingness to protect and save face for another person. The final dimension of trust is *openness*. That is, can you rely on the person to give you the full truth?

Trust and Leadership

As we have shown in discussing ethical and authentic leadership, trust is a primary attribute associated with leadership; and when this trust is broken, it can have serious negative effects on a group's performance.[44] When followers trust a leader, they are willing to be vulnerable to the leader's actions—confident that their rights and interests will not be abused.[45] People are unlikely to look up to or follow someone whom they see as dishonest or who is likely to take advantage of them. Honesty, for instance, consistently ranks at the top of most people's list

His Highness Sheikh Zayed bin Sultan Al Nahyan, former President of the UAE, was a truly authentic leader. He had a strong sense of values, great beliefs in his country and people, and motivated and encouraged his people at all times. The people had great trust in Sheikh Zayed and considered him as a father figure who always showed integrity.

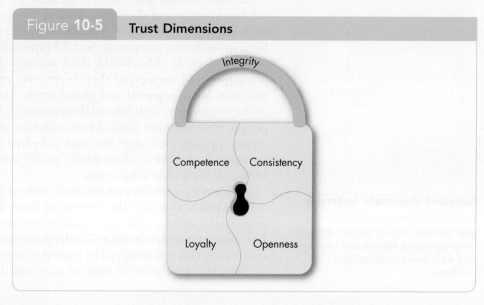

Figure 10-5 **Trust Dimensions**

of characteristics they admire in their leaders. "Honesty is absolutely essential to leadership. If people are going to follow someone willingly, whether it be into battle or into the boardroom, they first want to assure themselves that the person is worthy of their trust."[46]

Three Types of Trust

There are three types of trust in organizational relationships: *deterrence* based, *knowledge* based, and *identification* based.[47]

Deterrence-based trust
Trust based on fear of reprisal if the trust is violated.

Deterrence-Based Trust   The weakest relationships are contained in **deterrence-based trust**. One violation or inconsistency can destroy the relationship. This form of trust is based on fear if the trust is violated. Individuals who are in this type of relationship do what they do because they fear the consequences from not following through on their obligations.

Deterrence-based trust will work only to the degree that punishment is possible, consequences are clear, and the punishment is actually imposed if the trust is violated. To be sustained, the potential loss of future interaction with the other party must outweigh the profit potential that comes from violating expectations.

Knowledge-based trust
Trust based on behavioral predictability that comes from a history of interaction.

Knowledge-Based Trust   Most organizational relationships are found in **knowledge-based trust**—that is, trust is based on the behavioral predictability that comes from a history of interaction. It exists when you have adequate information about someone to understand them well enough to be able to accurately predict his or her behavior.

Knowledge-based trust relies on information rather than deterrence. Knowledge of the other party and predictability of behavior replaces the contracts, penalties, and legal arrangements more typical of deterrence-based trust. This knowledge develops over time, largely as a function of experience that builds confidence of trustworthiness and predictability. The better you know someone, the more accurately you can predict what he or she will do.

In an organizational context, most manager–employee relationships are knowledge based. Both parties have enough experience working with each other that they know what to expect. A long history of consistently open and honest interactions, for instance, is not likely to be destroyed by one error.

Identification-based trust
Trust based on a mutual understanding of each other's intentions and appreciation of each other's wants and desires.

Identification-Based Trust   The highest level of trust is achieved when there is an emotional connection between the parties. It allows one party to act as an agent for the other and substitute for that person in interpersonal transactions. This is called **identification-based trust**. Trust exists because the parties understand each other's intentions and appreciate each other's wants and desires. This mutual understanding is developed to the point that each can effectively act for the other. Controls are minimal at this level. You don't need to monitor the other party because there exists complete loyalty.

You see identification-based trust occasionally in organizations among people who have worked together for long periods of time and have a depth of experience that allows them to know each other inside and out. This is also the type of trust that managers ideally seek in teams. Team members are comfortable with and trusting of each other, and can anticipate each other and act freely in each other's absence.

Basic Principles of Trust

Research allows us to offer some principles for better understanding the creation of both trust and mistrust.[48]

Mistrust Drives Out Trust   People who are trusting demonstrate their trust by increasing their openness to others, disclosing relevant information, and expressing their true intentions. People who mistrust do not share information. A few mistrusting people can poison an entire organization.

Trust Leads to Trust   In the same way that mistrust drives out trust, exhibiting trust in others tends also to encourage more trust. Effective leaders increase trust in small parts and allow others to respond in kind.

Trust Can Be Regained   Once it is gone, trust can be regained, but only in certain situations. When an individual's trust in another is broken because the other party failed to do what was expected, it can be restored when the individual observes a consistent pattern of trustworthy behaviors. However, when the same untrustworthy behavior occurs with deception, trust never fully recovers, even when the deceived is given apologies, promises, or a consistent pattern of trustworthy actions.[49]

Mistrusting Groups Self-destruct   When group members mistrust each other, they pursue their own interests rather than the group's. Members of mistrusting groups tend to be suspicious of each other and remain aware of exploitation, and restrict communication with others in the group.

Mistrust Generally Reduces Productivity   Although we cannot say that trust necessarily *increases* productivity, though it usually does, mistrust almost always *reduces* productivity. Mistrust focuses attention on the differences in member interests, making it difficult for people to visualize common goals. People respond by concealing information and secretly pursuing their own interests.

Contemporary Leadership Roles

> 9 *Demonstrate the importance of mentoring, self-leadership, and virtual leadership to our understanding of leadership.*

Why are many effective leaders also active mentors? How can leaders develop self-leadership skills in their employees? And how does leadership work when face-to-face interaction is gone? In this section, we briefly address these three leadership roles—mentoring, self-leadership, and online leadership.

Mentoring

Mentor

A senior employee who sponsors and supports a less-experienced employee, called a protégé.

Many leaders create mentoring relationships. A **mentor** is a senior employee who sponsors and supports a less-experienced employee—a protégé—and this is becoming a common behavior in the Arab world. Although not all Arab countries exercise mentoring, some do believe that it can be an effective approach. Successful mentors are good teachers. They can present ideas clearly, listen well, and empathize with the problems of their protégés. As shown in Box 10-4, mentoring relationships have been described in terms of two broad categories of functions—career functions and psychosocial functions.[50]

Why would a leader want to be a mentor? There are personal benefits to the leader as well as benefits for the organization. The mentor–protégé relationship gives the mentor full access to the attitudes and feelings of lower-ranking employees, and protégés can be an excellent source of early-warning signals that identify potential problems. Research suggests that mentor commitment to a program is key to its effectiveness, so if a program is to be successful, it's critical that mentors be on board and see the relationship as beneficial to themselves and the protégé. It's also important that the protégés feel that they have input into the relationship; if it's something they feel is forced on them, they'll just go through the motions.[51]

BOX 10-4
Career and Psychosocial Functions of the Mentoring Relationship

Career Functions

- Lobbying to get the protégé challenging and visible assignments
- Coaching the protégé to help develop her skills and achieve work objectives
- Assisting the protégé by providing exposure to influential individuals within the organization
- Protecting the protégé from possible risks to her reputation
- Sponsoring the protégé by nominating her for potential advances or promotions
- Acting as a sounding board for ideas that the protégé might be hesitant to share with her direct supervisor

Psychosocial Functions

- Counseling the protégé about anxieties and uncertainty to help bolster her self-confidence
- Sharing personal experiences with the protégé
- Providing friendship and acceptance
- Acting as a role model

Self-Leadership

Self-leadership

A set of processes through which individuals control their own behavior.

Is it possible for people to lead themselves? An increasing body of research suggests that many can.[52] Proponents of **self-leadership** propose that there are a set of processes through which individuals control their own behavior. And effective leaders (or what advocates like to call *superleaders*) help their followers to lead themselves. They do this by developing leadership capacity in others and train followers so they no longer need to depend on formal leaders for direction and motivation.

To engage in effective self-leadership: (1) make your mental organizational chart horizontal rather than vertical; (2) focus on influence and not control (do your job *with* your colleagues, not *for* them or *to* them); and (3) don't wait for the right time to make your mark; create your opportunities rather than wait for them.[53]

Online Leadership

How do you lead people who are physically separated from you and with whom your interactions are basically reduced to written digital communications? This is a question that, to date, has received minimal attention from OB researchers.[54] Leadership research has been directed almost exclusively to face-to-face and verbal situations. But we can't ignore the reality that today's managers and their employees are increasingly being linked by networks rather than geographic distance. Examples include managers who regularly use e-mail to communicate with their staff, managers who oversee virtual projects or teams, and managers whose telecommuting employees are linked to the office by a computer and an internet connection.

In face-to-face communications, harsh *words* can be softened by nonverbal action. A smile and comforting gesture, for instance, can decrease the impact behind strong words like *disappointed, unsatisfactory, inadequate,* or *below expectations*. That nonverbal component doesn't exist with online interactions. The *structure* of words in a digital communication also has the power to motivate or demotivate the receiver.

In addition, online leaders confront unique challenges, the greatest of which appears to be developing and maintaining trust. Identification-based trust, for instance, is particularly difficult to achieve when there is a lack of intimacy and face-to-face interaction.[55] This discussion leads us to the tentative conclusion that, for an increasing number of managers, good interpersonal skills may include the abilities to communicate support and leadership through written words on a computer screen and to read emotions in others' messages. In this 'new world' of communications, writing skills are likely to become an extension of interpersonal skills.

Challenges to the Leadership Construct

10 Determine the challenges that leaders face.

In this section, we present two perspectives that challenge the widely accepted belief in the importance of leadership. The first argument proposes that leadership is more about appearances than reality. You don't have to *be* an effective leader as long as you *look* like one. The second argument directly attacks the idea that some leadership *will always be effective*, regardless of the situation.

Leadership as an Attribution

Attribution theory of leadership

A leadership theory that says that leadership is merely an attribution that people make about other individuals.

We introduced attribution theory in Chapter 4. As you may remember, it deals with the ways in which people try to make sense out of cause-and-effect relationships. We said that when something happens, we want to attribute it or relate it to something else. The **attribution theory of leadership** says that leadership is merely an attribution that people make about other individuals.[56]

The attribution theory has shown that people characterize leaders as having such traits as intelligence, outgoing personality, strong verbal skills, aggressiveness, understanding, and industriousness.[57] At the organizational level, the attribution framework accounts for the conditions under which people use leadership to explain organizational outcomes. Those conditions are extremes in organizational performance. That is, when an organization has either extremely negative or extremely positive performance, people tend to use leadership attributions as an explanation for the specific performance.

International OB

Cultural Variation in Charismatic Attributions

Do people from different cultures make different attributions about their leaders' charisma? One recent study attempted to answer this question.

A team of researchers conducted a study in which individuals from the United States and Turkey read short stories about a hypothetical leader. Each story portrayed the leader's behaviors and the performance of the leader's company differently. In both cultures, individuals believed that the leader possessed more charisma when displaying behaviors such as promoting the company's vision and involving subordinates *and* when the leader's company performed well. However, the participants from the United States, who are more individualistic, focused on the leader's behaviors when attributing charisma. In contrast, the participants from Turkey, who are more collectivistic, focused on the company's performance when attributing charisma.

Why do these differences exist? The researchers speculated that people from individualistic cultures place more emphasis on the person than on the situation and so they attribute charisma when a leader displays certain traits. People from collectivistic cultures, in contrast, place more emphasis on the situation and assume that the leader is charismatic when the company performs well. So whether others see you as charismatic may, in part, depend on what culture you work in.

Source: Based on N. Ensari and S. E. Murphy, "Cross-Cultural Variations in Leadership Perceptions and Attribution of Charisma to the Leader," *Organizational Behavior and Human Decision Processes*, September 2003, pp. 52–66.

Following the attribution theory of leadership, we'd say that what's important in being characterized as an "effective leader" is projecting the *appearance* of being a leader rather than focusing on *actual accomplishments*. Leader-wannabes can attempt to shape the perception that they're smart, personable, verbally competent, aggressive, hardworking, and consistent in their style. By doing so, they increase the probability that their bosses, colleagues, and employees will *view* them as effective leaders.

Substitutes for and Neutralizers of Leadership

Contrary to the arguments made throughout this chapter, leadership may not always be important. A theory of leadership suggests that, in many situations, whatever actions leaders exhibit are irrelevant. Certain individual, job, and organizational variables can act as *substitutes* for leadership or *neutralize* the leader's influence on his or her followers.[58]

Neutralizers make it impossible for leader behavior to make any difference to follower outcomes. They cancel the leader's influence. Substitutes, however, make a leader's influence not only impossible but also unnecessary. They act as a replacement for the leader's influence. For instance, characteristics of employees such as their experience, training, 'professional' orientation, or indifference toward organizational rewards can substitute for, or neutralize the effect of, leadership. Experience and training can replace the need for a leader's support or ability to create structure and reduce task uncertainty. Jobs that are clear and routine or that are satisfying may place fewer demands on the leadership variable. Organizational characteristics such as explicit, formalized goals, rigid rules and procedures, and cohesive work groups can also replace formal leadership (see Table 10-1).

This recognition that leaders don't always have an impact on follower outcomes should not be that surprising. It's important, therefore, to recognize explicitly that leadership is merely another independent variable in our overall OB model. In some situations, it may contribute a lot to explaining employee productivity, absence, turnover, satisfaction, and citizenship behavior, but in other situations, it may contribute little toward that end.

TABLE 10-1 Substitutes for Neutralizers of Leadership		
Defining Characteristics	**Relationship-Oriented Leadership**	**Task-Oriented Leadership**
Individual		
Experience/training	No effect on	Substitutes for
Professionalism	Substitutes for	Substitutes for
Indifference to rewards	Neutralizes	Neutralizes
Job		
Highly structured task	No effect on	Substitutes for
Provides its own feedback	No effect on	Substitutes for
Intrinsically satisfying	Substitutes for	No effect on
Organization		
Explicit formalized goals	No effect on	Substitutes for
Rigid rules and procedures	No effect on	Substitutes for
Cohesive work groups	Substitutes for	Substitutes for

Source: Based on S. Kerr and J. M. Jermier, "Substitutes for Leadership: Their Meaning and Measurement," *Organizational Behavior and Human Performance*, December 1978, p. 378.

Finding and Creating Effective Leaders

11 Explain how to find and create effective leaders.

We have covered a lot of material in this chapter on leadership. But the ultimate goal of our review is to answer this question: How can organizations find or create effective leaders? Let's try to be more specific in answering that question.

Selecting Leaders

The entire process that organizations go through to fill management positions is an exercise in trying to identify individuals who will be effective leaders. There are many associations, such as Young Arab Leaders (YAL), that are also involved in this process. Your search might begin by reviewing the specific requirements for the position to be filled. What knowledge, skills, and abilities (KSAs) are needed to do the job effectively? You should try to analyze the situation to find candidates who will make a proper match.

Testing is useful for identifying and selecting leaders. Personality tests can be used to look for traits associated with leadership—extraversion, conscientiousness, and openness to experience. Testing to find a leadership-candidate's score on self-monitoring also makes sense. High self-monitors are likely to outperform their low-scoring counterparts because the former are better at reading situations and adjusting their behavior accordingly.

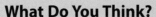

What Do You Think?

Can certain tests actually help to select effective leaders?

Interviews also provide an opportunity to evaluate leadership candidates. You can use an interview to determine whether a candidate's prior experience fits with the situation you're trying to fill. Similarly, the interview is a reasonably good vehicle for identifying the degree to which a candidate has leadership traits such as extraversion, self-confidence, a vision, the verbal skills to frame issues, or a charismatic physical presence.

The most important event organizations need to plan for is leadership changes. Nothing lasts forever, so it's always simply a matter of *when* a leader exits, not whether a leader exists.

Training Leaders

Organizations spend billions on leadership training and development.[59] These efforts take many forms, such as executive leadership programs offered by universities such as Harvard, in the US, and Notre Dame University, Lebanon.

Although much of the money spent on training may provide questionable benefits, our review suggests that there are some things managers can do to get the maximum effect from their leadership-training budgets.[60]

First, let's recognize the obvious. People are not equally trainable. Leadership training of any kind is likely to be more successful with individuals who are high self-monitors than with low self-monitors. Such individuals have the flexibility to change their behavior.

What kinds of things can individuals learn that might be related to higher leader effectiveness? It may be a bit optimistic to believe that we can teach 'vision creation,' but we can teach implementation skills. We can train people

Musa Freiji has led the Wadi Group of Companies into the twenty-first century. The story of success is a result of effective leadership. The success of Wadi is not a coincidence but the result of diligence, continuous learning, in-depth knowledge, sound vision, and wisdom in decision making. Freiji has led by example and taught employees to embrace the values of Wadi—honesty in word and deed, loyalty and dedication in behavior, faith and ambition in outlook, and integrity in practice. "What motivates our Group and drives our high ambitions is our strong and sincere desire to participate in the economic development of Egypt and other Arab countries in which we operate," stresses Freiji.

to develop "an understanding about content themes critical to effective visions."[61] We can also teach skills such as trust building and mentoring. And leaders can be taught situational-analysis skills.

In addition, they can learn how to evaluate situations, how to modify situations to make them fit better with their style, and how to assess which leader behaviors might be most effective in given situations. A number of companies have recently turned to executive coaches to help senior managers improve their leadership skills.[62] In particular, the banking sector provides professional training on a regular basis. Many well-known banks, such as Byblos Bank, Audi Bank, Bank of Beirut, and Arab Bank, ensure that their people in top management positions attend training to enhance their skills for better performance.

All the issues that have been discussed in this chapter about leadership are applicable to all cultures. They are concepts that leaders of all backgrounds can relate to and definitely consider. Being a leader in the Arab world is no different. Arab world leadership theories, issues and approaches are similar to those of any other country. What we do need to pay attention to, though, is the fact that leaders in the Arab world, or in any other culture, must stress their national culture when implementing their leadership duties and responsibilities. YAL and its partners present annual Arab American Business Fellowship programs aimed at helping people to break cultural barriers and improve the required skills for growth and development.

Global Implications

12 *Assess whether charismatic and transformational leadership generalize across cultures.*

Most of the research on the leadership theories discussed in this chapter has been conducted in English-speaking countries. Thus, we know very little about how culture might influence their validity, particularly in Eastern cultures. However, a recent analysis of the Global Leadership and Organizational Behavior Effectiveness (GLOBE) research project has produced some useful, if preliminary, insights into cultural issues that leaders need to consider.[63]

In this article, the authors sought to answer the practical question of how culture might affect a US manager if he or she had been given two years to lead a project in four prototypical countries, whose cultures diverged from that of the United States in different ways: Brazil, France, Egypt, and China. Let's consider each case in turn.

Brazil Based on the GLOBE study findings of the values of Brazilian employees, a US manager leading a team in Brazil would need to be team-oriented, participative, and humane. This would suggest that leaders who are high on consideration, who emphasize participative decision making, and who have high LPC scores would be best suited to managing employees in this culture. As one Brazilian manager said in the study, "We do not prefer leaders who take self-governing decisions and act alone without engaging the group. That's part of who we are."

France Compared with US employees, the French tend to have a more bureaucratic view of leaders and are less likely to expect them to be humane and considerate. Thus, a leader who is high on initiating structure, or relatively task-oriented, will do best, and he or she can make decisions in a relatively autocratic manner. A manager who scores high on consideration (people-oriented) leadership may find that style backfiring in France.

Egypt   Like those in Brazil, employees in Egypt are more likely to value team-oriented and participative leadership than US employees. However, Egypt is also a relatively high-power-distance culture, meaning that status differences between leaders and followers are expected. How would a US manager be participative and yet act in a manner that shows his or her high level of status? According to the authors, the leaders should ask employees for their opinions, try to minimize conflicts, but also not be afraid to take charge and make the final decision (after consulting team members).

China   According to the GLOBE study, Chinese culture emphasizes being polite, considerate, and unselfish. But the culture also has a high performance orientation. These two factors suggest that both consideration and initiating structure may be important. Although Chinese culture is relatively participative compared with that of the United States, there are also status differences between leaders and employees. This suggests that, as in Egypt, a moderately participative style may work best.

In sum, the GLOBE study suggests that leaders need to take culture into account whenever they are managing employees from different cultures.

We also noted in this chapter that while there is little cross-cultural research on the traditional theories of leadership, there is reason to believe that certain types of leadership behaviors work better in some cultures than in others. What about the more contemporary leadership roles covered in this chapter: Is there cross-cultural research on charismatic/transformational leadership? Does it generalize across cultures? Yes and yes. There has been cross-cultural research on charismatic/transformational leadership, and it seems to suggest that the leadership style works in different cultures.

What elements of transformational leadership appear universal? They are vision, foresight, providing encouragement, trustworthiness, dynamism, positiveness, and proactiveness. The results led two members of the GLOBE team to conclude that "effective business leaders in any country are expected by their subordinates to provide a powerful and proactive vision to guide the company into the future, strong motivational skills to stimulate all employees to fulfill the vision, and excellent planning skills to assist in implementing the vision."[64]

What might explain the universal appeal of these transformational leader attributes? It's been suggested that pressures toward common technologies and management practices, as a result of global competition and multinational influences, may make some aspects of leadership universally accepted. If that's true, we may be able to select and train leaders in a universal style and thus significantly raise the quality of leadership worldwide.

However, none of this is meant to suggest that a certain cultural sensitivity or adaptation in styles might not be important when leading teams in different cultures. A vision is important in any culture, but how that vision is formed and communicated may still need to vary by culture. This is true even for companies that are known worldwide for their emphasis on vision.

Summary and Implications for Managers

Leadership plays an important part in understanding group behavior, for it's the leader who usually provides the direction toward goal attainment.

The early search for a set of universal leadership traits failed. However, recent efforts using the Big Five personality framework (discussed in Chapter 2) have generated much more encouraging results. Specifically, the traits of extraversion, conscientiousness, and openness to experience show strong and consistent relationships to leadership.

The behavioral approach's major contribution was narrowing leadership into task-oriented (initiating structure) and people-oriented (consideration) styles. As with the trait approach, results from the behavioral school were initially dismissed. But recent efforts have confirmed the importance of task- and people-oriented leadership styles.

A major shift in leadership research came when we recognized the need to develop contingency theories that included situational factors. At present, the evidence indicates that relevant situational variables include: the task structure of the job; level of situational stress; level of group support; leader's intelligence and experience; and follower characteristics, such as personality, experience, ability, and motivation. Although contingency theories haven't lived up to their initial promise, the literature has provided basic support for Fiedler's LPC theory.

Two other theories—leader–member exchange (LMX) theory and the leader-participation model—also contribute to our understanding of leadership. LMX theory has proved influential for its analysis of followers—whether they are included in the leader's 'in-group' or were relegated to the 'out group.' Vroom's leader-participation model focuses on the leader's role as decision maker and considers *how* leaders make decisions (such as whether to involve followers in their decision making).

Moreover, organizations are increasingly searching for managers who can exhibit transformational leadership qualities. They want leaders with vision and the charisma to carry out their vision. And although true leadership effectiveness may be a result of exhibiting the right behaviors at the right time, the evidence is quite strong that people have a relatively uniform perception of what a leader should look like. They attribute 'leadership' to people who are smart, personable, verbally adept, and the like. To the degree that managers project these qualities, others are likely to name them as leaders. There is increasing evidence that the effectiveness of charismatic and transformational leadership crosses cultural boundaries.

Effective managers today must develop trusting relationships with those they seek to lead because, as organizations have become less stable and predictable, strong bonds of trust are likely to be replacing bureaucratic rules in defining expectations and relationships. Managers who aren't trusted aren't likely to be effective leaders.

Furthermore, for managers concerned with how to fill key positions in their organization with effective leaders, we have shown that tests and interviews help to identify people with leadership qualities. In addition to focusing on leadership selection, managers should also consider investing in leadership training. Many individuals with leadership potential can enhance their skills through formal courses, workshops, rotating job responsibilities, coaching, and mentoring.

Point ▶◀ Counterpoint

LEADERS ARE BORN, NOT MADE

That leaders are born, not made, isn't a new idea. Great leaders are what make teams, companies, and even countries great. These leaders are great leaders because they have the right stuff—stuff the rest of us don't have, or have in lesser quantities.

If you're not yet convinced, there is new evidence to support this position. One study was of several hundred identical twins separated at birth and raised in totally different environments. The researchers found that, despite their different environments, each pair of twins had striking similarities in terms of whether they became leaders.

A great part of leadership is a product of our genes. If we have the right stuff, we're destined to be effective leaders. If we have the wrong stuff, we're unlikely to excel in that role. Leadership cannot be for everyone, and we make a mistake in thinking that everyone is equally capable of being a good leader.[65]

On the other hand, personal qualities and characteristics matter to leadership, as they do to most other behaviors. But the real key is what you do with what you have.

First, if great leadership were just the possession of traits like intelligence and personality, we could simply give people a test and select those people to be leaders. Second, great leaders tell us that the key to their leadership success is not the characteristics they had at birth but what they learned along the way.

Finally, this focus on 'great men and great women' is not very productive. Even if it were true that great leaders were born, it's a very impractical approach to leadership. People need to believe in something, and one of those things is that they can improve themselves.[66]

Questions for Review

1 Are leadership and management different from one another? How?

2 What is the basis of trait theories? What traits are associated with leadership?

3 What are the characteristics and limitations of behavioral theories?

4 What is Fiedler's contingency model? Has it been supported in research?

5 How does leader–follower participation enhance employee performance?

6 What is charismatic leadership and how does it work?

7 What is transformational leadership? How is it different from transactional and charismatic leadership?

8 What is authentic leadership? Why do ethics and trust matter to leadership?

9 What are the importance of mentoring, self-leadership, and virtual leadership?

10 What are the challenges that leaders face and how can they be overcome?

11 How can organizations select and develop effective leaders?

12 How can leaders adapt to different cultures?

Discussion Exercise

Discuss what you think the adjectives are that describe a successful leader. Discuss them with the class and try to all agree on the most important 12 adjectives.

Ethical Considerations

The power that comes from being a leader can be used for evil as well as for good. When you assume the benefits of leadership, you also assume ethical burdens. But many highly successful leaders have relied on questionable tactics to achieve their ends. These include manipulation, verbal attacks, physical intimidation, lying, fear, and control.

Nawfal Hakim is the owner and manager of a fast growing chain of restaurants in Jordan. As an entrepreneur, he experienced very difficult times and had to sacrifice a lot to reach his present position. Because of all this, he has developed a rigid attitude. Nawfal feels that it is his right to control everything and everyone. His employees fear him and they complain that he doesn't trust them and won't give them any freedom. He expects excellence always and, as a result, has just fired 10 employees without giving them a chance to ask why.

What are the ethical implications of Hakim's actions? What do you think of Hakim's leadership style? Explain.

Critical Analysis

CULTURAL VARIATION IN CHARISMATIC ATTRIBUTIONS

Do people from different cultures make different attributions about their leaders' charisma? One recent study attempted to answer this question.

A team of researchers conducted a study in which individuals from the United States and Turkey read short stories about a hypothetical leader. Each story portrayed the leader's behaviors and the performance of the leader's company differently. In both cultures, individuals believed that the leader possessed more charisma when displaying behaviors such as promoting the company's vision and involving subordinates *and* when the leader's company performed well. However, the participants from the United States, who are more individualistic, focused on the leader's behaviors when attributing charisma. In contrast, the participants from Turkey, who are more collectivistic, focused on the company's performance when attributing charisma.

Why do these differences exist? The researchers speculated that people from individualistic cultures place more emphasis on the person than on the situation, and so they attribute charisma when a leader displays certain traits. People from collectivistic cultures, in contrast, place more emphasis on the situation and assume that the leader is charismatic when the company performs well. So whether others see you as charismatic may, in part, depend on what culture you work in.

Questions

1. Why do you think culture affects the attributes of charisma?

2. Compare the charismatic behavior of leaders from the East to those from the West.

3. How do you describe the charisma of leaders in your country?

Source: Based on N. Ensari and S. E. Murphy, "Cross-Cultural Variations in Leadership Perceptions and Attribution of Charisma to the Leader," *Organizational Behavior and Human Decision Processes*, September 2003, pp. 52–66.

Research Exercise

Many concepts, approaches and issues regarding leadership were discussed in this chapter, but not much research has been carried out on leadership in the Arab world. Do your own research and find out more about leadership practices in the Arab world by interviewing a leader of an organization in your country. Share your findings with the class.

LEARNING OBJECTIVES

This chapter will enable you to:

1 Define *power* and contrast leadership and power.

2 Contrast the five bases of power.

3 Identify nine power or influence tactics and their contingencies.

4 Show the connection between sexual harassment and the abuse of power.

5 Distinguish between legitimate and illegitimate political behaviour.

6 Identify the causes and consequences of political behavior.

7 Apply impression management techniques.

8 Determine whether a political action is ethical.

9 Show the influence of culture on the uses and perceptions of politics.

Power and Politics

That was my first lesson in leadership—that knowledge is power. —Abdallah S. Jum'ah

AL-WASTA

Nepotism is a form of power that people from all over the world constantly practice. We talk about selecting appropriate employees to fill positions because they have the qualifications and competencies that are required for the job. However, individuals are still employed on the basis of: 'Don't tell me who you are; tell me who you know.'

In Arabic, nepotism is '*al wasta.*' It is often referred to as 'vitamin W'—the magical power that smoothes the way to jobs and promotions. A truly cultural issue, wasta is considered to be behind almost all that happens in the Arab world. Wasta comes from the root 'w-s-t,' which means 'middle,' and wasta has come to mean the support of an intermediary who has connections and influence. As a result, the person who has received a favor because of wasta owes the intermediary gratitude and must repay it in an unspecified way whenever asked.

Dr. Adnan Badran states, "That's how wasta and nepotism spread and gave birth to thousands of unqualified and unproductive employees who do nothing but wait for their salaries at the end of the month."

Often, it seems that wasta has negative implications and is used for achieving things that one may not be entitled to without wasta. However, wasta is also considered to be the "poor people's weapon," whereby individuals can reach justice only through the influence and pressures that others have. Clearly, there are different opinions of wasta. In 2000, a survey conducted in Jordan found that 86 percent agreed that wasta was a form of corruption, and 87 percent wanted it to stop. Simultaneously, 90 percent expect to use wasta at some point in the future. Nevertheless, 42 percent felt the need would increase, whereas only 13 percent felt the need would decrease.

Many dream of, and hope for, equality among all that would allow those with potential the opportunity to progress. It is a dream, however, because no matter how much we want equal treatment, unfortunately nepotism and wasta will always exist. When Hakim Harb, a film producer, was interviewed by the Arab Archives Institute (AAI), he stressed, "When we live in a real society, progressive and civilized, and when we live in an atmosphere filled with freedoms, democracy and human rights, everyone will obtain his/her rights and the right people will be in the right places without the need for any form of help."

Source: Based on "Wasta: Vitamin W," *al-bab.com*, www.al-bab.com/arab/background/wasta.htm.

P ower and *politics* have been described as the last dirty words. As the opening text shows, power can have many forms; it can be used for both good and evil. However, the abuse can lead to inequalities among people and especially when influence is used, as nepotism or wasta imply. Wasta is considered to be a major part of all that happens in the Arab world. It is easier for most of us to talk about money than it is to talk about power or political behavior. People who have power deny it, people who want it try not to look like they're seeking it, and those who are good at getting it are secretive about how they do so.[1]

To see whether you think your work environment is political, take the following self-assessment.

Self **A**ssessment **L**ibrary ▶

IS MY WORKPLACE POLITICAL?

In the Self-Assessment Library (available online), take assessment IV.F.1 (Is My Workplace Political?); if you don't currently have a job, answer for your most recent job. Then answer the following questions:

1. *How does your score relate to those of your classmates? Do you think your score is accurate? Why or why not?*

2. *Do you think a political workplace is a bad thing? If yes, why? If no, why not?*

3. *What factors cause your workplace to be political?*

A major theme of this chapter is that power and political behavior are natural processes in any group or organization, and the opening case explains that wasta is part of the culture in the Arab world. Given that, you need to know how power is acquired and exercised if you are to fully understand organizational behavior. Although you may have heard the phrase "power corrupts, and absolute power corrupts absolutely," power is not always bad. As one author has noted, most medicines can kill if taken in the wrong amount, and thousands die each year in automobile accidents, but we don't abandon chemicals or cars because of the dangers associated with them. Rather, we consider danger an incentive to get training and information that will help us to use these forces productively.[2] The same applies to power. It's a reality of organizational life, and it's not going to go away. Moreover, by learning how power works in organizations, you'll be better able to use your knowledge to become a more effective manager.

Power

A capacity that A has to influence the behavior of B so that B acts in accordance with A's wishes.

A Definition of *Power*

1 Define power *and contrast leadership and power.*

Dependency

B's relationship to A when A possesses something that B requires.

Power refers to a capacity that *A* has to influence the behavior of *B* so that *B* acts in accordance with *A*'s wishes.[3] This definition implies a *potential* that need not be actualized to be effective, and a *dependency* relationship.

Power may exist but not be used. It is, therefore, a capacity or potential. Someone can have power but not impose it. Probably the most important aspect of power is that it is a function of **dependency**. The greater *B*'s dependence on *A*, the greater is *A*'s power in the relationship. Dependence, in turn, is based on alternatives that *B* perceives and the importance that *B* places on the alternative(s) that *A* controls. A person can have power over you only if he or she controls something you desire.

Contrasting Leadership and Power

A careful comparison of our description of power with our description of leadership in Chapter 10 reveals that the concepts are closely intertwined. Leaders use power as a means of attaining group goals. Leaders achieve goals, and power is a means of facilitating their achievement. The events that the Arab world experienced in 2011 definitely changed the way people view leadership and power. These transformations have allowed people the opportunity to witness history in the making. The Arab world will never be the same. We learned valuable lessons about how effective leadership and power, or the abuse of it, can completely change the attitudes of people.

What differences are there between the two terms? One difference relates to goal compatibility. Power does not require goal compatibility just dependence. Leadership, on the other hand, requires some equality between the goals of the leader and those being led. A second difference relates to the direction of influence. Leadership focuses on the downward influence on one's followers. It minimizes the importance of lateral and upward influence patterns. Power does not. Still another difference deals with research emphasis. Leadership research, for the most part, emphasizes style. It seeks answers to questions such as: How supportive should a leader be? How much decision making should be shared with followers? In contrast, the research on power focuses on tactics for gaining agreement. It has gone beyond the individual as the exerciser of power because power can be used by groups as well as by individuals to control other individuals or groups.

Bases of Power

 Contrast the five bases of power.

Where does power come from? What is it that gives an individual or a group influence over others? We answer these questions by dividing the bases or sources of power into two general groupings—formal and personal—and then breaking each of these down into more specific categories.[4]

Formal Power

Formal power is based on an individual's position in an organization. Formal power can come from the ability to coerce or reward, or it can come from formal authority.

Coercive power
A power base that is dependent on fear.

Coercive Power The **coercive power** base is dependent on fear. People react to this power out of fear of the negative results that might occur if they fail to comply. It rests on the application, or the threat of application, of physical authorization such as the infliction of pain, the generation of frustration through restriction of movement, or the controlling by force of basic physiological or safety needs.

Reward power

Compliance achieved based on the ability to distribute rewards that others view as valuable.

Reward Power   The opposite of coercive power is **reward power**. People comply with the wishes or directives of another because doing so produces positive benefits; therefore, one who can distribute rewards that others view as valuable will have power over those others. These rewards can be either financial—such as controlling pay rates, raises, and bonuses; or nonfinancial—including recognition, promotions, interesting work assignments, friendly colleagues, and preferred work shifts or sales territories.[5]

Coercive power and reward power are actually counterparts of each other. If you can remove something of positive value from another or inflict something of negative value, you have coercive power over that person. If you can give someone something of positive value or remove something of negative value, you have reward power over that person.

Legitimate power

The power a person receives as a result of his or her position in the formal hierarchy of an organization.

Legitimate Power   In formal groups and organizations, probably the most frequent access to one or more of the power bases is one's structural position. This is called **legitimate power**. It represents the formal authority to control and use organizational resources.

Positions of authority include coercive and reward powers. Legitimate power, however, is broader than the power to coerce and reward. Specifically, it includes acceptance by members in an organization of the authority of a position. For instance, when school principals, bank presidents, or army captains speak (assuming that their directives are viewed to be within the authority of their positions), teachers, tellers, and first lieutenants listen and usually comply.

Personal Power

You don't need a formal position in an organization to have power. Many of the most competent and productive chip designers at Intel, for instance, have power, but they aren't managers and have no formal power. What they have is personal power—power that comes from an individual's unique characteristics. In this section, we look at two bases of personal power—expertise and the respect and admiration of others.

Expert power

Influence based on special skills or knowledge.

Expert Power   **Expert power** is influence as a result of expertise, special skill, or knowledge. Expertise has become one of the most powerful sources of influence as the world has become more technologically oriented. As jobs become more specialized, we become increasingly dependent on experts to achieve goals. It is generally acknowledged that physicians have expertise and hence expert power—most of us follow the advice that our doctors give us. But it's also important to recognize that computer specialists, tax accountants, economists, industrial psychologists, and other specialists are able to wield power as a result of their expertise.

Referent power

Influence based on possession by an individual of desirable resources or personal traits.

Referent Power   **Referent power** is based on identification with a person who has desirable resources or personal traits. That is, if I like, respect, and admire you, you can exercise power over me because I want to please you.

Nike CEO Mark Parker has expert power. Since joining Nike in 1979 as a footwear designer, Parker has been involved in many of Nike's most significant design innovations. His primary responsibilities and leadership positions at Nike have been in product research, design, and development. Nike depends on Parker's expertise in leading the company's innovation initiatives and in setting corporate strategy to achieve the growth of its global business portfolio that includes Converse, Nike Golf, and Cole Haan. Parker is shown here introducing Nike's Considered Design during a news conference about the company's latest products that combine sustainability and innovation.

Referent power develops out of admiration of another and a desire to be like that person. It helps explain, for instance, why celebrities are paid millions of dollars to endorse products in commercials. Marketing research shows that the singers or actors such as Nancy Ajram and Omar Al Sharif that do commercials have the power to influence our choice of athletic shoes, drinks, and cars. With a little practice, you and I could probably deliver as smooth a sales pitch as these celebrities, but the buying public doesn't identify with you and me. One of the ways in which individuals acquire referent power is through charisma. Some people have referent power who, while not in formal leadership positions, nevertheless are able to exert influence over others because of their charismatic dynamism, likability, and emotional effects on us.

What Do You Think?

Is your choice of a particular product influenced by the person who is in an advertisement?

Which Bases of Power Are Most Effective?

Of the three bases of formal power (coercive, reward, legitimate) and two bases of personal power (expert, referent), which is most important to have? Interestingly, research suggests pretty clearly that the personal sources of power are most effective. Both expert and referent power are positively related to employees' satisfaction with supervision, their organizational commitment, and their performance, whereas reward and legitimate power seem to be unrelated to these outcomes. Moreover, one source of formal power—coercive power—actually can backfire in that it is negatively related to employee satisfaction and commitment.[6]

Dependency: The Key to Power

Earlier in this chapter we said that probably the most important aspect of power is that it is a function of dependency. In this section, we show how having an understanding of dependency is important to the understanding of power itself.

What Creates Dependency?

Dependency is increased when the resource you control is important, scarce, and nonsubstitutable.[7]

Importance   If nobody wants what you have, it's not going to create dependency. To create dependency, the thing(s) you control must be perceived as being important. Organizations such as Xerox, for instance, actively seek to avoid uncertainty.[8] We should, therefore, expect that the individuals or groups who can absorb an organization's uncertainty will be perceived as controlling an important resource. For instance, a study of industrial organizations found that the marketing departments in these firms were consistently rated as the most powerful.[9] The researcher concluded that the most critical uncertainty facing these firms was selling their products.

Scarcity   As noted previously, if something is plentiful, possession of it will not increase your power. A resource needs to be perceived as scarce or limited to create dependency. This can help explain how low-ranking members in an organization who have important knowledge not available to high-ranking members gain power over the high-ranking members. Possession of a scarce resource—in this case, important knowledge—makes the high-ranking member dependent on the low-ranking member.

The scarcity–dependency relationship can further be seen in the power of occupational categories. Individuals in occupations in which the supply of personnel is low relative to demand can negotiate compensation and benefits

Because Xerox Corporation has staked its future on development and innovation, Sophie Vandebroek is in a position of power at Xerox. As the company's chief technology officer, she leads the Xerox Innovation Group of 5,000 scientists and engineers at the company's global research centers. The group's mission is "to pioneer high-impact technologies that enable us to lead in our core markets and to create future markets for Xerox." Xerox depends on Vandebroek to make that mission a reality.

packages that are far more attractive than can those in occupations for which there is an abundance of candidates. For instance, college administrators have no problem today finding English instructors; however, the market for network systems analysts, in contrast, is extremely tight, with the demand high and the supply limited. The result is that the bargaining power of computer-engineering faculty allows them to negotiate higher salaries, lighter teaching loads, and other benefits.

Nonsubstitutability   The fewer feasible substitutes for a resource, the more power the control over that resource provides. Higher education again provides an excellent example. At universities in which there are strong pressures for the faculty to publish, we can say that a department head's power over a faculty member is inversely related to that member's publication record. The more recognition the faculty member receives through publication, the more mobile he or she is; that is, because other universities want faculty members who are highly published and visible, there is an increased demand for that person's services. Although the concept of tenure can act to alter this relationship by restricting the department head's alternatives, faculty members who have few or no publications have the least mobility and are subject to the greatest influence from their superiors.

What Do You Think?

Do you agree that market demand and supply can control power levels within the organization?

Power Tactics

3 *Identify nine power or influence tactics and their contingencies*

Power tactics

Ways in which individuals translate power bases into specific actions.

What **power tactics** do people use to translate power bases into specific actions? That is, what options do individuals have for influencing their bosses, coworkers, or employees? And are some of these options more effective than others? In this section, we review popular tactical options and the conditions under which one may be more effective than another.

Research has identified nine distinct influence tactics:[10]

- *Legitimacy.* Relying on one's authority position or stressing that a request is in accordance with organizational policies or rules.
- *Rational persuasion.* Presenting logical arguments and factual evidence to demonstrate that a request is reasonable.
- *Inspirational appeals.* Developing emotional commitment by appealing to a target's values, needs, hopes, and aspirations.
- *Consultation.* Increasing the target's motivation and support by involving him or her in deciding how the plan or change will be accomplished.
- *Exchange.* Rewarding the target with benefits or favors in exchange for following a request.
- *Personal appeals.* Asking for compliance based on friendship or loyalty.
- *Ingratiation.* Using flattery, praise, or friendly behavior prior to making a request.
- *Pressure.* Using warnings, repeated demands, and threats.
- *Coalitions.* Enlisting the aid of other people to persuade the target or using the support of others as a reason for the target to agree.

Without a doubt, some tactics are more effective than others. Specifically, evidence indicates that rational persuasion, inspirational appeals, and consultation tend to be the most effective. On the other hand, pressure tends to frequently backfire and is typically the least effective of the nine tactics.[11] You can also increase your chance of success by using more than one type of tactic at the same time or sequentially, as long as your choices are compatible.[12] For instance, using both ingratiation and legitimacy can lessen the negative reactions that might come from the appearance of being 'dictated to' by the boss.

To see how these tactics can work in practice, let's consider the most effective way of getting a raise. You can start with rational persuasion. That means doing your homework and carefully thinking through the best way to build your case: figure out how your pay compares with that of peers, or secure a competing job offer, or show objective results that testify to your performance. But the effectiveness of some influence tactics depends on the direction of influence.[13]

As shown in Table 11-1, studies have found that rational persuasion is the only tactic that is effective across organizational levels. Inspirational appeals work best as a downward-influencing tactic with subordinates. When pressure works, it's generally only to achieve downward influence. And the use of personal appeals and coalitions, as we see in the 'International OB' box opposite, are most effective with lateral influence attempts. In addition to the direction of influence, a number of other factors have been found to affect which tactics work best. These include the sequencing of tactics, a person's skill in using the tactic, and the culture of the organization.

Recently, research has shown that people differ in their **political skill**, or the ability to influence others in such a way as to enhance their own objectives. Those who are politically skilled are more effective in their use of influence tactics, regardless of the tactics they're using. Political skill also appears to be more effective when the stakes are high—such as when the individual is accountable for important organizational outcomes.

Finally, we know that cultures within organizations differ significantly—for example, some are warm, relaxed, and supportive; others are formal and conservative. The organizational culture in which a person works, therefore, will have an influence on defining which tactics are considered appropriate. Some cultures encourage the use of participation and consultation, some encourage reason, and still others rely on pressure. So the organization itself will influence which subset of power tactics is viewed as acceptable for use.

Political skill

The ability to influence others in such a way as to enhance one's objectives.

TABLE 11-1 Preferred Power Tactics by Influence Direction

Upward Influence	Downward Influence	Lateral Influence
Rational persuasion	Rational persuasion	Rational persuasion
	Inspirational appeals	Consultation
	Pressure	Ingratiation
	Consultation	Exchange
	Ingratiation	Legitimacy
	Exchange	Personal appeals
	Legitimacy	Coalitions

International OB

Influence Tactics in China

Researchers usually examine cross-cultural influences in business by comparing two very different cultures, such as those from Eastern and Western societies. However, it is also important to examine differences within a given culture because those differences can sometimes be greater than differences between cultures.

For example, although we might view all Chinese people as being alike due to their shared heritage and appearance, China is a big country, housing different cultures and traditions. A recent study examining Mainland Chinese, Taiwanese, and Hong Kong managers explored how the three cultural subgroups differ according to the influence tactics they prefer to use.

Though managers from all three places believe that rational persuasion and exchange are the most effective influence tactics, managers in Taiwan tend to use inspirational appeals and ingratiation more than managers from either Mainland China or Hong Kong. The study also found that managers from Hong Kong rate pressure as more effective in influencing others than do managers in Taiwan or Mainland China. Such differences have implications for business relationships. For example, Taiwanese or Mainland Chinese managers may be taken aback by the use of pressure tactics by a Hong Kong manager. Likewise, managers from Hong Kong may not be persuaded by managers from Taiwan, who tend to use ingratiating tactics. Such differences

in influence tactics may make business dealings difficult. Companies should address these issues, perhaps making their managers aware of the differences within cultures.

Managers need to know what variations exist within their local cultures so they can be better prepared to deal with others. Managers who fail to realize these differences may miss out on opportunities to deal effectively with others.

Source: Based on P. P. Fu, T. K. Peng, J. C. Kennedy, and G. Yukl, "A Comparison of Chinese Managers in Hong Kong, Taiwan, and Mainland China," *Organizational Dynamics*, February 2004, pp. 32–46.

Sexual Harassment: Unequal Power in the Workplace

> *4 Show the connection between sexual harassment and the abuse of power.*

Sexual harassment is wrong. It can also be costly to employers. Just ask executives at Philip Morris and UPS.[14] A US jury awarded US$2 million to a Philip Morris plant supervisor who suffered through more than a year of sexual harassment by men she supervised. In addition, a former UPS manager won an US$80 million suit against UPS for fostering a hostile work environment when it failed to listen to her complaints of sexual harassment. There have been similar cases in the Arab world; however, the culture does not allow for transparency about sexual harassment.

Not only are there legal dangers to sexual harassment, it obviously can have a negative impact on the work environment. Research shows that sexual harassment negatively affects job attitudes and leads those who feel harassed to withdraw from the organization. Moreover, in many cases, reporting sexual harassment doesn't improve the situation because the organization responds in a negative or unhelpful way. When organizational leaders make honest efforts to stop the harassment, the outcomes are much more positive.[15]

Sexual harassment

Any unwanted activity of a sexual nature that affects an individual's employment and creates a hostile work environment.

Sexual harassment is defined as any unwanted activity of a sexual nature that affects an individual's employment and creates a hostile work environment. But there continues to be disagreement as to what *specifically* constitutes sexual harassment. Organizations have generally made considerable progress in the past decade toward limiting open forms of sexual harassment. This includes unwanted physical touching, continuing requests for dates when it is made clear the person isn't interested, and threats that a person will lose their job if he or she refuses a sexual proposition. The problems today are likely to surface around more subtle forms of sexual harassment—unwanted looks or comments, off-color jokes, sexual artifacts like pin-ups posted in the workplace, or misinterpretations of where the line between being friendly ends and harassment begins.

In a regional study, it was estimated that between mid-2003 and mid-2005, 34 million Arab women may have suffered from sexual harassment at work.[16] Another recent review in the US concluded that 58 percent of women report having experienced potentially harassing behaviors, and 24 percent report having experienced sexual harassment at work.[17] As the authors of another study note, "Although progress has been made at defining sexual harassment, it is still unclear as to whose perspective should be taken."[18] Thus, although some behaviors constitute harassment, men and women continue to differ to some degree on what defines harassment. For you, the best approach is to be careful—stay away from any behavior that may be taken as harassing, even if that was not your intention. Always keep in mind that what you see as an innocent joke or hug may be seen as harassment by the other party.

Most studies confirm that the concept of power is central to understanding sexual harassment.[19] This seems to be true whether the harassment comes from a supervisor, a coworker, or an employee. And sexual harassment is more likely to occur when there are large power differentials. The supervisor–employee interaction best characterizes an unequal power relationship, where formal power gives the supervisor the capacity to reward and coerce. Because employees want favorable performance reviews, salary increases, and the like, it's clear that supervisors control resources that most employees consider important. Because of power inequities, sexual harassment by one's boss creates the greatest difficulty for those who are being harassed. If there are no witnesses, it is the victim's word against the harasser's. Are there others this boss has harassed, and, if so, will they come forward? Because of the supervisor's control over resources, many of those who are harassed are afraid of speaking out for fear of retaliation by the supervisor.

The topic of sexual harassment is about power. It's about an individual controlling or threatening another individual. It's wrong. And whether perpetrated against women or men, it's illegal. But you can understand how sexual harassment surfaces in organizations if you analyze it in terms of power.

A recent review of the literature shows the damage caused by sexual harassment. As you would expect, individuals who are sexually harassed report more negative job attitudes (lower job satisfaction, diminished organizational commitment) as a result. This review also revealed that sexual harassment undermines the victims' mental and physical health. However, sexual harassment also negatively affects the group in which the victim works, lowering its level of productivity. The authors of this study conclude that sexual harassment "is significantly and substantively associated with a host of harms."[20]

We have seen how sexual harassment can cause confusion in an organization, not to mention on the victims themselves. But it can be avoided. A manager's role in preventing sexual harassment is critical. Some ways managers can protect themselves and their employees from sexual harassment are to:

1. Make sure the policy that defines what constitutes sexual harassment is clear and informs employees that they can be fired for sexually harassing another employee, and that establishes procedures for how complaints can be made.
2. Ensure employees that they will not encounter revenge if they issue a complaint.
3. Investigate every complaint and include the legal and human resource departments.
4. Make sure that offenders are disciplined or terminated.
5. Set up in-house seminars to raise employee awareness of the issues surrounding sexual harassment.

The bottom line is that managers have a responsibility to protect their employees from a hostile work environment, but they also need to protect themselves. Managers may be unaware that one of their employees is being sexually harassed. But being unaware does not protect them or their organization. If investigators believe a manager could have known about the harassment, both the manager and the company can be held responsible.

Politics: Power in Action

> 5 *Distinguish between legitimate and illegitimate political behavior.*

When people get together in groups, power will be exerted. People want to have influence, to earn rewards, and to advance their careers.[21] When employees in organizations change their power into action, we describe them as being engaged in politics. That is, those with good political skills have the ability to use their bases of power effectively.[22]

Definition of *Organizational Politics*

Political behavior

Activities that are not required as part of a person's formal role in the organization but that influence, or attempt to influence, the distribution of advantages and disadvantages within the organization.

There are many definitions of *organizational politics*. Essentially, however, they have focused on the use of power to affect decision making in an organization or on behaviors by members that are self-serving.[23] For our purposes, we shall define **political behavior** in organizations as activities that are not required as part of one's formal role in the organization but that influence, or attempt to influence, the distribution of advantages and disadvantages within the organization.[24] This definition contains key elements from what most people mean when they talk about organizational politics. Political behavior is outside one's specified job requirements. The behavior requires some attempt to use one's power bases. In addition, our definition includes efforts to influence the goals, criteria, or processes used for *decision making* when we state that politics is concerned with "the distribution of advantages and disadvantages within the organization." Our definition is broad enough to include varied political behaviors such as keeping key information from decision makers, joining a coalition, whistle-blowing, spreading rumors, leaking confidential information about organizational activities to the media, exchanging favors with others in the organization for mutual benefit, and lobbying on behalf of or against a particular individual or decision alternative.

What Do You Think?

Is power a positive or negative force? Consider this on both a personal and an organizational level.

Legitimate political behavior
Normal everyday politics.

Illegitimate political behavior
Extreme political behavior that violates the implied rules of the game.

A final comment relates to what has been referred to as the 'legitimate–illegitimate' dimension in political behavior.[25] **Legitimate political behavior** refers to normal everyday politics—complaining to your supervisor, bypassing the chain of command, forming coalitions, obstructing organizational policies or decisions through inaction or excessive adherence to rules, and developing contacts outside the organization through one's professional activities. On the other hand, there is also **illegitimate political behavior** that violates the implied rules of the game. Illegitimate activities include sabotage, whistle-blowing, and symbolic protests such as wearing strange clothing or groups of employees calling in sick at the same time.

The Reality of Politics

Politics is a fact of life in organizations. People who ignore this fact of life do so at their own expense. But why, you may wonder, must politics exist? Isn't it possible for an organization to be politics free? It's *possible* but unlikely.

Organizations are made up of individuals and groups with different values, goals, and interests.[26] This sets up the potential for conflict over resources. Departmental budgets, space allocations, project responsibilities, and salary adjustments are just a few examples of the resources about whose allocation organizational members will disagree.

Resources in organizations are also limited, which often turns potential conflict into real conflict.[27] If resources were abundant, then all the various constituencies within the organization could satisfy their goals. But because they are limited, not everyone's interests can be provided for.

Maybe the most important factor leading to politics within organizations is the realization that most of the 'facts' that are used to allocate the limited resources are open to interpretation. What, for instance, is *good* performance? What's an *adequate* improvement? What constitutes an *unsatisfactory* job? One person's view that an act is a "selfless effort to benefit the organization" is seen by another as a "useless attempt to further one's interest."[28] It is in the large and ambiguous middle ground of organizational life—where the facts *don't* speak for themselves—that politics flourish (see Box 11-1).

Finally, because most decisions have to be made in a climate of uncertainty—where facts are rarely fully objective and thus are open to interpretation—people within organizations will use whatever influence they can to use the facts to support their goals and interests. That, of course, creates the activities we call *politicking*.

Therefore, to answer the earlier question of whether it is possible for an organization to be politics free, we can say "yes," if all members of that organization hold the same goals and interests, if organizational resources are not scarce, and if performance outcomes are completely clear and objective. But that doesn't describe the organizational world that most of us live in.

BOX 11-1
Politics in the Eye of the Beholder

A behavior that one person labels as 'organizational politics' is likely to be characterized as 'effective management' by another. The fact is not that effective management is necessarily political, although in some cases it might be. Rather, a person's reference point determines what he or she classifies as organizational politics. Take a look at the following labels used to describe the same phenomenon. These suggest that politics, like beauty, is in the eye of the beholder.

BOX 11-1 *continued*

'Political' Label		'Effective Management' Label
1. Blaming others	vs.	Fixing responsibility
2. 'Kissing up'	vs.	Developing working relationships
3. Apple polishing	vs.	Demonstrating loyalty
4. Passing the buck	vs.	Delegating authority
5. Covering your rear	vs.	Documenting decisions
6. Creating conflict	vs.	Encouraging change and innovation
7. Forming coalitions	vs.	Facilitating teamwork
8. Whistle-blowing	vs.	Improving efficiency
9. Scheming	vs.	Planning ahead
10. Overachieving	vs.	Competent and capable
11. Ambitious	vs.	Career minded
12. Opportunistic	vs.	Astute
13. Cunning	vs.	Practical minded
14. Arrogant	vs.	Confident
15. Perfectionist	vs.	Attentive to detail

Source: Based on T. C. Krell, M. E. Mendenhall, and J. Sendry, "Doing Research in the Conceptual Morass of Organizational Politics," paper presented at the Western Academy of Management Conference, Hollywood, CA, April 1987.

Causes and Consequences of Political Behavior

6 Identify the causes and consequences of political behavior.

Factors Contributing to Political Behavior

In the previous section, we learned more about the reality of politics. Now, let's understand what factors encourage political behavior. Not all groups or organizations are equally political. In some organizations, for instance, politicking is open and common, while in others, politics plays a small role in influencing outcomes. Why is there this variation? Recent research and observation have identified a number of factors that appear to encourage political behavior. Some are individual characteristics, derived from the unique qualities of the people the organization employs; others are a result of the organization's culture or internal environment. Figure 11-1 illustrates how both individual and organizational factors can increase political behavior and provide favorable outcomes (increased rewards and punishments) for both individuals and groups in the organization.

Individual Factors At the individual level, researchers have identified certain personality traits, needs, and other factors that are likely to be related to political behavior. In terms of traits, we find that employees who are high self-monitors,

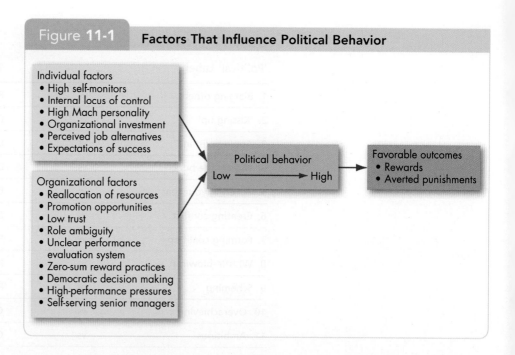

Figure **11-1**   **Factors That Influence Political Behavior**

possess an internal locus of control, and have a high need for power are more likely to engage in political behavior.[29] The high self-monitor is more sensitive to social cues, exhibits higher levels of social conformity, and is more likely to be skilled in political behavior than the low self-monitor. Individuals with an internal locus of control, because they believe they can control their environment, are more directed to take a proactive stance and attempt to manipulate situations in their favor. Not surprisingly, the Machiavellian personality—characterized by the will to manipulate and the desire for power—is comfortable using politics as a means to further self-interest.

In addition, an individual's investment in the organization, perceived alternatives, and expectations of success will influence the degree to which he or she will pursue illegitimate means of political action.[30] The more a person has invested in the organization in terms of expectations of increased future benefits, the more that person has to lose if forced out and the less likely he or she is to use illegitimate means. The more alternative job opportunities an individual has—due to a favorable job market or the possession of scarce skills or knowledge, a prominent reputation, or influential contacts outside the organization—the more likely that individual is to risk illegitimate political actions. Finally, if an individual has a low expectation of success in using illegitimate means, it is unlikely that he or she will attempt to do so. High expectations of success in the use of illegitimate means are most likely to be the province of both experienced and powerful individuals with polished political skills and inexperienced employees who misjudge their chances.

Organizational Factors   Political activity is probably more a function of an organization's characteristics than of individual difference variables. Why? Because many organizations have a large number of employees with the individual characteristics we listed, yet the extent of political behavior varies widely.

Although we acknowledge the role that individual differences can play in fostering politicking, the evidence more strongly supports the idea that certain situations and cultures promote politics. Specifically, when an organization's

Organizations foster politicking when they reduce resources in order to improve performance. As part of a restructuring program, Germany's Allianz AG announced plans to eliminate 5,000 jobs at its German insurance operation and 2,500 jobs at its banking subsidiary. The company stated that the job cuts were necessary to improve efficiency and to increase Allianz's competitiveness and would result in cost savings of between US$600 million and US$750 million. The company's cost-cutting measures stimulated conflict and political activity, as trade union workers joined Allianz employees in staging a token strike to safeguard their jobs.

resources are declining, when the existing pattern of resources is changing, and when there is opportunity for promotions, politicking is more likely to surface.[31] In addition, cultures characterized by low trust, role ambiguity, unclear performance evaluation systems, zero-sum reward allocation practices, democratic decision making, high pressures for performance, and self-serving senior managers will create reasons for politicking.[32]

When organizations downsize to improve efficiency, reductions in resources have to be made. Threatened with the loss of resources, people may engage in political actions to safeguard what they have. Promotion decisions have consistently been found to be one of the most political actions in organizations. The opportunity for promotions or advancement encourages people to compete for a limited resource and to try to positively influence the decision outcome.

The less trust there is within the organization, the higher the level of political behavior and the more likely that the political behavior will be of the illegitimate kind. Role ambiguity means that the prescribed behaviors of the employee are not clear. There are fewer limits, therefore, to the scope and functions of the employee's political actions. Because political activities are defined as those not required as part of one's formal role, the greater the role ambiguity, the more one can engage in political activity with little chance of it being visible.

The practice of performance evaluation is far from a perfect science. The more that organizations use subjective criteria in the appraisal, emphasize a single outcome measure, or allow significant time to pass between the time of an action and its appraisal, the greater the likelihood that an employee can get away with politicking. Subjective performance criteria create ambiguity. The use of a single outcome measure encourages individuals to do whatever is necessary to 'look good' on that measure, but often at the expense of performing well on other important parts of the job that are not being appraised. The more that an organization's culture emphasizes the zero-sum or win/lose approach to reward allocations, the more employees will be motivated to engage in politicking.

Picture This

The reward 'pie' is fixed so that any gain one person or group achieves has to come at the expense of another person or group. If I win, you must lose! If US$15,000 in annual raises is to be distributed among five employees, then any employee who gets more than US$3,000 takes money away from one or more of the others. How would you react to such a practice?

The more pressure that employees feel to perform well, the more likely they are to engage in politicking. When people are held strictly accountable for outcomes, this puts great pressure on them to 'look good.' If a person perceives that his or her entire career is riding on next quarter's sales figures or next month's plant productivity report, there is motivation to do whatever is necessary to make sure the numbers come out favorably.

Finally, when employees see the people on top engaging in political behavior, especially when they do so successfully and are rewarded for it, a climate is created that supports politicking. Politicking by top management, in a sense, gives permission to those lower in the organization to play politics by implying that such behavior is acceptable.

How Do People Respond to Organizational Politics?

In our discussion earlier in this chapter of factors that contribute to political behavior, we focused on the favorable outcomes for individuals who successfully engage in politicking. But for most people—who have modest political skills or are unwilling to play the politics game—outcomes tend to be negative. Figure 11-2 summarizes the extensive research on the relationship between organizational politics and individual outcomes.[33] There is, for instance, very strong evidence indicating that perceptions of organizational politics are negatively related to job satisfaction.[34] The perception of politics also tends to increase job anxiety and stress. This seems to be due to the perception that, by not engaging in politics, a person may be losing ground to others who are active

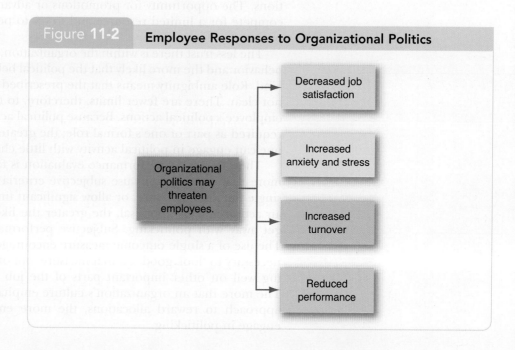

Figure **11-2** **Employee Responses to Organizational Politics**

Organizational politics may threaten employees.

- Decreased job satisfaction
- Increased anxiety and stress
- Increased turnover
- Reduced performance

politickers; or, conversely, because of the additional pressures individuals feel as a result of having entered into and competing in the political arena.[35]

Several interesting qualifiers have been noted. First, the politics–performance relationship appears to be moderated by an individual's understanding of the 'hows' and 'whys' of organizational politics. "An individual who has a clear understanding of who is responsible for making decisions and why they were selected to be the decision makers would have a better understanding of how and why things happen the way they do than someone who does not understand the decision-making process in the organization."[36] Second, when politics is seen as a threat and consistently responded to with defensiveness, negative outcomes are almost sure to surface eventually. When people perceive politics as a threat rather than as an opportunity, they often respond with **defensive behaviors**—reactive and protective behaviors to avoid action, blame, or change.[37] (Box 11-2 provides some examples of these defensive behaviors.) And defensive behaviors are often associated with negative feelings toward the job and work environment.[38] In the short run, employees may find that defensiveness protects their self-interest. But in the long run, it wears them down. People who consistently rely on defensiveness find that, eventually, it is the only way they know how to behave. At that point, they lose the trust and support of their peers, bosses, employees, and clients.

Defensive behaviors

Reactive and protective behaviors to avoid action, blame, or change.

BOX 11-2
Defensive Behaviors

Avoiding Action

Overconforming. Strictly interpreting your responsibility by saying things like, 'The rules clearly state . . .' or 'This is the way we've always done it.'

Buck passing. Transferring responsibility for the execution of a task or decision to someone else.

Playing dumb. Avoiding an unwanted task by falsely pleading ignorance or inability.

Stretching. Prolonging a task so that one person appears to be occupied—for example, turning a two-week task into a four-month job.

Stalling. Appearing to be more or less supportive publicly, while doing little or nothing privately.

Avoiding Blame

Buffing. This is a nice way to refer to 'covering your rear.' It describes the practice of rigorously documenting activity to project an image of competence and thoroughness.

Playing safe. Evading situations that may reflect unfavorably. It includes taking on only projects with a high probability of success, having risky decisions approved by superiors, qualifying expressions of judgment, and taking neutral positions in conflicts.

Justifying. Developing explanations that lessen one's responsibility for a negative outcome and/or apologizing to demonstrate remorse.

Scapegoating. Placing the blame for a negative outcome on external factors that are not entirely blameworthy.

Misrepresenting. Manipulation of information by distortion, embellishment, deception, selective presentation, or obfuscation.

Avoiding Change

Prevention. Trying to prevent a threatening change from occurring.

Self-protection. Acting in ways to protect one's self-interest during change by guarding information or other resources.

At this point, we must ask: Are our conclusions about responses to politics globally valid? Should we expect employees in Syria, for instance, to respond the same way to workplace politics that employees in the United States do? Almost all our conclusions on employee reactions to organizational politics are based on studies conducted in North America. The few studies that have included other countries suggest some minor modifications.[39] In countries that are more politically unstable, such as Egypt, employees seem to demonstrate greater tolerance of intense political processes in the workplace. This is likely to be because people in these countries are used to power struggles and have more experience in coping with them.[40] This suggests that people from politically turbulent countries in the Arab world or Latin America might be more accepting of organizational politics, and even more willing to use aggressive political tactics in the workplace, than people from countries such as the United Kingdom or Switzerland.

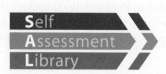

HOW GOOD AM I AT PLAYING POLITICS?

In the Self-Assessment Library (available online), take assessment II.C.3 (How Good Am I at Playing Politics?).

Impression Management

7   *Apply impression management techniques.*

Impression management (IM)

The process by which individuals attempt to control the impression others form of them.

We know that people have an ongoing interest in how others perceive and evaluate them. For example, North Americans spend billions of dollars on diets, health club memberships, cosmetics, and plastic surgery—all intended to make them more attractive to others.[41] This is something that Arabs are also becoming more aware of. Being perceived positively by others should have benefits for people in organizations. It might, for instance, help them initially to get the jobs they want in an organization and, once hired, to get favorable evaluations, superior salary increases, and more rapid promotions. In a political context, it might help sway the distribution of advantages in their favor. The process by which individuals attempt to control the impression others form of them is called **impression management (IM)**.[42] It's a subject that has gained the attention of OB researchers only recently.[43]

What Do You Think?

We live in a society that cares greatly about what other people think. Are you affected by other people's opinions of you; do you try hard to make a good impression?

Is everyone concerned with IM? No! Who, then, might we predict to engage in IM? No surprise here. It's our old friend, the high self-monitor.[44] Low self-monitors tend to present images of themselves that are consistent with their personalities, regardless of the beneficial or detrimental effects for them. In contrast, high self-monitors are good at reading situations and molding their appearances and behavior to fit each situation. If you want to control the impression others form of you, what techniques can you use? Box 11-3 summarizes some of the most popular IM techniques and provides an example of each.

BOX 11-3
Impression Management (IM) Techniques

Conformity

Agreeing with someone else's opinion in order to gain his or her approval.

Example: A manager tells his boss, "You're absolutely right on your reorganization plan for the Western regional office. I couldn't agree with you more."

Excuses

Explanations of a predicament-creating event aimed at minimizing the apparent severity of the predicament.

Example: Sales manager to boss, "We failed to get the ad in the paper on time, but no one responds to those ads anyway."

Apologies

Admitting responsibility for an undesirable event and simultaneously seeking to get a pardon for the action.

Example: Employee to boss, "I'm sorry I made a mistake on the report. Please forgive me."

Self-Promotion

Highlighting one's best qualities, downplaying one's deficits, and calling attention to one's achievements.

Example: A salesperson tells his boss: "Matt worked unsuccessfully for three years to try to get that account. I sewed it up in six weeks. I'm the best closer this company has."

Flattery

Complimenting others about their virtues in an effort to make oneself appear perceptive and likeable.

Example: New sales trainee to peer, "You handled that client's complaint so tactfully! I could never have handled that as well as you did."

Favors

Doing something nice for someone to gain that person's approval.

Example: Salesperson to prospective client, "I've got two tickets to the theater tonight that I can't use. Take them. Consider it a thank-you for taking the time to talk with me."

Association

Enhancing or protecting one's image by managing information about people and things with which one is associated.

Example: A job applicant says to an interviewer, "What a coincidence. Your boss and I were roommates in college."

Sources: Based on B. R. Schlenker, *Impression Management* (Monterey, CA: Brooks/Cole, 1980); W. L. Gardner and M. J. Martinko, "Impression Management in Organizations," *Journal of Management*, June 1988, p. 332; and R. B. Cialdini, "Indirect Tactics of Image Management Beyond Basking," in R. A. Giacalone and P. Rosenfeld (eds.), *Impression Management in the Organization* (Hillsdale, NJ: Lawrence Erlbaum, 1989), pp. 45–71.

Are there *situations* in which individuals are more likely to misrepresent themselves or more likely to get away with it? Yes—situations that are characterized by high uncertainty or ambiguity, as shown in the 'OB in the News' box on the next page provide relatively little information for challenging a false claim and reduce the risks associated with misrepresentation.[45]

Research indicates that some IM techniques work better than others in the interview. Researchers have compared applicants who used IM techniques

OB In the News

Excuses Are Everywhere

As we've noted, excuses are one means of managing impressions so as to avoid negative consequences of our actions. However, judging from some recent evidence on absenteeism, excuses are also a chance for workers to show their creative side.

A 2007 survey of nearly 7,000 employees and 3,000 hiring managers revealed some really creative excuses for being late for work or absent from work:

"Someone was following me and I drove all around town trying to lose them."

"My girlfriend got mad and destroyed all of my clothes."

"A tiger escaped from a zoo and kept running at me every time I tried to leave my house."

"My mother-in-law poisoned me."

"My mother-in-law is in jail."

"I blew my nose so hard, I hurt my back."

"My cow bit me."

"I'm too fat to get into my work pants."

Though you have to give the excuse makers high marks for originality, we seriously doubt supervisors believed these excuses. The making of excuses may be one of the few areas in which creativity is bad.

Sources: Based on K. Gurchiek, "'Sorry I'm Late; A Raccoon Stole My Shoe'," *HRWeek,* May 29, 2007, www.shrm.org/hrnews_published/archives/CMS_021684.asp; and K. Gurchiek, "Runaway Horses, Charging Buffalo Kept Workers Home in '06," *HRWeek,* December 28, 2006, www.shrm.org/hrnews_published/archives/CMS_019743.asp.

that focused on promoting one's accomplishments (called *self-promotion*) to applicants who used techniques that focused on complimenting the interviewer and finding areas of agreement (referred to as *ingratiation*). In general, applicants appear to use self-promotion more than ingratiation.[46] What's more, self-promotion tactics may be more important to interviewing success. Applicants who work to create an appearance of competence by enhancing their accomplishments, taking credit for successes, and explaining away failures do better in interviews. These effects reach beyond the interview: Applicants who use more self-promotion tactics also seem to get more follow-up job-site visits, even after adjusting for grade-point average, gender, and job type. Ingratiation also works well in interviews, meaning that applicants who compliment the interviewer, agree with his or her opinions, and emphasize areas of fit do better than those who don't.[47]

The Ethics of Behaving Politically

> **8** Determine whether a political action is ethical.

We conclude our discussion of politics by providing some ethical guidelines for political behavior. Although there are no clear-cut ways to differentiate ethical from unethical politicking, there are some questions you should consider. For example, what is the utility of engaging in politicking? Sometimes we engage in political behaviors for little good reason. For example, Farid or Maysa may declare that he or she has studied at the American University in Dubai, when in fact this is false. Direct lies like this may be a rather extreme example of impression management, but many of us have distorted information to make a favorable impression. The point is that, before we do so, one thing to keep in mind is whether it's really worth the risk. Another question to ask is an ethical one: How does the utility of engaging in the political behavior balance out any harm (or potential harm) it will do to others? For example, complimenting a supervisor on his or her appearance to win favor is probably much less harmful than accepting credit for a project that is deserved by others.

Finally, does the political activity conform to standards of equity and justice? Sometimes it is hard to weigh the costs and benefits of a political action, but its ethicality is clear. The department head who inflates the performance evaluation of a favored employee and deflates the evaluation of a disfavored employee—and then uses these evaluations to justify giving the former a big raise and nothing to the latter—has treated the disfavored employee unfairly.

Unfortunately, the answers to these questions are often argued in ways to make unethical practices seem ethical. Powerful people, for example, can become very good at explaining self-serving behaviors in terms of the organization's best interests. Similarly, they can persuasively argue that unfair actions are really fair and just. Our point is that immoral people can justify almost any behavior. Those who are powerful, articulate, and persuasive are most vulnerable because they are likely to be able to get away with unethical practices successfully. When faced with an ethical dilemma regarding organizational politics, try to consider the preceding issues (is playing politics worth the risk, and will others be harmed in the process?). If you have a strong power base, recognize the ability of power to corrupt. Remember that it's a lot easier for the powerless than the powerful to act ethically, if for no other reason than they typically have very little political discretion to exploit.

Global Implications

9 *Show the influence of culture on the uses and perceptions of politics.*

Although culture might enter any of the topics we've covered to this point, three questions are particularly important: (1) Does culture influence politics perceptions? (2) Does culture affect the power of influence tactics people prefer to use? and (3) Does culture influence the effectiveness of different tactics?

Politics Perceptions

We noted earlier that when people see their work environment as political, negative consequences in their overall work attitudes and behaviors generally result. Most of the research on politics perceptions has been conducted in the United States. A recent study, however, suggested that politics perceptions have the same negative effects in Nigeria. When employees of two agencies in Nigeria viewed their work environments as political, they reported higher levels of job distress and were less likely to help their coworkers.

Preference for Power Tactics

Evidence indicates that people in different countries tend to prefer different power tactics.[48] For instance, a study comparing managers in the United States and China found that US managers prefer rational appeal, whereas Chinese managers prefer coalition tactics.[49] These differences tend to be consistent with the values in these two countries. Research also has shown that individuals in Western, individualistic cultures tend to engage in more self-enhancement (such as self-promotion) behaviors than individuals in Eastern, more collectivistic cultures.[50]

Effectiveness of Power Tactics

Unfortunately, while we know people in different cultures seem to have different preferences for the use of power or influence tactics, there is much less evidence as to whether these tactics work better in some cultures than in others. One study of managers in US culture and three Chinese cultures (People's Republic of China, Hong Kong, Taiwan) found that US managers evaluated 'gentle persuasion' tactics such as consultation and inspirational appeal as more effective than did their Chinese counterparts.[51]

Summary and Implications for Managers

If you want to get things done in a group or an organization, it helps to have power. As a manager who wants to maximize your power, you will want to increase others' dependence on you. You can, for instance, increase your power in relation to your boss by developing knowledge or skills that are needed. But power is a two-way street. You will not be alone in attempting to build your power bases. Others, particularly employees and peers, will be seeking to make you dependent on them. The result is a continual battle. While you seek to maximize others' dependence on you, you will be seeking to minimize your dependence on others. And, of course, others you work with will be trying to do the same.

Few employees enjoy being powerless in their job and organization. It's been argued, for instance, that when people in organizations are difficult, argumentative, and temperamental, it may be because they are in positions of powerlessness in which the performance expectations placed on them exceed their resources and capabilities.[52]

There is evidence that people respond differently to the various power bases.[53] Expert and referent power are derived from an individual's personal qualities. In contrast, coercion, reward, and legitimate power are essentially organizationally derived. Because people are more likely to enthusiastically accept and commit to an individual whom they admire or whose knowledge they respect (rather than someone who relies on his or her position for influence), the effective use of expert and referent power should lead to higher employee motivation, performance, commitment, and satisfaction.[54] Competence especially appears to offer wide appeal, and its use as a power base results in high performance by group members. The message for managers seems to be "Develop and use your expert power base!"

The power of your boss may also play a role in determining your job satisfaction. "One of the reasons many of us like to work for and with people who are powerful is that they are generally more pleasant—not because it is their native disposition, but because the reputation and reality of being powerful permits them more discretion and more ability to delegate to others."[55]

In addition, an effective manager accepts the political nature of organizations. By assessing behavior in a political framework, you can better predict the actions of others and use that information to formulate political strategies that will gain advantages for you and your work unit.

Finally, those who are good at playing politics can be expected to get higher performance evaluations and, hence, larger salary increases and more promotions than the politically naive or inept.[56] The politically alert are also likely to exhibit higher job satisfaction and be better able to neutralize job stressors.[57] For employees with poor political skills or who are unwilling to play the politics game, the perception of organizational politics is generally related to lower job satisfaction and self-reported performance, increased anxiety, and higher turnover.

Point >>> << Counterpoint

MANAGING IMPRESSIONS IS UNETHICAL

Managing impressions is wrong for both ethical and practical reasons.

First, managing impressions is just another name for lying. Don't we have a responsibility, both to ourselves and to others, to present ourselves as we really are? If you want to know whether telling a lie is justifiable, you must try to imagine what would happen if everyone were to lie. Surely you would agree that a world in which no one lies is preferable to one in which lying is common because in such a world we could never trust anyone.

Practically speaking, impression management generally backfires in the long run. People are most satisfied with their jobs when their values match the culture of the organizations. If either side misrepresents itself in the interview process, the odds are, people won't fit in in the organizations they choose. It is better to exhibit qualities that are good, while still being honest.

Oh, come on. *Everybody* fudges to some degree in the process of applying for a job. If you really told the interviewer what your greatest weakness or worst mistake was, you'd never get hired. What if you answered, "I find it hard to get up in the morning and get to work"?

These sorts of 'white lies' are expected and act as a kind of social lubricant. If we really knew what people where thinking, we'd go crazy. Sometimes it's necessary to lie. You mean you wouldn't lie to save the life of your family?

Sometimes a bit of deception is necessary to get a job. When an interviewer asks you what you earned on your previous job, that information will be used against you, to pay you a salary lower than you deserve. Is it wrong to boost your salary a bit?

Of course you can go too far. What we are talking about here is a reasonable amount of enhancement. If we can help ourselves without doing any real harm, then impression management is not the same as lying and actually is something we should teach others.

Questions for Review

1 How would you define *power*? How is it different from leadership?

2 What are the five bases of power?

3 What are the nine power or influence tactics?

4 In what way is sexual harassment about the abuse of power?

5 What is political behavior and how would you distinguish between legitimate and illegitimate political behavior?

6 What are the causes and consequences of political behavior?

7 What is impression management and what are the techniques for managing impressions?

8 How can one determine whether a political action is ethical?

9 How does culture influence politics perceptions, preferences for different power or influence tactics, and the effectiveness of those tactics?

Discussion Exercise

Wasta may be considered a misuse of power and political connections in some organizations. Discuss the positives and negatives of Wasta. Do you think that Wasta will ever be eliminated?

Ethical Considerations

What is a scapegoat? A scapegoat is someone who is made to take the blame for someone else's failure or wrongdoing. In Arabic, this person is referred to as '*kebsh al mahraka.*' Unfortunately, one way that power is abused in an organization is by using scapegoats.

Amani was the new assistant to the Director of Finance at a shipping company in Tunis. Rima was jealous because she wanted this position. In addition, Rima knew all the ins and outs of the company and she was not a nice person. She used her influence to convince Bahaa, the Assistant Director of Finance, to help her with 'a plan.' Bahaa couldn't resist the offer.

Three weeks later, the company was in chaos. Then, Amani was fired. She tried to talk to her boss but he wouldn't listen. As Amani left the office, Rima and Bahaa exchanged glances. What do you think happened? Discuss the ethical implications.

Critical Analysis

THE POLITICS OF BACKSTABBING

Samir Reshdi believed that he was making progress as an assistant manager of a financial-services company in Saudi Arabia—until he noticed that his colleague, Walid, another assistant manager, was attempting to push him aside. On repeated occasions, Samir would observe Walid speaking with their manager behind closed doors. It wasn't until much later that Samir discovered that Walid was telling the supervisor that he (Samir) was incompetent and was not managing his job effectively. Samir remembered other instances of Walid's disloyal behavior; for example, once when a subordinate asked Samir a question to which he did not know the answer, Walid had said to their supervisor, "I can't believe he didn't know something like that."

On other occasions, after instructing a subordinate to complete a specific task, Walid would say, "I wouldn't make you do something like that." What was the end result of such illegitimate political tactics? Samir was demoted, an action that led him to resign shortly after, while his colleague was promoted. "Whatever I did, I lost," Samir recalls.

What leads individuals to behave this way? According to Judith Briles, a management consultant who has extensively studied the practice of backstabbing, a tight job-market is often a contributing factor. Fred Nader, another management consultant, believes that backstabbing is the result of "some kind of character disorder."

One executive at a technology company in Seattle, in the US, admits that blind ambition was responsible for the backstabbing he did. In 1999, he was appointed as an external sales representative, partnered with a colleague who worked internally at their client's office. The executive wanted the internal sales position for himself. To reach this goal, he systematically engaged in backstabbing to destroy his colleague's credibility. Each time he heard a complaint, however small, from the client, he would ask for it in an e-mail and then forward the information to his boss. He'd include a short message about his colleague, such as: "I'm powerless to deal with this. She's not being responsive and the customer is beating on me." In addition, he would fail to share important information with her before presentations with their boss, to convey the impression that she did not know what she was talking about. He even went so far as to schedule meetings with their boss on an electronic calendar but then altered her version so that she was late. Eventually, he convinced his boss that she was overworked. He was transferred to the client's office, while his colleague was moved back to the main office.

Questions

1. What factors, in addition to those cited here, do you believe lead to illegitimate political behaviors such as backstabbing?

2. Imagine that a colleague is engaging in illegitimate political behavior toward you. What steps might you take to reduce or eliminate this behavior?

3. Do you believe that it is ever justifiable to engage in illegitimate political behaviors such as backstabbing? If so, what are some conditions that might justify such behavior?

Source: Based on J. Sandberg, "Sabotage 101: The Sinister Art of Backstabbing," *Wall Street Journal*, February 11, 2004, p. B1.

Research Exercise

There is little evidence to say whether some power or influences tactics work better in some cultures than others. Carry out some research to determine which of the nine influences tactics are most likely to be successful in the Arab culture and how this may differ from the Western culture.

LEARNING OBJECTIVES

This chapter will enable you to:

1 Define *conflict*.

2 Differentiate between the traditional, human relations, and interactionist views of conflict.

3 Outline the conflict process.

4 Define *negotiation*.

5 Contrast distributive and integrative bargaining.

6 Apply the five steps of the negotiation process.

7 Show how individual differences influence negotiations.

8 Assess the roles and functions of third-party negotiations.

9 Describe cultural differences in negotiations.

Conflict and Negotiation

12

When involved in business negotiation, a key skill is to listen to what the other party is trying to achieve and to try to understand their personal motivations during the negotiation process. —Naz Daud

CCC Faces Conflict in the GCC

Consolidated Contractor's Company (CCC), a multinational construction firm, was founded by Said Khoury and has established itself as a reputable company in the Arab world. Now one of the largest contractors in the Arab world, CCC has not only been involved in construction projects but has also been active with education programs. CCC has employed over 700 students from the American University of Beirut (AUB) and has signed a memorandum of understanding with the AUB to finance a Green Building Training Program.

However, despite the good that CCC is doing, it has faced major problems, and its reputation has suffered because liability payments have not been settled. In fact, at the time of writing, the firm is facing court action over a failure to pay a US$64.5 million liability settlement to its former partner Munib Masri.

A British high court judge expressed extreme disappointment when CCC did not commit and implement the court's decision to pay Masri for his share in a joint project involving Yemeni oil revenues. A joint venture partner of CCC in Yemen, Masri was assured he would receive 10 percent of the profits from an oilfield that the firm had developed in the south of Yemen.

Consequently, the court approved orders to freeze all CCC assets in the United Kingdom, Bermuda, and Switzerland. Moreover, CCC assets in Nigeria, Palestine, and the Cayman Islands were also frozen. The best of companies are open to conflict despite their credibility and reliable market reputation. It is only the most cautious of companies that are able to overcome any obstacles through negotiation.

Source: Based on "Real Estate & Development FYIs—Lebanon & the GCC," *The Executive*, Issue No. 140, March 2011, p. 92.

The opening case about Consolidated Contractor's Company (CCC) clearly shows how conflict can affect credibility and reputation. It can create chaotic conditions that can only be resolved through litigation, and this can reflect negatively on the overall performance of the company. This is commonplace in all countries around the world, including the Arab world. Experiences of such conflict within companies can often turn ugly, and make it nearly impossible for employees to work as a team if it is not managed well.

Nevertheless, conflict does have a less-well-known positive side; it can bring out the best in some people, as one of the duties of a manager is managing conflict effectively.

We'll explain the difference between negative and positive conflicts in this chapter and provide a guide to help you understand how conflicts develop. We'll also present a topic closely related to conflict: negotiation. But first, understand how you handle conflict by taking the following self-assessment.

Self Assessment Library

WHAT'S MY PREFERRED CONFLICT-HANDLING STYLE?

In the Self-Assessment Library (available online), take assessment II.C.5 (What's My Preferred Conflict-Handling Style?) and answer the following questions:

1. *Judging from your highest score, what's your primary conflict-handling style?*

2. *Do you think your style varies, depending on the situation?*

3. *Would you like to change any aspects of your conflict-handling style?*

A Definition of *Conflict*

1 *Define conflict.*

Conflict

A process that begins when one party perceives that another party has negatively affected, or is about to negatively affect, something that the first party cares about.

There have been several definitions of *conflict.*[1] Conflict must be perceived by the parties to it; whether or not conflict exists is a perception issue. If no one is aware of a conflict, then it is generally agreed that no conflict exists.

We can define **conflict**, then, as a process that begins when one party observes that another party has negatively affected, or is about to negatively affect, something that the first party cares about.[2] This definition describes that point in any ongoing activity when an interaction "crosses over" to become an interparty conflict. It includes the wide range of conflicts that people experience in organizations such as incompatibility of goals, differences over interpretations of facts, disagreements based on behavioral expectations, and the like.

Conflict can lead to demotivation of employees and thus performance is negatively affected. What are the legal implications for employers and employees in the event of conflict? Dr. Charbel Aoun, Attorney at Law specializes in business law and practises employment law. He says that:[3]

> The constitutions and laws of most of the Arab countries generally guarantee employees' rights (right to work, leaves rights, etc. . .). Most of these rights are not positively guaranteed or respected. Some of the Arab countries have amended their laws in order to be in agreement with the minimum standards imposed by (1) the International Labour Organization and (2) the International and Arab Work Conventions. Some countries have not amended their laws and have left that task to public authorities or ministries such as the Ministry of Labour or the Ministry of Social Affairs. When employers refuse to follow the minimum standards and the additional benefits set by public authorities or ministries, then conflicts pressure the employer–employee relationship and often negotiation is not enough.

Transitions in Conflict Thought

2 *Differentiate between the traditional, human relations, and interactionist views of conflict.*

It is appropriate to say there has been conflict over the role of conflict in groups and organizations. One school of thought known as the *traditional* view has argued that conflict indicates a malfunctioning within the group. Another school of thought, the *human relations* view, argues that conflict is a natural and inevitable outcome in any group and that it need not be evil but rather has the potential to be a positive force in determining group performance. The third, and most recent perspective proposes not only that conflict can be a positive force in a group but explicitly argues that some conflict is *absolutely necessary* for a group to perform effectively. We label this third school the *interactionist* view. Let's take a closer look at each of these views.

The Traditional View of Conflict

Traditional view of conflict
The belief that all conflict is harmful and must be avoided.

The early approach to conflict assumed that all conflict is bad. Conflict was viewed negatively, and it was used synonymously with such terms as *violence, destruction,* and *irrationality* to reinforce its negative connotation. Conflict, by definition, was harmful and was to be avoided. The **traditional view of conflict** was consistent with the attitudes that prevailed about group behavior in the 1930s and 1940s. Conflict was seen as a dysfunctional outcome, as we saw with CCC, resulting from poor communication, a lack of openness and trust between people, and the failure of managers to be responsive to the needs and aspirations of their employees.

The view that all conflict is bad certainly offers a simple approach to looking at the behavior of people who create conflict. Because all conflict is to be avoided, we need to direct our attention to the causes of conflict and correct those errors to improve group and organizational performance.

The Human Relations View of Conflict

Human relations view of conflict
The belief that conflict is a natural and inevitable outcome in any group.

The **human relations view of conflict** argued that conflict is a natural occurrence in all groups and organizations. Because conflict is inevitable, the human relations school advocated acceptance of conflict. Supporters rationalized its existence: it cannot be eliminated, and there are even times when conflict may benefit a group's performance. The human relations view dominated conflict theory from the late 1940s through the mid-1970s.

The Interactionist View of Conflict

Interactionist view of conflict
The belief that conflict is not only a positive force in a group but that it is also an absolute necessity for a group to perform effectively.

Functional conflict
Conflict that supports the goals of the group and improves its performance.

Dysfunctional conflict
Conflict that hinders group performance.

While the human relations view accepted conflict, the **interactionist view of conflict** encourages conflict on the grounds that a harmonious, peaceful, tranquil, and cooperative group is prone to becoming static, indifferent, and nonresponsive to needs for change and innovation.[4] The major contribution of the interactionist view, therefore, is encouraging group leaders to maintain an ongoing minimum level of conflict—enough to keep the group viable, self-critical, and creative.

The interactionist view does not propose that all conflicts are good. Rather, some conflicts support the goals of the group and improve its performance; these are **functional**, constructive, forms of conflict. In addition, there are conflicts that hinder group performance; these are **dysfunctional**, or destructive, forms of conflict. What differentiates functional from dysfunctional conflict?

The evidence indicates that you need to look at the *type* of conflict.[5] Specifically, there are three types: task, relationship, and process.

Task conflict relates to the content and goals of the work. **Relationship conflict** focuses on interpersonal relationships. **Process conflict** relates to how the work gets done. Studies demonstrate that relationship conflicts are almost always dysfunctional.[6] Why? It appears that the friction and interpersonal hostilities found in relationship conflicts increase personality clashes and decrease mutual understanding, which hinders the completion of organizational tasks. Unfortunately, managers spend a lot of their time resolving personality conflicts; one survey indicated that 18 percent of managers' time is spent trying to resolve personality conflicts among staff members.[7]

On the other hand, low levels of process conflict and low to moderate levels of task conflict are functional. For process conflict to be productive, it must be kept low. Intense arguments about who should do what become dysfunctional when they create uncertainty about task roles, increase the time to complete tasks, and lead to members working at cross purposes. Low-to-moderate levels of task conflict consistently demonstrate a positive effect on group performance because it stimulates discussion of ideas that helps groups perform better. The next section will discuss the conflict process.

Task conflict

Conflict over content and goals of the work.

Relationship conflict

Conflict based on interpersonal relationships.

Process conflict

Conflict over how work gets done.

> ## What Do You Think?
>
> *What does conflict mean to you? Do you agree that different people identify conflict in different ways? In other words, what may be a serious situation to you may not mean much to someone else.*

The Conflict Process

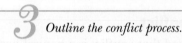
Outline the conflict process.

The **conflict process** has five stages: potential opposition or incompatibility, cognition and personalization, intentions, behavior, and outcomes. The process is shown in Figure 12-1.

Stage I: Potential Opposition or Incompatibility

The first step in the conflict process is the presence of conditions that create opportunities for conflict to arise. They *need not* lead directly to conflict, but one of these conditions is necessary if conflict is to surface. For simplicity's sake, these conditions (which we can also look at as causes or sources of conflict) have been reduced to three general categories: communication, structure, and personal variables.

Conflict process

A process that has five stages: potential opposition or incompatibility, cognition and personalization, intentions, behavior, and outcomes.

Communication   Salwa had worked in supply-chain management for three years. She enjoyed her work in large part because her boss, Talal Badr, was a great guy to work for. Then Talal got promoted, and Bilal Nasser took his place. Salwa says her job is a lot more frustrating now; "Talal and I were on the same wavelength. It's not that way with Bilal. He tells me something and I do it. Then he tells me I did it wrong. I think he means one thing but says something else. It's been like this since the day he arrived. I don't think a day goes by when he isn't yelling at me for something. You know, there are some people you just find it easy to communicate with. Well, Bilal isn't one of those!"

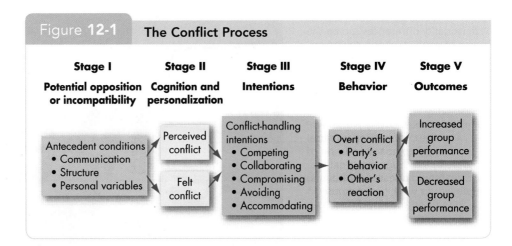

Figure **12-1**   **The Conflict Process**

Stage I	Stage II	Stage III	Stage IV	Stage V
Potential opposition or incompatibility	Cognition and personalization	Intentions	Behavior	Outcomes

Antecedent conditions
• Communication
• Structure
• Personal variables → Perceived conflict / Felt conflict → Conflict-handling intentions
• Competing
• Collaborating
• Compromising
• Avoiding
• Accommodating → Overt conflict
• Party's behavior
• Other's reaction → Increased group performance / Decreased group performance

Salwa's comments illustrate that communication can be a source of conflict.[8] They represent the opposing forces that arise from misunderstandings and 'noise' in the communication channels. Much of this discussion can be related to our comments on communication in Chapter 9.

A review of the research suggests that differing word connotations, jargon, insufficient exchange of information, and noise in the communication channel are all barriers to communication and can lead to conflict. Research has further demonstrated a surprising finding: the potential for conflict increases when either too little or too much communication takes place. Apparently, an increase in communication is functional up to a point, whereupon it is possible to over communicate, with a resultant increase in the potential for conflict.

Structure   Carla and Tarub both work at a furniture store in Rabat, Morocco. Carla is a salesperson on the floor, and Tarub is the company credit manager. The two women have known each other for years and have much in common: They live in the same neighborhood, and their oldest daughters attend the same middle school and are best friends. In reality, if Carla and Tarub had different jobs, they might be best friends themselves, but these two women are consistently fighting battles with each other. Carla's job is to sell furniture, and she does a great job. But most of her sales are made on credit. Because Tarub's job is to make sure the company minimizes credit losses, she regularly has to turn down the credit application of a customer with whom Carla has just closed a sale. It's nothing personal between Carla and Tarub; the requirements of their jobs just bring them into conflict.

The conflicts between Carla and Tarub are structural in nature. The term *structure* is used, in this context, to include variables such as size, degree of specialization in the tasks assigned to group members, legal clarity, member-goal compatibility, leadership styles, reward systems, and the degree of dependence between groups.

Research indicates that size and specialization act as forces to stimulate conflict. The larger the group and the more specialized its activities, the greater the likelihood of conflict. Tenure and conflict have been found to be inversely related. The potential for conflict tends to be greatest when group members are younger and when turnover is high.

Personal Variables   Have you ever met someone to whom you took an immediate dislike? You disagreed with most of the opinions they expressed. Even insignificant characteristics—the sound of their voice, the way they

Personal variables such as personality differences can be the source of conflict among coworkers. To reduce conflict resulting from personality differences, Vertex Pharmaceuticals teaches employees how to identify other people's personality types and then how to communicate effectively with them. At Vertex, innovation is critical to the company's mission of developing drugs that treat life-threatening diseases. By training employees to work harmoniously in spite of personality differences, Vertex hopes to eliminate unproductive conflict that limits innovation.

smiled, their personality—annoyed you. We've all met people like that. When you have to work with such individuals, there is often the potential for conflict.

Our last category of potential sources of conflict is personal variables, which include personality, emotions, and values. Evidence indicates that certain personality types—for example, individuals who are highly authoritarian—lead to potential conflict. Emotions can also cause conflict. For example, an employee who shows up to work angry because of morning traffic may carry that anger with her to her 9 A.M. meeting. The problem? Her anger can annoy her colleagues, which may lead to a tension-filled meeting.[9]

What Do You Think?

Is it professional to bring your personal feelings or problems to work?

Stage II: Cognition and Personalization

If the conditions cited in Stage I negatively affect something that one party cares about, then the potential for opposition or incompatibility becomes actualized in the second stage.

As we noted in our definition of conflict, perception is required. Therefore, one or more of the parties must be aware of the existence of the antecedent conditions. However, because a conflict is **perceived conflict** does not mean that it is personalized. In other words, "*A* may be aware that *B* and *A* are in serious disagreement . . . but it may not make *A* tense or anxious, and it may have no effect whatsoever on *A*'s affection toward *B*."[10] It is at the **felt conflict** level, when individuals become emotionally involved, that parties experience anxiety, tension, frustration, or hostility.

Keep in mind two points. First, Stage II is important because it's where conflict issues tend to be defined. This is the place in the process where the parties decide what the conflict is about.[11] Our second point is that emotions play a

Perceived conflict

Awareness by one or more parties of the existence of conditions that create opportunities for conflict to arise.

Felt conflict

Emotional involvement in a conflict that creates anxiety, tenseness, frustration, or hostility.

major role in shaping perceptions.[12] For example, negative emotions have been found to produce oversimplification of issues, reductions in trust, and negative interpretations of the other party's behavior.[13] In contrast, positive feelings have been found to increase the tendency to see potential relationships among the elements of a problem, to take a broader view of the situation, and to develop more innovative solutions.[14]

Stage III: Intentions

Intentions intervene between people's perceptions and emotions and their open behavior. These intentions are decisions to act in a given way.[15]

Intentions are separated out as a separate stage because you have to infer the other's intent to know how to respond to that other's behavior. A lot of conflicts are escalated merely by one party attributing the wrong intentions to the other party. In addition, there typically are many differences between intentions and behavior, so behavior does not always accurately reflect a person's intentions.

Figure 12-2 represents one author's effort to identify the primary conflict-handling intentions. Using two dimensions—*cooperativeness* (the degree to which one party attempts to satisfy the other party's concerns) and *assertiveness* (the degree to which one party attempts to satisfy his or her own concerns)—five conflict-handling intentions can be identified: **competing** (assertive and uncooperative), such as winning a bet and your opponent losing; **collaborating** (assertive and cooperative), such as attempting to find a win–win solution that allows both parties' goals to be completely achieved; **avoiding** (unassertive and uncooperative), such as ignoring a conflict and avoiding others with whom you disagree; **accommodating** (unassertive and cooperative), such as supporting someone else's opinion despite your reservations about it; and **compromising** (midrange on both assertiveness and cooperativeness), such as each party intending to give up something.[16]

Intentions are not always fixed. During the course of a conflict, they might change because of reconceptualization or because of an emotional reaction to the behavior of the other party. However, research indicates that people handle conflicts in certain ways.[17] Specifically, individuals have preferences among the five conflict-handling intentions just described above; these preferences tend to be relied on quite consistently, and a person's intentions can be predicted rather well from a combination of intellectual and personality characteristics.

Intentions
Decisions to act in a given way.

Competing
A desire to satisfy one's interests, regardless of the impact on the other party to the conflict.

Collaborating
A situation in which the parties to a conflict each desire to satisfy fully the concerns of all parties.

Avoiding
The desire to withdraw from or suppress a conflict.

Accommodating
The willingness of one party in a conflict to place the opponent's interests above his or her own.

Compromising
A situation in which each party to a conflict is willing to give up something.

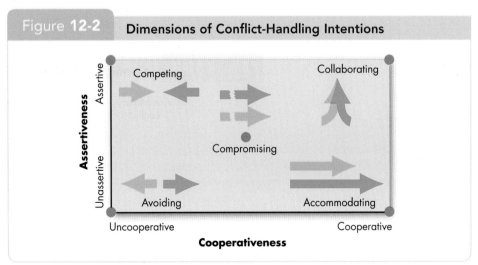

Figure 12-2 — Dimensions of Conflict-Handling Intentions

Source: K. Thomas, "Conflict and Negotiation Processes in Organizations," in M. D. Dunnette and L. M. Hough (eds.), *Handbook of Industrial and Organizational Psychology*, 2nd ed., vol. 3 (Palo Alto, CA: Consulting Psychologists Press, 1992), p. 668. Used with permission.

Stage IV: Behavior

When most people think of conflict situations, they tend to focus on Stage IV because this is where conflicts become visible. The behavior stage includes the statements, actions, and reactions made by the conflicting parties. These conflict behaviors are usually direct attempts to implement each party's intentions. But these behaviors have a stimulus quality that is separate from intentions. As a result of miscalculations or bad acts, open behaviors sometimes change from original intentions.[18]

It helps to think of Stage IV as a dynamic process of interaction. For example, you make a demand on me, I respond by arguing, you threaten me, I threaten you back, and so on. Figure 12-3 provides a way of visualizing conflict behavior. All conflicts exist somewhere along this continuum. At the lower part of the continuum are conflicts characterized by subtle, indirect, and highly controlled forms of tension. An illustration might be a student questioning in class a point the instructor has just made. Conflict intensities escalate as they move upward along the continuum until they become highly destructive. For the most part, you should assume that conflicts that reach the upper ranges of the continuum are almost always dysfunctional. Functional conflicts are typically confined to the lower range of the continuum.

If a conflict is dysfunctional, what can the parties do to correct it? Or, on the other hand, what options exist if conflict is too low and needs to be increased? This brings us to **conflict-management** techniques. Table 12-1 lists the major resolution and stimulation techniques that allow managers to control conflict levels. Note that several of the resolution techniques were described earlier as conflict-handling intentions. This, of course, shouldn't be surprising. Under ideal conditions, a person's intentions should translate into comparable behaviors.

Stage V: Outcomes

The action–reaction interplay between the conflicting parties results in consequences. As our model (see Figure 12-1) demonstrates, these outcomes may be functional in that the conflict results in an improvement in the group's performance or dysfunctional in that it hinders group performance.

Functional Outcomes How might conflict act as a force to increase group performance? Although people often find it difficult to think of instances in which conflict can be constructive, there are a number of instances in which it's

Conflict management

The use of resolution and stimulation techniques to achieve the desired level of conflict.

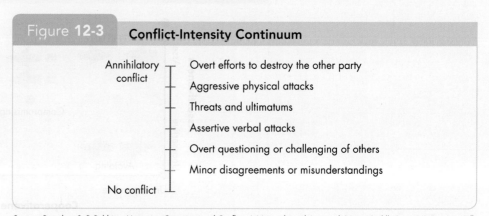

Figure 12-3	Conflict-Intensity Continuum

Annihilatory conflict
— Overt efforts to destroy the other party
— Aggressive physical attacks
— Threats and ultimatums
— Assertive verbal attacks
— Overt questioning or challenging of others
— Minor disagreements or misunderstandings
No conflict

Sources: Based on S. P. Robbins, *Managing Organizational Conflict: A Nontraditional Approach* (Upper Saddle River, NJ: Prentice Hall, 1974), pp. 93–97; and F. Glasi, "The Process of Conflict Escalation and the Roles of Third Parties," in G. B. J. Bomers and R. Peterson (eds.), *Conflict Management and Industrial Relations* (Boston: Kluwer-Nijhoff, 1982), pp. 119–140.

TABLE 12-1 Conflict-Management Techniques

Conflict-Resolution Techniques

Problem solving	Face-to-face meeting of the conflicting parties for the purpose of identifying the problem and resolving it through open discusssion.
Superordinate goals	Creating a shared goal that cannot be attained without the cooperation of each of the conflicting parties.
Expansion of resources	When a conflict is caused by the scarcity of a resource—say, money, promotion, opportunities, office space—expansion of the resource can create a win–win solution.
Avoidance	Withdrawal from or suppression of the conflict.
Smoothing	Playing down differences while emphasizing common interests between the conflicting parties.
Compromise	Each party to the conflict gives up something of value.
Authoritative command	Management uses its formal authority to resolve the conflict and then communicates its desires to the parties involved.
Altering the human variable	Using behavioral change techniques such as human relations training to alter attitudes and behaviors that cause conflict.
Altering the structural variables	Changing the formal organization structure and the interaction patterns of conflicting parties through job redesign, transfers, creation of coordinating positions, and the like.

Conflict-Stimulation Techniques

Communication	Using ambiguous or threatening messages to increase conflict levels.
Bringing in outsiders	Adding employees to a group whose backgrounds, values, attitudes, or managerial styles differ from those of present members.
Restructuring the organization	Realigning work groups, altering rules and regulations, increasing interdependence, and making similar structural changes to disrupt the status quo.
Appointing a devil's advocate	Designating a critic to purposely argue against the majority positions held by the group.

Source: Based on S. P. Robbins, *Managing Organizational Conflict: A Nontraditional Approach* (Upper Saddle River, NJ: Prentice Hall, 1974), pp. 59–89.

possible to envision how low or moderate levels of conflict could improve the effectiveness of a group.

> ### Picture This
> Imagine a situation in which open or violent aggression could be functional or productive.

Conflict is constructive when it improves the quality of decisions, stimulates creativity and innovation, encourages interest and curiosity among group members, provides the medium through which problems can be aired and tensions released, and fosters an environment of self-evaluation and change. The evidence suggests that conflict can improve the quality of decision making by allowing all points, particularly the ones that are unusual or held by a minority, to be weighed in important decisions.[19]

It was demonstrated that, among established groups, performance tended to improve more when there was conflict among members than when there was fairly close agreement. The investigators observed that when groups analyzed

A lack of functional conflict among General Motors (GM) management in past decades resulted in concessions to union demands for generous health benefits and pensions. Today, burdened by health costs that GM provides to more than 1 million employees, retirees, and dependents, the automaker is eliminating jobs and closing assembly plants as part of a cost-cutting strategy. The two employees shown here embrace as the last automobile rolls off the assembly line at GM's plant in Linden, New Jersey, which GM closed after 68 years of operation.

decisions that had been made by the individual members of that group, the average improvement among the high-conflict groups was 73 percent greater than that of those groups characterized by low-conflict conditions.[20] In addition, groups composed of members with different interests tend to produce higher-quality solutions to a variety of problems than do homogeneous groups.

The above leads us to predict that the increasing cultural diversity of the workforce should provide benefits to organizations. And that's what the evidence indicates. Research demonstrates that heterogeneity among group and organization members can increase creativity, improve the quality of decisions, and facilitate change by enhancing member flexibility.[21]

Dysfunctional Outcomes   The destructive consequences of conflict on a group's or an organization's performance are generally well known. A reasonable summary might state: Uncontrolled opposition leads to discontent, which acts to break common ties and eventually leads to the destruction of the group. And, of course, there is a substantial body of literature to document how conflict—the dysfunctional varieties—can reduce group effectiveness.[22] Among the more undesirable consequences are a retarding of communication, reductions in group cohesiveness, and subordination of group goals to the primacy of infighting among members. At the extreme, conflict can bring group functioning to a stop and potentially threaten the group's survival.

Creating Functional Conflict   If managers accept the interactionist view toward conflict, what can they do to encourage functional conflict in their organizations?[23]

There seems to be general agreement that creating functional conflict is a tough job. As one consultant put it, "A high proportion of people who get to the top are conflict avoiders. They don't like hearing negatives; they don't like saying or thinking negative things. They frequently make it up the ladder in part because they don't irritate people on the way up." Another suggests that at least 7 out of 10 people in US business stay quiet when their opinions are different to those of their superiors, allowing bosses to make mistakes even when they know better.

Such anticonflict cultures may have been tolerable in the past but are not in today's competitive global economy. Organizations that don't encourage and support disagreement may find their survival threatened.

One common ingredient in organizations that successfully create functional conflict is that they reward opposition and punish conflict avoiders. The real challenge for managers, however, is when they hear news they don't want to hear. The news may make their blood boil or their hopes collapse, but they can't show it. They have to learn to take the bad news without reaction. Managers should ask calm, even-tempered questions: 'Can you tell me more about what happened?' 'What do you think we ought to do?' A sincere 'Thank you for bringing this to my attention' will probably reduce the likelihood that managers will be cut off from similar communications in the future.

Having considered conflict—its nature, causes, and consequences—we now turn to negotiation. Negotiation and conflict are closely related because negotiation often resolves conflict.

Negotiation

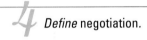

4 *Define* negotiation.

Negotiation filters through the interactions of almost everyone in groups and organizations. There's the obvious: labor bargains with management. There's the not-so-obvious: managers negotiate with employees, peers, and bosses; salespeople negotiate with customers; purchasing agents negotiate with suppliers. And there's the subtle: an employee agrees to answer a colleague's phone for a few minutes in exchange for some past or future benefit. In today's loosely structured organizations, in which members are increasingly finding themselves having to work with colleagues over whom they have no direct authority and with whom they may not even share a common boss, negotiation skills become critical.

Negotiation

Interaction between two or more parties for the purpose of reaching a mutually beneficial agreement.

We can define **negotiation** as a process in which two or more parties exchange goods or services, and attempt to agree on the exchange rate for them.[24] Note that we use the terms *negotiation* and *bargaining* interchangeably. In this section, we contrast two bargaining strategies, provide a model of the negotiation process, ascertain the role of moods and personality traits on bargaining, review gender and cultural differences in negotiation, and take a brief look at third-party negotiations.

Bargaining Strategies

5 *Contrast distributive and integrative bargaining.*

There are two general approaches to negotiation—*distributive bargaining* and *integrative bargaining*.[25] As Table 12-2 shows, distributive and integrative bargaining differ in their goal and motivation, focus, interests, information sharing, and duration of relationship. We now define distributive and integrative bargaining and illustrate the differences between these two approaches.

Distributive Bargaining   You see a used car advertised for sale in the newspaper. It appears to be just what you've been looking for. You go out to see the car. It's great, and you want it. The owner tells you the asking price. You don't want to pay that much. The two of you then negotiate over the price.

TABLE 12-2   Distributive Versus Integrative Bargaining

Bargaining Characteristic	Distributive Bargaining	Integrative Bargaining
Goal	Get as much of the pie as possible	Expand the pie so that both parties are satisfied
Motivation	Win/lose	Win/win
Focus	Positions ('I can't go beyond this point on this issue.')	Interests ('Can you explain why this issue is so important to you?')
Interests	Opposed	Congruent
Information sharing	Low (sharing information will only allow other party to take advantage)	High (sharing information will allow each party to find ways to satisfy interests of each party)
Duration of relationship	Short term	Long term

Distributive bargaining

Negotiation that seeks to divide up a fixed amount of resources; a win–lose situation.

Fixed pie

The belief that there is only a set amount of goods or services to be divided up between the parties.

The negotiating strategy you're engaging in is called **distributive bargaining**. Its most identifying feature is that it operates under zero-sum conditions. That is, any gain I make is at your expense and vice versa. In the used-car example, every dollar you can get the seller to cut from the car's price is a dollar you save. Conversely, every dollar more the seller can get from you comes at your expense. So the essence of distributive bargaining is negotiating over who gets what share of a fixed pie. By **fixed pie**, we mean that the bargaining parties believe there is only a set amount of goods or services to be divided up. Therefore, fixed pies are zero-sum games in that every dollar in one party's pocket is a dollar out of their counterpart's pocket. When parties believe the pie is fixed, they tend to bargain distributively.

When engaged in distributive bargaining, one of the best things you can do is to make the first offer, and to make it an aggressive one. Research consistently shows that the best negotiators are those who make the first offer, and whose initial offer has very favorable terms. Why is this so? One reason is that making

In March 2011, Qatar International Islamic Bank (QIIB), a sharia-compliant bank, negotiated to purchase an increased stake in the Islamic Bank of Britain (IBB). QIIB made the first offer of one pence per share—even though it represented a 70 percent discount on the British bank's market price—ensuring that their first bid offered favourable terms. They thus demonstrated their power, a power further demonstrated by the fact that they already owned 81 percent of IBB. Their initial offer also created an anchoring bias, so that the parties later focused on that initial information when negotiating the deal.

the first offer shows power; research shows that individuals in power are much more likely to make initial offers, speak first at meetings, and thereby gain the advantage. Another reason was mentioned in Chapter 4; recall that we discussed the anchoring bias, which is the tendency for people to focus on initial information. Once that anchoring point is set, people fail to adequately adjust it based on subsequent information. A smart negotiator sets an anchor with the initial offer, and scores of negotiation studies show that such an anchor greatly favor the person who sets it.[26]

Another distributive bargaining tactic is revealing a deadline. Why? Negotiators who reveal deadlines speed concessions from their negotiating counterparts, making them reconsider their position. And even though negotiators don't *think* this tactic works, in reality, negotiators who reveal deadlines do better.[27]

Picture This

You have a job offer, and your prospective employer asks what sort of starting salary you'd be looking for. You are afraid of scaring off the employer so you settle for too little. If you had suggested what you thought was the highest salary that you think the employer could reasonably offer, you would have likely negotiated a higher salary.

Integrative Bargaining   A sales representative for a women's sportswear manufacturer has just closed a US$15,000 order from a small clothing retailer. The sales rep calls in the order to her firm's credit department. She is told that the firm can't approve credit to this customer because of a past slow-payment record. The next day, the sales rep and the firm's credit manager meet to discuss the problem. The sales rep doesn't want to lose the business. Neither does the credit manager, but he also doesn't want to get stuck with an uncollectible debt. The two openly review their options. After considerable discussion, they agree on a solution that meets both their needs: The credit manager will approve the sale, but the clothing store's owner will provide a bank guarantee that will ensure payment if the bill isn't paid within 60 days.

Integrative bargaining

Negotiation that seeks one or more settlements that can create a win–win solution.

This is an example of **integrative bargaining**. In contrast to distributive bargaining, integrative bargaining operates under the assumption that there are one or more settlements that can create a win–win solution.

Why, then, don't we see more integrative bargaining in organizations? The answer lies in the conditions necessary for this type of negotiation to succeed. These include parties who are open with information and honest about their concerns, a sensitivity by both parties to the other's needs, the ability to trust one another, and a willingness by both parties to maintain flexibility.[28] Because these conditions often don't exist in organizations, it isn't surprising that negotiations often take on a win-at-any-cost dynamic.

There are some ways to achieve more integrative outcomes. For example, individuals who bargain in teams reach more integrative agreements than those who bargain individually. This happens because more ideas are generated when more people are at the bargaining table. So try bargaining in teams.[29]

Finally, you should realize that compromise may be your worst enemy in negotiating a win–win agreement. This is because compromising reduces the pressure to bargain integratively. After all, if you or your opponent gives in easily, it doesn't require anyone to be creative to reach a settlement. Thus, people end up settling for less than they could have obtained if they had been forced to consider the other party's interests, trade-off issues, and be creative.[30] Think of the classic example where two sisters are arguing over who gets an orange. They don't know but one sister wants orange juice whereas the other sister

United Auto Workers President Ron Gettelfinger (left in the photograph) shakes hands with Ford Motor Company Executive Chairman Bill Ford at the opening of negotiations for a new union contract. Both the union and Ford say they are committed to integrative bargaining in finding mutually acceptable solutions to issues such as funding retiree health care and pensions that will boost Ford's competitiveness with Japanese automakers.

wants the orange peel to bake a cake. If one sister simply gives the other sister the orange, then they would not be forced to explore their reasons for wanting the orange, and thus they will never find the win–win solution: They could *each* have the orange because one wants the inside and the other wants the outside!

The Negotiation Process

6   *Apply the five steps of the negotiation process.*

Figure 12-4 provides a simplified model of the negotiation process. It views negotiation as made up of five steps: (1) preparation and planning, (2) definition of ground rules, (3) clarification and justification, (4) bargaining and problem solving, and (5) closure and implementation.[31]

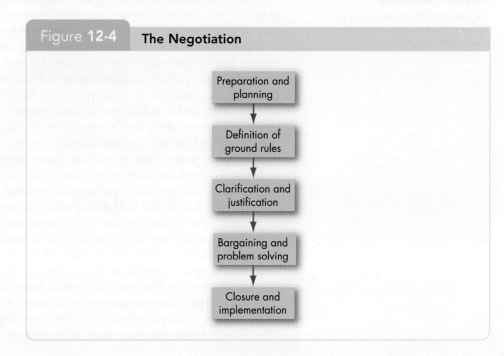

Figure **12-4**	**The Negotiation**

Preparation and planning

↓

Definition of ground rules

↓

Clarification and justification

↓

Bargaining and problem solving

↓

Closure and implementation

Preparation and Planning   Before you start negotiating, you need to do your homework. What's the nature of the conflict? What's the history leading up to this negotiation? Who's involved and what are their perceptions of the conflict? What do you want from the negotiation? What are *your* goals?

You also want to prepare an assessment of what you think the other party's goals are. What are they likely to ask for? How attached are they likely to be in their position? What hidden interests may be important to them? What might they be willing to settle on? When you can anticipate your opponent's position, you are ready to counter arguments with the facts and figures that support your position.

Definition of Ground Rules   Once you've done your planning and developed a strategy, you're ready to begin defining the ground rules and procedures with the other party over the negotiation itself. Who will do the negotiating? Where will it take place? What time constraints, if any, will apply? To what issues will negotiation be limited? Will there be a specific procedure to follow if an agreement is reached? During this phase, the parties will also exchange their initial proposals or demands.

Clarification and Justification   When initial positions have been exchanged, both you and the other party will explain, amplify, clarify, and justify your original demands. This needn't be confrontational. Rather, it's an opportunity for educating and informing each other on the issues, why they are important, and how each arrived at their initial demands. This is the point at which you might want to provide the other party with any documentation that helps support your position.

Bargaining and Problem Solving   The essence of the negotiation process is the actual give-and-take in trying to reach an agreement. This is where both parties will undoubtedly need to bargain and may need to make compromises.

What Do You Think?

Are you a good negotiator? Do you think culture plays a part?

Closure and Implementation   The final step in the negotiation process is formalizing the agreement that has been worked out and developing any procedures that are necessary for implementation and monitoring. For major negotiations—which would include everything from labor-management negotiations to bargaining over lease terms to buying a piece of real estate to negotiating a job offer for a senior management position—this requires paying close attention to the specifics in a formal contract. For most cases, however, closure of the negotiation process is nothing more formal than a handshake.

Individual Differences in Negotiation Effectiveness

7   Show how individual differences influence negotiations.

Are some people better negotiators than others? Though the answer to this question might seem obvious, as it turns out it's more complex than you might think. Here we discuss three factors that influence how effectively individuals negotiate: personality, mood/emotions, and gender.

In 2011, the Association of Banks in Lebanon (ABL) and the Association of Banks in Jordan, signed a cooperation agreement to promote and strengthen both parties. The agreement was made in an attempt to improve collaboration efforts through joint initiatives, the exchange of information, and the sharing of economic and financial data. Both parties agreed to the terms and conditions and jointly determined the specific details that would dictate the formal contract between them.

Personality Traits in Negotiation   Can you predict an opponent's negotiating tactics if you know something about his or her personality? It's tempting to answer 'yes' to this question. For instance, you might assume that high-risk takers would be more aggressive bargainers who make fewer concessions. Surprisingly, the evidence hasn't always supported this intuition.[32]

Assessments of the personality–negotiation relationship have been that personality traits have no significant direct effect on either the bargaining process or the negotiation outcomes. However, recent research has started to question the theory that personality and the negotiation process aren't connected. In fact, it appears that several of the Big Five traits that were discussed in Chapter 2 are related to negotiation outcomes. For example, negotiators who are agreeable or extraverted are not very successful when it comes to distributive bargaining. Why? Because extraverts are outgoing and friendly, they tend to share more information than they should. And agreeable people are more interested in finding ways to cooperate rather than to disagree. These traits, while slightly helpful in integrative negotiations, are liabilities when interests are opposed. So the best distributive bargainer appears to be a disagreeable introvert—that is, someone who is interested in his own outcomes versus pleasing the other party and having a pleasant social exchange.

Though personality and intelligence do appear to have some influence on negotiation, it's not a strong effect. In a sense, that's good news because it means even if you're an agreeable extrovert, you're not severely disadvantaged when it comes time to negotiate. Thus, we all can learn to be better negotiators.

Moods/Emotions in Negotiation   Do moods and emotions influence negotiation? They do, but the way they do appears to depend on the type of negotiation. In distributive negotiations, it appears that negotiators who show anger negotiate better outcomes, because their anger encourages concessions from their opponents. This appears to hold true even when the negotiators are instructed to show anger despite not being truly angry.

In integrative negotiations, in contrast, positive moods and emotions appear to lead to more integrative agreements (higher levels of joint gain). This may happen because, as we noted in Chapter 4, positive mood is related to creativity.[33]

Gender Differences in Negotiations   Do men and women negotiate differently? And does gender affect negotiation outcomes? The answer to the first question appears to be no.[34] The answer to the second is a qualified yes.[35]

A popular stereotype is that women are more cooperative and pleasant in negotiations than are men. The evidence doesn't support this belief. However, men have been found to negotiate better outcomes than women, although the difference is relatively small.

The belief that women are 'nicer' than men in negotiations is probably due to a confusion between gender and the lower degree of power women typically hold in most large organizations. Because women are expected to be 'nice' and men 'tough,' research shows that, relative to men, women are penalized when they initiate negotiations.[36] What's more, when women and men actually do conform to these stereotypes—women act 'nice' and men 'tough'—it becomes a self-fulfilling prophecy, reinforcing the stereotypical gender differences between male and female negotiators.[37] Thus, one of the reasons why negotiations favor men is that women are 'damned if they do, damned if they don't.' Negotiate tough and they are penalized for violating a gender stereotype. Negotiate nice and it only reinforces the stereotype (and is taken advantage of).

Test your negotiation style in the following self-assessment exercise.

In addition to the other party's attitudes and behaviors, the evidence also suggests that women's own attitudes and behaviors hurt them in negotiations. Managerial women demonstrate less confidence in anticipation of negotiating and are less satisfied with their performance after the process is complete, even when their performance and the outcomes they achieve are similar to those for men.[38] This latter conclusion suggests that women may penalize themselves by failing to engage in negotiations when such action would be in their best interests.

Third-Party Negotiations

8 *Assess the roles and functions of third-party negotiations.*

To this point, we've discussed bargaining in terms of direct negotiations. Occasionally, however, individuals or group representatives reach a situation where they are unable to resolve their differences through direct negotiations. In such cases, they may turn to a third party to help them find a solution. There are four basic third-party roles: mediator, arbitrator, conciliator, and consultant.[39]

International OB

Negotiating Across Cultures

Obtaining a favorable outcome in a negotiation may in part depend on the cultural characteristics of your opponent. A study of negotiators in the United States, China, and Japan found that culture plays an important role in successful negotiation. The study found that, overall, negotiators who had both a self-serving 'egoistic' orientation and a high goal level came out best overall compared with negotiators with an other-serving 'prosocial' orientation and a low goal level. In other words, the strategy combining a self-serving negotiation position, where one is focused only on maximizing one's . own outcomes, coupled with a strong desire to obtain the best outcomes, led to the most favorable negotiation results.

However, the degree to which this particular strategy resulted in better outcomes depended on the negotiating partner. The results showed that being self-serving and having a high negotiation goal level resulted in higher outcomes (in this case, profits) only when the negotiating opponent was other-serving. Negotiators from the United States are more likely to be self-serving and have high goal levels. In China and Japan, however, there is a greater likelihood that negotiators are other-serving and thus are more concerned with others' outcomes. Consequently, negotiators from the United States are likely to obtain better outcomes for themselves when negotiating with individuals from China and Japan because American negotiators tend to be more concerned with their own outcomes, sometimes at the expense of the other party.

Though this study suggests that being self-serving can be beneficial in some situations, negotiators should be wary of being too self-serving. US negotiators may benefit from a self-serving negotiation position and a high goal level when negotiating with individuals from China or Japan, but being too self-serving may result in damaged relationships, leading to less favorable outcomes in the long run.

Source: Based on Y. Chen, E. A. Mannix, and T. Okumura, "The Importance of Who You Meet: Effects of Self-Versus Other-Concerns Among Negotiators in the United States, the People's Republic of China, and Japan," *Journal of Experimental Social Psychology*, January, 2003, pp. 1–15.

Mediator

A neutral third party who facilitates a negotiated solution by using reasoning, persuasion, and suggestions for alternatives.

Arbitrator

A third party to a negotiation who has the authority to dictate an agreement.

Conciliator

A trusted third party who provides an informal communication link between the negotiator and the opponent.

Consultant

An impartial third party, skilled in conflict management, who attempts to facilitate creative problem solving through communication and analysis.

First, a **mediator** is a neutral third party who facilitates a negotiated solution by using reasoning and persuasion, suggesting alternatives, and the like. Mediators are widely used in labor-management negotiations and in civil court disputes. The overall effectiveness of mediated negotiations is fairly impressive. The settlement rate is approximately 60 percent, with negotiator satisfaction at about 75 percent. But the situation is the key to whether or not mediation will succeed; the conflicting parties must be motivated to bargain and resolve their conflict. In addition, conflict intensity can't be too high; mediation is most effective under moderate levels of conflict. Finally, perceptions of the mediator are important; to be effective, the mediator must be perceived as neutral and noncoercive.

Second, an **arbitrator** is a third party with the authority to dictate an agreement. Arbitration can be voluntary (requested by the parties) or compulsory (forced on the parties by law or contract). The big plus of arbitration over mediation is that it always results in a settlement. If one party is left feeling defeated, that party is certain to be dissatisfied and unlikely to accept the arbitrator's decision. Therefore, the conflict may resurface at a later time.

A **conciliator** is a trusted third party who provides an informal communication link between the negotiator and the opponent. Comparing its effectiveness to mediation has proven difficult because the two overlap a great deal. In practice, conciliators typically act as more than mere communication channels. They also engage in fact-finding, interpreting messages, and persuading parties to develop agreements.

Finally, a **consultant** is a skilled and objective third party who attempts to facilitate problem solving through communication and analysis, aided by a

OB in the News

'Marriage Counseling' for the Top Bosses

That the two top executives of a company conflicted with one another is no surprise. What's surprising is what they did about it.

When Watermark, a struggling maker of kayaks and car racks, brought in a new executive team, the top two executives came from very different backgrounds. CEO Jim Clark, 43, was an avid hunter and outdoorsman. COO Thomas Fumarelli, 50, was an urbane professional used to high finance in New York and Paris. Because the organization was struggling, with anxious employees who were playing them off one another, the two executives knew their differences were likely to overwhelm them. So they headed off personality conflicts at the pass with two-and-a-half years of joint executive-coaching sessions.

Although such joint coaching sessions are highly unusual, both Clark and Fumarelli (it was his idea) credit the weekly sessions for helping them work through their differences. "It was like marriage counseling," said Clark. "You get all the issues on the table."

Early on, the coaches asked Clark and Fumarelli what they needed from one another. Clark said that he needed Fumarelli to be his eyes and ears for the company and to "cover his back." Fumarelli replied that he needed Clark to support him. "I can check my ego at the door," he recalls saying, "But I need validation and support from you for the role I'm playing to support you."

The two discovered a conflict, though, when the coaches asked

them separately how much time they should spend on various corporate activities. Both Clark and Fumarelli thought that development of the annual budget was his responsibility. After getting this out in the open, Clark realized the budget should primarily be Fumarelli's responsibility. "Very early on, we knew we were going to be stepping on each other's toes," Clark said.

When a private equity company bought Watermark, both left the company. But even then, the two used coaches to handle what they called their "divorce."

Source: Based on P. Dvorak, "CEO and COO Try 'Marriage Counseling,'" *Wall Street Journal*, July 31, 2006, p. B1, B3.

knowledge of conflict management. In contrast to the previous roles, the consultant's role is not to settle the issues, but, rather, to improve relations between the conflicting parties so that they can reach a settlement themselves. Instead of putting forward specific solutions, the consultant tries to help the parties learn to understand and work with each other. Therefore, this approach has a longer-term focus: to build new and positive perceptions and attitudes between the conflicting parties.

Global Implications

9 Describe cultural differences in negotiations.

Conflict and Culture

There is relatively little research on cross-cultural differences in conflict resolution strategies. Some research indicates that individuals in Japan and in the United States view conflict differently. Compared with Japanese negotiators, their US counterparts are more likely to see offers from their counterparts as unfair and to reject them. Another study revealed that whereas US managers are more likely to use competing tactics in the face of conflicts, compromising and avoiding are the most preferred methods of conflict management in China.[40]

There are no significant studies on cross-cultural differences in conflict resolution between Arab countries and others. However, the fact that the Beirut-based contractor Arabian Construction Company (ACC) has landed an estimated US$98.7 million contract to build India's highest skyscraper, World One,[41] suggests that Arabs are able to adapt and interact well with people from different cultures, and are equally able to overcome any possible conflicts that may arise. This is a joint venture partnership with the Indian contractor Simplex Infrastructures, and World One will be the tallest residential tower in the world. The expected completion date is 2014, and the 117-story Mumbai tower will stand half a kilometer high. Imagine how much negotiation must have been involved in this deal!

Cultural Differences in Negotiations

Compared to the research on conflict, there is a lot more research on how negotiating styles vary across national cultures.[42] One study compared US and Japanese negotiators. These researchers found that the Japanese negotiators tended to communicate indirectly and adapt their behaviors to the situation. A follow-up study showed that whereas among US managers making early offers led to the anchoring effect we noted when discussing distributive negotiation, for Japanese negotiators, early offers led to more information sharing and better integrative outcomes.[43]

Another study compared North American, Arab, and Russian negotiators.[44] North Americans tried to persuade by relying on facts and appealing to logic. They countered opponents' arguments with objective facts. They made small concessions early in the negotiation to establish a relationship and usually reciprocated opponents' concessions. North Americans treated deadlines as very important. The Arabs tried to persuade by appealing to emotion. They countered opponents' arguments with subjective feelings. They made concessions throughout the bargaining process and almost always reciprocated opponents' concessions. Arabs approached deadlines very casually. The Russians based their arguments on asserted ideals. They made few, if any, concessions.

Any concession offered by an opponent was viewed as a weakness and almost never reciprocated. Finally, the Russians tended to ignore deadlines.

Another study looked at verbal and nonverbal negotiation tactics exhibited by North Americans, Japanese, and Brazilians during half-hour bargaining sessions.[45] Some of the differences were particularly interesting. For instance, the Brazilians on average said 'no' 83 times, compared with 5 times for the Japanese and 9 times for the North Americans. The Japanese displayed more than 5 periods of silence lasting longer than 10 seconds during the 30-minute sessions. North Americans averaged 3.5 such periods; the Brazilians had none. The Japanese and North Americans interrupted their opponent about the same number of times, but the Brazilians interrupted 2.5 to 3 times more often than the North Americans and the Japanese. Finally, the Japanese and the North Americans had no physical contact with their opponents during negotiations except for handshaking, but the Brazilians, like Arabs, touched each other almost 5 times every half hour.

Summary and Implications for Managers

Many people automatically assume that conflict is related to lower group and organizational performance. This chapter has demonstrated that this assumption is frequently incorrect. Conflict can be either constructive or destructive to the functioning of a group or unit.

What advice can we give managers faced with excessive conflict and the need to reduce it? Don't assume that one conflict-handling intention will always be best! You should select an intention appropriate for the situation. The following are some guidelines:[46]

- Use *competition* when quick, decisive action is vital (in emergencies), on important issues, where unpopular actions need to be implemented (in cost cutting, enforcing unpopular rules, discipline), on issues vital to the organization's welfare when you know you're right, and against people who take advantage of noncompetitive behavior.
- Use *collaboration* to find an integrative solution when both sets of concerns are too important to be compromised, when your objective is to learn, to merge insights from people with different perspectives, to gain commitment by incorporating concerns into a consensus, and to work through feelings that have interfered with a relationship.
- Use *avoidance* when an issue is trivial or when more important issues are pressing, when you perceive no chance of satisfying your concerns, when potential disruption outweighs the benefits of resolution, to let people cool down and regain perspective, when gathering information is more important than the immediate decision, and when others can resolve the conflict more effectively.
- Use *accommodation* when you find that you're wrong and to allow a better position to be heard, to learn, and to show your reasonableness; when issues are more important to others than to yourself and to satisfy others and maintain cooperation; to build social credits for later issues; to minimize loss when you are losing; when harmony and stability are especially important; and to allow employees to develop by learning from mistakes.
- Use *compromise* when goals are important but not worth the effort of potential disruption of more assertive approaches; when opponents with equal power are committed to mutually exclusive goals; to achieve temporary settlements to complex issues; to arrive at solutions under time pressure; and as a backup when collaboration or competition is unsuccessful.

Finally, negotiation is an ongoing activity in groups and organizations. Distributive bargaining can resolve disputes, but it often negatively affects the satisfaction of one or more negotiators because it is focused on the short term and because it is confrontational. Integrative bargaining, in contrast, tends to provide outcomes that satisfy all parties and that build lasting relationships. When engaged in negotiation, make sure you set aggressive goals and try to find creative ways to achieve the goals of both parties, especially when you value the long-term relationship with the other party. That doesn't mean 'giving in' on your self-interest; rather, it means trying to find creative solutions that give both parties what they really want.

Point > < Counterpoint

CONFLICT BENEFITS ORGANIZATIONS

*C*onflict can provide benefits to the organization:

- **Conflict is a means to solve problems and bring about change.** If there is no conflict, it means the real problems aren't being addressed.
- **Conflict facilitates group cohesiveness.** Conflict with another group brings together those within each group.
- **Conflict improves group and organizational effectiveness.** In fact, more organizations probably fail because they have *too little* conflict, not because they have too much. Though most of us don't like conflict, it often is the last best hope of saving an organization.

*I*n general, conflicts are dysfunctional, and it is one of management's major responsibilities to keep conflict intensity as low as possible. A few points support this case:

- **The negative consequences from conflict can be devastating.** The most obvious negatives are increased turnover, decreased employee satisfaction, inefficiencies between work units, sabotage, and labor grievances and strikes. One study estimated that managing conflict at work costs the average employer nearly 450 days of management time a year.[47]
- **Effective managers build teamwork.** A good manager builds a coordinated team. Conflict works against such an objective. Management creates teamwork by minimizing internal conflicts and facilitating internal coordination.
- **Conflict is avoidable.** It may be true that conflict is inevitable when an organization is in a downward spiral, but the goal of good leadership and effective management is to avoid the spiral to begin with.

Questions for Review

1 What is conflict?

2 What are the differences among the traditional, human relations, and interactionist views of conflict?

3 What are the steps of the conflict process?

4 What is negotiation?

5 What are the differences between distributive and integrative bargaining?

6 What are the five steps in the negotiation process?

7 How do the individual differences of personality and gender influence negotiations?

8 What are the roles and functions of third-party negotiations?

9 How does culture influence negotiations?

Discussion Exercise

Consider these two statements: "Conflict may motivate people to appreciate each other's positions more fully," and "Conflict may encourage people to consider new ideas, thereby facilitating change." Discuss and share your thoughts with the class.

Ethical Considerations

Is lying acceptable when it comes to negotiation? Most ethicists would probably agree that lies during negotiation are wrong. However, there is a universal dilemma around the 'little white lie'—the small omissions and evasions that may be necessary to get your way.

During negotiations, when is a lie a *lie*? Is exaggerating benefits, downplaying negatives, ignoring errors, or saying "I don't know" when in reality you do, considered lying? Rather than being considered unethical, the use of these 'lies' is considered by many as an indicator that a negotiator is strong, smart, and savvy. Is it ever ethically acceptable to use deception and evasion in negotiations? Where would you draw the line?

Critical Analysis

ETISALAT-ZAIN DEAL BLOCKED

The giant communication company Etisalat, based in Abu-Dhabi, had had plans to acquire 46 percent of the Kuwait telecom giant Zain, at an estimated US$12 billion. However, from the beginning, in November, 2010, the negotiations faced many obstacles, and they continued all the way through. An official statement from Etisalat determined that due diligence, political instability, and Zain shareholder conflicts were the main reasons behind the decision to stop the talks.

There had originally been a commitment by National Investments Company to act as an intermediary and to see the deal through to the end. This happened after Zain had turned down three bids for a stake in its Saudi Arabia unit, valued at US$750 million. In addition, Etisalat was stopped by authorities from taking ownership of its Saudi affiliates Mobily and Zain KSA.

In March, 2011, Zain's board accepted an offer by Kingdom Holding and Bahrain Telecom Company (Batelco) for its Saudi assets, and made a separate deal with Etisalat, offering Zain Group shares for US$6.11 each. This offer was valued at US$5 billion; Kingdom and Batelco would pay US$950 million in cash and cover US$3.8 billion of debt. Zain KSA would pay the remaining US$250 million. Both Kingdom and Batelco still intend to buy Zain's Saudi operations. Accordingly, all three companies signed a preliminary contract that included payments to be made in case the group decided to break up.

Questions

1. Do you think the breakup fee is ethical? Explain.
2. What kind of conflicts do you think this deal may face? Explain.

Source: "Multi-billion Dollar Etisalat–Zain Deal Falls Through," *The Executive*, Issue No. 141, April, 2011, p. 56.

Research Exercise

We saw in this chapter that when negotiating, Arabs differ from some other cultures. Do some research into what cultural differences may influence negotiation styles. Compare the Arab culture with one other that interests you.

Part 4 The Organization System

LEARNING OBJECTIVES

This chapter will enable you to:

1 Identify the six elements of an organization's structure.

2 Identify the characteristics of a bureaucracy.

3 Describe a matrix organization.

4 Identify the characteristics of a virtual organization.

5 Show why managers want to create boundaryless organizations.

6 Demonstrate how organizational structures differ, and contrast mechanistic and organic structural models.

7 Analyze the behavioral implications of different organizational designs.

8 Show how globalization affects organizational structure.

Foundations of Organizational Structure

13

Every company has two organizational structures: The formal one is written on the charts; the other is the everyday relationship of the men and women in the organization.

—Harold S. Geneen

Aramex—Empowerment Through Organizational Structure

What began in 1982 as a small entrepreneurial endeavor by two friends, rapidly evolved into a global brand recognized for its customized and innovative services, broke traditional boundaries as the first Arab-based international company to list on the NASDAQ, and today has become one of the leading global logistics and express service providers, competing with giants such as DHL, FedEx, and UPS.

One of the key factors in the growth of Aramex has been the company's flexible customer-centric approach, with a promise to deliver everything from the smallest package to fully fledged logistics and supply-chain solutions, all the while ensuring that each is customized to meet the diverse needs of its customers.

This posed a challenge: How do you maintain the flexibility to deliver solutions that are customized to local market-needs in a globally expanding organization? The founder and CEO of Aramex, Fadi Ghandour, decided that Aramex would operate as a federation of interdependent business units, with a decentralized organization structure: Each region is empowered to make its own business decisions, emphasizing entrepreneurship and innovation led by the front lines.

Management is structured by type of service and by geographical location. Each main service line and geographical area is assigned a chief executive officer (CEO). This leads to greater flexibility and ability to respond to changing needs; "if you want to do business here, then you have to have an organization that is capable of structuring itself to adapt quickly to the changes and conflicts that happen in the neighborhood. This has been the story of our life for the past twenty years," says Fadi Ghandour.

Meanwhile, the company's expanding global network, with its flexible and empowered structure, is tightly knit by a corporate culture and shared core values that focus on people as the company's most valuable asset. As a demographically young organization—81 percent of its workforce are aged between 18 and 40 years—Aramex actively promotes career development and professional growth within the company through talent management programs, an internal corporate university, as well as partnering with leading academic institutions to build a generation of future company leaders. In 2010, 60 percent of all new team leaders, managers, and senior managers were promoted internally, and that number is increasing year-over-year.

This focus on people is bolstered by the company's stand on creativity and entrepreneurship: it views creativity not as a revelation, but rather as the fruit of hard work and a relentless formula of trial and error; and it asserts that entrepreneurial employees can achieve a sense of ownership inside the organization.

Source: Case study contributed by the marketing team at Aramex International.

Structural decisions are arguably the most fundamental ones a leader, such as Fadi Ghandour in the opening case, has to make. This chapter talks about organizational structure in organizations. Before we discuss the elements of an organization's structure and how they can affect behavior, consider how you might react to one type of organizational structure—the bureaucratic structure—by taking the following self-assessment.

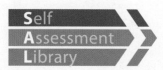

DO I LIKE BUREAUCRACY?

In the Self-Assessment Library (available online), take assessment IV.F.2 (Do I Like Bureaucracy?) and answer the following questions:

1. *Judging from the results, how willing are you to work in a bureaucratic organization?*
2. *Do you think scores on this measure matter? Why or why not?*
3. *Do you think people who score very low (or even very high) on this measure should try to adjust their preferences based on where they are working?*

What Is Organizational Structure?

1 *Identify the six elements of an organization's structure.*

Organizational structure

The way in which job tasks are formally divided, grouped, and coordinated within an organization.

An **organizational structure** defines how job tasks are formally divided, grouped, and coordinated. There are six key elements that managers need to address when they design their organization's structure: work specialization, departmentalization, chain of command, span of control, centralization and decentralization, and formalization.[1] Table 13-1 presents each of these elements as answers to an important structural question. The following sections describe these six elements of structure.

Work Specialization

Early in the twentieth century, Henry Ford became rich and famous by building automobiles on an assembly line. Every Ford worker was assigned a specific, repetitive task. For instance, one person would just put on the right-front wheel, and someone else would install the right-front door. By breaking jobs up into small standardized tasks, which could be performed over and over again, Ford

TABLE 13-1 Key Design Questions and Answers for Designing the Proper Organizational Structure	
The Key Question	**The Answer Is Provided By**
1. To what degree are activities subdivided into separate jobs?	Work specialization
2. On what basis will jobs be grouped together?	Departmentalization
3. To whom do individuals and groups report?	Chain of command
4. How many individuals can a manager efficiently and effectively direct?	Span of control
5. Where does decision-making authority lie?	Centralization and decentralization
6. To what degree will there be rules and regulations to direct employees and managers?	Formalization

Work is specialized at the Russian factories that manufacture the wooden nesting dolls called matryoshkas. At this factory outside Moscow, individuals specialize in doing part of the doll production, from the craftsmen who carve the dolls to the painters who decorate them. Work specialization brings efficiency to doll production, as some 50 employees can make 100 matryoshkas every 2 days.

was able to produce cars at the rate of one every 10 seconds, while using employees who had relatively limited skills.

Ford demonstrated that work can be performed more efficiently if employees are allowed to specialize. Today we use the term **work specialization**, or *division of labor*, to describe the degree to which activities in the organization are subdivided into separate jobs. The essence of work specialization is that rather than an entire job being done by one individual, it is broken down into a number of steps, with each step being completed by a separate individual. In essence, individuals specialize in doing part of an activity rather than the entire activity.

For much of the first half of the twentieth century, managers viewed work specialization as an unending source of increased productivity. But by the 1960s, there came increasing evidence that a good thing can be carried too far. The point had been reached in some jobs at which the human diseconomies from specialization—which surfaced as boredom, fatigue, stress, low productivity, poor quality, increased absenteeism, and high turnover—more than offset the economic advantages. In such cases, productivity could be increased by enlarging, rather than narrowing, the scope of job activities. In addition, a number of companies found that by giving employees a variety of activities to do, allowing them to do a whole and complete job, and putting them into teams with interchangeable skills, they often achieved significantly higher output, with increased employee satisfaction.

Departmentalization

Once you've divided jobs up through work specialization, you need to group these jobs together so that common tasks can be coordinated. The basis by which jobs are grouped together is called **departmentalization**.

One of the most popular ways to group activities is by *functions* performed. A manufacturing manager might organize a plant by separating engineering, accounting, manufacturing, personnel, and supply specialists into common

Work specialization

The degree to which tasks in an organization are subdivided into separate jobs.

Departmentalization

The basis by which jobs in an organization are grouped together.

departments. Of course, departmentalization by function can be used in all types of organizations. Only the functions change to reflect the organization's objectives and activities. A hospital might have departments devoted to research, patient care, accounting, and so forth. The major advantage to this type of grouping is obtaining efficiencies from putting similar specialists together. Functional departmentalization seeks to achieve economies of scale by placing people with common skills and orientations into common units.

Jobs can also be departmentalized by the type of *product* the organization produces. The major advantage to this type of grouping is increased accountability for product performance since all activities related to a specific product are under the direction of a single manager. If an organization's activities are service related rather than product related, each service would be autonomously grouped.

Another way to departmentalize is on the basis of *geography*, or territory, as we saw in the opening case on Aramex. If an organization's customers are scattered over a large geographic area and have similar needs based on their location, then this form of departmentalization can be valuable. In addition, process departmentalization can be used for processing customers as well as products.

A final category of departmentalization is to use the particular type of *customer* the organization seeks to reach. Microsoft, for instance, is organized around four customer markets: consumers, large corporations, software developers, and small businesses. The assumption underlying customer departmentalization is that customers in each department have a common set of problems and needs that can best be met by having specialists for each.

Large organizations may use all of the forms of departmentalization that we've described. Across organizations of all sizes, one strong trend has developed over the past decade. Rigid, functional departmentalization is being increasingly complemented by teams that cross over traditional departmental lines. As we described in Chapter 8, as tasks have become more complex and more diverse, skills are needed to accomplish those tasks; management has turned to cross-functional teams.

Chain of Command

Thirty-five years ago, the chain-of-command concept was a basic cornerstone in the design of organizations. As you'll see, it has far less importance today.[2] But contemporary managers should still consider its implications when they decide how best to structure their organizations. The **chain of command** is an unbroken line of authority that extends from the top of the organization to the lowest levels and clarifies who reports to whom. It answers questions for employees such as 'To whom do I go if I have a problem?' and 'To whom am I responsible?'

Chain of command

The unbroken line of authority that extends from the top of the organization to the lowest echelon and clarifies who reports to whom.

What Do You Think?

Do you think that employees function more effectively when they are aware of who they are responsible to and what they are responsible for?

Authority

The rights inherent in a managerial position to give orders and to expect the orders to be obeyed.

You can't discuss the chain of command without discussing two complementary concepts: *authority* and *unity of command*. **Authority** refers to the rights inherent in a managerial position to give orders and to expect the orders to be obeyed. To facilitate coordination, each managerial position is given a place in the chain of command, and each manager is given a degree of authority in order to meet his or her responsibilities, a model adopted in many countries across the region, including Saudi Aramco.

Unity of command

The idea that a subordinate should have only one superior to whom he or she is directly responsible.

The **unity-of-command** principle helps preserve the concept of an unbroken line of authority. It states that a person should have one and only one superior to whom that person is directly responsible. If the unity of command is broken, an employee might have to cope with conflicting demands or priorities from several superiors.

Span of Control

Span of control

The number of subordinates a manager can efficiently and effectively direct.

How many employees can a manager efficiently and effectively direct? This question of **span of control** is important because, to a large degree, it determines the number of levels and managers an organization has. All things being equal, the wider or larger the span, the more efficient the organization. An example can illustrate the validity of this statement.

Assume that we have two organizations, each of which has approximately 4,100 operative-level employees. As Figure 13-1 illustrates, if one has a uniform span of four and the other a span of eight, the wider span would have two fewer levels and approximately 800 fewer managers. If the average manager made US$50,000 a year, the wider span would save US$40 million a year in management salaries! Obviously, wider spans are more efficient in terms of cost. However, at some point, wider spans reduce effectiveness. That is, when the span becomes too large, employee performance suffers because supervisors no longer have the time to provide the necessary leadership and support.

Narrow, or small, spans have their supporters. By keeping the span of control to five or six employees, a manager can maintain close control.[3] But narrow spans have three major drawbacks. First, as already described, they're expensive because they add levels of management. Second, they make vertical communication in the organization more complex. The added levels of hierarchy slow down decision making and tend to isolate upper management. Third, narrow spans of control encourage overly tight supervision and discourage employee autonomy.

The trend recently has been toward wider spans of control.[4] They're consistent with recent efforts by companies to reduce costs, cut overheads, speed up decision making, increase flexibility, get closer to customers, and empower employees. However, to ensure that performance doesn't suffer because of these wider spans, organizations have been investing heavily in employee training. Managers recognize that they can handle a wider span when employees know their jobs inside and out, or can turn to their coworkers when they have questions.

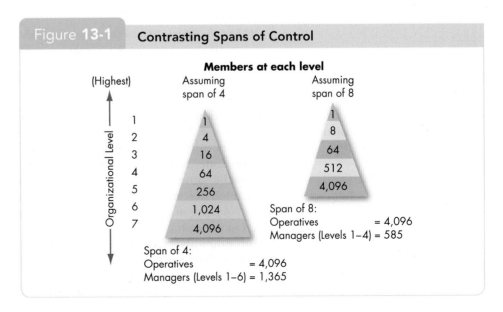

Figure **13-1** **Contrasting Spans of Control**

Centralization and Decentralization

In some organizations, top managers make all the decisions. Lower-level managers merely carry out top management's directions. At the other extreme, there are organizations in which decision making is pushed down to the managers who are closest to the action. The former organizations are highly centralized; the latter are decentralized.

Centralization

The degree to which decision making is concentrated at a single point in an organization.

The term **centralization** refers to the degree to which decision making is concentrated at a single point in the organization. The concept includes only formal authority—that is, the rights relative to one's position. Typically, it's said that if top management makes the organization's key decisions with little or no input from lower-level personnel, then the organization is centralized. In contrast, the more that lower-level personnel provide input or are actually given the discretion to make decisions, the more decentralization there is. An organization characterized by centralization is a different structure from one that is decentralized. In a decentralized organization, action can be taken more quickly to solve problems, more people provide input into decisions, and employees are less likely to feel left out from those who make the decisions that affect their work lives.

Consistent with recent management efforts to make organizations more flexible and responsive, there has been a marked trend toward decentralizing decision making. In large companies, lower-level managers are closer to 'the action' and typically have more detailed knowledge about problems than top managers have. Take the following self-assessment exercise to determine how willing you may be to delegate others.

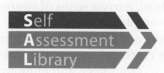

HOW WILLING AM I TO DELEGATE?

In the Self-Assessment Library (available online), take assessment III.A.2 (How Willing Am I to Delegate?).

What Do You Think?

Will you be the type of business person who believes in delegation of authority?

Formalization

Formalization

The degree to which jobs within an organization are standardized.

Formalization refers to the degree to which jobs within the organization are standardized. If a job is highly formalized, then the employee has a minimum amount of influence over what is to be done, when it is to be done, and how it is to be done. Employees can be expected always to handle the same input in exactly the same way, resulting in a consistent and uniform output. There are explicit job descriptions, lots of organizational rules, and clearly defined procedures covering work processes in organizations in which there is high formalization. On the other hand, where formalization is low, job behaviors are relatively nonprogrammed, and employees have a great deal of freedom to exercise discretion in their work. Because an individual's discretion on the job is negatively related to the amount of behavior in that job that is preprogrammed by the organization, the greater the standardization, the less input the employee has

OB in the News

Siemens Simple Structure—Not

There is perhaps no tougher task for an executive than to restructure a European organization. Ask former Siemens CEO Klaus Kleinfeld.

Siemens, with US$114 billion in revenues in 2006 and branches in 190 countries, is one of the largest electronics companies in the world. Although the company has long been respected for its engineering prowess, it's also derided for its sluggishness and mechanistic structure. So when Kleinfeld took over as CEO, he sought to restructure the company along the lines of what Jack Welch did at General Electric. He has tried to make the structure less bureaucratic so that decisions are made faster. He spun off underperforming businesses. And he simplified the company's structure.

Kleinfeld's efforts drew angry protests from employee groups,

with constant picket lines outside his corporate offices. One of the challenges of transforming European organizations is the active participation of employees in executive decisions. Half the seats on the Siemens board of directors are allocated to labor representatives. Not surprisingly, the labor groups did not react positively to Kleinfeld's GE-like restructuring efforts. In his attempts to speed those efforts, labor groups alleged, Kleinfeld secretly bank-rolled a business-friendly workers' group to try to undermine Germany's main industrial union.

Due to this and other allegations, Kleinfeld was forced out in June 2007 and replaced by Peter Löscher. Löscher has found the same tensions between inertia and the need for restructuring. Only a month after becoming CEO, Löscher was faced with a decision whether to spin off its

underperforming US$14 billion auto parts unit, VDO. Löscher had to weigh the forces for stability, who wish to protect worker interests, with US-style pressures for financial performance. One of VDO's possible buyers is a US company, TRW, the controlling interest of which is held by US private equity firm Blackstone. Private equity firms have been called "locusts" by German labor representatives, so, more than most CEOs, Löscher had to balance worker interests with pressure for financial performance. When Löscher decided to sell VDO to German tire giant Continental Corporation, Continental promptly began to downsize and restructure operations.

Sources: Based on M. Esterl and D. Crawford, "Siemens CEO Put to Early Test," *Wall Street Journal*, July 23, 2007, p. A8; and J. Ewing, "Siemens' Culture Clash," *BusinessWeek*, January 29, 2007, pp. 42–46.

into how the work is to be done. Standardization not only eliminates the possibility of employees engaging in alternative behaviors, but it even removes the need for employees to consider alternatives.

The degree of formalization can vary widely between organizations and within organizations. Certain jobs, for instance, are well known to have little formalization. For instance, college book travelers—the representatives of publishers who call on professors to inform them of their company's new publications—have a great deal of freedom in their jobs. They have no standard sales talk and the extent of rules and procedures governing their behavior may be little more than the requirement that they submit a weekly sales report and some suggestions on what to emphasize for the various new titles. At the other extreme, there are clerical and editorial positions in the same publishing houses for which employees are required to be at their desks by 8:00 A.M., following a set of precise procedures dictated by management.

Common Organizational Designs

We now turn to describing three of the more common organizational designs found in use: the *simple structure*, the *bureaucracy*, and the *matrix structure*.

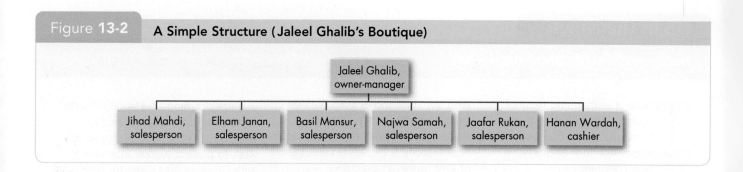

Figure 13-2 **A Simple Structure (Jaleel Ghalib's Boutique)**

The Simple Structure

What do a small retail store, an electronics firm run by a hard-driving entrepreneur, and an airline with a pilots' strike have in common? They probably all use the **simple structure**.

The simple structure is said to be characterized most by what it is not rather than by what it is. The simple structure is not elaborate.[5] It has a low degree of departmentalization, wide spans of control, authority centralized in a single person, and little formalization. The simple structure is a 'flat' organization; it usually has only two or three vertical levels, a few employees, and one individual in whom the decision-making authority is centralized.

The simple structure is most widely practiced in small businesses in which the manager and the owner are one and the same. This, for example, is illustrated in Figure 13-2, an organization chart for a boutique. Jaleel Ghalib owns and manages this store. Although he employs five full-time salespeople, a cashier, and extra personnel for weekends and holidays, he 'runs the show.' But large companies, in times of crisis, often simplify their structures as a means of focusing their resources.

The strength of the simple structure lies in its simplicity. It's fast, flexible, and inexpensive to maintain, and accountability is clear. One major weakness is that it's difficult to maintain in anything other than small organizations. It becomes increasingly inadequate as an organization grows because its low formalization and high centralization tend to create information overload at the top. As size increases, decision making typically becomes slower and can eventually stop as the single executive tries to continue making all the decisions. However, when an organization begins to employ 50 or 100 people, it's very difficult for the owner-manager to make all the choices. If the structure isn't changed and made more elaborate, the firm can eventually fail. The simple structure's other weakness is that it's risky—everything depends on one person. One heart attack can literally destroy the organization's information and decision-making center.

Simple structure

A structure characterized by a low degree of departmentalization, wide spans of control, authority centralized in a single person, and little formalization.

The Bureaucracy

Standardization! That's the key concept that underlies all bureaucracies.

② Identify the characteristics of a bureaucracy.

Picture This

Consider the bank where you keep your checking account, the department store where you buy your clothes, or the government offices that collect your taxes, enforce health regulations, and provide local fire protection. What do they all have in common? They all rely on standardized work processes for coordination and control.

Bureaucracy

A structure with highly routine operating tasks achieved through specialization, very formalized rules and regulations, tasks that are grouped into functional departments, centralized authority, narrow spans of control, and decision making that follows the chain of command.

The **bureaucracy** is characterized by highly routine operating tasks achieved through specialization, very formalized rules and regulations, tasks that are grouped into functional departments, centralized authority, narrow spans of control, and decision making that follows the chain of command. The primary strength of the bureaucracy lies in its ability to perform standardized activities in a highly efficient manner. Putting like specialties together in functional departments results in economies of scale, minimum duplication of personnel and equipment, and employees who have the opportunity to talk "the same language" among their peers. Furthermore, bureaucracies can continue with less talented—and, hence, less costly—middle- and lower-level managers. Standardized operations, coupled with high formalization, allow decision making to be centralized. There is little need, therefore, for innovative and experienced decision makers below the level of senior executives.

One of the major weaknesses of a bureaucracy is illustrated in the following dialogue among four executives in one company: "You know, nothing happens in this place until we *produce* something," said the production executive. "Wrong," commented the research and development manager. "Nothing happens until we *design* something!" "What are you talking about?" asked the marketing executive. "Nothing happens here until we *sell* something!" Finally, the frustrated accounting manager responded, "It doesn't matter what you produce, design, or sell. No one knows what happens until we *calculate the results!*" This conversation shows that specialization creates subunit conflicts. Functional unit goals can override the overall goals of the organization.

International OB

Structural Considerations in Multinationals

When bringing out a business innovation in any country, trudging through corporate bureaucracy can cause delays that result in a competitive disadvantage. This is especially true in China, one of the world's fastest-growing economies. Successful multinational corporations operating in China are realizing that the optimal structure is decentralized with a relatively high degree of managerial autonomy. Given that more than 1.3 billion people live in China, the opportunity for businesses is tremendous and, as a result, competition is increasing. To take advantage of this opportunity, companies must be able to respond to changes before their competitors.

For example, Tyson Foods gives its vice-president and head of the company's China operations, James Rice, the freedom to build the company's business overseas. While walking past a food vendor in Shanghai, Rice got the idea for cumin-flavored chicken strips. Without the need to obtain approval from upper management, Rice and his team immediately developed the recipe, tested it, and, after receiving a 90 percent customer-approval rating, began selling the product within two months of coming up with the idea.

Other companies that have implemented more formalized, bureaucratic structures have fared less well. One manager of a consumer electronics company who wanted to reduce the package size of a product to lower its cost and attract lower-income Chinese customers had to send the idea to his boss. His boss, the vice-president of Asian operations, then sent the idea to the vice-president of international operations, who in turn sent the idea to upper management in the United States. Although the idea was approved, the process took five months, during which a competitor introduced a similarly packaged product.

So, when it comes to innovating in a dynamic, fast-paced economy such as China, decentralization and autonomy can be major competitive advantages for multinational companies. To gain this competitive advantage, companies like Tyson are empowering their overseas managers to make their own decisions.

Source: Based on C. Hymowitz, "Executives in China Need Both Autonomy and Fast Access to Boss," *Wall Street Journal*, May 10, 2005, p. B1.

The other major weakness of a bureaucracy is something we've all experienced at one time or another when having to deal with people who work in these organizations: obsessive concern with following the rules. When cases arise that don't precisely fit the rules, there is no room for modification. The bureaucracy is efficient only as long as employees confront problems that they have previously encountered and for which programmed decision rules have already been established.

The Matrix Structure

> **3**   *Describe a matrix organization.*

Matrix structure

A structure that creates dual lines of authority and combines functional and product departmentalization.

Another popular organizational design option is the **matrix structure**. You'll find it being used in advertising agencies, research and development laboratories, construction companies, hospitals, government agencies, universities, management consulting firms, and entertainment companies.[6] Essentially, the matrix combines two forms of departmentalization: functional and product departmentalization.

The strength of functional departmentalization lies in putting similar specialists together, which minimizes the number necessary, while allowing the pooling and sharing of specialized resources across products. Its major disadvantage is the difficulty of coordinating the tasks of diverse functional specialists so that their activities are completed on time and within budget. Product departmentalization, on the other hand, has exactly the opposite benefits and disadvantages. It facilitates coordination among specialties to achieve on-time completion and to meet budget targets. Furthermore, it provides clear responsibility for all activities related to a product, but with duplication of activities and costs. The matrix attempts to gain the strengths of each, while avoiding their weaknesses.

The most obvious structural characteristic of the matrix is that it breaks the unity-of-command concept. That is, employees in the matrix have two bosses—their functional department managers and their product managers. Therefore, the matrix has a dual chain of command.

Figure 13-3 shows the matrix form as used in a college of business administration. The academic departments of accounting, decision and information systems, marketing, and so forth are functional units. In addition, specific

| Figure **13-3** | Matrix Structure for a College of Business Administration |

Programs / Academic Departments	Undergraduate	Master's	PhD	Research	Executive Development	Community Service
Accounting						
Finance						
Decision and Information Systems						
Management						
Marketing						

programs (that is, products) are overlaid on the functions. In this way, members in a matrix structure have a dual assignment—to their functional department and to their product groups. For instance, a professor of accounting who is teaching an undergraduate course may report to the director of undergraduate programs as well as to the chairperson of the accounting department.

The strength of the matrix lies in its ability to facilitate coordination when the organization has a multiplicity of complex and interdependent activities. As an organization gets larger, its information-processing capacity can become overloaded. In a bureaucracy, complexity results in increased formalization. The direct and continuous contact between different specialties in the matrix can make for better communication and more flexibility. Information spreads throughout the organization and more quickly reaches the people who need to take account of it. Another advantage to the matrix is that it facilitates the efficient allocation of specialists. When individuals with highly specialized skills are located in one functional department or product group, their talents are monopolized and underused. The matrix achieves the advantages of economies of scale by providing the organization with both the best resources and an effective way of ensuring their efficient deployment.

The major disadvantages of the matrix lie in the confusion it creates, its encouragement of power struggles, and the stress it places on individuals.[7] When you dispense with the unity-of-command concept, ambiguity is significantly increased, and ambiguity often leads to conflict. For example, it's frequently unclear who reports to whom, and it is not unusual for product managers to fight over getting the best specialists assigned to their products. Confusion and ambiguity also create the seeds of power struggles. Bureaucracy reduces the potential for power grabs by defining the rules of the game. When those rules are 'open for all,' power struggles between functional and product managers result. For individuals who desire security and absence from ambiguity, this work climate can produce stress. Reporting to more than one boss introduces role conflict, and unclear expectations introduce role ambiguity. The comfort of bureaucracy's predictability is absent, replaced by insecurity and stress.

New Design Options

4 *Identify the characteristics of a virtual organization.*

Over the past decade or two, senior managers in a number of organizations have been working to develop new structural options that can better help their firms to compete effectively. In this section, we'll describe two such structural designs: the *virtual organization* and the *boundaryless organization*.

The Virtual Organization

Virtual organization

A small, core organization that outsources major business functions.

Why own when you can rent? That question captures the essence of the **virtual organization** (also sometimes called the *network*, or *modular*, organization), typically a small, core organization that outsources major business functions.[8] In structural terms, the virtual organization is highly centralized, with little or no departmentalization.

The best example of the virtual structure is today's movie-making organization. In Hollywood's golden era, movies were made by huge, vertically integrated corporations. Studios such as MGM, Warner Brothers, and 20th Century Fox owned large movie lots and employed thousands of full-time specialists— set designers, camera people, film editors, directors, and even actors. Today,

The Boeing Company outsourced the production of about 70 percent of the components of its new 787 Dreamliner passenger jet aircraft. For example, the Italian firm Alenia Aeronautica produced the plane's rear fuselage and horizontal stabilizer, and Tokyo-based Mitsubishi Motors Corporation created the wings. Global outsourcing helped Boeing reduce the plane's development and production costs, enabling it to offer the plane at a price attractive to buyers. Before the Dreamliner's maiden flight, Boeing had a record-breaking 500 orders for the plane, many of which came from the countries that made parts for the aircraft that was assembled at Boeing's Everett, Washington, plant.

most movies are made by a collection of individuals and small companies who come together and make films project by project.[9] This structural form allows each project to be staffed with the talent most suited to its demands, rather than having to choose just from the people employed by the studio. It minimizes bureaucratic overhead because there is no lasting organization to maintain. And it lessens long-term risks and their costs because there is no long term—a team is assembled for a specific period and then broken up.

What's going on here? It is the search for maximum flexibility. These virtual organizations have created networks of relationships that allow them to contract out manufacturing, distribution, marketing, or any other business function for which management feels that others can do better or more cheaply. The virtual organization stands in sharp contrast to the typical bureaucracy that has many vertical levels of management and where control is sought through ownership. In such organizations, research and development are done in-house, production occurs in company-owned plants, and sales and marketing are performed by the company's own employees. To support all this, management has to employ extra staff, including accountants, human resource specialists, and lawyers. The virtual organization, however, outsources many of these functions and concentrates on what it does best.

Figure 13-4 shows a virtual organization in which management outsources all of the primary functions of the business. The core of the organization is a small group of executives whose job is to oversee directly any activities that are done in-house and to coordinate relationships with the other organizations that manufacture, distribute, and perform other important functions for the virtual organization. The dotted lines in Figure 13-4 represent the relationships typically maintained under contracts. In essence, managers in virtual structures spend most of their time coordinating and controlling external relations, typically by way of computer-network links.

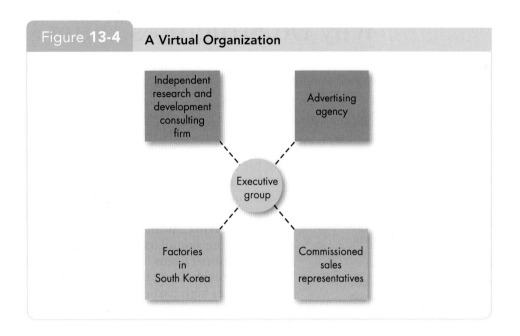

Figure **13-4**   **A Virtual Organization**

The major advantage to the virtual organization is its flexibility. The primary drawback to this structure is that it reduces management's control over key parts of its business.

The Boundaryless Organization

5 *Show why managers want to create boundaryless organizations.*

Boundaryless organization

An organization that seeks to eliminate the chain of command, have limitless spans of control, and replace departments with empowered teams.

General Electric's former chairman, Jack Welch, coined the term **boundaryless organization** to describe his idea of what he wanted GE to become. Welch, a well-known name in the Arab world, wanted to turn his company into a "family grocery store."[10] That is, in spite of its monstrous size (2010 revenues were US$150.2 billion)[11] he wanted to eliminate *vertical* and *horizontal* boundaries within GE and break down *external* barriers between the company and its customers and suppliers. The boundaryless organization seeks to eliminate the chain of command, have limitless spans of control, and replace departments with empowered teams. And because it relies so heavily on information technology, some have turned to calling this structure the *T-form* (or technology-based) organization.[12]

By removing vertical boundaries, management flattens the hierarchy. Status and rank are minimized. Cross-hierarchical teams (which include top executives, middle managers, supervisors, and operative employees), participative decision-making practices, and the use of 360-degree performance appraisals (in which peers and others above and below the employee evaluate performance) are examples of what GE is doing to break down vertical boundaries.

Functional departments create horizontal boundaries. And these boundaries can limit interaction between functions, product lines, and units. The way to reduce these barriers is to replace functional departments with cross-functional teams and to organize activities around processes. Another way management can cut through horizontal barriers is to use lateral transfers, rotating people into and out of different functional areas. This approach turns specialists into generalists.

Why Do Structures Differ?

6 *Demonstrate how organizational structures differ, and contrast mechanistic and organic structural models.*

Mechanistic model

A structure characterized by extensive departmentalization, high formalization, a limited information network, and centralization.

Organic model

A structure that is flat, uses cross-hierarchical and cross-functional teams, has low formalization, possesses a comprehensive information network, and relies on participative decision making.

In the previous sections, we described a variety of organizational designs ranging from the highly structured and standardized bureaucracy to the loose boundaryless organization. The other designs we discussed tend to exist somewhere between these two extremes.

Figure 13-5 supports our previous discussions by presenting two extreme models of organizational design. One extreme we'll call the **mechanistic model**. It is synonymous with the bureaucracy in that it has extensive departmentalization, high formalization, a limited information network (mostly downward communication), and little participation by low-level members in decision making. At the other extreme is the **organic model**. This model looks a lot like the boundaryless organization. It's flat, uses cross-hierarchical and cross-functional teams, has low formalization, possesses a comprehensive information network (using lateral and upward communication as well as downward), and involves high participation in decision making.[13]

What Do You Think?

Why are some organizations structured along more mechanistic lines, whereas others follow organic characteristics? What are the forces that influence the design that is chosen?

In the following sections, we present the major forces that have been identified as causes or determinants of an organization's structure.[14]

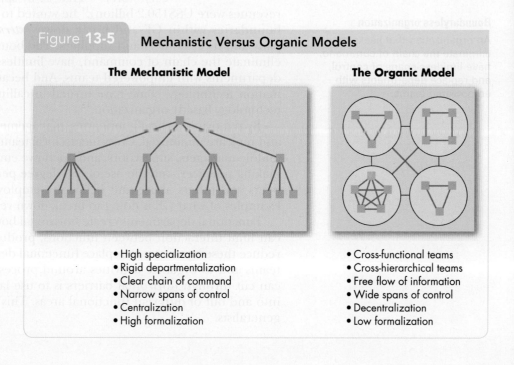

| Figure **13-5** | Mechanistic Versus Organic Models |

The Mechanistic Model

The Organic Model

- High specialization
- Rigid departmentalization
- Clear chain of command
- Narrow spans of control
- Centralization
- High formalization

- Cross-functional teams
- Cross-hierarchical teams
- Free flow of information
- Wide spans of control
- Decentralization
- Low formalization

Strategy

An organization's structure is a means to help management achieve its objectives. Because objectives are derived from the organization's overall strategy, it's only logical that strategy and structure should be closely linked. More specifically, structure should follow strategy. If management makes a significant change in its organization's strategy, the structure will need to be modified to accommodate and support this change.[15]

Most current strategy frameworks focus on three strategy dimensions, cost minimization, and imitation—and the structural design that works best with each.[16]

To what degree does an organization introduce major new products or services? An **innovation strategy** does not mean a strategy just for simple changes from previous offerings but rather one for meaningful and unique innovations. However, not all firms want innovation. An organization that is pursuing a **cost-minimization strategy** tightly controls costs, tries to stop unnecessary innovation or marketing expenses, and cuts prices in selling a basic product.

Organizations following an **imitation strategy** try to capitalize on the best of both of the previous strategies. They seek to minimize risk and maximize opportunity for profit. Their strategy is to move into new products or new markets. They take the successful ideas of innovators and copy them. Manufacturers of mass-marketed fashion goods that copy designer styles follow the imitation strategy.

Table 13-2 describes the structural option that best matches each strategy. Innovators need the flexibility of the organic structure, whereas cost minimizers seek the efficiency and stability of the mechanistic structure. Imitators combine the two structures. They use a mechanistic structure in order to maintain tight controls and low costs in their current activities, while at the same time they create organic subunits in which to pursue new ideas.

Organization Size

There is considerable evidence to support the idea that an organization's size significantly affects its structure.[17] For instance, large organizations—those that typically employ 2,000 or more people—tend to have more specialization, more departmentalization, more vertical levels, and more rules and regulations than do small organizations. However, the relationship isn't linear. Rather, size affects structure at a decreasing rate. The impact of size becomes less important as an organization expands. Why is this? Essentially, once an organization has around 2,000 employees, it's already fairly mechanistic. An additional 500 employees will not have much impact. On the other hand, adding

Innovation strategy

A strategy that emphasizes the introduction of major new products and services.

Cost-minimization strategy

A strategy that emphasizes tight cost controls, avoidance of unnecessary innovation or marketing expenses, and price cutting.

Imitation strategy

A strategy that seeks to move into new products or new markets only after their viability has already been proven.

TABLE 13-2 The Strategy–Structure Relationship	
Strategy	**Structural Option**
Innovation	**Organic:** A loose structure; low specialization, low formalization, decentralized
Cost minimization	**Mechanistic:** Tight control; extensive work specialization, high formalization, high centralization
Imitation	**Mechanistic and organic:** Mix of loose with tight properties; tight controls over current activities and looser controls for new undertakings

500 employees to an organization that has only 300 members is likely to result in a significant shift toward a more mechanistic structure.

However, we must realize that organization size is relevant. The numbers mentioned above may be typical of US organizations but are large for most Arab organizations. In other words, what may be considered an organic or flat structure in the US may be considered as mechanistic or tall in the Arab world because the relativity of size of organization differs from one country to another.

Technology

The term **technology** refers to how an organization transfers its inputs into outputs. Every organization has at least one technology for converting financial, human, and physical resources into products or services. The Ford Motor Co., for instance, predominantly uses an assembly-line process to make its products. On the other hand, colleges may use a number of instruction technologies— the ever-popular formal lecture method, the case-analysis method, the experiential exercise method, the programmed learning method, and so forth. In this section we want to show that organizational structures adapt to their technology.

Numerous studies have been carried out on the technology–structure relationship.[18] The details of those studies are quite complex, so we'll go straight to 'the point' and attempt to summarize what we know.

The common theme that differentiates technologies is their *degree of routineness*. By this we mean that technologies tend toward either routine or nonroutine activities. The former are characterized by automated and standardized operations. Nonroutine activities are customized. They include varied operations such as furniture restoring, custom shoemaking, and genetic research.

What relationships have been found between technology and structure? Although the relationship is not overwhelmingly strong, we find that routine tasks are associated with taller and more departmentalized structures.

The relationship between technology and formalization, however, is stronger. Studies consistently show routineness to be associated with the presence of rule

The degree of routineness differentiates technologies. At Wallstrip.com, nonroutineness characterizes the customized work of employees who create an entertaining daily Web video show and accompanying blog about the stock market. The show relies heavily on the knowledge of specialists such as host Lindsay Campbell and writer/producer Adam Elend, who are shown here in the production studio, where they're getting ready to film an episode of their show.
Source: Dima Gavrysh
New York Times.

manuals, job descriptions, and other formalized documentation. Finally, an interesting relationship has been found between technology and centralization. It seems logical that routine technologies would be associated with a centralized structure, while nonroutine technologies, which rely more heavily on the knowledge of specialists, would be characterized by delegated decision authority. This position has met with some support. However, a more general conclusion is that the technology-centralization relationship is moderated by the degree of formalization. Formal regulations and centralized decision making are both control mechanisms and management can substitute one for the other. Routine technologies should be associated with centralized control if there is a minimum of rules and regulations. However, if formalization is high, routine technology can be accompanied by decentralization. Thus, we would predict that routine technology would lead to centralization, but only if formalization is low.

Environment

Environment

Institutions or forces outside an organization that potentially affect the organization's performance.

An organization's **environment** is composed of institutions or forces outside the organization that potentially affect the organization's performance. These typically include suppliers, customers, competitors, government agencies, public pressure groups, and the like.

Why should an organization's structure be affected by its environment? Because of environmental uncertainty. Some organizations face relatively stable environments—few forces in their environment are changing. There are, for example, no new competitors, no new technological breakthroughs by current competitors, or little activity by public pressure groups to influence the organization. Other organizations face very dynamic environments—rapidly changing government regulations affecting their business, new competitors, difficulties in acquiring raw materials, continually changing product preferences by customers, and so on. Static environments create significantly less uncertainty for managers than do dynamic ones. And because uncertainty is a threat to an organization's effectiveness, management will try to minimize it. One way to reduce environmental uncertainty is through adjustments in the organization's structure.[19]

Recent research has helped clarify what is meant by environmental uncertainty. It's been found that there are three key dimensions to any organization's environment: capacity, volatility, and complexity.[20]

The *capacity* of an environment refers to the degree to which it can support growth. Rich and growing environments generate excess resources, which can protect the organization in times of relative scarcity.

The degree of instability in an environment is captured in the *volatility* dimension. When there is a high degree of unpredictable change, the environment is dynamic. This makes it difficult for management to predict accurately the probabilities associated with various decision alternatives. Because information technology changes at such a rapid place, more organizations' environments are becoming volatile.

Finally, the environment needs to be assessed in terms of *complexity*—that is, the degree of heterogeneity and concentration among environmental elements. Simple environments—like in the tobacco industry—are homogeneous and concentrated. In contrast, environments characterized by heterogeneity—think of companies in the broadband industry, such as Etisalat—are called complex, meaning the environment is diverse and the competitors numerous.

Some general conclusions show that there is evidence that relates the degrees of environmental uncertainty to different structural arrangements. Specifically, the more scarce, dynamic, and complex the environment, the more organic a structure should be. The more abundant, stable, and simple the environment, the more the mechanistic structure will be preferred.

The work environment at Etisalat offers a continually challenging and professionally rewarding experience. "As information and communication technologies continue to develop and the business environment constantly changes, enterprises need to enable the facilitation for employees' self-learning and capability development activities; to support corporate strategies while improving employee and organizational performance. Huawei Learning Service aims to associate with Etisalat's strength in that area and with the search for continuous competence improvement", said Mr. Frank Guo, vice-president of Huawei Learning Services.

Source: http://ea.ae/index.php/en/news-topmenu-19/615-huawei-etisalat-alumni-association.

Organizational Designs and Employee Behavior

> **7** *Analyze the behavioral implications of different organizational designs.*

We opened this chapter by implying that an organization's structure can have significant effects on its members. In this section, we want to assess directly just what those effects might be.

A review of the evidence linking organizational structures to employee performance and satisfaction leads to a clear conclusion—you can't generalize! Not everyone prefers the freedom and flexibility of organic structures. Some people are most productive and satisfied when work tasks are standardized and ambiguity is minimized—that is, in mechanistic structures. So any discussion of the effect of organizational design on employee behavior has to address individual differences. To illustrate this point, let's consider employee preferences for work specialization, span of control, and centralization.[21]

The evidence generally indicates that *work specialization* contributes to higher employee productivity but at the price of reduced job satisfaction. However, this statement ignores individual differences and the type of job tasks people do. As we noted previously, work specialization is not an unending source of higher productivity. Problems arise, and productivity begins to suffer, when repetitive and narrow tasks overtake the economies of specialization. As the workforce has become more highly educated and desirous of jobs that are intrinsically rewarding, the point at which productivity begins to decrease seems to be reached more quickly than in the past years.

Although more people today are demotivated by overly specialized jobs than were their parents or grandparents, it would be wrong to ignore the reality that there is still a part of the workforce that prefers the routine and repetitiveness of highly specialized jobs. Some individuals want work that makes minimal intellectual demands and provides the security of routine and a study conducted by IPSOS shows how Arabs behavior is affected by certain jobs. For these people, high work specialization is a source of job satisfaction. The empirical question, of course, is whether this represents 2 percent of the workforce or 52 percent. Given that there is some self-selection operating in the choice of careers, we might conclude that negative behavioral outcomes from high specialization are most likely to surface in professional jobs occupied by individuals with high needs for personal growth and diversity.

A review of the research indicates that it is probably safe to say there is no evidence to support a relationship between *span of control* and employee performance. Although it is intuitively attractive to argue that large spans might lead to higher employee performance because they provide more distant supervision and more opportunity for personal initiative, the research fails to support this idea. At this point, it's impossible to state that any particular span of control is best for producing high performance or high satisfaction among employees. Again, the reason is probably individual differences. That is, some people like to be left alone, while others prefer the security of a boss who is quickly available at all times. Consistent with several of the contingency theories of leadership discussed in Chapter 10, we would expect factors such as employees' experiences and abilities and the degree of structure in their tasks to explain when wide or narrow spans of control are likely to contribute to their performance and job satisfaction. However, there is some evidence indicating that a manager's job satisfaction increases as the number of employees supervised increases.

We also find fairly strong evidence linking *centralization* and job satisfaction. In general, organizations that are less centralized have a greater amount of autonomy. And the evidence suggests that autonomy is positively related to job satisfaction. But, again, individual differences surface. While some employees may value freedom, others may find autonomous environments ambiguous.

What Do You Think?

Do you agree with the notion 'never generalize' when referring to the effect that organizational structure can have on employee behavior.

The tasks of these women making cookies at a factory in South Korea are highly standardized. Individual differences influence how these employees respond to their high work specialization. For these women, specialization may be a source of job satisfaction because it provides the security of routine and gives them the chance to socialize on the job because they work closely with coworkers.

In conclusion, to maximize employee performance and satisfaction, individual differences, such as experience, personality, and the work task, should be taken into account. As we'll note in the next section about the global implications, culture needs to be taken into consideration, too.

Before we leave this topic, one obvious point needs to be made: People don't select employers randomly. There is strong evidence that individuals are attracted to, selected by, and stay with organizations that suit their personal characteristics.[22] Job candidates who prefer predictability, for instance, are likely to seek out and take employment in mechanistic structures, and those who want autonomy are more likely to end up in an organic structure. So the effect of structure on employee behavior is undoubtedly reduced when the selection process facilitates proper matching of individual characteristics with organizational characteristics, as was discussed in Chapter 2 when we spoke about the 'person-organization fit'.

Global Implications

8 *Show how globalization affects organizational structure.*

When we think about how culture influences organization structure, several questions come to mind. First, does culture really matter to organizational structure? Second, do employees in different countries vary in their perceptions of different types of organizational structures? Finally, how do cultural considerations fit with our discussion of the boundaryless organization? Let's tackle each of these questions in turn.

Culture and Organizational Structure Does culture really affect organizational structure? The answer might seem obvious—yes!—but there are reasons culture may not matter as much as you think. The US model of business has been very influential, so much so that the organizational structures in other countries may mirror those of US organizations. Moreover, US structures themselves have been influenced by structures in other countries and regions (especially Japan, the Arab world, the United Kingdom, and Germany). However, cultural concerns still might be important. Bureaucratic structures still dominate in many parts of Europe, the Arab world and Asia. It could be said that management in the Arab world today places too much emphasis on individual leadership, which may be a problem in countries where decision making has previously been decentralized.[23]

Culture and Employee Structure Preferences Although there isn't a great deal of research out there, it does suggest that national culture influences the preference for structure, so it, too, needs to be considered.[24] For instance, organizations that operate with people from high power distance cultures, such as those found in Greece, France, the Arab countries and most of Latin America, find employees much more accepting of mechanistic structures than where employees come from low power distance countries. So you need to consider cultural differences along with individual differences when making predictions on how structure will affect employee performance and satisfaction.

Culture and the Boundaryless Organization When fully operational, the boundaryless organization also breaks down barriers created by geography. As a result, many companies struggle with the problem of how to incorporate geographic regions into their structure. The boundaryless organization provides one solution to this problem because geography is considered more of a tactical, logistical issue than a structural issue. In short, the goal of the boundaryless organization is to break down cultural barriers.

One way to break down barriers is through strategic alliances. These alliances limit the distinction between one organization and another as employees work on joint projects. And some companies are also allowing customers to perform functions that previously were done by management.

Summary and Implications for Managers

The theme of this chapter has been that an organization's internal structure contributes to explaining and predicting behavior. That is, in addition to individual and group factors, the structural relationships in which people work has an impact on employee attitudes and behavior.

What's the basis for the argument that structure has an impact on both attitudes and behavior? To the degree that an organization's structure reduces ambiguity for employees and clarifies concerns such as "What am I supposed to do?" "How am I supposed to do it?" "To whom do I report?" and "To whom do I go if I have a problem?" it shapes their attitudes and facilitates and motivates them to higher levels of performance.

Of course, structure also restricts employees to the extent that it limits and controls what they do. For example, organizations structured around high levels of formalization and specialization, strict adherence to the chain of command, limited delegation of authority, and narrow spans of control give employees little autonomy. Controls in such organizations are tight, and behavior tends to vary within a narrow range. In contrast, organizations that are structured around limited specialization, low formalization, and wide spans of control provide employees greater freedom and, thus, are characterized by greater behavioral diversity.

Figure 13-6 visually summarizes what we've discussed in this chapter. Strategy, size, technology, and environment determine the type of structure an organization will have. For simplicity's sake, we can classify structural designs around one of two models: mechanistic or organic. The specific effect of structural designs on performance and satisfaction is moderated by employees' individual preferences and cultural norms.

Finally, increasingly, technology is reshaping work such that organizational structures may be increasingly disorganized. This allows a manager the flexibility of taking into account things like employee preferences, experience, and culture so as to design work systems that truly motivate employees.

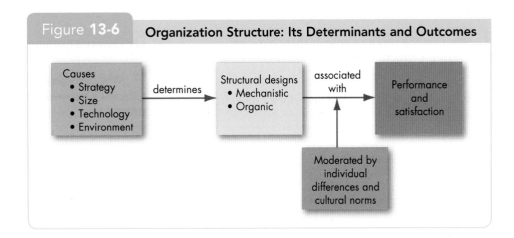

Figure 13-6   Organization Structure: Its Determinants and Outcomes

Point >< Counterpoint

DOWNSIZING IMPROVES ORGANIZATIONAL PERFORMANCE

There aren't many leaders who like to downsize. But if there is one thing we have learned in the past 20 years, it's that downsizing has been an indispensable factor in making companies more competitive.

Look at IBM, once one of the largest employers in the world. But in the 1980s and 1990s, it became quite clear that IBM was too big, too complex, and spread too thin. Today, IBM is profitable again, but only after it shed nearly 100,000 jobs. Here is what former IBM CEO Lou Gerstner said about the need to restructure the company:[25]

It got stuck because it fell victim to what I call the success syndrome. The more successful enterprises are, the more they try to replicate, duplicate, codify what makes us great. And suddenly they're inward thinking. They're thinking how can we continue to do what we've done in the past without understanding that what made them successful is to take risks, to change and to adapt and to be responsive. And so in a sense success breeds its own failure. And I think it's true of a lot of successful businesses.

Layoffs and restructuring are rarely the popular things to do. But without them, most organizations would not survive, much less remain competitive.

Downsizing has become a sort of rite of passage for business leaders: you're not a real leader unless you've downsized a company. Do companies that have downsized perform better as a result?

To study this, a research team found that downsizing strategies did *not* result in improved long-term financial performance. It's important to remember that the results control for prior financial performance and reflect financial performance after the downsizing efforts occurred.

The authors of this study don't argue that downsizing is always a bad strategy. Rather, the upshot is that managers shouldn't assume layoffs are a quick fix to what ails a company. In general, downsizing does *not* improve performance, so the key is to do it only when needed and to do it in the right way.

What are some ways organizations can do this? First, they should use downsizing only as a last resort. Second, and related, they should inform employees about the problem, and give them a chance to contribute alternative restructuring solutions. Third, organizations need to bend over backward to ensure that employees see the layoff process as fair. Finally, make sure downsizing is done to good effect—not just to cut costs, but to reallocate resources to where they can be most effective.[26]

Questions for Review

1 What are the six key elements that define an organization's structure?

2 What is a bureaucracy, and how does it differ from a simple structure?

3 What is a matrix organization?

4 What are the characteristics of a virtual organization?

5 How can managers create a boundaryless organization?

6 Why do organizational structures differ, and what is the difference between a mechanistic structure and an organic structure?

7 What are the behavioral implications of different organizational designs?

8 How does globalization affect organizational structure?

Discussion Exercise

Think about the organization in which you work, have worked or would like to work in. In particular, consider the department that you are affiliated with. How would you want to characterize this unit with respect to division of labor, span of control, and centralization? Discuss how these issues can either 'make or break' the organization.

Ethical Considerations

One critical structural element of most corporations is the board of directors. Nearly any organization has a board of directors. And formally at least, chief executives often report to the directors. Informally, however, many boards defer to the CEO and *advise* more than *direct*.

You might think an active board is always good for an organization. However, like most structural decisions, it has disadvantages and risks. When directors are empowered, they can become 'free agents' who follow their own agendas, including some that may even have conflict with the CEO's. Or they may make statements or disclose information that goes against company interests. A final danger is the possibility that board members will micromanage a CEO's strategy. Give your comments on the above from the ethical point of view.

Critical Analysis

ORGANIZATIONAL STRUCTURE AT FOOD & CO.

Food & Co. was established in 1960 as a family business that caters to the Lebanese market. The company imports and distributes food items in various countries in the Arab world and has over 900 items in its inventory. Because of the great demand, Food & Co. opened branches in Syria, Jordan, and the Kingdom of Saudi Arabia, which proved to be its largest niche. To start with, the products were all from Europe and America, but then they began to distribute local Lebanese produce.

There were so many limitations at the time of its establishment that Food & Co. developed an unusual organizational structure. It looked like a group of companies owned by a single holding company rather than a company with regional branches. Today, a design like that seems to be ineffective.

In 2009, the founder of Food & Co. retired and appointed his son, who had only ten years of financial experience, as CEO. The son was a consultant with a firm that specialized in organizational design, and he wanted to take the company to new levels of success by considering the market position. Food & Co. took into account the competing Asian brands that were showing up on the market and the present, revised structure of Food & Co. is a result of political and regulatory issues in the region.

Consequently, the new CEO utilized his past experience as an organizational design consultant and his finance background to create a structure that would remain decentralized. The major objective, though, was to ensure savings that would help Food & Co. to meet the challenges of the economy and global competition.

Questions

1. How would a more decentralized structure help Food & Co. meet the challenges of the economy and global competition?

2. Do you think that organizations are better off following a decentralized structure, like the one at Food & Co? Why or why not?

Source: Adapted from Jerald Greenberg, 2011, "The Changing Economic and Regulatory Factors Influencing Organizational Design," *Behavior in Organizations* (10th ed., Global Edition), p. 577.

Research Exercise

Fawwaz Inc. is a medium-size manufacturing company that uses standard assembly lines to produce its products. Its employees are not very educated and have routine tasks to perform. Yahyah Inc., on the other hand, develops programs to solve its customer's internet problems. Its employees are educated and have interesting and innovative jobs. Both these companies want to restructure their organizations. Conduct some research across the Arab world to identify companies that follow the two different approaches—mechanistic and organic—and look at their organizational structures. As a consultant what would you advise Fawwaz Inc. and Yahyah Inc. as to their optimum organizational structure?

LEARNING OBJECTIVES

This chapter will enable you to:

1 Relate institutionalized culture to organizational culture.

2 Define *organizational culture* and describe its common characteristics.

3 Compare the functional and dysfunctional effects of organizational culture on people and the organization.

4 Explain the factors that create and sustain an organization's culture.

5 Show how culture is transmitted to employees.

6 Demonstrate how an ethical culture can be created.

7 Describe a positive organizational culture.

8 Identify characteristics of a spiritual culture.

9 Show how national culture may affect the way organizational culture is transported to a different country.

Organizational Culture

14

I believe that national culture not only influences organizational cultures and the behavior of employees, but it also affects our perception toward understanding organizational culture. —Mohammed Al Suwaidi

The Culture at Arab World Companies

Numerous companies in the Arab world provide a comfortable organizational culture—that is, a work environment that offers employees the physical and emotional facilities to perform effectively. It is the incentives that organizations offer that encourage employees to want to be members of such organizations. The aim is to create an organizational culture that is friendly and empathetic. Employees will assess employers on the basis of criteria such as work environment, leadership, pay, and organizational culture.

A study carried out by Hewitt Association in collaboration with the Mohammed bin Rashid Al Maktoum Foundation investigated what made certain organizations in the Arab world more attractive for people to work at. These companies are likely to retain their talent because individuals consider them to be outstanding places to work.

The objective of the study was to understand the employee practices of the best companies to work for, so as to create a benchmark for work practices in the Arab world and make it a better place to work in.

The scope of the study covered multinational companies (MNCs), local organizations, and government organizations. The study examined issues such as: employee commitment and engagement; work environment; pay; benefits; leadership; training and development; recruitment; employee retention; cultural factors; diversity; and demographic differences.

After careful analysis of files and information, the judges selected the following Best Employers in the Middle East for 2009:

Alghanim Industries	Kuwait
BankMuscat SAOG	Oman
Deloitte & Touche (ME)	Middle East
FineHygienic Paper FZE	UAE
First Gulf Bank	UAE
Jones Lang LaSalle—Middle East & North Africa	Middle East
Marriott International, UAE	UAE
Microsoft Gulf FZ LLC and Microsoft Egypt	UAE and Egypt
Procter & Gamble Near East—Beirut Office	Lebanon
The Ritz-Carlton, Dubai	UAE

The judges recognized two organizations for *Special Recognition*. One was the Jumeirah Group, UAE, for Emerging International Best Employer from the Middle East. The other went to Magrudy Enterprises LLC, UAE, as Emerging SME Best Employer in the Middle East.

Source: Mohammed bin Rashid Al Maktoum Foundation, www.mbrfoundation.ae.

As the chapter opener suggests, organizational culture can cross national boundaries. A strong culture provides stability to an organization since it affects organizational performance. But for some organizations, it can also be a major barrier to change. In this chapter, we show that every organization has a culture and, depending on its strength, that culture can have a significant influence on the attitudes and behaviors of organization members. The opening text highlights those Arab-world companies that employees would prefer to work for. Among the reasons why employees seek employment at these companies is that they offer a comfortable work environment, and an organizational culture that motivates people in the most effective manner.

What kind of organizational culture would you prefer? Take the self-assessment exercise below to find out.

WHAT'S THE RIGHT ORGANIZATIONAL CULTURE FOR ME?

In the Self-Assessment Library (available online), take assessment III.B.1 (What's the Right Organizational Culture for Me?) and answer the following questions:

1. *Judging from your results, do you fit better in a more formal and structured culture or in a more informal and unstructured culture?*

2. *Did your results surprise you? Why do you think you scored as you did?*

3. *How might your results affect your career path?*

Institutionalization: A Forerunner of Culture

> *1* *Relate institutionalized culture to organizational culture.*

The idea of viewing organizations as cultures—where there is a system of shared meaning among members—is a relatively recent phenomenon. Until the mid-1980s, organizations were, for the most part, simply thought of as rational means by which to coordinate and control a group of people. They had vertical levels, departments, authority relationships, and so forth. But organizations are more. They have personalities, too, just like individuals. They can be rigid or flexible, unfriendly or supportive, innovative or conservative. Organizational theorists now acknowledge this by recognizing the important role that culture plays in the lives of organization members. Interestingly, though, the origin of culture as an independent variable affecting an employee's attitudes and behavior can be traced back more than 50 years to the concept of **institutionalization**.[1]

Institutionalization

A condition that occurs when an organization takes on a life of its own, apart from any of its members, and acquires immortality.

When an organization becomes institutionalized, it becomes valued for itself, not merely for the goods or services it produces. It acquires immortality. If its original goals are no longer relevant, it doesn't go out of business. Rather, it redefines itself.

Institutionalization operates to produce common understandings among members about what is appropriate and meaningful behavior.[2] So when an organization takes on institutional permanence, acceptable modes of behavior become largely self-evident to its members. As we'll see, this is essentially the same thing that organizational culture does. So an understanding of what makes up an organization's culture and how it is created, sustained, and learned will enhance our ability to explain and predict the behavior of people at work.

What Is Organizational Culture?

2 *Define* organizational culture *and describe its common characteristics.*

Organizational culture

A system of shared meaning held by members that distinguishes the organization from other organizations.

Facebook stresses the characteristics of innovation and risk taking and describes itself as "a cutting-edge technology company, constantly taking on new challenges in the worlds of milliseconds and terabytes." The vast majority of the company's employees are under 40, and enjoy the excitement of working in a fast-paced environment with considerable change and ambiguity. Facebook says it encourages employees to interact in a creative climate that encourages experimentation and tolerates conflict and risk. Facebook fosters a fun-loving, casual, and collegial culture in its employees.

Previously, an executive was asked what he thought *organizational culture* meant. One particular definition stated, "I can't define it, but I know it when I see it." This approach to defining organizational culture isn't acceptable for our purposes. We need a basic definition to provide a point of departure for our objective to better understand the concept. In this section, we propose a specific definition and review several issues that revolve around this definition.

A Definition of *Organizational Culture*

There seems to be wide agreement that **organizational culture** refers to a system of shared meaning held by members that distinguishes the organization from other organizations.[3] This system of shared meaning is, on closer examination, a set of key characteristics that the organization finds valuable, such as is the case at Facebook. The research suggests that there are seven primary characteristics that capture the essence of an organization's culture:[4] innovation and risk taking; attention to detail; outcome orientation; people orientation; team orientation; aggressiveness; and stability.

Each of these characteristics exists on a continuum from low to high. Appraising the organization on these seven characteristics, then, gives a composite picture of the organization's culture. This picture becomes the basis for feelings of shared understanding that members have about the organization, how things are done in it, and the way members are supposed to behave. Box 14-1 demonstrates how these characteristics can be mixed to create highly diverse organizations.

Culture Is a Descriptive Term

Organizational culture is concerned with how employees perceive the characteristics of an organization's culture, not with whether they like them. That is, it's a descriptive term. This is important because it differentiates this concept from job satisfaction.

Research on organizational culture has tried to measure how employees see their organization. In contrast, job satisfaction seeks to measure affective responses to the work environment. It's concerned with how employees feel about the organization's expectations, reward practices, and the like. Although the two terms undoubtedly have overlapping characteristics, keep in mind that the term *organizational culture* is descriptive, whereas *job satisfaction* is evaluative.

What Do You Think?

Does the organizational culture where you work encourage teamwork? Does it reward innovation? Does it limit initiative?

BOX 14-1
Contrasting Organizational Cultures

Organization A

This organization is a manufacturing firm. Managers are expected to fully document all decisions, and 'good managers' are those who can provide detailed data to support their recommendations. Creative decisions that incur significant change or risk are not encouraged. Because managers of failed projects are openly criticized and penalized, managers try not to implement ideas that deviate much from the status quo. One lower-level manager quoted an often-used phrase in the company: "If it ain't broke, don't fix it."

There are extensive rules and regulations in this firm that employees are required to follow. Managers supervise employees closely to ensure there are no deviations. Management is concerned with high productivity, regardless of the impact on employee morale or turnover.

Work activities are designed around individuals. There are distinct departments and lines of authority, and employees are expected to minimize formal contact with other employees outside their functional area or line of command. Performance evaluations and rewards emphasize individual effort, although seniority tends to be the primary factor in the determination of pay raises and promotions.

Organization B

This organization is also a manufacturing firm. Here, however, management encourages and rewards risk taking and change. Decisions based on intuition are valued as much as those that are well rationalized. Management prides itself on its history of experimenting with new technologies and its success in regularly introducing innovative products. Managers or employees who have a good idea are encouraged to 'run with it.' And failures are treated as 'learning experiences.' The company prides itself on being market-driven and rapidly responsive to the changing needs of its customers.

There are few rules and regulations for employees to follow, and supervision is loose because management believes that its employees are hardworking and trustworthy. Management is concerned with high productivity, but believes that this comes through treating its people right. The company is proud of its reputation as being a good place to work.

Job activities are designed around work teams, and team members are encouraged to interact with people across functions and authority levels. Employees talk positively about the competition between teams. Individuals and teams have goals, and bonuses are based on achievement of these outcomes. Employees are given considerable autonomy in choosing the means by which the goals are attained.

Do Organizations Have Uniform Cultures?

Organizational culture represents a common perception held by the organization's members. This was made explicit when we defined culture as a system of *shared* meaning. We should expect, therefore, that individuals with different backgrounds or at different levels in the organization will tend to describe the organization's culture in similar terms.[5]

Acknowledgment that organizational culture has common properties does not mean, however, that there cannot be subcultures within any given culture. Most large organizations have a dominant culture and numerous sets of subcultures.[6] A **dominant culture** expresses the core values that are shared by

Dominant culture

A culture that expresses the core values that are shared by a majority of the organization's members.

Subcultures

Minicultures within an organization, typically defined by department designations and geographical separation.

Core values

The primary or dominant values that are accepted throughout the organization.

a majority of the organization's members. **Subcultures** tend to develop in large organizations to reflect common problems, situations, or experiences that members face. These subcultures are likely to be defined by department designations and geographical separation. The purchasing department, for example, can have a subculture that is shared by members of that department. It will include the **core values** of the dominant culture plus additional values unique to members of the purchasing department.

If organizations had no dominant culture and were composed only of numerous subcultures, the value of organizational culture as an independent variable would be significantly lessened because there would be no uniform interpretation of what represented appropriate and inappropriate behavior. It is the 'shared meaning' aspect of culture that makes it such a strong tool for guiding and shaping behavior.

Strong versus Weak Cultures

It has become increasingly popular to differentiate between strong and weak cultures.[7] The argument here is that strong cultures have a greater impact on employee behavior and are more directly related to reduced turnover.

Strong culture

A culture in which the core values are intensely held and widely shared.

In a **strong culture**, the organization's core values are both intensely held and widely shared.[8] The more members who accept the core values and the greater their commitment to those values, the stronger the culture. Consistent with this definition, a strong culture will have a great influence on the behavior of its members because the high degree of sharing and intensity creates an internal atmosphere of high behavioral control.

One specific result of a strong culture should be lower employee turnover. A strong culture demonstrates high agreement among members about what the organization stands for. Such agreement of purpose builds cohesiveness, loyalty, and organizational commitment. These qualities, in turn, decrease employees' intentions to leave the organization.[9]

Culture versus Formalization

A strong organizational culture increases behavioral consistency. In this sense, we should recognize that a strong culture can act as a substitute for formalization.[10]

In the previous chapter, we discussed how formalization's rules and regulations act to regulate employee behavior. High formalization in an organization creates predictability, order, and consistency. Our point here is that a strong culture achieves the same result without the need for written documentation. Therefore, we should view formalization and culture as two different roads to a common destination. The stronger an organization's culture, the less management needs to be concerned with developing formal rules and regulations to guide employee behavior. Those guides will be internalized in employees when they accept the organization's culture.

What Do You Think?

Box 14-1 shows contrasting organizational cultures and mentions the saying, "If it ain't broke, don't fix it." Do you agree with this statement?

Another manifestation of culture is as a feature of a country or group of countries. An obvious question for multinational corporations then is whether it is better to establish a single strong organizational culture across different countries or to adopt different cultural practices in each country. Research suggests the best management practice is to develop a strong unifying mission, while allowing teams to accomplish their work in ways that suit each country's culture.

In a study of 230 organizations in different industries from regions including North America, Asia, Europe, the Middle East, and Africa, having a strong and positive organizational culture was associated with increased organizational effectiveness. The study found that the strong and positive aspects of organizational culture that were most critical to success across all countries included empowerment, team orientation, establishing a clear strategic direction, and providing a recognized vision. However, the practices were not equally important. Empowerment appeared more important in individualistic than in collectivistic countries.

Another study of 115 teams in five different multinational corporations found that when companies emphasized a unified global integration of business operations, teams shared less information. The reason might be that home office culture was dictating policies, leading teams to be less proactive about making changes. On the other hand, encouraging local teams to find their own solutions for their own cultural context resulted in greater learning and performance.

Overall, these studies show a productive organizational culture is associated with increased sales growth, profitability, employee satisfaction, and overall organizational performance. Part of this effective management strategy means empowering managers to take local context into account.

Sources: Based on D. R. Denison, S. Haaland, and P. Goelzer, "Corporate Culture and Organizational Effectiveness: Is Asia Different from the Rest of the World?" *Organizational Dynamics*, February 2004, pp. 98–109; and M. Zellmer-Bruhn and C. Gibson, "Multinational Organizational Context: Implications for Team Learning and Performance," *Academy of Management Journal* 49, no. 3 (2006), pp. 501–518.

What Do Cultures Do?

> **3** Compare the functional and dysfunctional effects of organizational culture on people and the organization.

We have discussed the impact of organizational culture on behavior. We've also directly argued that a strong culture should be associated with reduced turnover. In this section, we will more carefully review the functions that culture performs and determine if culture can be a problem for an organization.

Culture's Functions

Culture performs a number of functions within an organization. First, it has a boundary-defining role; that is, it creates distinctions between one organization and others. Second, it gives a sense of identity for organization members. Third, culture facilitates the generation of commitment to something larger than one's individual self-interest. Fourth, it enhances the stability of the social system. Culture is the social glue that helps hold the organization together by providing appropriate standards for what employees should say and do. Finally, culture serves as a sense-making and control mechanism that guides and shapes the attitudes and behavior of employees. It is this last function that is of particular interest to us.[11]

The role of culture in influencing employee behavior appears to be increasingly important in today's workplace.[12] As organizations have wider spans of control, flattened structures, introduced teams, reduced formalization, and empowered employees, the *shared meaning* provided by a strong culture ensures that everyone is aiming to the same direction.

As we show later in this chapter, who receives a job offer to join the organization, who is appraised as a high performer, and who gets a promotion are strongly influenced by the individual–organization 'fit'—that is, whether the applicant's or employee attitudes and behavior are compatible with the culture. It's not a coincidence that employees at Disneyland appear to be attractive, clean, and with bright smiles. That's the image Disney wants. The company selects employees who will maintain that image. And once on the job, a strong culture, supported by formal rules and regulations, ensures that Disney employees will act in a uniform and predictable way.

Culture as a Liability

We are treating culture in a nonjudgmental manner. We haven't said that it's good or bad, only that it exists. Many of its functions are valuable for both the organization and the employee. Culture enhances organizational commitment and increases the consistency of employee behavior. These are clearly benefits to an organization. From an employee's standpoint, culture is valuable because it reduces ambiguity. It tells employees how things are done and what's important. But we shouldn't ignore the negative aspects of culture, especially a strong one, on an organization's effectiveness.

Barriers to Change   Culture is a liability when the shared values are not in agreement with those that will increase the organization's effectiveness. This is most likely to occur when an organization's environment is dynamic.[13] When an environment is undergoing rapid change, an organization's culture may no longer be appropriate. So consistency of behavior is an asset to an organization when it faces a stable environment. It may, however, burden the organization and make it difficult to respond to changes in the environment.

Barriers to Diversity   Hiring new employees who, because of race, age, gender, disability, or other differences, are not like the majority of the organization's members creates confusion.[14] Management wants new employees to accept the organization's core cultural values. Otherwise, these employees are unlikely to fit in or be accepted. But at the same time, management wants to openly acknowledge and demonstrate support for the differences that these employees bring to the workplace.

Barriers to Acquisitions and Mergers   Historically, the key factors that management looked at in making acquisition or merger decisions were related to financial advantages or product synergy. In recent years, cultural compatibility has become the primary concern.[15] While a favorable financial statement or product line may be the initial attraction of an acquisition candidate, whether the acquisition actually works seems to have more to do with how well the two organizations' cultures match up.

Many acquisitions and mergers may fail if the issues of cultural 'fit' are not addressed. This is applicable to all industries and especially in the banking sector. In the Arab world, many banks are merging or being acquired and the challenge is to ensure that there is a smooth reallocation of the employees of both banks and that they are able to integrate themselves into the new culture of the bank. This would have been an important consideration when Societe

Generale de Banque au Liban (SGBL) acquired the Lebanese Canadian Bank in 2011. The challenge would have been to make the acquisition as smooth as possible and for the CEO of SGBL, Antoun Sehnaoui, to keep the employees of both banks in their positions for an initial period until people became familiar with the new culture of the bank.[16]

Creating and Sustaining Culture

4 Explain the factors that create and sustain an organization's culture.

An organization's culture doesn't just happen. Once established, it shouldn't go away.

What Do You Think?

What forces influence the creation of a culture? What reinforces and sustains these forces once they're in place?

We answer both questions mentioned above in this section.

How a Culture Begins

An organization's current customs, traditions, and general way of doing things are largely due to what it has done before and the degree of success it has had with those endeavors. This leads us to the ultimate source of an organization's culture: its founders.[17]

The founders of an organization traditionally have a major impact on that organization's early culture. They have a vision of what the organization should be. They do not limit themselves to previous customs or ideologies. Culture creation occurs in three ways.[18] First, founders hire and keep only employees

The Ritz-Carlton Hotel Company entered an agreement on July, 2011, with the Ministry of Tourism from the Sultanate of Oman, to acquire the full management of Al Bustan Palace in Muscat, Oman. To make sure there was a smooth transition, all employees were retained by The Ritz-Carlton under the new management. "The Ritz-Carlton is [. . .] strongly committed to all the Omani ladies and gentlemen at the hotel and we welcome the existing Al Bustan Palace team to The Ritz-Carlton family. I know that we shall do our utmost to make them feel comfortable within our corporate culture," said Mr. Humler, President and Chief Operating Officer of the hotel.

Source: "The Ritz-Carlton Hotel Company, LLC assumes management of Al Bustan Palace in Muscat," *Hozpitality.com*, July 2011.

who think and feel the same way they do. Second, they train and socialize these employees to their way of thinking and feeling. And finally, the founders' own behavior acts as a role model that encourages employees to identify with them and thereby internalize their beliefs, values, and assumptions. When the organization succeeds, the founders' vision becomes seen as a primary determinant of that success. At this point, the founders' entire personality becomes embedded in the culture of the organization.

Keeping a Culture Alive

Once a culture is in place, there are practices within the organization that act to maintain it by giving employees a set of similar experiences.[19] For example, many of the human resource practices we discuss in the next chapter reinforce the organization's culture. The selection process, performance evaluation criteria, training and development activities, and promotion procedures ensure that those hired fit in with the culture, reward those who support it, and penalize those who challenge it. Three forces play a particularly important part in sustaining a culture: selection practices, the actions of top management, and socialization methods. Let's take a closer look at each.

Selection   The explicit goal of the selection process is to identify and hire individuals who have the knowledge, skills, and abilities to perform the jobs within the organization successfully. Typically, more than one candidate will be identified who meets any given job's requirements. When that point is reached, it would be wrong to ignore the fact that the final decision as to who is hired will be significantly influenced by the decision-maker's judgment of how well the candidates will fit into the organization. To ensure a proper match, we should hire people who have values essentially consistent with those of the organization.[20]

Top Management   The actions of top management also have a major impact on the organization's culture.[21] Through what they say and how they behave, senior executives establish norms that filter down through the organization as to whether risk taking is desirable; how much freedom managers should give their employees; what is appropriate dress; what actions will pay off in terms of pay raises, promotions, and other rewards; and the like.

Socialization   No matter how good a job the organization does in recruiting and selection, new employees are not fully part of the organization's culture. Because they are unfamiliar with the organization's culture, new employees are potentially likely to disturb the beliefs and customs that are in place. The organization will, therefore, want to help new employees adapt to its culture. This adaptation process is called **socialization**.[22]

Socialization

A process that adapts employees to the organization's culture.

As we discuss socialization, keep in mind that the most critical socialization stage is at the time of entry into the organization. This is when the organization seeks to mold the outsider into a good employee. The organization socializes employees during their entire career and stay in the organization. This further contributes to sustaining the culture.

Socialization can be seen as a process made up of three stages: prearrival, encounter, and metamorphosis.[23] The first stage includes all the learning that occurs before a new member joins the organization. In the second stage, the new employee sees what the organization is really like and confronts the possibility that expectations and reality may be separate issues. In the third stage, the relatively long-lasting changes take place. The new employee masters the skills required for the job, successfully performs the new roles, and makes the

Prearrival stage

The period of learning in the socialization process that occurs before a new employee joins the organization.

Encounter stage

The stage in the socialization process in which a new employee sees what the organization is really like and confronts the possibility that expectations and reality may diverge.

Metamorphosis stage

The stage in the socialization process in which a new employee changes and adjusts to the job, work group, and organization.

adjustments to the work group's values and norms.[24] This three-stage process has an impact on the new employee's work productivity, commitment to the organization's objectives, and decision to stay with the organization. Figure 14-1 shows this process.

The **prearrival stage** explicitly recognizes that each individual arrives with a set of values, attitudes, and expectations. These cover both the work to be done and the organization. For instance, in many jobs, particularly professional work, new members will have undergone a considerable degree of socialization in training and in school. One major purpose of a business school, for example, is to socialize business students to the attitudes and behaviors that business firms want. If business executives believe that successful employees value the profit ethic, are loyal, will work hard, and desire to achieve, they can hire individuals out of business schools who have been premolded in this pattern. Moreover, most people in business realize that no matter how well they think they can socialize newcomers, the most important predictor of newcomers' future behavior is their past behavior. Research shows that what people know before they join the organization, and how proactive their personality is, are critical predictors of how well they adjust to a new culture.[25]

One way to capitalize on the importance of prehire characteristics in socialization is to select employees with the 'right stuff' and to use the selection process to inform prospective employees about the organization as a whole. In addition, as noted previously, the selection process also acts to ensure the inclusion of the 'right type'—those who will fit in. "Indeed, the ability of the individual to present the appropriate face during the selection process determines his ability to move into the organization in the first place.

On entry into the organization, the new member enters the **encounter stage**. Here the individual confronts the possible relationship between expectations—about the job, the coworkers, the boss, and the organization in general—and reality. If expectations prove to have been more or less accurate, the encounter stage merely provides a confirmation of the perceptions gained earlier. However, this is often not the case. Where expectations and reality differ, new employees must undergo socialization that will separate them from previous assumptions and replace them with another set that the organization considers desirable. Also, an employee's network of friends and coworkers can play a critical role in helping them 'learn the ropes,' that is, to become familiar with how things are done within the organization. So organizations can help newcomers socialize by encouraging friendship ties in organizations.[26]

Finally, the new member must work out any problems discovered during the encounter stage. This may mean going through changes that we call the **metamorphosis stage**. The options presented in Box 14-2 are alternatives designed to bring about the desired metamorphosis. Note, for example, that the more management relies on socialization programs that are formal, collective, fixed, serial, and emphasize diversity, the greater the likelihood that newcomers' differences and perspectives will be replaced by standardized and predictable behaviors.

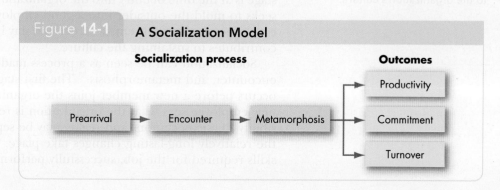

Figure **14-1** A Socialization Model

Socialization process

Outcomes

Prearrival → Encounter → Metamorphosis

Productivity

Commitment

Turnover

BOX 14-2

Entry Socialization Options

Formal vs. Informal The more a new employee is segregated from the ongoing work setting and differentiated in some way to make explicit his or her newcomer's role, the more formal socialization is. Specific orientation and training programs are examples. Informal socialization puts the new employee directly into the job, with little or no special attention.

Individual vs. Collective New members can be socialized individually. This describes how it's done in many professional offices. They can also be grouped together and processed through an identical set of experiences, as in military boot camp.

Fixed vs. Variable This refers to the time schedule in which newcomers make the transition from outsider to insider. A fixed schedule establishes standardized stages of transition. This characterizes rotational training programs. It also includes probationary periods, such as the 8- to 10-year 'associate' status used by accounting and law firms before deciding on whether or not a candidate is made a partner. Variable schedules give no advance notice of their transition timetable. Variable schedules describe the typical promotion system, in which one is not advanced to the next stage until one is 'ready.'

Serial vs. Random Serial socialization is characterized by the use of role models who train and encourage the newcomer. Apprenticeship and mentoring programs are examples. In random socialization, role models are deliberately withheld. New employees are left on their own to figure things out.

Investiture vs. Divestiture Investiture socialization assumes that the newcomer's qualities and qualifications are the necessary ingredients for job success, so these qualities and qualifications are confirmed and supported. Divestiture socialization tries to strip away certain characteristics of the recruit. Fraternity and sorority 'pledges' go through divestiture socialization to shape them into the proper role.

We can say that metamorphosis and the entry socialization process are complete when new members have become comfortable with the organization and their job. They have internalized the norms of the organization and their work group, and understand and accept those norms. New members feel accepted by their peers as trusted and valued individuals. They are self-confident that they have the competence to complete the job successfully. They understand the system—not only their own tasks but the rules, procedures, and informally accepted practices as well. Finally, they know how they will be evaluated; that is, what criteria will be used to measure and appraise their work. They know what is expected of them and what constitutes a job 'well done.' As Figure 14-1 shows, successful metamorphosis should have a positive impact on new employees' productivity and their commitment to the organization and reduce their desire to leave the organization.

Summary: How Cultures Form

Figure 14-2 summarizes how an organization's culture is established and sustained. The original culture is derived from the founder's philosophy. This, in turn, strongly influences the criteria used in hiring. The actions of the current top management establish the general climate of what is acceptable behavior and what is not.

How employees are to be socialized will depend both on the degree of success achieved in matching new employees' values to those of the organization's in the selection process and on top management's preference for socialization methods.

Figure 14-2   **How Organization Cultures Form**

How Employees Learn Culture

5 Show how culture is transmitted to employees.

Culture is transferred to employees in a number of forms, the most effective being stories, rituals, material symbols, and language.

Stories

Nike has a number of senior executives who spend much of their time as storytellers. And the stories they tell are meant to convey what Nike is about.[27] When they tell the story of how co-founder (and Oregon running coach) Bill Bowerman went to his workshop, experimented and then created a better running shoe by pouring rubber into his wife's waffle iron, they're talking about Nike's spirit of innovation. When new employees hear the stories of Oregon running star Steve Prefontaine's battles to make running a professional sport and to have better-performance equipment, they learn of Nike's commitment to helping athletes.

Stories such as these circulate through many organizations. They typically contain a narrative of events about the organization's founders, rule breaking, financial successes, reductions in the workforce, relocation of employees, reactions to past mistakes, and organizational coping.[28] These stories link the present in the past and provide explanations and legitimacy for current practices.

Rituals

Rituals
Repetitive sequences of activities that express and reinforce the key values of the organization, which goals are most important, which people are important, and which are expendable.

Rituals are repetitive sequences of activities that express and reinforce the key values of the organization—which goals are most important, which people are important and which are not.[29] For instance, at a business meeting in an Arab company, traditional Arabic coffee or kahwa will be served. A common ritual in the Arab world is for people to share coffee at social gatherings, and it's considered bad manners not to drink some coffee. The coffee cup is usually held in the right hand. When one requires more coffee, one either leaves some coffee in the bottom of one's cup or gently moves the cup from side to side.

Material Symbols

The headquarters of Google doesn't look like your typical head-office operation. It is essentially made up of common areas and meeting rooms, and offers all the sports, entertainment, and comfort facilities you could imagine. This shows employees that Google values openness, equality, creativity, and flexibility, and wants to create an environment where employees can be as productive as possible. Some corporations even provide their top executives with chauffeur-driven limousines and, when they travel by air, unlimited use of the corporate jet. Others may not get to ride in limousines or private jets, but they might still get a car and air transportation paid for by the company. Only the car is a Chevrolet (with no driver), and the jet seat is in the economy section of a commercial airliner.

The layout of corporate headquarters, the types of automobiles top executives are given, and the presence or absence of corporate aircraft are a few examples of material symbols. Others include the size of offices, the elegance of furnishings, executive benefits, and clothing.[30] These material symbols convey to employees who is important, the degree of equality desired by top management, and the kinds of behavior (for example, risk taking, conservative, authoritarian, participative, individualistic, social) that are appropriate.

Language

Many organizations and units within organizations use language as a way to identify members of a culture or subculture. By learning this language, members are agreeing to accept the culture of their organization. That is, certain organizations develop language and expressions that become significant only to that organization, something like a secret code. For example, if you're a new employee at Boeing Airlines, you'll find yourself learning a special vocabulary of acronyms, including *BOLD* (Boeing online data), *CATIA* (computer-graphics-aided three-dimensional interactive application), *MAIDS* (manufacturing assembly and installation data system), *POP* (purchased outside production), and *SLO* (service-level objectives).[31]

Organizations, over time, often develop unique terms to describe equipment, offices, key personnel, suppliers, customers, or products that relate to its business. New employees are frequently overwhelmed with acronyms and jargon (special language) that, after six months on the job, have become fully part of their language. Once learned, this terminology unites members of a given culture or subculture.

OB in the News

Change Jobs, and You May Be in for a Culture Shock

When Lyria Charles, a project manager, changed jobs, she didn't check her e-mail on weekends. Eventually, a fellow manager pulled her aside and told her that managers were expected to read e-mail over the weekend. "I didn't know," Charles said. "No one told me."

Employees have to learn the ropes when they change jobs. But unlike many aspects of business, organizational culture has few written rules. Very often, people learn the new culture only after stumbling into barriers and violating unwritten rules. "It's like going to a different country," says Michael Kanazawa of Dissero Partners, a management consulting firm.

There are myriad ways in which one organization's culture differs from another. To paraphrase Tolstoy, in certain ways, organizations are all alike, but each develops its culture in its own way.

Some of the differences—such as dress codes—are pretty easy to detect. Others are much harder to discern. In addition to weekend e-mails, another unwritten rule Charles learned was that she shouldn't have meetings with subordinates in her own office. How did she learn that? When Charles asked to meet with them, her assistant kept scheduling the meetings in the subordinates' cubicles. When Charles asked why,

her assistant told her, "That's how it's done."

One way to decode the maze is to astutely observe unwritten rules and customs and to ask lots of questions. Some learning of organization's culture, though, is pure trial and error. When Kevin Hall started a new job as a mortgage banker, he had to make his own travel arrangements because the first person he asked said it wasn't her job. When he observed colleagues getting help, though, he asked someone else, who was happy to oblige. "You feel your way as you go," Hall said.

Source: Based on E. White, "Culture Shock: Learning Customs of a New Office," *Wall Street Journal*, November 28, 2006, p. B6.

Creating an Ethical Organizational Culture

> *6 Demonstrate how an ethical culture can be created.*

The content and strength of a culture influence an organization's ethical climate and the ethical behavior of its members.[32] An organizational culture most likely to shape high ethical standards is one that's high in risk tolerance, low to moderate in aggressiveness, and focuses on means as well as outcomes. Managers in such a culture are supported for taking risks and innovating, engage in healthy competition, and will pay attention to *how* goals are achieved as well as to *what* goals are achieved.

What Do You Think?

What is your understanding of 'healthy' competition?

A strong organizational culture will exert more influence on employees than a weak one. If the culture is strong and supports high ethical standards, it should have a very powerful and positive influence on employee behavior. Johnson & Johnson, for example, has a strong culture that has long stressed corporate obligations to customers, employees, the community, and shareholders, in that order. When poisoned Tylenol (a Johnson & Johnson product) was found on store shelves in the United States, all employees at Johnson & Johnson across the US independently pulled the product from these stores before management had even issued a statement concerning the problems. No one had to tell these individuals what was morally right; they knew what Johnson & Johnson would expect them to do. On the other hand, a strong culture that encourages pushing the limits can be a powerful force in shaping unethical behavior. For instance, Enron's aggressive culture, with pressure on executives to rapidly expand earnings, encouraged unethical dealings and eventually contributed to the company's collapse.[33]

What can management do to create a more ethical culture? We suggest a combination of the following practices:

- *Be a visible role model.* Employees will look to the behavior of top management as a benchmark for defining appropriate behavior. When senior management is seen as taking the ethical road, it provides a positive message for all employees.
- *Communicate ethical expectations.* Ethical ambiguities can be minimized by creating an organizational code of ethics. It should state the organization's primary values and the ethical rules that employees are expected to follow.
- *Provide ethical training.* Set up seminars, workshops, and similar ethical training programs. Use these training sessions to reinforce the organization's standards of conduct, to clarify what practices are and are not allowed, and to address possible ethical problems.
- *Visibly reward ethical acts and punish unethical ones.* Performance appraisals of managers should include a point-by-point evaluation of how his or her decisions measure up against the organization's code of ethics. Appraisals must include the means taken to achieve goals as well as the ends themselves. People who act ethically should be visibly rewarded for their behavior. Just as importantly, unethical acts should be punished.
- *Provide protective mechanisms.* The organization needs to provide formal mechanisms so that employees can discuss ethical dilemmas and report unethical behavior without fear of punishment. This might include creation of ethical counselors or ethical officers.

Creating a Positive Organizational Culture

Describe a positive organizational culture.

It's often difficult to separate management concepts from lasting changes in management thinking. In this book, we have tried to stay current while staying away from ideas that might die. There is one early trend, though, that we think is here to stay: creating a positive organizational culture.

The one thing that makes us believe that creating a positive culture is here to stay is that there are signs that management practice and OB research are joining forces.

A **positive organizational culture** is defined as a culture that emphasizes building on employee strengths, rewards more than it punishes, and emphasizes individual vitality and growth.[34] Let's consider each of these areas.

Positive organizational culture

A culture that emphasizes building on employee strengths, rewards more than punishes, and emphasizes individual vitality and growth.

Building on Employee Strengths   Both OB and management practices are concerned with how to fix employee problems. Although a positive organizational culture does not ignore problems, it does emphasize showing workers how they can capitalize on their strengths. It is sad but true, most people do not know what their strengths are. When you ask them, they look at you with a blank stare, or they respond in terms of subject knowledge, which is the wrong answer.

> **Picture This**
>
> Imagine you work for a company that takes little interest in you or your development. Wouldn't it be better to belong to an organizational culture that helped you discover those, and learn ways to make the most of them?

One top CEO said, "If you really want to [excel], you have to know yourself—you have to know what you're good at, and you have to know what you're not so good at."[35]

Rewarding More Than Punishing   There is, of course, a time and place for punishment, but there is also a time and place for rewards. Although most organizations are sufficiently focused on extrinsic rewards like pay and promotions, they often forget about the power of smaller rewards like praise. Creating a positive organizational culture means that managers 'catch employees doing something right.' Part of creating a positive culture is giving praise. Many managers don't give praise either because they're afraid employees will change as a result, or because they think praise is not valued. Failing to praise can become a 'silent killer' like escalating blood pressure. Because employees generally don't ask for praise, managers usually don't realize the costs of failing to do it.

Emphasizing Vitality and Growth   A positive organizational culture emphasizes not only organizational effectiveness, but individuals' growth as well. No organization will get the best out of employees if the employees see themselves as just tools or parts of the organization. A positive culture can make the difference between a job and a career, and reflects not only what the employee does to contribute to organizational effectiveness, but also what the organization does and values.

Limits of Positive Culture   Is a positive culture the solution? There are people who may doubt the benefits of positive organizational culture. To be sure, even

With more than 8,500 employees worldwide, the Lebanese-based multinational INDEVCO group believes that people are a company's greatest asset. Driven by its values (Modesty, Honesty, Precision, Hard Work, Entrepreneurial Drive, Servant Leadership and Family Spirit) the group strives to nurture organizational effectiveness and instill a positive organizational culture through initiatives in Human Resources, Learning & Development, Quality Management and Best Practices. The goal is to train and develop employees in order to sustain an atmosphere of growth, integrity, dedication and mutual caring. As a result, employees are happier, more motivated, and more likely to focus on production and delivery of quality products.

though some companies such as GE, Xerox, and Boeing implement aspects of a positive organizational culture, it is a new enough area that there is some uncertainty about how and when it works best. Moreover, any OB scholar or manager needs to make sure he is objective about the benefits—and risks—of cultivating a positive organizational culture.

There may be benefits to establishing a positive culture, but an organization also needs to be careful to be objective, and not continue past the point of effectiveness.

Spirituality and Organizational Culture

> **8** *Identify characteristics of a spiritual culture.*

There are many organizations such as Ford and INDEVCO that have embraced workplace spirituality.

What Is Spirituality?

Workplace spirituality

The recognition that people have an inner life that nourishes and is nourished by meaningful work that takes place in the context of community.

Workplace spirituality is *not* about organized religious practices. It's not about God or theology. **Workplace spirituality** recognizes that people have an inner life that values and is valued by meaningful work that takes place in the context of community.[36] Organizations that promote a spiritual culture recognize that people have both a mind and a spirit, seek to find meaning and purpose in their work, and desire to connect with other human beings and be part of a community.

Why Spirituality Now?

Concern about an employee's inner life had no role in the perfectly rational model. But just as we've now come to realize that the study of emotions, as we discussed in Chapter 6, improves our understanding of organizational behavior, an awareness of spirituality can help you to better understand employee behavior in the twenty-first century.

Of course, employees have always had an inner life. So why has the search for meaning and purposefulness in work appeared now? There are a number of reasons. We summarize them in Box 14-3.

Characteristics of a Spiritual Organization

The concept of workplace spirituality draws on our previous discussions of topics such as values, ethics, motivation, leadership, and work–life balance. Spiritual organizations are concerned with helping people develop and reach their full potential. Similarly, organizations that are concerned with spirituality are more likely to directly address problems created by work–life conflicts. What differentiates spiritual organizations from others? Although research on this question is only preliminary, our review identified four cultural characteristics that tend to be clear in spiritual organizations:[37]

- *Strong sense of purpose.*   Spiritual organizations build their cultures around a meaningful purpose. Although profits may be important, they're not the primary values of the organization. People want to be inspired by a purpose that they believe is important and worthwhile.
- *Trust and respect.*   Spiritual organizations are characterized by mutual trust, honesty, and openness. Managers aren't afraid to admit mistakes.
- *Humanistic work practices.*   These practices embraced by spiritual organizations include flexible work schedules, group- and organization-based rewards, narrowing of pay and status differentials, guarantees of individual worker rights, employee empowerment, and job security.
- *Toleration of employee expression.*   The final characteristic that differentiates spiritually based organizations is that they don't limit employee emotions. They allow people to be themselves—to express their moods and feelings without guilt or fear of reprimand.

How spiritual are you? Take the following Self-Assessment exercise to find out.

HOW SPIRITUAL AM I?

In the Self-Assessment Library (available online), take assessment IV.A.4 (How Spiritual Am I?). Note: People's scores on this measure vary from time to time, so take that into account when interpreting the results.

BOX 14-3

Reasons for the Growing Interest in Spirituality

- As a counterbalance to the pressures and stress of a turbulent pace of life. Contemporary lifestyles—single-parent families, geographic mobility, the temporary nature of jobs, new technologies that create distance between people—underscore the lack of community many people feel and increase the need for involvement and connection.
- Formalized religion hasn't worked for many people, and they continue to look for anchors to replace lack of faith and to fill a growing feeling of emptiness.
- Job demands have made the workplace dominant in many people's lives, yet they continue to question the meaning of work.
- The desire to integrate personal life values with one's professional life.
- An increasing number of people are finding that the pursuit of more material acquisitions leaves them unfulfilled.

Mark Trang, an employee of Salesforce.com, teaches business basics to fifth-grade students at an elementary school. Salesforce.com encourages every employee to donate 1 percent of his or her working time to the community. Through volunteer work, Salesforce.com gives employes the opportunity to experience the joy and satisfaction that comes from helping others. Employees give to the community by feeding the homeless, tutoring kids, gardening in community parks, lending computer expertise to nonprofit organizations, and providing disaster relief.

Criticisms of Spirituality

We must understand that there are always people who argue any concept. Critics of the spirituality movement in organizations have focused on three issues. First is the question of scientific foundation. What really is workplace spirituality? Is it just a new management word? Second, are spiritual organizations legitimate? Specifically, do organizations have the right to impose spiritual values on their employees? Third is the question of economics: Are spirituality and profits compatible?

First, as you might imagine, there is very little research on workplace spirituality. We don't know whether the concept will have lasting power. Do the cultural characteristics just identified really separate spiritual organizations? What is a nonspiritual organization, anyway? Do employees of so-called spiritual organizations perceive that they work in spiritual organizations? Although there is some research suggesting support for workplace spirituality (as we discuss later), before the concept of spirituality gains full credibility, the questions we've just posed need to be answered.

On the second question, there is clearly the potential for an emphasis on spirituality to make some employees uneasy. Critics might argue that secular institutions, especially business firms, have no business imposing spiritual values on employees. This criticism is undoubtedly valid when spirituality is defined as bringing religion and God into the workplace.[38] However, the criticism seems less stinging when the goal is limited to helping employees find meaning in their work lives. If the concerns listed in Box 14-3 truly characterize a growing segment of the workforce, then perhaps the time is right for organizations to help employees find meaning and purpose in their work and to use the workplace as a source of community.

Finally, the issue of whether spirituality and profits are compatible objectives is certainly relevant for managers and investors in business. The evidence, although limited, indicates that the two objectives may be very compatible. A recent research study by a major consulting firm found that companies that introduced spiritually based techniques improved productivity and significantly reduced turnover.[39] Another study found that organizations that provided their employees with opportunities for spiritual development outperformed those that didn't.[40] Other studies also report that spirituality in organizations is positively related to creativity, employee satisfaction, team performance, and organizational commitment.[41]

In the Arab world, spirituality does not only mean an understanding of 'who you are' as an individual but also welcomes religion into the workplace. In fact, God and religious issues are dominant in most organizations. And as we know, the expressions '*Inshallah*' and 'God willing' are part of almost every sentence.

Global Implications

9 Show how national culture may affect the way organizational culture is transported to a different country.

We considered global cultural values (collectivism–individualism, power distance, and so on) in Chapter 2. Here our focus is more specific: How is organizational culture affected by a global context? Organizational cultures are powerful and often rise above national boundaries but that doesn't mean that organizations should be ignorant of local culture.

This is becoming a bigger issue. In 2007, half of General Electric's revenue came from outside the United States. GE even moved the headquarters of its health care division to the United Kingdom, and the number of non-US citizens among GE's top 500 managers has tripled since 2001. GE is hardly alone. Large and small organizations alike are often heavily dependent on foreign product markets, labor markets, or both. This is also very apparent in the Arab world, where a large percentage of the workforce are foreigners.

All managers need to be culturally sensitive and tolerant. Accordingly, employees must also respect each other regardless of any diversity. Companies such as Microsoft have implemented training programs to sensitize their managers to cultural differences. Some ways in which managers can be culturally sensitive include talking in a low tone of voice, speaking slowly, listening more, and avoiding discussions of religion and politics.

Summary and Implications for Managers

Figure 14-3 shows organizational culture as an intervening variable. Employees form an overall subjective perception of the organization based on factors such as degree of risk tolerance, team emphasis, and support of people. This overall perception becomes, in effect, the organization's culture or personality. These

| Figure **14-3** | **How Organizational Cultures Have an Impact on Employee Performance and Satisfaction** |

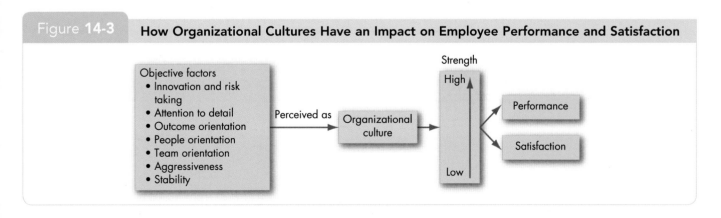

favorable or unfavorable perceptions then affect employee performance and satisfaction, with the impact being greater for stronger cultures.

Just as people's personalities tend to be stable over time, so too do strong cultures. This makes strong cultures difficult for managers to change. When a culture becomes mismatched to its environment, management will want to change it. But as the Point/Counterpoint demonstrates, changing an organization's culture is a long and difficult process. The result, at least in the short term, is that managers should treat their organization's culture as relatively fixed.

One of the most important managerial implications of organizational culture relates to selection decisions. Hiring individuals whose values don't align with those of the organization is likely to lead to employees who lack motivation and commitment and who are dissatisfied with their jobs and the organization.[42] Not surprisingly, employee "misfits" have considerably higher turnover rates than individuals who perceive a good fit.[43]

We should also not overlook the influence socialization has on employee performance. An employee's performance depends to a considerable degree on knowing what he should or should not do. Understanding the right way to do a job indicates proper socialization.

Finally, as a manager, you can shape the culture of your work environment. That is particularly the case with some of the cultural aspects we discussed in the latter part of this chapter—all managers can do their part to create an ethical culture, and spirituality and a positive organizational culture should be considered, too. Often you can do as much to shape your organizational culture as the culture of the organization shapes you.

Point >> << Counterpoint

ORGANIZATIONAL CULTURES CAN'T BE CHANGED

An organization's culture is made up of relatively stable characteristics. It develops over many years and is rooted in deeply held values to which employees are strongly committed. In addition, there are a number of forces continually operating to maintain a given culture. These include written statements about the organization's mission and philosophy, the design of physical spaces and buildings, the dominant leadership style, hiring criteria, past promotion practices, entrenched rituals, popular stories about key people and events, the organization's historic performance evaluation criteria, and the organization's formal structure.

Our argument should not be viewed as saying that culture can *never* be changed. In the unusual case in which an organization confronts a survival-threatening crisis, members of the organization will be responsive to efforts at cultural change. However, anything less than that is unlikely to be effective in bringing about cultural change.

Changing an organization's culture is extremely difficult, but cultures *can* be changed. The evidence suggests that cultural change is most likely to take place when most or all of the following conditions exist:

- a dramatic crisis
- turnover in leadership
- young and small organizations
- weak culture.

If all or most of these conditions exist, the following management actions may lead to change: initiating new stories and rituals, selecting and promoting employees who support the new values, changing the reward system to support the new values, and undermining current subcultures through transfers, job rotation, and terminations. Therefore, cultures can be changed.

Questions for Review

1 What is institutionalization and how does it affect organizational culture?

2 What is organizational culture and what are its common characteristics?

3 What are the functional and dysfunctional effects of organizational culture?

4 What factors create and sustain an organization's culture?

5 How is culture transmitted to employees?

6 How can an ethical culture be created?

7 What is a positive organizational culture?

8 What are the characteristics of a spiritual culture?

9 How does national culture affect how organizational culture is transported to a different country?

Discussion Exercise

Does culture provide a sense of belongingness and identity? The more clearly an organization's shared perceptions and values are defined, the more strongly people can associate with its mission and feel a vital part of it. Do you agree? Discuss.

Ethical Considerations

Many organizations spy on their employees—sometimes with and sometimes without their knowledge or consent. Organizations differ in their culture of surveillance. Some differences are due to the type of business.

Consider the following surveillance actions and for each action, decide whether it would never be ethical (mark N), would sometimes be ethical (mark S), or would always be ethical (mark A). For those you mark S, indicate on what factors your judgment would depend.

1. Looking through an employee's trash for evidence of wrongdoing.
2. Periodically reading e-mail messages for disclosure of confidential information or inappropriate use.
3. Conducting video surveillance of workspace.
4. Monitoring websites visited by employees and determining the appropriateness and work-relatedness of those visited.
5. Taping phone conversations.
6. Posing as a job candidate, an investor, a customer, or a colleague when the real purpose is to get information.

Would you be less likely to work for an employer that engaged in some of these methods? Why or why not? Do you think use of surveillance says something about an organization's culture?

Critical Analysis

GHOSN TURNS NISSAN AROUND

Carlos Ghosn was the man who turned Nissan around, taking it from a downward direction to one that changed the company in an exceptional manner. He observed and discovered the problems, and realized that strict measures needed to be taken or Nissan would be on its way out of the market. In particular, he knew that he had to establish an effective organizational culture—one that would involve all members of the organization—to encourage trust and understanding.

Even though Nissan was a prominent Japanese company during the 1990s, it had huge debts. To the surprise of many, however, Renault acquired 36.8 percent of Nissan in 1999. It was no surprise, though, when Renault appointed Ghosn as CEO at Nissan—they knew that he was the only person who could deal with Nissan's debts and he had a reputation for making effective decisions in difficult situations. The most complicated issue was addressing the different cultures: Japan is known for its collectivist culture, whereas that of France was individualistic. However, Ghosn was known for his readiness and willingness to deal with challenging situations.

Among the many obstacles that Ghosn found were affecting Nissan was the Japanese system of *Keiretsu*, which establishes close relations with suppliers and manufacturers. This practice was found to be the main obstacle to the company's growth and it was generating a loss. As a result, some contracts with *Keiretsu* suppliers were stopped.

What action did Carlos Ghosn then take to turn Nissan around? He took some very harsh decisions, but only because he knew this would be the best way to start. First, he educated his staff on the importance of culture and values. Then he established a merit-based promotion scale. Naturally, many criticized his methods, but he continued and was extremely content when Nissan employees responded positively.

Moreover, Ghosn stressed cultural training and team building to encourage synergy between Renault and Nissan at all levels. He also wanted to increase knowledge-sharing among employees and transparency at top levels. The biggest shock came when Ghosn took action to cut costs, closed down assembly plants, and laid off 21,000 employees—in a country where people were used to being employed for life.

The rest is history, and the famous case study about Nissan is one that all students learn about when studying management and organizational behavior. The success of Renault-Nissan continues to this day by making profit and looking for emerging markets. Ghosn's appointment as CEO was definitely in line with the saying, "The Right Person in the Right Place."

Questions

1. In what ways were the cultures of Renault and Nissan similar and different?

2. How do you react to the methods that Ghosn took to deal with the problems at Nissan?

3. Do you think that culture is important to the success of a company? Why or why not?

Research Exercise

Within this chapter, there was a section that discussed how employees learn culture. One particular way was through material symbols. Do your research and find organizations in the Arab world that also apply this concept.

LEARNING OBJECTIVES

This chapter will enable you to:

1 Describe the recruitment process.

2 Understand the selection process and its significance.

3 Compare and contrast training and development techniques.

4 Describe the purposes of performance evaluation and list the various methods.

5 Explain how diversity can be managed in organizations.

6 Show how managers can improve their employees' work–life balance.

7 Show how a global context affects human resource management.

Human Resource Policies and Practices in the Arab World

15

To manage people well, companies should [. . .] elevate HR to a position of power and primacy in the organization.

—Former General Electric CEO, Jack Welch

Human Resource Policy at Azadea

Azadea Group Holding is the owner and operator of 40 leading international franchise retail concepts in the Middle East and North Africa. The company's mission is to provide its customers and people with an entertaining and exciting way of life.

The group currently employs 6,700 men and women of diverse nationalities to manage its portfolio of retail brands, which add up to 378 stores in a dozen different countries.

As a retail and lifestyle company, Azadea's highest priority is to engage with its customers by upholding a strong two-way communication channel, open to receiving feedback on a continuous basis. In order to achieve this, the company requires competent management for the brands it represents. Hence it is the brand managers who play a crucial role in the success of all the stores within their respective retail concept and in the prosperity of the company as a whole, and consequently in maintaining a high level of customer satisfaction.

Each brand manager is responsible for a unique retail concept, from planning, developing and directing marketing efforts to coordinating with specialists on sales, advertising, promotions, all the way to gaining customers' loyalty for a particular brand. Therefore, one of the company's main challenges is to ensure

that brand managers are properly trained and have the necessary tools to organize and handle its retail business in the realm of its rapid development and growth. The more understanding brand managers have of the retail scene, the better they are able to ensure customer satisfaction, which is at the core of Azadea's business. And that is why they strongly believe that promotion to the position of brand manager must be from within employee ranks, namely from store managers, as their mission is deeply instilled in each and every member of their family from the onset.

As in any competitive business, there are several other challenges, typical of retail companies, with regard to securing employees with the right competencies. One of the issues is that of high employee turnover, due to the stressful nature of the industry. Another is the need to elaborate a meaningful career development plan to retain talent and preserve intellectual capital. It is also essential to sustain the motivation and performance of store employees and brand managers.

To overcome these challenges and because it is inherently a people's company, inside and out, Azadea invests heavily in training and developing everyone, from retail staff to back office employees. Furthermore, specifically for preparing the next generation of brand managers, the company established the Executive Retail Management Program (ERMP), to which qualified store managers wanting to pursue careers as brand managers may apply. Applicants go through a selection process and meet rigorous requirements that include a certain level of education, reasoning ability, retail experience and a history of excellent professional performance within the group. ERMP's goal is to increase trainees' overall knowledge of the retail industry and to provide the necessary tools and skills that will enhance their future careers as brand managers, all with the ultimate goal of ensuring the finest client brand relationship.

On one hand, the program consists of technical training in areas such as finance, logistics, stock management, marketing, human resource management, fashion and visual merchandizing. On the other hand, it delivers behavioral skills training (managerial and interpersonal) to teach trainees how to manage a team that is both geographically and ethnically diverse. Azadea operates in over 12 countries and its employees span nearly 80 different nationalities.

The 11-month program is delivered in the form of 15 four-day segments at Azadea's headquarters in Lebanon. Each four-day segment focuses on a specific topic, on which trainees are given an assignment to hand in at the beginning of the following segment, at which time they will also have to pass an assessment test on the particular topic. At the end of the program, trainees have to complete a final comprehensive three-month project that covers all the topics studied and is graded collectively by all the instructors. Each trainee receives an overall grade, based on a weighted average of each topic and the final project grades, which will determine whether he or she graduates and becomes eligible for promotion to the next available brand manager vacancy.

ERMP's benefits are manifold and became apparent from the moment the program's first class graduated. With the eligibility requirements used in the selection process and the proper training, rising brand managers were armed with the knowledge and skills needed to fulfill their new roles. Moreover, the graduates received positive feedback from their peers for their improvement in managerial skills and technical knowledge, and this translated into a more positive approach toward and from their clientele.

ERMP is a model of Azadea's commitment to nurturing a culture of continuous learning. The program helps define a career path for store employees, from stock keeper leading up to brand manager, ultimately motivating store managers to continuously perform better in the hope of gaining entry into the coveted ERMP program, seeking a long-term career within the organization. Furthermore, ERMP has increased brand managers' diversity and smashed the glass ceiling for minorities, attracting more talent and retaining employees' loyalty by providing equal opportunity to reach the highest levels in the organization.

Source: Case study contributed by AZADEA Group, © Azadea Group Holding SAL, 2011.

The message of this chapter is that human resource (HR) policies and practices—such as employee selection, training, and performance management—influence an organization's effectiveness.[1] However, studies show that many managers—even HR managers—often don't know which HR practices work and which don't.

The opening case about Azadea talks about such HR practices, in particular, training and development and their effects on employee behavior in the organization. Specifically, the case stresses the importance of recruiting talented and competent people who are willing and able to maximize organizational performance. When people are allowed to get more involved in the system, they feel more committed and their behavior is likely to improve and so benefit the organization.

This chapter covers the basics of human resource practices and policies and the issues to consider when implementing them in *different countries around the world*. In particular, we will see how HR works in the countries of the Arab world. However, before you start, see how much you know by taking the self-assessment test that follows.

HOW MUCH DO I KNOW ABOUT HRM?

In the Self-Assessment Library (available online), take assessment IV.G.2 (How Much Do I Know About HRM?) and answer the following questions:

1. *How did you score compared with your classmates? Did the results surprise you?*

2. *How much of effective HRM is common sense?*

3. *Do you think your score will improve after reading this chapter?*

Many textbooks will tell you that HRM revolves around six domains: recruitment, selection, training, development, compensation, and rewards. These are the basic themes that should lead to satisfaction and motivation at work, as we discussed in Chapter 5.

The issues related to HRM, recruitment and selection—training and development, rewards and compensation—are similar in context worldwide. However, the applications and implementations of policies and practices do differ according to the culture of the country, as discussed in Chapter 14.

Human Resource Management Societies

The Society for Human Resource Management (SHRM), formerly called the American Society for Personnel Administration (ASPA), was founded in 1948 by a group of just 28 individuals who anticipated the need for a national organization to represent the personnel profession. Their goal was to provide continued professional development opportunities, and promote national networking. Today, SHRM includes a global membership of more than 250,000 in over 140 countries and has offices in the US, India, and China.[2]

SHRM exists to build and sustain partnerships with human resource professionals and to address people management challenges that influence the effectiveness and sustainability of their organizations and communities. In addition, SHRM provides a community for human resource professionals to share expertise and create innovative solutions on people management issues. It also proactively provides leadership, education and research to human resource professionals in businesses and academic institutions.

In the Arab world, the Arabian Society for Human Resource Management (ASHRM) was founded in 1991 to provide guidelines and share experiences, with diversity, creativity, and motivation being the keys for membership. ASHRM is committed to advancing the human resource profession in the Arab world and the capabilities of all human resource professionals to ensure that HR is an essential and effective partner in developing and executing the strategy of organizations.

Beyond that, ASHRM cooperates with other human resource organizations in the region, such as the Bahrain Society for Training and Development, which has co-sponsored several events with ASHRM for the mutual benefit of both groups. The Society does not limit its outreach to regional partners, however. It also strives to maintain close working relationships with the US-based Society for Human Resource Management, Institute for International Human Resources, and American Society for Training and Development. Another group that helps the Arab world to acknowledge human resources as assets and is willing to encourage and support is the Human Resource Association of Lebanon (HRAL).

The Recruitment Process

1   *Describe the recruitment process.*

Recruitment
Locating, identifying, and attracting capable applicants.

Recruitment is the act of finding the most appropriate and qualified person for a particular job. This typically involves assessing the KSAs—Knowledge, Skills, Attitude. This is done by matching the requirements of the job with the candidates' skills and qualifications, so that the right person is selected. This is known as the "*fit*" and will be discussed in a later section of this chapter.

Following recruitment, employees will often be expected to follow a training and development program throughout their time in the organization. Training is a learning process and is about teaching people new skills, whereas development helps people to improve upon existing skills. Finally, performance—whether positive or negative—must be acknowledged, and this is where rewards are addressed. The objective is to ensure that people are treated fairly and equally when compensated. The focus of this section, however, is on recruitment.

If implemented effectively, recruitment will allow us to choose the most appropriate person for the job so that we put the right person in the right position.[3] Notice the word 'choose' in the previous sentence; this stresses the selection practices involved in recruiting someone and these will be covered in the following section.

Picture This

Farah has been the assistant manager in the marketing department of a big insurance company in Amman for seven years. She has had a productive relationship with her boss and has always received positive performance evaluations. Unfortunately, Mr. Abdul-Latif now has to resign from his position as Manager for health reasons. What action should now be taken to address this situation?

When Mr. Abdul-Latif leaves, the office will no longer have a manager, which means it will have a vacancy—an empty position that must be filled. Where would we go to find the right people to fill this position? There are two sources of potential candidates: either we can look for them amongst those currently employed within the organization—*internal recruitment*; or we can look for them outside the organization—*external recruitment*. Once a pool of candidates has been found, it is necessary to think about how to select the best among these.

Selection Practices

It's been said the most important HR decision you can make is who you hire. That makes sense—if you can figure out who the right people are. The objective of effective selection is to figure out who these right people are, by matching individual characteristics such as ability and experience with the requirements of the job.[4] When management fails to get a proper match, both employee performance and satisfaction suffer.

How the Selection Process Works

A clear outline showing how the selection process works in most organizations is shown in Figure 15-1. Applicants go through several stages once they have decided to apply for a specific job. In practice, some organizations do not follow all of these steps, in order to save time, but this also depends on the type of job. That is, a meat-packing factory may hire the first person who walks in the door because not everyone would be excited about the job specifications, whereas an announcement for the position of public relations officer may attract more candidates. Whatever the case, most organizations follow a process

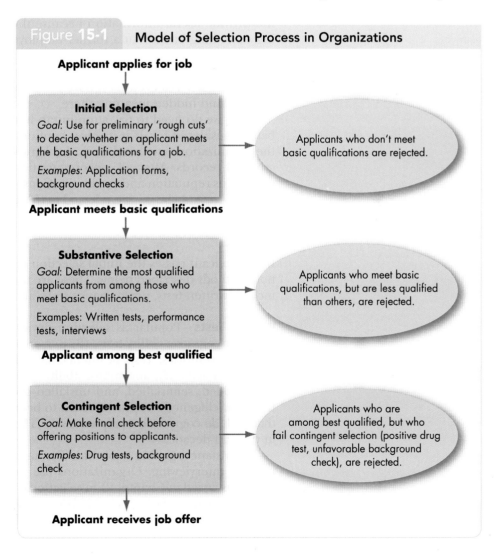

Figure 15-1   Model of Selection Process in Organizations

Applicant applies for job

Initial Selection

Goal: Use for preliminary 'rough cuts' to decide whether an applicant meets the basic qualifications for a job.

Examples: Application forms, background checks

Applicants who don't meet basic qualifications are rejected.

Applicant meets basic qualifications

Substantive Selection

Goal: Determine the most qualified applicants from among those who meet basic qualifications.

Examples: Written tests, performance tests, interviews

Applicants who meet basic qualifications, but are less qualified than others, are rejected.

Applicant among best qualified

Contingent Selection

Goal: Make final check before offering positions to applicants.

Examples: Drug tests, background check

Applicants who are among best qualified, but who fail contingent selection (positive drug test, unfavorable background check), are rejected.

Applicant receives job offer

similar to the one in Figure 15-1 so let's go into a bit more detail about each of the stages.

Initial Selection

Initial selection tools are the first information applicants submit and these are used to decide whether an applicant meets the basic qualifications for a job. Examples of initial selection devices are application forms and background checks.

Application Forms   These can be a good initial screen, since they supply information about the qualifications of the applicant. For example, there's no sense in spending time interviewing an applicant for a registered nurse position if he or she doesn't have the proper credentials (education, certification, experience). Today, more and more organizations encourage applicants to submit applications online. It is also important that organizations be careful about the questions they ask on applications to avoid any legal problems. For example, there should be no questions about race, gender, or nationality.

Background Checks   These allow the organization to know more about an applicant and what they did in past jobs, and whether former employers would recommend hiring the person. The problem is that previous employers may not provide useful information because they are afraid of being sued for saying something bad about a former employee. Letters of recommendation are another form of background check, but applicants may select those who write good letters, so almost all letters of recommendation are positive. In the end, readers of such letters either ignore them altogether or read 'between the lines' to try to find hidden meaning there.

What we do need to pay attention to here is the type of job the applicant is being considered for. If it involves confidentiality, honesty, and integrity, then the organization may need to do background checks on credit history or on criminal records. After all, no organization wants to hire someone who may damage its reputation and credibility. Consequently, applicants who do not pass the background checks are rejected at this point.

Substantive Selection

If an applicant passes the initial selection phase, next are the substantive selection methods described below. These are the heart of the selection process and include written tests, performance tests, and interviews.

Written Tests   Popular as selection devices, written tests include (1) intelligence or cognitive ability tests, (2) personality tests, (3) integrity tests, and (4) interest inventories. Tests of intellectual ability, spatial and mechanical ability, perceptual accuracy, and motor ability have proven to be valid predictors for many skilled, semiskilled, and unskilled operative jobs in industrial organizations.[5] Intelligence tests have proven to be particularly good predictors for jobs that include cognitively complex tasks.[6] The use of personality tests has grown in the past decade.

For instance, getting a job with Toyota can require up to three days of testing and interviewing. Organizations use numerous measures of the Big Five traits (discussed in Chapter 2) in selection decisions. The traits that best predict job performance are conscientiousness and positive self-concept.[7] This makes sense in that conscientious people tend to be motivated and dependable, and positive people are 'can-do' oriented and persistent. As ethical problems have increased in organizations, integrity tests measure factors such as dependability, carefulness, responsibility, and honesty.

Performance-Simulation Tests   What better way to find out whether applicants can do a job successfully than by having them do it? That's precisely the logic of performance-simulation tests.

The two best-known performance-simulation tests are work samples and assessment centers. **Work sample tests** are hands-on simulations of part or all of the job that must be performed by applicants. By carefully devising work samples based on specific job tasks, management determines the knowledge, skills, and abilities needed for each job. Then each work sample element is matched with a corresponding job performance element. To illustrate, job candidates for production jobs at BMW's factory in South Carolina have 90 minutes to perform a variety of typical work tasks on a specially built simulated assembly line.[8] **Assessment centers** are places where line executives, supervisors, and/or trained psychologists evaluate candidates as they go through one to several days of exercises that simulate real problems they would confront on the job.[9] For instance, a candidate might be required to play the role of a manager who must decide how to respond to ten memos in an in-basket within a two-hour period.

> **Work sample test**
>
> A test that is a miniature replica of a job that is used to evaluate the performance abilities of job candidates.

> **Assessment centers**
>
> A place where job candidates are evaluated as they go through one to several days of exercises that simulate real problems they would confront on the job.

Interviews   Of all the selection devices organizations around the globe use to decide between candidates, the interview continues to be the most common.[10] Not only is the interview widely used, it also seems to carry a great deal of weight. The candidate who performs poorly in the employment interview is likely to be cut from the applicant pool regardless of experience, test scores, or letters of recommendation. There are two types of interview: the structured interview and the unstructured interview. The unstructured interview is short in duration, casual, made up of random questions, and as such is not very effective. The structured interview involves a standard set of questions. The effectiveness of the interview also improves when employers use a behavioral structured interview.[11] This interview technique requires applicants to describe how they handled specific problems and situations in previous jobs. It's built on the assumption that past behavior offers the best predictor of future behavior. So in addition to specific, job-relevant skills, organizations are looking at candidates' personality characteristics, personal values, and the like to find individuals who fit with the organization's culture and image.

What Do You Think?

Have you ever been interviewed for a job? Think about your experience. Does it relate to what we have just discussed? Do you feel that interviews conducted in your Arab country may differ from those conducted in the US, for example?

Contingent Selection

If applicants pass the substantive selection methods, they are basically ready to be hired after a final check, such as a drug test. The job offer is contingent (or depends) on passing the final check. There are organizations in the Arab world that make job offers contingent on applicants passing a drug test, but they prefer to remain anonymous. For example, many universities such as Notre Dame University, Lebanon, require potential students to have a medical exam and a drug test before the final acceptance is made.

Wheeler Landscaping in Chagrin Falls, Ohio, US, uses the contingent selection method of drug testing before hiring new employees. A growing number of small businesses like Wheeler, which has 76 employees, are using drug tests to help reduce insurance costs, workers' compensation claims due to workplace accidents, absenteeism, and employee theft.

Source: Amy E. Voigt/ *New York Times*.

Drug testing is controversial. Many applicants think it is unfair to test them without reasonable suspicion. Such individuals likely believe that drug use is a private matter and applicants should be tested on factors that directly bear on job performance, not lifestyle issues that may or may not be job relevant. Drug tests typically screen out individuals who have used marijuana but not alcohol (for both legal and practical reasons—alcohol is legal and leaves the system in 24 hours).

In brief, even though applicants may be among the best qualified, if they fail the contingent selection, they will be rejected. Once the conditions of the job are agreed upon and the candidate becomes an employee, we can presume that a proper 'fit' has been made.

Training and Development Programs

3 *Compare and contrast training and development techniques.*

Employees don't remain qualified forever. Skills can change and then new skills need to be learned. That's why organizations spend billions of dollars each year on formal training. Thereafter, learned skills need to improve and advance, and this is where development programs come into the picture. That is, employees are given the opportunity to improve themselves, their skills and competencies, and this, in turn, allows people to perform better on the job. Organizations in the Arab world are becoming more aware of the importance of employee training and development. They realize that even though these programs are costly, they will result in a return on investment that will ensure higher productivity and enhanced performance. One such organization is INDEVCO, which allocates a large annual budget for employee training and development. Another example is IBM, a multinational organization that is well established in the Arab world, which spends in excess of US$300 million per year on employee training.

What Do You Think?

Many companies spend millions of dollars on training. Is all this money worth investing in employees?

Types of Training

Training can include everything from teaching employees basic reading skills to conducting advanced courses in executive leadership. Let's look at four general skill categories identified as basic literacy, technical, interpersonal, and problem-solving, and we will briefly discuss ethics training (training individuals to consider moral questions when making decisions or taking actions at work).

Basic Literacy Skills   Statistics show that nearly 40 percent of the US labor force and more than 50 percent of US high school graduates don't possess the basic work skills needed to perform in today's workplace.[12] This problem, of course, isn't unique to the United States. It's a worldwide problem—from the most developed countries to the least.[13] For many developing countries, where few workers can read or have gone beyond the equivalent of the third grade, widespread illiteracy means there is almost no hope of competing in a global economy.

There is great awareness in the Arab countries of the high levels of illiteracy. This concern is at both the governmental and organizational levels. A major plan of action in the area was the establishment of the regional program for universalization and renewal of primary education and eradication of illiteracy in the Arab world. In particular, the pressure is on developing the Arab educational systems at the level of literacy and primary education through improving the curriculum, teaching methods, teacher training, and enhanced administrative structures to ensure that workers possess the basic skills for employment.[14]

Technical Skills   Technical training is becoming increasingly important today because of new technology and new structural designs in the organization. For instance, computer-controlled equipment has required millions of production employees to learn a whole new set of skills.[15]

In addition, because of changes in organization design employees need to master a wider variety of tasks and to increase their knowledge of how their organization operates.

Interpersonal Skills   All employees belong to a work unit, and their work performance depends on their ability to effectively interact with their coworkers and their boss. Some employees have excellent interpersonal skills, but others require training to improve theirs. This includes learning how to be a better listener, how to communicate ideas more clearly, and how to be a more effective team player.

Problem-Solving Skills   Managers, as well as many employees who perform nonroutine tasks, have to solve problems in their jobs. When people require these skills but are weak in them, they can participate in problem-solving training. This can include activities to sharpen their logic, reasoning, and problem-defining skills.

What Do You Think?

Which of the four skills do you excel in? Which do you feel you need training in?

International OB

Cultural Training

In a global economy, employee training is no longer limited to the specific tasks of the job. As more and more positions in the information technology and service industries move to India from the United States, many companies are training their Indian employees to improve their cultural skills when dealing with American clients.

For example, the Hyderabad offices of Sierra Atlantic, a California-based software company, trains its Indian employees in various aspects of US culture, including addressing colleagues as Mr. or Ms., learning how to interact with others during a conference call, and even how to sip wine. According to Lu Ellen Schafer, executive director at Global Savvy, a consulting firm based in California, "The training in American culture is not to make Indian software professionals less Indian. It is to make them more globally competent."

Some companies are benefiting from cultural training. Sierra Atlantic's offices in Hyderabad, for example, won a bid with an American firm over an Indian competitor because the Sierra employees were viewed as a better cultural fit. Such successes make it likely that companies with foreign clients will either adopt or continue to use cultural training.

Source: Based on S. Rai, "Indian Companies Are Adding Western Flavor," *New York Times*, August 19, 2003, p. W1.

What About Ethics Training?   There is still a debate on whether you can actually teach ethics.[16] Critics argue that ethics is based on values, and value systems are fixed at an early age. By the time employers hire people, their ethical values have already been established. The critics also claim that ethics cannot be formally 'taught' but must be learned by example. However, training could be effective because it would help employees to recognize ethical dilemmas and become more aware of the ethical issues underlying their actions.

There are certain banks in the Arab world countries such as Saudi Arabia and Bahrain that have asked the Edcomm Group Banker's Academy to offer ethics training to their employees.[17]

Training Methods

Training methods are classified as formal or informal and as on-the-job or off-the-job training.

Historically, training meant *formal training*. That is, it's planned in advance and has a structured format. In reality, a lot of training is informal—unstructured, unplanned, and easily adapted to situations and individuals. In reality, informal training is nothing other than employees helping each other out. They share information and solve work-related problems with one another. For example, at a Siemens plant, management now recognizes that people needn't be on the production line to be working.[18] Discussions around the water cooler or in the cafeteria weren't, as managers thought, about nonwork topics such as sports or politics. They largely focused on solving work-related problems. So now Siemens's management encourages such casual meetings.

What Do You Think?

Do employees in the Arab world discuss work-related issues during breaks and at the cafeteria?

On-the-job training includes job rotation, apprenticeships, and formal mentoring programs; these are effective but may interrupt the flow of work. So organizations may invest in *off-the-job training* such as classroom lectures, video-tapes, public seminars, self-study programs, internet courses, and group activities that use role play and case studies.

Individualizing Formal Training to Fit the Employee's Learning Style

Individuals learn and process, and remember new and difficult information in different ways. This fact means that effective formal training should be individualized to reflect the learning style of the employee.[19] Some examples of different learning styles are reading, watching, listening, and participating. Some people absorb information better when they read about it. Others need to observe or watch and then imitate or even listen to instructions.

The existence of different learning styles means that different people have to use different learning methods. To maximize learning, readers should be given books; watchers should get the opportunity to observe individuals; listeners will benefit from hearing lectures or audiotapes; and participants will benefit most from experiential opportunities in which they can simulate and practice the new skills.

What Do You Think?

What is your learning style? Why does that work for you?

Evaluating Effectiveness of Training Programs

Most training programs work rather well because the majority of people who have training learn more than those who do not, and change their behavior in response to the training.

ARAMEX International is a major provider of total transportation solutions in the Middle East and Indian subcontinent. In 2003 it announced that it was introducing a web-based training initiative for its staff. This programme aimed to sharpen essential business skills, through a number of specialized training courses and modules, supported by an internet chat service, whiteboard, video and audio conferencing. Progress reports also allow supervisors to monitor the course of training for each employee.

The success of training depends on the individual as much as on the quality of the training itself. If individuals are unmotivated to learn, they will benefit very little. What factors determine training motivation? Personality and training climate are important. In other words, when trainees believe that there are opportunities on the job to apply their newly learned skills and enough resources to apply what they have learned, they are more motivated to learn and do better in training programs.[20]

Training and development give employees a chance to build new skills and improve performance. Let's now turn our attention to how performance is evaluated and how these evaluations benefit both the employer and the organization.

OB in the News

Awareness of Human Capital From Within: 'Project Emiratization'

It is largely understood that the Arab world countries have limited resources for competition within a global context. These countries are well aware of the importance of competing with all the right tools, and human capital is one such instrument. As one example, the United Arab Emirates (UAE) is making great efforts to enhance nationalization by stressing that their human resources should be locals. They have engaged in recruiting and training their own people and have launched 'project Emiratization.'

Training is at the heart of this project, with organizations from both the private and public sectors offering employment opportunities for UAE graduates. There are many programs that have been initiated to allow people to develop their skills and competencies. For example, 'Ruwad,' a three-year intensive training program, prepares people from the UAE for leadership positions. The National Bank of Dubai (NBD) is also giving leadership training through the 'Program for Accelerated Learning' (PAL) that prepares

employees for supervisory or managerial roles.

Several sectors have joined forces to promote the campaign of 'project Emiratization,' and accordingly offer all UAE nationals the opportunity for training and development. The organizers of the project take the view that there should be no need to import the skills that are already available in the country. To illustrate, Dubai International Airport (DIA) has a great need for skilled fuel operators and so the Emirates Nationals Development Program (ENDP) has developed the 'Tamheed' training program in collaboration with BP, Shell and Emarat. This program aims to train UAE nationals for work as fuelling operators.

Emaar construction developers are also involved in the Emiratization process. This program began in 2005 and is called 'Afaq,' or horizon, and covers four areas: (1) the 'Emaar Leadership Programme;' (2) the 'Management Associate Program;' (3) a program for experienced Emirati professionals; and (4) the 'Employer Choice Program.' These four programs each

aim to develop skills, competencies, and motivate people so as to enhance their performance and productivity.

One of the major domains of Human Resource Management (HRM) is Training and Development. The aim is to train and retain employees, that is, to keep talent in the organization. Managers need to pay attention to employee needs and keep them satisfied so that they do not seek employment elsewhere and leave the organization, after money and time has been spent training them. As you can see from the above, recruiting, training, developing, and retaining qualified UAE nationals remains a challenging task, which will only be accomplished through careful planning.

Sources: "UAE: Recent Developments," *Arab Law Quarterly* 11(1), 1996, pp. 50–68; K. Randeree and A. G. Chaudhry, 2007, "Leadership in project managed environments: Employee perceptions of leadership styles within infrastructure development in Dubai," *International Review of Business Research Papers* 3(4); The National Human Resource Development & Employment Authority, United Arab Emirates, www.tanmia.ae.

Performance Evaluation

> ## Picture This
>
> You are taking a course on a pass–fail basis. Would you study differently or put in more effort for a course graded on a pass–fail basis than you would for one awarded letter grades from A to F?

> 4   *Describe the purposes of performance evaluation and list the various methods.*

Your answer illustrates how performance evaluation systems influence behavior. Major determinants of your in-class behavior and out-of-class studying effort in college are the criteria and techniques your instructor uses to evaluate your performance. What applies in the college context also applies to employees at work. In this section, we look at how the choice of a performance evaluation system and the way it's administered can be important to influence employee behavior in any culture.

Some research has suggested that 91 percent of companies worldwide conduct performance appraisals.[21] Interestingly, an online poll of performance appraisal in the Middle East conducted between October 27, 2008 and January 4, 2009 by Bayt.com found that 28 percent of employees do not receive an evaluation. The regional manager of Bayt.com, Amer Zureikat said:[22]

> It is well known that performance appraisals are an intrinsic part of employee development, and in the Middle East's dynamic work places, employers can gain a competitive edge by nurturing and mentoring their staff, through regular discussions and meetings about their progress. This kind of data can be very useful for HR professionals and industry stakeholders by serving as a relevant indicator of what employees really think about something as simple as an appraisal.

Purposes of Performance Evaluation

Performance evaluation serves a number of purposes.[23] One purpose is to help management make general *human resource decisions*. Evaluations provide input into important decisions such as promotions, transfers, and terminations. Evaluations also *identify training and development needs*. They identify employee skills and competencies that are currently inadequate but for which remedial programs can be developed. Evaluations also fulfill the purpose of *providing feedback to employees* on how the organization views their performance. Furthermore, performance evaluations are the *basis for reward allocations*. Decisions as to who gets merit pay increases based on their output and other rewards are frequently determined by performance evaluations.

Performance evaluation has five main steps:[24]

1. Define expected levels of performance
2. Define how outcomes will be measured
3. Measure actual outcomes
4. Give rewards based on the outcomes
5. Redefine future objectives and activities

Each of these steps of performance evaluation is valuable and clearly relevant to human resource management decisions, as we mentioned above. However, our interest is in organizational behavior and thus we shall emphasize performance evaluation as a mechanism for providing feedback and as a determinant of reward allocations.

What Do We Evaluate?

The criteria that management chooses to evaluate when appraising employee performance will have a major influence on what employees do. The three most popular sets of criteria are individual task outcomes, behaviors, and traits.

Individual Task Outcomes   If management is not concerned only with how a job is accomplished, then employees should be evaluated on task outcomes and final results. For example, a plant manager could be judged on criteria such as quantity produced and cost per unit of production. Similarly, a salesperson could be assessed on overall sales volume, dollar increase in sales, and number of new accounts established.

> ### Picture This
> You are a member of a group that is working on an end-of-semester project. The group also includes Ameena, Rashid, and Nafez. However, Rashid is known for his lack of cooperation. You are worried about the final grade. What do you do?

Behaviors   We may evaluate a group's performance but have difficulty distinguishing clearly the contribution of each group member. In such instances, it's not unusual for management to evaluate the employees' behavior. Remember the examples given in the previous section. Behaviors of a plant manager that could be used for performance evaluation might include promptness in submitting monthly reports or the leadership style the manager exhibits. Relevant salesperson behaviors could be the average number of contact calls made per day or sick days used per year.

Traits   The weakest set of criteria, yet one that is still widely used by organizations, is individual traits.[25] We say they're weaker than either task outcomes or behaviors because they're farthest removed from the actual performance of the job itself. Traits such as having a good attitude, showing confidence, being

General Electric Company (GE) evaluates the performance of its corporate managers, including the group of top executives shown here, on five 'growth traits.' The traits are inclusiveness, imagination/ courage, expertise, external focus, and clear thinking/decisiveness. By evaluating its 5,000 top managers on these traits, GE believes it will generate corporate leaders who will help the company achieve its goal of building the revenue growth of its business units that operate throughout the world.

dependable, looking busy, or possessing a wealth of experience may or may not be highly correlated with positive task outcomes, but such traits are frequently used as criteria for assessing an employee's level of performance.

Who Should Do the Evaluating?

Who should evaluate an employee's performance? By tradition, the task has fallen on the manager, on the grounds that managers are held responsible for their employees' performance. But others may actually be able to do the job better.

An employee's immediate superior may not be the most reliable judge of that employee's performance. Thus, in an increasing number of cases, peers and even subordinates are being asked to participate in the performance evaluation process. Also, increasingly, employees are participating in their own performance evaluation. In many situations it is advisable to use multiple sources of ratings. By averaging across raters, we can obtain a more reliable, unbiased, and accurate performance evaluation. Needless to say, each one of these methods of evaluation can have drawbacks.

A study conducted in the United Arab Emirates found that employees tend to give themselves a much higher rating in comparison than that given by their supervisors. Possible reasons for this are:[26]

1. Even though they are weak, employees overrate themselves because they know that rewards are connected to higher performance.
2. The Arab culture contributes greatly to the way employees measure their own performance.
3. Employees know that even though they are members of a group, they will only be evaluated based on their individual performance. Thus, employees increase their performance evaluation to reflect the individual motivation system rather than the group motivation system that is one of the basic pillars of Arabic management.

What Do You Think?

How honest would you be if you were asked to evaluate yourself? Do you know your strengths and weaknesses?

The latest approach to performance evaluation is the use of 360-degree evaluations.[27] It provides for performance feedback from the full circle of daily contacts that an employee might have and these are shown in Figure 15-2. By relying on feedback from coworkers, customers, and subordinates, organizations hope to give everyone more of a sense of participation in the review process and gain more accurate readings on employee performance.

Methods of Performance Evaluation

The previous sections explained *what* we evaluate and *who* should do the evaluating. Now we ask: *How* do we evaluate an employee's performance? That is, what are the specific techniques for evaluation?

Written Essays   Probably the simplest method of evaluation is to write a narrative describing an employee's strengths, weaknesses, past performance, potential, and suggestions for improvement. But in this method a good or bad appraisal may be determined as much by the evaluator's writing skill as by the employee's actual level of performance.

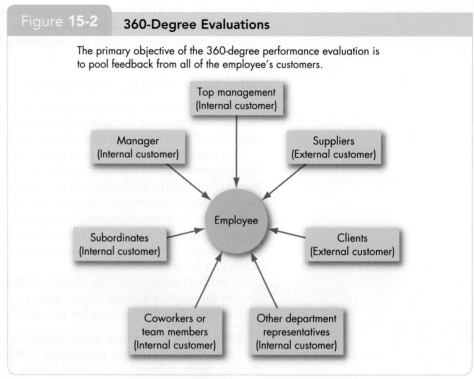

Figure 15-2   360-Degree Evaluations

The primary objective of the 360-degree performance evaluation is to pool feedback from all of the employee's customers.

- Top management (Internal customer)
- Manager (Internal customer)
- Suppliers (External customer)
- Employee
- Subordinates (Internal customer)
- Clients (External customer)
- Coworkers or team members (Internal customer)
- Other department representatives (Internal customer)

Source: Adapted from *Personnel Journal*, November 1994, p. 100.

Critical Incidents   These focus the evaluator's attention on the behaviors that are important in making the difference between completing a job effectively and ineffectively. A list of **critical incidents** provides a rich set of examples from which the employee can be shown the behaviors that are desirable and those that need improvement.

Graphic Rating Scales   One of the oldest and most popular methods of evaluation is a **graphic rating scale**. A set of performance factors, such as quantity and quality of work, depth of knowledge, cooperation, attendance, and initiative, is listed. The evaluator then goes down the list and rates each on incremental scales. The scales may specify five points, so a factor such as *job knowledge* might be rated 1 (poorly informed about work duties) to 5 (has complete mastery of all phases of the job).

Behaviorally Anchored Rating Scales   Behaviorally anchored rating scales **(BARS)** combine major elements from the critical incident and graphic rating scale approaches: The appraiser rates the employees based on items along a continuum, but the points are examples of actual behavior on the given job rather than general descriptions or traits. Examples of job-related behavior and performance dimensions are found by asking participants to give specific illustrations of effective and ineffective behavior regarding each performance dimension.

Forced Comparisons   Forced comparisons evaluate one individual's performance against the performance of another or others and we can use group order ranking or individual ranking.

The **group order ranking** requires the evaluator to place employees into a particular classification, such as top ten or top twenty. This method is often used in recommending students to graduate schools. Evaluators are asked whether the student ranks in the top 5 percent of the class, the next 5 percent,

Critical incidents

A way of evaluating the behaviors that are key in making the difference between executing a job effectively and executing it ineffectively.

Graphic rating scales

An evaluation method in which the evaluator rates performance factors on an incremental scale.

Behaviorally anchored rating scales (BARS)

Scales that combine major elements from the critical incident and graphic rating scale approaches: the appraiser rates the employees based on items along a continuum, but the points are examples of actual behavior on the given job rather than general descriptions or traits.

Group order ranking

An evaluation method that places employees into a particular classification, such as quartiles.

Individual ranking

An evaluation method that rank-orders employees from best to worst.

the next 15 percent, and so forth. But in this type of performance appraisal, managers deal with all their subordinates. Therefore, if a rater has 20 employees, only 4 can be in the top fifth and, of course, 4 must also be relegated to the bottom fifth. The **individual ranking** approach rank-orders employees from best to worst. If the manager is required to appraise 30 employees, this approach assumes that the difference between the first and second employee is the same as that between the twenty-first and twenty-second. The result is a clear ordering of employees, from the highest performer down to the lowest.

Providing Performance Feedback

For many managers, few activities are more unpleasant than providing performance feedback to employees.[28] In fact, unless pressured by organizational policies and controls, managers are likely to ignore this responsibility.[29]

Why the reluctance to give performance feedback? There seem to be at least three reasons. First, managers are often uncomfortable discussing performance weaknesses directly with employees. Even though almost every employee could stand to improve in some areas, managers fear a confrontation when presenting negative feedback.

Second, many employees tend to become defensive when their weaknesses are pointed out. Instead of accepting the feedback as constructive and a basis for improving performance, some employees challenge the evaluation by criticizing the manager or redirecting blame to someone else.

Finally, employees tend to have an inflated assessment of their own performance. Statistically speaking, half of all employees must be below-average performers. But the evidence indicates that the average employee's estimate of his or her own performance level generally falls around the 75th percentile.[30] So even when managers are providing good news, employees are likely to perceive it as not good enough.

Once the performance evaluation is conducted, the intention is that the performance gap will be minimized and corrected.[31] In addition, communication channels will improve and trust will increase not only in the system but also in the management. As a result, it is likely that overall productivity will be enhanced.

In sum, the solution to the performance feedback problem is not to ignore it, but to confront it and train managers to conduct constructive feedback sessions with employee involvement.

Suggestions for Improving Performance Evaluations

The performance evaluation process is not without problems. For instance, evaluators can unconsciously overrate evaluations (positive tolerance), underrate performance (negative tolerance), or allow the assessment of one characteristic to influence the assessment of others (the halo error). Some appraisers bias their evaluations by unconsciously favoring people who have qualities and traits similar to their own (the similarity error). And, of course, some evaluators see the evaluation process as a political opportunity to overtly reward or punish employees they like or dislike. Although there are no *guarantees*, for accurate performance evaluations, the following suggestions can help to make the process more objective and fair.

Use Multiple Evaluators   As the number of evaluators increases, the probability of more accurate information increases. For example, if an employee has had 10 supervisors, 9 have rated her excellent and 1 poor, we can safely discount the one poor evaluation.

Evaluate Selectively   Appraisers should evaluate only in areas in which they have some expertise.[32] In general, appraisers should be as close as possible to the individual being evaluated. Conversely, the more levels that separate the evaluator and the person being evaluated, the less opportunity the evaluator has to observe the individual's behavior and, not surprisingly, the greater the possibility for inaccuracies.

Train Evaluators   If you can't *find* good evaluators, the alternative is to *make* good evaluators. There is substantial evidence that training evaluators can make them more accurate raters.[33]

Provide Employees with Due Process   The concept of *due process* can be applied to appraisals to increase the perception that employees are being treated fairly.[34] Three features characterize due process systems: (1) Individuals are provided with adequate notice of what is expected of them; (2) all evidence relevant to a proposed violation is given in a fair hearing so the individuals affected can respond; and (3) the final decision is based on the evidence and free of bias.

When due process has been part of the evaluation system, employees report positive reactions to the appraisal process, perceive the evaluation results as more accurate, and express increased intent to remain with the organization.

To summarise, the studies on performance appraisal referred to in this section suggest that organizations in the UAE and other parts of the Arab world should change their ways and encourage open performance appraisals. Evaluations should be discussed with employees so that they understand why they are rewarded and why they may be punished. However, you should also be aware that certain ideologies in the Arab world may not encourage people to follow ideas of fairness, equality, and ethics in management.

Supervisors in all cultures must monitor the outcomes of their employees on a regular basis. In doing so, they will give employees a feeling of being involved, which will ultimately lead to greater work commitment and loyalty.

Managing Diversity in Organizations

 **5** *Explain how diversity can be managed in organizations.*

David Morris and his father, Saul, started Habitat International in 1981. The company manufactures a grass-like indoor/outdoor carpet. From the beginning, the Morrises hired refugees from Cambodia, Bosnia, and Laos, many of whom didn't speak English. But when a social-service worker suggested in 1984 that the company hire mentally challenged people, Saul was concerned. Hiring someone with a condition such as Down's syndrome seemed too risky. But David thought otherwise and convinced his dad into giving it a try.[35]

The first group of eight mentally disabled workers came in with their job coach from the social-services agency and went straight to work packing mats in boxes. Two weeks later, says Saul, employees were coming to him and wondering why the company couldn't "hire more people like this, who care, do their work with pride, and smile?"

Today, 75 percent of Habitat's employees have some kind of disability. People with schizophrenia, for instance, are driving forklifts next to employees with autism or cerebral palsy. Meanwhile, the Morris father-and-son team is doing good things both for these people and for themselves. The disabled employees have enhanced self-esteem and are now self-sufficient enough to be off government aid, and the Morrises enjoy the benefits of a dedicated, hard-working labor force. "We have practically zero absenteeism and very little turnover," says David.

Habitat International illustrates the role of employee selection in increasing diversity. But effective diversity programs go well beyond merely hiring a diverse workforce. They also include managing work–life conflicts and providing diversity training. These seem to be common characteristics among major organizations that have developed reputations as diversity leaders—including Avon, McDonald's, PepsiCo, Coca-Cola, and Xerox.[36]

The concept of globalization has changed the lives of people from all around the world and thus, today we live in a global village. Accordingly, people must be more open and flexible to 'adopt and adapt' to new ideas, new people, new methods of doing things and therefore, embrace diversity.

Diversity can be defined in terms of acknowledging, understanding, accepting, valuing, and observing differences between people in relation to their age, class, ethnicity, gender, physical and mental ability, race, sexual orientation, and spiritual practices.[37] Accordingly, any country around the world is liable to face problems when it comes to any of these diversity-related issues. The Arab world is no exception. In fact, the Arab world countries experience great challenges with respect to these differences, as we will see later.

Diversity has nothing to do with how we look at ourselves but is about how we perceive others, and human nature tells us that people find difficulty accepting 'the other.' The major challenges of diversity are the language barrier, the effectiveness of interpersonal communication, acceptability of others and the resistance to change, the last of which will be considered in the next chapter.

There are also many advantages to diversity. Employment approaches that encourage diversity include the ability to value differences of opinion, to generate more ideas, to increase productivity, to promote innovation and creativity, and to overcome bias and discrimination.

Diversity training or awareness includes cultural programs that improve relationships. The training should focus on developing interpersonal skills such as active listening and appreciating the differences in the cultural, religious, and ethnic population. For example, the American Arab Chamber of Commerce (AACC) conducts Diversity Training programs that enlighten individuals and companies about cultural differences and how we can learn to tolerate them for more effective business interaction.

Remember, diversity is a 'way of thinking.' Once we are able to establish this mindset and promote awareness, then it should be much easier to accept the differences between people.

> ## What Do You Think?
>
> *What is your standpoint with respect to diversity? Are you a flexible person? Or do you have difficulty accepting others?*

Work–Life Conflicts

6 Show how managers can improve their employees' work–life balance.

We introduced work–life balance in Chapter 1, and discussed the forces that confuse the lines between work life and personal life and the ways in which we can overcome the barriers that may interfere with the lines.

Work–life conflicts grabbed management's attention in the 1980s, largely as a result of the growing number of women with dependent children entering the workforce. In response, most major organizations took actions to make their workplaces more family friendly.[38] They introduced programs such as on-site child care, summer day camps, flextime, job sharing, telecommuting, and part-time employment. In the Arab world, National Child Care Centers is an initiative set up to provide nurseries for mothers working in Dubai government departments and organizations.[39] Both the community and the workplace realized that there was an urgent need to support working mothers; people in Arab countries have strong family ties, and if the working mother is worried about her child, her performance and productivity may decrease. Thus, the presence of such professional and attractive nurseries in Dubai is a relief for mothers *and* benefits the organization.

But organizations quickly realized that work–life conflicts were not experienced only by female employees with children. Male workers and women without children were also facing this problem. Heavy workloads and increased travel demands, for instance, were making it increasingly hard for a wide range of employees to meet both work and personal responsibilities. A study by Harvard University in the US found that 82 percent of men between the ages of 20 and 39 said a 'family-friendly' schedule was their most important job criterion.[40]

Certain paths contribute to the ways in which people see their lives and how they determine the outcomes of their performance. When we talk about work–life balance, we refer to healthy means of enriching our lives both at work and at home. In other words, we should not sacrifice one for the other but try to find an equilibrium between the two. Five such balanced paths and the characteristics of each path are shown below.[41] It's probably quite clear how they apply to work, but it is also useful to think about them in relation to home life. For example, a person with a strong home life will often have a rich family history, strong values and a strong sense of purpose for their life as part of a family.

1. Mission, Values, and Pride – noble purpose; rich history; strong values; group cohesion.
2. Process and Metrics – clear measures and standards; focused processes; performance transparency; collaborative and collective effort.
3. Entrepreneurial Spirit – high-earning opportunity; strong ownership interests; personal risk.

4. Individual Achievement – lots of opportunity; individuals given freedom to act; focus on individual performance; performance-based advancement; healthy competitiveness.
5. Recognition and Celebration – widespread recognition/reward; lots of special events; visible high energy; social interaction and fun.

The above-mentioned paths can act as guidelines for organizations to reduce work–life conflicts.

In the Arab world, work–life conflict mostly applies to women because they experience more difficulty when trying to juggle their responsibilities in both the home and the workplace. As we mentioned above, in many circumstances, females may be largely responsible for their jobs, households, and children, and this can cause great stress (we will discuss the issue of stress in the next chapter). Many Arab countries have hosted international conferences on this topic. For example, the annual Arab Women Leadership Forum of 2010 revolved around the theme "Women's Leadership in Organizations: Towards New Conceptions of Work–Life Balance." The Forum focused on addressing all conflicts that both men and women face in the workplace and, put simply, 'making it work at work.'

Many of these work–life initiatives are illustrated below in Table 15-1.

TABLE 15-1   Work–Life Initiatives

Strategy	Program or Policy
Time-based strategies	Flextime
	Job sharing
	Part-time work
	Leave for new parents
	Telecommuting
	Closing plants/offices for special occasions
Information-based strategies	Intranet work–life website
	Relocation assistance
	Eldercare resources
Money-based strategies	Vouchers for child care
	Flexible benefits
	Adoption assistance
	Discounts for child-care tuition
	Leave with pay
Direct services	On-site child care
	Emergency back-up care
	On-site health/beauty services
	Concierge services
	Takeout dinners
Culture-change strategies	Training for managers to help employees deal with work–life conflicts
	Tie manager pay to employee satisfaction
	Focus on employees' actual performance, not 'face time'

Sources: Based on C. A. Thompson, "Managing the Work–Life Balance Act: An Introductory Exercise," *Journal of Management Education,* April 2002, p. 210; and R. Levering and M. Maskowitz, "The Best in the Worst of Times," *Fortune,* February 4, 2002, pp. 60–90.

Organizations are modifying their workplaces to accommodate the varied needs of a diverse workforce. This includes providing a wide range of scheduling options and benefits that allow employees more flexibility at work and permit them to better balance or integrate their work and personal lives.

Recent research on work–life conflicts has provided new insights for managers into what works and when. For instance, evidence indicates that time pressures aren't the primary problem underlying work–life conflicts.[42] People are worrying about personal problems at work and thinking about work problems at home. So dad may physically make it home in time for dinner, but his mind is elsewhere while he's at the dinner table. This suggests that organizations should spend less effort helping employees with time-management issues and more helping them clearly segment their lives. Keeping workloads reasonable, reducing work-related travel, and offering on-site quality child care are examples of practices that can help in this effort.

Diversity Training

The focus of most diversity programs is training. For instance, a relatively recent survey found that 93 percent of large corporations in the US with diversity initiatives used training as part of their programs.[43] Diversity training programs are generally intended to provide a means for increasing awareness and examining stereotypes. Participants learn to value individual differences, increase their cross-cultural understanding, and confront stereotypes.[44]

One piece of research studied the potential conflict caused by diversity between Arab locals and expatriates in the workplace. The survey first identified the key issues of division and social cohesion. It then showed how these factors may interact, and looked at how the negative impact of cultural difference can be neutralized to acheive improved working relations. This pioneer study of Arab–expatriate work relations in a public sector organization in Oman shows how the organization developed good working relations and maintained a positive and high-performing organizational climate.[45]

Having looked at all the issues related to HR practices, training, performance appraisals and managing diversity in an organization, we should now have a clearer picture of how employee relations are determined in organizations in the Arab world.

Global Implications

> 7 *Show how a global context affects human resource management.*

Many of the human resource policies and practices discussed in this chapter have to be modified to reflect cultural differences.[46] To illustrate this point, let's briefly look at the universality of selection practices and the importance of performance evaluation in different cultures.

Selection

A recent study of 300 large organizations in 22 countries demonstrated that selection practices differ by country.[47] A few common procedures were found. For instance, the use of educational qualifications in screening candidates seems to be a universal practice. For the most part, however, different countries tend to emphasize different selection techniques.

This study, when combined with earlier research, tells us that there are no universal selection practices. Moreover, global firms that attempt to implement

Executives of ImageNet Company (in red jackets), one of Japan's top internet clothing retailers, conducted job interviews atop Mount Fuji, Japan's highest mountain. Of the 20 candidates who applied for one of four job openings, 11 succeeded in reaching the summit of the 12,388-foot mountain for the interview. ImageNet staged the unique interview setting to identify candidates who are highly motivated, determined to succeed, and prepared for unusual challenges. In many other nations this type of interview would contravene equal employment opportunity laws.

standardized worldwide selection practices can expect to face considerable resistance from local managers. Policies and practices need to be modified to reflect culture-based norms and social values, as well as legal and economic differences.

Performance Evaluation

We've looked at the role performance evaluation plays in motivating and affecting behavior. We must be careful, however, in generalizing across cultures. Why? Because many cultures are not particularly concerned with performance appraisal as we saw in this chapter when we focused on performance appraisals in organizations in the Middle East.

Let's look at performance evaluation in the context of four cultural dimensions: individualism/collectivism, a person's relationship to the environment, time orientation, and focus of responsibility.

Individual-oriented cultures emphasize formal performance evaluation systems more than informal systems. On the other hand, the collectivist cultures that dominate the Arab world, Asia and much of Latin America are characterized by more informal systems—downplaying formal feedback and disconnecting reward allocations from performance ratings.

In Arab countries, performance evaluations are not often used. It is extremely urgent to make HR practitioners in the Arab world realize that performance appraisals are an important way of improving employee performance and retention. The online poll (October, 2008–January, 2009) conducted by Bayt.com that we mentioned in the section about performance evaluation gives surprising results. Even though 71 percent of all workers received either quarterly, half-yearly or yearly performance appraisals, 50 percent stated that they had no feedback, whereas 14 percent said that they had informal meetings with their supervisors but 'that was it.'

Equally important was that 43 percent felt that the appraisals served no purpose, compared with 35 percent who felt that their organization's system was effective, while 22 percent strongly believed that significant changes needed to be made in the process.

Furthermore, some countries, such as the United States, have a short-term time orientation. Performance evaluations are likely to be frequent in such a culture—at least once a year. In Japan, however, where people hold a long-term time frame, performance appraisals may occur only every 5 or 10 years.

Summary and Implications for Managers

An organization's human resource policies and practices represent important forces for shaping employee behavior and attitudes. In this chapter, we specifically discussed the influence of selection practices, training and development programs, performance evaluation systems, diversity, and work–life balance initiatives.

Selection Practices   An organization's selection practices will determine who gets hired. If properly designed, they will identify competent candidates and accurately match them to the job and the organization. The use of the proper selection devices will increase the probability that the right person will be chosen to fill a position.

Some organizations fail to design a selection system that will increase the likelihood of achieving the right person–job fit. When hiring errors are made, the chosen candidate's performance may be less than satisfactory and training may be necessary to improve the candidate's skills. At worst, the candidate will prove unacceptable, and the firm will need to find a replacement. Similarly, when the selection process results in the hiring of less-qualified candidates or individuals who don't fit into the organization, those chosen are likely to feel anxious, tense, and uncomfortable. This, in turn, is likely to increase dissatisfaction with the job.

Training and Development Programs   Training programs can affect work behavior in two ways. The most obvious is by directly improving the skills necessary for the employee to successfully complete the job. An increase in ability improves the employee's potential to perform at a higher level. Of course, whether that potential becomes realized is largely an issue of motivation.

A second benefit of training is that it increases an employee's self-efficacy. Employees with high self-efficacy have strong expectations about their abilities to perform successfully in new situations. They're confident and expect to be successful.

Performance Evaluation   A major goal of performance evaluation is to assess an individual's performance accurately as a basis for making reward allocation decisions. If the performance evaluation process emphasizes the wrong criteria or inaccurately appraises actual job performance, employees will be over-rewarded or under-rewarded. Specifically, performance and satisfaction are increased when the evaluation is based on behavioral, results-oriented criteria, when career issues as well as performance issues are discussed, and when the employee has an opportunity to participate in the evaluation.

Diversity and Work–Life Balance   Diversity can be defined in terms of acknowledging, understanding, accepting, valuing, and observing differences between people in relation to their age, class, ethnicity, gender, physical and mental ability, race, sexual orientation, and spiritual practices. Diversity training or awareness includes cultural programs that improve relationships. The training should focus on developing interpersonal skills such as active listening and appreciating the differences in the cultural, religious, and ethnic population.

Work–life conflict mostly applies to women, but can affect anyone who has to juggle their responsibilities in both the home and the workplace. A number of different strategies are available to help people to find a suitable balance.

In sum, an organization's human resource policies and practices represent important forces for shaping employee behavior and attitudes.

Point >< Counterpoint

TELECOMMUTING MAKES GOOD BUSINESS SENSE

More and more companies are turning to flexible work schedules, for good reasons.

The first and most obvious reason is changes in how, and where, work is done. Today's virtual organizations realize that where people work is becoming less and less important.

Second, organizations are realizing that offering telecommuting and other flexible schedules allows them to attract and retain the best talent. Third, research shows that while managers are a main source of opposition to telework, when managers are exposed to telecommuting, they become much more positive in their attitudes toward it.

There are too many arguments in favor of telecommuting and flexible schedules for organizations to ignore. Nearly half of all organizations now offer flexible schedules; those that do are ahead of the curve.

There are other managers, however, who don't view tele-commuters very positively. When surveyed, more than two-thirds (68 percent) of employees thought that working at home made them more productive. However, when managers were surveyed, more than one-third (37 percent) thought that, if allowed to work at home, staff would use their so-called working hours for personal activities.

The 'Telecommuting in the Middle East Workplace' October/November online poll series conducted by Bayt.com sought to understand from employees whether they believe telecommuting is beneficial in the Middle East, what the perceived advantages of telecommuting are, and how widespread its use is in the region.

Forty percent of respondents agreed that self-disciplined employees with excellent performance records would be able to telecommute, while another 18 percent agreed that employees who do not have to interact face-to-face with customers or colleagues would suit telecommuting. A further 11 percent said that telecommuting would be appropriate for working mothers, while another 24 percent of respondents said that telecommuting would be ideal for all three of these groups.[48]

Of course, employees want flexible schedules and may rationalize their preferences by arguing that it helps them get more done. But a lot of managers suspect that they know better—that while some of 'working at home' does involve work, another part of it involves 'wasting time' doing non-work stuff like chores, personal or family activities, and so on.

Questions for Review

1 What is human resource management?

2 What is the recruitment process and its sources?

3 What is selection and what are the most useful initial selection methods?

4 How can training and development methods affect organizations?

5 What are the main purposes of performance evaluation?

6 How can managers improve work–life balance?

7 How can diversity be managed in organizations?

8 How is human resource management affected by a global context?

Discussion Exercise

Research has identified seven performance dimensions to the college instructor's job: (1) instructor knowledge, (2) testing procedures, (3) student–teacher relations, (4) organizational skills, (5) communication skills, (6) subject relevance, and (7) utility of assignments.

Discuss these performance dimensions with your instructor. Are there other dimensions that you feel are also important for evaluating the performance of college instructors?

Ethical Considerations

Does a résumé have to be 100 percent truthful? Apparently, a lot of people don't think so. Studies have found that nearly half of all résumés contain at least one lie.[49] To help clarify your ethical views on this issue, consider the following three situations and answer the questions for each.

1. Talal left a job for which his title was 'credit clerk.' When looking for a new job, he lists his previous title as 'credit analyst.' He thinks it sounds more impressive. Is this 'retitling' of a former job wrong? Why or why not?

2. About eight years ago, Mounira took nine months off between jobs to travel overseas. Afraid that people might consider her unstable or lacking in career

motivation, she put down on her résumé that she was engaged in 'independent consulting activities' during the period. Was she wrong? How else could she have described this time period on her résumé?

3. Omar is the 46-year-old CEO of a prominent company. He enrolled in a college 20 years ago, but he never got a degree. Just nine months after he was appointed CEO, a local newspaper reported that he had lied on his résumé. His résumé indicated that he had a bachelor's degree in psychology, but neither he nor the college can produce any evidence of that. Should his contract be terminated? If yes, why, and if not, what should his employer do about Omar's missing credentials?

Source: Based on M. Conlin, "You Are What You Post," *BusinessWeek*, March 27, 2006, pp. 52–53.

Critical Analysis

SO7I WA SARI3

Monique Bassila Zaarour, a registered dietitian and McGill graduate, has over 18 years of experience in the field of dietetics and established So7i Wa Sari3 (SWS) in 2008.

SWS is a successful chain of diet clinics all over Lebanon, employing a group of experienced and well-trained dietitians who have followed an intensive training program with Monique. The company has developed an interactive website where professional experience with diet and food is shared, and the professional dietitians also prepare educational wellness days for schools and companies, where students and employees are instructed about healthy eating at school and work.

The employee selection process at SWS is one of ultimate importance. Monique insists on ensuring a proper 'fit' is established between the person and the job. Applications are very carefully screened and narrowed down to a shortlist. Thereafter, dietitians on the shortlist are interviewed by Monique and the head dietitian.

Successful applicants then undergo a series of assessment tests. These include a 3-hour written clinical exam, a PowerPoint presentation, oral interaction on frequently asked questions, and consultation role play.

If they pass the exams, the new recruits start training and are provided with a detailed and rigorous two-month training program. There are various issues that these recruits must become aware of; for instance, a thorough comprehension of the So7i Wa Sari3 dietitian manual is required. Meticulous readings and interpretations of the So7i Wa Sari3 diet sheets is also crucial.

The new recruits then experience an observation rotation with assistants from all clinics. This includes answering the phone, checking missed calls, preparing clients' files and sheets, preparing the dietitian's daily schedule, taking anthropometric measurements, doing fat tests and blood pressure tests arranging appointments and scheduling, selling SWS products (membership, cookbook, elliptical lunchbox etc.), sending clients SMSs, using diet program software, reporting results and progress, cash handling, and archiving. The recruit eventually replaces the assistants once they have acquired all the necessary information and competencies.

Finally, the new dietitian will start doing first and follow-up consultations in all clinics under the supervision of a dietitian. After successful completion of the training, reviews and evaluation feedback are provided.

By the end of the training and orientation period, the recruited dietitian should be qualified to manage an SWS clinic and assistant, give consultations and meet the clinic's monthly sales targets. They should also be able to answer Facebook fan questions. Most importantly, the recruit must meet with the head dietitian at least twice a month to sign and evaluate client files and discuss clinical cases. At this point, the recruited dietician will also start attending the monthly general meeting with Monique and other dietitians, where they will attend presentations and discuss cases, SWS clinics issues, and sales.

Questions

1. How does SWS ensure that a proper 'fit' is established between the person and the job?

2. This chapter discusses both substantive and contingent selection. Which of these does SWS focus on?

3. Given the information you have about SWS, do you believe that the recruits of SWS receive enough training? Explain your answer.

Research Exercise

Do your own research and find a case study or incident that talks about any of the various topics we have discussed in this chapter about HR practices and policies. Make sure that you find some information that is relevant to any of the Arab world countries and their HR practices. Discuss with your classmates.

Part 5 Organization Dynamics

LEARNING OBJECTIVES

This chapter will enable you to:

1 Identify forces that act as stimulants to change and contrast planned and unplanned change.

2 List the sources for resistance to change.

3 Compare the four main approaches to managing organizational change.

4 Demonstrate two ways of creating a culture for change.

5 Define *stress* and identify its potential sources.

6 Understand Emotional Intelligence.

7 Identify the consequences of stress.

8 Contrast the individual and organizational approaches to managing stress.

9 Explain global differences in organizational change and work stress.

Organizational Change and Stress Management

16

Change is a door that can only be opened from the inside.

—Terry Neil

'A Crisis is a Terrible Thing to Waste'

Richard Clark doesn't have an Ivy League pedigree. He's not particularly charismatic. It took him more than 30 takes to tape a short commercial advertisement. 'Low key' might be the positive way to describe his personality.

Yet, Clark is CEO of one of America's largest companies.

We must be writing about Clark here to tell the story of someone who's led his company to greatness against the odds, right? Well, not really.

Financially, the company Richard Clark leads has been a bit of a dog. Its stock price trades at 20 percent below its level four years ago and less than *half* what it was in 2000. Its profits have declined for three years in a row. And the company has been the target of 27,000 claims and more than 9,200 active lawsuits, all for a single product that has allegedly killed people.

Richard Clark is CEO of Merck, one of the largest drug companies in the world, and also one of the most troubled companies you'll find listed among the Fortune 500 (it was number 57 as of 2012). Clark is noteworthy not because he's leading a successful company but because he's leading a company that's fighting for its survival.

Any drug company is one launch away from instant success—think Viagra or Prozac—or financial ruin. Sometimes they're both, like Merck. When Merck launched the anti-arthritis drug Vioxx in 1999, it quickly rose to sales of US$2.5 billion per year. However,

problems with the drug soon became apparent, and lawsuits started to accumulate. In 2004, Merck pulled Vioxx from the market, and it now budgets US$1 billion per year to fight lawsuits against the product.

Clark's predecessor shrugged off Merck's problems. Not Clark. He's trying to make changes in the company that reach well beyond the Vioxx debacle. He argues to employees that without dramatic changes, Merck will not survive.

Clark's vision for transforming Merck includes streamlining the company—eliminating its hierarchical organizational structure, which he felt worked against innovation—and gathering more input from patients, doctors, and employees. He also set new goals for bringing drugs to market as well as establishing other markers of performance. Increased accountability is a big part of how Clark hopes to change the culture at Merck.

Many analysts have applauded his efforts. "At least we can measure whether the company is meeting its goals or not," said one industry analyst.

"It's very important for us to be able to respond and say, 'Here's our scorecard of how we're doing', vs. saying, 'Trust me," Clark says.

In addition to setting high aspirations, and transforming Merck's structure, Clark has also attacked the complacency that, he argues, has put the entire industry in a rut. "If you ever feel comfortable that your model is the right model, you end up where the industry is today," he says. "It's always going to be continuous improvement. We will never declare victory."

It's not clear whether Clark and Merck will be successful. But it is clear that Clark does not see the status quo as an option. "A crisis is a terrible thing to waste," says the CEO.

Sources: Based on "Is Merck's Medicine Working?" *BusinessWeek*, June 30, 2007, pp. 1–3; and K. McKay, "Merck CEO Sets Sights on Change," *USA Today*, February 27, 2006, pp. 1B, 2B.

This chapter is about change and stress. We describe environmental forces that require managers to implement comprehensive change programs. We also consider why people and organizations often resist change and how this resistance can be overcome. We review various processes for managing organizational change. We also discuss change issues for today's managers. Then we move to the topic of stress. We elaborate on the sources and consequences of stress. Finally, we conclude this chapter with a discussion of what individuals and organizations can do to better manage stress levels.

Before we dive into the subject of change, see how well you handle change by taking the following self-assessment.

HOW WELL DO I RESPOND TO TURBULENT CHANGE?

In the Self-Assessment Library (available online), take assessment III.C.1 (How Well Do I Respond to Turbulent Change?) and answer the following questions:

1. *How did you score? Are you surprised by your score?*

2. *During what time of your life have you experienced the most change? How did you deal with it? Would you handle these changes in the same way today? Why or why not?*

3. *Are there ways you might reduce your resistance to change?*

Forces for Change

1 Identify forces that act as stimulants to change and contrast planned and unplanned change.

No company today is in a stable environment. Even traditionally stable industries such as energy and utilities have witnessed—and will continue to experience—turbulent change. Companies that occupy a dominant market share in their industries must change, sometimes radically.

Thus, the dynamic and changing environments that organizations face today require adaptation, sometimes calling for deep and quick responses. 'Change or die!' is the cry among today's managers worldwide. Table 16-1 below summarizes six specific forces that are acting as drivers for change.

The *nature of the workforce* is the essence of this textbook, since we are dealing with organizational behavior. Almost every organization needs to adjust to a

TABLE 16-1 Forces for Change	
Force	**Examples**
Nature of the workforce	More cultural diversity
	Aging population
	Many new entrants with inadequate skills
Technology	Faster, cheaper, and more mobile computers
	Online music sharing
	Deciphering of the human genetic code
Economic shocks	Rise and fall of dot-com stocks
	2008 recession
	Record low interest rates
Competition	Global competitors
	Mergers and consolidations
	Growth of e-commerce
Social trends	Internet chat rooms
	Retirement of baby boomers
	Rise in discount and 'big box' retailers

multicultural environment. Demographic changes, immigration, and outsourcing have also affected the nature of the workforce.

Technology is changing jobs and organizations because as an organization adapts to one technological change, other technological challenges and opportunities appear.

Economic shocks have continued to impose changes on organizations. In recent years, for instance, new dot-com businesses have been created, turned tens of thousands of investors into overnight millionaires, then crashed, and opened the door for others to rise.

What Do You Think?

How well do you adapt to change?

Competition is changing. The global economy means that competitors are as likely to come from across the ocean as from accross town. Successful organizations will be the ones that can change in response to the competition, since they'll be capable of developing new products rapidly and getting them to market quickly. They will require a flexible and responsive workforce that can adapt to rapidly changing conditions.

Social trends don't remain constant. For instance, in contrast to just 15 years ago, people are meeting and sharing information in internet chat rooms; Baby Boomers have begun to retire; and consumers are increasingly doing their shopping at 'big box' retailers and online at websites like eBay.

This textbook argues strongly for the importance of seeing OB in a global context. The keyword here being global, which automatically means that there will be continuous change. 'Change is healthy' is true but easier said than implemented. It is required that changes happen to keep up with the world around us. Every culture needs change for improvement.

Planned Change

Fiat Group Automobiles hired an outsider as a change agent to return the ailing company to profitability. As Fiat's new CEO, Sergio Marchionne led a turnaround by changing a hierarchical, status-driven firm into a market-driven one. Marchionne reduced the layers of Fiat's management and fired 10 percent of its 20,000 white-collar employees. He improved relationships with union employees, reduced car-development time, and introduced new car designs. Marchionne is shown here with the redesigned version of the compact Fiat 500, which he hopes will be for the company what the iPod was for Apple.

Change
Making things different.

Planned change
Change activities that are intentional and goal oriented.

Change agents
People who act as catalysts and assume the responsibility for managing change activities.

A group of housekeeping employees who work for a small hotel confronted the owner: "It's very hard for most of us to maintain rigid 7-to-4 work hours," said their spokeswoman. "Each of us has significant family and personal responsibilities. And rigid hours don't work for us. We're going to begin looking for someplace else to work if you don't set up flexible work hours." The owner listened thoughtfully to the group and agreed to its request. The next day, the owner introduced a flextime plan for these employees.

A major automobile manufacturer spent several billion dollars to install state-of-the-art robotics. One area that would receive the new equipment was quality control. Sophisticated computer-controlled equipment would be put in place to significantly improve the company's ability to find and correct problems. Because the new equipment would change the jobs of the people working in the quality-control area, and because management anticipated considerable employee resistance to the new equipment, executives were developing a program to help people become familiar with the equipment and to deal with any anxieties they might be feeling.

Both of the previous scenarios are examples of **change**. That is, both are concerned with making things different. However, only the second scenario describes a **planned change**. Many changes in organizations are like the one that occurred at the hotel—they just happen. Some organizations treat all change as an accidental occurrence. We're concerned with change activities that are proactive and purposeful. In this chapter, we address change as an intentional, goal-oriented activity.

What are the goals of planned change? First, it seeks to improve the ability of the organization to adapt to changes in its environment. Second, it seeks to change employee behavior.

If an organization is to survive, it must respond to changes in its environment. Efforts to stimulate innovation, empower employees, and introduce work teams are examples of planned-change activities directed at responding to changes in the environment.

Because an organization's success or failure is essentially due to the things that its employees do or fail to do, planned change is also concerned with changing the behavior of individuals and groups within the organization.

Who in organizations is responsible for managing change activities? The answer is **change agents**.[1] Change agents can be managers or nonmanagers, current employees of the organization, newly hired employees, or outside consultants.

An example of a change agent is Lawrence Summers, former president of Harvard University.[2] When he accepted the presidency in 2001, Summers took decisions to shake up the institution by reshaping the undergraduate curriculum, proposing that the university be more directly engaged with problems in education and public health, and reorganizing to get more power in the president's office. His change efforts generated tremendous resistance, particularly among Harvard faculty. Finally, in 2006, when Summers made comments suggesting that women were less able to excel in science than men, the Harvard faculty revolted, and in a few weeks, Summers was forced to resign. In 2007, he was replaced with Drew Gilpin Faust, Harvard's first female president, who promised to be less aggressive in instituting changes.[3]

What Do You Think?

If the president of your university behaved in the same way as the president of Harvard, what do you think the reaction of all members of the university would be? Why do you think the people at Harvard reacted as they did?

Summers's case shows that many change agents fail because organizational members resist change. In the next section, we discuss resistance to change and what can be done about it.

Resistance to Change

2 *List the sources for resistance to change.*

One of the most well-documented findings from studies of individual and organizational behavior is that organizations and their members resist change. One recent study showed that even when employees are shown data that suggest they need to change, they hold onto whatever data they can find that suggests they are okay and don't need to change. Our egos are fragile, and we often see change as threatening.[4]

In some ways, resistance to change is positive. It provides a degree of stability and predictability to behavior. If there weren't some resistance, organizational behavior would take on the characteristics of chaos. Resistance to change can also be a source of functional conflict. For example, resistance to a reorganization plan or a change in a product line can stimulate a healthy debate over the merits of the idea and result in a better decision. But there is a definite disadvantage to resistance to change. It blocks adaptation and progress.

Resistance to change doesn't necessarily surface in standardized ways. Resistance can be overt, implicit, immediate, or delayed. It's easiest for management to deal with resistance when it is open and immediate. For instance, a change is proposed and employees quickly respond by voicing complaints, engaging in a work slowdown, threatening to go on strike, or the like. The greater challenge is managing resistance that is implicit or deferred. Implicit resistance efforts are more careful—loss of loyalty to the organization, loss of motivation to work, increased errors or mistakes, increased absenteeism due to 'sickness'—and hence are more difficult to recognize.

Box 16-1 summarizes major forces for resistance to change, categorized by individual and organizational sources. Individual sources of resistance are found in basic human characteristics such as perceptions, personalities, and needs, whereas organizational sources are found in the structural makeup of organizations themselves.

Before we move on to ways to overcome resistance to change, it's important to note that not all change is good. Research has shown that sometimes an emphasis on making speedy decisions can lead to bad decisions. Sometimes the line between resisting needed change and falling into a 'speed trap' is a fine one indeed.

Overcoming Resistance to Change

Seven tactics have been suggested for use by change agents in dealing with resistance to change.[5] Let's review them briefly.

BOX 16-1
Sources of Resistance to Change

Individual Sources

Habit—To cope with life's complexities, we rely on habits or programmed responses. But when confronted with change, this tendency to respond in our accustomed ways becomes a source of resistance.

Security—People with a high need for security are likely to resist change because it threatens their feelings of safety.

Economic factors—Changes in job tasks or established work routines can arouse economic fears if people are concerned that they won't be able to perform the new tasks or routines to their previous standards, especially when pay is closely tied to productivity.

Fear of the unknown—Change substitutes ambiguity and uncertainty for the unknown.

Selective information processing—Individuals are guilty of selectively processing information in order to keep their perceptions intact. They hear what they want to hear and they ignore information that challenges the world they've created.

Organizational Sources

Structural inertia—Organizations have built-in mechanisms—like their selection processes and formalized regulations—to produce stability. When an organization is confronted with change, this structural inertia acts as a counterbalance to sustain stability.

Limited focus of change—Organizations are made up of a number of interdependent subsystems. One can't be changed without affecting the others. So limited changes in subsystems tend to be nullified by the larger system.

Group inertia—Even if individuals want to change their behavior, group norms may act as a constraint.

Threat to expertise—Changes in organizational patterns may threaten the expertise of specialized groups.

Threat to established power relationships—Any redistribution of decision-making authority can threaten long-established power relationships within the organization.

Threat to established resource allocations—Groups in the organization that control sizable resources often see change as a threat. They tend to be content with the way things are.

Education and Communication   Resistance can be reduced through communicating with employees to help them see the logic of a change. Communication can reduce resistance on two levels. First, it fights the effects of misinformation and poor communication: If employees receive the full facts and get any misunderstandings cleared up, resistance should decrease. Second, communication can be helpful in 'selling' the need for change and explaining that there is an urgent necessity for change.

Participation   It's difficult for individuals to resist a change decision in which they participated. Prior to making a change, those opposed can be brought into the decision process. Assuming that the participants have the expertise to make a meaningful contribution, their involvement can reduce resistance, obtain commitment, and increase the quality of the change decision. However, this could be time-consuming.

Building Support and Commitment   Change agents can offer a range of supportive efforts to reduce resistance. Research on middle managers has shown that when managers or employees have low emotional commitment to change, they favor the status quo and resist it.[6]

Implementing Changes Fairly   Most people simply don't like change. But one way organizations can minimize the negative impact of change is to make sure the change is implemented fairly. Fairness becomes especially important when employees perceive an outcome as negative, so when implementing changes, it's crucial that organizations make sure employees see the reason for the change, and perceive that the changes are being implemented consistently and fairly.[7]

Manipulation and Cooptation   *Manipulation* refers to open influence attempts. Twisting and distorting facts to make them appear more attractive, withholding undesirable information, and creating false rumors to get employees to accept a change are all examples of manipulation. *Cooptation*, on the other hand, is a form of both manipulation and participation. It seeks to 'buy off' the leaders of a resistance group by giving them a key role in the change decision. The leaders' advice is asked for, not to seek a better decision, but to get their support.

Selecting People Who Accept Change   Research suggests that the ability to easily accept and adapt to change is related to personality—some people simply have more positive attitudes about change than others.[8] It appears that people who adjust best to change are those who are open to experience, take a positive attitude toward change, are willing to take risks, and are flexible in their behavior.

Coercion   Last on the list of tactics is coercion, that is, the application of direct threats or force on the resisters. Other examples of coercion are threats of transfer, loss of promotions, negative performance evaluations, and a poor letter of recommendation.

The Politics of Change

No discussion of resistance to change would be complete without a brief mention of the politics of change. Because change invariably threatens the status quo, it inherently implies political activity.[9]

Internal change agents are individuals high in the organization who have a lot to lose from change. They have, in fact, risen to their positions of authority by developing skills and behavioral patterns that are favored by the organization. Change is a threat to those skills and patterns. What if they are no longer the ones the organization values? Change creates the potential for others in the organization to gain power at their expense.

Politics suggests that change is more likely to come from outside change agents, employees who are new to the organization, or from managers removed from the main power structure. Managers who have spent their entire career with a single organization and eventually achieve a senior position in the hierarchy are often major obstacles to change.

Power struggles within the organization will determine the speed and quantity of change. You should expect that long-time career executives will be sources of resistance. This explains why boards of directors that recognize the imperative for the rapid introduction of radical change in their organizations frequently turn to outside candidates for new leadership.[10]

What Do You Think?

What is your position on internal politics and its effects on organizational behavior?

Approaches to Managing Organizational Change

3 *Compare the four main approaches to managing organizational change.*

Now let's turn to the approaches to managing change; the most significant are Lewin's classic three-step model of the change process, Kotter's eight-step plan, action research, and organizational development.

Lewin's Three-Step Model

Unfreezing

Changing to overcome the pressures of both individual resistance and group conformity.

Movement

A change process that transforms the organization from the status quo to a desired end state.

Refreezing

Stabilizing a change intervention by balancing driving and restraining forces.

Driving forces

Forces that direct behavior away from the status quo.

Restraining forces

Forces that hinder movement from the existing equilibrium.

Kurt Lewin argued that successful change in organizations in all cultures should follow three steps: **unfreezing** the status quo, **movement** to a desired end state, and **refreezing** the new change to make it permanent.[11] These steps are clearly shown in Figure 16.1.

The status quo or existing situation can be considered to be an equilibrium state. To move from this equilibrium, unfreezing is necessary. One way that this can be achieved is that the **driving forces**, which direct behavior away from the status quo, can be increased. Another way that this can be achieved is that the **restraining forces**, which stop movement from the existing equilibrium, can be decreased. A third alternative is to combine the first two approaches. Companies that have been successful in the past are likely to encounter restraining forces because people question the need for change.[12]

If resistance is extremely high, management may have to resort to both reducing resistance and increasing the attractiveness of the alternative if the unfreezing is to be successful.

Once the consolidation change has been implemented, if it is to be successful, the new situation needs to be refrozen so that it can be sustained over time. Unless this last step is taken, there is a very high chance that the change will be short-lived and that employees will attempt to revert to the previous equilibrium state. The objective of refreezing, then, is to stabilize the new situation by balancing the driving and restraining forces.

Kotter's Eight-Step Plan for Implementing Change

John Kotter of the Harvard Business School built on Lewin's three-step model to create another more detailed approach for implementing change.[13] Kotter began by listing common failures that managers make when trying to initiate change. These included the inability to create a sense of urgency about the need for change, failure to create a coalition for managing the change process, the absence of a vision for change and to effectively communicate that vision, not removing obstacles that could impede the achievement of the vision, failure to provide short-term and achievable goals, the tendency to declare victory too soon, and not anchoring the changes into the organization's culture.

Thereafter, Kotter established eight steps to overcome these problems, as listed in Box 16-2 are the fine-tuning of the list mentioned above.

Figure **16.1** **Lewin's Three-Step Change Model**

Unfreezing ▸ Movement ▸ Refreezing

BOX 16-2
Kotter's Eight-Step Plan for Implementing Change

1. Establish a sense of urgency by creating a compelling reason for why change is needed.

2. Form a coalition with enough power to lead the change.

3. Create a new vision to direct the change and strategies for achieving the vision.

4. Communicate the vision throughout the organization.

5. Empower others to act on the vision by removing barriers to change and encouraging risk taking and creative problem solving.

6. Plan for, create, and reward short-term 'wins' that move the organization toward the new vision.

7. Consolidate improvements, reassess changes, and make necessary adjustments in the new programs.

8. Reinforce the changes by demonstrating the relationship between new behaviors and organizational success.

Source: Based on J. P. Kotter, *Leading Change* (Boston: Harvard Business School Press, 1996).

Notice how Box 16-2 builds on Lewin's model. Kotter's first four steps essentially extrapolate on the 'unfreezing' stage. Steps 5 through 7 represent 'movement.' And the final step works on 'refreezing.' So Kotter's contribution lies in providing managers and change agents with a more detailed guide for successfully implementing change.

Action Research

Action research *refers to a third change process based on the systematic collection of data and then selection of a change action based on what the analyzed data indicate.*[14] The process of action research consists of five steps: diagnosis, analysis, feedback, action, and evaluation.

The change agent, often an outside consultant in action research, begins by gathering information about problems, concerns, and needed changes from members of the organization. This *diagnosis* is analogous to the physician's search to find specifically what is wrong with a patient. In action research, the change agent asks questions, interviews employees, reviews records, and listens to the concerns of employees.

Diagnosis is followed by *analysis*. What problems do people key in on? What patterns do these problems seem to take? The change agent then divides this information into primary concerns, problem areas, and possible actions.

People who will be involved in any change program must be actively involved in determining what the problem is and participating in creating the solution. So the third step—*feedback*—requires sharing with employees what has been found from steps one and two. The employees, with the help of the change agent, develop action plans for bringing about any needed change.

Now the *action* part of action research is set in motion. Accordingly, the employees and the change agent carry out the specific actions to correct the problems that have been identified.

The final step is *evaluation* of the action plan's effectiveness. Using the initial data gathered as a benchmark, any changes that follow can be compared and evaluated.

Action research provides at least two specific benefits for an organization. First, it is problem focused. The change agent objectively looks for problems, and the type of problem determines the type of change action. Second, because

Action research

A change process based on systematic collection of data and then selection of a change action based on what the analyzed data indicate.

action research so heavily involves employees in the process, resistance to change is reduced. In fact, once employees have actively participated in the feedback stage, the change process typically takes on a momentum of its own. The employees and groups that have been involved become an internal source of pressure to bring about the change.

Organizational Development

No discussion of managing change would be complete without including organizational development. **Organizational development (OD)** is not an easily defined concept. It is a collection of planned-change interventions built on humanistic-democratic values that seeks to improve organizational effectiveness and employee wellbeing.[15] This is exactly what The World Bank aimed to do for Lebanon.

OD values human and organizational growth, collaborative and participative processes, and a spirit of inquiry.[16] The change agent may be directive in OD; however, there is a strong emphasis on collaboration.

The following briefly identifies the values in most OD efforts:

1. *Respect for people.* Individuals are perceived as being responsible, conscientious, and caring. They should be treated with dignity and respect.
2. *Trust and support.* An effective and healthy organization is characterized by trust, authenticity, openness, and a supportive climate.
3. *Power equalization.* Effective organizations deemphasize hierarchical authority and control.
4. *Confrontation.* Problems shouldn't be swept under the rug. They should be openly confronted.
5. *Participation.* The more that people who will be affected by a change are involved in the decisions surrounding that change, the more they will be committed to implementing those decisions.

What are some of the OD techniques or interventions for bringing about change? In the following sections, we shall briefly present six interventions that change agents might consider using.

Organizational development (OD)

A collection of planned change interventions, built on humanistic-democratic values, that seeks to improve organizational effectiveness and employee wellbeing.

Organizational development at Wal-Mart includes a new voluntary program called the Personal Sustainability Project that seeks to improve employee wellbeing and organizational effectiveness. Through workshops, retreats, and seminars, Wal-Mart informs employees about the benefits of issues ranging from physical fitness to energy conservation and then gives them the freedom to make positive changes in their personal lives and in their workplace. Wal-Mart employees in this photo sample healthy food as part of a seminar promoting the benefits of fitness and lifestyle improvements.

Michael Stravato/
The New York Times

Sensitivity training

Training groups that seek to change behavior through unstructured group interaction.

Survey feedback

The use of questionnaires to identify discrepancies among member perceptions; discussion follows, and remedies are suggested.

Process consultation (PC)

A meeting in which a consultant assists a client in understanding process events with which he or she must deal and identifying processes that need improvement.

Team building

High interaction among team members to increase trust and openness.

Intergroup development

OD efforts to change the attitudes, stereotypes, and perceptions that groups have of each other.

Sensitivity Training   It can have many names—**sensitivity training**, laboratory training, encounter groups, or T-groups (training groups)—but all refer to a method of changing behavior through unstructured group interaction.[17] Members are brought together in a free and open environment in which participants discuss themselves and their interactive processes. Individuals learn through observing and participating rather than being told.

Greater sensitivity to the behavior of others and increased understanding of group processes are specific results in addition to the increased ability to empathize with others, improved listening skills, greater openness, increased tolerance of individual differences, and improved conflict-resolution skills.

Survey Feedback   One tool for assessing attitudes held by organizational members, identifying discrepancies among member perceptions, and solving these differences is the **survey feedback** approach.[18]

Everyone in an organization can participate in survey feedback, but of key importance is the organizational family—the manager of any given unit and the employees who report directly to him or her. A questionnaire is usually completed by all members in the organization or unit. Organization members may be asked to suggest questions or may be interviewed to determine what issues are relevant. The questionnaire typically asks members for their perceptions and attitudes on a broad range of topics, including: decision-making practices; communication effectiveness; coordination between units; and satisfaction with the organization, job, peers, and their immediate supervisor.

Process Consultation   No organization operates perfectly. Managers often sense that their unit's performance can be improved, but they're unable to identify what can be improved and how it can be improved. The purpose of **process consultation (PC)** is for an outside consultant to assist a client, usually a manager, "to perceive, understand, and act upon process events" with which the manager must deal.[19] These might include work flow, informal relationships among unit members, and formal communication channels.

Team Building   As we've noted in numerous places throughout this book, organizations are increasingly relying on teams to accomplish work tasks. **Team building** uses high-interaction group activities to increase trust and openness among team members.[20] Team building can be applied within groups or at the intergroup level, at which activities are interdependent. The objective is to improve coordinative efforts of members, which will result in increasing the team's performance.

The activities considered in team building typically include goal setting, development of interpersonal relations among team members, role analysis to clarify each member's role and responsibilities, and team process analysis. Team building can also address itself to clarifying each member's role on the team. Each role can be identified and clarified. Previous ambiguities can be brought to the surface. For some individuals, it may offer one of the few opportunities they have had to think about what their job is all about and what specific tasks they are expected to carry out if the team is to optimize its effectiveness.

Intergroup Development   A major area of concern in OD is the dysfunctional conflict that exists between groups. As a result, this has been a subject to which change efforts have been directed. **Intergroup development** seeks to change the attitudes, stereotypes, and perceptions that groups have of each other. Groups meets independently to develop lists of their perceptions, the other group, and how they believe other groups perceive them. The groups then share their lists, after which similarities and differences are discussed. Differences are clearly articulated, and the groups look for the causes of the differences.

Appreciative inquiry (AI)

An approach that seeks to identify the unique qualities and special strengths of an organization, which can then be built on to improve performance.

Appreciative Inquiry (AI)   Most OD approaches are problem-centered. They identify a problem or set of problems, then look for a solution. **Appreciative inquiry (AI)** accentuates the positive.[21] Rather than looking for problems to fix, this approach seeks to identify the unique qualities and special strengths of an organization, which can then be built on to improve performance. That is, it focuses on an organization's successes rather than on its problems.

The AI process consists of four steps. The first step is *discovery*. The idea is to find out what people think are the strengths of the organization. For instance, employees are asked to remember the times they felt the organization worked best or when they specifically felt most satisfied with their jobs. The second step is *dreaming*. The information from the discovery phase is used to speculate on possible futures for the organization. For instance, people are asked to envision the organization in 5 years and to describe what's different. The third step is *design*. Based on the dream articulation, participants focus on finding a common vision of how the organization will look and agree on its unique qualities. The fourth stage seeks to define the organization's *destiny*. In this final step, participants discuss how the organization is going to fulfill its dream. This typically includes the writing of action plans and development of implementation strategies.

Creating a Culture for Change

4 *Demonstrate two ways of creating a culture for change.*

We've considered how organizations can adapt to change. Now we need to consider how organizations can embrace and accept change by transforming their cultures. What we need to contemplate is that change is common to all cultures; organizations in all countries experience change in one way or another and the techniques of approach, the way in which we can prepare people, and how people deal with change is similar. In this section we review two approaches for preparing people for change: stimulating a culture of innovation and creating a learning organization.

Stimulating a Culture of Innovation

How can an organization become more innovative?

Although there is no guaranteed formula, certain characteristics surface again and again when researchers study innovative organizations. We've grouped them into structural, cultural, and human resource categories. Our message to change agents is that they should consider introducing these characteristics into their organization if they want to create an innovative climate. Before we look at these characteristics, however, let's clarify what we mean by innovation.

Innovation

A new idea applied to initiating or improving a product, process, or service.

Definition of *Innovation*   We said change refers to making things different. **Innovation** is a more specialized kind of change. Innovation is a new idea applied to initiating or improving a product, process, or service.[22] So all innovations involve change, but not all changes necessarily involve new ideas or lead to significant improvements. Innovations in organizations can range from small improvements to radical breakthroughs.

Sources of Innovation   *Structural variables* have been the most studied potential source of innovation.[23] First, organic structures positively influence innovation. Second, long tenure in management is associated with innovation. Third, innovation is nurtured when there are slack resources. Finally, interunit communication is high in innovative organizations.[24] These organizations are high

Respected as one of the world's most innovative companies, Starbucks turned a commodity product that was declining in sales and invented specialty coffees as a major new product category. Starbucks relies on its employees to share customer insights with managers and takes product development teams on inspirational field trips to view customer behavior, local cultures, and fashion trends. Starbucks has extended its coffee shops from American college campuses and urban sites to locations throughout the world, including the shop shown here at a shopping center in Ramadan, Dubai.

users of committees, task forces, cross-functional teams, and other mechanisms that facilitate interaction across departmental lines.

Innovative organizations tend to have similar *cultures*. They encourage experimentation. They reward both successes and failures. They celebrate mistakes. Unfortunately, in too many organizations, people are rewarded for the absence of failures rather than for the presence of successes. Such cultures extinguish risk taking and innovation. People will suggest and try new ideas only when they feel such behaviors exact no penalties. Managers in innovative organizations recognize that failures are a natural byproduct of venturing into the unknown.

Within the *human resources* category, we find that innovative organizations actively promote the training and development of their members so that they keep current, offer high job security so employees don't fear getting fired for making mistakes, and encourage individuals to become champions of change. Once a new idea is developed, **idea champions** actively and enthusiastically promote the idea, build support, overcome resistance, and ensure that the innovation is implemented.[25] They inspire and energize others with their vision of the potential of an innovation and through their strong personal conviction in their mission. They are also good at gaining the commitment of others to support their mission. In addition, idea champions have jobs that provide considerable decision-making discretion. As a result, this autonomy helps them introduce and implement innovations in organizations.[26]

Idea champions

Individuals who take an innovation and actively and enthusiastically promote the idea, build support, overcome resistance, and ensure that the idea is implemented.

Creating a Learning Organization

Another way organizations can proactively manage change is to make continuous growth part of its culture—to become a learning organization.[27] In this section, we describe what a learning organization looks like and the methods for managing learning.

What's a Learning Organization?   A **learning organization** is an organization that has developed the continuous capacity to adapt and change. Just as individuals

Learning organization

An organization that has developed the continuous capacity to adapt and change.

Single-loop learning

A process of correcting errors using past routines and present policies.

Double-loop learning

A process of correcting errors by modifying the organization's objectives, policies, and standard routines.

learn, so too do organizations. "All organizations learn, whether they consciously choose to or not—it is a fundamental requirement for their sustained existence."[28] However, some organizations just do it better than others.

Most organizations engage in what has been called **single-loop learning**.[29] When errors are detected, the correction process relies on past routines and present policies. In contrast, learning organizations use **double-loop learning**. When an error is detected, it's corrected in ways that involve the modification of the organization's objectives, policies, and standard routines. In this way, it provides opportunities for radically different solutions to problems and dramatic jumps in improvement.

Box 16-3 summarizes the five basic characteristics of a learning organization. It's an organization in which people put aside their old ways of thinking, learn to be open with each other, understand how their organization really works, form a plan or vision that everyone can agree on, and then work together to achieve that vision.[30]

Managing Learning   How do you change an organization to make it into a continual learner? What can managers do to make their firms learning organizations? The following are some suggestions:

- *Establish a strategy.*   Management needs to make explicit its commitment to change, innovation, and continuous improvement.
- *Redesign the organization's structure.*   The formal structure can be a serious impediment to learning. By flattening the structure, eliminating or combining departments, and increasing the use of cross-functional teams, interdependence is reinforced and boundaries between people are reduced.
- *Reshape the organization's culture.*   To become a learning organization, managers need to demonstrate by their actions that taking risks and admitting failures are desirable traits. That means rewarding people who take chances and make mistakes. And management needs to encourage functional conflict. "The key to unlocking real openness at work," says one expert on learning organizations, "is to teach people to give up having to be in agreement."

An excellent illustration of a learning organization is what is being done at Merck, a top pharmaceutical company that is well known in the Arab countries. In addition to changing Merck's structure so that innovation can come from customers—patients and doctors—Merck is also trying to reward researchers for taking risks, even if their risky ideas end in failure. Merck's transformed strategy, structure, and culture may or may not succeed, but that's part of the risk of stimulating change through creating a learning organization.

BOX 16-3
Characteristics of a Learning Organization

1. There exists a shared vision that everyone agrees on.
2. People discard their old ways of thinking and the standard routines they use for solving problems or doing their jobs.
3. Members think of all organizational processes, activities, functions, and interactions with the environment as part of a system of interrelationships.
4. People openly communicate with each other (across vertical and horizontal boundaries) without fear of criticism or punishment.
5. People sublimate their personal self-interest and fragmented departmental interests to work together to achieve the organization's shared vision.

Source: Based on P. M. Senge, *The Fifth Discipline* (New York: Doubleday, 1990).

Work Stress and Its Management

5 *Define* stress *and identify its potential sources.*

Most of us are aware that employee stress is an increasing and common problem in all types of organizations and in all cultures. Friends tell us they're stressed out from greater work-loads. Parents talk about the lack of job stability in today's world and remember a time when a job with a large company meant lifetime security. We read surveys in which employees complain about the stress created in trying to balance work and family responsibilities.[31] In this section we'll look at the causes and consequences of stress, and then consider what individuals and organizations can do to reduce it and how cultures deal with stress.

It has been determined that there is a strong correlation between stress and satisfaction leading to organizational commitment.[32] That is, higher stress leads to lower satisfaction and lower satisfaction leads to lower commitment. Similarly, research in the United Arab Emirates shows that job role conflict and ambiguity are different facets of stress that affects organizational commitment,[33] and this will be discussed further in the coming sections.

What Is Stress?

Stress

A dynamic condition in which an individual is confronted with an opportunity, a demand, or a resource related to what the individual desires and for which the outcome is perceived to be both uncertain and important.

Challenge stressors

Stressors associated with workload, pressure to complete tasks, and time urgency.

Hindrance stressors

Stressors that keep you from reaching your goals (red tape, office politics, confusion over job responsibilities).

Demands

Responsibilities, pressures, obligations, and even uncertainties that individuals face in the workplace.

Resources

Things within an individual's control that can be used to resolve demands.

Stress is a condition that causes pressure and can be the result of a combination of factors. Today, it has become common to hear the word 'stress.' Young, old, married, employed, unemployed, single—all are in a state of stress because of the environment that we either live or work in. If someone is not feeling well without any significant reason, most doctors blame stress.

Some stress can be good, and some can be bad. Recently, researchers have argued that **challenge stressors**—or stressors associated with workload, pressure to complete tasks, and time urgency—operate quite differently from **hindrance stressors**—or stressors that keep you from reaching your goals (red tape, office politics, confusion over job responsibilities). Although research on challenge and hindrance stress is just starting to accumulate, early evidence suggests that challenge stressors are less harmful (produce less strain) than hindrance stressors.[34]

More typically, stress is associated with **demands** and **resources**. Demands are responsibilities, pressures, obligations, and even uncertainties that individuals face in the workplace. Resources are things within an individual's control that can be used to resolve the demands. This demands–resources model has received increasing support in the literature.[35]

Stress is part of any environment—academic or professional, and whilst there are certain studies that suggest that the academic environment does not cause stress at all, many do highlight a strong link.[36]

A recent study by Elzubeir *et al.* was undertaken into the area of stress and coping among medical students in the Arab world. It looked at various studies conducted in the Arab world in order to identify what implications this had for future research into the area.[37] The following paragraphs highlight some of the more notable studies they uncovered.

One study, conducted in the UAE and looking at students' self-reported stress levels, identified concerns over the high actual and perceived stress levels of these students, compared with their US college counterparts.[38] At a Saudi Arabian medical school, another study showed that 57 percent of the male students surveyed reported that they experienced stress, and 19.6 percent reported severe stress levels. The most significant sources of stress in this study were issues relating to courses (60.3 percent) and the home environment (3.8 percent).[39] In a survey comparing stress levels among male medical students in Egypt and Saudi Arabia it was found that 95 percent of the Egyptian and 92 percent of the

Saudi students reported one or more stressors.[40] The most common stressors for Egyptian students were congested classrooms (71 percent), inconsiderate and insensitive instructors (33 percent), fear of the future (27 percent), limited time for recreational activities (25 percent), and anxiety and depression (25 percent). They were also more likely than their Saudi counterparts to mention relationship, academic and environmental problems as being stressful.

How do these students cope with these stress factors? Elzubeir *et al.* found that the genral consensus among the studies they researched recommended the use of coping mechanisms such as student support systems, wellness, counseling and preventive mental health services, stress management programmes, and training workshops. In the US, some medical schools provide treatment services and wellness programs to address students' mental health issues—for example at one university, an elective called 'Mindfulness-based Stress Reduction' reportedly reduced stress and enhanced coping. Furthermore, Elzubeir *et al.* found that certain medical schools in the Arab world are emulating their Western counterparts; some of the methods being used include innovative teaching and assessment styles and, in Saudi Arabia, some medical schools are turning to student-centered, small-group learning.

> ### Picture This
>
> You have an annual performance review at work coming up. A good performance review may lead to a promotion, greater responsibilities, and a higher salary. A poor review may prevent you from getting a promotion. An extremely poor review might even result in your being fired. Are you stressed?

Potential Sources of Stress

What causes stress? As the model in Figure 16.2 shows, there are three categories of potential stressors: environmental, organizational, and personal. Let's take a look at each.[41]

Environmental Factors　Just as environmental uncertainty influences the design of an organization's structure, it also influences stress levels among

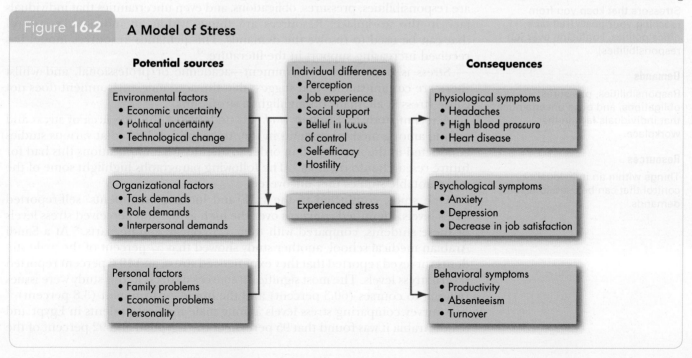

Figure 16.2　A Model of Stress

Potential sources

Environmental factors
• Economic uncertainty
• Political uncertainty
• Technological change

Organizational factors
• Task demands
• Role demands
• Interpersonal demands

Personal factors
• Family problems
• Economic problems
• Personality

Individual differences
• Perception
• Job experience
• Social support
• Belief in locus of control
• Self-efficacy
• Hostility

Experienced stress

Consequences

Physiological symptoms
• Headaches
• High blood pressure
• Heart disease

Psychological symptoms
• Anxiety
• Depression
• Decrease in job satisfaction

Behavioral symptoms
• Productivity
• Absenteeism
• Turnover

employees in that organization. Indeed, evidence indicates that uncertainty is the biggest reason people have trouble coping with organizational changes.[42] The three main types of environmental uncertainty are economic, political, and technological.

Changes in the business cycle create *economic uncertainties*. When the economy is contracting, for example, people become increasingly anxious about their job security. *Political uncertainties* don't tend to create stress among Americans as they do for employees in Arab countries. The obvious reason is that the United States has a stable political system, in which change is typically implemented in an orderly manner. Yet political threats and changes in the Arab world lead to political uncertainty that becomes stressful to people in these countries.[43] *Technological change* is a third type of environmental factor that can cause stress. Because new innovations can make an employee's skills and experience obsolete in a very short time, computers, robotics, automation, and similar forms of technological innovation are a threat to many people and cause them stress.

Organizational Factors   There is no shortage of factors within an organization that can cause stress. Pressures to avoid errors or complete tasks in a limited time, work overload, a demanding and insensitive boss, and unpleasant coworkers are a few examples. We've categorized these factors around task, role, and interpersonal demands.[44]

Task demands are factors related to a person's job. They include the design of the individual's job, working conditions, and the physical work layout. Assembly lines, for instance, can put pressure on people when the line's speed is perceived as excessive. Similarly, working in an overcrowded room or in a visible location where noise and interruptions are constant can increase anxiety and stress.[45]

Role demands relate to pressures placed on individuals as a function of the particular role they play in the organization. *Interpersonal demands* are pressures created by other employees. Lack of social support from colleagues and poor interpersonal relationships can cause stress, especially among employees with a high social need.

Personal Factors   The typical individual works about 40 to 50 hours a week. But the experiences and problems that people encounter in the other 120-plus nonwork hours each week can spill over to the job. Our final category is related to the employee's personal life. Primarily, these factors are family issues, personal economic problems, and inherent personality characteristics. Even though we always talk about leaving 'personal problems at home,' it is often easier said than done and, as a result, performance and behavior changes within the workplace.

National surveys in general show that people hold *family* and personal relationships dear. Marital difficulties, the breaking off of a relationship, and discipline troubles with children are examples of relationship problems that create stress for employees that aren't left at the front door when they arrive at work.[46]

Economic problems created by individuals overextending their financial resources is another set of personal troubles that can create stress for employees and distract their attention from their work. Stress symptoms expressed on the job may actually originate in the person's *personality*.

Stressors Are Additive   A fact that tends to be overlooked when stressors are reviewed individually is that stress is an additive phenomenon.[47] Stress builds up. Each new and persistent stressor adds to an individual's stress level. So a single stressor may be relatively unimportant in and of itself, but if it's added to an already high level of stress, it can become too heavy a burden to carry. If we want to appraise the total amount of stress an individual is under, we have to sum up his or her opportunity stresses, constraint stresses, and demand stresses.

Individual Differences

Some people thrive on stressful situations, while others are overwhelmed by them.

What Do You Think?

What is it that differentiates people in terms of their ability to handle stress? What individual difference variables balance the relationship between potential stress and experienced stress?

At least four variables—perception, job experience, social support, and personality—have been found to be relevant moderators.

The evidence indicates that *experience* on the job tends to be negatively related to work stress. Why? Two explanations have been offered.[48] First is the idea of selective withdrawal. Voluntary turnover is more probable among people who experience more stress. Therefore, people who remain with an organization longer are those with more stress-resistant traits or those who are more resistant to the stress characteristics of their organization. Second, people eventually develop coping mechanisms to deal with stress. Because this takes time, senior members of the organization are more likely to be fully adapted and should experience less stress.

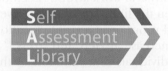

HOW STRESSFUL IS MY LIFE?

In the Self-Assessment Library (available online), take assessment III.C.2 (How Stressful Is My Life?).

Emotional Intelligence and Stress

6 *Understand Emotional Intelligence.*

Emotional intelligence (EI)
The ability to detect and to manage emotional cues and information.

Emotional Intelligence (EI) is a popular concept these days. What does EI refer to and what is its relationship to stress?

Emotional Intelligence (EI) is the ability to perceive, control, and evaluate emotions. In 1987, Keith Beasley used the term 'emotional quotient' and determined that "Emotional intelligence is an array of noncognitive capabilities, competencies, and skills that influence one's ability to succeed in coping with environmental demands and pressures."

Thereafter, Peter Salovey and John D. Mayer have been the leading researchers on this topic and in 1990, they gave the following definition, "Emotional Intelligence (EI) is the subset of social intelligence that involves the ability to monitor one's own and others' feelings and emotions, to discriminate among them and to use this information to guide one's thinking and actions."[49]

The consequences of stress are discussed in detail in the following section; however, to clarify the concept of this section, we need to mention the common responses to stress. In general, people usually become very aggressive, agitated, depressed, and unable to express their feelings. Because stress has become part of our everyday lifestyle, many of us have forgotten how to relax. It is not easy, but we need to achieve a state of balance by maintaining a calm state of energy, alertness, and focus.

Accordingly, one way of reaching this state is through EI. Emotional Intelligence training teaches you how to connect to the power of your emotions and use them to enhance your relationships, your career, and your self-confidence. Consequently, EI allows you to overcome stress, anxiety, and depression.

Consequences of Stress

> *7* *Identify the consequences of stress.*

Stress shows itself in a number of ways. For instance, an individual who is experiencing a high level of stress may develop high blood pressure, ulcers, irritability, difficulty making routine decisions, loss of appetite, accident-proneness, and the like. These symptoms can be subsumed under three general categories: physiological, psychological, and behavioral symptoms.[50]

Physiological Symptoms   Most of the early concern with stress was directed at physiological symptoms. This was because the topic was researched by specialists in the health and medical sciences. This research led to the conclusion that stress could create changes in metabolism, increase heart and breathing rates, increase blood pressure, bring on headaches, and induce heart attacks.

Psychological Symptoms   Stress can cause dissatisfaction. Job-related stress can cause job-related dissatisfaction. Job dissatisfaction, in fact, is "the simplest and most obvious psychological effect" of stress.[51] But stress shows itself in other psychological states—for instance, tension, anxiety, irritability, boredom, and procrastination.

OB in the News

The Ten Most Stressful Jobs—and One More That Didn't Make the List

According to the US Centers for Disease Control and Prevention (CDC) and *Health* magazine, the top ten most and least stressful jobs are:

10 Most Stressful Jobs	10 Least Stressful Jobs
1. Inner-city high school teacher	1. Forester
2. Police officer	2. Bookbinder
3. Miner	3. Telephone line worker
4. Air traffic controller	4. Toolmaker
5. Medical intern	5. Millwright
6. Stockbroker	6. Repairperson
7. Journalist	7. Civil engineer
8. Customer service/ complaint worker	8. Therapist
9. Secretary	9. Natural scientist
10. Waiter	10. Sales representative

One job that certainly seems like it should be on the list is flight attendant. Planes are more full than ever, passengers are grumpier than ever (due to full planes, smaller seats, fewer perks, and more delays), and the pay and job security seems to decline with every passing year.

Of these factors, perhaps none is more stressful than the increasingly tense relationship between passengers and flight attendant. Lori Sheridan, Northwest Airlines flight attendant since 1968,' said her job description used to be all about providing "whatever the passenger wanted." Now, she said, "It's all about telling them what they can and can't do." "It's one more level of stress on top of several years of pretty severe stress," said Patricia Friend, president of the largest flight attendant's union.

It is no surprise to find that stressful jobs can result in lower productivity as well as mental and physical health problems.

A study conducted by CareerCast (and reported in *Jordan Directions*) looked at five criteria—environment, income, stress, outlook, physical demands—when identifying the most and least stressful jobs.

In 2010, the most stressful jobs were found to be Firefighter, Senior Corporate Executive, Taxi Driver, Surgeon, Public Relations Officer, and Real Estate Agent. The same researchers listed the least stressful jobs as Musical Instrument Repairer, Records Technician, Forklift Operator, Librarian, Medical Secretary, Bookkeeper, and Janitor.

Source: Based on *Helicobacter pylori and Peptic Ulcer Disease*, Centers for Disease Control and Prevention, US Department of Health and Human Services; M. Maynard, "Maybe the Toughest Job Aloft," *New York Times*, August 15, 2006, pp. C1, C6; and "Most and least stressful jobs," *Jordan Directions*, August 09, 2010, www.jordandirections.com.

Similarly, the less control people have over the pace of their work, the greater the stress and dissatisfaction.

Behavioral Symptoms Behavior-related stress symptoms include changes in productivity, absence, and turnover, as well as changes in eating habits, increased smoking or consumption of alcohol, rapid speech, fidgeting, and sleep disorders.[52]

Managing Stress

8 *Contrast the individual and organizational approaches to managing stress.*

From the organization's standpoint, management may not be concerned when employees experience low to moderate levels of stress. The reason, as we showed earlier, is that such levels of stress may be functional and lead to higher employee performance. But high levels of stress, or even low levels over long periods, can lead to reduced employee performance and, thus, require action by management.

Although a limited amount of stress may benefit an employee's performance, don't expect employees to see it that way. From the individual's standpoint, even low levels of stress are likely to be perceived as undesirable. It's not unlikely, therefore, for employees and management to have different ideas of what leads to an acceptable level of stress on the job. What management may consider to be "a positive stimulus that keeps the adrenalin running" is very likely to be seen as "excessive pressure" by the employee. Keep this in mind as we discuss individual and organizational approaches toward managing stress.[53]

Individual Approaches An employee can take personal responsibility for reducing stress levels. Individual strategies that have proven effective include implementing time-management techniques, increasing physical exercise, relaxation training, and expanding the social support network.

Many people manage their time poorly. The well-organized employee, like the well-organized student, can often accomplish twice as much as the person who is poorly organized. So an understanding and utilization of basic *time-management* principles can help individuals better cope with tensions created by job demands.[54]

Physicians have recommended noncompetitive physical exercise, such as aerobics, walking, jogging, swimming, and riding a bicycle as a way to deal with excessive stress levels. These forms of *physical exercise* increase heart capacity, lower the at-rest heart rate, provide a mental diversion from work pressures, and offer a means to 'let off steam.'[55]

Individuals can teach themselves to reduce tension through *relaxation techniques* such as meditation, hypnosis, and biofeedback. Deep relaxation for 15 or 20 minutes a day releases tension and provides a person with a pronounced sense of peacefulness. Importantly, significant changes in heart rate, blood pressure, and other physiological factors result from achieving the condition of deep relaxation.

As we noted earlier in this chapter, having friends, family, or work colleagues to talk to provides an outlet when stress levels become excessive. Expanding your *social support network*, therefore, can be a means for tension reduction. It provides you with someone to hear your problems and to offer a more objective perspective on the situation.

Organizational Approaches Several of the factors that cause stress—particularly task and role demands—are controlled by management. As such, they can

International OB

Coping with Stress: Cultural Differences

Stress is a common complaint of workers worldwide. But how workers manage that stress, and whether they seek social support for relief, varies from one culture to another. A recent study examined this issue. Moreover, stress is part of life for it is anything that causes mental, physical, or spiritual tension. Thus, we can not run away from it; stress is inevitable.

The study compared the tendency to seek social support to relieve stress among some Asian groups (Koreans and Asian Americans) to that of European Americans. Given that Asians tend to be more collectivist than European Americans (who tend to be more individualist), two possibilities arise. First, a collectivist orientation might increase the likelihood that one would want to talk about stressful problems, in essence seeking social support. Second, because collectivists strive for group harmony, they may keep problems to themselves and fail to use social support as a means of coping with stress.

The study found support for the latter suggestion: Koreans and Asian Americans reported using social support less often than European Americans because they were concerned about maintaining group harmony. What's the upshot? Collectivists experiencing stress may be limiting themselves in terms of coping mechanisms and may need to find other means of coping with work-related stress.

For many in the Arab world, the number one way to reduce stress and anxiety is through prayer and full dependence on God. Patience is also important, for it allows them the feeling of control. They aim to remember that life is short and understand what their priorities are and not get caught up in their stress patterns. In addition, keeping contact with others and communicating with them is crucial. That is, they feel a support network around them that encourages them to continue in the face of problems.

Finally, Arabs should always give thanks to God and be thankful for everything around them. For many, this proves to be a source of comfort and consolation. These are but a few of the ways in which people can cope with stress, but ultimately we must have the will to face this issue with an open mind.

Source: Based on S. Taylor, D. K. Sherman, H. S. Kim, J. Jarcho, K. Takagi, and M. Dunagan, "Culture and Social Support: Who Seeks It and Why?" *Journal of Personality and Social Psychology*, September, 2004, pp. 354–362.

be modified or changed. Strategies that management might want to consider include improved personnel selection and job placement, training, use of realistic goal setting, redesigning of jobs, increased employee involvement, improved organizational communication, offering employee sabbaticals, and establishment of corporate wellness programs.

Certain jobs are more stressful than others but, as we learned earlier in this chapter, individuals differ in their response to stressful situations. The use of goals can reduce stress as well as provide motivation. Specific goals that are perceived as attainable clarify performance expectations. In addition, goal feedback reduces uncertainties about actual job performance. The result is less employee frustration, role ambiguity, and stress.

Redesigning jobs to give employees more responsibility, more meaningful work, more autonomy, and increased feedback can reduce stress because these factors give the employee greater control over work activities and lessen dependence on others. But as we noted in our discussion of work design, not all employees want enriched jobs. The right redesign, then, for employees with a low need for growth might be less responsibility and increased specialization. If individuals prefer structure and routine, reducing skill variety should also reduce uncertainties and stress levels.

Increasing formal *organizational communication* with employees reduces uncertainty by lessening role ambiguity and role conflict. Given the importance that perceptions play in moderating the stress–response relationship, management

Xerox Corporation employee Joanne Belknap took a four-month sabbatical to work as a volunteer for the American Cancer Society, where she visited businesses and informed managers and employees about the society's programs. Xerox grants employees fully paid sabbaticals to work on community service projects. Sabbaticals are one way that organizations can rejuvenate employees by allowing them to work on meaningful projects in the community.

can also use effective communications as a means to shape employee perceptions. Remember that what employees categorize as demands, threats, or opportunities are merely an interpretation, and that interpretation can be affected by the symbols and actions communicated by management.

Our final suggestion is to offer organizationally supported **wellness programs**. These programs focus on the employee's total physical and mental condition.[56] For example, they typically provide workshops to help people quit smoking, control alcohol use, lose weight, eat better, and develop a regular exercise program.

Wellness programs

Organizationally supported programs that focus on the employee's total physical and mental condition.

Global Implications

9 *Explain global differences in organizational change and work stress.*

Organizational Change   A number of change issues we've discussed in this chapter are culture-bound. To illustrate, let's briefly look at five questions:

1. Do people believe change is possible?
2. If it's possible, how long will it take to bring it about?
3. Is resistance to change greater in some cultures than in others?
4. Does culture influence how change efforts will be implemented?
5. Do successful idea champions do things differently in different cultures?

Do people believe change is possible? Remember that cultures vary in terms of beliefs about their ability to control their environment. In cultures in which people believe that they can dominate their environment, individuals will take a proactive view of change. This, for example, would describe the United States and Canada. In many other countries, such as Saudi Arabia, people see themselves as governed by their environment and thus will tend to take a passive approach toward change.

Is resistance to change greater in some cultures than in others? Resistance to change will be influenced by a society's reliance on tradition. Italians, like Arabs for example, focus on the past, and thus are more resistant to change, whereas US adults emphasize the present. Another important difference between cultures has to do with how certain cultures influence how change efforts will be implemented?

Finally, do successful idea champions do things differently in different cultures? Yes.[57] People in collectivist cultures prefer appeals for cross-functional support for innovation efforts; people in high-power-distance cultures prefer champions to work closely with those in authority to approve innovative activities before work is begun; and the higher the uncertainty avoidance of a society, the more champions should work within the organization's rules and procedures to develop the innovation.

Stress   In considering global differences in stress, there are three questions to answer:

1. Do the causes of stress vary across countries?
2. Do the outcomes of stress vary across cultures?
3. Do the factors that lessen the effects of stress vary by culture?

Let's deal with each of these questions in turn. First, research suggests that the job conditions that cause stress show some differences across cultures. One study of US and Chinese employees revealed that whereas US employees were stressed by a lack of control, Chinese employees were stressed by job evaluations and lack of training. Another study conducted by Bayt.com in the Middle East shows that employees were stressed by lack of communication and involvement within the organization.[58]

Second, evidence tends to suggest that stressors are associated with perceived stress and strains among employees in different countries. In other words, stress is equally bad for employees of all cultures.[59]

Third, although not all factors that reduce stress have been compared across cultures, research does suggest that, whereas the demand to work long hours leads to stress, this stress can be reduced by the resource of social support, such as having friends or family to talk to.

Summary and Implications for Managers

The need for change has been implied throughout this text. "A casual reflection on change should indicate that it encompasses almost all of our concepts in the organizational behavior literature."[60] For instance, think about attitudes, motivation, work teams, communication, leadership, organizational structures, human resource practices, and organizational cultures. Change was an integral part in the discussion of each of these topics.

The real world is turbulent, requiring organizations and their members to undergo dynamic change if they are to perform at competitive levels.

Managers are the primary change agents by the decisions they make and their role-modeling behaviors; they shape the organization's change culture. For instance, management decisions related to structural design, cultural factors, and human resource policies largely determine the level of innovation within the organization. Similarly, management decisions, policies, and practices will determine the degree to which the organization learns and adapts to changing environmental factors.

We found that the existence of work stress does not necessarily lower performance. The evidence indicates that stress can be either a positive or a negative influence on employee performance. However, a high level of stress, or even a moderate amount sustained over a long period, eventually takes its toll, and performance declines. The impact of stress on satisfaction is far more straightforward and job-related tension tends to decrease general job satisfaction.[61]

Point ⟫ ⟪ Counterpoint

MANAGING CHANGE IS AN EPISODIC ACTIVITY

Organizational change is an activity that starts at some point, proceeds through a series of steps, and culminates in some outcome that those involved hope is an improvement over the starting point. In other words, it has a beginning, a middle, and an end.

Lewin's three-step model represents a classic illustration of this perspective. Change is seen as a break in the organization's equilibrium. The status quo has been disturbed, and change is necessary to establish a new equilibrium state. The objective of refreezing is to stabilize the new situation by balancing the driving and restraining forces.

Some experts have argued that organizational change should be thought of as balancing a system made up of five interacting variables within the organization—people, tasks, technology, structure, and strategy.

Another way to look at change is to think of managing change as captaining a ship. The organization is like a large ship traveling across the calm Mediterranean Sea to a specific port. Like this ship's voyage, managing an organization should be seen as a journey with a beginning and an end, and implementing change as a response to a break in the status quo and needed only occasionally.

Change is considered as the occasional disturbance in an otherwise peaceful world. However, it bears little resemblance to today's environment of constant and chaotic change.[62]

If you want to understand what it's like to manage change in today's organizations, think of it as equivalent to permanent white-water rafting.[63] The organization is not a large ship, but more similar to a 40-foot raft moving across a raging river made up of an uninterrupted flow of permanent white-water rapids. Change is a natural state and managing change is a continual process. That is, managers never get the luxury of escaping the white-water rapids.

Consequently, disruptions in the status quo are not occasional, temporary, and followed by a return to an equilibrium state. There is, in fact, no equilibrium state. Managers today face constant change, bordering on chaos. They're being forced to play a game they've never played before, governed by rules that are created as the game progresses.

Questions for Review

1 What forces act as stimulants to change and what is the difference between planned and unplanned change?

2 What forces act as sources of resistance to change?

3 What are the main approaches to managing organizational change?

4 How can managers create a culture for change?

5 What is stress and what are the possible sources of stress?

6 What is emotional intelligence?

7 What are the consequences of stress?

8 What are the individual and organizational approaches to managing stress?

9 What does research tell us about global differences in organizational change and work stress?

Discussion Exercise

Read each of the scenarios below and then, for each, identify and discuss how these could trigger organizational changes, and how these could affect people's stress levels in light of the new conditions.

1. Management have made a strategic cost-cutting decision to outsource more labor abroad.

2. An external consultant is hired to assess the efficiency of teams and processes.

3. The company is merging with another company.

Ethical Considerations

Some of the most admired business leaders argue that the only way to get the most out of people is to stretch them. This view would seem to be backed by both business situations and research evidence. "If you do know how to get there, it's not a stretch target," former General Electric CEO Jack Welch has said. "We have found that by reaching for what appears to be the impossible, we often actually do the impossible; and even when we don't quite make it, we inevitably wind up doing much better than we would have done."[64]

The implication is that to be the most effective manager you need to push, push, and push more.

But is this an ethical dilemma for managers? What if you learned that pushing employees to the maximum comes at the expense of their health or their family life? While it seems true that managers get the performance they expect, it also seems likely that some people push themselves too hard. If your stretch goals mean that your best employees are those who give it all for the organization—even putting aside their own personal or family interests—is that what you wish for as a manager?

Critical Analysis

EMBRACING CHANGE THROUGH OPERATIONAL LEADERSHIP

From a Lebanese family-owned small business to a leading multi-line conglomerate in the Middle East and North Africa (MENA) region, Khalil Fattal & Fils (KFF) Holding is the exclusive agent and distributor of many multinational brands within the following categories: food and beverages, home and personal care, beauty and accessories, household and office equipment, consumer electronics, and pharmaceuticals. The corporation now employs more than 2,100 individuals with a turnover of approximately US$650 million.

Over the course of 112 years (1897–2009), the corporation has gone through many successful structural changes that have shaped the business and contributed to its success. At the base of this success is the owners' philosophy, which drove the corporation toward its vision and instilled solid corporate values that have increased performance and created a spirit of unity among its members.

At the beginning of 2002, the owners gathered 30 of their top managers in a retreat to define the corporate culture in the coming years. The team succeeded in drafting a mission that enlarged the scope of the corporation's activities to 'reach out to millions of consumers in the Levant and North African countries.' (The Levant is comprised of Lebanon, Syria, Jordan, and Iraq.) The team also adopted a set of corporate values that were disseminated to all other employees through workshops and group discussions.

The corporation's core values revolve around trust, respect, sharing, and courage, with a specific set of expected behaviors for each value. Under the value of courage, embracing change was selected as the main behavior for individuals who aspire to succeed in their careers with the group. This is now stated in the corporate manual as "embrace change as an opportunity to grow," and employees are invited to accept rotation in their assignments every four to five years, or whenever needed, not only in Lebanon but also throughout the region where the corporation operates.

To conduct business in the MENA region, it is a legal requirement that local partners and employees be engaged. Hence, to ensure the operation's success, the corporation decided to relocate part of the management team to its subsidiaries in Syria, Jordan, Iraq, Sudan, Algeria, and Egypt. Although these countries share a common language (Arabic) with Lebanon, their social, economic, and political systems differ. As a result, some managers were reluctant to relocate outside their home country. This became a major obstacle that needed to be resolved.

To overcome this impediment, the KFF's CEO took the initiative and moved ahead of everyone else to ensure a satisfactory setup, and even asked some members of his family to accept these new foreign assignments, thereby setting the example for others to follow suit—and many managers did. To further motivate these managers, an attractive financial package was offered, including fringe benefits such as housing, schooling for children, expatriate allowances, and longer vacations. This rotational path has since become part of KFF management's recognized fast track for career progression within the group.

KFF's expansion throughout the region exposed the corporation to new kinds of customers, such as hypermarket chains. This necessitated a change in the business model, which required new knowledge and techniques, and raised awareness of the need to enhance employee skills. Accordingly, the corporation took the initiative and provided employees with intensive training and workshops aimed at improving the competences and skills of its workforce. As a result, it was better able to meet the expectations of its customers and suppliers alike.

Questions

1. What were the forces that necessitated change in the organization?
2. Why is it so difficult for individuals to accept change?
3. What were the forces that helped make the change process smoother?

Source: KFF Holding Manual. Special thanks to Samir Messarra for his valuable suggestions.

Research Exercise

Despite the information that has been presented in this chapter, there are very few studies and surveys conducted on the topic of change and stress in the Arab world. Do some research by contacting individuals and asking about these issues in the local workplace. Share your findings in class.

LEARNING OBJECTIVES

This chapter will enable you to:

1 Define a family business and its three stages.

2 Identify the characteristics of a family business.

3 Identify the significance of the family business in the Arab world.

4 Understand the advantages of the family business.

5 Understand the disadvantages of the family business.

6 Describe the succession plan.

7 Demonstrate how the family business should be transferred.

8 Determine the future of family businesses.

9 Understand family business in a global context.

Organizational Behavior in the Family Business

17

Family businesses always have a core competence in what they do which makes them successful. They do not require the same bureaucratic processes, and are ready to implement the necessary changes, which other companies may be slow to do. —Dr. Khalid Maniar

Family Business Success Stories from the Region: The Habtoor Empire

Khalaf Al Habtoor, the founder and chairman of the Al Habtoor empire, was proactive and had enough vision to realize the significance of setting a well-established succession plan to ensure a smooth transition into the coming generations. He was ready and willing to confront the challenges of competition and globalization, but was aware that guidelines had to be available for the incoming new blood.

Accordingly, Khalaf put family emotions aside and considered the purely business perspective. He decided to determine the proper structures and rules that would reserve rights and allocate responsibilities among the siblings who decided to continue the family business. This was a very courageous step on the part of Khalaf because succession plans are usually not addressed until conflicts emerge and threaten family ties.

"Family businesses don't survive that long for some inherent structural issues," says Mohammad Al Habtoor, Khalaf Al Habtoor's son. "There is a general perception that as family size increases, the pie sometimes does not grow commensurately and different members have different views and objectives."

At 60, Khalaf Al Habtoor, is concerned about how succeeding generations will take over the family business and meet the market challenges. After all, it is running effectively and efficiently, and Khalaf wants this to continue.

Rashid, the eldest son initially worked with his father for three years but, in 1993, decided to establish his own business—Al Habtoor Trading Enterprises. Rashid today operates a diversified business in the Middle East and the former states of the Soviet Union. Mohammad and Ahmad, both educated in the US, and Amna, with a law degree, manage different segments of the group.

The Al Habtoor Group, with its construction, hospitality and car sales businesses, is one of the biggest diversified business consortiums in the UAE and also has interests in the UK. Mohammad (41) is CEO, Ahmad (32) is chief of Habtoor Motors, and Amna looks after the education sector.

None of the children have had it easy; they have all worked very hard to gain not only their father's respect and confidence, but also their positions in the Habtoor empire.

Source: Based on Z. Bitar, "Keeping it all in the family," *Gulf News*, June 14, 2010, http://gulfnews.com/business/features/keeping-it-all-in-the-family-1.640715.

The opening case highlights one of the Arab world's most prominent family businesses. It shows the concerns that the father—owner, founder, CEO, chairman, entrepreneur—usually has regarding the continuity of the business. The succession plan is something not often addressed in the Arab culture, although it is a major source of conflict for following generations. Khalaf Al Habtoor knew that he could only overcome any difficulties by setting clear lines of communication and structure that would facilitate the continuity process. These details will be discussed throughout this chapter, where we will consider other profiles of prominent family businesses in the Arab world. In addition, the characteristics of the family business and the secrets of their success will be discussed.

Before we continue, take the self-assessment exercise below to see if you are experiencing work/family conflict.

Self **A**ssessment **L**ibrary »

AM I EXPERIENCING WORK/FAMILY CONFLICT?

In the Self-Assessment Library (available online), take assessment III.B.3 (Am I Experiencing Work/Family Conflict?) and answer the following questions:

1. *How did you score? Are you surprised by your score?*
2. *Do you think the types of conflict you face might change throughout your career? Why/why not?*
3. *How do you think you could manage/reduce your work/family conflicts?*

What Is a Family Business?

1 Define a family business and its three stages.

Family business

A complex dual system that is made up of the family and the business.

Non-family business

A business system that is usually governed by contract.

Family-owned businesses are an essential and distinct type of organization in the world economy. Many people think of the family business as that small, informal business run by members of a family. However, this impression is wrong—most of the world's largest organizations started as family businesses and many now only have a few family members in senior positions. A few of the well-established examples include Ford Motors, Motorola, Marriott, Levi Strauss, L'Oreal, BMW, LG, Peugeot, Benetton, Fiat, and Gucci. The family business is crucial to the economic wellbeing of the world, and is considered to be the engine for economic development.[1]

The **family business** is a complex dual system that is made up of the *family* and the *business*. Family businesses provide the only location where family issues and business issues overlap. Family members are part of a task system as well as the family system. This is where the danger lies: it is inevitable that conflict will arise since each of the systems has its own rules, roles, and requirements. For instance, the family can have emotional bonds since it stresses relationships and rewards loyalty. Entry into a family business is by birth, membership is permanent, and there are certain responsibilities and expectations. On the other hand, the **non-family business** system may be governed by *contract*. Entry is dependent on experience, expertise, and potential. Membership is contingent on performance, which, in turn, is rewarded in material terms.

Figure 17-1 shows the system of a family business. The numbers determine the dynamics of a family business by identifying five significant roles of family members as defined by family legacy advisors. Person one is a member of all three subsystems, and is often the founder or current leader of the business.

Dr. Juma Khalfan Belhoul is a physician and the founder of the Belhoul Group, a collection of companies specializing in healthcare, pharmaceuticals, education, construction, garment manufacturing, and travel and tourism. As chairman, he maintains an effective business governance plan that separates ownership and management. Juma's eldest son, Faisal Bin Juma Belhoul, has gained his father's trust and was made Chief Executive of the group. All the siblings are shareholders and have all the rights that come with that position. "We tried to institutionalize and professionalize the management role," Faisal says. Most of the brothers are on the board of directors and they are consulted on key decisions. On a case-by-case basis, and dependant on their qualifications and availability, family members are offered an active role as senior director, supporting the manager.

Source: Z. Bitar, "Keeping it all in the family," *Gulf News*, June 2010, http://gulfnews.com/business/features/keeping-it-all-in-the-family-1.640715.

Entrepreneurial stage

The first stage in the evolution of the family business, whereby development is driven by personal and family goals.

Managerial stage

The second stage in the evolution of the family business, whereby development requires expertise, financial discipline, structure, and accountability.

Professional stage

The third stage in the evolution of the family business, whereby development is driven by what is best for the business.

Person two is a family member who is an inactive owner and may or may not participate in decision making, and may or may not share in the financial benefits of ownership. Person three is a family member who is active in the business, but does not have any ownership and receives compensation as an employee. Person four is a non-family owner working in the business. Person five is a family member and uninvolved in the business or ownership.

Family businesses typically evolve through three stages, and the business focus at each stage is different. The **entrepreneurial stage** is designed around the founder or leader and driven by personal and family goals. Next, the business should reach the **managerial stage**, where it is more organized but still based on the family; that is, the company requires expertise, financial discipline, structure, and accountability. Finally the company enters the **professional stage** and is directed by what is best for the business and specific goal-setting. It is important to identify what stage the family-owned business has reached, in order to be able to determine the corresponding leadership style and the

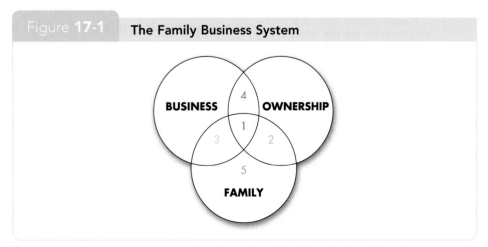

Figure 17-1 **The Family Business System**

Source: Based on information from Family Legacy Advisors LLC website: http://familylegacyadvisorsllc.com/family-business-succession-planning.htm

Besides being profitable, family business can also prove to be socially responsible. Georges Frem, founder of the Georges N. Frem Foundation (GNFF), maintained a strong commitment to community welfare, believing that private companies with social spirit can, in many areas, contribute more effectively than public institutions to solving the problems that hamper the social and economic development of the community. Today, in line with Frem's philosophy "What is good for the community is good for the company," the non-profit organization strives to foster economic development for job creation, nurture civic education and advance steward leadership and collective good. Promoting human dignity and social responsibility are the pillars on which the foundation stands; GNFF translates the Frem family's ongoing commitment to the well-being of the Lebanese community.

most likely strengths and characteristics, which will be discussed in a coming section.

Furthermore, families develop unique styles of communication and resolving conflicts that have taken years to perfect. These particular styles may be appropriate for family situations; however, they may not be the best methods to apply to business situations.[2]

The method of interaction between individual family members and the actual firm creates an environment that determines the performance outcomes of all members. Business leaders have always been confused by the distinction between the performance requirements of the family firm versus the non-family firm.[3] Many times these leaders attempt to discount, ignore, or separate the family factors from the business and refer to the traditional strategy models. As a result, there is usually a failure to consider the specific factors that influence performance within the organization.

What Do You Think?

Do you belong to a family business, or have you observed one in action? Think about the methods of interaction within such a business.

Family firms experience an evolutionary process as they grow from infancy to mature businesses. During this process, business leaders find themselves facing great challenges, such as market competition. If, however, they are not proactive and don't anticipate such threats, then problems emerge; among the consequences could be the collapse of the firm.

When we discussed change management in the previous chapter, it became clear that many businesses have difficulty accepting and adapting to change. Similarly, the family institution may have challenges because the culture of most family businesses does not adapt well to change. In addition, family business leaders tend to create unwanted and unnecessary conflicts and, most importantly, they fail to establish succeeding generations of leaders.[4]

Definitions of the Family Business

The family business has been defined in many different ways. In fact, a review of 250 studies on family businesses shows the use of about 21 different definitions.[5] However, certain common criteria are often used to formulate the definitions, including the percentage of ownership, voting power, degree of involvement in strategy, involvement of the generations, and active management by family members.[6]

One possible definition is that a family business is one in which the majority of ownership or control lies within a family because two or more family members are directly involved in the business. Another definition of a family business is a business that includes two or more relatives and has at least two generations working together. A related definition is of a business that will be passed on for the family's next generation to manage and control.[7]

The above-mentioned definitions highlight the key terms of a family business. They can be combined to define a family business as a business where control is by members of a single family, in which both ownership and policy making are dominated by members of an emotional kinship group, and which has experienced at least one transition between generations.[8]

Statistics about the Family Business

Gross Domestic Profit (GDP)

The market value of all the goods and services produced within a country's borders within a given period of time.

Family businesses account for about 80 percent of businesses worldwide[9], contribute about 50 percent of the **Gross Domestic Product (GDP)**, employ more than 75 percent of the working population, and create about 78 percent of new jobs. Family businesses represent 80 to 90 percent of the world's businesses—90 percent of all businesses in the US, 80 percent of businesses in Germany, France, and Spain, and 90 to 98 percent of the businesses in Italy, India, and Latin America. In addition, family businesses play a vital role in the Arab world, where at least 80 percent of all businesses are family-run and family-owned. In Bahrain, 70 percent of all businesses are family businesses and in Oman 57 percent of the businesses are family-owned.

Since family businesses are a major part of the overall economic system, they generate 49 percent of the GDP in the United States, and over 75 percent of the GDP in other countries. They employ 80 percent of the US workforce, and more than 75 percent of the working population around the world. Moreover, family businesses create 86 percent of all new jobs in the US. In the Gulf region, family businesses control more than 90 percent of commerce.

The average age of a family business in the Middle East is usually a little longer than the world average. The average life-span of the family business is 40 years, and 75 percent of those businesses are managed by the second generation. Certain family businesses in the Arab world have survived for over 100 years.

Even though females in the Middle East are entering the workplace, about 17 percent of family businesses still deny them ownership in the business, and 37 percent are undecided. The reason for this is that the family regards people who have married into the family as a major threat to the stability of the family business. One way to limit any problems that may arise is to ensure that organizational structure is clear, channels of communication are determined, and policy is implemented without any favoritism toward family members. Organizational design will be discussed in the next section.

Planning the Family Business

Planning

A process that includes defining goals, establishing strategy, and developing plans to coordinate activities.

Planning is more crucial to the family business than to any other type of business because most families have a majority of their assets tied up in their business. Consequently, **planning** becomes essential and is related to *succession planning*, *business planning*, and *family planning* (channels of communication among the family).

Succession planning, which will be covered in detail later in this chapter, is a long process that owners usually wait too long to address. The grooming, training, and development of talent in the next generation should start early in the business. Most family businesses do not have a succession plan and this can cause problems in the future.

Lack of planning is often the fault of the founder himself. The founder may consider that the business is an extension of his life and have few outside interests, but if the remaining family members have a different view, the business may die with the founder. Family planning addresses the needs and interests of all family members involved in the business and a family council may be established to guide the communication process between family members and management.

Organizational Structure of the Family Business

In Chapter 13, we discussed the organizational structure of all types of businesses. Let's consider the family business in particular. Does the structure of family organizations differ from others? The actual structure of a family business should not be different from that of any other type of business. Similarly, the **organizational structure** of a family business describes how tasks are formally divided, grouped, and coordinated. The six elements that managers of both family and non-family businesses need to address when they design their organization's structure are *work specialization, departmentalization, chain of command, span of control, centralization and decentralization, and formalization.* Table 17-1 shows each of these elements as answers to an important structural question that a family business may ask.

Individual Differences Evidence relating organizational structures to employee performance and satisfaction stress that we can never generalize. Individuals differ in their needs and preferences and not everyone prefers the freedom and flexibility of organic structures. Some people are most productive and satisfied when work tasks are standardized and ambiguity is minimized, as it is in mechanistic structures. So any discussion of the effect of organizational design on employee behavior has to address individual differences.

Work Specialization The term **work specialization**, or *division of labor*, describes the degree to which activities in the organization are subdivided into separate jobs. The essence of work specialization is that rather than an entire job being done by one individual, it is broken down into a number of steps, with each step being completed by a separate individual who is an expert in a particular area. *Work specialization* contributes to higher employee productivity but at the price of reduced job satisfaction. We must be aware of what motivates people: highly specialized jobs, and the security of routine. A family business will succeed when the members are allocated work according to their specialization. For instance, if a family member is appointed a managerial position even though he or she is not qualified, the consequences could be harmful for the organization.

Organizational structure

The way in which job tasks are formally divided, grouped, and coordinated within an organization.

Work specialization

The degree to which tasks in an organization are subdivided into separate jobs.

TABLE 17-1   Key Questions and Answers for Designing the Proper Organizational Structure for a Family Business

The Key Question	The Answer Is Provided By
1. To what degree are activities subdivided into separate jobs in a family business?	Work specialization
2. On what basis will jobs be grouped together in a family business?	Departmentalization
3. To whom do individuals and groups report in a family business?	Chain of command
4. How many individuals can a manager efficiently and effectively direct in a family business?	Span of control
5. Where does decision-making authority lie in a family business?	Centralization and decentralization
6. To what degree will there be rules and regulations to direct employees and managers in a family business?	Formalization

Departmentalization

The basis by which jobs in an organization are grouped together.

Departmentalization Once you've divided jobs up through work specialization, you need to group these jobs together so that common tasks can be coordinated. The basis by which jobs are grouped together is called **departmentalization**. One of the most popular ways to group activities is by *functions*, type of *product* the organization produces, the basis of *geography*, or territory, and particular type of *customer* the organization serves. The family business can function more effectively once it determines how it should group its jobs.

Chain of command

The unbroken line of authority that extends from the top of the organization to the lowest echelon and clarifies who reports to whom.

Authority

The rights inherent in a managerial position to give orders and to expect the orders to be obeyed.

Unity of command

The idea that a subordinate should have only one superior to whom he or she is directly responsible.

Chain of Command The **chain of command** is a continuous line of authority that extends from the top of the organization to the lowest levels and explains who reports to whom. It answers questions for employees such as "To whom do I go if I have a problem?" and "To whom am I responsible?" The chain of command has two complementary concepts: *Authority* and *unity of command*. **Authority** is the ability to give direction and expect people to implement the decisions; it comes with a managerial position. The **unity of command** states that a person should have only one superior to whom they report. The major problem of chain of command with family businesses lies in the unity of command because if the channels of communication are not clearly determined and articulated, then overlap of authority can pose as a threat to the stability of the organization.

Span of control

The number of subordinates a manager can efficiently and effectively direct.

Span of Control How many employees can a manager efficiently and effectively direct? The answer to this question identifies the **span of control** of a manager. It's impossible to know what span of control is best for producing high performance or high satisfaction among employees. Again, the reason is probably individual differences. That is, some people like to be left alone, while others prefer the security of a boss who is quickly available at all times.

Consistent with several of the contingency theories of leadership discussed in Chapter 10, we would expect factors such as employees' experiences and abilities and the degree of structure in their tasks to explain when wide or narrow spans of control are likely to contribute to their performance and job satisfaction. The family business is no exception, and the span of control will definitely contribute to a more effective and efficient outcome.

Centralization and Decentralization In some organizations, whether family businesses or not, top managers make all the decisions and lower-level managers just carry out top management's directions. At the other extreme, there are organizations in which decision making is pushed down to the managers who are closest to the action. The former organizations are highly centralized; the latter are known to be decentralized.

Centralization

The degree to which decision making is concentrated at a single point in an organization.

We find fairly strong evidence linking **centralization** and job satisfaction. In general, organizations that are less centralized have a greater amount of autonomy. And the evidence suggests that autonomy is positively related to job satisfaction. But, again, individual differences must be addressed here. Many family businesses tend to be centralized and thus employees have less autonomy, and this can be demotivating and frustrating to many people.

Formalization

The degree to which jobs within an organization are standardized.

Formalization The degree to which jobs within the organization are standardized is known as **formalization**. If a job is highly formalized, then the employee has a minimum amount of influence over what is to be done, when it is to be done, and how it is to be done. On the other hand, where formalization is low, job behaviors are relatively nonprogrammed, and employees have a great deal of freedom to exercise discretion in their work. The family business may restrict the degree to which family members or non-family members are able to influence direction or decision making within the organization.

The Characteristics of the Family Business

2 Identify the characteristics of a family business.

In a previous section, we mentioned that a family business deals with both family issues and business issues and it is this significant overlap between the family and the business that is considered to be a **major characteristic** of a family business. Other noteworthy characteristics of a family business are:[10]

1. The family members themselves, with all they have to offer the business.
2. If the family business stops growing, then the overlap of family, management, and ownership will leave the business helpless during succession.
3. The unique competitive advantage that a family business can gain if the family members remain unified.
4. The dream of the owner to ensure the business remains in the family and a strong will to continue from one generation to another.

Because of the family presence, a family business may show a more positive and encouraging corporate culture than does a business not affiliated with a particular family. The 3 Ps (Parsimony, Personalism and Particularism) as characteristics of family businesses are more relevant than others.[11]

Parsimony, is relevant because family businesses have to be careful about their financial resources, as they are owned by the family. Second, **personalism** dictates that the family business does not have to account for all its decisions to external bodies, since ownership and control belong to the family members. Third, **particularism** means that the family business can set goals that are different from those of a profit-maximizing non-family business.

We will be discussing various issues related to the family business in the rest of this chapter, but what we really need to keep in mind as we proceed is that the family business has its specifications. Still, we need to remember that the organizational structure and culture of any business is determined by its framework, as we saw in Chapter 13, and the family business is no exception. We have discussed the characteristics of a family business, so let's now take a look at some specific examples of prominent family businesses in the Arab world.

Major characteristic

The significant overlap between the family and the business that is considered to be a major characteristic of a family business.

Parsimony

The unwillingness of a business to use its financial resources.

Personalism

A doctrine that emphasises the value of the individual person within his or her social, political or familial environment.

Particularism

Exclusive commitment to the interests of one's own group or family.

Organizational Behavior in the Family Business

Now, we turn to the question of organizational behavior in family-owned versus non-family-owned businesses.

OB in the News

The Family Business: The Foundation of Arab World Success

After the death of their father Ali Abdul Wahab Al Mutawa, in 1946, the first-born son, Abdul Aziz Ali Al Mutawa, and his brother Abdullah continued to manage the business. The company has gained widespread acknowledgement and a clean reputation through the affiliation of the family name with many prominent institutions and companies. A few of these are Kuwait Overland Transport Company, Jordan Kuwait Bank, Kuwait Chamber of Commerce and Industry, and American–Kuwaiti Friendship Association. Moreover, another brother, Faisal Ali Al Mutawa, established Bayan Investment Company, a Kuwait shareholding company, in 1997 to provide various consultancy and investment services; it was listed on the Kuwait Stock Exchange in 2003, and then in the Dubai Financial Market in 2006.

The three sons, Abdul Aziz, Abdullah, and Faisal jointly managed the business and established a trade system under the name of their father, Ali Abdulwahab Sons & Co. Faisal, who acquired a bachelor degree in Business Administration and Political Sciences from the American University of Beirut (AUB), has held different positions such as vice-president and managing director. Today, Faisal is general manager and chief executive officer, following the death of his brother Abdullah in 2006.

Today, Ali Abdulwahab Sons & Co. ranks among the top trading companies in Kuwait, dealing with a diversified range of products. It is one of the leading and most prominent Kuwaiti companies in retail and wholesale. The company has over 90 years of established experience in the marketplace and is an agent for over 40 US and European commercial brands.

What is noteworthy is that the good name of Ali Abdulwahab Sons & Co. was established not only through the company's own activities, but also through the family's involvement in various of the world's most well-known brand names, such as Procter & Gamble, Kelvinator of the US, and Bosch and Siemens of Germany. Furthermore, Ali Abdulwahab Sons & Co. owns more than 22 pharmacies and distributes pharmaceuticals to a large number of the pharmacies in Kuwait. This successful family business also possesses a significant share in the real estate residential and investment sector in Kuwait.

Source: Based on Family Business Profile: Ali Abdulwahab Sons & Co, Kuwait, June, 2010, www.zawya.com/story.cfm/sidZAWYA201002222090023?ar.

Every business depends on individuals, groups, and its structure and their impact on the effectiveness and efficiency of the organization. The family business is no exception to this definition of organizational behavior.

The absence of a clear organizational structure and a board to oversee the day-to-day activities and management of the firm is likely to result in problems and ultimately affect performance. Family owners who are not involved in the running of the firm are in a position to observe the business in an objective fashion. One of the issues that they may be concerned about is whether the firm is progressing as efficiently as it would be if it had a formal organization. In short, an effective board and a logical management structure are necessary conditions for retaining family loyalty in a growing family firm and for the continued success of the firm itself.[12]

The survival of family businesses is dependent on how they manage the complex interaction of the family, the business, and individual family members as part of the family business system. Family businesses are unique. They offer a real sense of mission and legacy, while providing both flexibility and success. It follows that owners, managers, employees, and family members must learn to balance their roles, expectations, and communication channels for the 'common good' of the family and the business. However, often the balance is tough to keep and leads to obstacles to success. Finally, the family business does not stand in a category by itself. It is still an organization and must have the system, processes, and structure of an effective organization. As a result, organizational behavior in family businesses will be directed by the ways in which individuals are treated and strategy is implemented.

Family Businesses Are Dominant in the Arab World

3 Identify the significance of the family business in the Arab world.

We have defined the family business and looked at its characteristics, so now let's see *why* the family business is so significant in any culture, paying particular attention to Arab culture. The family is a vital part of the society and community, as explained by Geert Hofstede[13] when he talks about the cultural dimensions that influence individuals and groups. From this explanation, we can understand why the family is so important specifically in the Arab world and, as an extension, why the family business is dominant in the Arab world. Box 17-1 provides some examples of prominent family businesses across the region.

BOX 17-1

Some Examples of Family Businesses in the Arab World

Trama. Founded in 1983 by Mr. Tony E. Hanna in Lebanon, Trama's objective was to import and distribute disposable plastic articles for daily use. Within a short period, the firm had acquired a reputation in the marketplace and spread to all regions of Lebanon. Thereafter, management decided to follow a path of structured expansion to reach the KSA, UAE, and Turkey.

M. A. Kharafi & Sons. Kuwait's Nasser Al-Kharafi's family business, M. A. Kharafi & Sons, is one of the Arab world's oldest and most prominent family businesses, with interests that include hospitality, construction, manufacturing, and marketing.

The Gargash Group. Founded by Ali Gargash in the UAE, The Gargash Group is now run by his son, Anwar Muhammad Gargash. Anwar has established himself in the insurance, financial, and real estate sectors and the Group also has the dealership of Mercedes-Benz for Dubai and the northern Emirates.

Ajmal Perfumes. Abdulla A. Ajmal is Deputy-General Manager of Ajmal Perfumes in Dubai, and a third generation family member. In 1951, the Ajmal family business established itself with the ambitious vision of its founder, Ali Ajmal. Ali moved from a small Indian village to the capital Mumbai, and then sent one of his sons to the UAE where the family established what is today one of the most popular fragrance houses in the Middle East. Abdullah explains that the internationalization of their brands reflects the best of both worlds from the East and West.

The Nasser Bin Khaled Holding. The late Sheikh Nasser Bin Khaled Al Thani founded the Nasser Bin Khaled Holding over 50 years ago. Upon its establishment, the company sold and distributed reputable international brands in the Qatari market, and then went on to expand its activities to include investment, industrial, and trade sectors. Thereafter, the Nasser Bin Khaled Holding became a significant player in the rapidly developing economy of Qatar.

Anwar Gargash, shown here carrying out his duties as the UAE Minister of State for Foreign Affairs, is also a prominent scholar and businessman. He runs the family business that his father, Ali Haji Abdulla Gargash, started in 1918 and which now makes up the expansive Gargash Group. In addition to insurance, construction, real estate and hospitality operations, the Gargash empire includes Gargash Enterprises: *the* Mercedes-Benz dealership for Dubai and the northern Emirates, of which Answar Gargash is the executive director.

Any family business life cycle involves four stages: (1) creation of the business; (2) growth and development; (3) succession to the second generation; (4) ensuring of public ownership and professional management. However, while the older members of a family may be less concerned with financial needs and more interested in the family's legacy, the younger members may have no strong connection to the business other than their name, some shares and perhaps participation in a trust fund.

"Lessons learned from family businesses could prove to be very apt during this unprecedented time and non-family owned businesses could take some strategic insight from this most enduring model of family businesses," says Soha Nashaat, CEO of Barclays Wealth Middle East.[14] Family businesses are an important source of wealth, creation, and employment and the statistics show that 95 percent of businesses in Asia, the Middle East, Italy and Spain are family controlled.[15]

The Family Business in the Arab World

Most family businesses in the Arab world are not dependent on structured management systems but rather on bloodlines and trust. Accordingly, credibility and reputation is the most valuable asset that the family business can hold. The family name is an integral part of the business: even if it is sold or the name is changed to a professional name in place of the family name, the company will always be known by its family name.

One concern of the family business in the Arab world is the possibility of conflicts among family members that may threaten the stability of the business. In particular, father–son disagreements are common when the father doesn't retire even though the next generation has taken over the business.[16] The fathers usually consider themselves to be indispensable and have difficulty letting go of the reins.

The dominance of the family business in the Arab world has been identified. However, we must realize that family businesses do have advantages and disadvantages, just like any other type of business. The next sections will discuss these pros and cons.

International OB

Globalization: The Direction of Arab Family Businesses

Globalization is a great challenge; however, any well-established business should be able to overcome any challenge. "Thirty to 40 percent of family businesses in the Arab world have an international footprint or are in the process of going global." This statement was made by Dr. Hischam El Agamy, who is the founder and board member of Tharawat Family Business Forum, the Arab network for family-run and family-owned companies. This forum provides a platform for the mutual exchange of knowledge and insights on management, growth, continuity, strategy, and other business-related topics. These regional companies are well aware of the positive consequences of being affiliated with an international company, and of being located in another international destination.

A recent study by Booz & Company found that the Arab family-run business had all the requirements and specifications to effectively compete in the global economy, even though it faces many obstacles in a region where so many factors are often against progress. El Agamy insists that "There is a trend of acquiring or entering into strategic alliances." There are also opportunities available to show the potential and quality of local production. Accordingly, El Agamy continues, "The market is more open than ever before. You can't rely on your local market and be protected. Cross-border competition is there. This is a challenge and also opportunity."

In fact, family businesses in the Arab world are growing and witnessing transitions from one generation to another: new blood is entering to offer fresh ideas. Often, this results in a clash between the old school of thought and the new school. This may be inevitable, but these businesses need to be aware of the consequences and thus keep an open mind and become more innovative. It comes as no surprise, then, that so many family businesses in this part of the world show flexibility and innovation.

Family businesses also play a significant role in the US economy. According to the Family Firm Institute in Brookline, Massachusetts, family businesses contribute to 78 percent of job creation and 60 percent of national employment. In addition, about 35 percent of the Fortune 500 companies are family firms. Among the most prominent family businesses that are still controlled by their founding families are Ford, Johnson & Johnson, Marriott, Motorola, Philip Morris, and Wal-Mart. In Canada, one of the largest businesses, Cara, is a family-owned company that operates about 1,200 restaurants and employs over 39,000 people.

Nevertheless, there are risks involved, and it is these risks that should encourage these firms to make sure that all their people are in harmony and working as a team to enhance the image of the business. "They are encouraging their employees to come up with ideas and their top management is implementing the ideas to improve products, market presence, processes. There is a shift, which is also due to economic crisis. But it is a gradual shift. Family businesses are risk averse and at the same time they want to grow. So they have to balance risk and growth," says El Agamy.

Finally, it is important to note that family firms outperformed non-family firms in shareholder creation by 15 percent between January 2005 and October 2008, according to an index compiled by Credit Suisse. This enhanced performance of family businesses encouraged and attracted international shareholders, as the index used is known for its credibility worldwide.

Sources: S. Pathak, "Arab Family Businesses Go Global," *Emirates 24/7*, June 7, 2010, www.emirates247.com/eb247/economy/regional-economy/arab-family-businesses-go-global-2010-06-07-1.252487; N. Stein, "The Age of the Scion," *Fortune*, April 2001, p. 21; M. Brown, "Inside an Empire," *Canadian Business*, May–June, 2004, p. 61; and www.booz.com/media/uploads/GCC_Family_Businesses_Face_New_Challenges.pdf

Advantages of the Family Business

> 4 *Understand the advantages of the family business.*

Psychological contract

An unwritten agreement that sets out what management expects from an employee and vice versa.

In general, family businesses work for a number of reasons but most importantly, they add social and emotional dimensions to the art of making money. The traditional **psychological contract** between individual and organization is breaking down and the family business represents a safe place to be. We must always remember that families have their own loyalties and culture that non-family businesses usually have more difficulty in creating. Such loyalty is the emotional glue that holds the family together, no matter what comes its way, and it also develops a sense of corporate identity and commitment.

> **Picture This**
>
> You are part of a family business but have some personal problems with your cousin, Rabih. The chairman of one of your major competitors, Mr. Abd Al Razzak, has just finished a meeting with Rabih. As he leaves the office, you hear Razzak threatening Rabih. As a family member, how do you react?

A publicly owned business will always be thinking about the next quarterly or annual financial results to keep shareholders happy, whereas a family-controlled business will have an eye on the next generation. Additionally, the family's reputation will play an important role in the decision-making process and as a result will promote a sense of continuity through financial considerations.

The founders of the family business create organizations to fulfill their needs and desires, and establish structures and motivate employees to carry out their vision. This is also true for other types of businesses, but the founders of family businesses can focus on continuity into the coming generations. In other words, these founders have the incentive for long-term success right from setting up of the business. Nevertheless, in the case of illness or sudden death, followers may be lost and this dependency can leave the organization and the family in a weak position.[17]

In other words, family-owned firms can offer employees the communication, care, dependability, and security that are all too often missing in companies that focus day-to-day on stock prices. Other unique advantages include stability, trust, resilience, speed, and the ability to sacrifice short-term considerations for long-term benefits.[18]

Family businesses offer freedom, independence, and control in addition to many lifestyle benefits such as flexibility, prestige, community pride, and creativity. Family businesses normally allow closer interaction with management, are less bureaucratic, have a built-in trust factor with established relationships, and provide for hands-on training and early exposure of the next generation to the business.

There is no doubt that any business will contribute great effort, time and expertise to remain successful in today's turbulent environment. The family business will also operate in a similar fashion but perhaps to a higher degree, because the family name and reputation is at stake. Consequently, family businesses may think more long-term, put in longer hours, become more flexible and efficient, may focus on quality goods and services, and act more ethically.

Thus, loyalty and pride should motivate family members to persevere and overcome obstacles, and put aside their self-interest and pay attention to the common good of the business.

Disadvantages of the Family Business

> 5 Understand the disadvantages of the family business.

Family businesses do experience many problems that may be very intense but the hope is that family members will be able to work through them because, as the proverb goes, "blood is thicker than water." One major disadvantage relates to lines of succession: these may not benefit the organization since the different generations will have different needs and demands. In fact, while the founder may be driven to succeed, members of the next generation may simply feel trapped in the family business and may feel no commitment. In addition, those people who are not family members may not feel an emotional attachment to the company.[19]

Another problem that family businesses tend to face is the issue of change. Resistance to change is especially strong in family firms because certain family members see change as a threat to their power and security.[20] Founders may look at change as a sign of decline and death of their family business. In addition, decision making is often delayed because founders have difficulty delegating decision making to employees. Yet another obstacle is the fact that non-family members are generally not considered for top management positions, and this in turn demotivates people and decreases their loyalty and commitment, and thus affects performance and productivity.

Family businesses are often sources of difficulty when it comes to succession issues, identity development, and sibling relationships. Succession—discussed in the next section—is one of the largest challenges facing family businesses. Succession becomes an issue when the senior generation does not allow the junior generation the necessary room to grow, effectively develop, and eventually assume the leadership of the business. Often business relationships deteriorate because of lack of communication within the family and this develops into ongoing criticism, judgments, lack of support, and lack of trust.

Non-family members in managerial positions may be discouraged when they are not involved in the decision-making process and when all business-related issues are addressed by either the owner or only family members. Additionally, the concerns and interests of family members may not be aligned with those of the business and this can threaten the business. Family members should possess the qualifications, commitment, ability, and willingness to reach a balance.[21]

Family-owned businesses have a set of shared traditions and values that are rooted in the history of the firm. Family businesses can honor their traditions if they allow the business to grow, but it wouldn't be logical to let traditions block the road to progress and change. Family communication, conflict with relatives, and sibling relationships typically rank among the top ten concerns among family-owned businesses, and they should be confronted and resolved. Other keys to a successful family business include mutual respect, good role models within the family, the ability not to take business issues personally, and the patience and ability to listen to others.

Family businesses do have several advantages and disadvantages in common with non-family businesses; however, the way in which the family business is transferred to the next generation differs from non-family businesses, as we will determine in the following section.

The Succession Plan

6 Describe the succession plan.

As the next generation prepares itself to enter the family business, existing management has difficult decisions to make to determine who would make good leaders. Thus, the succession crisis emerges and many issues need to be considered.

Usually, only about one-third of family businesses are successfully transferred to the second generation, with about 10 to 20 percent making it to the third generation.[22] Fewer than 13 percent stay in the family for more than 60 years. At one of the Arab-German Family Business Summits that was held recently in Cairo, it was mentioned that only 6 percent of family businesses survive past the third generation.

Smooth transitions can fail for many reasons, the most common of which is that the children may not be interested in the family business. Parents just assume that they will pass it on to the children regardless of their feelings. Another reason is rivalry between the various brothers and sisters, which can destroy a family business. Finally, the founder may find it difficult to release control of the business, something that can become increasingly difficult if there are business partners.[23]

The process of transferring leadership to the next generation is known as **succession** and will only be effective if there is a plan of action.

A particular survey by PwC Belgium of more than 1,600 family business executives in 35 countries found that only 50 percent have decided who will take over the top job. Since over 80 percent of Middle Eastern companies are run by families, succession planning becomes an issue of urgency. The authors of the study commented: "One of the biggest risks facing any family-owned business is the transition from one generation to the next. Twenty-seven percent of survey respondents said they expect their business to change hands within the next five years, with 53 percent of these companies expecting the business to remain in the family. Yet 48 percent of all companies have no succession plan, a similar percentage to the last survey two years ago. Of those that do have a succession plan, only 50 percent have decided who will take over the top job."[24]

In most cultures, succession does not take place until the retirement or death of the entrepreneur, and this is still the case in most Arab world countries. However, the Eastern ideology is starting to change and become aware that children should be able to decide on their own career paths, and, most importantly, of the need to avoid any conflict among the siblings. One attorney who specializes in family businesses states, "The easiest part of a succession plan is transferring the hard assets; the most difficult part is transferring leadership and values."[25]

Succession

The process of transferring leadership to the next generation.

What Do You Think?

If you were a member of a family business, would you find it easy to talk to your father about inheritance issues?

How and When Should the Business Be Transferred?

7 Demonstrate how the family business should be transferred.

There are many options for transferring ownership. Ownership may be transferred to family members as a gift or it may be sold to them. Equally, it may be transferred while the entrepreneur is still living or after death. Some transfers may even be combinations of several options. Whatever the case, the decision should be made with the tax implications of the country in mind and, therefore, legal and financial advice is essential.

Many family-owned companies in the GCC were founded in the mid-twentieth century and accordingly they are now between their second and third generation of family control. Of course, these firms are governed by a patriarch who is not easily going to give up control of the company he founded and built up. In addition, tradition dictates that transfer of responsibility follows a set pattern— for example, to the oldest son—even though other siblings may be more capable of carrying out the duties.[26]

Sometimes what happens is that the business is divided among the siblings to ensure that everyone has some level of authority, as was shown in the opening case about the Habtoor family. However, the problem here is that certain members may feel that they have been treated unfairly and this will have negative effects on management, and may threaten the stability of both the company and the family. As Ahmed Youssef, a partner at Booz & Company, says: "The solution is to establish clear lines between governance of the family and management of the business . . . It's crucial that the company recruits managers from outside the family, ensuring that responsibility for its future goes to those most qualified, not merely those best positioned because of their family ties."[27]

It is evident that a major source of conflict for family businesses in the Arab world is the issue of succession and ownership because it creates misunderstandings among family members. Family business planning advisors stress the need to address the issue of succession planning and resolve any problems with parents, siblings, uncles and cousins in a friendly manner.

Nasser Saidi, chief economist of the Dubai International Financial Centre, listed five major challenges with regard to succession planning in the GCC[28]. These can be summarized as follows:

1. Difficulties of bringing the younger generation into the business.
2. Controlling the crisis of succession planning.
3. Addressing the issue of dilution in big families.
4. How to face up to the crisis of competition, with the opening of markets and having more players, both regional and global.
5. Businesses facing pressure amid the latest economic crises.

Many family businesses don't survive very long, with only 5 percent surviving into the fourth generation. Only around 15 percent survive into the third generation. Saidi says the reasons for this are: the inherent structural issues of informal management structures; ineffective oversight and control mechanism; and non-alignment of incentives among family members—all of which result in conflict and lack of discipline.

Family Business Continuity

Business continuity

The ability of a business to continue during and after a setback.

When a business continues even after the founders have gone, this is known as **business continuity**. In fact, in a family business, continuity is maintained only if the family and the business stay together for many generations. Earlier, we spoke about the set of values and goals that family businesses establish; it is these values and goals that should be preserved.

There are several aspects that can be used to focus on continuity; at least one of the following should be maintained to ensure business continuity:[29]

1. *Strategy*: continuing the value proposition of the business.
2. *Ownership and/or governance*: preserving the memory, legacy, or the founder's and/or leader's wishes about the family and the business.

The Tharawat Family Business Forum is a non-profit organization that manages a network of family-owned enterprises in the MENA region; it has made an effort to strengthen connections between family businesses and advocate their interests in the business world at large. Founded in 2006 by Dr. Hischam El Agamy along with several Arab family businesses, it provides a platform for the exchange of knowledge and insights on management, growth, continuity, strategy, and other family business-related topics.

3. *Family leadership of the business*: keeping the business in the family and maybe with certain family members.
4. *Family cohesion*: using the business as a vehicle for cohesion; that is, family first.
5. *The business culture*: preserving the values set by the founder, leader, or family. These values include approaches used with employees, suppliers, customers, community, and other stakeholders.
6. *Mission*: conserving the mission; why the business performs such activities.
7. *Independence*: exercising independent judgment. This cannot be achieved unless the business remains in the hands of the same family.

Continuity is not the objective but the result of retaining the original spirit of the organization.

The Future of the Family Business

8 Determine the future of the family businesses.

Family businesses will continue to play a great role in world economies into the next century. They will become more recognized as business organizations, and be studied and written about in increasing depth. Schools and colleges will recognize the family business as a career option of choice and provide direction and resources for students to pursue opportunities there.

To pursue those opportunities, family businesses should prepare themselves for the future in a better fashion because certain statistics lead to concern:[30]

- 62 percent haven't prepared for the possible sickness or death of a key manager or stakeholder.
- 56 percent haven't established any procedures for purchasing the shares of incapacitated or deceased shareholders.
- 50 percent either lack the liquidity to buy out family members who want to dispose of their stakes in the business, or haven't considered the possibility.

- 37 percent don't know how much domestic capital gains tax they or their companies might be liable for, while 58 percent don't know the international implications.

Over 50 percent of the leaders of family businesses in the United States think their businesses will be owned and managed by two or more of their children, so the future looks bright. Even in Eastern Europe entrepreneurs are emerging and rekindling family businesses from years ago. They are starting family businesses for the next generation, and others are using family support systems to launch new enterprises. In Italy, family businesses are so common that the Chamber of Commerce tracks each family member and their position in the firm, along with the traditional business information that is regularly collected. Asians have a legacy of passing on their family traditions in business and of all working together with a central business focus. The next century will bring more research on how ethnicity affects families in business.

Global Implications

9 *Understand family business in a global context.*

Some significant global data, such as the fact that family businesses create an estimated 70 to 90 percent of global GDP annually, can clarify matters more. The majority (two-thirds) of family business owners in a Barclays/Economist poll want to ensure a livelihood for their dependents by running the business.[31] In addition, the environment for innovation in family businesses improves when more generations of the owning family are actively involved in it.

Many small- and medium-sized family companies have trouble fully participating in global markets, due to the lack of necessary resources, other personal factors, and because of political influences. Thus, internationalization becomes more likely when younger family members are involved in managing the company. Family businesses in developing countries are often owned by foreign minorities—known as middleman minorities—and tend to be the dominant force in those economies.

In 2010, the Dubai International Financial Centre (DIFC) hosted a seminar to discuss how family businesses can sustain and enhance their growth in the current economic environment. Abdulla Mohammed Al Awar, CEO of DIFC, said: "Family businesses constitute the heart of the region's economy. To help family businesses negotiate today's economic challenges and take better advantage of new business opportunities, DIFC has created a platform for families to establish dedicated Family Offices. We have created specific regulations to enable family businesses to set up holding companies at DIFC for managing their private wealth. Such resources are critical to family-run institutions in negotiating the critical challenges they face in sustaining and growing their business in today's economic environment."

Source: Press Release by Dubai International Financial Centre Authority, April 2010, http://www.ameinfo.com/229467.html

DIFC Knowledge Series 8: CREATING SUSTAINABLE FAMILY BUSINESSES IN THE MIDDLE EAST

In the light of globalization, we need to enhance and clarify the image of the family business to get rid of any queries that may arise and misunderstandings that may lead to conflicts for which there are no solutions.

Summary and Implications for Managers

The theme of this chapter has been family businesses and their significance in the Arab world. It is not practical to think that the children will automatically want to become part of the business, so failure of the business in the future cannot be ruled out. The reasons for the possible failure must be addressed to avoid them. Reasons include lack of business knowledge, skills, and commitment on the part of successor generations, lack of planning for succession, and family problems that may impact business operations. It takes the right ingredients and the appropriate combination of entrepreneurial spirit and family unity, and the result can be a powerful family force.

The issue of trust is very important in a family business for it reflects the reputation and credibility of the company's name. These are usually an extension of the founder's belief patterns and values. In particular, we must note that the family business deals with both the family-related issues and the business-related issues, and the overlap of these issues can cause conflict if structure is not clear and channels of communication identified.

If we create a family-business-friendly environment, then all members—family and non-family—of the organization will become committed to the mission. The firm's survival is a major matter that must be addressed by facilitating transfer through a well-structured succession plan. Individuals must learn how to place the interests of the company ahead of their own personal interests.

Final statistics that can sum up the family business in the Arab world are:[32]

1. Around 75 percent of the Middle East's private economy is controlled by 5,000 high-net-worth families, with their companies creating 70 percent of the region's employment.
2. Family businesses control over 90 percent of commercial activity.
3. In the region, it is estimated that family businesses worth more than US$1 trillion will be handed down to the next generation within the next five to ten years.
4. With charity being a requirement of Islam, business families in the Muslim-Arab world have begun to structure their charitable endeavors to improve their support of the poor.
5. All but about 2 percent of Gulf companies are family controlled. Largely because owners have a variety of religious affiliations, management styles differ widely among the various businesses. The array of Islam's sectarian groups means that owners adopt different management styles, from authoritarian to consultative.

Point >< Counterpoint

IS STRUCTURE NEEDED?

Any type of organization requires structure; the family business is no exception. Many family businesses in the region have informal channels of communication. However, these informal structures can be damaging to the business. Employees feel they are scapegoats because any conflict among family members is taken out on them. There will also be an overlap of authority because every person will want to give 'orders.' Clearly then, the chain of disagreements will continue and ultimately the business will suffer.

With formal structure, though, not all family members may be involved in problem solving and decision making. Because there may be many generations within the business, it is more fruitful to allow for informal channels of communication so that all members can offer suggestions.

Informal structure allows more flexibility and freedom of speech and this can help managers to interact more openly and without restrictions.

Questions for Review

1 What are the three stages that a family business experiences?

2 What are the characteristics of a family business?

3 Why are family businesses significant in the Arab world?

4 What are the advantages of a family business?

5 What are the disadvantages of a family business?

6 How can the succession of a family business be as smooth as possible?

7 What are issues to consider when transferring a family business?

8 How do you see the future of family businesses in the Arab world?

Discussion Exercise

What would be the advantages and disadvantages of growing up in a family in which one parent owns a business and the other parent works as an employee in another firm?

On the other hand, what would be the advantages and disadvantages of having both parents working in the family business? Discuss.

Ethical Considerations

Muneer Abdul Hakim continued in his father's footsteps and ran the successful family bakery. Muneer and Haifa had only one child, Nawal. Unfortunately, Muneer passed away, and Haifa, a devoted wife and mother, carried on with the family business. Nawal was only seven when her father died, and spent all her time at the bakery, cleaning tables, taking orders, and working at the counter and interacting with customers. As a result, she became very involved and attached to the bakery.

When it was time, Nawal went away to college to study restaurant management because she had great ambitions of expanding the business and introducing innovative ideas when she came back home. Meanwhile, Haifa remarried, and her new husband had two teenaged daughters: Lubna and Rabihya. Since the girls were still at school and she needed help, Haifa encouraged them to work in the business part time.

It followed that Nawal became very concerned about this situation; she now had stepsisters. The ownership of the bakery was now an issue, and similarly, Nawal was worried that if she took a job after graduation, her mother might think that she was no longer interested in the family business. So when Nawal came home between semesters, she spoke to her mother about the future of the business. It came as a surprise when her mother's response was, "I'm only 44 years old and I'm not going to retire for a long time. Don't worry about anything."

Discuss the ethical implications of Nawal's situation. Do you think Nawal has reason to be worried? Explain.

Critical Analysis

FROM LONDON TO LEBANON

In June 2009, whilst on a trip to the UK, business partners Bassam Michel Sleiman and Jean Johnston came up with the concept of bringing the 'London Taxi' to Lebanon. They established contact with the London Taxi Company in Coventry, UK, and prepared a business plan explaining their concept. To their delight, three months later contracts were signed and, at last, an idea became reality.

"The venture meant much effort and sacrifice, especially as we wanted to remain a family-run business, eventually leading to a franchise system with acknowledged standards. It is well known that a family business is one of the hardest to achieve and with our family this was to prove even harder, as no one had any experience in the taxi business. However, we took this venture as a challenge and decided that the sky was the limit.

Preparations for acquiring the first ten taxis started in earnest. We assessed our family and delegated to them certain jobs, since our work commitments obliged us to be abroad. Accordingly, Michel Sleiman, Bassam's father, was asked to oversee all the work; Elie Sleiman, a cousin, had the responsibility of finding a location for the showroom; and Bassam's sister, Nelly Sleiman, was asked to recruit people with a commercial/marketing background, who believed in what we were doing. The design of the showroom was a mixture of everyone's ideas as we had to take into account a garage that would not only service the taxis but also bring other business in by servicing other cars. We needed builders, electricians, plumbers, equipment, drivers, and operators, and so we used friends of friends to help build our showroom.

Looking back it seemed so simple, but in reality our troubles were just beginning. It seemed everyone had a cousin, uncle, or brother-in-law that needed a job, and how could we please everyone from the family? More importantly, how do we not upset anyone in the family? So we took a stand and set out the criteria that all drivers had to speak English, be smart in appearance, and above all believe in the ethos of the 'London driver'. This was a safe haven for us where family was concerned, as we made sure everyone knew what was expected and that we could not employ anyone who did not meet these criteria. The plan worked, although we still had family commitments which we kept by employing family members whenever we could.

Everything was now ready for the big launch of 'National New Dawn: London Taxi'—now generally known as 'London Taxi'. Our marketing manager, Rabih Dib, is a true believer in the concept and set about arranging interviews with television stations and newspapers, as well as preparing a marketing campaign that had the London Taxi on display in key locations around Lebanon. Soon everyone was talking about London Taxi.

Today, after two years, we are still growing. Yes, the old cliché about working with family is correct, but nonetheless we have decided to pass the chain of command to our elder sister, Gisele Sleiman. Although Gisele has no previous experience, she has proved without any shadow of a doubt that if you believe in something, the strength to move it forward comes from within and the strength of the whole family wanting it to succeed carries you onward and upward. In time, London Taxi will become an icon of Lebanon."

Questions

1. With reference to the concepts discussed in this chapter, discuss the challenge that the Sleiman family faced.

2. What advantages and disadvantages of family business are apparent from this case?

3. What advice would you give the Sleiman family for continued success?

Source: Case study contributed by Bassem M. Sleiman, National New Dawn: London Taxi.

Research Exercise

Visit a family business in your area and do some research, and ask about the structure at that organization. Collect more information about the channels of communication and the challenges that the family members are facing, and how they try to overcome them. Share your findings with the class, and comment.

Part 6 Specifics in OB

LEARNING OBJECTIVES

This chapter will enable you to:

1 Define *intercultural management.*

2 Understand Hofstede's cultural dimensions and their implications for the Arab world.

3 Understand what intercultural managers do.

4 Determine the significance of communication for intercultural managers.

5 Identify the role of the intercultural manager in international business practice.

6 Realize that intercultural managers need to be global managers.

Intercultural Management: The Significance to Organizational Behavior

18

The present and future offer opportunities for more synergistic relationships if both Europeans and Arabs learn to appreciate each other's cultural heritages and differences.

—Philip R. Harris, Robert T. Moran, and Sarah V. Moran

'Our Visions Are Sky High'

Dr. Anthony Said Hasham is an entrepreneur of Lebanese origin, born in Australia, who conducts business in numerous countries around the world, and this requires excellent communication skills and tolerance. Dr. Hasham established Australian Consulting Engineers Pty Ltd (ACE) in 1998. Since then, and as a result of Dr. Hasham's exceptional people skills, the company has expanded and established a prominent name for itself, providing civil, structural, architectural and building services, as well as project management consultation services for projects throughout New South Wales, Australia, and the Arab world. In 2009 Dr. Hasham went on to be a founding member of Futurebuild, an engineering consulting and contracting company in Abu Dhabi that caters for the Arab world, and an offshore Australian company called Australian Lebanese Design Services, established in Beirut in 2011.

Dr. Hasham's multicultural background and vast experience have enabled him to lecture on civil and structural engineering at top universities and publish several articles in local and international journals. Dr. Hasham is highly regarded and respected in his field for his unique style of intercultural management and professional ethics, and he has thus established an impeccable reputation. Moreover, Dr. Hasham has won several prestigious awards for his contributions to engineering and is an advocate of engineering education. He has established excellent rapport through his articulate communication skills, and cooperates with professional organizations to cultivate social networks.

The teams of dedicated professionals at each of the locations are motivated to consistently deliver innovative and cost-effective solutions to all clients in Australia and the Arab world. Dr. Hasham says:

Our philosophy is clear and simple; we practice proactive management and are 'people oriented.' We focus on our clientele and their needs to enable us to deliver innovative and sustainable solutions to engineering problems. We are advocates of Total Quality Management and, accordingly, ongoing improvement is at the top of our agenda. In addition, we provide mentoring to all employees and opportunities for self-development. Accordingly, clients express unanimous satisfaction and consistently rate us as accessible, friendly, helpful, and ethical.

Although Dr. Hasham realizes the significance of open communication channels, he is also aware of the cultural implications and respects the diversity of channels that he has to deal with, and all staff are trained to do the same.

Dr. Hasham adheres to three basic principles: building trust, encouraging change, and measuring

the performance of people through intercultural competence. ACE's aim is to transform customer dreams into reality, while guiding people every step of the way. Its customers value ACE's high-quality engineering services, which are backed by integrity and honesty. Ultimately, the staff at ACE are committed to high service standards and take pride in the work they do.

Source: Case study provided by Dr. Anthony S. Hasham, 2011, entrepreneur and engineer.

Culture

The values, beliefs, behavior and customs of a particular group of people.

The opening case clearly shows that intercultural managers do not have easy jobs. Dr. Hasham creates conditions that will make it possible for employees from different nationalities and cultures to work as a team and to interact with a diverse clientele. However, there will always be conflicts and an effective manager is one who has the characteristics to deal with all situations. This chapter will discuss the importance of intercultural management and the qualities that managers must possess to be successful.

But first, how well could you manage people from different cultures? Take the following self-assessment test.

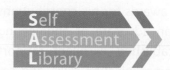

AM I WELL-SUITED FOR A CAREER AS A GLOBAL MANAGER?

In the Self-Assessment Library (available online), take assessment III.B.5 (Am I Well-Suited for a Career as a Global Manager?) and answer the following questions:

1. *How did you score compared to your classmates? Are you surprised by your score?*
2. *Do you think that the skills needed to become a Global Manager can be learned?*

What Is Intercultural Management?

1   Define intercultural management.

Integration

The process of uniting different groups or parts of an organization to form a larger group or whole, in order to create better workplaces, products and services.

Before we start the discussion of intercultural management, we need to understand the essence of culture itself. So, what is culture? **Culture** identifies who we are, where we come from, and how we behave. Culture explains our values, beliefs, attitudes, and actions. Culture defines us and what we represent.

We need to understand globalization as a concept that can 'melt the ice' between countries. Globalization is a worldwide system that has affected everyone and everything. How do we go about accepting it? **Integration** can best describe this concept; countries and cultures open up to one another by accepting differences, and cooperating and coordinating to create better workplaces, products, and services.

For example, among the well-established brand names that have expanded their operations into different cultures are Nestlé, The Four Seasons, Henkel,

Procter & Gamble, and McDonalds. The secret of their success is, at least in part, related to intercultural management.

What Do You Think?

What is your understanding of culture? How does it define you as an individual?

Every country has its own culture and guiding forces and, as a result, individuals behave in their own way depending on the country and area they come from. For instance, we are each citizens of a particular country but we also know that every country has various regions and areas, and each of them has its own style of behaving, its own beliefs, and so on.

This is where intercultural management comes in to play. Intercultural management is concerned with the management and understanding of a workforce's cultural differences. The key if organizations and people are to interact effectively is for people to accept and respect all the differences that exist. This respect and tolerance should not only be applicable to people within our own countries, but also to people from other countries. As a result, we develop what is known as intercultural tolerance and respect, and learn to 'adopt and adapt to' the other.

Unless we accept others regardless of their differences—educational, religious, social, racial—we will not be able to achieve harmony within the workplace, which will lead to conflict that in turn will affect the behavior of individuals within the organization.

Stephen Green, Group CEO at HSBC says,[1] "We don't look so much at what and where people have studied, but rather at their drive, initiative, cultural sensitivity. . ." This statement is significant because it shows the importance that HSBC gives to cultural sensitivity as a characteristic for success.

Picture This

A new student has joined your class this year. You like this new student but your friend does not because they are from a different culture. Your friend makes you choose. What do you do?

Hofstede's Cultural Dimensions

2 Understand Hofstede's cultural dimensions and their implications for the Arab world.

We cannot talk about intercultural issues without reference to Dr. Geert Hofstede and his cultural dimensions.[2] Geert Hofstede is an influential Dutch social psychologist and anthropologist who is a well-known pioneer in his research of cross-cultural groups and organizations. Hofstede has played a major role in developing a systematic framework for assessing and differentiating national cultures and organizational cultures. His most notable work has been in developing the cultural dimensions theory that demonstrates that there are national and regional cultural groups that influence the behavior of societies and organizations.

Hofstede is a firm believer that 'culture counts.' He identified five dimensions of national culture that he explains have an impact on the way individuals behave: *power distance, uncertainty avoidance, individualism versus collectivisim, masculinity versus femininity,* and *short-term versus long-term orientation* (for full definitions of each, see Chapter 2, page 61). These dimensions are critical for intercultural management, as we will see when we explore the characteristics of an intercultural manager.

Hofstede's Dimensions and the Arab World

Hofstede conducted an analysis on these dimensions in the Arab world that included the countries of Egypt, Iraq, Kuwait, Lebanon, Libya, Saudi Arabia, and the United Arab Emirates.

He revealed significant findings with respect to four of the cultural dimensions mentioned in the previous section—power distance index (PDI), uncertainty avoidance index (UAI), individualism index (IDV), and masculinity index (MAS). These four indexes showed that the countries of the Arab world are dominated by tradition and culture.

The assessment of these cultural dimensions identifies the styles of interaction of intercultural managers. Hofstede conducted studies in the Arab world to identify the cultural dimensions of the region and how they affect the behavior of people in organizations. For instance, the Arab world is considered to be a collectivist society because of its strong social ties. It is also considered to be a masculine society as the male figure is dominant and the 'head of the house.'

The results and interpretations of this study are very important and reveal to both the Arab world itself and to other cultures the specifics of Arab culture. These findings can clarify and facilitate issues for those individuals who are sent to work in the Arab world countries and thus can help them understand how to interact with the locals.

Managing Diversity

Diversity

The differences that people bring to an organization or group.

The concept of diversity was discussed in Chapter 15, but let's look at the importance of understanding this concept in relation to intercultural management. As we mentioned previously, differences exist both between individuals and between organizations; no two are ever identical. **Diversity** is existence of differences between the various people in an organization or group.[3] For this reason, managing diversity requires a full understanding of these differences so as to contribute to the wellbeing of the organization as a whole.

What Do Intercultural Managers Do?

3 *Understand what intercultural managers do.*

We have discussed intercultural management and the importance of managing diversity, so now let's focus on intercultural managers and what characteristics and skills they must possess to succeed and enhance organizational behavior and productivity. As we discussed above, culture is a set of norms, beliefs, values, and attitudes that people have which govern the way they behave in particular situations. Individuals interpret events in their own way, and thus people see, hear, and understand what they want to. Individuals have their own 'cultural glasses.'

Because of all these differences, it becomes more challenging for managers to deal with a diverse workforce. So, what are the skills that intercultural managers must have to enable them to cope with such obstacles?

Intercultural Managers' Competencies

The competencies and skills that intercultural managers need are specific. The following six characteristics are significant to the behavior of intercultural managers in the Arab world. In particular, because of the constant economic and political uncertainty in the region, great tolerance, flexibility and understanding are required.

Dr. Carol Kfouri is the Dean of Humanities at Notre Dame University in Lebanon. Carol has held many academic and administrative positions, and has acquired wide experience in intercultural management. Kfouri has come to realize that appreciation of foreign culture is necessary, but that a theoretical knowledge about the culture of the other is not in itself sufficient to ensure a healthy work atmosphere in which coworkers work in harmony. Nor is it enough to help a foreigner feel at ease in a diverse community; it is also important to *interact* with other cultures, to learn more about them: "Living and working abroad in another culture has me made more insightful of myself first of all, and then of others. I feel as though I have been given the gift of a sixth sense, that of anticipating my reaction in many new situations and learning to control them."

1. *Tolerance of uncertainty.* Can the manager deal with unclear situations and take suitable actions?
2. *Behavioral flexibility.* Can the manager vary his or her behavior so that it suits different situations?
3. *Awareness.* Is the manager aware of the communication barriers that may exist; can he or she understand people from other cultures?
4. *Knowledge management.* Can the manager collect and interpret new knowledge about a culture and its practices?
5. *Respect.* Does the manager respect other people and their beliefs?
6. *Empathy.* Can the manager see situations from the viewpoints of people very different from him- or herself?

Dr. Carol Kfouri, the Dean of Humanities at Notre Dame University, in Lebanon, is a Canadian working and living in Lebanon. Kfouri says that because you have chosen the option to work abroad in an international environment as an intercultural manager, it is necessary to devise a list of qualities in the other culture that you admire. The qualities on this list must also be obvious to coworkers. It is crucial to learn to live within the culture of the new country and accept the significant cultural issues. If a workplace has a more formal hierarchy than we are used to, then we must learn to adapt to it. If people insist on titles, address them as they wish. If meetings do not always start as punctually as you would wish, bring along some extra reading so as not to feel stressed. In general, it is enough to show people from other cultures appreciation and respect.

We can summarize by saying that intercultural managers can be most effective only by increasing their own general cultural awareness. By improving their cultural understanding and sensitivity, managers can then minimize cultural clashes and maximize professional development and organizational effectiveness. The most effective method of improving cultural awareness is cross-cultural learning or training and we'll look at this in detail later in the chapter.

What Do You Think?

Do you feel you have the skills to become an intercultural manager? How sensitive are you to cultural differences?

Cultural Awareness Framework

We have discussed many of the skills that intercultural managers require to have a positive influence on the organization and encourage the full commitment and loyalty of people. Many researchers have covered this topic in depth and offered certain guidelines; however one study, which will be described below, stands out. In a study by Harris *et al.*, a set of ten concepts were identified as an ultimate framework for cultural awareness and favorable global performance:[4]

1. *Global leadership.* This critical skill can only be achieved if the manager respects cultural diversity, and is able to accept change and differences between people and cultures.
2. *Cross-cultural communication skills.* Intercultural managers must try to avoid misinterpretations in verbal and non-verbal messages, even though there will be cultural and language barriers.
3. *Cultural sensitivity.* This involves showing understanding and having respect for other cultures, as discussed earlier in the chapter.
4. *Acculturation* **Acculturation** is about managers being able to adjust their own behavior to adapt to other cultures.
5. *Acting appropriately.* Beng able to understand is important, but the manager must be able to translate that understanding into action. Intercultural managers must be able to act on the cultural influences that they experience.
6. *Effective intercultural performance.* Managers need to identify which specific cultural issues will ultimately affect the performance of individuals within the organization.
7. *Changing international business.* Intercultural managers need to understand how cultural differences will affect a person's commitment and loyalty to the organization.
8. *Cultural synergy.* This is the increased effectiveness that results from combining the perceptions, knowledge, and practices of people from different cultures.

Acculturation

Adaptation and integration into another culture.

Claire Kfouri has worked in a development organization as a water and sanitation engineer for many years. "My guiding principle has always been that people around the world, regardless of language, race or gender, want the same things: respect, fairness and acknowledgment. So whether managing a team of ten people who speak at least as many languages, or meeting a client for the first time who is not quite sure of the role of female engineers, applying my guiding principle unfailingly leads to results."

9. *Corporate culture* (also known as 'work culture' or 'organizational culture') is yet another factor that intercultural managers must consider. Managers will work with different work professions, styles, and environments, and they must realize the possible effects of those factors on the work environment and organizational behavior.

10. *Global culture.* There will be interactions between the national and corporate culture. Both of them relate to values, norms, and beliefs, but the culture a person experiences within a country will often differ from the culture that exists within an organization.

In general, effective intercultural managers are individuals who can cope in all situations and circumstances, and understand that their behavior will interact with that of all members of the organization.

The Intercultural Manager as a Problem Solver

The intercultural manager must be a problem solver because in dealing with differences and diversity, there will definitely be conflict. Conflict can only be resolved with caution and understanding, and through excellent communication skills.

The managers of every country contribute something to a multinational organization. Competent intercultural managers are able to recognize the contributions made by employees of different nationalities. They are also able to develop solutions for problems by considering these contributions and the value of diversity as resources rather than barriers.

Managers from both the East and the West may need to use the 5 Cs—continuity, commitment, connections, compassion, and cutural sensitivity—and the 5 Es—expertise, ethos, eagerness, **esprit de corps**, and endorsement—to enable them to behave effectively in a multicultural environment and solve problems. The summary in Box 18-1 is based on Bedi,[5] who studied managers in Hong Kong and found that Asian managers tended to focus on the 5 Cs, whereas Western managers generally focus on the 5 Es.

Esprit de corps

Teamspirit among colleagues or co-workers.

BOX 18-1

The 5 Cs

1. Continuity, being aware of the organization's history and tradition
2. Commitment to the success and growth of the organization
3. Connections with others, based on social skills and social standing
4. Compassion, basing decisions and actions on all the personal and organizational issues
5. Cultural sensitivity, having respect for other people and their ways

The 5 Es

1. Expertise, based on knowledge and experience; managerial and technical theory
2. Ethos, having practical experience of the organization and its environment
3. Eagerness, having the enthusiasm of an entrepreneur
4. 'Esprit de corps,' a technical term similar in meaning to 'teamspirit'
5. Endorsement, looking out for unusual opportunities that will benefit the organization

Negotiation

Interaction between two or more parties for the purpose of reaching a mutually beneficial agreement.

The Intercultural Manager as a Negotiator

The act of **negotiation** is a basis for effective communication and interaction. In fact, people negotiate all the time—with children, partners, friends, colleagues, bosses, employees, and customers. When negotiations are taking place with any of these people in your own country, one thing that may facilitate the process is that you are both familiar with the cultural context. However, the individuals mentioned above may be from a different country or background to you, or the negotiation may even be taking place in another country. If this is the case, then there will be a gap between the negotiating parties because they have different values, beliefs, interests, attitudes, and behavioral styles.

The common key words in all definitions of negotiation can be combined as follows: "Two or more parties, who have both common and conflicting interests, interact with one another for the purpose of reaching a mutually beneficial agreement."[6] Intercultural managers must realize that successful negotiations require an in-depth understanding of the different cultures and especially the culture of the negotiating party. In fact, each party needs to be aware of the other's cultural background in order to have an active interaction. The intercultural managers must recognize that communication is a two-way street and that each side must carry the responsibilities of cultural responsiveness.

No two negotiating situations are ever alike, but there are certain guidelines that can lead the way. The intercultural manager or global negotiator should be prepared and should: (a) concentrate on building long-term relationships rather than short-term contracts; (b) focus on the interests that lay behind the positions; (c) avoid overdependence on cultural generalizations; (d) develop a sensitivity to timing; (e) remain flexible; (f) prepare carefully ahead of time; (g) learn to listen effectively; and (h) know when to use interpreters.[7] In addition, managers need to remember that each party in the negotiation will have differing views and beliefs. It's essential to treat those views and beliefs with respect. Overall, effective intercultural communication can only occur if there is a spirit of mutual respect and cooperation.[8]

At times the two sides of the negotiating table are like two persons in a canoe who must combine their skills and strength if they are to make headway against powerful currents, through dangerous rapids, and around hidden rocks. Alone they can make no progress and will probably lose control. Unless they cooperate, they risk wrecking or overturning the canoe on the obstacles in the river. Similarly, unless global deal-makers find ways of working together, their negotiations will founder on the many barriers encountered in putting together an international business transaction.

Picture This

Barry Moody was in charge of cultural affairs at the Kuwaiti Embassy for many years and was familiar with the traditions and culture of the country. Barry had retired but was still active as a consultant with a reputable construction company in New York, and they were negotiating a joint venture with a company in Saudi Arabia. He had a meeting with the Saudi representative, Mr. Mehdi, but knew that he should socialize first. Barry asked about work and the family in general, and then Mehdi asked the same about Barry, who explained that his elderly father was doing fine at the nursing home. Suddenly, Mehdi's attitude changed from warm to cool and the company was asked to appoint another person to finish the negotiations. Why do you think Mehdi did not want to continue the talks with Barry?

The Significance of Communication for the Intercultural Manager

4 Determine the significance of communication for intercultural managers.

Communication
The transfer and understanding of meaning through verbal and nonverbal messages.

Cultural synergy
Increased effectiveness within an organization or environment as a result of combining the perceptions, knowledge, and practices of people from different cultures.

There are many definitions of **communication**, but they all have similarities in that they stress that it is a process of sharing information, meanings, and feelings through the exchange of verbal and nonverbal messages. However, the individual working and communicating in a multicultural environment should also note the important point that the message that really counts is the one that the other person creates in their mind, which may not be the one we send.[9]

Communication across cultural boundaries can be difficult. Differences in customs, behavior, and values result in obstacles that can only be resolved through effective intercultural communication. A cross-cultural misunderstanding tends to occur when people from different cultural backgrounds fail to recognize and appreciate the various goals, customs, values, and styles of thinking that exist in other cultures. Now when we talk about cross-cultural environments, it does not only apply to countries from one region to another, but it may also apply to countries in the same region.

Not all the countries of the Arab world have the same language, accent, values, and beliefs. Consequently, effective intercultural managers need to learn about these differences and, most importantly, have the willingness to accept, respect, and deal with them; this, in turn, should facilitate the communication process. "The global leader, sensitive to cultural differences, appreciates a people's distinctiveness and seeks to make allowances for such factors when communicating with representatives of that cultural group."[10]

Previously, cultural differences were considered as barriers to productivity and performance within the organization. However, today efficient intercultural managers should be more aware that if cultural differences are managed well, they can be utilized as resources to enhance communication and interaction. Members of an organization can be taught how to create **cultural synergy** through training and adequate preparation; individuals who will be dealing with different cultures must 'do their homework.'

Preparation in its many forms will definitely make things easier, but it may not be the final solution; the skills of the intercultural manager as an effective communicator play an important role here. For example, an effective communicator working with American nationals in the United States may not necessarily be an effective communicator working with Japanese or Saudi Arabians in the US, Japan, or Saudi Arabia.

Nevertheless, communication is at the heart of all organizational operations and international relations. It is an essential tool when announcing and implementing plans and strategies and the foundation for understanding, cooperation, and action. In fact, the very existence of an organization depends on the degree of effective communication that takes place. The intercultural manager in aiming to achieve synergy must act as a practical problem solver, a decision maker, a conflict resolver, and an effective negotiator—having the characteristics we discussed in a previous section. To be able to fulfill each of these roles is not a simple task and that is why communication skills are so vital—because sometimes even the most articulate individual may be misunderstood.

Similarly, people are part of different groups that have their own identity and perceptions. It is these very differences, as we discussed previously, that cause conflicts and misunderstandings. This is what intercultural management tries to avoid by making people aware of the methods of dealing with the differences. Thus, the roles—problem solver, decision maker, conflict resolver and negotiator—can only be played by intercultural managers if they understand the challenges and keep an open mind as to how to interact to overcome these barriers. That is, tolerance of the other is a major requirement for success in this scenario.

We have been talking about creating cultural synergy—that force that allows people who work in intercultural environments to understand, share, and be in complete harmony, and this synergy results in organizational behavior that is effective and productive. To solve problems and make good decisions for the benefit of the organization, managers must have total knowledge and input. One explanation that explains this idea well is presented by Bennett and states:[11]

> When we travel to another culture or interact with people from another culture in our culture, we cannot base our predictions of their behavior on our cultural rules and norms. This inevitably leads to misunderstanding. If we want to communicate effectively, we must use our knowledge of the other culture to make predictions. If we have little or no knowledge of the other person's culture, we have no basis for making predictions.

High versus Low Culture Contexts

We cannot make predictions without enough information and cues to help us. Hence, when communicating across cultures, in addition to Hofstede's five cultural dimensions, which we discussed earlier in the chapter, we must also consider Edward Hall's distinction between high and low culture contexts. Hall found that Japan, Saudi Arabia, Spain, and China are high-context cultures. That is, they do not depend on explicit words but on physical gestures and body language to communicate a message. On the other hand, Canada, the United States and many European countries engage in low-context cultures. That is, they depend on words alone as a means of communication.

In the Middle East, many leaders are aware of the crucial role of communication. However, there is still much to be done in order to enhance such skills in a way that does not make them seem weak. The objective should be to reach the highest level of competency. "A person's aptitude to properly communicate and express himself, effectively reaching his audiences and speaking a language that strikes a chord with them, both through his physical demeanor and messages, can determine whether he truly is a leader."[12]

What Do You Think?

How do people in the Arab world communicate? Is it through words alone? What is your style?

As we discussed earlier, international negotiations must result in long-term synergy and not just short-term solutions, and the only way this can be achieved is through awareness and acceptance of the differences in cultural issues. To illustrate methods of cross-cultural negotiation, let's examine some, inevitably oversimplified, perceptions. For example, the Chinese are likely to come well-prepared and proceed slowly and formally and have an interpreter ready. Only senior officials are expected to talk and background information is exchanged without joking. With the Japanese, the group is expected to be homogeneous and they want more information than you plan to give. They focus on middle managers, who make recommendations to senior managers, who then make the decisions. As for the Arabs, they expect to mix business and personal information to establish individual rapport, trust, and commitments but will not give a final decision without consultation.

As a result, all means of communication must finally encourage synergy—the act of collaboration, cooperation and team management regardless of cultural differences so that both sides feel they have benefited.

How to Enhance Communication

How do intercultural managers overcome barriers, and what are the synergistic skills that will enhance channels of communication within the organization? Ruben says that there are six synergistic skills that can enhance intercultural communication:[13]

1. *Respect.* People want to believe that they themselves, their ideas, and their achievements are respected and appreciated.
2. *Tolerating ambiguity.* Managers need to adapt to different environments and work effectively with managers who have a different set of values.
3. *Relating to people.* Managers need to make people feel that they belong in the organization, and that their work-related needs will be satisfied. Only then will they give the organization a sense of commitment and loyalty.
4. *Being nonjudgmental.* Communication is more effective if the manager can be objective and not judge people without justification.
5. *Empathy.* This involves looking at things from another person's perspective and so trying to understand their feelings; it is the ability to "put yourself in another's shoes."
6. *Persistence.* Effective communication often involves being patient and persevering despite difficulties.

The above skills are among the most effective in establishing channels of communication that intercultural managers can apply with positive results.

OB in the News

Yahoo! Talks Arabic; Maktoob Talks English!

Wishing to obtain a higher share of the Arab world market, and weaken the hold of market leader Google, Yahoo! and Microsoft acquired the Jordan-based Arabic internet portal, Maktoob. As a result, Yahoo! will gain its first portal dedicated to the Arab world and access to more than 16.5 million unique users of Maktoob.

A significant share of Maktoob had previously been owned by the Dubai-based private equity company Abraaj Capital, which then sold its share to the US company Tiger Global Management.

"Maktoob is a terrific local brand," said Yahoo's senior vice-president and head of emerging markets, Keith Nilsson. "Yahoo will be combining its global technology and Maktoob's local Arabic content."

Samih Toukan, founder of Maktoob, stated, "Yahoo! and Maktoob are natural partners and this combination should help energize the internet market in the region as a whole. We are excited about Yahoo! building a stronger presence in the East and bringing its compelling suite of services to Arab users in Arabic."

Source: "Yahoo! Buys Maktoob," *Executive Magazine*, September 2009, Issue No. 122, p. 111.

Monique Bassila Zaarour, pictured here with her employees, is founder and manager of So7i Wa Sari3 (SWS). Monique believes that the fundamental principle of her company's success is the excellent communication she has with her employees—"As SWS becomes increasingly multicultural, addressing the Lebanese and Arabic population through television shows and the social media, I work on maintaining an effective intercultural communication between SWS dietitians and customers." she says. "I always make sure that people understand our messages." One technique that Monique uses is to *write instructions down*, to ensure that a message is fully understood. "Writing down instructions allows our customers to re-read requests and is also a good back-up to show that instructions were delivered properly." Monique's management style ensures that the SWS spirit is understood across various cultural boundaries.

The Intercultural Manager as Global Manager

Whilst there have been various discussions on what defines global management, the following two viewpoints may help to shed more light on the meaning of the *intercultural manager* as a global manager. In his book, *A Manager's Guide to Globalization*, Rhinesmith states that:[14]

> Global managers must reframe the boundaries of their world [. . .] of space, time, scope, structure, geography and function; of functional, professional, and technical skills from a past age; of thinking and classification relative to rational to intuitive, national versus foreign, we versus they; of cultural assumptions, values and beliefs about your relations with others, and your understanding of yourself.

Additionally, as Bartlett and Ghoshal wrote in the *Harvard Business Review*:[15]

> Clearly, there is no single model for the global manager. Neither the old-line international specialist nor the more recent global generalist can cope with the complexities of cross-border strategies. Indeed, the dynamism of today's marketplace calls for managers with diverse skills. Responsibility for worldwide operations belongs to senior business, country, and functional executives who focus on the intense interchanges and subtle negotiations required. In contrast, those in middle management and front-line jobs need well-defined responsibilities, a clear understanding of their organization's transnational mission, and a sense of accountability.

The above comments highlight the importance of accepting, knowing, and dealing with different cultures. Intercultural managers must understand themselves and the people around them so that they can interact with others effectively and for the benefit of the organization to ensure maximum performance.

In the introduction to this chapter, we discussed the issues related to intercultural management and explained that we cannot talk about this issue without referring to Geert Hofstede, who has conducted a series of studies

International OB

Intercultural Action at Hillcrest!

Hillcrest coaches individuals, trains teams and offers consulting services to organizations for building InterCultural Competence (ICC), a combination of knowledge and skill to enhance leadership, teamwork, customer care, motivation and programs such as Emiratization. Hillcrest is the sole provider of multicultural workplace solutions in the Middle East, with a unique, comprehensive regional research base, and training programs endorsed by the Institute of Leadership and Management.

"People often talk about difficulties with colleagues or customers of other nationalities, however there is very little information available about why misunderstandings and frustrations are to be expected, nor how to manage diversity in this region," said Dr. Rodney Hills, managing director of Hillcrest. "On the other hand, people who have had some intercultural training explain how it has helped them become more successful in their jobs, in winning deals, and to thrive among people of other cultures," he said. "On a corporate scale, companies can reap great rewards by building InterCultural Competence among their staff—their customers will be happier too," he continued.

InterCultural Competence involves:

- Recognizing the impact culture has on workplace behaviour
- Understanding how what is valued and believed 'normal' differs between cultures
- Developing skills to disable our cultural 'autopilot'
- Learning key concepts, management tools, techniques and theory developed from over 30 years of international research.

Hillcrest augments existing intercultural management research undertaken by pioneers such as Fons Trompenaars and Charles Hampden-Turner, with a comprehensive study on cultural norms and values of people working in the Middle East region. "For our clients, this means we can quickly diagnose strengths and potential trouble spots for an individual manager, across a team, or throughout an organization," Hills said. "We can then customise practical and relevant ICC training, applying it where it will be most beneficial."

Hillcrest is engaged in initial discussions with leading companies across the business sectors in the UAE about the application of ICC to enhance management excellence, customer service, sales, marketing, human resources management, and Emiratization.

Source: Press Release, UAE, "Hillcrest Establishes Dubai Office", March 2005, www.ameinfo.com/55266.html. Reproduced with permission of Hillcrest Business Association.

across various regions of the world to clarify the cultural dimensions that he has specified.

Once we understand how to behave with others and respect their differences, then interaction becomes more effective and organizational behavior becomes more efficient. Intercultural managers need to understand that the more they know about the culture they are operating within, the more productive they become in performing their own duties and in motivating their coworkers.

What does Hofstede say about the cultural dimensions and their contributions to the workplace in the Arab world? The Power Distance Index (PDI) in the Arab world is high at 80, which means that the Arab society experiences inequality of power and wealth and these are increasing. The high Uncertainty Avoidance Index (UAI) of 68 indicates that the Arab society has very low tolerance and acceptance of uncertainty, and thus strict rules, laws, policies, and regulations must be adopted and implemented. Moreover, these people have a tendency to control everything so as to avoid the unexpected. Consequently, Arabs do not accept change easily.

Even though many feel that the Arab world is individualistic, the results translate into a collectivist society that believes in long-term commitment to the group, family, extended family, or extended relationships, and ultimately enhancing loyalty. The above information can be extremely helpful for intercultural managers in general, and for those operating in the Arab world in particular.

Zaatar w Zeit (ZwZ) is a fast-food restaurant business that started in Lebanon and has expanded through franchises in Jordan, Qatar, Kuwait, and Dubai. The corporate culture of Zaatar w Zeit stresses team spirit, communication, respect, and trust, which have been the fuel for the company's expansion. The first branch of ZwZ opened in Beirut in 1999. Today there are seven outlets across Lebanon. "What distinguishes ZwZ from other restaurants is the great service and friendly atmosphere; it's like a home away from home," says Walid Hajj, CEO of ZwZ's parent company, Cravia.

Source: *"Zaatar w Zeit continues expansion with opening of two new outlets,"* www.ameinfo.com/161407.html.

Corporate culture

The internal culture that determines the atmosphere and work environment of an organization.

Foreign labor

Work carried out by people who are nationals of a foreign country.

Expatriates

People who live outside of their native country.

As an example of the type of training available in the region, study the International OB box, which contains a press release from one training organization.

Corporate Culture

What we want to determine here is that intercultural managers should differentiate between the national culture of every country and the corporate or organizational culture that determines the internal culture—beliefs, norms, values—of the company.

Corporate culture—internal culture—determines the atmosphere and work environment of an organization. It ultimately clarifies and explains that this is 'how we do things here'. That is, this is how we communicate, treat our employees and customers, and interact with one another at both the internal and external levels. Every organization creates its own corporate culture, and this is usually determined by the owner and/or top management.

To illustrate, Levi's corporate culture was set by the creator and founder Levi himself, and he wanted all employees to be comfortable at work in order to produce quality output. As a result, he wanted employees to dress casually. In addition, Google has a very friendly and comfortable corporate culture where employees are offered facilities such as sports services, cafeterias and entertainment of all kinds to put them at ease and enhance their innovative productivity. The overall aim for employers of people in the technology industry is to enable them to be as creative and innovative as possible.

Foreign Labour

One of the biggest issues facing intercultural managers is **foreign labor**, particularly in the Gulf Cooperation Council (GCC) countries, where foreign workers make up 80 percent of the workforce. Intercultural management involves managing local workers as well as **expatriates** (foreign workers), and in order to do the best job, managers need to be aware of the regulations.

Labor market regulation, particularly of foreign labor, is a crucial concern for the GCC countries. There are fears of unemployment for locals owing to the large influx of foreign workers in the domestic sector. But why do GCC countries need to import workers? The simple answer is that it is cheaper. However, 'Westernization' accompanies this process, and the small Gulf Countries (SGCs) become concerned about loss of local identity. Migrant workers are thus seen as a 'threat to local society.'[16]

For instance, expatriate labor accounts for nearly 80 percent of the workforce in Dubai, with over 50 percent being Indian. As a result, unemployment among UAE nationals is estimated to be 36,000, with currently more than 50 percent of them benefiting from social security. For these reasons, the Ministry of Labor aims to have nationals make up over 50 percent of the whole workforce in the UAE by 2015.

To address problems in Bahrain's labor market, one option being considered by the Labor Market Regulatory Authority (LMRA) is increasing the cost of foreign workers. This would benefit nationals by giving them more opportunity for employment in their own country. Reform could be achieved by increasing the cost especially of unskilled workers and therefore improving the competitiveness of Bahrain's own population.

All SGCs are worried about their strong reliance an foreign labor and the threat it brings of increasing local unemployment. Most managers are focused on securing their economic growth and are reluctant to risk their competitiveness by raising the cost of foreign labor. As a result, intercultural managers encourage local workers to develop their skills and realize their potential.

Domains of International Business Practice

5 *Identify the role of the intercultural manager in international business practice.*

International business practice is based on good intercultural management and on the issues that we have discussed in this chapter—acceptance, tolerance, respect, cultural understanding, interaction, and effective communication. Maybe the best way to explain this is by showing the history of how one prominent international organization, Nestlé, established itself in the Arab world.

Nestlé was established in 1867 by Henri Nestlé, who developed the first milk food for babies, as a substitute for breast milk. Today, Nestlé is the world's leader in food and beverages designed to promote nutrition, health and wellness. Henri Nestlé was a visionary and understood the importance of diversification. The company ventured into many other products, such as soups and sauces (Maggi), chocolate milk (Milo), and coffee (Nescafé), and, in 1974, Henri Nestlé became a major shareholder in L'Oreal. The international operations of the Nestlé group have been successful, at least in part, because they have been able to meet the demands and preferences of intercultural management.

What Do You Think?

Nestlé has established itself well in the Arab world. The company has also founded ventures in many other countries around the world. What is the secret of Nestlé's success?

Cross-Cultural Training

Cross-cultural training (CCT)

Training given so that employees can communicate and interact more successfully with different cultures.

Cross-cultural Training (CCT) is vital to international business success. After all, training is a learning process. When employees, at any level, are called upon to leave their home country and travel to another country to continue working for their organization, the very first thing that comes to mind is the cross-cultural challenges that will be faced. Such employees, known as expatriates, must become aware of the different style of living, thinking, and communicating that the destination country practices to avoid any cultural clash. Expatriates are individuals from other cultures who may be found at all levels of the organization.

Understanding the differences in cross-cultural settings and applying them to expatriates (intercultural individuals)[17] will allow for a better understanding of local employees. A study of 409 expatriates, on assignment in over 51 countries around the world, found that it took 6 to 12 months for them to feel comfortable living in their new cultural settings and adjusting to the work environment. There are many ways in which individuals can prepare themselves for overseas assignments but the only effective method is cross-cultural training (CCT). The goal of CCT is to minimize 'cultural shock' when on a foreign assignment, and to enhance the employee's cross-cultural experience.

In brief, the most important criteria for selecting the suitable expatriate to travel and work abroad should be cultural awareness, tolerance and adjustment. Equally important is that there should be complete familiarity with the customs, culture and work habits of the local people, and all this can only be acquired through training.

Global Implications

> *6 Realize that intercultural managers need to be global managers.*

The managers who are most likely to succeed in operating in leading world organizations are those who are able to adapt to change and transform their organization's systems and their managers' and employees' behavior to enable people to effectively and efficiently work and compete in any country around the world. However, accepting international standards does not mean that the organization should compromise its key values and culture. Rather, integration is required here. Consequently, intercultural managers are those competent and skilled individuals who can go from the local marketplace to become leaders with strong international awareness and experience.

Intercultural managers travel all around the world looking for healthy business relationships. Some of the individuals are buyers, others are sellers; in some instances they are both. The truth of the matter is that no matter what their objective is, executives that go global must learn to walk—like a baby—by trial and error. They will fall many times along the way until they finally are able to stand on both feet. That is, global leaders need to develop a pattern of interaction and a style of behavior that will give them effective results.

Intercultural managers must also communicate and work with individuals who have developed in a different cultural environment. Their customs, values, lifestyles, beliefs, management practices, and other aspects of their personal and professional life are different. To be effective, the intercultural manager must try to understand the various values and beliefs of the different cultures and so gain a better insight into that country's management practices and strategies. If they can achieve these aims, intercultural managers will be able to transfer knowledge and collaborate more productively.[18]

"Being an effective global manager in the twenty-first century requires more than technical competence alone. It also requires a full understanding of the international business environment, the use of culturally diverse teams, and a heavy dose of cultural and linguistic sensitivity."[19]

According to Ferraro, the major competencies required for intercultural managers in the twenty-first century are:[20]

1. *Broad perspective*. The intercultural manager must be able to see the big picture and view situations from the widest possible perspective.
2. *Appreciate other perspectives*. The intercultural manager accepts that others will quite reasonably adopt other perspectives.
3. *Balance contradictions*. An effective intercultural manager must see contradictions and conflicts as opportunities rather than as liabilities or problems.
4. *Emphasize global teamwork*. The intercultural manager must focus on cross-cultural teamwork and cultural awareness, rather than on individual objectives.
5. *Cognitive complexity*. The intercultural manager must be able to differentiate between people and cultures, integrate them, and adapt to the differences.
6. *Emotional resilience*. The intercultural manager must be able to cope with the stress of dealing with different people.
7. *Cognitive flexibility*. The intercultural manager must be ready and willing to learn and increase his or her understanding and knowledge.
8. *Personal autonomy*. The intercultural manager must be open-minded, flexible and non-judgmental.
9. *Perceptual acuity*. The successful intercultural manager must be attentive, listening carefully to try to understand the verbal and nonverbal communication of people from various cultures.
10. *Willingness to make risky decisions*. The intercultural manager must be ready to face ambiguous situations, and make what might be risky decisions in the uncertain situations.

Summary and Implications for Managers

Culture determines the uniqueness of humans and their attitudes and behavior. Intercultural managers are required to effectively manage international organizations by promoting synergy that will accept the differences in people and simultaneously encourage them to integrate skills and competencies into the workplace. When cultural differences are understood and used as a *resource*, then everyone will benefit.[21]

Cultural Dimensions   Geert Hofstede believes that 'culture counts,' and has identified five dimensions of national culture that have an impact on the way individuals behave. These dimensions are critical for intercultural management— power distance, uncertainty avoidance, individualism/collectivism, femininity/ masculinity, and short-term/long-term direction.

Characteristics of Intercultural Managers   Characteristics significant to the behavior of intercultural managers in the Arab countries and worldwide are tolerance, flexibility, awareness, knowledge, respect, and empathy.

Problem Solver and Negotiator   Intercultural managers must possess excellent communication skills and patience to deal with the differences that people of diverse backgrounds bring into the workplace. These differences will cause conflicts that must be addressed. In addition, business deals require articulate managers who can work under pressure and negotiate with the other party to reach an agreement that is accepted by all parties.

Communication   Intercultural managers must give high priority to intercultural communication and skills. As you have seen earlier, every cultural world operates according to its own internal principles and laws (both written and unwritten). The culture itself is primarily a system for creating, sending, storing, and processing information about norms of behavior and beliefs. Within that culture, communication underlies everything.[22]

Corporate Culture   Corporate culture dictates how an organization deals with competition and change. Similarly, intercultural managers must be tuned in or aware of their national culture, business culture, and corporate culture.[23] Managers find themselves under great pressure to 'adopt and adapt,' and "managers are also under pressure to adapt their organization to the local characteristics of the market, the legislation, the socio-political system, and the cultural system. This balance between consistency and adaptation is essential for corporate success."

Foreign Labor   Intercultural managers must manage foreign labor, particularly in the Gulf Cooperation Council (GCC) countries, where foreign workers make up 80 percent of the workforce. The large percentage of foreign workers is considered by many to have negatively affected the workplace by decreasing the employment of locals.

Cross-cultural Training (CCT)   Cross-cultural Training (CCT) is important to international business success. When employees are called upon to leave their home country and travel to another country to continue working for an organization, a key consideration is the cross-cultural challenges that will be faced. Such employees, known as expatriates, must become aware of the different style of living, thinking, and communication channels.

Point ⟩⟩ ⟨⟨ Counterpoint

"WHEN IN ROME, DO AS THE ROMANS DO"

Individuals must 'go with the flow' and behave as the people of a particular culture do. There is an obligation to adapt and accept the values and traditional behavioral patterns of the culture one is in. One must adapt to the styles of communication and interaction of individuals of certain cultures so as to fit into the system. Otherwise, newcomers will feel like outsiders and will have difficulty in establishing themselves in the organization. Accordingly, we can stress that individuals must 'adopt and adapt' in order to succeed, and encourage others to do the same.

On the other hand, 'doing as the Romans do' will often be extremely difficult and against one's values. We must also remember that some cultures are more accepting of outsiders than others. It depends on both the individual and the culture that the individual is trying to become a part of. As an outsider, rarely do you become an insider. Often, the best an outsider can expect is to be an employee who does his/her job without question.

Questions for Review

1 What is intercultural management?

2 How does culture affect the behavior of the intercultural manager?

3 What are the characteristics of an intercultural manager?

4 What is the importance of cultural synergy?

5 What are the different roles that an intercultural manager plays as a communicator?

6 How does the intercultural manager act as a problem solver, or as a negotiator?

7 How does the intercultural manager become a global knowledge manager?

8 What significance does foreign labor have on the intercultural manager?

9 How can the intercultural manager act as a global manager?

Discussion Exercise

Global managers are made, not born. This is not a natural process. We are herd animals. We like people who are like us. But there are many things you can do. Obviously, you rotate people around the world. There is no substitute for line experience in three or four countries to create global perspective. You also encourage people to work in mixed nationality teams. You *force* them to create personal alliances across borders, which means that sometimes you interfere in hiring decisions.

Discuss the views expressed above.

Source: P. Banevik, former President and CEO of Asea Brown Boveri, as quoted in Harris *et al.*, *Managing Cultural Differences: Global Leadership Strategies for the 21st Century*, p. 25.

Ethical Considerations

Culture often influences managerial behavior and the ethical considerations behind the choices managers make. When a manager has to take a particular ethical stand on an issue, it is quite possible that colleagues who do not share the same ethical viewpoint will object. Explaining the reasoning behind such decisions may be very difficult, and the conflict that arises has the potential

to result in divides between colleagues with different cultural beliefs.

Do you think managers should let cultural beliefs (both their own and those of others) affect the organizational decisions they make, or should they remain impartial? How might a manager deal with conflict that arises from opposing ethical viewpoints?

Critical Analysis

WHAT'S TRUST GOT TO DO WITH IT?

What is trust? It may be difficult to define it in one term, but it could be explained as a combination of feelings such as confidence, reliance, dependence, and faith. It is absolutely essential to have trust, especially in an intercultural context. After all, we are dealing with people of different cultures; that is, people with different values and beliefs, and these values and beliefs are what lead us to have confidence and faith in others. In fact, a high level of trust is essential for organizational effectiveness, particularly in culturally diverse industries.

A breakdown in communication may be due to the language barrier. In fact, language difficulties can create many misunderstandings in multinational/multicultural environments. Another reason people find it hard to trust others is related to cultural barriers. To clarify, cultural differences play a major role in the creation of trust and, ultimately, trust means different things around the world.

How do we overcome this difficulty in trusting people? Naturally, we need to build trust, but how do we achieve this? It can only be done by showing goodwill and good

intentions towards others. This cannot happen overnight; it takes time, so we need patience. Once trust is reached between two or more people, we need to maintain it because it can disappear if the intentions do not continue to be positive.

We can establish trust through emotional bonding and conceptual understanding. The key to achieving both of these is effective communication to avoid any misinterpretations. We do not want misunderstandings. We want to maintain credibility with others.

Questions

1. How can intercultural managers build trust in their employees?
2. What does trust have to do with intercultural management?
3. Are the rules of establishing trust unique, or do they change in different cultural environments?

For more on the question of trust, study Asherman *et al.*: *Building Trust Across Cultural Boundaries*.[24]

Research Exercise

Do actions really speak louder than words? The most important barrier of intercultural management is communication, both verbal and non-verbal. The body language is what stresses the message. However, we must be aware of

the signs and gestures we use because one particular gesture can have different interpretations in different countries. Do your own research and discuss the meanings of hand and arm gestures in different cultures.

LEARNING OBJECTIVES

This chapter will enable you to:

1 Determine the need for females in the workplace.

2 Define the role of women in business in the Arab world.

3 Determine what motivates women.

4 Understand the challenges that face women in the Arab world.

5 Determine how men react to successful women.

6 Realize that tradition can be broken: it is time for change.

7 Understand the global implications of the female in the Arab workplace.

Female Entrepreneurs in the Arab World

19

Economic growth and political democracy cannot achieve their full potential unless the female half of humanity participates on an equal footing with the male.

—Muhammad Yunus, 2006 Nobel Peace Prize Winner

A Sheikha and a Queen

There are two women who have enchanted the Arab world with their grace, intelligence, and elegance. In addition to being first ladies, they are extremely productive in their roles as businesswomen, entrepreneurs, and nation-builders. Born into ordinary families, these two ladies were destined to rule: Sheikha Mozah of Qatar, and Queen Rania of Jordan.

Sheikha Mozah Bint Nasser Al-Missned's charm and intellect so attracted the Emir that he gave her powers like no other 'sheikha' ever had before. She had vision—and her first accomplishment was helping to establish Education City, which houses five prominent US universities. Mozah is also special envoy for UNESCO on Basic and Higher Education, President of the Supreme Council for Family Affairs in Qatar, and Vice-President of the Supreme Education Council.

Sheikha Mozah teaches her children respect and treats them as ordinary teenagers and not as royals. She is very proud of her Arab identity, and says, "People tend to believe that to be modern you have to disengage from your heritage. We see the global citizen as someone who has confidence and is proud of his culture and history—and open to the modern world."

Rania, the Queen consort of Jordan, has revolutionized Jordanian society and has enchanted the world with her eloquence and elegance. Queen Rania has been awarded the honorary rank of colonel in the Jordanian Army by King Abdullah. Domestically, she promotes education reforms, mandatory English at schools, and finance for entrepreneurs with ideas.

Queen Rania has been ranked as number 80 in Forbes' list of Most Powerful Women in the World. She tours the world speaking on behalf of Jordan and defending the Arab woman's rights. In 2006, she made headlines by appearing on the Oprah Winfrey Show and breaking the stereotyped image of Arab women, because we rarely see the Arab woman as a guest on foreign talk shows.

Queen Rania maintains balance in her life: "My official activities take account of the children's school day and their plans and programs, and extensive periods of time on overseas engagements are limited."

Source: S. Moubayed, "A Sheikha, a Queen and a First Lady," *Asia Times online*, March 2008, www.atimes.com/atimes/Middle_East/JC28Ak01.html.

The focus of this chapter is female entrepreneurs in the Arab world and the challenges they face. Most importantly, the chapter highlights the achievements of the Arab woman and the potential she holds. We will learn about prominent women in various sectors in the Arab world countries, and also about the many organizations, forums, and associations that exist for women's rights. Before we commence, though, take the self-assessment test below.

WHAT ARE MY GENDER ROLE PERCEPTIONS?

In the Self-Assessment Library (available online), take assessment IV.C.2 (What Are My Gender Role Perceptions?) and answer the following questions:

1. *Did you score as high as you thought you would?*

2. *Do you think a problem with measures like this is that people aren't honest in responding?*

3. *If others, such as friends, classmates, and family members rated you, would they rate you differently? Why or Why not?*

4. *Research has shown that people's gender-role perceptions are becoming less traditional over time. Why do you suppose this is so?*

Self
Assessment
Library

The Need for Women in the Workplace

1 *Determine the need for females in the workplace.*

Equality is the issue: We must acknowledge that women can do whatever men can. The role of the female is no longer limited to housework and childcare. Women have proven to be just as competent as men and have the potential to succeed in any domain. Women have decided to enter the world of business by joining the family business, by working for various organizations, or by establishing their own businesses to become entrepreneurs.

Women are an important part of the workforce. This is applicable to countries all over the world and the Arab world is no exception. Despite tradition and culture, the Arab female is being given opportunities and is using them extremely well. A person with a good head for business or the requirements of an entrepreneur can be either male or female. Gender should not be an issue. What is important is the ability and skills of the person. Consequently, there is a need for qualified persons whether male or female.

What Do You Think?

Her Excellency Queen Rania of Jordan has accomplished so much for her country and encourages women in Jordan to participate in all aspects of work. What is the secret of her success? Are there influential women in your country?

Characteristics of Entrepreneurs

There are so many characteristics that individuals—both male and female—must have in order to succeed in life and achieve their goals. Female entrepreneurs and businesswomen are likely to require similar qualities to their male counterparts, but it may be that females must make more effort and sacrifice.[1] They must be highly ambitious about transforming their ideas into reality. In addition, these women must have complete confidence in themselves and their abilities. They must also attach great value to teamwork and loyalty, and must

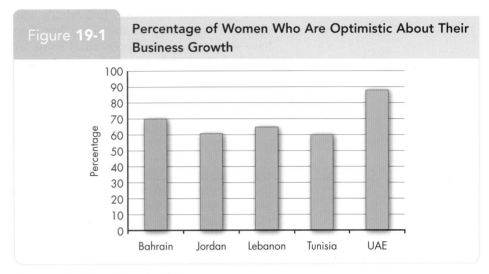

Figure **19-1**   **Percentage of Women Who Are Optimistic About Their Business Growth**

Source: International Finance Corporation, 2007.

be open to all opinions and interact well with different types of people. Equally important, these women must balance home and work by controlling their passion for work. Moreover, they must be committed to helping others, which enhances their business image. Finally, successful businesswomen must always be optimistic. That is, they should always look at the 'glass half full.' Thus, they should see failure as just a stepping stone to success.

Growth of Women-Owned Businesses in the Arab World

Figure 19-1 shows the degree of optimism that women have for business growth in the Arab world. Sixty percent of the women in Tunisia and 88 percent of females in the United Arab Emirates are optimistic about their business growth. Lebanon, Jordan, and Bahrain have very similar percentages. Research has found that the percentage of firms with female participation in ownership is 17.43 percent in the MENA region, compared with 28.61 percent across the world.[2] What is worth noting is that in these countries 60 percent of businesswomen are optimistic about business growth despite the problems the countries may face. For instance, Lebanon continuously faces political and economic instability, yet

Wassila Hamdi Ben Amor is a woman from Tunisia with a great passion for the cause of women's rights in the Arab world. Ben Amor holds a top managerial position at Tunis International Bank (TIB). Tunisia has long been supportive of women's rights, according to Ben Amor, and the state is a pioneer in establishing laws to protect females, such as those against sexual discrimination. "Women in Tunisia have been lucky," Ben Amor says. However, even though many women enter the workforce, they may not reach senior posts.

Source: Shyamantha Asokan and David Patrikarakos, "Who's Who: Extended version of our list of personalities," *Financial Times*, June, 2008.

there are many successful individuals who have their own companies. Such success is expected from the males, but, despite the obstacles, many females also have shown their entrepreneurial spirit and have prospered. A few Lebanese females who have achieved great fortune are May El Khalil, founder and President of the Beirut Marathon; Nawale Yaghi Fakhri, founder and owner of Taxi Banet (or Taxis for Women); Josephine Zhgeib, who is bringing youth back to an appreciation of nature through a project named Beity; and Mayada Baydas, co-founder and Managing Director of Development Innovations Group.

It is interesting to know that the percentage of female entrepreneurs in the Arab world is the highest in the world. In fact, 20 to 30 percent of CEOs in the region are female.[3] Successful women from other Arab countries include Reem Badran from Jordan, a chief executive of Kuwaiti Jordanian Holding Company; Sheikha Al-Bahar from Kuwait, general manager at National Bank of Kuwait (NBK); and Wassila Hamdi Ben Amor from Tunisia, an advocate of women's rights—to name but a few.

In 2007, the Oman Economic Review reported that the previous decade had seen an increase in female entrepreneurship in the MENA region, and that women entrepreneurs had become more visible. Women-owned businesses were said to be contributing to the economic growth and wealth creation and they were also creating employment opportunities for other women. Finally, the article commented that economically active women represented a potentially profitable market segment for the financial sector.[4] Enabling women to work secures an income for them and their families. They definitely have the potential to start and manage their own businesses, but may lack the resources and support they need. Thus, women do still face some barriers, and these will be discussed in more detail later in the chapter.

The Role of Women in Business

> 2 *Define the role of women in business in the Arab world.*

Men used to be considered the only individuals who could become entrepreneurs or prosperous businesspersons. However, women started to establish themselves in the field, and by the 1990s in the United States the number of women who owned businesses doubled, female employment in these companies increased fourfold, and sales grew fivefold.[5] In 1997, fewer than 5.5 million businesses in the US were owned by women. By 2011, there were an estimated 8.1 million women-owned businesses in the US.[6]

In the Arab world, there have also been significant developments over the past 50 years. For example, in the 1960s women comprised about 5 percent of the full-time labor force in Bahrain (compared with nearly 30 percent in the US), but by 2001 this figure had risen to 40 percent. Furthermore, in the UAE in 2007, 33 percent of female-owned companies were earning annual revenues of more than US$100,000, compared to just 13 percent in the US.[7]

See Figure 19-2 for details of the growth rate in the US over the past decade or so.

What do you think?

Do you know, or have you read about, any female entrepreneurs? Describe their performance.

Next, we look at some statistics about women entrepreneurs in the Arab world, as well as the numerous associations that have been established for the purpose of encouraging and supporting women in their quest for equal opportunity.

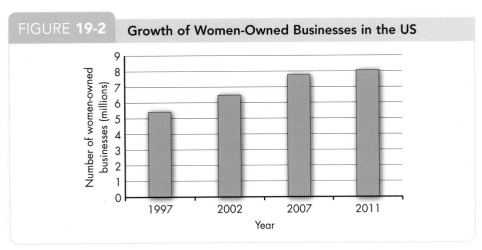

FIGURE **19-2**   **Growth of Women-Owned Businesses in the US**

Source: Figures based on the American Express OPEN "State of Women-owned Businesses" Report, March 2011, www.openforum.com.

The Female Entrepreneur in the Arab World

Nadereh Chamlou is a senior advisor to the chief economist at the World Bank's Middle East and North Africa (MENA) Region, and Reem Kettaneh Yared is a consultant. In their paper, "Women Entrepreneurs in the Middle East and North Africa: Building on Solid Beginnings,"[8] they revealed the following facts (we have added some up-dated figures):

- In Bahrain, women entrepreneurs increased from 193 in 1991 to 815 in 2001. For example, Standard Chartered Bank encourages females and, in 2011, 35 percent of its 565 employees in Bahrain were women, and 37 percent of its executive positions across the region were held by women.
- In Iraq, many women are self-employed, members of the Chamber of Commerce, and hold leadership positions in major trade unions.
- In Lebanon, 7 percent of the female labor force is self-employed and own businesses.
- In Morocco, 5 percent of women were self-employed in 1999.
- In Syria, in the 1990s, 7.1 percent of all economically active females were running their own businesses.

Many surveys have been conducted to understand the characteristics of female-owned businesses and their contributions to economic development and job creation. Chamlou and Yared's study investigated 1,228 women in five Arab countries: Bahrain, Jordan, Lebanon, Tunisia and the UAE. They found that women entrepreneurs in the Arab region are ahead of their counterparts in Western Europe and North America with respect to size of company and revenue generation. Female-owned businesses in this region are also able to create jobs just as well as their Western counterparts.

In addition, Chamlou and Yared's study showed that women are able to manage and maintain their firms for a long period. For example, women have owned businesses in Lebanon for 10.6 years on average, in Bahrain for 10.2 years, in Tunisia for 8.6 years, in Jordan for 6.1 years, and in the UAE for 5.9 years. Moreover, women entrepreneurs in the five surveyed countries use information and communication technology for their businesses at rates above the per capita average worldwide.

Numerous international associations and organizations have been established for female professionals and businesswomen (see Box 19-1). There are also many international conferences and forums that support the Arab woman and offer her more opportunities for advancement and development.

Mrs. Nadereh Chamlou is an extremely active female with extraordinary competencies. Chamlou is senior advisor to the chief economist at the World Bank's Middle East and North Africa Region. This position authorizes Chamlou to lead the region's gender agenda and she also advises on the bank's policy and consultancy work.

BOX 19-1

Associations for Businesswomen in the Arab world

World Women Entrepreneurs World Women Entrepreneurs or *Leading Women Entrepreneurs of the World* represents the world's most powerful and successful female entrepreneurs. This not-for-profit organization was established to identify, honor, promote, and encourage female entrepreneurial excellence. The organization currently has women representing over 56 countries worldwide.

Women Employment Enterprise and Training Unit (WEETU) The Women Employment Enterprise and Training Unit (WEETU) was established in 1987, in Norwich, in the UK. WEETU is an innovative not-for-profit company that assists women to take control of their economic lives by giving them advice and training to support themselves.

Organization of Mediterranean Businesswomen The Organization of Mediterranean Businesswomen is composed of 23 Associations. Members are located throughout the Mediterranean from Spain to Syria, passing through Morocco, Algeria, France, Italy, Croatia, Albania, Greece, Malta, Cyprus, Turkey, Lebanon, Egypt, and Jordan. The Organization focuses on gender equality and business issues.

Lebanese League for Women in Business (LLWB) The Lebanese League for Women in Business (LLWB) aims to bring together professional women by providing them with a forum in which they can exchange experiences and expertise, discuss common challenges and issues, provide specialized training through vocational development programs, and facilitate the exchange of information. The mission of the LLWB is to encourage women in business to 'take the lead and succeed.' The LLWB also endorses women's issues in the business world and advances entrepreneurial opportunities and access to resources.

Center for Arab Women Training and Research (CAWTAR) The Center for Arab Women Training and Research (CAWTAR) was established in 1993 in Tunisia to support gender equality in the Arab world. CAWTAR provides information that enables Arab women to become fully empowered and to enjoy their human rights as part of the development of their communities and societies. CAWTAR offers programs in the form of training and internships.

Lebanese Council of Women (LCW) The Lebanese Council of Women (LCW) is a nongovernmental organization (NGO) founded in 1952 to secure women's right to vote and employment rights. Its objectives now are to lead and give direction to the Lebanese feminist movement.

The New Arab Woman Forum (NAWF) The New Arab Woman Forum (NAWF) considers the trend towards openness and economic and social reform across the Arab world and the exposure of the new Arab woman after years of underrepresentation in all walks of life. Today, the new Arab woman is more educated, empowered, and engaged. The forum aims at discussing the path-breaking transformation underway, analyzing its future impact on Arab society, and the economic role of women,

The Arab Women Leadership Forum The Arab Women Leadership Forum is a platform for the Arab woman to express herself. H.H. Sheikha Manal bint Mohammed bin Rashid Al Maktoum, President of Dubai Women Establishment (DWE), wife of H.H. Sheikh Mansour bin Zayed Al Nahyan, Minister of Presidential Affairs, says, "Our goal in the establishment is to provide women in the Arab world with the advanced skill sets and best practices for assuming leadership roles, on par with top-tier achievers worldwide."[9] Mona Al Marri, chairperson of DWE's board, confirmed the importance of the forum to local and Arab women by saying, "The Arab Women Leadership Forum will provide women from across the region with an avenue to voice their opinions and share diverse perspectives on what it takes to be a results-oriented leader and create a new generation of leaders."

Motivation

3 *Determine what motivates women.*

In this section, we will look at some prominent business-women and their achievements from around the world and in particular in the Arab world. We can't say that women are more ambitious or motivated than men, but we can show that women can be just as successful as men when they are given the opportunity.

The meaning of motivation and what motivates people was discussed in Chapter 5. We saw that all people can be motivated. However, we developed an idea about what drives individuals to perform to their full potential. It is only natural that we face challenges, but we need to understand how to overcome them no matter what our gender is.

The identification of those factors that motivate women in the Arab world is actually challenging in itself. However, four motivating factors that facilitate the process for women in the Arab region to start their own businesses, have been identified. They have even been referred to as *opportunities*:

1. *High-end services* such as software development, call-service centers, and advertising offer self-motivated women great opportunities.
2. *Untapped domains* such as childcare centers, care for the elderly, and cleaning services can offer women competitive advantage because they tend to be more understanding in these markets.
3. *Franchising* can allow women to overcome challenges by giving them access to a whole existing business system.
4. *Information and communication* technologies allow women to reach international markets with less difficulty.

We cannot say that women are naturally more motivated than men—there is no actual proof or evidence—but we can refer to statistics and studies that imply this. A particular study of seven Middle Eastern countries, 'The Environment for Women Entrepreneurship in the Middle East and North Africa Region,' conducted by the World Bank in 2007, found that women owned 13 percent of the 4,000 companies that were investigated. These companies were shown to be well-established, productive, and highly involved in the global economy. In addition, the study found that the number of firms employing more than 100 employees is higher (31 percent) among female-owned firms compared with firms owned by men (24 percent).

Successful Female Entrepreneurs

The following profiles are of well-established female entrepreneurs from around the world who have become extremely successful. They all have one thing in common: they are driven by self-motivation and a will to achieve their goals in life because they believe in themselves. Motivation can be contagious because one win leads to another.

Oprah Winfrey   Oprah Winfrey started reading the news on the air at the age of 17. At the age of 30, she discovered her talent in presenting talk shows and started a career in this field. The major milestone was the 'AM Chicago' show, which was renamed in September 1985 to become the 'Oprah Winfrey Show.' She built an empire—website, book club, magazine, and shows such as 'Dr. Phil,' and then her own production house, Harpo. In 2003, Winfrey became the first African-American female billionaire, because she knew how to diversify her businesses, to surround herself with a qualified team, and to promote social activities.

FOCUS magazine was established in February 2006 by entrepreneur Nadine Fayad Comair. Comair realized the needs of women and thus started a French luxury magazine in Lebanon and the Middle East. Comair's vision enabled her to focus on particular subjects of interest to her readership, and the magazine is distinguished by its high quality and the richness of its contents. As an Arab female herself, Comair understands what Arab women want, and offers them the opportunity to expand their knowledge about many issues, such as Beauty, Health, Fashion, Travel and Leisure, Architecture and Art, Sports, Kids, Stars, Technology, and Cars.

Tamara Abdel-Jaber   Jordanian Tamara Abdel-Jaber was a speaker at the 2009 Fortune Most Powerful Women Summit. She is a co-founder and an executive board member of business and information technology for the consulting firm Palma. Abdel-Jaber oversees strategy, corporate governance, performance management, and business development. Founded in 1997, Amman-based Palma delivers strategic management business consulting services to large- and medium-size organizations in Arab countries, including Saudi Arabia, the United Arab Emirates, Libya, Sudan, and Qatar. As a member of Young Arab Leaders, Abdel-Jaber is promoting a more positive future for the region.

Dr. Maha Al Muneef   Dr. Al Muneef, from Saudi Arabia, is the executive director of the Family Protection Program. She went to medical school in Riyadh and then completed her residency training in Pediatrics at the University of Alabama. She possesses many esteemed qualifications in the medical field. Al Muneef continues to be extremely active in both her profession and with academic positions at King Saud Bin Abdulaziz University.

Dr. Aysha Binbraik   Dr. Binbraik is from the United Arab Emirates and is a human resource manager. She is the strategic resourcing manager for Shell Exploration and Production International Ltd. She has held other prestigious posts such as director of human capital at Tatweer, and HR manager for Shell Markets, Middle East. Binbraik participates annually as a key speaker at GCC summits and conferences on Emiratization and Regionalization. She also participates as a coach for selected candidates on the Ashridge Leadership program run in the UAE.

Anita Roddick   Although Anita Roddick is no longer with us, The Body Shop continues to be a well-known brand worldwide, and is especially popular in the Arab world. How did it start? Before starting the Body Shop, Anita Roddick was an educator. In 1976, at the age of 34, she had a need to create a source of revenue for herself and two daughters, and entrepreneurship was the only survival tool that nurtured Roddick's innovative thinking. Her experiences with nature in different countries around the world gave her the idea for the environmentally oriented Body Shop. The company went public in 1984 and today the Body Shop operates in more than 50 markets, with over 2,000 stores.

The above-mentioned profiles speak for themselves and give us a taste of what women can achieve. However, there are barriers to their success, as we shall see.

Picture This

You have been asked to write a profile of a successful female you know. What would you stress?

The Barriers for Women in the Arab World

4 Understand the challenges that face women in the Arab world.

Women in business in the Arab world face many problems and barriers. These may include low income, the 'glass ceiling,' gender discrimination, time shifts, and nepotism, among others.

Low Income

Even though we talk about equality and equal opportunity, significant differences in wages between men and women still exist. Women continue to earn less than their male counterparts in the same occupations. This is due mainly to the short career paths of women as they leave the workplace, or to part-time schedules, because their family commitments are their priority.

Many people think that if women work in male-dominated occupations, the wage gap will disappear. The fact is that there is a gender-related wage gap in every job. However, the gap is more apparent in part-time employment. Women working 41 to 44 hours per week earn 84.6 percent of what men working similar hours earn; women working more than 60 hours per week earn only 78.3 percent of what men in the same time category earn.[10] In addition, women may need to work longer to be promoted and accordingly to get an increase in salary. For example, a female school-principal would need to work three years more than a male.[11]

Education also contributes to the income gap. To illustrate, educated Canadian females earn lower incomes than their male counterparts within identical occupations.[12] Other interesting statistics from Canada include:[13]

- Women aged 25 to 29, holding a graduate or professional diploma and working on a full-time, full-year basis, earned 96 cents for every dollar (100 cents) earned by their male counterparts in 2005.
- Women with a bachelor's degree earned 89 cents for every dollar earned by their male counterparts.
- Women with a registered apprenticeship or trades certificate earned only 65 cents for every dollar earned by their male counterparts.
- Young women with no high school diploma earned 67 cents for every dollar earned by young men with the same level of education.

Similarly, the Arab world experiences great gaps between males and females at all levels. A particular study in the United Arab Emirates determined the ratio of estimated female to male earned income, as shown in Figure 19-3.

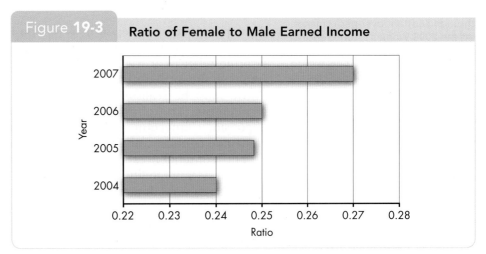

Figure 19-3   Ratio of Female to Male Earned Income

Source: Figures based on United Nations Development Programme "Sustainability and Equity: A Better Future for All," Human Development Report, 2011.

One woman who has managed to break through the glass ceiling very successfully is CEO of PepsiCo, Indra Nooyi. After graduating from Yale, south-Indian born Nooyi worked her way up the career ladder to join PepsiCo in 1994 as senior vice-president of strategy and development. After being promoted several times she eventually became CEO in 1996, and is now one of the most powerful women in the corporate world. Nooyi has many significant qualities that have enabled her to succeed where others haven't, but believes that one of the biggest keys to success is to focus on proving yourself through constant over-performance. At the 2008 Women's Conference in California, Nooyi explained her belief that the only way to permanently remove the glass ceiling is for women to work together.

Glass ceiling

An unacknowledged barrier that prevents women and minorities from advancing to higher levels in their profession.

Nepotism

The showing of favoritism in business toward relatives and friends, based upon that relationship, rather than on an objective evaluation of ability, merit or suitability.

Glass Ceiling

Is there a **glass ceiling**? That is, even if women are being given more chances, will there still be problems, obstacles, and limits to their success and progress? The culture in the Arab world, as we discussed in the previous chapter, is such that men are viewed as the main breadwinners of the household. Recall the masculinity domain that Hofstede presents as one of the five cultural dimensions (p. 61). As a result, in some countries, men can forbid women from working at all, or during certain hours of the day, or from going on business trips.

Gender Discrimination

In the Arab world, the tradition is that 'man is the head of the household.' We talk about equality, but cultural issues can often dominate and we often witness men reacting negatively to successful women. But we do not wish to generalize; there are exceptions to this rule. However, females must work harder and put in more effort than males to achieve their goals. The transition of business from local to global operations will result in increasing the trend of women entrepreneurship and help to break tradition. Masculine societies will be obliged to become open to other countries where gender equality exists and women operate on a business-level equal to men.

Time Shifts

Time shifts are important especially for the female workforce because they need flexible work hours so that they can do a good job and at the same time take care of the family. If individuals are required to take late-night shifts, for example, then they will be exhausted, since the sleep routine will be interrupted. This is bad enough for males but for females it can be even more tiring and impact on their output, since females need also to take care of the household needs and the children.

In addition, extended working hours negatively affect the amount of time available for sleep and social activities. If individuals work more than 48 hours within a week, this results in sleep of a limited quality and length, which causes fatigue, and ultimately affects health and safety and performance.

Nepotism

Some people refer to nepotism as the 'business cancer.'[14] The *Oxford Dictionary* describes **nepotism** as, "the practice among those with power or influence of favoring relatives or friends, especially by giving them jobs".[15] This is known as '*wasta*' in the Arab world, and is very common (see p. 289).

We must be realistic and realize that every organization has some form of nepotism. The obvious forms of nepotism are: relative nepotism, friend nepotism, connection nepotism, contribution nepotism, referral nepotism, credential nepotism, and favoritism. They are always with us.

The consequences of employee favoritism and nepotism include: low personal accountability, low employee accountability, low productivity, poor employee morale, low trust relationships, diminished customer experiences, and high-performer turnover.

Managers should implement a strict 'no nepotism' policy to allow for equal opportunity and, in particular, to prevent gender discrimination. Even if the outcome of the nepotism seems likely to benefit the firm, it should not be used. Females should be given the chance to prove themselves and nepotism should not be used against them.

Other Challenges

The most common challenges faced by business women in the Arab region have been identified[16] as follows: accessing capital, new markets, and business training. In addition, learning financial management skills and establishing networks and informal business relationships pose problems for women. Moreover, finding and keeping good employees, balancing between business and social roles, as well as dealing with bureaucracy and paperwork, can be barriers that may be difficult to overcome.

Despite these barriers, females are needed in the Arab region to diversify the economy and create jobs for a workforce estimated to reach 174 million by the year 2030. Nadereh Chamlou, senior advisor at World Bank's Middle East and North Africa region, says, "Female entrepreneurs can become an engine of growth. Women entrepreneurship could help the region meet its challenges, because empowering women and diversifying the economy can go together—and help the region meet the critical challenge of creating more and better jobs."[17]

This brings us to the question of the role that the woman plays in the Arab world culture. She may be wife, mother, sister, and she can also be a business-woman. Thus, women can engage in responsibilities other than housework and childcare. One issue is that some men may feel threatened when they see that their women are becoming more successful than them, and may feel uncomfortable that women are starting to orient their interests towards new fields that were previously assigned to men, and are expressing themselves more strongly in terms of their personality and intellect.

International OB

The World Supports the Middle Eastern Woman

The Middle East Partnership Initiative (MEPI) is a US State Department program that encourages reform efforts in the Middle East and North Africa (MENA). MEPI was established in 2002 to strengthen civil society and the rule of law; empower women and youth; improve and expand education; encourage economic reform; and increase political participation.

In 2005, the US State Department announced that 40 women from the MENA region would take part in a program that combines academic training and internship at prestigious companies and law firms such as Microsoft, Boeing Company, and Verizon. The program is a unique combination of both the study of US business culture and internships that allow participants to practice and enhance their management and business skills.

Many Arab women started their own business after their internship and thus were able to benefit themselves and help other women. For example, one Saudi woman founded a club to empower young Saudi women; a Palestinian woman advises women entrepreneurs in Palestine; and a third woman from Morocco cites recent legal reforms in her country to help women express their voice. Alaa Naseif from Saudi Arabia explains that empowerment begins with education. Empowerment is not just having an opportunity, but "having a choice in selecting among various opportunities," she says.

Other organizations for empowering women were started in Jordan and Egypt. The International Republican Institute and the National Democratic Institute, with MEPI support, regularly offer training courses for women from Bahrain, Kuwait, Oman, Qatar, the United Arab Emirates, and Yemen. Yet another partnership is between the Center for Development and Population Activity and the National Council for Women.

Source: Based on K. McConnell, "Middle East Women Discuss Importance of Empowerment," *Washington Files*, March 2006.

How Do Males React to Successful Females?

5 Determine how men react to successful women.

Women entrepreneurs can have a large impact on the economy and employment of their countries and also they can stimulate development. Women and men are equal in their managerial abilities and overall capacity to succeed. However, the promotion of women to senior positions is often hindered by the existence of discrimination, since the Arab male may not encourage female success.

According to Femeo, a web-based community for working women in the Middle East, there are several factors that cause men to feel threatened by successful women:[18]

1. *Self-esteem issues.* People who struggle with a lack of self-esteem will sometimes project those feelings onto others.
2. *Feeling threatened.* It's common for some men to feel threatened by women who are more successful than they are. Arab men especially prefer to be in control, and some of them may feel that a woman's success would undermine their authority.
3. *Fear of independence.* The idea of financially and emotionally self-sufficient women can be scary to some men. They grow concerned that their partners no longer need them.
4. *Shortcomings.* Some men might feel they're a disappointment to their society if their spouse is successful at her career. It makes them feel as though they've fallen short of being a real man.
5. *Ego complex.* Those who are self-centered have a very difficult time coping with the idea that there could possibly exist someone (let alone a woman!) more accomplished than them.
6. *Losing control.* Men want to be in command of all aspects in their lives, including their home and their family. The idea of that control slipping from their hands can cause a dramatic reaction.

Every country of the Arab world has successful females who have proven themselves in all domains, despite the obstacles they face from the community and from males. For example, there is the aspiring Qatari businesswomen Buthaina Al-Ansari, who created Qatariat to help those Qatari women who had the potential but were not climbing the corporate ladder. Qatariat runs three different firms—Qatariat Training and Development, Qatariat Media and Advertising, and Qatariat Magazine. A member of the Qatari Business Women Forum and the Arab International Women's Forum, Al-Ansari admits she faces many challenges as she tries to advance the cause of female entrepreneurship in Qatar. Strangely, "The biggest challenge is not being a woman in Qatar, but convincing others to believe in what local entrepreneurs do," Al-Ansari says. However, it's in her role as founder and chairwoman of Qatariat that she is able to encourage and train Qatari entrepreneurs and business professionals. "Nothing is impossible, but you have to start your business with a unique idea," Al-Ansari says. Although many women thought that starting Qatariat would be impossible, Al-Ansari persisted, showing a determination to succeed. She adds, "You will find that, step by step, you can make it happen."[19]

Sheikha al-Bahar from Kuwait has been given the title of "the billion dollar banker." She started as a trainee at National Bank of Kuwait (NBK) and now, as group general manager of corporate banking, oversees more than US$12bn of assets and almost 150 employees. She is so passionate about encouraging young women to become professionals that she addresses them at their schools and universities. "If you want to succeed, you need a clear goal of what you want," she says. "When I first arrived at the bank I told them that I wanted to be the general manager; they thought I was just this crazy 20-year old. But I did it. And there are many young women out there who can as well."

Source: Shyamantha Asokan and David Patrikarakos, "Who's Who: Extended version of our list of personalities," *Financial Times*, June, 2008.

Stereotypes Can Be Broken: Time for Change

> **6** *Realize that tradition can be broken: It is time for change.*

Although women have advanced, they still have a long way to go to overcome the gender bias in the workforce. Why is it that only 15 female CEOs currently lead Fortune 500 companies? Can the female change the stereotype? Over 70 years ago, Eleanor Roosevelt was right when she said, "No one can make you feel inferior without your consent."

Lois Frankel's book *Nice Girls Don't Get the Corner Office*, talks about the mistakes women make that affect their careers. Frankel writes, "Our tendencies to collaborate rather than compete, listen more than talk, and use relationships rather than muscle to influence are the very same behaviors I coach men to acquire. But it's all about balance. Just as men can overuse their stereotypical characteristics, so can women."[20]

Many changes have started to appear in the Arab world. Females are being given opportunities to show their potential and, in some instances, the traditional role is breaking.[21] A significant change happened in Saudi Arabia when a woman was appointed to the Council of Ministers. For the first time in the history of the country, Noor Al-Fayez became Deputy Minister for Women's Education in Saudi Arabia—a country where women are still not allowed to drive a car. This step came as a surprise not only for the region, but also for the world.

Surprisingly, women in the United Arab Emirates are also breaking stereotypes and 30 percent of public-sector management positions are held by

OB in the News

Female Leaders in Business

Sheikha Lubna Al Qasimi is the female Chief Executive Officer (CEO) of Tejari.com, an online business-to-business (B2B) environment. Tejari.com is based in the United Arab Emirates (UAE), where Arabic is the official language; for business purposes, English and other languages are spoken widely. Islam is the official religion of the UAE, and other faiths are tolerated. The national (Emirati) population is 2.4 million, approximately 25 percent of the total population. The remainder of the population are non-nationals (expatriates). Females comprised about 19.4 percent of the total workforce in 1995, when the literacy rate among women in the UAE was 88.7 percent. Employees at Tejari.com are from 12 different

countries, thus bringing cultural diversity to a working environment.

Sheikha Lubna has faced challenges to her role as CEO from outside the region, which she believes are due to negative assumptions held about Muslim women because of the way they dress. She (like many others of her religion) wears an abaya (a black garment that covers her hair and body) in public. Although her face is not veiled, her hair is covered. In 2004, Sheikha Lubna was appointed as the Minister of Economy and Planning and was the first woman in the UAE to assume a cabinet position.

Sheikha Lubna Al Qasimi has broken barriers both as a female leader in a geographical area not renowned for its gender equality and as a female business leader in

the field of technology, where women are underrepresented. As such she represents a positive role model. Her husband, Sheikh Mohammed, said, "Arab women are half our community. . . . Perhaps in the past we lagged behind, but today she is growing to better heights in our society and is able to achieve goals within our communities."

Sources: UAE interact, "UAE Population Growth Highest in Arab world," February 7, 2004, www.uaeinteract.com/news/default.asp?cntDisplay=10&ID=134; Miniwatts International "Internet World Statistics," www.internetworldstats.com/stats5.htm; UNESCO, *Statistical Yearbook*, 1999; S. L. Al Qasimi, "I Have Earned My Desk," www.womenone.org/faceslubna04.htm; and H. H. S. Mohammad bin Rashed Al Maktoum, www.sheikhmohammed.co.ae/english/history/history_women.asp.

During a gala dinner at Lebanon's Horeca 2010 Exhibition, five pioneering women pictured here were recognized for their successful achievements in the hospitality and catering industry. Hotelier Mirna Boustany of Hotel Al Bustan was given a Lifetime Achievement Award, and four other women were given Women Achievers in the Hospitality Industry awards: Sawsan Al Wazzan, proprietor of The Nutrition and Diet Center; Christine Sfeir, CEO of Meeting Point S.A.L.; Lina Lteif, proprietor of La Mie Dorée restaurant; and Maya Bekhaazi, proprietor of Acquisition.

Source: Executive Magazine, Issue No. 131, June 2010, p. 28.

women. This is confirmed by Hoda Kanoo, founder of the world-class Abu Dhabi Music & Arts Festival, and Anita Mehra, marketing and communications vice-president for Dubai International Airport, one of the fastest growing air hubs on the planet.

Global Implications

> **7** *Understand the global implications of the female in the Arab workplace.*

Globalization has encouraged the expansion of woman-owned businesses and the emergence of entrepreneurs. The growing economic power and influence of businesses owned by women are changing the shape of the global economy. For example, women produce more than 80 percent of the food for sub-Saharan Africa, 50 to 60 percent for Asia, 26 percent for the Caribbean, 34 percent for North America and the Middle East, and more than 30 percent for Latin America. Female entrepreneurs are active at all levels domestically, regionally, and globally. A recent United Nations report concluded that economic development is closely related to the advancement of women: "Global markets and women are not often used in the same sentence but increasingly, statistics show that women have economic clout—most visibly as entrepreneurs and most powerfully as customers."[22]

All issues related to women around the world are of importance to heads of states and decision makers. That is why so many international organizations and committees have been established to address these concerns. For instance, the Economic and Social Commission for Western Asia (ESCWA) Committee on Women was established in 2003. This committee follows up on women-related regional and international conferences, considers all recommendations, and implements the decisions that are taken. The first session of the Committee was held in 2003, and Session Two convened in 2004. Session Three of the Committee on Women was held in Abu Dhabi, UAE, in March, 2007.

Three of the goals of that third session can be summarized as follows:[23]

- The priorities for 2015 are to put forward initiatives and measures to accelerate the implementation of the Arab Plan of Action for the Advancement of Women and to overcome all challenges.

- To investigate ways of implementing the Beirut Declaration: "Arab Women Ten Years after Beijing: Call for Peace," which took into consideration the Millennium goals of eliminating all forms of gender discrimination.
- To explore the best ways of advancing and improving the lot of Arab women living in conditions of war and armed conflict.

A survey conducted by Catalyst and MacKenzie[24] of the US and UK found that there is a direct relationship between organizational profit and the presence of women in top management positions. Another study by Nick Wilson from the Faculty of Economics at Leeds University, in the UK, found that the presence of females on the board of directors can decrease the risks of bankruptcy by 20 percent[25].

Summary and Implications for Managers

The problems that Arab women are facing are many, but they can be overcome. Today, there is greater acceptance and awareness of the importance of women in all professions and business sectors. Women represent more than half the world's population, yet in no country do they represent anywhere near half the corporate managers.

The Need for Females in the Workplace   Women have proven to be just as competent as men and have the potential to succeed in any domain. Women have decided to enter the world of business by joining the family business, or by working for various organizations, or by establishing their own businesses to become entrepreneurs. Men used to be considered the only individuals who could become entrepreneurs or prosperous businesspersons. However, women started to establish themselves in the field and by the 1990s, the number of woman-owned businesses in the United States had increased dramatically, and has continued to do so. Similar trends have been noticeable in recent decades in the Arab world.

What Motivates Individuals   We can't say that women are more ambitious or motivated than men, but we can show that women can be just as successful as men when they are given the opportunity. The identification of those factors that motivate women in the Arab world is actually challenging itself. There are many motivating factors, or opportunities, that can facilitate the process for women in the Arab region to start their own businesses.

The Challenges Females Face   Women in business in the Arab world face many problems and barriers. These may include low income, the glass ceiling, gender discrimination, time shifts, and nepotism. In addition, some men may feel threatened when they see that women are becoming more successful, and this makes them feel uncomfortable. What women are starting to do is orient their interests towards new fields that were previously assigned to men, and strengthening their personalities and intellectual levels.

The Stereotype Can Be Changed   Many changes have started to appear in the Arab world. Females are being given opportunities to show their potential and, in some instances, the traditional role is breaking. For example, females from Yemen, Saudi Arabia, and the United Arab Emirates have not only managed to break the stereotype of the traditional woman, but have also challenged many of the preconceptions that people had about what women could do.

Point >> << Counterpoint

FEMALES CAN FIND A BALANCE

Women should be given a positive choice to stay at home and give children the best possible start in life. Many religions and cultures view a women's place as being in the home. Facilitating women to stay at home with their children respects these beliefs and helps to foster the culture of respect towards women's special role that identifies them as mothers who want the best care for their children.

By staying at home, women are doing the best for their family.

Mothers should have as much freedom as anyone else in society to decide what is best for them and their children. If they would rather work, then they should be given the opportunity so that they are not dependent upon their partners. Encouraging females to work increases the number of people in the workforce and thus increases the productivity of the country.

A woman's place is not necessarily at home; it is anywhere she has the competencies to be.

Questions for Review

1 Why is there a need to encourage women to enter the workplace?

2 What is the significance of the Arab businesswoman?

3 Can motivation differ according to gender? Explain.

4 What are the main challenges that female entrepreneurs face?

5 What are the reactions of males to the success of the female? Do men feel threatened?

6 What is the glass ceiling?

7 How has tradition been broken?

8 What are the global implications of females in the workplace?

Discussion Exercise

Here in the Middle East, . . . [a] long hopeful process of democratic change is now beginning to unfold. Millions of people are demanding freedom for themselves and democracy for their countries. There are those who say that democracy is for men alone. In fact, the opposite is true; half a democracy is not a democracy. One Arab female leader said, "Society is like a bird. It has two wings. And a bird cannot fly if one wing is broken." (Condoleezza Rice, 2005)[26]

Do you agree with this statement? Discuss.

Ethical Considerations

Economic development in the Gulf Cooperation Council (GCC) countries—Bahrain, Kuwait, Oman, Qatar, Saudi Arabia, and the United Arab Emirates—is exploding. The ruling elite, anxious to tap the resources of all their citizens, are encouraging women to step up and take on leadership roles as businesswomen, heads of financial firms, teachers, scholars, and writers.

Sheikha Hanadi Al-Thani, a member of Qatar's ruling family and a prominent businesswoman, points out, "In many ways, the Gulf offers more opportunities for women. It is a rapidly growing economy, and with growth comes opportunities that would otherwise not be there . . . One advantage is that there are no glass ceilings because people are a scarce resource."

Arab women continue to balance individual advancement and service to their countries against cultural expectations; this balancing act is a skill they have long practiced and continue to embrace.

Contrary to many Western assumptions, women in the Gulf are encouraged to study, work outside the home, marry partners who share their personal and professional goals, seek out mentors and leadership opportunities, and contribute to the welfare of their countries, both through traditional roles as mothers and wives *and* as businesswomen, financial leaders, and teachers. Indeed, many Arab businesses are family business – a fact that helps women blend the professional and personal with less conflict.

Professor Amal Mohammed Al-Malki, who teaches at Carnegie Mellon University's campus in Qatar, explains that women carefully negotiate their power and authority within age-old constructs of the family. For example, "women in business often refer to the men in their lives, be that a father or a husband, with gratitude. It is crucial for a woman to have such acceptance, because our societies are still male-dominated societies, and a man is still the head of his family."

Arab societies and governments must learn to balance ways to reward women for working outside the home while affirming their roles within the home.

What are the ethical implications here?

Source: Extracts from M. Momaya, "Women's Empowerment, Arab Style: Women in the Middle East Break New Ground", *International Museum of Women*, www.imow.org/economica/stories/viewStory?storyID=3644.

Critical Analysis

NO MATTER WHAT, THE BOARDROOM IS STILL OFF LIMITS TO FEMALES!

Even though the Arab woman has made her mark and has entered most professions and owns huge amounts of wealth, her presence in the boardroom is minimal. One study of the Gulf Cooperation Council (GCC) countries was conducted by The National Investor and Hawkamah, the Dubai-based Institute for Corporate Governance. It found that only 63 out of 4,254 board seats across the Gulf belonged to females. The results did, however, reveal that Kuwait and Oman broke the tradition by having more women on their boards than Italy and Japan.

Nadereh Chamlou, a senior advisor at the World Bank states, "There are both explicit and implicit hurdles for women to exercise the same kind of control as men do." For example, in Saudi Arabia, one woman made it to the boardroom in 2004: Lubna Olayan, a prominent businesswoman, was appointed to the board of the Saudi Hollandi Bank.

With family businesses, females also face many problems. When the head of the family passes away, there may be a conflict between brothers and sisters; that is, if sisters are able to get involved. Their rights are often not considered. What is ironic is that if the situation gets worse and the sister wants to take legal action, she needs the permission of a male of the family.

Reem Badran, a Jordanian businesswoman and chief executive of Kuwaiti Jordanian Holding Company, stresses, "We have to empower women to become more aggressive in reaching senior positions." Badran continues, "We are usually shy about taking our rights. Also the business community, which is male-dominated, has to give women a chance to prove themselves."

It is not a matter of changing laws but of changing social outlooks. Women need to work so much harder than men to reach higher positions and prove they are capable of being effective leaders.

"Men ask for positions and they strive for them," says Neveen Al-Taheri. "We [women] think it is our right to get these jobs because we are efficient. We don't fight for them."

Moreover, what is apparent is that there are more and more female university graduates in the Arab world. With the establishment of associations for females and the potential they are showing, women are starting their own businesses and aiming to reach leadership positions. Ultimately, the boardroom will be decorated with competent females who will gain the respect of their male counterparts.

Questions

1. What do you think are the 'explicit' and 'implicit' hurdles faced by women in business?

2. What specific challenges face women in family businesses?

3. What do you think Noveen Al-Taheri means when she says that women don't fight for higher positions?

Source: H. Saleh, "Corporate Governance: Boardroom Is Still Male Territory," *Financial Times*, June 2008, p. 3.

Research Exercise

Unfortunately, there is little research on female employment rates and the specifics of their employment in the Arab world. Nonetheless, we can still find some information and data. Do your own research and discuss the findings in class. Try to find answers to questions such as: What is the employment rate of men to women in different sectors? Is there a difference in salary scale? What motivates women? Are they more emotional as leaders?

Appendix A Research in Organizational Behavior

For every complex problem, there is a solution that is simple, neat, and wrong.

—H. L. Mencken

A number of years ago, a friend of mine was excited because he had read about the findings from a research study that finally, once and for all, resolved the question of what it takes to make it to the top in a large corporation. I doubted there was any simple answer to this question but, not wanting to dampen his enthusiasm, I asked him to tell me of what he had read. The answer, according to my friend, was *participation in college athletics*. To say I was skeptical of his claim is a gross understatement, so I asked him to tell me more.

The study encompassed 1,700 successful senior executives at the 500 largest US corporations. The researchers found that half of these executives had played varsity-level college sports.[1] My friend, who happens to be good with statistics, informed me that since fewer than 2 percent of all college students participate in intercollegiate athletics, the probability of this finding occurring by mere chance is less than 1 in 10 million! He concluded his analysis by telling me that, based on this research, I should encourage my management students to get into shape and to make one of the varsity teams.

My friend was somewhat perturbed when I suggested that his conclusions were likely to be flawed. These executives were all males who attended college in the 1940s and 1950s. Would his advice be meaningful to females in the twenty-first century? These executives also weren't your typical college students. For the most part, they had attended elite private colleges in the US such as Princeton and Amherst, where a large proportion of the student body participates in intercollegiate sports. And these 'jocks' hadn't necessarily played football or basketball; many had participated in golf, tennis, baseball, cross-country running, crew, rugby, and similar minor sports. Moreover, maybe the researchers had confused the direction of causality. That is, maybe individuals with the motivation and ability to make it to the top of a large corporation are drawn to competitive activities like college athletics.

My friend was guilty of misusing research data. Of course, he is not alone. We are all continually bombarded with reports of experiments that link certain substances to cancer in mice and surveys that show changing attitudes toward sex among college students, for example. Many of these studies are carefully designed, with great caution taken to note the implications and limitations of the findings. But some studies are poorly designed, making their conclusions at best suspect, and at worst meaningless.

Rather than attempting to make you a researcher, the purpose of this appendix is to increase your awareness as a consumer of behavioral research. A knowledge of research methods will allow you to appreciate more fully the care in data collection that underlies the information and conclusions presented in this text. Moreover, an understanding of research methods will make you a more skilled evaluator of the OB studies you will encounter in business and professional journals. So an appreciation of behavioral research is important because (1) it's the foundation on which the theories in this text are built, and (2) it will benefit you in future years when you read reports of research and attempt to assess their value.

Purposes of Research

Research is concerned with the systematic gathering of information. Its purpose is to help us in our search for the truth. Although we will never find ultimate truth—in our case, that would be to know precisely how any person or group would behave in any organizational context—ongoing research adds to our body of OB knowledge by supporting some theories, contradicting others, and suggesting new theories to replace those that fail to gain support.

Research Terminology

Researchers have their own vocabulary for communicating among themselves and with outsiders. The following briefly defines some of the more popular terms you're likely to encounter in behavioral science studies.[2]

Variable

A *variable* is any general characteristic that can be measured and that changes in amplitude, intensity, or both. Some examples of OB variables found in this textbook are job satisfaction, employee productivity, work stress, ability, personality, and group norms.

Hypothesis

A tentative explanation of the relationship between two or more variables is called a *hypothesis*. My friend's statement that participation in college athletics leads to a top executive position in a large corporation is an example of a hypothesis. Until confirmed by empirical research, a hypothesis remains only a tentative explanation.

Dependent Variable

A *dependent variable* is a response that is affected by an independent variable. In terms of the hypothesis, it is the variable that the researcher is interested in explaining. Referring back to our opening example, the dependent variable in my friend's hypothesis was executive succession. In organizational behavior research, the most popular dependent variables are productivity, absenteeism, turnover, job satisfaction, and organizational commitment.[3]

Independent Variable

An *independent variable* is the presumed cause of some change in the dependent variable. Participating in varsity athletics was the independent variable in my friend's hypothesis. Popular independent variables studied by OB researchers include intelligence, personality, job satisfaction, experience, motivation, reinforcement patterns, leadership style, reward allocations, selection methods, and organization design.

You may have noticed we said that job satisfaction is frequently used by OB researchers as both a dependent and an independent variable. This is not an error. It merely reflects that the label given to a variable depends on its place in the hypothesis. In the statement "Increases in job satisfaction lead to reduced turnover," job satisfaction is an independent variable. However, in the statement "Increases in money lead to higher job satisfaction," job satisfaction becomes a dependent variable.

Moderating Variable

A *moderating variable* abates the effect of the independent variable on the dependent variable. It might also be thought of as a contingency variable: If X (independent variable), then Y (dependent variable) will occur, but only under conditions Z (moderating variable). To translate this into a real-life example, we might say that if we increase the amount of direct supervision in the work area (X), then there will be a change in worker productivity (Y), but this effect will be moderated by the complexity of the tasks being performed (Z).

Causality

A hypothesis, by definition, implies a relationship. That is, it implies a presumed cause and effect. This direction of cause and effect is called *causality*. Changes in the independent variable are assumed to cause changes in the dependent variable. However, in behavioral research, it's possible to make an incorrect assumption of causality when relationships are found. For example, early behavioral scientists found a relationship between employee satisfaction and productivity. They concluded that a happy worker was a productive worker. Follow-up research has supported the relationship, but disconfirmed the direction of the arrow. The evidence more correctly suggests that high productivity leads to satisfaction rather than the other way around.

Correlation Coefficient

It's one thing to know that there is a relationship between two or more variables. It's another to know the *strength* of that relationship. The term *correlation coefficient* is used to indicate that strength, and is expressed as a number between –1.00 (a perfect negative relationship) and +1.00 (a perfect positive correlation).

When two variables vary directly with one another, the correlation will be expressed as a positive number. When they vary inversely—that is, one increases as the other decreases—the correlation will be expressed as a negative number. If the two variables vary independently of each other, we say that the correlation between them is zero.

For example, a researcher might survey a group of employees to determine the satisfaction of each with his or her job. Then, using company absenteeism reports, the researcher could correlate the job satisfaction scores against individual attendance records to determine whether employees who are more satisfied with their job have better attendance records than their counterparts who indicated lower job satisfaction. Let's suppose the researcher found a correlation coefficient of +0.50 between satisfaction and attendance. Would that be a strong association? There is, unfortunately, no precise numerical cutoff separating strong and weak relationships. A standard statistical test would need to be applied to determine whether the relationship was a significant one.

A final point needs to be made before we move on: A correlation coefficient measures only the strength of association between two variables. A high value does *not* imply causality. The length of women's skirts and stock market prices, for instance, have long been noted to be highly correlated, but one should be careful not to infer that a causal relationship between the two exists. In this instance, the high correlation is more happenstance than predictive.

Theory

The final term we introduce in this section is *theory*. Theory describes a set of systematically interrelated concepts or hypotheses that purports to explain and predict phenomena. In OB, theories are also frequently referred to as *models*. We use the two terms interchangeably.

There are no shortages of theories in OB. For instance, we have theories to describe what motivates people, the most effective leadership styles, the best way to resolve conflicts, and how people acquire power. In some cases, we have half a dozen or more separate theories that purport to explain and predict a given phenomenon. In such cases, is one right and the others wrong? No! They tend to reflect science at work—researchers testing previous theories, modifying them, and, when appropriate, proposing new models that may prove to have higher explanatory and predictive powers. Multiple theories attempting to explain common phenomena merely attest that OB is an active discipline, still growing and evolving.

Evaluating Research

As a potential consumer of behavioral research, you should follow the dictum of *caveat emptor*—let the buyer beware! In evaluating any research study, you need to ask three questions.[4]

Is it valid? Is the study actually measuring what it claims to be measuring? A number of psychological tests have been discarded by employers in recent years because they have not been found to be valid measures of the applicants' ability to do a given job successfully. But the validity issue is relevant to all research studies. So, if you find a study that links cohesive work teams with higher productivity, you want to know how each of these variables was measured and whether it is actually measuring what it is supposed to be measuring.

Is it reliable? Reliability refers to consistency of measurement. If you were to have your height measured every day with a wooden yardstick, you'd get highly reliable results. On the other hand, if you were measured each day by an elastic tape measure, there would probably be considerable disparity between your height measurements from one day to the next. Your height, of course, doesn't change from day to day. The variability is due

to the unreliability of the measuring device. So if a company asked a group of its employees to complete a reliable job satisfaction questionnaire, and then repeat the questionnaire six months later, we'd expect the results to be very similar—provided nothing changed in the interim that might significantly affect employee satisfaction.

Is it generalizable? Are the results of the research study generalizable to groups of individuals other than those who participated in the original study? Be aware, for example, of the limitations that might exist in research that uses college students as subjects. Are the findings in such studies generalizable to full-time employees in real jobs? Similarly, how generalizable to the overall work population are the results from a study that assesses job stress among 10 nuclear power plant engineers in the hamlet of Mahone Bay, Nova Scotia?

Research Design

Doing research is an exercise in trade-offs. Richness of information typically comes with reduced generalizability. The more a researcher seeks to control for confounding variables, the less realistic his or her results are likely to be. High precision, generalizability, and control almost always translate into higher costs. When researchers make choices about who they'll study, where their research will be done, the methods they'll use to collect data, and so on, they must make some concessions. Good research designs are not perfect, but they do carefully reflect the questions being addressed. Keep these facts in mind as we review the strengths and weaknesses of five popular research designs: Case studies, field surveys, laboratory experiments, field experiments, and aggregate quantitative reviews.

Case Study

You pick up a copy of Soichiro Honda's autobiography. In it he describes his impoverished childhood; his decisions to open a small garage, assemble motorcycles, and eventually build automobiles; and how this led to the creation of one of the largest and most successful corporations in the world. Or you're in a business class and the instructor distributes a 50-page handout covering two companies: Wal-Mart and Kmart. The handout details the two firms' histories; describes their corporate strategies, management philosophies, and merchandising plans; and includes copies of their recent balance sheets and income statements. The instructor asks the class members to read the handout, analyze the data, and determine why Wal-Mart has been so much more successful than Kmart in recent years.

Soichiro Honda's autobiography and the Wal-Mart and Kmart handouts are case studies. Drawn from real-life situations, case studies present an in-depth analysis of one setting. They are thorough descriptions, rich in details about an individual, a group, or an organization. The primary source of information in case studies is obtained through observation, occasionally backed up by interviews and a review of records and documents.

Case studies have their drawbacks. They're open to the perceptual bias and subjective interpretations of the observer. The reader of a case is captive to what the observer/case writer chooses to include and exclude. Cases also trade off generalizability for depth of information and richness of detail. Because it's always dangerous to generalize from a sample of one, case studies make it difficult to prove or reject a hypothesis. On the other hand, you can't ignore the in-depth analysis that cases often provide. They are an excellent device for initial exploratory research and for evaluating real-life problems in organizations.

Field Survey

A lengthy questionnaire was created to assess the use of ethics policies, formal ethics structures, formalized activities such as ethics training, and executive involvement in ethics programs among billion-dollar corporations. The public affairs or corporate communications office of all *Fortune* 500 industrial firms and 500 service corporations were contacted to get the name and address of the 'officer most responsible for dealing with ethics and conduct issues' in each firm. The questionnaire, with a cover letter explaining the nature of the study, was mailed to these 1,000 officers. Of the total, 254 returned a completed questionnaire, for a response rate just above 25 percent. The results of the survey found, among other things, that 77 percent had formal codes of ethics and 54 percent had a single officer specifically assigned to deal with ethics and conduct issues.[5]

The preceding study illustrates a typical field survey. A sample of respondents (in this case, 1,000 corporate officers in the largest US publicly held corporations) was selected to represent a larger group that was under examination (billion-dollar US business firms). The respondents were then surveyed using a questionnaire or interviewed to collect data on particular characteristics (the content and structure of ethics programs and practices) of interest to the researchers. The standardization of response items allows for data to be easily quantified, analyzed, and summarized, and for the researchers to make inferences from the representative sample about the larger population.

The field survey provides economies for doing research. It's less costly to sample a population than to obtain data from every member of that population. (There are, for instance, more than 5,000 US business firms with sales in excess of a billion dollars; and

since some of these are privately held and don't release financial data to the public, they are excluded from the *Fortune* list). Moreover, as the ethics study illustrates, field surveys provide an efficient way to find out how people feel about issues or how they say they behave. These data can then be easily quantified.

But the field survey has a number of potential weaknesses. First, mailed questionnaires rarely obtain 100 percent returns. Low response rates call into question whether conclusions based on respondents' answers are generalizable to nonrespondents. Second, the format is better at tapping respondents' attitudes and perceptions than behaviors. Third, responses can suffer from social desirability; that is, people saying what they think the researcher wants to hear. Fourth, since field surveys are designed to focus on specific issues, they're a relatively poor means of acquiring depth of information. Finally, the quality of the generalizations is largely a factor of the population chosen. Responses from executives at *Fortune* 500 firms, for instance, tell us nothing about small- or medium-sized firms or not-for-profit organizations. In summary, even a well-designed field survey trades off depth of information for breadth, generalizability, and economic efficiencies.

Laboratory Experiment

The following study is a classic example of the laboratory experiment. A researcher, Stanley Milgram, wondered how far individuals would go in following commands. If subjects were placed in the role of a teacher in a learning experiment and told by an experimenter to administer a shock to a learner each time that learner made a mistake, would the subjects follow the commands of the experimenter? Would their willingness to comply decrease as the intensity of the shock was increased?

To test these hypotheses, Milgram hired a set of subjects. Each was led to believe that the experiment was to investigate the effect of punishment on memory. Their job was to act as teachers and administer punishment whenever the learner made a mistake on the learning test.

Punishment was administered by an electric shock. The subject sat in front of a shock generator with 30 levels of shock—beginning at zero and progressing in 15-volt increments to a high of 450 volts. The demarcations of these positions ranged from 'Slight Shock' at 15 volts to 'Danger: Severe Shock' at 450 volts. To increase the realism of the experiment, the subjects received a sample shock of 45 volts and saw the learner—a pleasant, mild-mannered man about 50 years old—strapped into an 'electric chair' in an adjacent room. Of course, the learner was an actor, and the electric shocks were phony, but the subjects didn't know this.

Taking his seat in front of the shock generator, the subject was directed to begin at the lowest shock level and to increase the shock intensity to the next level each time the learner made a mistake or failed to respond.

When the test began, the shock intensity rose rapidly because the learner made many errors. The subject got verbal feedback from the learner: At 75 volts, the learner began to grunt and moan; at 150 volts, he demanded to be released from the experiment; at 180 volts, he cried out that he could no longer stand the pain; and at 300 volts, he insisted that he be let out, yelled about his heart condition, screamed, and then failed to respond to further questions.

Most subjects protested and, fearful they might kill the learner if the increased shocks were to bring on a heart attack, insisted they could not go on with their job. Hesitations or protests by the subject were met by the experimenter's statement, "You have no choice, you must go on! Your job is to punish the learner's mistakes." Of course, the subjects did have a choice. All they had to do was stand up and walk out.

The majority of the subjects dissented. But dissension isn't synonymous with disobedience. Sixty-two percent of the subjects increased the shock level to the maximum of 450 volts. The average level of shock administered by the remaining 38 percent was nearly 370 volts.[6]

In a laboratory experiment such as that conducted by Milgram, an artificial environment is created by the researcher. Then the researcher manipulates an independent variable under controlled conditions. Finally, since all other things are held equal, the researcher is able to conclude that any change in the dependent variable is due to the manipulation or change imposed on the independent variable. Note that, because of the controlled conditions, the researcher is able to imply causation between the independent and dependent variables.

The laboratory experiment trades off realism and generalizability for precision and control. It provides a high degree of control over variables and precise measurement of those variables. But findings from laboratory studies are often difficult to generalize to the real world of work. This is because the artificial laboratory rarely duplicates the intricacies and nuances of real organizations. In addition, many laboratory experiments deal with phenomena that cannot be reproduced or applied to real-life situations.

Field Experiment

The following is an example of a field experiment. The management of a large company is interested in determining the impact that a four-day workweek would have on employee absenteeism. To be more specific, management wants to know if employees working four 10-hour days have lower absence rates than similar employees working the traditional five-day week of 8 hours each day. Because the company is large, it has a number of manufacturing plants that employ essentially similar workforces. Two of these are chosen for the experiment, both located in the greater Cleveland area. Obviously, it would not be appropriate to compare two similar-sized plants if one is in rural Mississippi and the other is in urban Copenhagen because factors such as national culture, transportation, and weather might be more likely to explain any differences found than changes in the number of days worked per week.

In one plant, the experiment was put into place—workers began the four-day week. At the other plant, which became the control group, no changes were made in the employees' five-day week. Absence data were gathered from the company's records at both locations for a period of 18 months. This extended time period lessened the possibility that any results would be distorted by the mere novelty of changes being implemented in the experimental plant. After 18 months, management found that absenteeism had dropped by 40 percent at the experimental plant, and by only 6 percent in the control plant. Because of the design of this study, management believed that the larger drop in absences at the experimental plant was due to the introduction of the compressed workweek.

The field experiment is similar to the laboratory experiment, except it is conducted in a real organization. The natural setting is more realistic than the laboratory setting, and this enhances validity but hinders control. In addition, unless control groups are maintained, there can be a loss of control if extraneous forces intervene—for example, an employee strike, a major layoff, or a corporate restructuring. Maybe the greatest concern with field studies has to do with organizational selection bias. Not all organizations are going to allow outside researchers to come in and study their employees and operations. This is especially true of organizations that have serious problems. Therefore, since most published studies in OB are done by outside researchers, the selection bias might work toward the publication of studies conducted almost exclusively at successful and well-managed organizations.

Our general conclusion is that, of the four research designs we've discussed to this point, the field experiment typically provides the most valid and generalizable findings and, except for its high cost, trades off the least to get the most.[7]

Aggregate Quantitative Reviews

What's the overall effect of organizational behavior modification (OB Mod) on task performance? There have been a number of field experiments that have sought to throw light on this question. Unfortunately, the wide range of effects from these various studies makes it hard to generalize.

To try to reconcile these diverse findings, two researchers reviewed all the empirical studies they could find on the impact of OB Mod on task performance over a 20-year period.[8] After discarding reports that had inadequate information, had nonquantitative data, or didn't meet all conditions associated with principles of behavioral modification, the researchers narrowed their set to 19 studies that included data on 2,818 individuals. Using an aggregating technique called *meta-analysis*, the researchers were able to synthesize the studies quantitatively and to conclude that the average person's task performance will rise from the 50th percentile to the 67th percentile after an OB Mod intervention.

The OB Mod–task performance review done by these researchers illustrates the use of meta-analysis, a quantitative form of literature review that enables researchers to look at validity findings from a comprehensive set of individual studies, and then apply a formula to them to determine if they consistently produced similar results.[9] If results prove to be consistent, it allows researchers to conclude more confidently that validity is generalizable. Meta-analysis is a means for overcoming the potentially imprecise interpretations of qualitative reviews and to synthesize variations in quantitative studies. In addition, the technique enables researchers to identify potential moderating variables between an independent and a dependent variable.

In the past 25 years, there's been a surge in the popularity of this research method. Why? It appears to offer a more objective means for doing traditional literature reviews. Although the use of meta-analysis requires researchers to make a number of judgment calls, which can introduce a considerable amount of subjectivity into the process, there is no arguing that meta-analysis reviews have now become widespread in the OB literature.

Ethics in Research

Researchers are not always tactful or candid with subjects when they do their studies. For instance, questions in field surveys may be perceived as embarrassing by respondents or as an invasion of privacy. Also, researchers in laboratory studies have been known to deceive participants about the true purpose of their experiment "because they felt deception was necessary to get honest responses."[10]

The 'learning experiments' conducted by Stanley Milgram, which were conducted more than 30 years ago, have been widely criticized by psychologists on ethical grounds. He lied to subjects, telling them his study was investigating learning, when, in fact, he was concerned with obedience. The shock machine he used was a fake. Even the 'learner' was an accomplice of Milgram's who had been trained to act as if he were hurt and in pain. Yet ethical lapses continue. For instance, in 2001, a professor of organizational behavior at Columbia University sent out a common letter on university letterhead to 240 New York City restaurants in which he detailed how he had eaten at this restaurant with his wife in celebration of their wedding anniversary, how he had gotten food poisoning, and that he had spent the night in his bathroom throwing up.[11] The letter closed with: "Although it is not my intention to file any reports with the Better Business Bureau or the Department of Health, I want you to understand what I went through in anticipation that you will respond accordingly. I await your response." The fictitious letter was part of the professor's study to determine how restaurants responded to complaints. But it created culinary chaos among many of the restaurant owners, managers, and chefs as they reviewed menus and produce deliveries for possibly spoiled food, and questioned kitchen workers about possible lapses. A follow-up letter of apology from the university for "an egregious error in judgment by a junior faculty member" did little to offset the distress it created for those affected.

Professional associations like the American Psychological Association, the American Sociological Association, and the Academy of Management have published formal guidelines for the conduct of research. Yet the ethical debate continues. On one side are those who argue that strict ethical controls can damage the scientific validity of an experiment and cripple future research. Deception, for example, is often necessary to avoid contaminating results. Moreover, proponents of minimizing ethical controls note that few subjects have been appreciably harmed by deceptive experiments. Even in Milgram's highly manipulative experiment, only 1.3 percent of the subjects reported negative feelings about their experience. The other side of this debate focuses on the rights of participants. Those favoring strict ethical controls argue that no procedure should ever be emotionally or physically distressing to subjects, and that, as professionals, researchers are obliged to be completely honest with their subjects and to protect the subjects' privacy at all costs.

Summary

The subject of organizational behavior is composed of a large number of theories that are research based.

Research studies, when cumulatively integrated, become theories, and theories are proposed and followed by research studies designed to validate them. The concepts that make up OB, therefore, are only as valid as the research that supports them.

The topics and issues in this book are for the most part research-derived. They represent the result of systematic information gathering rather than merely hunch, intuition, or opinion. This doesn't mean, of course, that we have all the answers to OB issues. Many require far more corroborating evidence. The generalizability of others is limited by the research methods used. But new information is being created and published at an accelerated rate. To keep up with the latest findings, we strongly encourage you to regularly review the latest research in organizational behavior. The more academic work can be found in journals such as the *Academy of Management Journal, Academy of Management Review, Administrative Science Quarterly, Human Relations, Journal of Applied Psychology, Journal of Management, Journal of Organizational Behavior,* and *Leadership Quarterly.* For more practical interpretations of OB research findings, you may want to read the *Academy of Management Execuive, California Management Review, Harvard Business Review, Organizational Dynamics,* and the *Sloan Management Review.*

Comprehensive Cases

Being Lean, Not Mean

Even by the standards of the worst financial crisis for at least a generation, the events of Sunday September 14th and the day before were extraordinary. The weekend began with hopes that a deal could be struck, with or without government backing, to save Lehman Brothers, America's fourth-largest investment bank. Early Monday morning Lehman filed for Chapter 11 bankruptcy protection. It has more than $613 billion of debt.[1]

The news hit hard, and redundancies started to roll down at the company where Dr Olga Kampaxi worked in Dubai. On November 7, 2008, a meeting was held to announce the intended changes within the division. The tension was evident. Everyone was wondering whose job would be next on the list of redundancies after the company announced cancellations and delays to projects. No official announcements were made—just private meetings in the lobby of a city-centre hotel informing employees who would be next. Dr. Kampaxi was one of these employees, and she had been as shocked by the news of the fall of Lehman Brothers as the rest of the world was. Sensing the threat to her position from the knock-on effects in the financial world, she went home and started contacting people she knew in the Human Resources community. In December 2008 an opportunity was offered, and she signed a contract with Rotana.

Trusted with an area human resources position and in charge of the human resources department of Al Bustan Rotana, the new year looked challenging. Bad news continued to flood the meeting rooms and morning briefings: "Occupancy rates for hotels in Dubai have fallen by 4% in 2008 to October as a result of the global economic downturn . . . ;"[2] "Hotel occupancy rates in Dubai fell to 84.9% in November 2008, down from 90 percent in November 2007, according to figures by STR Global."[3]

The news from other hotel companies was not encouraging either. No one really knew what was going to happen. Uncertainty was the dominant feeling, with statements in the media such as: "Luxury Dubai hotel [. . .] has announced 70 staff have lost their jobs;" and

"The company expects that the number of staff will be reduced, which reflects the current economic conditions."[4]

With all this news swirling around, the obvious questions started to surface unofficially during lunch breaks, meetings, and employee gatherings: Will Rotana cut jobs? Will employees be sent on unpaid leave? Will merit increases happen? Will salary reviews be carried out? What will happen to promotion plans? Will the new hotels open or will inter-property transfers be halted? The list went on. Employees from two of the Rotana hotels that were expected to open in Dubai were already in their posts when delays were announced, and candidates with signed offer letters, who were waiting to travel to join Rotana, were on standby.

Decisions had to be made fast. At that time, the spontaneous and mechanical reaction was to save on expenses, as was the case with most companies. Rotana had already experienced crises in other cities across the region, so was all too familiar with these fluctuations; once again they had to apply the same principles, but this time to a much broader audience.

Although a management company, with the owners seeing their bottom line reduced compared with previous years, and feeling the pressure, the plan had to be right. The necessary steps had to be taken to prevent the erosion of profit.

"Measures had to be taken," said Mr. El Zyr, President and CEO of Rotana. "We have, like everyone else, become fully alert to the economic situation. However, we stayed confident while remaining realistic. Also, we were aware of what our competitors were and are still doing, we listened to our customers, and we were lean."

In January 2009, and following several meetings and studies done at a corporate level, Mr. El Zyr announced 'Operation Swordfish' to all the Rotana properties. He informed all the hotel general managers: "Operating revenues are constantly affected by the local, national, and global events where the hotel management has no control. The purpose of Operation Swordfish is to support how costs and expenses are managed when a shortfall in revenue is anticipated. This is not to pre-empt the judgment of the general manager and his team, rather to encourage the process where savings may be achieved."

'Operation Swordfish' was cascaded down to all the properties, and an action plan was set for each, with the aim of achieving the following objectives:

- Exceed fair market share in revenues
- Reduce costs and expenses (as appropriate) according to the level of business activity.

The following criteria were a must in preparing the action plans for each property:

- Protect and maximize the operating profit
- Protect the company image
- Maintain service and product quality
- Maintain employee morale
- Protect cash flow.

Operational efficiency and costs reduction, but with no jobs losses, were the top priorities. Looking at the medium and long term, Rotana could not afford to lose any of its workforce, especially with the expansion plans in place. Mr. El Zyr said:

> It is our people that make all the difference to Rotana's continued success. I believe that the lowest paid job at any hotel is very often the most important for its success. You can go to the best hotel in the world, but if your plate is not polished, your glass is not clean, or the bellboy not as friendly as the manager, you may not want to head back there.
>
> We strongly believe that our people are the ones who bring flair into a hotel and are directly associated with the success of a place or company, and for this reason, we focused on the training and development of the skills. This culture was aggressively cascaded from the top across all the Rotana properties.
>
> Swordfish are known to be vigorous, powerful fighters as well as impressive jumpers. This is what we were aiming for: to surface, fight through the crisis, and not just survive but sustain the business for medium- to long-term growth, balancing between our stakeholders, customers, and colleagues.

Looking back at that time, when Dr Kampaxi gave a speech to a group of students, she admitted that "Operation Swordfish was at first difficult: Difficult to acknowledge, communicate, and implement to the team in the operation. However, great emphasis was put on the morale of the employees and on engaging them with the process, which was the primary measure used to turn the crisis into an opportunity. Everything revolved around words, starting with re-reform, then redeploy, reorganize, and, above all, rethink the way they were operating."

Things like renegotiating with suppliers, renegotiating the rents, contracts, assessing manning needs, and revising budgets to ensure profitability would not be negatively affected. When other companies pressed the panic button and looked at cutting marketing budgets, drastically reducing manpower and cutting training, Rotana took a more holistic approach.

All department heads were made owners in the process; they had to embrace the new way of operating and had to rethink whether they really needed to outsource services, such as security or casual staff for events; they had to plan for clearing pending vacation days and set a good example by planning some days of unpaid vacation in relation to the forecasted occupancy, so that the payroll cost would not be too high if the business was not advantageous. Why outsource training when you can tap on the internal knowledge and cater internally for the needs required? Recruitment agencies were not a priority to source talent, especially as more candidates were available in the market.

Rotana was expanding at a phenomenal rate, and because of this its resources were well focused on its own employees and their retention, in addition to the centralization of recruitment through rotanacareers.com. The company had 10,000 employees and planned to increase its manning by 150 percent by 2012.

Rotana focused its efforts to ensure the retention and accommodation of its existing employees rather than looking out and recruiting new employees. In fact for all its pre-opening properties during 2009, the numbers of new recruits versus Rotana Inter Property Transfers were quite limited, as the company wanted to reduce payroll expenses within its running hotels and avoid over recruitment for its new developments, while awaiting the further economic and business trends.

Rotana participated in job fairs across the region in search for local talent to embrace the Rotana **LIFE** and to plan a **L**ong-term career and join an **I**nnovative, **F**riendly and **E**thical team, in line with the Rotana values.

Manning budgets were revised, when at the same time a big logistical exercise was planned and closely monitored by Corporate Office, to redeploy employees as an alternative to downsizing. With new properties opening up in Syria, Saudi Arabia, and Abu Dhabi, Rotana started redeploying employees to new hotels. Priority was given to existing colleagues, and while some candidates who already had signed offer-letters were put on hold, every human resources colleague had to communicate and ensure that prospective colleagues were updated on any developments if they chose to wait for a position to become available. That was another sign of Rotana's long-term vision. A crisis lived now might not need to hurt the image and the future of the company and its employer branding image. Every colleague whose position was revised was closely counseled about alternative options; this was a time-consuming and sometimes emotional exercise, but the overall efforts had a human-centric goal: To preserve jobs and employment continuity. Although for some employees it was hard to persuade them that the company had their best interests in mind and were doing everything they could to safeguard their jobs, a high percentage did take advantage of the beneficial inter-property transfer policy and managed to join other pre-opening properties.

During the global financial crisis, economists were asking whether we have learned enough from past crises. During the Great Depression, a series of bank panics took place and between 1930 and 1933 more than 9,000 banks were closed.[5]

Operating in the Middle East, you learn to expect the unexpected, but whether you decide to be reactive rather than look at the long-term impact of the brand, your reputation to the key stakeholders is based on the company culture and clarity of strategy, focus, and vision. Rotana was versatile, it looked at all areas to

monitor and reduce expenses and this operation was for the benefit of the group as a whole. It embraced uncertainty and change by 'being lean, not mean,' because, at the end of the day, one is judged by the legacy left behind.

Questions for Discussion

1. How would you describe the corporate culture of Rotana and how is it aligned with the Rotana Company values? Justify your answer with examples.
2. Would you consider that the financial crisis had a positive impact on Rotana? If so, explain what the impact was.
3. If you were to take action during this critical period, what would you have done differently and why? Base your answer on findings from the market situation of the Middle East region during this period.

Case study written and provided by Dr. Olga Kampaxi and Amal Harb of Rotana Hotel Management Corporation.

CASE 2 She Loves a Challenge!

The President of Louise University had discussed his new appointment with Dr. Marie Shaheen, but she was traveling and told him they would clarify all the details when she returned. Dr. Shaheen was leaving for London to meet with her Ph.D. supervisor. She was pursuing a second thesis in Educational Leadership, Administration, and Management entitled 'The Extent to which Satisfaction is a Prerequisite to Enhance Employee Performance and Productivity in Institutions of Higher Education: A Case Study of Louise University.' Apparently, the president could not wait and to her surprise the appointment was announced in her absence which obliged Dr. Shaheen to return immediately to prepare for the coming academic year. Dr. Shaheen had been assigned to head one of the most critical offices in any institution of higher education.

All offices in any educational institution are important, especially those that require personnel to be in direct contact with students, parents, and educators. The office that Dr. Shaheen now headed was Admissions, and she considered it to be the backbone of the university. The objective of this office is to promote the image of the university and to recruit students. Thus, coordinated effort was necessary, and personnel are required to possess excellent people skills as a must for success.

The Admissions Office is the very first office that students, parents, and visitors are in contact with. Accordingly, it is crucial that all members of this office are in agreement with reference to goals, attitude, and mission. To say that the success of this office depends on how effectively the personnel perform as team players and on their communication skills is an understatement. Consequently, the alignment of employees' competencies was going to be a challenge for the director.

Upon Dr. Shaheen's appointment as director, there were four employees in the office: May, Mehdi, Chirine, and Aisha. Apart from introducing herself and asking the employees to introduce themselves, Dr. Shaheen simply observed performance and the office dynamics during the first week. The dominant culture was 'I' and not 'we.' There was no productive interaction, and it was evident that there was absolutely no team spirit. She needed to clarify that team spirit was a prerequisite for teamwork, which is all about trust. Dr. Shaheen realized the scope of the challenge ahead of her, but she had a deep sense of commitment to the institution and her loyalty and self-motivation triggered an ultimate acceptance.

Dr. Shaheen took refuge in her office to contemplate and prepare her plan of action. As she thought about the strategy and stamina she would need to ensure the accomplishment of the office objectives, she pondered on the characteristics of each of the employees she had inherited. As a result, she was reminded of something she had previously read by Barbara Coloroso, which had left a lasting impression: "In today's world, many influences push kids in the direction of thinking in terms of 'Me, Mine, and More.' What we want is to offer supports that encourage our children to be thinking about 'Us, Ours, and Enough.'" This quotation was so typical of the admissions staff and Dr. Shaheen was definitely not going to ignore the problem at hand.

There was just no synergy, and this was definitely triggered by the negative energy that was being generated and, in particular, from the lack of trust. Dr. Shaheen noticed this and decided to meet with each employee and then have a joint gathering. The one-on-one sessions with each of the personnel were quite informative and enlightening. Ironically, there were both overlaps and contradictions that were all identified and clarified. Each one of them had issues with the other that had accumulated intensely. Every employee explained that problems had arisen repeatedly but no one ever took the time to investigate or to solve the matters.

During the confrontation of all employees—May, Mehdi, Chirine, and Aisha—they were all asked to be honest and 'lay their cards on the table' so that we could 'clear the air' and move on with their duties. The interaction was quite tense and Dr. Shaheen noticed that the negative feelings had been accumulating and were bottled up. However, the meeting proved to be fruitful and it was very healthy to have them talk about their grievances and to have them listen to one another. They were aware of Dr. Shaheen's presence, and mindful that she was attentive and patient with their outbursts. Deep down, they were very grateful that someone finally was concerned enough to take the time to talk, and listen to them, in the attempt to enhance their relationship with one another in the office.

After a lengthy assembly, the director set all her ground rules. She emphasized that there was not to be any gossip and that if there were any problems, even with her, they were to approach her personally; her door would always be open: "We are here to be as productive as possible as we have a great responsibility to fulfill." Dr. Shaheen went on to explain that they needed to trust one another so that they can share and cooperate for the welfare of the office. She also determined that she was an advocate of participative management and management by walking around (MBWA). She emphasized her willingness to encourage employee involvement and that she welcomed their constructive feedback. "You are the people on the ground and your direct contact with students can be an enlightening experience if you work hand-in-hand." Dr. Shaheen

then reminded them of the acronym TEAM, which means 'Together Everyone Achieves More'.

Moreover, the mission of the institution was revised and the goals of the office specified. Thereafter, duties and responsibilities were distributed with delegation according to seniority and the determination of accountability. Meetings would be held on a regular basis to inform them of plans and activities, and to share information, as well as listen to recommendations and input. Furthermore, Dr. Shaheen described how they needed to demonstrate more commitment, and that it was only through this sense of belonging that they would experience self-satisfaction.

It must be highlighted that the director did not say that everything would be easy-going and foolproof. "There will be obstacles; there will be resistance; there will be lack of cooperation from other offices; however, if we unify and solidify our efforts, we can overcome the hurdles," she explained. "We have the option to choose our attitude; let's go for the positive preference." Dr. Shaheen continued, "I can't succeed alone, I need you all to help me and as they say 'one hand alone can't clap', so let's make a lot of noise together and, God willing, we can make a difference."

Dr. Shaheen was delighted to notice the signs of relaxation on the faces of her staff, and they all expressed their willingness to work together.

The office required more personnel and so three new employees were recruited—Ahmad, George, and Nawal. On their first day, a meeting was held with all seven people and the framework was explained, this time not by Dr. Shaheen but by each of the office staff—May, Mehdi, Chirine, and Aisha.

For the next couple of weeks, Dr. Shaheen carefully observed the interaction in the office. Moreover, she encouraged them to come and speak to her about anything that was bothering them. She was delighted to sense the positive attitudes. As she sat in her office, a broad smile shaped on Dr. Shaheen's face and she felt pleased with her achievements in bringing these people closer together.

Questions for Discussion

1. Identify each of the four stages of team development and explain how the director described each to the staff.
2. This case has stressed both team spirit and teamwork. What is the difference?
3. Describe the MBWA concept and what this tells you about the director's personality. Do you think the results were productive?
4. How did Dr. Shaheen motivate the employees? If you were a consultant observing Dr. Shaheen's performance, what more would you recommend?

A New Way to Change

Zaatar w Zeit (ZwZ) is a 'hip' Lebanese baked wrap concept. Launched in May of 1999, ZwZ took its love for the mankousheh (Lebanese pizza) to a whole new level, opening its first branch in Sodeco, Beirut, to offer a new spin on this Lebanese favorite to mankousheh lovers all over Lebanon. The ultimate mission was to offer the traditional, fluffy pizza-like delicacy (with an infinite choice of delicious toppings) in a comfortable and cozy environment, with a friendly service and a smile. The concept rapidly witnessed a huge success and expanded massively, opening in Zalka, Kaslik, ABC Ashrafieh, Bliss, and Jeita.

During its ten years of existence, ZwZ's cutomers have got used to delicious, quality food. That, along with a friendly atmosphere and fun image, has turned the restaurant into a genuine favorite. A true crowd pleaser, ZwZ updates its menu regularly, offering all kinds of tempting new items from appetizers and salads, to wraps and desserts. ZwZ is also a restaurant with a conscience; that's why it gladly sponsors student events and NGOs, and has even taken on a new recycling initiative!

ZwZ is now a huge success story in other Arab countries as well, and has franchises in the UAE, Kuwait, Jordan, and Qatar. The success of Zaatar w Zeit throughout the years has always been based on people. By people, we mean internal customers (employees) and external customers. Zaatar w Zeit aims to make its customers enjoy their experience in the restaurants and continuously strives to provide its team members with the best working environment and adequate coaching.

Zaatar w Zeit has acquired the Food Safety Management System Certification, ISO 22,000, and has developed and implemented a system that links food safety practices to people management practices. The values communicated to the clients and ZwZ employees are:

- People—attract retain and recruit talent.
- Standards—uphold the highest standards.
- Customers—offer high quality of service.
- Community—work and help the community.
- Profitability—strive for profitability and continuous success.

Since its opening, ZwZ has had a Clan culture, comprising shared values, goals cohesion, participations, and the sense of 'we-ness.' ZwZ culture seems to represent more of an extended family than an economic entity. Instead of the rules and procedures of hierarchies, or the competitive profit centers of markets, the typical characteristics in ZwZ culture are teamwork, employee involvement programs, and customers considered as partners. In this type of culture, the turbulent and changing environment makes it difficult for managers to plan in advance. When decision making is uncertain, it is generally thought that an effective way to coordinate organizational activity is to ensure that all employees share the same values, beliefs, and goals.

In 2010, ZwZ faced fierce competition from the copy cat (Me Too) restaurants, which sold the same products but with less quality, and the added attraction of being able to smoke hookah. ZwZ was much attached to its brand identity and to its health and safety measures on behalf of its customers; therefore, such new products were not compatible with the ZwZ concept, brand and values. Sales started to decrease, so the management had to come up with new ways to bring customers back. They decided to act quickly and take strategic corrective actions, such as:

- recruiting an executive team of directors on its management board
- valuing the HR director as an important business partner in ZwZ, given that he is also managing the organizational development division
- developing a strategy based on differentiation (new concept, new food innovative products, new brand)
- training the restaurant operations managers on the Management by Objectives process, and leadership skills
- reassessing the values and preparing the shift from Clan culture to Market culture, based on sales, bottom-line results, dominance in market shares, stretched targets, and securing customer bases as primary objectives of the organization. The dominating factors in this culture should be competiveness and productivity
- developing, in coordination with the finance director, tools to monitor the budget and control expenses, with long-term planning and financial analysis
- developing, in coordination with the OD/HR director, tools to monitor performance and objectives results
- developing a reward strategy for innovation in work and results achievement
- developing a new internal communication plan to manage change and monitor the values implementation.

These corrective actions resulted in a new set of values:

- leadership
- operations excellence
- growth
- accountability
- commitment
- integrity.

Based on these corrective actions and the monthly results, the executive committee started implementing the new strategy by the end of the third quarter of 2010. The decline in sales stopped in all branches except for one ('Branch A'), which had previously been ranked in second place in terms of sales.

Fady joined ZwZ 11 years ago as a kitchen employee. He was later promoted to 'waiter,' then to 'floor manager.' In 2005, he was transferred to ZwZ Qatar franchise as a restaurant manager. In 2010, he came back to Lebanon as restaurant manager of Branch A. Fady was well known for his integrity, teamwork, and commitment. However, after his transfer, Branch A started losing customers. Management realized that Fady's management style was one of the reasons for the decrease of sales at Branch A and the increase in employee turnover.

In order to fulfill the implementation of the new strategy and change the management program, the operations director had to take immediate action to improve sales. He realized that Fady was not a results-oriented person and could not cope with the new culture (standards, key performance indicators, audits). He proposed to him an expatriation opportunity or a termination option with financial indemnities.

Fady chose the second option and resigned in March 2011—six months after the implementation of the new strategy.

Questions for Discussion

1. In your opinion, was ZwZ's decision to implement a change management program, develop new values, and establish a new executive committee, to enhance the company's strategy?
2. In your opinion, when employees, like Fady, do not fulfill their role in implementing a company's strategy, should they be expatriated or have their contract terminated? Explain.
3. What are your suggestions, if any, for ZwZ to better implement its new strategy?

Case study provided by Khaled Tayara, Human Resources and Organizational Development Director at Zaatar w Zeit.

CASE 4

What a Strange Man!

The Situation According to Mr. Hussni

Our parent company in Germany recently sent us a young German marketing director, Mr. Müller, to work in our marketing department. What a strange man! He seems to be more a robot than a human being. Whenever we meet in the morning, he starts talking right away about work. Sometimes I try to break the ice and ask him about his family and how he enjoys his stay in Egypt. He immediately changes the subject and goes back to work topics. I do not understand why he refuses to speak about himself. We are colleagues after all and should know each other better to develop trust and a better relationship.

Our company manufactures forklifts and construction vehicles. We have been assigned a new project. We will have to introduce a new product on the Egyptian market. It is a new forklift with exceptional high technology and several new functionalities. The first meeting we had showed what kind of person Mr. Müller is. He just began by saying that he did not want to lose time and directly presented the meeting agenda. I offered him a coffee, but he refused it. He is so unfriendly and seems to feel superior towards his Egyptian colleagues.

He wants everything to be written. He wants minutes for every meeting. Every small detail, every procedure, every plan must be precisely documented. He wants to develop new procedures to reorganize our department— a kind of re-engineering. As if we were not doing our job right before his arrival. Everyone has been given a detailed job description and must present on a monthly basis the accomplished tasks, allocated time for every task, and even tasks to do for the following month. We will spend our time filling sheets and writing reports just because he wants to know what everyone is doing.

When he talks to me, he never looks me straight in the eyes. I have the feeling that he is hiding something or maybe he just does not respect me. Nor does he seem to respect our customers. Every time we have meetings with important customers, he comes wearing his old and informal clothes. How could our customers take him seriously? He is reflecting a bad image of the company. He does not even wear a tie.

When we are negotiating with our clients, he makes an unnecessarily long presentation about the product. Several times, I have felt that clients are bored and fed-up. It is enough to show them our portfolio of international customers and they will buy right away. The reputation of our client companies speaks for the quality and features of our products. I have always had an excellent relationship with our clients, some of whom are even friends of mine. Once we had the husband of my cousin in a meeting and Müller was presenting the product to him in detail, but I had the courage to interfere and told him that the customer trusts us and will buy the product without a long presentation. He became angry.

What a strange man! He does not even care about family issues. Last week I had to go to my sister's wedding in Upper Egypt. I had to leave on Thursday and came back on Tuesday. He seemed to be angry about my trip and said to me, clearly, that I had neglected my duties by prioritizing family issues. I got angry as well. He should respect my family. It was my sister's wedding! It happens once in a lifetime and my village is 700 kilometers from Cairo. What could I do? I am 20 years older than him and he should at least respect my age.

Two weeks ago, we had another problem: one of our engineers had a death in the family. He was absent for one week, receiving people for condolences. Because of his absence, a delivery was delayed by two days, and Mr. Müller went crazy and started shouting at me.

He doesn't seem to understand us at all. I hope that in the future, inshallah, he will get more used to our work environment or go back to Germany.

The Situation According to Mr. Müller

Our company is a multinational with subsidiaries all over the world. The company owns a subsidiary in Egypt that is also the regional office for the Middle East and North Africa region. As a promotion, and based on my exceptional performance in our headquarters in Munich, I have been given an international assignment to relocate to Egypt to control our marketing activity in this area. After all, Egypt and the MENA is a huge market and the company depends a lot on this market, especially as there are many opportunities and new markets to penetrate. Although I am only 35 years old, I have been working since my graduation, ten years ago, in the marketing department of our company. I have excellent credentials. I have learned that accuracy and respect for deadlines are two important qualities in our business.

I arrived six months ago in Cairo and my first assignment was to introduce a new product, a high-tech forklift, into the Egyptian market. Before my arrival, I had checked the profiles of employees in the marketing department. They are all well qualified and I thought things would go according to the marketing plan I had prepared. The marketing plan is clear and detailed enough. Even the brochures and the specifications about the product are very detailed and give accurate information to prospective customers.

Mr. Hussni is the customer relationship manager at the subsidiary, as well the deputy marketing director. I am not sure that Mr. Hussni likes having a boss. What a strange man! I cannot find a way to discuss anything with him longer than 20 minutes face to face. He leaves the door of his office permanently open, and we are subject to all types of interruptions. People go in and out, interrupt us for petty matters, shake hands, propose a cup of coffee. . . It is just impossible to concentrate and to discuss an issue, to make clear decisions. Sometime I suggest that he makes a decision and he just remains silent. At department meetings, we spend half of the time talking about silly things from sports to family issues, even food and the weather. I decided to have an agenda for every meeting and asked for written minutes and reports to structure the communication. But it does not really work, so far.

The productivity of the department should be improved; they seem to spend too much time discussing, joking, and receiving private phone calls many times a day. Things go so slowly here. People tend to postpone their work all the time. If I ask them about deadlines or tasks to be accomplished, they always answer with 'inshallah' or as God wills. It is the first Arabic word I learned from Mr. Hussni. This word does not mean that they will do what they promise to do. It is rather to tell me that events are not controlled by man but by God and only God can know the unexpected events. That is the expression they use to justify absenteeism. I have never seen such an absenteeism as they have here. Last month, we had an employee absent for one week because a member of his family had passed away. Although he knew that his presence was essential at this time, and that his absence would delay the whole project, he left for a whole week after seeking permission from Mr. Hussni. Nobody cares here about the clients; the company seems to be the least of their concerns. When I asked Mr. Hussni about the absence of this employee, he reacted with an aggressive attitude. I think that he did not understand my point. How could he understand my concerns? He has himself been absent for five days to attend his sister's wedding two months ago. As a deputy director, he should be a role model. But he does not seem to understand what good management is.

Questions for Discussion

1. What is the nature of the problem between Mr. Müller and Mr. Hussni?

2. What are the main cultural differences that you can observe?

3. How could this problem be resolved?

4. What should the company do in future to avoid this kind of situation?

Case study Written by Eric Davoine and Samer Nakhle, University of Fribourg, Switzerland, 2010.

A Question of Motivation

Abbas and Salwa have a few things in common. Both are students at the same university, and both work full-time at a local supermarket to make ends meet and help pay for college. Though the pay isn't great, it's a steady job that allows them some flexibility, which helps when scheduling classes. Both students joined the supermarket two years ago, and, given their similar situations, became friends quickly.

Although Salwa seems to enjoy her job, arriving and leaving work each day with a smile on her face, Abbas often grumbles and complains about his work. Much of the time, Abbas complains about his boss, Sa'eed, who oversees the produce department. Salwa works for Jalal, who everyone generally admires for his friendly attitude and relaxed management style.

Most employees want to work for Jalal, as he often assigns his employees different duties each week so workers don't get bored. Salwa, for instance, can be working at the checkout counter one week, stocking shelves the next, and working in the store's culinary center the following week.

The culinary center is a new service that the store is test-marketing. Employees show customers how to create exciting recipes from start to finish. It is Salwa's favorite place in the store to work. She is also responsible for taking customers around the store to locate ingredients for a culinary center recipe, many of the ingredients being some of the store's finest. And she enjoys allowing customers to sample what she cooks. So far, the culinary center is a success, and many of the store's more expensive ingredients are becoming difficult to keep in stock. To help with this issue, Jalal encourages his employees to notify him immediately when an item is running low, and even empowers employees to reorder items from vendors. By doing this, Salwa has quickly grasped how the supermarket operates.

Abbas's supervisor, in contrast, prefers most of his employees to work in the same area each day—Abbas is one of those employees. Sa'eed believes that the best way to master a job is to do it over and over again. This means that Abbas has to stock the same produce areas each day. As boxes of produce are delivered to the store's supply room, Abbas unloads their contents onto the shelves. Abbas also has to constantly reorganize the items already on the shelves to make them look as orderly as possible. Most of the time, though, he doesn't feel inclined to do either task.

After a particularly boring morning of restocking apples (the store had apples on sale that day), Abbas met Salwa for lunch in the break room. After sitting down, Abbas reached into his lunchbox and pulled out an apple, a look of disgust on his face. . . "If I have to look at another apple, I'm going to be sick."

"Bad day again?" asked Salwa, as Abbas stuffed the apple back into his lunchbox.

"I stocked apples all morning—what do you think?" Abbas retorted.

"Why don't you tell Sa'eed you want to do something else?" Salwa inquired. "I see that he lets Dunia work in other areas." Salwa leaned closer. "I've even heard that she gets paid more than you. Is that true?" she whispered.

"Apparently, she gets paid US\$2.00 more an hour, but I do the same things that she does. Oh, that's right. One thing I don't do is tell Sa'eed what a cool shirt he has on or how awesome his car is. They're both pathetic if you ask me," frowned Abbas.

"Two dollars more an hour, but she's been here for only three months!" Salwa exclaimed. "And I know that you work just as hard as she does. No wonder you're so irritated all the time."

"I don't even care any more. What's the point? If I stock more apples, or something meaningless like that, what does that get me—another sticker that says 'good job'? Oooh, that's really great. Thanks a bunch, Sa'eed!" replied Abbas, punctuating his last sentence with a sarcastic thumbs-up. "Anyway, enough about my day. How's yours going?"

"Pretty good, actually. Jalal and I met earlier today, and we both set a goal for me to sell ten bottles of truffle oil next week."

"Wow. That stuff is pretty expensive, isn't it?" asked Abbas.

"Thirty-five dollars for four ounces," replied Salwa. "It'll be tough, but I've found a pretty good recipe that I'll be making for customers who stop by the culinary center." She paused, then said, "I think I'll be able to do it. I've made quite a few similar recipes before, and even though this one is more difficult, it shouldn't be too bad. Besides, if I sell the oil, Jalal said that he'll give me a US$75 bonus. So I'm definitely going to give it a shot. The nice thing is that I'll be able to do this on my own, without someone breathing down my neck."

"Well that's certainly more than I'll be making this week," said Abbas. "This job is okay, but I'd probably leave if I could. It's too risky right now to just quit. If I can't find something, then I'll be in trouble when that next tuition bill comes around."

"Look on the bright side. At least you make more than Joumana. She's been here for seven years, still working in the deli," replied Salwa.

"That's true," sighed Abbas as he returned to his lunch. He looked up at the clock. They had been at lunch for a half hour already. Sa'eed was quite the stickler about keeping lunch to a minimum. Although store policy allowed employees 45 minutes for lunch, Sa'eed often pushed his employees to keep it to 30 minutes. As Abbas quickened his chewing, Sa'eed strolled into the break room and opened the refrigerator, his back to Abbas and Salwa.

Walking around with a soda in hand, Sa'eed commented, "Bit of a long lunch, hey Abbas?"

Abbas could feel the blood rising to his face. "It's been exactly a half hour, and I'm almost finished," he said.

"Well, we're running low on apples again. So quit lying around and get back to work." Sa'eed walked toward the door, stopped, and turned around. "I thought that college students were supposed to be smarter than this. At the very least I would hope that they could tell the time." He added, "I guess the university must have glossed over your application." And with that, Sa'eed left.

"What an idiot," said Salwa after Sa'eed left.

"What's new," said Abbas. "I'd guess I'd better get back to work." Abbas got up and returned what was left of his lunch to the refrigerator. When he opened the door, he noticed a sandwich labeled with a post-it note that read "Sa'eed's." After glancing quickly to the door, he casually swept the sandwich onto the floor. Salwa turned round at the sound.

"Oops," said Abbas. He paused, staring down at the sandwich. "Five-second rule!" he said as he picked up the sandwich, being sure to smear the underside of it on the floor. After putting it neatly back on the shelf, Abbas turned to Salwa. "Well Salwa, have a good one. I think maybe I'll take my time on those apples."

Questions for Discussion

1. How can expectancy theory be used to explain the differences in motivation between Abbas and Salwa? What specifics from the case apply to expectancy theory?

2. Abbas states that he is underpaid for the work he does. What motivational theory does this apply to, and how would it explain Abbas's behavior?

3. Using concepts from organizational justice (Chapter 5), explain why Abbas knocks his boss's lunch to the floor. What should Abbas's boss do to improve the fairness of his treatment?

4. Using concepts from the chapter on emotions and moods (Chapter 6), explain why Abbas retaliates toward his supervisor. Was his behavior driven purely by emotion, or did cognition also play a role? How so?

5. Compare and contrast Abbas and Salwa in terms of each person's level of work stress. How might stress affect their attitudes and behaviors within their work environment?

6. Discuss Abbas and Salwa in terms of each person's job attitudes (for example, job satisfaction, organizational commitment). What factors might be responsible for any differences?

CASE
6 ## The Big Promotion

Kareem and Reema arrived outside their boss's office at the same time and took a seat. Both exchanged a friendly "Hello," but they didn't say much else as they waited outside. Moving nervously in their seats, the two knew that only one of them was going to receive what would be the biggest promotion of their career.

Kareem and Reema worked for a large software company and each was responsible for managing one of the company's largest divisions. Both had been in their current position for years, hoping that a spot at the company's corporate headquarters would open up. That time had arrived a month earlier when one of the company's senior executives retired. Such positions did not open frequently, so Kareem and Reema knew that this was a tremendous opportunity.

For the past month, they had prepared for their meeting with the company's CEO, Wasim Al Kadi. Although Wasim already knew Kareem and Reema well, he wanted to meet with them at the same time to see how they handled the pressure of being interviewed in front of each other.

After waiting for what seemed like an eternity, Kareem and Reema looked up simultaneously as Wasim opened the door to his office.

"Reema. Kareem. Good to see you. Come on in," said Wasim.

Kareem and Reema entered Wasim's office and took the chairs ready for them at the front of his desk.

Wasim broke the silence by saying, "Well, you both know why you are here, so there's no need to waste time. I already know your résumés backwards and forwards, and I've gathered as much information as possible from those who know you best, so now it comes down to hearing it directly from you. I'm going to ask you both one question only, and it's the same question for both of you. Let me flip a coin to see who will respond first." He flipped the coin. "Kareem, you're first."

Kareem sat up with confidence, eyeing Wasim.

Wasim began. "To function effectively in an executive position requires strong leadership skills. Both of you have gained valuable experience as managers of your respective divisions, making decisions that have resulted in strong performances from those divisions. But you have also, as managers, followed directives that this corporate office has handed down. As an executive, this will change. You will no longer take directives—you will give them. In short, you will be responsible for guiding the future of this company, and its success will depend greatly on you. So my question to you both is: How do you plan to succeed as a leader if you are offered this position?"

"Well Wasim," responded Kareem, "That is an excellent question. I believe that, to be a successful leader, one must be able to exert influence. When you get down to it, that is what leadership is all about—the ability to influence others. I have demonstrated that I have this ability since I joined the ranks of management." Kareem stopped, collecting his thoughts. "It is my opinion that leadership boils down to what actions you take with your employees. For me, leadership is all about rewarding and punishing appropriately. I try to make my employees' jobs less complicated by stating exactly what they need to do, assigning particular tasks, setting appropriate goals, and ensuring that my subordinates have the resources they need."

Wasim listened carefully as Kareem continued. "Basically, I am an organizer. When employees accomplish a given task or goal, I reward them appropriately for their work. When employees fail to accomplish an assignment, an appropriate response from me is needed. If it is clear that the employee did not try to accomplish the task, then punishment is necessary, and this punishment could range from a verbal reprimand to termination, depending, of course, on the circumstances. If the employee did not have the necessary skills or resources to complete a task, then my job is to provide those skills and resources. By rewarding and punishing employees based on their performance, I am able not only to influence employee behavior to match the goals of the organization but also to send a clear message as to what I expect."

Kareem added, "I also want to add that a strong sense of fairness guides all of my decisions—I reward and punish justly. As a result, my employees are satisfied with their work and perform at high levels. So I will bring my ability to influence behavior with me if I am offered this position, and in doing so will be able to shape the future of our company."

"Thank you, Kareem," responded Wasim. "Reema, how would you answer this question?"

"Well, Wasim," said Reema, "I think you'll find that my perspective on leadership is different from Kareem's. Although I certainly agree with Kareem that giving clear guidance to employees, setting appropriate goals, and rewarding employees for accomplishing tasks is a fundamental leadership quality, I believe that it takes more than that to be a successful leader. You see, I do not believe that just anyone can be a leader. To be a leader requires a certain 'something' that not all people possess."

"And you believe that you possess that certain something?" interrupted Wasim.

Reema grinned. "I think you'll find that my record suggests that I do, in fact. You see, successful leadership is about motivating people beyond the formal requirements of their jobs. It is not enough in today's global economy to simply ensure that employees are completing their tasks. To survive, and moreover to grow, leaders must challenge employees to look ahead, to contribute ideas, and to make sacrifices for the good of the company. My job as a leader of this company is to create a vision of where we will be 5, 10, and 15 years from now. I see us creating new technologies, as well as merging existing technologies, to give our company the competitive advantage it needs to sustain growth in the long term. By sharing this vision with my employees, we will all be able to pursue the same goals."

Reema continued, "I inspire my subordinates to see the company as their own, rather than as a means to a paycheck. I consider employee input and the different needs of each worker, and I challenge each and every one of them to think outside the box and develop innovative solutions to the problems facing us. The end result is, in my opinion, a highly motivated workforce with a common goal—to make sure our company is the industry leader."

Wasim nodded, thinking about both answers. He had studied each person's record carefully, and both were qualified for the job. However, the two candidates differed in important ways. Kareem had built a strong reputation for being a traditional, straightforward leader, motivating his employees well, setting appropriate goals, and ensuring that employees accomplished tasks on time—even ahead of schedule. However, Kareem was not known for developing the most creative solutions, and he lacked the vision that Wasim knew was an important competency to have as an executive.

Reema, in contrast, had built a reputation as being a visionary leader. Though her ideas were a bit unconventional at times, in many cases they were directly responsible for getting the company out of a jam. In addition, her magnetic personality made her a favorite among employees. However, Reema often revealed a somewhat egotistical personality, and Wasim was unsure whether this egoism would be amplified if she were in a more authoritative position.

Wasim had to make a tough decision. He thought about his company's future. Things were relatively stable now, and business was good, but he knew that stability was not always certain.

"I would like to thank you both for coming today. You're making this a tough decision for me," said Wasim. "I need to think about this a bit more, but I'll be getting back to you soon." He paused, then added, "You'll have my answer tomorrow morning."

Questions for Discussion

1. Using terms from the text, how would you describe Kareem's leadership style? How would you describe Reema's leadership style?

2. Whose leadership style do you believe would be more effective, Reema's or Kareem's? Why? What, if any, situational factors might their effectiveness depend on?

3. If you were Wasim, who would you hire and why?

4. What are some potential downsides to each candidate's leadership style?

5. Whose employees do you think are likely to be more motivated, Kareem's or Reema's? Whose employees are likely to have higher job satisfaction, trust in leadership, and organizational commitment? Why?

6. Based on their leadership styles, in what type of organizational structure would Kareem be most effective? What about Reema? Why?

Credits

References

Chapter 1

1. Cited in R. Alsop, "Playing Well with Others," *Wall Street Journal*, September 9, 2002.
2. See, for instance, C. Penttila, "Hiring Hardships," *Entrepreneur*, October 2002, pp. 34–35.
3. *The 2002 National Study of the Changing Workforce* (New York: Families and Work Institute, 2002).
4. I. S. Fulmer, B. Gerhart, and K. S. Scott, "Are the 100 Best Better? An Empirical Investigation of the Relationship Between Being a 'Great Place to Work' and Firm Performance," *Personnel Psychology*, Winter 2003, pp. 965–993.
5. H. Fayol, *Industrial and General Administration* (Paris: Dunod, 1916).
6. H. Mintzberg, *The Nature of Managerial Work* (Upper Saddle River, NJ: Prentice Hall, 1973).
7. "GE and Mubadala Launch Multi-Billion Dollar Global Business Partnership," *GE News Centre*, July 22, 2008, www.genewscenter.com/content/detail.aspx?releaseid=3873&newsareaid=2&menusearchcategoryid=.
8. R. L. Katz, "Skills of an Effective Administrator," *Harvard Business Review*, September–October 1974, pp. 90–102.
9. F. Luthans, "Successful vs. Effective Real Managers," *Academy of Management Executive*, May 1988, pp. 127–132; and F. Luthans, R. M. Hodgetts, and S. A. Rosenkrantz, *Real Managers* (Cambridge, MA: Ballinger, 1988). See also F. Shipper and J. Davy, "A Model and Investigation of Managerial Skills, Employees' Attitudes, and Managerial Performance," *Leadership Quarterly* 13 (2002), pp. 95–120.
10. P. H. Langford, "Importance of Relationship Management for the Career Success of Australian Managers," *Australian Journal of Psychology*, December 2000, pp. 163–169; and A. M. Konrad, R. Kashlak, I. Yoshioka, R. Waryszak, and N. Toren, "What Do Managers Like to Do? A Five-Country Study," *Group & Organization Management*, December 2001, pp. 401–433.
11. "Employee Motivation in the Middle East Study," *bayt.com*, September 2009, www.bayt.com/en/research-report-5601/.
12. See, for instance, C. Heath and S. B. Sitkin, "Big-B Versus Big-O: What Is *Organizational* about Organizational Behavior?" *Journal of Organizational Behavior*, February 2001, pp. 43–58. For a review of what one eminent researcher believes *should* be included in organizational behavior, based on survey data, see J. B. Miner, "The Rated Importance, Scientific Validity, and Practical Usefulness of Organizational Behavior Theories: A Quantitative Review," *Academy of Management Learning & Education*, September 2003, pp. 250–268.
13. See L. A. Burke and J. E. Moore, "A Perennial Dilemma in OB Education: Engaging the Traditional Student," *Academy of Management Learning & Education*, March 2003, pp. 37–52.
14. See www.thegff.com/Articles/75959/Global_Futures_and/Reports/The_Future_of.aspx, accessed 30th March 2012.
15. Knight Ridder/Tribune Business News, May 5, 2010, "Ageing workforce 'a threat to oil sector,'" www.aarpinternational.org/news/news_show.htm?doc_id=1237886.
16. "Putting the Middle East to Work," *Business Management*, Issue 2, www.busmanagementme.com/article/Putting-the-Middle-East-to-work.
17. ibid.
18. O. C. Richard, "Racial Diversity, Business Strategy, and Firm Performance: A Resource-Based View," *Academy of Management Journal*, April 2000, pp. 164–177.
19. This section is based on M. Toosi, "A Century of Change: The US Labor Force, 1950–2050," *Monthly Labor Review*, May 2002, pp. 15–27; and *CBO's Projections of the Labor Force* (Washington, DC: Congressional Budget Office, September 2004).
20. Global Employment Trends (January, 2010). International Labor Organization (ILO), www.oit.org/wcmsp5/groups/public/---ed_emp/---emp_elm/---trends/documents/publication/wcms_120471.pdf.
21. See M. E. A. Jayne and R. L. Dipboye, "Leveraging Diversity to Improve Business Performance: Research Findings and Recommendations for Organizations," *Human Resource Management*, Winter 2004, pp. 409–424; S. E. Jackson and A. Joshi, "Research on Domestic and International Diversity in Organizations: A Merger That Works?" in N. Anderson *et al.* (eds), *Handbook of Industrial, Work & Organizational Psychology*, vol. 2 (Thousand Oaks, CA: Sage, 2001), pp. 206–231; and L. Smith, "The Business Case for Diversity," *Fortune*, October 13, 2003, pp. S8–S12.
22. "Putting the Middle East to Work," *Business Management*, Issue 2, www.busmanagementme.com/article/Putting-the-Middle-East-to-work.
23. S. Rahman, "Services Sector is Key Driver of Growth," *Al Nisr Publishing LLC (Gulf News)*, May 3, 2009, http://gulfnews.com/business/general/services-sector-is-key-driver-of-growth-1.159861.
24. See, for instance, S. D. Pugh, J. Dietz, J. W. Wiley, and S. M. Brooks, "Driving Service Effectiveness Through Employee-Customer Linkages," *Academy of Management Executive*, November 2002, pp. 73–84; and H. Liao and A. Chuang, "A Multilevel Investigation of Factors Influencing Employee Service Performance and Customer Outcomes," *Academy of Management Journal*, February 2004, pp. 41–58.
25. See www.patagonia.com/jobs/retail_asst_mgr.shtml; and "Patagonia Sets the Pace for Green Business," *Grist Magazine*, October 22, 2004, www.grist.org.
26. Reproduced by permission of Aramex International.
27. See, for instance, M. Workman and W. Bommer, "Redesigning Computer Call Center Work: A Longitudinal Field Experiment," *Journal of Organizational Behavior*, May 2004, pp. 317–337.
28. See, for instance, V. S. Major, K. J. Klein, and M. G. Ehrhart, "Work Time, Work Interference with Family, and Psychological Distress," *Journal of Applied Psychology*, June 2002, pp. 427–436; D. Brady, "Rethinking the Rat Race," *Business Week*, August 26, 2002, pp. 142–143; J. M. Brett and L. K. Stroh, "Working 61 Plus Hours a Week: Why Do Managers Do It?" *Journal of Applied Psychology*, February 2003, pp. 67–78.
29. "Employee Motivation in the Middle East Study", *bayt.com*, September 2009, www.bayt.com/en/research-report-5601/.
30. Cited in S. Armour, "Workers Put Family First Despite Slow Economy, Jobless Fears."

31. L. M. Roberts, G. Spreitzer, J. Dutton, R. Quinn, E. Heaphy, and B. Barker, "How to Play to Your Strengths," *Harvard Business Review*, January 2005, pp. 1–6; and L. M. Roberts, J. E. Dutton, G. M. Spreitzer, E. D. Heaphy, and R. E. Quinn, "Composing the Reflected Best-Self Portrait: Becoming Extraordinary in Work Organizations," *Academy of Management Review* 30, no. 4 (2005), pp. 712–736.

32. J. Merritt, "For MBAs, Soul-Searching 101," *Business Week*, September 16, 2002, pp. 64–66; and S. Greenhouse, "The Mood at Work: Anger and Anxiety," *New York Times*, October 29, 2002, p. E1.

33. See, for instance, G. R. Weaver, L. K. Trevino, and P. L. Cochran, "Corporate Ethics Practices in the Mid-1990's: An Empirical Study of the Fortune 1000," *Journal of Business Ethics*, February 1999, pp. 283–294; and C. De Mesa Graziano, "Promoting Ethical Conduct: A Review of Corporate Practices," *Strategic Investor Relations*, Fall 2002, pp. 29–35.

34. United Arab Emirates: "Employee Turnover Remains Regional Business's Invisible Enemy, Despite Global Crisis, Says Management Expert," December 13, 2008, www.ameinfo.com/178478.html.

35. See, for example, M. C. Sturman and C. O. Trevor, "The Implications of Linking the Dynamic Performance and Turnover Literatures," *Journal of Applied Psychology*, August 2001, pp. 684–696.

36. Cited in "You Often Lose the Ones You Love," *Industry Week*, November 21, 1988, p. 5.

37. D. W. Organ, *Organizational Citizenship Behavior: The Good Soldier Syndrome* (Lexington, MA: Lexington Books, 1988), p. 4; and J. A. LePine, A. Erez, and D. E. Johnson, "The Nature and Dimensionality of Organizational Citizenship Behavior: A Critical Review and Meta-Analysis," *Journal of Applied Psychology*, February 2002, pp. 52–65.

38. T. A. Judge, C. J. Thoresen, J. E. Bono, and G. R. Patton, "The Job Satisfaction–Job Performance Relationship: A Qualitative and Quantitative Review," *Psychological Bulletin* 127 (2001), pp. 376–407.

Chapter 2

1. M. D. Dunnette, "Aptitudes, Abilities, and Skills," in M. D. Dunnette (ed.), *Handbook of Industrial and Organizational Psychology* (Chicago: Rand McNally, 1976), pp. 478–483.

2. J. F. Salgado, N. Anderson, S. Moscoso, C. Bertua, F. de Fruyt, and J. P. Rolland, "A Meta-analytic Study of General Mental Ability Validity for Different Occupations in the European Community," *Journal of Applied Psychology*, December 2003, pp. 1068–1081; and F. L. Schmidt and J. E. Hunter, "Select on Intelligence," in E. A. Locke (ed.), *Handbook of Principles of Organizational Behavior* (Malden, MA: Blackwell, 2004).

3. Y. Ganzach, "Intelligence and Job Satisfaction," *Academy of Management Journal* 41, no. 5 (1998), pp. 526–539; and Y. Ganzach, "Intelligence, Education, and Facets of Job Satisfaction," *Work and Occupations* 30, no. 1 (2003), pp. 97–122.

4. E. A. Fleishman, "Evaluating Physical Abilities Required by Jobs," *Personnel Administrator*, June 1979, pp. 82–92.

5. K. Greene, "Older Workers Can Get a Raw Deal—Some Employers Admit to Promoting, Challenging Their Workers Less," *Wall Street Journal*, April 10, 2003, p. D2; and K. A. Wrenn and T. J. Maurer, "Beliefs About Older Workers' Learning and Development Behavior in Relation to Beliefs About Malleability of Skills, Age-Related Decline, and Control," *Journal of Applied Social Psychology* 34, no. 2 (2004), pp. 223–242.

6. D. R. Davies, G. Matthews, and C. S. K. Wong, "Ageing and Work," in C. L. Cooper and I. T. Robertson (eds.), *International Review of Industrial and Organizational Psychology*, vol. 6 (Chichester, UK: Wiley, 1991), pp. 183–187.

7. R. D. Hackett, "Age, Tenure, and Employee Absenteeism," *Human Relations*, July 1990, pp. 601–619.

8. See G. M. McEvoy and W. F. Cascio, "Cumulative Evidence of the Relationship Between Employee Age and Job Performance," *Journal of Applied Psychology*, February 1989, pp. 11–17; and F. L. Schmidt and J. E. Hunter, "The Validity and Utility of Selection Methods in Personnel Psychology: Practical and Theoretical Implications of 85 Years of Research Findings," *Psychological Bulletin* 124 (1998), pp. 262–274.

9. See, for instance, F. J. Landy, *et al.*, *Alternatives to Chronological Age in Determining Standards of Suitability for Public Safety Jobs* (University Park, PA: Center for Applied Behavioral Sciences, Pennsylvania State University, 1992).

10. R. Lee and E. R. Wilbur, "Age, Education, Job Tenure, Salary, Job Characteristics, and Job Satisfaction: A Multivariate Analysis," *Human Relations*, August 1985, pp. 781–791.

11. K. M. Kacmar and G. R. Ferris, "Theoretical and Methodological Considerations in the Age–Job Satisfaction Relationship," *Journal of Applied Psychology*, April 1989, pp. 201–207; and W. A. Hochwarter, G. R. Ferris, P. L. Perrewe, L. A. Witt, and C. Kiewitz, "A Note on the Nonlinearity of the Age–Job Satisfaction Relationship," *Journal of Applied Social Psychology*, June 2001, pp. 1223–1237.

12. See E. M. Weiss, G. Kemmler, E. A. Deisenhammer, W. W. Fleischhacker, and M. Delazer, "Sex Differences in Cognitive Functions," *Personality and Individual Differences*, September 2003, pp. 863–875; and A. F. Jorm, K. J. Anstey, H. Christensen, and B. Rodgers, "Gender Differences in Cognitive Abilities: The Mediating Role of Health State and Health Habits," *Intelligence*, January 2004, pp. 7–23.

13. S. Shellenbarger, "More Job Seekers Put Family Needs First," *Wall Street Journal*, November 15, 1991, p. B1.

14. R. W. Griffeth, P. W. Hom, and S. Gaertner, "A Meta-analysis of Antecedents and Correlates of Employee Turnover: Update, Moderator Tests, and Research Implications for the Next Millennium," *Journal of Management* 26, no. 3 (2000), pp. 463–488.

15. See, for instance, K. D. Scott and E. L. McClellan, "Gender Differences in Absenteeism," *Public Personnel Management*, Summer 1990, pp. 229–253; and A. Vanden Heuvel and M. Wooden, "Do Explanations of Absenteeism Differ for Men and Women?" *Human Relations*, November 1995, pp. 1309–1329.

16. P. Bobko, P. L. Roth, and D. Potosky, "Derivation and Implications of a Meta-Analytic Matrix Incorporating Cognitive Ability, Alternative Predictors, and Job Performance," *Personnel Psychology*, Autumn 1999, pp. 561–589.

17. M. A. Quinones, J. K. Ford, and M. S. Teachout, "The Relationship Between Work Experience and Job Performance:

A Conceptual and Meta-analytic Review," *Personnel Psychology*, Winter 1995, pp. 887–910.

18. I. R. Gellatly, "Individual and Group Determinants of Employee Absenteeism: Test of a Causal Model," *Journal of Organizational Behavior*, September 1995, pp. 469–485.

19. See H. M. Weiss, "Learning Theory and Industrial and Organizational Psychology," in M. D. Dunnette and L. M. Hough (eds.), *Handbook of Industrial & Organizational Psychology*, 2nd ed., vol. 1 (Palo Alto, CA: Consulting Psychologists Press, 1990), pp. 172–173.

20. W. McGehee, "Are We Using What We Know About Training? Learning Theory and Training," *Personnel Psychology*, Spring 1958, p. 2.

21. "The Leadership Development Program (LDP)", *The Arab Leadership Academy*, www.ala.com.kw

22. I. P. Pavlov, *The Work of the Digestive Glands*, trans. W. H. Thompson (London: Charles Griffin, 1902). See also the special issue of *American Psychologist*, September 1997, pp. 933–972, commemorating Pavlov's work.

23. A. Bandura, *Social Learning Theory* (Upper Saddle River, NJ: Prentice Hall, 1977).

24. A. D. Stajkovic and F. Luthans, "A Meta-analysis of the Effects of Organizational Behavior Modification on Task Performance, 1975–95," *Academy of Management Journal*, October 1997, pp. 1122–1149.

25. See F. Luthans and A. D. Stajkovic, "Reinforce for Performance: The Need to Go Beyond Pay and Even Rewards," *Academy of Management Executive*, May 1999, pp. 49–57; and A. D. Stajkovic and F. Luthans, "Differential Effects of Incentive Motivators on Work Performance," *Academy of Management Journal* 44, no. 3 (2001), pp. 580–590.

26. G. W. Allport, *Personality: A Psychological Interpretation* (New York: Holt, Rinehart & Winston, 1937), p. 48. For a brief critique of current views on the meaning of personality, see R. T. Hogan and B. W. Roberts, "Introduction: Personality and Industrial and Organizational Psychology," in B. W. Roberts and R. Hogan (eds.), *Personality Psychology in the Workplace* (Washington, DC: American Psychological Association, 2001), pp. 11–12.

27. K. I. van der Zee, J. N. Zaal, and J. Piekstra, "Validation of the Multicultural Personality Questionnaire in the Context of Personnel Selection," *European Journal of Personality* 17 (2003), pp. S77–S100.

28. See, for instance, M. B. Stein, K. L. Jang, and W. J. Livesley, "Heritability of Social Anxiety-Related Concerns and Personality Characteristics: A Twin Study," *Journal of Nervous and Mental Disease*, April 2002, pp. 219–224; and S. Pinker, *The Blank Slate: The Modern Denial of Human Nature* (New York: Viking, 2002).

29. See A. H. Buss, "Personality as Traits," *American Psychologist*, November 1989, pp. 1378–1388; R. R. McCrae, "Trait Psychology and the Revival of Personality and Culture Studies," *American Behavioral Scientist*, September 2000, pp. 10–31; and L. R. James and M. D. Mazerolle, *Personality in Work Organizations* (Thousand Oaks, CA: Sage, 2002).

30. R. B. Kennedy and D. A. Kennedy, "Using the Myers-Briggs Type Indicator in Career Counseling," *Journal of Employment Counseling*, March 2004, pp. 38–44.

31. See, for instance, D. J. Pittenger, "Cautionary Comments Regarding the Myers-Briggs Type Indicator," *Consulting Psychology Journal: Practice and Research*, Summer 2005, pp. 210–221; L. Bess and R. J. Harvey, "Bimodal Score Distributions and the Myers-Briggs Type Indicator: Fact or Artifact?" *Journal of Personality Assessment*, February 2002, pp. 176–186; R. M. Capraro and M. M. Capraro, "Myers-Briggs Type Indicator Score Reliability Across Studies: A Meta-analytic Reliability Generalization Study," *Educational & Psychological Measurement*, August 2002, pp. 590–602; and R. C. Arnau, B. A. Green, D. H. Rosen, D. H. Gleaves, and J. G. Melancon, "Are Jungian Preferences Really Categorical? An Empirical Investigation Using Taxometric Analysis," *Personality & Individual Differences*, January 2003, pp. 233–251.

32. See, for example, J. M. Digman, "Personality Structure: Emergence of the Five-Factor Model," in M. R. Rosenzweig and L. W. Porter (eds.), *Annual Review of Psychology*, vol. 41 (Palo Alto, CA: Annual Reviews, 1990), pp. 417–440; R. R. McCrae, "Special Issue: The Five-Factor Model: Issues and Applications," *Journal of Personality*, June 1992; D. B. Smith, P. J. Hanges, and M. W. Dickson, "Personnel Selection and the Five-Factor Model: Reexamining the Effects of Applicant's Frame of Reference," *Journal of Applied Psychology*, April 2001, pp. 304–315; and M. R. Barrick and M. K. Mount, "Yes, Personality Matters: Moving on to More Important Matters," *Human Performance* 18, no. 4 (2005), pp. 359–372.

33. See, for instance, M. R. Barrick and M. K. Mount, "The Big Five Personality Dimensions and Job Performance: A Meta-analysis," *Personnel Psychology*, Spring 1991, pp. 1–26; G. M. Hurtz and J. J. Donovan, "Personality and Job Performance: The Big Five Revisited," *Journal of Applied Psychology*, December 2000, pp. 869–879; J. Hogan and B. Holland, "Using Theory to Evaluate Personality and Job-Performance Relations: A Socioanalytic Perspective," *Journal of Applied Psychology*, February 2003, pp. 100–112; and M. R. Barrick and M. K. Mount, "Select on Conscientiousness and Emotional Stability," in E. A. Locke (ed.), *Handbook of Principles of Organizational Behavior* (Malden, MA: Blackwell, 2004), pp. 15–28.

34. M. K. Mount, M. R. Barrick, and J. P. Strauss, "Validity of Observer Ratings of the Big Five Personality Factors," *Journal of Applied Psychology*, April 1994, p. 272. Additionally confirmed by G. M. Hurtz and J. J. Donovan, "Personality and Job Performance: The Big Five Revisited;" and M. R. Barrick, M. K. Mount, and T. A. Judge, "The FFM Personality Dimensions and Job Performance: Meta-analysis of Meta-analyses," *International Journal of Selection and Assessment* 9 (2001), pp. 9–30.

35. A. Elanain and M. Hossam, "The Five-Factor Model of Personality and Organizational Citizenship Behavior in United Arab Emirates", *Advanced Management Journal* 72(3), 2007, pp. 47–57.

36. T. A. Judge and J. E. Bono, "A Rose by Any Other Name . . . Are Self-Esteem, Generalized Self-Efficacy, Neuroticism, and Locus of Control Indicators of a Common Construct?" in B. W. Roberts and R. Hogan (eds.), *Personality Psychology in the Workplace* (Washington, DC: American Psychological Association), pp. 93–118.

37. U. Malmendier and G. Tate, "CEO Overconfidence and Corporate Investment," *Journal of Finance* 60, no. 6 (2005), pp. 2661–2700.

38. R. G. Vleeming, "Machiavellianism: A Preliminary Review," *Psychological Reports*, February 1979, pp. 295–310.

39. R. Christie and F. L. Geis, *Studies in Machiavellianism* (New York: Academic Press, 1970), p. 312; and N. V. Ramanaiah, A. Byravan, and F. R. J. Detwiler, "Revised Neo Personality Inventory Profiles of Machiavellian and Non-Machiavellian People," *Psychological Reports*, October 1994, pp. 937–938.

40. Christie and Geis, *Studies in Machiavellianism*.

41. W. K. Campbell and C. A. Foster, "Narcissism and Commitment in Romantic Relationships: An Investment Model Analysis," *Personality and Social Psychology Bulletin* 28, no. 4 (2002), pp. 484–495.

42. T. A. Judge, J. A. LePine, and B. L. Rich, "The Narcissistic Personality: Relationship with Inflated Self-Ratings of Leadership and with Task and Contextual Performance," *Journal of Applied Psychology* 91, no. 4 (2006), pp. 762–776.

43. See M. Snyder, *Public Appearances/Private Realities: The Psychology of Self-Monitoring* (New York: W. H. Freeman, 1987); and S. W. Gangestad and M. Snyder, "Self-Monitoring: Appraisal and Reappraisal," *Psychological Bulletin*, July 2000, pp. 530–555.

44. Snyder, *Public Appearances/Private Realities*.

45. D. V. Day, D. J. Shleicher, A. L. Unckless, and N. J. Hiller, "Self-Monitoring Personality at Work: A Meta-Analytic Investigation of Construct Validity," *Journal of Applied Psychology*, April 2002, pp. 390–401.

46. M. Kilduff and D. V. Day, "Do Chameleons Get Ahead? The Effects of Self-Monitoring on Managerial Careers," *Academy of Management Journal*, August 1994, pp. 1047–1060; and A. Mehra, M. Kilduff, and D. J. Brass, "The Social Networks of High and Low Self-Monitors: Implications for Workplace Performance," *Administrative Science Quarterly*, March 2001, pp. 121–146.

47. R. N. Taylor and M. D. Dunnette, "Influence of Dogmatism, Risk-Taking Propensity, and Intelligence on Decision-Making Strategies for a Sample of Industrial Managers," *Journal of Applied Psychology*, August 1974, pp. 420–423.

48. M. Friedman and R. H. Rosenman, *Type A Behavior and Your Heart* (New York: Alfred A. Knopf, 1974), p. 84.

49. Ibid., pp. 84–85.

50. K. W. Cook, C. A. Vance, and E. Spector, "The Relation of Candidate Personality with Selection-Interview Outcomes," *Journal of Applied Social Psychology* 30 (2000), pp. 867–885.

51. J. M. Crant, "Proactive Behavior in Organizations," *Journal of Management* 26, no. 3 (2000), p. 436.

52. S. E. Seibert, M. L. Kraimer, and J. M. Crant, "What Do Proactive People Do? A Longitudinal Model Linking Proactive Personality and Career Success," *Personnel Psychology*, Winter 2001, p. 850.

53. See, for instance, R. C. Becherer and J. G. Maurer, "The Proactive Personality Disposition and Entrepreneurial Behavior Among Small Company Presidents," *Journal of Small Business Management*, January 1999, pp. 28–36.

54. S. E. Seibert, J. M. Crant, and M. L. Kraimer, "Proactive Personality and Career Success," *Journal of Applied Psychology*, June 1999, pp. 416–427; Seibert, Kraimer, and Crant, "What Do Proactive People Do?" p. 850; and J. D. Kammeyer-Mueller and C. R. Wanberg, "Unwrapping the Organizational Entry Process: Disentangling Multiple Antecedents and Their Pathways to Adjustment," *Journal of Applied Psychology* 88, no. 5 (2003), pp. 779–794.

55. See, for instance, B. M. Meglino and E. C. Ravlin, "Individual Values in Organizations: Concepts, Controversies, and Research," *Journal of Management* 24, no. 3 (1998), p. 355, pp. 351–389.

56. Rokeach, *The Nature of Human Values*, p. 6.

57. J. M. Munson and B. Z. Posner, "The Factorial Validity of a Modified Rokeach Value Survey for Four Diverse Samples," *Educational and Psychological Measurement*, Winter 1980, pp. 1073–1079; and W. C. Frederick and J. Weber, "The Values of Corporate Managers and Their Critics: An Empirical Description and Normative Implications," in W. C. Frederick and L. E. Preston (eds.), *Business Ethics: Research Issues and Empirical Studies* (Greenwich, CT: JAI Press, 1990), pp. 123–144.

58. W. C. Frederick and J. Weber, "The Values of Corporate Managers and Their Critics: An Empirical Description and Normative Implications," in W. C. Frederick and L. E. Preston (eds.), *Business Ethics: Research Issues and Empirical Studies* (Greenwich, CT: JAI Press, 1990), pp. 123–144.

59. J. L. Holland, *Making Vocational Choices: A Theory of Vocational Personalities and Work Environments* (Odessa, FL: Psychological Assessment Resources, 1997).

60. See B. Schneider, "The People Make the Place," *Personnel Psychology*, Autumn 1987, pp. 437–453; B. Schneider, H. W. Goldstein, and D. B. Smith, "The ASA Framework: An Update," *Personnel Psychology*, Winter 1995, pp. 747–773; A. L. Kristof, "Person–Organization Fit: An Integrative Review of Its Conceptualizations, Measurement, and Implications," *Personnel Psychology*, Spring 1996, pp. 1–49; B. Schneider, D. B. Smith, S. Taylor, and J. Fleenor, "Personality and Organizations: A Test of the Homogeneity of Personality Hypothesis," *Journal of Applied Psychology*, June 1998, pp. 462–470; W. Arthur, Jr., S. T. Bell, A. J. Villado, and D. Doverspike, "The Use of Person–Organization Fit in Employment Decision-Making: An Assessment of Its Criterion-Related Validity," *Journal of Applied Psychology* 91, no. 4 (2006), pp. 786–801; and J. R. Edwards, D. M. Cable, I. O. Williamson, L. S. Lambert, and A. J. Shipp, "The Phenomenology of Fit: Linking the Person and Environment to the Subjective Experience of Person–Environment Fit," *Journal of Applied Psychology* 91, no. 4 (2006), pp. 802–827.

61. Based on T. A. Judge and D. M. Cable, "Applicant Personality, Organizational Culture, and Organization Attraction," *Personnel Psychology*, Summer 1997, pp. 359–394.

62. M. L. Verquer, T. A. Beehr, and S. E. Wagner, "A Meta-analysis of Relations Between Person–Organization Fit and Work Attitudes," *Journal of Vocational Behavior* 63, no. 3 (2003), pp. 473–489.

63. G. Hofstede, *Culture's Consequences: International Differences in Work-Related Values* (Beverly Hills, CA: Sage, 1980); G. Hofstede, *Cultures and Organizations: Software of the Mind* (London: McGraw-Hill, 1991); G. Hofstede, "Cultural Constraints in Management Theories," *Academy of Management Executive* 7, no. 1 (1993), pp. 81–94; G. Hofstede and M. F. Peterson, "National Values and Organizational Practices," in N. M. Ashkanasy, C. M. Wilderom, and M. F. Peterson (eds.), *Handbook of Organizational Culture and Climate* (Thousand Oaks, CA: Sage, 2000), pp. 401–416; and G. Hofstede, *Culture's Consequences: Comparing Values,*

Behaviors, Institutions, and Organizations Across Nations, 2nd ed. (Thousand Oaks, CA: Sage, 2001). For criticism of this research, see B. McSweeney, "Hofstede's Model of National Cultural Differences and Their Consequences: A Triumph of Faith—A Failure of Analysis," *Human Relations* 55, no. 1 (2002), pp. 89–118.

64. M. Javidan and R. J. House, "Cultural Acumen for the Global Manager: Lessons from Project GLOBE," *Organizational Dynamics* 29, no. 4 (2001), pp. 289–305; and R. J. House, P. J. Hanges, M. Javidan, and P. W. Dorfman (eds.), *Leadership, Culture, and Organizations: The GLOBE Study of 62 Societies* (Thousand Oaks, CA: Sage, 2004).

65. M. H. Bond, "Reclaiming the Individual from Hofstede's Ecological Analysis—A 20-Year Odyssey: Comment on Oyserman *et al.* (2002). *Psychological Bulletin* 128, no. 1 (2002), pp. 73–77; G. Hofstede, "The Pitfalls of Cross-National Survey Research: A Reply to the Article by Spector *et al.* on the Psychometric Properties of the Hofstede Values Survey Module 1994," *Applied Psychology: An International Review* 51, no. 1 (2002), pp. 170–178; and T. Fang, "A Critique of Hofstede's Fifth National Culture Dimension," *International Journal of Cross-Cultural Management* 3, no. 3 (2003), pp. 347–368.

66. M. Javidan and R. J. House, "Cultural Acumen for the Global Manager: Lessons from Project GLOBE," *Organizational Dynamics* 29, no. 4 (2001), pp. 289–305; and R. J. House, P. J. Hanges, M. Javidan, and P. W. Dorfman (eds.), *Leadership, Culture, and Organizations: The GLOBE Study of 62 Societies* (Thousand Oaks, CA: Sage, 2004).

67. P. C. Early, "Leading Cultural Research in the Future: A Matter of Paradigms and Taste," *Journal of International Business Studies,* September 2006, pp. 922–931; G. Hofstede, "What Did GLOBE Really Measure? Researchers' Minds Versus Respondents' Minds," *Journal of International Business Studies,* September 2006, pp. 882–896; and M. Javidan, R. J. House, P. W. Dorfman, P. J. Hanges, and M. S. de Luque, "Conceptualizing and Measuring Cultures and Their Consequences: A Comparative Review of GLOBE's and Hofstede's Approaches," *Journal of International Business Studies,* September 2006, pp. 897–914.

68. N. Barber, "Educational and Ecological Correlates of IQ: A Cross-National Investigation," *Intelligence,* May–Jun 2005, pp. 273–284.

69. See, for instance, J. E. Williams *et al.,* "Cross-Cultural Variation in the Importance of Psychological Characteristics: A Seven-Country Study," *International Journal of Psychology,* October 1995, pp. 529–550; R. R. McCrae and P. T. Costa, Jr., "Personality Trait Structure as a Human Universal," *American Psychologist,* May 1997, pp. 509–516; R. R. McCrae, "Trait Psychology and the Revival of Personality-and-Culture Studies," *American Behavioral Scientist,* September 2000, pp. 10–31; S. V. Paunonen *et al.,* "The Non-verbal Assessment of Personality in Five Cultures," *Journal of Cross-Cultural Psychology,* March 2000, pp. 220–239; H. C. Triandis and E. M. Suh, "Cultural Influences on Personality," in S. T. Fiske, D. L. Schacter, and C. Zahn-Waxler (eds.), *Annual Review of Psychology,* vol. 53 (Palo Alto, CA: Annual Reviews, 2002), pp. 133–160; R. R. McCrae and J. Allik, *The Five-Factor Model of Personality Across Cultures* (New York: Kluwer Academic/Plenum, 2002); and R. R. McCrae *et al.,*

"Consensual Validation of Personality Traits Across Cultures," *Journal of Research in Personality* 38, no. 2 (2004), pp. 179–201.

70. A. T. Church and M. S. Katigbak, "Trait Psychology in the Philippines," *American Behavioral Scientist,* September 2000, pp. 73–94.

71. L. A. Witt, "The Interactive Effects of Extraversion and Conscientiousness on Performance," *Journal of Management* 28, no. 6 (2002), p. 836.

72. R. P. Tett and D. D. Burnett, "A Personality Trait-Based Interactionist Model of Job Performance," *Journal of Applied Psychology,* June 2003, pp. 500–517.

73. Points in this argument are based on N. Nicholson, "How Hardwired Is Human Behavior?" *Harvard Business Review,* July–August 1998, pp. 135–147; and B. D. Pierce and R. White, "The Evolution of Social Structure: Why Biology Matters," *Academy of Management Review,* October 1999, pp. 843–853.

Chapter 3

1. S. J. Breckler, "Empirical Validation of Affect, Behavior, and Cognition as Distinct Components of Attitude," *Journal of Personality and Social Psychology,* May 1984, pp. 1191–1205; and S. L. Crites, Jr., L. R. Fabrigar, and R. E. Petty, "Measuring the Affective and Cognitive Properties of Attitudes: Conceptual and Methodological Issues," *Personality and Social Psychology Bulletin,* December 1994, pp. 619–634.

2. L. Festinger, *A Theory of Cognitive Dissonance* (Stanford, CA: Stanford University Press, 1957).

3. See, for instance, I. R. Newby-Clark, I. McGregor, and M. P. Zanna, "Thinking and Caring About Cognitive Consistency: When and for Whom Does Attitudinal Ambivalence Feel Uncomfortable?" *Journal of Personality & Social Psychology,* February 2002, pp. 157–166; and D. J. Schleicher, J. D. Watt, and G. J. Greguras, "Reexamining the Job Satisfaction-Performance Relationship: The Complexity of Attitudes," *Journal of Applied Psychology* 89, no. 1 (2004), pp. 165–177.

4. See, for instance, J. Nocera, "If It's Good for Philip Morris, Can It also Be Good for Public Health?" *New York Times,* June 18, 2006.

5. See L. R. Glasman and D. Albarracín, "Forming Attitudes That Predict Future Behavior: A Meta-analysis of the Attitude–Behavior Relation," *Psychological Bulletin,* September 2006, pp. 778–822; I. Ajzen, "The Directive Influence of Attitudes on Behavior," in M. Gollwitzer and J. A. Bargh (eds.), *The Psychology of Action: Linking Cognition and Motivation to Behavior* (New York: Guilford, 1996), pp. 385–403; and I. Ajzen, "Nature and Operation of Attitudes," in S. T. Fiske, D. L. Schacter, and C. Zahn-Waxler (eds.), *Annual Review of Psychology,* vol. 52 (Palo Alto, CA: Annual Reviews, Inc., 2001), pp. 27–58.

6. D. A. Harrison, D. A. Newman, and P. L. Roth, "How Important Are Job Attitudes? Meta-analytic Comparisons of Integrative Behavioral Outcomes and Time Sequences," *Academy of Management Journal* 49, no. 2 (2006), pp. 305–325.

7. Based on G. J. Blau and K. R. Boal, "Conceptualizing How Job Involvement and Organizational Commitment Affect Turnover and Absenteeism," *Academy of Management Review,* April 1987, p. 290.

8. K. W. Thomas and B. A. Velthouse, "Cognitive Elements of Empowerment: An 'Interpretive' Model of Intrinsic Task Motivation," *Academy of Management Review* 15, no. 4 (1990), pp. 666–681; G. M. Spreitzer, "Psychological Empowerment in the Workplace: Dimensions, Measurement, and Validation," *Academy of Management Journal* 38, no. 5 (1995), pp. 1442–1465; G. Chen and R. J. Klimoski, "The Impact of Expectations on Newcomer Performance in Teams as Mediated by Work Characteristics, Social Exchanges, and Empowerment," *Academy of Management Journal* 46, no. 5 (2003), pp. 591–607; A. Ergeneli, G. Saglam, and S. Metin, "Psychological Empowerment and Its Relationship to Trust in Immediate Managers," *Journal of Business Research,* January 2007, pp. 41–49; and S. E. Seibert, S. R. Silver, and W. A. Randolph, "Taking Empowerment to the Next Level: A Multiple-Level Model of Empowerment, Performance, and Satisfaction," *Academy of Management Journal* 47, no. 3 (2004), pp. 332–349.

9. J. M. Diefendorff, D. J. Brown, A. M. Kamin, and R. G. Lord, "Examining the Roles of Job Involvement and Work Centrality in Predicting Organizational Citizenship Behaviors and Job Performance," *Journal of Organizational Behavior,* February 2002, pp. 93–108.

10. G. J. Blau, "Job Involvement and Organizational Commitment as Interactive Predictors of Tardiness and Absenteeism," *Journal of Management,* Winter 1986, pp. 577–584; K. Boal and R. Cidambi, "Attitudinal Correlates of Turnover and Absenteeism: A Meta Analysis," paper presented at the meeting of the American Psychological Association, Toronto, Canada, 1984; and M. R. Barrick, M. K. Mount, and J. P. Strauss, "Antecedents of Involuntary Turnover Due to a Reduction in Force," *Personnel Psychology* 47, no. 3 (1994), pp. 515–535.

11. Blau and Boal, "Conceptualizing," p. 290.

12. J. P. Meyer, N. J. Allen, and C. A. Smith, "Commitment to Organizations and Occupations: Extension and Test of a Three-Component Conceptualization," *Journal of Applied Psychology* 78, no. 4 (1993), pp. 538–551.

13. L. Rhoades, R. Eisenberger, and S. Armeli, "Affective Commitment to the Organization: The Contribution of Perceived Organizational Support," *Journal of Applied Psychology* 86, no. 5 (2001), pp. 825–836.

14. Z. X. Chen, S. Aryee, and C. Lee, "Test of a Mediation Model of Perceived Organizational Support," *Journal of Vocational Behavior,* June 2005, pp. 457–470; and J. A. M. Coyle-Shapiro and N. Conway, "Exchange Relationships: Examining Psychological Contracts and Perceived Organizational Support," *Journal of Applied Psychology,* July 2005, pp. 774–781.

15. L. Rhoades and R. Eisenberger, "Perceived Organizational Support: A Review of the Literature," *Journal of Applied Psychology* 87, no. 4 (2002), pp. 698–714; and R. L. Payne and D. Morrison, "The Differential Effects of Negative Affectivity on Measures of Well-Being Versus Job Satisfaction and Organizational Commitment," *Anxiety, Stress & Coping: An International Journal* 15, no. 3 (2002), pp. 231–244.

16. The Wyatt Company's 1989 national WorkAmerica study identified 12 dimensions of satisfaction: work organization, working conditions, communications, job performance and performance review, coworkers, supervision, company management, pay, benefits, career development and training, job content and satisfaction, and company image and change.

17. See E. Spector, *Job Satisfaction: Application, Assessment, Causes, and Consequences* (Thousand Oaks, CA: Sage, 1997), p. 3.

18. J. Wanous, A. E. Reichers, and M. J. Hudy, "Overall Job Satisfaction: How Good Are Single-Item Measures?" *Journal of Applied Psychology,* April 1997, pp. 247–252.

19. W. K. Balzer, J. A. Kihm, P. C. Smith, J. L. Irwin, P. D. Bachiochi, C. Robie, E. F. Sinar, and L. F. Parra, *Users' Manual for the Job Descriptive Index (JDI; 1997 Revision) and the Job In General Scales* (Bowling Green, OH: Bowling Green State University, 1997).

20. J. Barling, E. K. Kelloway, and R. D. Iverson, "High-Quality Work, Job Satisfaction, and Occupational Injuries," *Journal of Applied Psychology* 88, no. 2 (2003), pp. 276–283; F. W. Bond and D. Bunce, "The Role of Acceptance and Job Control in Mental Health, Job Satisfaction, and Work Performance," *Journal of Applied Psychology* 88, no. 6 (2003), pp. 1057–1067.

21. E. Diener and M. E. P. Seligman, "Beyond Money: Toward an Economy of Well-Being," *Psychological Science in the Public Interest* 5, no. 1 (2004), pp. 1–31; and A. Grant, "Money=Happiness? That's Rich: Here's the Science Behind the Axiom," *The (South Mississippi) Sun Herald,* January 8, 2005.

22. See D. Farrell, "Exit, Voice, Loyalty, and Neglect as Responses to Job Dissatisfaction: A Multidimensional Scaling Study," *Academy of Management Journal,* December 1983, pp. 596–606; C. E. Rusbult, D. Farrell, G. Rogers, and A. G. Mainous III, "Impact of Exchange Variables on Exit, Voice, Loyalty, and Neglect: An Integrative Model of Responses to Declining Job Satisfaction," *Academy of Management Journal,* September 1988, pp. 599–627; M. J. Withey and W. H. Cooper, "Predicting Exit, Voice, Loyalty, and Neglect," *Administrative Science Quarterly,* December 1989, pp. 521–539; J. Zhou and J. M. George, "When Job Dissatisfaction Leads to Creativity: Encouraging the Expression of Voice," *Academy of Management Journal,* August 2001, pp. 682–696; J. B. Olson-Buchanan and W. R. Boswell, "The Role of Employee Loyalty and Formality in Voicing Discontent," *Journal of Applied Psychology,* December 2002, pp. 1167–1174; and A. Davis-Blake, J. P. Broschak, and E. George, "Happy Together? How Using Nonstandard Workers Affects Exit, Voice, and Loyalty Among Standard Employees," *Academy of Management Journal* 46, no. 4 (2003), pp. 475–485.

23. T. A. Judge, C. J. Thoresen, J. E. Bono, and G. K. Patton, "The Job Satisfaction–Job Performance Relationship: A Qualitative and Quantitative Review," *Psychological Bulletin,* May 2001, pp. 376–407.

24. C. Ostroff, "The Relationship Between Satisfaction, Attitudes, and Performance: An Organizational Level Analysis," *Journal of Applied Psychology,* December 1992, pp. 963–974; A. M. Ryan, M. J. Schmit, and R. Johnson, "Attitudes and Effectiveness: Examining Relations at an Organizational Level," *Personnel Psychology,* Winter 1996, pp. 853–882; and J. K. Harter, F. L. Schmidt, and T. L. Hayes, "Business-Unit Level Relationship Between Employee Satisfaction, Employee Engagement, and Business Outcomes: A Meta-analysis," *Journal of Applied Psychology,* April 2002, pp. 268–279.

25. See T. S. Bateman and D. W. Organ, "Job Satisfaction and the Good Soldier: The Relationship Between Affect and

Employee 'Citizenship'," *Academy of Management Journal*, December 1983, pp. 587–595; P. Podsakoff, S. B. MacKenzie, J. B. Paine, and D. G. Bachrach, "Organizational Citizenship Behaviors: A Critical Review of the Theoretical and Empirical Literature and Suggestions for Future Research," *Journal of Management* 26, no. 3 (2000), pp. 513–563.

26. E. A. Locke, "The Nature and Causes of Job Satisfaction," in M. D. Dunnette (ed.), *Handbook of Industrial and Organizational Psychology* (Chicago: Rand McNally, 1976), p. 1331; R. D. Hackett and R. M. Guion, "A Reevaluation of the Absenteeism–Job Satisfaction Relationship," *Organizational Behavior and Human Decision Processes*, June 1985, pp. 340–381; K. D. Scott and G. S. Taylor, "An Examination of Conflicting Findings on the Relationship between Job Satisfaction and Absenteeism: A Meta-analysis," *Academy of Management Journal*, September 1985, pp. 599–612; R. Steel and J. R. Rentsch, "Influence of Cumulation Strategies on the Long-Range Prediction of Absenteeism," *Academy of Management Journal*, December 1995, pp. 1616–1634; and G. Johns, "The Psychology of Lateness, Absenteeism, and Turnover," p. 237.

27. W. Hom and R. W. Griffeth, *Employee Turnover* (Cincinnati, OH: South-Western Publishing, 1995); R. W. Griffeth, P. W. Hom, and S. Gaertner, "A Meta-analysis of Antecedents and Correlates of Employee Turnover: Update, Moderator Tests, and Research Implications for the Next Millennium," *Journal of Management* 26, no. 3 (2000), p. 479; G. Johns, "The Psychology of Lateness, Absenteeism, and Turnover," p. 237.

28. D. G. Spencer and R. M. Steers, "Performance as a Moderator of the Job Satisfaction–Turnover Relationship," *Journal of Applied Psychology*, August 1981, pp. 511–514.

29. See, for instance, B. Schneider and D. E. Bowen, "Employee and Customer Perceptions of Service in Banks: Replication and Extension," *Journal of Applied Psychology*, August 1985, pp. 423–433; D. J. Koys, "The Effects of Employee Satisfaction, Organizational Citizenship Behavior, and Turnover on Organizational Effectiveness: A Unit-Level, Longitudinal Study," *Personnel Psychology*, Spring 2001, pp. 101–114; and J. Griffith, "Do Satisfied Employees Satisfy Customers? Support-Services Staff Morale and Satisfaction Among Public School Administrators, Students, and Parents," *Journal of Applied Social Psychology*, August 2001, pp. 1627–1658.

30. M. J. Bitner, B. H. Booms, and L. A. Mohr, "Critical Service Encounters: The Employee's Viewpoint," *Journal of Marketing*, October 1994, pp. 95–106.

31. K. Holland, "Inside the Minds of Your Employees," *New York Times*, January 28, 2007, p. B1; "Study Sees Link Between Morale and Stock Price," *Workforce Management*, February 27, 2006, p. 15; and "The Workplace as a Solar System," *New York Times*, October 28, 2006, p. B5.

32. M. J. Gelfand, M. Erez, and Z. Aycan, "Cross-Cultural Organizational Behavior," *Annual Review of Psychology* 58 (2007), pp. 479–514; A. S. Tsui, S. S. Nifadkar, and A. Y. Ou, "Cross-National, Cross-Cultural Organizational Behavior Research: Advances, Gaps, and Recommendations," *Journal of Management*, June 2007, pp. 426–478.

33. M. Benz and B. S. Frey, "The Value of Autonomy: Evidence from the Self-Employed in 23 Countries," working paper 173, Institute for Empirical Research in Economics, University of

Zurich, November 2003, http://ssrn.com/abstract=475140; and P. Warr, *Work, Happiness, and Unhappiness* (Mahwah, NJ: Laurence Erlbaum, 2007).

34. Harrison, Newman, and Roth, "How Important Are Job Attitudes?" pp. 320–321.

35. Judge, *et al.*, "Job Satisfaction: A Cross-Cultural Review;" T. A. Judge and A. H. Church, "Job Satisfaction: Research and Practice," in C. L. Cooper and E. A. Locke (eds.), *Industrial and Organizational Psychology: Linking Theory with Practice* (Oxford, UK: Blackwell, 2000), pp. 166–198; L. Saari and T. A. Judge, "Employee Attitudes and Job Satisfaction," *Human Resource Management* 43, no. 4 (2004), pp. 395–407.

36. See, for instance, R. D. Arvey *et al.*, "Genetic Influences on Job Satisfaction and Work Values," *Personality and Individual Differences*, July 1994, pp. 21–33; D. Lykken and A. Tellegen, "Happiness Is a Stochastic Phenomenon," *Psychological Science*, May 1996, pp. 186–189; and D. Lykken and M. Csikszentmihalyi, "Happiness—Stuck with What You've Got?" *Psychologist*, September 2001, pp. 470–472; and "Double Take," *UNH Magazine*, Spring 2000, www.unhmagazine.unh.edu/sp00/twinssp00.html.

Chapter 4

1. H. H. Kelley, "Attribution in Social Interaction," in E. Jones *et al.* (eds.), *Attribution: Perceiving the Causes of Behavior* (Morristown, NJ: General Learning Press, 1972).

2. See L. Ross, "The Intuitive Psychologist and His Short Comings," in L. Berkowitz (ed.), *Advances in Experimental Social Psychology*, vol. 10 (Orlando, FL: Academic Press, 1977), pp. 174–220; and A. G. Miller and T. Lawson, "The Effect of an Informational Option on the Fundamental Attribution Error," *Personality and Social Psychology Bulletin*, June 1989, pp. 194–204.

3. See, for instance, G. Johns, "A Multi-Level Theory of Self-Serving Behavior in and by Organizations," in R. I. Sutton and B. M. Staw (eds.), *Research in Organizational Behavior*, vol. 21 (Stamford, CT: JAI Press, 1999), pp. 1–38; N. Epley and D. Dunning, "Feeling 'Holier Than Thou': Are Self-Serving Assessments Produced by Errors in Self-or Social Prediction?" *Journal of Personality and Social Psychology*, December 2000, pp. 861–875; and M. Goerke, J. Moller, S. Schulz-Hardt, U. Napiersky, and D. Frey, "'It's Not My Fault—But Only I Can Change It': Counterfactual and Prefactual Thoughts of Managers," *Journal of Applied Psychology*, April 2004, pp. 279–292.

4. D. C. Dearborn and H. A. Simon, "Selective Perception: A Note on the Departmental Identification of Executives," *Sociometry*, June 1958, pp. 140–144. Some of the conclusions in this classic study have recently been challenged in J. Walsh, "Selectivity and Selective Perception: An Investigation of Managers' Belief Structures and Information Processing," *Academy of Management Journal*, December 1988, pp. 873–896; M. J. Waller, G. Huber, and W. H. Glick, "Functional Background as a Determinant of Executives' Selective Perception," *Academy of Management Journal*, August 1995, pp. 943–974; and J. M. Beyer, P. Chattopadhyay, E. George, W. H. Glick, D. T. Ogilvie, and D. Pugliese, "The Selective Perception of Managers Revisited," *Academy of Management Journal*, June 1997, pp. 716–737.

5. See K. R. Murphy and R. L. Anhalt, "Is Halo a Property of the Rater, the Ratees, or the Specific Behaviors Observed?" *Journal of Applied Psychology*, June 1992, pp. 494–500; K. R. Murphy, R. A. Jako, and R. L. Anhalt, "Nature and Consequences of Halo Error: A Critical Analysis," *Journal of Applied Psychology*, April 1993, pp. 218–225; P. Rosenzweig, *The Halo Effect* (New York: The Free Press, 2007); and C. E. Naquin and R. O. Tynan, "The Team Halo Effect: Why Teams Are Not Blamed for Their Failures," *Journal of Applied Psychology*, April 2003, pp. 332–340.

6. S. E. Asch, "Forming Impressions of Personality," *Journal of Abnormal and Social Psychology*, July 1946, pp. 258–290.

7. J. L. Hilton and W. von Hippel, "Stereotypes," in J. T. Spence, J. M. Darley, and D. J. Foss (eds.), *Annual Review of Psychology*, vol. 47 (Palo Alto, CA: Annual Reviews, 1996), pp. 237–271.

8. H. G. Heneman III and T. A. Judge, *Staffing Organizations* (Middleton, WI: Mendota House, 2006).

9. J. Willis and A. Todorov, "First Impressions: Making Up Your Mind After a 100ms Exposure to a Face," *Psychological Science*, July 2006, pp. 592–598.

10. See, for example, D. Eden, *Pygmalion in Management* (Lexington, MA: Lexington Books, 1990); D. Eden, "Leadership and Expectations: Pygmalion Effects and Other Self-Fulfilling Prophecies," *Leadership Quarterly*, Winter 1992, pp. 271–305; D. B. McNatt, "Ancient Pygmalion Joins Contemporary Management: A Meta-analysis of the Result," *Journal of Applied Psychology*, April 2000, pp. 314–322; O. B. Davidson and D. Eden, "Remedial Self-Fulfilling Prophecy: Two Field Experiments to Prevent Golem Effects Among Disadvantaged Women," *Journal of Applied Psychology*, June 2000, pp. 386–398; and D. Eden, "Self-Fulfilling Prophecies in Organizations," in J. Greenberg (ed.), *Organizational Behavior: The State of the Science*, 2nd ed. (Mahwah, NJ: Lawrence Erlbaum, 2003), pp. 91–122.

11. D. Eden and A. B. Shani, "Pygmalion Goes to Boot Camp: Expectancy, Leadership, and Trainee Performance," *Journal of Applied Psychology*, April 1982, pp. 194–199; and D. B. McNatt and T. A. Judge, "Boundary Conditions of the Galatea Effect: A Field Experiment and Constructive Replication," *Academy of Management Journal*, August 2004, pp. 550–565.

12. See, for example, R. D. Bretz, Jr., G. T. Milkovich, and W. Read, "The Current State of Performance Appraisal Research and Practice: Concerns, Directions, and Implications," *Journal of Management*, June 1992, pp. 323–324; and S. E. DeVoe and S. S. Iyengar, "Managers' Theories of Subordinates: A Cross-Cultural Examination of Manager Perceptions of Motivation and Appraisal of Performance," *Organizational Behavior and Human Decision Processes*, January 2004, pp. 47–61.

13. R. Sanders, *The Executive Decisionmaking Process: Identifying Problems and Assessing Outcomes* (Westport, CT: Quorum, 1999).

14. See H. A. Simon, "Rationality in Psychology and Economics," *Journal of Business*, October 1986, pp. 209–224; and E. Shafir and R. A. LeBoeuf, "Rationality," in S. T. Fiske, D. L. Schacter, and C. Zahn-Waxler, eds., *Annual Review of Psychology*, vol. 53 (Palo Alto, CA: Annual Reviews, 2002), pp. 491–517.

15. For a review of the rational model, see E. F. Harrison, *The Managerial Decision-Making Process*, 5th ed. (Boston: Houghton Mifflin, 1999), pp. 75–102.

16. J. G. March, *A Primer on Decision Making* (New York: The Free Press, 1994), pp. 2–7; and D. Hardman and C. Harries, "How Rational Are We?" *Psychologist*, February 2002, pp. 76–79.

17. M. Bazerman, *Judgment in Managerial Decision Making*, 3rd ed. (New York: Wiley, 1994), p. 5.

18. D. Kahneman, "Maps of Bounded Rationality: Psychology for Behavioral Economics," *The American Economic Review* 93, no. 5 (2003), pp. 1449–1475; J. Zhang, C. K. Hsee, and Z. Xiao, "The Majority Rule in Individual Decision Making," *Organizational Behavior and Human Decision Processes* 99 (2006), pp. 102–111.

19. See H. A. Simon, *Administrative Behavior*, 4th ed. (New York: The Free Press, 1997); and M. Augier, "Simon Says: Bounded Rationality Matters," *Journal of Management Inquiry*, September 2001, pp. 268–275.

20. See T. Gilovich, D. Griffin, and D. Kahneman, *Heuristics and Biases: The Psychology of Intuitive Judgment* (New York: Cambridge University Press, 2002).

21. E. Dane and M. G. Pratt, "Exploring Intuition and Its Role in Managerial Decision Making," *Academy of Management Review* 32, no. 1 (2007), pp. 33–54.

22. See, for instance, L. A. Burke and M. K. Miller, "Taking the Mystery Out of Intuitive Decision Making," *Academy of Management Executive*, November 1999, pp. 91–99; N. Khatri and H. A. Ng, "The Role of Intuition in Strategic Decision Making," *Human Relations*, January 2000, pp. 57–86; J. A. Andersen, "Intuition in Managers: Are Intuitive Managers More Effective?" *Journal of Managerial Psychology* 15, no. 1–2 (2000), pp. 46–63; D. Myers, *Intuition: Its Powers and Perils* (New Haven, CT: Yale University Press, 2002); and L. Simpson, "Basic Instincts," *Training*, January 2003, pp. 56–59.

23. See, for instance, Burke and Miller, "Taking the Mystery Out of Intuitive Decision Making," pp. 91–99.

24. S. P. Robbins, *Decide & Conquer: Making Winning Decisions and Taking Control of Your Life* (Upper Saddle River, NJ: Financial Times/Prentice Hall, 2004), p. 13.

25. S. Plous, *The Psychology of Judgment and Decision Making* (New York: McGraw-Hill, 1993), p. 217.

26. J. Kruger and D. Dunning, "Unskilled and Unaware of It: How Difficulties in Recognizing One's Own Incompetence Lead to Inflated Self-Assessments," *Journal of Personality and Social Psychology*, November 1999, pp. 1121–1134.

27. B. Fischhoff, P. Slovic, and S. Lichtenstein, "Knowing with Certainty: The Appropriateness of Extreme Confidence," *Journal of Experimental Psychology* 3 (1977), pp. 552–564.

28. Kruger and Dunning, "Unskilled and Unaware of It: How Difficulties in Recognizing One's Own Incompetence Lead to Inflated Self-Assessments."

29. See, for instance, A. Tversky and D. Kahneman, "Judgment Under Uncertainty: Heuristics and Biases," *Science*, September 1974, pp. 1124–1131.

30. J. S. Hammond, R. L. Keeney, and H. Raiffa, *Smart Choices* (Boston: HBS Press, 1999), p. 191.

31. See R. S. Nickerson, "Confirmation Bias: A Ubiquitous Phenomenon in Many Guises," *Review of General Psychology*,

June 1998, pp. 175–220; and E. Jonas, S. Schultz-Hardt, D. Frey, and N. Thelen, "Confirmation Bias in Sequential Information Search After Preliminary Decisions," *Journal of Personality and Social Psychology*, April 2001, pp. 557–571.

32. See A. Tversky and D. Kahneman, "Availability: A Heuristic for Judging Frequency and Probability," in D. Kahneman, P. Slovic, and A. Tversky (eds.), *Judgment Under Uncertainty: Heuristics and Biases* (Cambridge, UK: Cambridge University Press, 1982), pp. 163–178; and B. J. Bushman and G. L. Wells, "Narrative Impressions of Literature: The Availability Bias and the Corrective Properties of Meta-analytic Approaches," *Personality and Social Psychology Bulletin*, September 2001, pp. 1123–1130.

33. See B. M. Staw, "The Escalation of Commitment to a Course of Action," *Academy of Management Review*, October 1981, pp. 577–587; K. Fai, E. Wong, M. Yik, and J. Y. Y. Kwong, "Understanding the Emotional Aspects of Escalation of Commitment: The Role of Negative Affect," *Journal of Applied Psychology* 91, no. 2 (2006), pp. 282–297; H. Moon, "Looking Forward and Looking Back: Integrating Completion and Sunk-Cost Effects Within an Escalation-of-Commitment Progress Decision," *Journal of Applied Psychology*, February 2001, pp. 104–113; and A. Zardkoohi, "Do Real Options Lead to Escalation of Commitment? Comment," *Academy of Management Review*, January 2004, pp. 111–119.

34. B. M. Staw, "Knee-Deep in the Big Muddy: A Study of Escalating Commitment to a Chosen Course of Action," *Organizational Behavior and Human Performance* 16 (1976), pp. 27–44.

35. R. L. Guilbault, F. B. Bryant, J. H. Brockway, and E. J. Posavac, "A Meta-analysis of Research on Hindsight Bias," *Basic and Applied Social Psychology*, September 2004, pp. 103–117; and L. Werth, F. Strack, and J. Foerster, "Certainty and Uncertainty: The Two Faces of the Hindsight Bias," *Organizational Behavior and Human Decision Processes*, March 2002, pp. 323–341.

36. H. Moon *et al.*, "The Tripartite Model of Neuroticism and the Suppression of Depression and Anxiety within an Escalation of Commitment Dilemma," *Journal of Personality* 71 (2003), pp. 347–368; and H. Moon, "The Two Faces of Conscientious ness: Duty and Achievement Striving in Escalation of Commitment Dilemmas," *Journal of Applied Psychology* 86 (2001), pp. 535–540.

37. J. Musch, "Personality Differences in Hindsight Bias," *Memory* 11 (2003), pp. 473–489.

38. W. K. Campbell and C. Sedikides, "Self-Threat Magnifies the Self-Serving Bias: A Meta-analytic Integration," *Review of General Psychology* 3 (1999), pp. 23–43.

39. This section is based on S. Nolen-Hoeksema, J. Larson, and C. Grayson, "Explaining the Gender Difference in Depressive Symptoms," *Journal of Personality & Social Psychology*, November 1999, pp. 1061–1072; S. Nolen-Hoeksema and S. Jackson, "Mediators of the Gender Difference in Rumination," *Psychology of Women Quarterly*, March 2001, pp. 37–47; S. Nolen-Hoeksema, "Gender Differences in Depression," *Current Directions in Psychological Science*, October 2001, pp. 173–176; and S. Nolen-Hoeksema, *Women Who Think Too Much* (New York: Henry Holt, 2003).

40. A. Wildavsky, *The Politics of the Budgetary Process* (Boston: Little, Brown, 1964).

41. G. F. Cavanagh, D. J. Moberg, and M. Valasquez, "The Ethics of Organizational Politics," *Academy of Management Journal*, June 1981, pp. 363–374.

42. T. M. Amabile, "A Model of Creativity and Innovation in Organizations," in B. M. Staw and L. L. Cummings (eds.), *Research in Organizational Behavior*, vol. 10 (Greenwich, CT: JAI Press, 1988), p. 126; and J. E. Perry-Smith and C. E. Shalley, "The Social Side of Creativity: A Static and Dynamic Social Network Perspective," *Academy of Management Review*, January 2003, pp. 89–106.

43. Cited in C. G. Morris, *Psychology: An Introduction*, 9th ed. (Upper Saddle River, NJ: Prentice Hall, 1996), p. 344.

44. This section is based on T. M. Amabile, "Motivating Creativity in Organizations: On Doing What You Love and Loving What You Do," *California Management Review* 40, no. 1 (Fall 1997), pp. 39–58.

45. See T. M. Amabile, *KEYS: Assessing the Climate for Creativity* (Greensboro, NC: Center for Creative Leadership, 1995); N. Madjar, G. R. Oldham, and M. G. Pratt, "There's No Place Like Home? The Contributions of Work and Nonwork Creativity Support to Employees' Creative Performance," *Academy of Management Journal*, August 2002, pp. 757–767; and C. E. Shalley, J. Zhou, and G. R. Oldham, "The Effects of Personal and Contextual Characteristics on Creativity: Where Should We Go from Here?" *Journal of Management*, November 2004, pp. 933–958.

46. See, for instance, G. R. Semin, "A Gloss on Attribution Theory," *British Journal of Social and Clinical Psychology*, November 1980, pp. 291–230; M. W. Morris and K. Peng, "Culture and Cause: American and Chinese Attributions for Social and Physical Events," *Journal of Personality and Social Psychology*, December 1994, pp. 949–971; and D. S. Krull, M. H.-M. Loy, J. Lin, C.-F. Wang, S. Chen, and X. Zhao, "The Fundamental Attribution Error: Correspondence Bias in Individualistic and Collectivist Cultures," *Personality & Social Psychology Bulletin*, October 1999, pp. 1208–1219.

47. S. Nam, "Cultural and Managerial Attributions for Group Performance," unpublished doctoral dissertation; University of Oregon. Cited in R. M. Steers, S. J. Bischoff, and L. H. Higgins, "Cross-Cultural Management Research," *Journal of Management Inquiry*, December 1992, pp. 325–326.

48. M. J. Gelfand, M. Erez, and Z. Aycan, "Cross-Cultural Organizational Behavior," *Annual Review of Psychology*, January 2007, pp. 479–514, and A. S. Tsui, S. S. Nifadkar, and A. Y. Ou, "Cross-National, Cross-Cultural Organizational Behavior Research: Advances, Gaps, and Recommendations," *Journal of Management*, June 2007, pp. 426–478.

49. N. J. Adler, *International Dimensions of Organizational Behavior*, 4th ed. (Cincinnati, OH: SouthWestern Publishing, 2002), pp. 182–189.

50. T. Jackson, "Cultural Values and Management Ethics: A 10-Nation Study," *Human Relations*, October 2001, pp. 1267–1302; see also J. B. Cullen, K. P. Parboteeah, and M. Hoegl, "Cross-National Differences in Managers' Willingness to Justify Ethically Suspect Behaviors: A Test of Institutional Anomie Theory," *Academy of Management Journal*, June 2004, pp. 411–421.

51. P. Digh, "Shades of Gray in the Global Marketplace," *HR Magazine*, April 1997, p. 91.

52. Based on T. Gilovich, V. H. Medvec, and D. Kahneman, "Varieties of Regret: A Debate and Partial Resolution," *Psychological Review* 105 (1998), pp. 602–605; see also M. Tsiros and V. Mittal, "Regret: A Model of Its Antecedents and Consequences in Consumer Decision Making," *Journal of Consumer Research*, March 2000, pp. 401–417.

Chapter 5

1. C. A. O'Reilly III, "Organizational Behavior: Where We've Been, Where We're Going," in M. R. Rosenzweig and L. W. Porter (eds.), *Annual Review of Psychology*, vol. 42 (Palo Alto, CA: Annual Reviews, 1991), p. 431. See also M. L. Ambrose and C. T. Kulik, "Old Friends, New Faces: Motivation Research in the 1990s," *Journal of Management* 25, no. 3 (1999), pp. 231–292.

2. Cited in D. Jones, "Firms Spend Billions to Fire Up Workers—With Little Luck," *USA Today*, May 10, 2001, p. 1A.

3. "Wasted Time at Work Costs Employers Billions," *IPMA-HR Bulletin*, August 11, 2006, pp. 1–7.

4. See, for instance, T. R. Mitchell, "Matching Motivational Strategies with Organizational Contexts," in L. L. Cummings and B. M. Staw (eds.), *Research in Organizational Behavior*, vol. 19 (Greenwich, CT: JAI Press, 1997), pp. 60–62.

5. A. Maslow, *Motivation and Personality* (New York: Harper & Row, 1954).

6. See, for example, E. E. Lawler III and J. L. Suttle, "A Causal Correlation Test of the Need Hierarchy Concept," *Organizational Behavior and Human Performance*, April 1972, pp. 265–287; D. T. Hall and K. E. Nougaim, "An Examination of Maslow's Need Hierarchy in an Organizational Setting," *Organizational Behavior and Human Performance*, February 1968, pp. 12–35; A. K. Korman, J. H. Greenhaus, and I. J. Badin, "Personnel Attitudes and Motivation," in M. R. Rosenzweig and L. W. Porter (eds.), *Annual Review of Psychology* (Palo Alto, CA: Annual Reviews, 1977), pp. 178–179; and J. Rauschenberger, N. Schmitt, and J. E. Hunter, "A Test of the Need Hierarchy Concept by a Markov Model of Change in Need Strength," *Administrative Science Quarterly*, December 1980, pp. 654–670.

7. C. P. Alderfer, "An Empirical Test of a New Theory of Human Needs," *Organizational Behavior and Human Performance*, May 1969, pp. 142–175.

8. C. P. Schneider and C. P. Alderfer, "Three Studies of Measures of Need Satisfaction in Organizations," *Administrative Science Quarterly*, December 1973, pp. 489–505; and I. Borg and M. Braun, "Work Values in East and West Germany: Different Weights, but Identical Structures," *Journal of Organizational Behavior* 17, special issue (1996), pp. 541–555.

9. M. A. Wahba and L. G. Bridwell, "Maslow Reconsidered: A Review of Research on the Need Hierarchy Theory," *Organizational Behavior and Human Performance*, April 1976, pp. 212–240.

10. D. McGregor, *The Human Side of Enterprise* (New York: McGraw-Hill, 1960). For an updated analysis of Theory X and Theory Y constructs, see R. J. Summers and S. F. Cronshaw, "A Study of McGregor's Theory X, Theory Y and the Influence of Theory X, Theory Y Assumptions on Causal Attributions for Instances of Worker Poor Performance," in S. L. McShane (ed.), Organizational Behavior, *ASAC 1988 Conference Proceedings*, vol. 9, Part 5. Halifax, Nova Scotia, 1988, pp. 115–123.

11. F. Herzberg, B. Mausner, and B. Snyderman, *The Motivation to Work* (New York: Wiley, 1959).

12. D. C. McClelland, *The Achieving Society* (New York: Van Nostrand Reinhold, 1961); J. W. Atkinson and J. O. Raynor, *Motivation and Achievement* (Washington, DC: Winston, 1974); D. C. McClelland, *Power: The Inner Experience* (New York: Irvington, 1975); and M. J. Stahl, *Managerial and Technical Motivation: Assessing Needs for Achievement, Power, and Affiliation* (New York: Praeger, 1986).

13. D. C. McClelland and D. G. Winter, *Motivating Economic Achievement* (New York: The Free Press, 1969); and J. B. Miner, N. R. Smith, and J. S. Bracker, "Role of Entrepreneurial Task Motivation in the Growth of Technologically Innovative Firms: Interpretations from Follow-up Data," *Journal of Applied Psychology*, October 1994, pp. 627–630.

14. D. G. Winter, "The Motivational Dimensions of Leadership: Power, Achievement, and Affiliation," in R. E. Riggio, S. E. Murphy, and F. J. Pirozzolo (eds.), *Multiple Intelligences and Leadership* (Mahwah, NJ: Lawrence Erlbaum, 2002), pp. 119–138.

15. J. B. Miner, *Studies in Management Education* (New York: Springer, 1965).

16. R. de Charms, *Personal Causation: The Internal Affective Determinants of Behavior* (New York: Academic Press, 1968).

17. E. L. Deci, R. Koestner, and R. M. Ryan, "A Meta-analytic Review of Experiments Examining the Effects of Extrinsic Rewards on Intrinsic Motivation," *Psychological Bulletin* 125, no. 6 (1999), pp. 627–668.

18. J. P. Meyer, T. E. Becker, and C. Vandenberghe, "Employee Commitment and Motivation: A Conceptual Analysis and Integrative Model," *Journal of Applied Psychology* 89, no. 6 (2004), pp. 991–1007.

19. E. A. Locke and G. P. Latham, "Building a Practically Useful Theory of Goal Setting and Task Motivation: A 35-Year Odyssey," *American Psychologist* 57, no. 9 (2002), pp. 705–717.

20. J. M. Ivancevich and J. T. McMahon, "The Effects of Goal Setting, External Feedback, and Self-Generated Feedback on Outcome Variables: A Field Experiment," *Academy of Management Journal*, June 1982, pp. 359–372; and E. A. Locke, "Motivation through Conscious Goal Setting," *Applied and Preventive Psychology* 5 (1996), pp. 117–124.

21. H. J. Klein, M. J. Wesson, J. R. Hollenbeck, P. M. Wright, and R. D. DeShon, "The Assessment of Goal Commitment: A Measurement Model Meta-analysis," *Organizational Behavior and Human Decision Processes* 85, no. 1 (2001), pp. 32–55.

22. See R. E. Wood, A. J. Mento, and E. A. Locke, "Task Complexity as a Moderator of Goal Effects: A Meta-analysis," *Journal of Applied Psychology*, August 1987, pp. 416–425; R. Kanfer and P. L. Ackerman, "Motivation and Cognitive Abilities: An Integrative/Aptitude-Treatment Interaction Approach to Skill Acquisition," *Journal of Applied Psychology (monograph)*, vol. 74, 1989, pp. 657–690; T. R. Mitchell and W. S. Silver, "Individual and Group Goals When Workers Are Interdependent: Effects on Task Strategies and Performance," *Journal of Applied Psychology*, April 1990, pp. 185–193; and A. M. O'Leary-Kelly, J. J. Martocchio, and D. D. Frink, "A Review of the Influence of Group Goals on Group

Performance," *Academy of Management Journal*, October 1994, pp. 1285–1301.

23. S. Taylor, "Geert Hofstede Analysis", www.cyborlink.com/besite/saudi-arabia.htm.

24. See, for instance, S. J. Carroll and H. L. Tosi, *Management by Objectives: Applications and Research* (New York: Macmillan, 1973); and R. Rodgers and J. E. Hunter, "Impact of Management by Objectives on Organizational Productivity," *Journal of Applied Psychology*, April 1991, pp. 322–336.

25. See, for instance, C. H. Ford, "MBO: An Idea Whose Time Has Gone?" *Business Horizons*, December 1979, p. 49; R. Rodgers and J. E. Hunter, "Impact of Management by Objectives on Organizational Productivity," *Journal of Applied Psychology*, April 1991, pp. 322–336; R. Rodgers, J. E. Hunter, and D. L. Rogers, "Influence of Top Management Commitment on Management Program Success," *Journal of Applied Psychology*, February 1993, pp. 151–155; and M. Tanikawa, "Fujitsu Decides to Backtrack on Performance-Based Pay," *New York Times*, March 22, 2001, p. W1.

26. A. Bandura, *Self-Efficacy: The Exercise of Control* (New York: Freeman, 1997).

27. A. D. Stajkovic and F. Luthans, "Self-Efficacy and Work-Related Performance: A Meta-analysis," *Psychological Bulletin*, September 1998, pp. 240–261; and A. Bandura, "Cultivate Self-Efficacy for Personal and Organizational Effectiveness," in E. Locke (ed.), *Handbook of Principles of Organizational Behavior* (Malden, MA: Blackwell, 2004), pp. 120–136.

28. A. Bandura and D. Cervone, "Differential Engagement in Self-Reactive Influences in Cognitively-Based Motivation," *Organizational Behavior and Human Decision Processes*, August 1986, pp. 92–113.

29. A. Bandura, *Self-Efficacy: The Exercise of Control* (New York: Freeman, 1997).

30. J. L. Komaki, T. Coombs, and S. Schepman, "Motivational Implications of Reinforcement Theory," in R. M. Steers, L. W. Porter, and G. Bigley (eds.), *Motivation and Work Behavior*, 6th ed. (New York: McGraw-Hill, 1996), pp. 87–107.

31. C. T. Kulik and M. L. Ambrose, "Personal and Situational Determinants of Referent Choice," *Academy of Management Review*, April 1992, pp. 212–237.

32. See, for example, E. Walster, G. W. Walster, and W. G. Scott, *Equity: Theory and Research* (Boston: Allyn & Bacon, 1978); and J. Greenberg, "Cognitive Reevaluation of Outcomes in Response to Underpayment Inequity," *Academy of Management Journal*, March 1989, pp. 174–184.

33. P. S. Goodman and A. Friedman, "An Examination of Adams' Theory of Inequity," *Administrative Science Quarterly*, September 1971, pp. 271–288; R. P. Vecchio, "An Individual-Differences Interpretation of the Conflicting Predictions Generated by Equity Theory and Expectancy Theory," *Journal of Applied Psychology*, August 1981, pp. 470–481; J. Greenberg, "Approaching Equity and Avoiding Inequity in Groups and Organizations," in J. Greenberg and R. L. Cohen (eds.), *Equity and Justice in Social Behavior* (New York: Academic Press, 1982), pp. 389–435; R. T. Mowday, "Equity Theory Predictions of Behavior in Organizations," in R. Steers, L. W. Porter, and G. Bigley (eds.), *Motivation and Work Behavior*, 6th ed. (New York: McGraw-Hill, 1996), pp. 111–131; S. Werner and N. P. Mero, "Fair or Foul? The Effects of External, Internal, and Employee Equity on Changes in

Performance of Major League Baseball Players," *Human Relations*, October 1999, pp. 1291–1312; R. W. Griffeth and S. Gaertner, "A Role for Equity Theory in the Turnover Process: An Empirical Test," *Journal of Applied Social Psychology*, May 2001, pp. 1017–1037; and L. K. Scheer, N. Kumar, and J.-B. E. M. Steenkamp, "Reactions to Perceived Inequity in US and Dutch Interorganizational Relationships," *Academy of Management* 46, no. 3 (2003), pp. 303–316.

34. See, for example, R. C. Huseman, J. D. Hatfield, and E. W. Miles, "A New Perspective on Equity Theory: The Equity Sensitivity Construct," *Academy of Management Journal*, April 1987, pp. 222–234; K. S. Sauley and A. G. Bedeian, "Equity Sensitivity: Construction of a Measure and Examination of Its Psychometric Properties," *Journal of Management* 26, no. 5 (2000), pp. 885–910; M. N. Bing and S. M. Burroughs, "The Predictive and Interactive Effects of Equity Sensitivity in Teamwork-Oriented Organizations," *Journal of Organizational Behavior*, May 2001, pp. 271–290; and J. A. Colquitt, "Does the Justice of One Interact with the Justice of Many? Reactions to Procedural Justice in Teams," *Journal of Applied Psychology* 89, no. 4 (2004), pp. 633–646.

35. See, for instance, J. Greenberg, *The Quest for Justice on the Job* (Thousand Oaks, CA: Sage, 1996); R. Cropanzano and J. Greenberg, "Progress in Organizational Justice: Tunneling through the Maze," in C. L. Cooper and I. T. Robertson (eds.), *International Review of Industrial and Organizational Psychology*, vol. 12 (New York: Wiley, 1997); J. A. Colquitt, D. E. Conlon, M. J. Wesson, C. O. L. H. Porter, and K. Y. Ng, "Justice at the Millennium: A Meta-Analytic Review of the 25 Years of Organizational Justice Research," *Journal of Applied Psychology*, June 2001, pp. 425–445; T. Simons and Q. Roberson, "Why Managers Should Care About Fairness: The Effects of Aggregate Justice Perceptions on Organizational Outcomes," *Journal of Applied Psychology*, June 2003, pp. 432–443; and G. P. Latham and C. C. Pinder, "Work Motivation Theory and Research at the Dawn of the Twenty-First Century," *Annual Review of Psychology* 56 (2005), pp. 485–516.

36. D. P. Skarlicki and R. Folger, "Retaliation in the Workplace: The Roles of Distributive, Procedural, and Interactional Justice," *Journal of Applied Psychology* 82, no. 3 (1997), pp. 434–443.

37. V. H. Vroom, *Work and Motivation* (New York: Wiley, 1964).

38. For criticism, see H. G. Heneman III and D. P. Schwab, "Evaluation of Research on Expectancy Theory Prediction of Employee Performance," *Psychological Bulletin*, July 1972, pp. 1–9; T. R. Mitchell, "Expectancy Models of Job Satisfaction, Occupational Preference and Effort: A Theoretical, Methodological and Empirical Appraisal," *Psychological Bulletin*, November 1974, pp. 1053–1077; and W. Van Eerde and H. Thierry, "Vroom's Expectancy Models and Work-Related Criteria: A Meta-analysis," *Journal of Applied Psychology*, October 1996, pp. 575–586. For support, see L. W. Porter and E. E. Lawler III, *Managerial Attitudes and Performance* (Homewood, IL: Irwin, 1968); and J. J. Donovan, "Work Motivation," in N. Anderson *et al.* (eds.), *Handbook of Industrial, Work & Organizational Psychology*, vol. 2 (Thousand Oaks, CA: Sage, 2001), pp. 56–59.

39. Vroom refers to these three variables as expectancy, instrumentality, and valence, respectively.

40. J. R. Hackman and G. R. Oldham, "Motivation Through the Design of Work: Test of a Theory," *Organizational Behavior and Human Performance*, August 1976, pp. 250–279; and J. R. Hackman and G. R. Oldham, *Work Redesign* (Reading, MA: Addison-Wesley, 1980).

41. J. R. Hackman, "Work Design," in J. R. Hackman and J. L. Suttle (eds.), *Improving Life at Work* (Santa Monica, CA: Goodyear, 1977), p. 129.

42. See "Job Characteristics Theory of Work Redesign," in J. B. Miner, *Theories of Organizational Behavior* (Hinsdale, IL: Dryden Press, 1980), pp. 231–266; B. T. Loher, R. A. Noe, N. L. Moeller, and M. P. Fitzgerald, "A Meta-analysis of the Relation of Job Characteristics to Job Satisfaction," *Journal of Applied Psychology*, May 1985, pp. 280–289; W. H. Glick, G. D. Jenkins, Jr., and N. Gupta, "Method Versus Substance: How Strong Are Underlying Relationships Between Job Characteristics and Attitudinal Outcomes?" *Academy of Management Journal*, September 1986, pp. 441–464; Y. Fried and G. R. Ferris, "The Validity of the Job Characteristics Model: A Review and Meta-analysis," *Personnel Psychology*, Summer 1987, pp. 287–322; S. J. Zaccaro and E. F. Stone, Incremental Validity of an Empirically Based Measure of Job Characteristics," *Journal of Applied Psychology*, May 1988, pp. 245–252; J. R. Rentsch and R. P. Steel, "Testing the Durability of Job Characteristics as Predictors of Absenteeism over a Six-Year Period," *Personnel Psychology*, Spring 1998, pp. 165–190; S. J. Behson, E. R. Eddy, and S. J. Lorenzet, "The Importance of the Critical Psychological States in the Job Characteristics Model: A Meta-analytic and Structural Equations Modeling Examination," *Current Research in Social Psychology*, May 2000, pp. 170–189; and T. A. Judge, "Promote Job Satisfaction Through Mental Challenge," in E. A. Locke (ed.), *Handbook of Principles of Organizational Behavior*, pp. 75–89.

43. T. A. Judge *et al.*, "Job Satisfaction: A Cross-Cultural Review," in N. Anderson, D. S. Ones (eds.), *Handbook of Industrial, Work and Organizational Psychology*, vol. 2 (Thousand Oaks, CA: Sage Publications, 2002), pp. 25–52.

44. C. Ansberry, "In the New Workplace, Jobs Morph to Suit Rapid Pace of Change," *Wall Street Journal*, March 22, 2002, p. A1.

45. J. Ortega, "Job Rotation as a Learning Mechanism," *Management Science*, October 2001, pp. 1361–1370.

46. Hackman and Oldham, *Work Redesign*.

47. Bayt.com Survey, "Employee Motivation in MENA," 2009, www.bayt.com/en/research-report-5601.

48. D. R. Dalton and D. J. Mesch, "The Impact of Flexible Scheduling on Employee Attendance and Turnover," *Administrative Science Quarterly*, June 1990, pp. 370–387; K. S. Kush and L. K. Stroh, "Flextime: Myth or Reality," *Business Horizons*, September–October 1994, p. 53; and L. Golden, "Flexible Work Schedules: What Are We Trading Off to Get Them?" *Monthly Labor Review*, March 2001, pp. 50–55.

49. S. Shellenbarger, "Two People, One Job: It Can Really Work," *Wall Street Journal*, December 7, 1994, p. B1.

50. "Job-Sharing: Widely Offered, Little Used," *Training*, November 1994, p. 12.

51. Shellenbarger, "Two People, One Job," p. B1.

52. See, for example, T. H. Davenport and K. Pearlson, "Two Cheers for the Virtual Office," *Sloan Management Review*, Summer 1998, pp. 61–65; E. J. Hill, B. C. Miller, S. P. Weiner, and J. Colihan, "Influences of the Virtual Office on Aspects of Work and Work/Life Balance," *Personnel Psychology*, Autumn 1998, pp. 667–683; K. E. Pearlson and C. S. Saunders, "There's No Place Like Home: Managing Telecommuting Paradoxes," *Academy of Management Executive*, May 2001, pp. 117–128; S. J. Wells, "Making Telecommuting Work," *HR Magazine*, October 2001, pp. 34–45; and E. J. Hill, M. Ferris, and V. Martinson, "Does It Matter Where You Work? A Comparison of How Three Work Venues (Traditional Office, Virtual Office, and Home Office) Influence Aspects of Work and Personal/Family Life," *Journal of Vocational Behavior* 63, no. 2 (2003), pp. 220–241.

53. Cited in R. W. Judy and C. D'Amico, *Workforce 2020* (Indianapolis: Hudson Institute, 1997), p. 58.

54. *Business Intelligence Middle East*, December, 2009, www.bi-me.com.

55. J. M. Stanton and J. L. Barnes-Farrell, "Effects of Electronic Performance Monitoring on Personal Control, Task Satisfaction, and Task Performance," *Journal of Applied Psychology*, December 1996, pp. 738–745; B. Pappas, "They Spy," *Forbes*, February 8, 1999, p. 47; S. Armour, "More Bosses Keep Tabs on Telecommuters," *USA Today*, July 24, 2001, p. 1B; and D. Buss, "Spies Like Us," *Training*, December 2001, pp. 44–48.

56. See, for example, the increasing body of literature on empowerment, such as: W. A. Randolph, "Re-Thinking Empowerment: Why Is It So Hard to Achieve?" *Organizational Dynamics*, 29, no. 2 (2000), pp. 94–107; K. Blanchard, J. P. Carlos, and W. A. Randolph, *Empowerment Takes More Than a Minute*, 2nd ed. (San Francisco: Berrett-Koehler, 2001); D. P. Ashmos, D. Duchon, R. R. McDaniel, Jr., and J. W. Huonker, "What a Mess! Participation as a Simple Managerial Rule to 'Complexify' Organizations," *Journal of Management Studies*, March 2002, pp. 189–206; and S. E. Seibert, S. R. Silver, and W. A. Randolph, "Taking Empowerment to the Next Level: A Multiple-Level Model of Empowerment, Performance, and Satisfaction" *Academy of Management Journal* 47, no. 3 (2004), pp. 332–349.

57. F. Heller, E. Pusic, G. Strauss, and B. Wilpert, *Organizational Participation: Myth and Reality* (Oxford, UK: Oxford University Press, 1998).

58. J. L. Cotton, *Employee Involvement* (Newbury Park, CA: Sage, 1993), p. 114.

59. See, for example, M. Gilman and P. Marginson, "Negotiating European Works Council: Contours of Constrained Choice," *Industrial Relations Journal*, March 2002, pp. 36–51; J. T. Addison and C. R. Belfield, "What Do We Know About the New European Works Council? Some Preliminary Evidence from Britain," *Scottish Journal of Political Economy*, September 2002, pp. 418–444; and B. Keller, "The European Company Statute: Employee Involvement—And Beyond," *Industrial Relations Journal*, December 2002, pp. 424–445.

60. E. White, "Opportunity Knocks, and It Pays a Lot Better," *Wall Street Journal*, November 13, 2006, p. B3.

61. Bayt.com Survey (2011), "Middle East Salary Survey."

62. Based on J. R. Schuster and P. K. Zingheim, "The New Variable Pay: Key Design Issues," *Compensation & Benefits Review*, March–April 1993, p. 28; K. S. Abosch, "Variable Pay: Do We Have the Basics in Place?" *Compensation & Benefits Review*, July–August 1998, pp. 12–22; and K. M. Kuhn and M. D. Yockey, "Variable Pay as a Risky Choice: Determinants of the Relative Attractiveness of Incentive Plans," *Organizational Behavior and Human Decision Processes*, March 2003, pp. 323–341.

63. G. E. Ledford, Jr., "Paying for the Skills, Knowledge, and Competencies of Knowledge Workers," *Compensation & Benefits Review*, July–August 1995, pp. 55–62; B. Murray and B. Gerhart, "An Empirical Analysis of a Skill-Based Pay Program and Plant Performance Outcomes," *Academy of Management Journal*, February 1998, pp. 68–78; J. R. Thompson and C. W. LeHew, "Skill-Based Pay as an Organizational Innovation," *Review of Public Personnel Administration*, Winter 2000, pp. 20–40; and J. D. Shaw, N. Gupta, A. Mitra, and G. E. Ledford, Jr., "Success and Survival of Skill-Based Pay Plans," *Journal of Management*, February 2005, pp. 28–49.

64. "Tensions of a New Pay Plan," *New York Times*, May 17, 1992, p. F5.

65. See, for instance, D.-O. Kim, "Determinants of the Survival of Gainsharing Programs," *Industrial & Labor Relations Review*, October 1999, pp. 21–42; "Why Gainsharing Works Even Better Today Than in the Past," *HR Focus*, April 2000, pp. 3–5; L. R. Gomez-Mejia, T. M. Welbourne, and R. M. Wiseman, "The Role of Risk Sharing and Risk Taking Under Gainsharing," *Academy of Management Review*, July 2000, pp. 492–507; W. Atkinson, "Incentive Pay Programs That Work in Textile," *Textile World*, February 2001, pp. 55–57; M. Reynolds, "A Cost-Reduction Strategy That May Be Back," *Healthcare Financial Management*, January 2002, pp. 58–64; and M. R. Dixon, L. J. Hayes, and J. Stack, "Changing Conceptions of Employee Compensation," *Journal of Organizational Behavior Management* 23, no. 2–3 (2003), pp. 95–116.

66. A. A. Buchko, "The Effects of Employee Ownership on Employee Attitudes: A Test of Three Theoretical Perspectives," *Work and Occupations* 19, no. 1 (1992), 59–78.

67. J. L. Pierce and C. A. Furo, "Employee Ownership: Implications for Management," *Organizational Dynamics* 18 no. 3 (1990), pp. 32–43.

68. See data in D. Stamps, "A Piece of the Action," *Training*, March 1996, p. 66.

69. C. G. Hanson and W. D. Bell, *Profit Sharing and Profitability: How Profit Sharing Promotes Business Success* (London: Kogan Page, 1987); M. Magnan and S. St-Onge, "Profit-Sharing and Firm Performance: A Comparative and Longitudinal Analysis," paper presented at the 58th annual meeting of the Academy of Management, San Diego, August 1998; and D. D'Art and T. Turner, "Profit Sharing, Firm Performance, and Union Influence in Selected European Countries," *Personnel Review* 33, no. 3 (2004), pp. 335–350.

70. T. M. Welbourne and L. R. Gomez-Mejia, "Gainsharing: A Critical Review and a Future Research Agenda," *Journal of Management* 21, no. 3 (1995), pp. 559–609.

71. C. B. Cadsby, F. Song, and F. Tapon, "Sorting and Incentive Effects of Pay for Performance: An Experimental Investigation," *Academy of Management Journal* 50, no. 2 (2007), pp. 387–405.

72. See, for instance, M. W. Barringer and G. T. Milkovich, "A Theoretical Exploration of the Adoption and Design of Flexible Benefit Plans: A Case of Human Resource Innovation," *Academy of Management Review*, April 1998, pp. 305–324; D. Brown, "Everybody Loves Flex," *Canadian HR Reporter*, November 18, 2002, p. 1; J. Taggart, "Putting Flex Benefits Through Their Paces," *Canadian HR Reporter*, December 2, 2002, p. G3; and N. D. Cole and D. H. Flint, "Perceptions of Distributive and Procedural Justice in Employee Benefits: Flexible Versus Traditional Benefit Plans," *Journal of Managerial Psychology* 19, no. 1 (2004), pp. 19–40.

73. D. A. DeCenzo and S. P. Robbins, *Human Resource Management*, 7th ed. (New York: Wiley, 2002), pp. 346–348.

74. S. E. Markham, K. D. Scott, and G. H. McKee, "Recognizing Good Attendance: A Longitudinal, Quasi-Experimental Field Study," *Personnel Psychology*, Autumn 2002, p. 641; and S. J. Peterson and F. Luthans, "The Impact of Financial and Nonfinancial Incentives on Business Unit Outcomes over Time," *Journal of Applied Psychology* 91, no. 1 (2006), pp. 156–165.

75. M. Littman, "Best Bosses Tell All," *Working Woman*, October 2000, p. 54.

76. Cited in S. Caudron, "The Top 20 Ways to Motivate Employees," *IndustryWeek*, April 3, 1995, pp. 15–16. See also B. Nelson, "Try Praise," *INC.*, September 1996, p. 115.

77. A. D. Stajkovic and F. Luthans, "Differential Effects of Incentive Motivators on Work Performance," *Academy of Management Journal*, June 2001, p. 587. See also F. Luthans and A. D. Stajkovic, "Provide Recognition for Performance Improvement," in E. A. Locke (ed.), *Handbook of Principles of Organizational Behavior* (Malden, MA: Blackwell, 2004), pp. 166–180.

78. Cited in K. J. Dunham, "Amid Shrinking Workplace Morale, Employers Turn to Recognition," *Wall Street Journal*, November 19, 2002, p. B8.

79. Bayt.com Survey, "Employee Motivation Study," 2009.

80. Cited in K. J. Dunham, "Amid Shrinking Workplace Morale, Employers Turn to Recognition," *Wall Street Journal*, November 19, 2002, p. B8.

81. G. Hofstede, "Motivation, Leadership, and Organization: Do American Theories Apply Abroad?" *Organizational Dynamics*, Summer 1980, p. 55.

82. J. K. Giacobbe-Miller, D. J. Miller, and V. I. Victorov, "A Comparison of Russian and US Pay Allocation Decisions, Distributive Justice Judgments, and Productivity Under Different Payment Conditions," *Personnel Psychology*, Spring 1998, pp. 137–163.

83. I. Harpaz, "The Importance of Work Goals: An International Perspective," *Journal of International Business Studies*, First Quarter 1990, pp. 75–93.

84. G. E. Popp, H. J. Davis, and T. T. Herbert, "An International Study of Intrinsic Motivation Composition," *Management International Review*, January 1986, pp. 28–35.

85. P. Peters and L. den Dulk, "Cross Cultural Differences in Managers' Support for Home-Based Telework: A Theoretical Elaboration," *International Journal of Cross Cultural Management*, December 2003, pp. 329–346.

86. S. C. L. Fong and M. A. Shaffer, "The Dimensionality and Determinants of Pay Satisfaction: A Cross-Cultural Investigation of a Group Incentive Plan," *International Journal of Human Resource Management*, June 2003, pp. 559–580.

87. D. Brown, "Everybody Loves Flex.," *Canadian HR Reporter*, December 2002, p. 1.

88. See, for instance, A. Sagie and Z. Aycan, "A Cross-Cultural Analysis of Participative Decision-Making in Organizations," *Human Relations*, April 2003, pp. 453–473; and J. Brockner, "Unpacking Country Effects: On the Need to Operationalize the Psychological Determinants of Cross-National

Differences," in R. M. Kramer and B. M. Staw (eds.), *Research in Organizational Behavior*, vol. 25 (Oxford, UK: Elsevier, 2003), pp. 336–340.

89. C. Robert, T. M. Probst, J. J. Martocchio, R. Drasgow, and J. J. Lawler, "Empowerment and Continuous Improvement in the United States, Mexico, Poland, and India: Predicting Fit on the Basis of the Dimensions of Power Distance and Individualism," *Journal of Applied Psychology*, October 2000, pp. 643–658.

90. E. S. Hasham, "The Extent to which Satisfaction is a Prerequisite to Employee Performance and Productivity in Institutions of Higher Education: A Case Study of Notre Dame University, Lebanon," Ph.D. Thesis, Leicester University, 2003.

Chapter 6

1. See, for instance, C. D. Fisher and N. M. Ashkanasy, "The Emerging Role of Emotions in Work Life: An Introduction," *Journal of Organizational Behavior*, Special Issue 2000, pp. 123–129; N. M. Ashkanasy, C. E. J. Hartel, and W. J. Zerbe (eds.), *Emotions in the Workplace: Research, Theory, and Practice* (Westport, CT: Quorum Books, 2000); N. M. Ashkanasy and C. S. Daus, "Emotion in the Workplace: The New Challenge for Managers," *Academy of Management Executive*, February 2002, pp. 76–86; and N. M. Ashkanasy, C. E. J. Hartel, and C. S. Daus, "Diversity and Emotion: The New Frontiers in Organizational Behavior Research," *Journal of Management* 28, no. 3 (2002), pp. 307–338.

2. See, for example, L. L. Putnam and D. K. Mumby, "Organizations, Emotion and the Myth of Rationality," in S. Fineman (ed.), *Emotion in Organizations* (Thousand Oaks, CA: Sage, 1993), pp. 36–57; and J. Martin, K. Knopoff, and C. Beckman, "An Alternative to Bureaucratic Impersonality and Emotional Labor: Bounded Emotionality at the Body Shop," *Administrative Science Quarterly*, June 1998, pp. 429–469.

3. B. E. Ashforth and R. H. Humphrey, "Emotion in the Workplace: A Reappraisal," *Human Relations*, February 1995, pp. 97–125.

4. S. G. Barsade and D. E. Gibson, "Why Does Affect Matter in Organizations?" *Academy of Management Perspectives*, February 2007, pp. 36–59.

5. See N. H. Frijda, "Moods, Emotion Episodes and Emotions," in M. Lewis and J. M. Haviland (eds.), *Handbook of Emotions* (New York: Guilford Press, 1993), pp. 381–403.

6. H. M. Weiss and R. Cropanzano, "Affective Events Theory: A Theoretical Discussion of the Structure, Causes and Consequences of Affective Experiences at Work," in B. M. Staw and L. L. Cummings (eds.), *Research in Organizational Behavior*, vol. 18 (Greenwich, CT: JAI Press, 1996), pp. 17–19.

7. Frijda, "Moods, Emotion Episodes and Emotions," p. 381.

8. See Ekman and Davidson (eds.), *The Nature of Emotions: Fundamental Questions* (Oxford, UK: Oxford University Press, 1994).

9. See, for example, P. Ekman, "An Argument for Basic Emotions," *Cognition and Emotion*, May/July 1992, pp. 169–200; C. E. Izard, "Basic Emotions, Relations Among Emotions, and Emotion–Cognition Relations," *Psychological Bulletin*, November 1992, pp. 561–565; and J. L. Tracy and R. W. Robins, "Emerging Insights into the Nature and Function of Pride," *Current Directions in Psychological Science* 16, no. 3 (2007), pp. 147–150.

10. R. C. Solomon, "Back to Basics: On the Very Idea of 'Basic Emotions,'" *Journal for the Theory of Social Behaviour* 32, no. 2 (June 2002), pp. 115–144.

11. R. Descartes, *The Passions of the Soul* (Indianapolis: Hackett, 1989).

12. P. Ekman, *Emotions Revealed: Recognizing Faces and Feelings to Improve Communication and Emotional Life* (New York: Times Books/Henry Holt and Co., 2003).

13. P. R. Shaver, H. J. Morgan, and S. J. Wu, "Is Love a 'Basic' Emotion?" *Personal Relationships* 3, no. 1 (March 1996), pp. 81–96.

14. Solomon, "Back to Basics."

15. Weiss and Cropanzano, "Affective Events Theory," pp. 20–22.

16. D. Watson, L. A. Clark, and A. Tellegen, "Development and Validation of Brief Measures of Positive and Negative Affect: The PANAS Scales," *Journal of Personality and Social Psychology*, 1988, pp. 1063–1070.

17. A. Ben-Ze'ev, *The Subtlety of Emotions* (Cambridge, MA: MIT Press, 2000), p. 94.

18. "Flight Attendant War Stories . . . Stewardess," AboutMyJob.com, www.aboutmyjob.com/main.php3?action=displayarticle&artid=2111.

19. Cited in Ibid., p. 99.

20. J. T. Cacioppo and W. L. Gardner, "Emotion," in *Annual Review of Psychology*, vol. 50 (Palo Alto, CA: Annual Reviews, 1999), pp. 191–214.

21. FYI Health Writer, "Mood Linked to Beginning of Day," May, 2011 www.fyiliving.com/research/mood-linked-to-beginning-of-day.

22. L. Cosmides and J. Tooby, "Evolutionary Psychology and the Emotions," in M. Lewis and J. M. Haviland-Jones (eds.), *Handbook of Emotions*, 2nd ed. (New York: Guilford Press, 2000), pp. 91–115.

23. R. J. Larsen and E. Diener, "Affect Intensity as an Individual Difference Characteristic: A Review," *Journal of Research in Personality* 21 (1987), pp. 1–39.

24. Information in this section taken from D. Watson, *Mood and Temperament* (New York: Guilford Press, 2000).

25. Ibid., p. 100.

26. Ibid., p. 73.

27. J. A. Fuller, J. M. Stanton, G. G. Fisher, C. Spitzmüller, S. S. Russell, and P. C. Smith, "A Lengthy Look at the Daily Grind: Time Series Analysis of Events, Mood, Stress, and Satisfaction," *Journal of Applied Psychology* 88, no. 6 (December 2003), pp. 1019–1033.

28. M. Isen, "Positive Affect as a Source of Human Strength," in L. G. Aspinwall and U. Staudinger (eds.), *The Psychology of Human Strengths* (Washington, DC: American Psychological Association, 2003), pp. 179–195.

29. Watson, *Mood and Temperament* (2000).

30. *Sleep in America Poll* (Washington, DC: National Sleep Foundation, 2005).

31. M. Lavidor, A. Weller, and H. Babkoff, "How Sleep Is Related to Fatigue," *British Journal of Health Psychology* 8 (2003), pp. 95–105; and J. J. Pilcher and E. Ott, "The Relationships Between Sleep and Measures of Health and Well-Being in College Students: A Repeated Measures Approach," *Behavioral Medicine* 23 (1998), pp. 170–178.

32. E. K. Miller and J. D. Cohen, "An Integrative Theory of Prefrontal Cortex Function," *Annual Review of Neuroscience* 24 (2001), pp. 167–202.

33. P. R. Giacobbi, H. A. Hausenblas, and N. Frye, "A Naturalistic Assessment of the Relationship Between Personality, Daily Life Events, Leisure-Time Exercise, and Mood," *Psychology of Sport & Exercise* 6, no. 1 (January 2005), pp. 67–81.

34. L. L. Carstensen, M. Pasupathi, M. Ulrich, and J. R. Nesselroade, "Emotional Experience in Everyday Life Across the Adult Life Span," *Journal of Personality and Social Psychology* 79, no. 4 (2000), pp. 644–655.

35. K. Deaux, "Sex Differences," in M. R. Rosenzweig and L. W. Porter (eds.), *Annual Review of Psychology*, vol. 26 (Palo Alto, CA: Annual Reviews, 1985), pp. 48–82; M. LaFrance and M. Banaji, "Toward a Reconsideration of the Gender–Emotion Relationship," in M. Clark (ed.), *Review of Personality and Social Psychology*, vol. 14 (Newbury Park, CA: Sage, 1992), pp. 178–197; and A. M. Kring and A. H. Gordon, "Sex Differences in Emotion: Expression, Experience, and Physiology," *Journal of Personality and Social Psychology*, March 1998, pp. 686–703.

36. L. R. Brody and J. A. Hall, "Gender and Emotion," in M. Lewis and J. M. Haviland (eds.), *Handbook of Emotions* (New York: Guilford Press, 1993), pp. 447–460; M. G. Gard and A. M. Kring, "Sex Differences in the Time Course of Emotion," *Emotion* 7, no. 2 (2007), pp. 429–437; and M. Grossman and W. Wood, "Sex Differences in Intensity of Emotional Experience: A Social Role Interpretation," *Journal of Personality and Social Psychology*, November 1992, pp. 1010–1022.

37. N. James, "Emotional Labour: Skill and Work in the Social Regulations of Feelings," *Sociological Review*, February 1989, pp. 15–42; A. Hochschild, *The Second Shift* (New York: Viking, 1989); and F. M. Deutsch, "Status, Sex, and Smiling: The Effect of Role on Smiling in Men and Women," *Personality and Social Psychology Bulletin*, September 1990, pp. 531–540.

38. A. Rafaeli, "When Clerks Meet Customers: A Test of Variables Related to Emotional Expression on the Job," *Journal of Applied Psychology*, June 1989, pp. 385–393; and LaFrance and Banaji, "Toward a Reconsideration of the Gender–Emotion Relationship."

39. See J. A. Morris and D. C. Feldman, "Managing Emotions in the Workplace," *Journal of Managerial Issues* 9, no. 3 (1997), pp. 257–274; S. Mann, *Hiding What We Feel, Faking What We Don't: Understanding the Role of Your Emotions at Work* (New York: HarperCollins, 1999); and S. M. Kruml and D. Geddes, "Catching Fire Without Burning Out: Is There an Ideal Way to Perform Emotion Labor?" in N. M. Ashkansay, C. E. J. Hartel, and W. J. Zerbe, *Emotions in the Workplace* (New York: Quorum Books, 2000), pp. 177–188.

40. P. Ekman, W. V. Friesen, and M. O'Sullivan, "Smiles When Lying," in P. Ekman and E. L. Rosenberg (eds.), *What the Face Reveals: Basic and Applied Studies of Spontaneous Expression Using the Facial Action Coding System (FACS)* (London: Oxford University Press, 1997), pp. 201–216.

41. A. Grandey, "Emotion Regulation in the Workplace: A New Way to Conceptualize Emotional Labor," *Journal of Occupational Health Psychology* 5, no. 1 (2000), pp. 95–110; and R. Cropanzano, D. E. Rupp, and Z. S. Byrne, "The Relationship of Emotional Exhaustion to Work Attitudes, Job Performance, and Organizational Citizenship Behavior," *Journal of Applied Psychology*, February 2003, pp. 160–169.

42. A. R. Hochschild, "Emotion Work, Feeling Rules, and Social Structure," *American Journal of Sociology*, November 1979, pp. 551–575; W.-C. Tsai, "Determinants and Consequences

of Employee Displayed Positive Emotions," *Journal of Management* 27, no. 4 (2001), pp. 497–512; M. W. Kramer and J. A. Hess, "Communication Rules for the Display of Emotions in Organizational Settings," *Management Communication Quarterly*, August 2002, pp. 66–80; and J. M. Diefendorff and E. M. Richard, "Antecedents and Consequences of Emotional Display Rule Perceptions," *Journal of Applied Psychology*, April 2003, pp. 284–294.

43. Solomon, "Back to Basics."

44. C. M. Brotheridge and R. T. Lee, "Development and Validation of the Emotional Labour Scale," *Journal of Occupational & Organizational Psychology* 76, no. 3 (September 2003), pp. 365–379.

45. T. M. Glomb, J. D. Kammeyer-Mueller, and M. Rotundo, "Emotional Labor Demands and Compensating Wage Differentials," *Journal of Applied Psychology* 89, no. 4 (August 2004), pp. 700–714.

46. H. M. Weiss and R. Cropanzano, "An Affective Events Approach to Job Satisfaction," *Research in Organizational Behavior* 18 (1996), pp. 1–74.

47. J. Basch and C. D. Fisher, "Affective Events–Emotions Matrix: A Classification of Work Events and Associated Emotions," in N. M. Ashkanasy, C. E. J. Hartel, and W. J. Zerbe (eds.), *Emotions in the Workplace* (Westport, CT: Quorum Books, 2000), pp. 36–48.

48. See, for example, H. M. Weiss and R. Cropanzano, "Affective Events Theory"; and C. D. Fisher, "Antecedents and Consequences of Real-Time Affective Reactions at Work," *Motivation and Emotion*, March 2002, pp. 3–30.

49. Based on H. M. Weiss and R. Cropanzano, "Affective Events Theory," p. 42.

50. N. M. Ashkanasy, C. E. J. Hartel, and C. S. Daus, "Diversity and Emotion: The New Frontiers in Organizational Behavior Research," *Journal of Management* 28, no. 3 (2002), p. 324.

51. This section is based on Daniel Goleman, *Emotional Intelligence* (New York: Bantam, 1995); P. Salovey and D. Grewal, "The Science of Emotional Intelligence," *Current Directions in Psychological Science* 14, no. 6 (2005), pp. 281–285; M. Davies, L. Stankov, and R. D. Roberts, "Emotional Intelligence: In Search of an Elusive Construct," *Journal of Personality and Social Psychology*, October 1998, pp. 989–1015; D. Geddes and R. R. Callister, "Crossing the Line(s): A Dual Threshold Model of Anger in Organizations," *Academy of Management Review* 32, no. 3 (2007), pp. 721–746; and J. Ciarrochi, J. P. Forgas, and J. D. Mayer (eds.), *Emotional Intelligence in Everyday Life* (Philadelphia: Psychology Press, 2001).

52. J. Freedman, J. Morrison & A. Olsson, "Leadership Success and Emotional Intelligence in the Middle East," 2010, www.6seconds.org/blog/2010/08/leadership-success-and-emotional-intelligence-in-the-middle-east.

53. F. I. Greenstein, *The Presidential Difference: Leadership Style from FDR to Clinton* (Princeton, NJ: Princeton University Press, 2001).

54. K. S. Law, C. Wong, and L. J. Song, "The Construct and Criterion Validity of Emotional Intelligence and Its Potential Utility for Management Studies," *Journal of Applied Psychology* 89, no. 3 (2004), pp. 483–496.

55. H. A. Elfenbein and N. Ambady, "Predicting Workplace Outcomes from the Ability to Eavesdrop on Feelings," *Journal of Applied Psychology* 87, no. 5 (October 2002), pp. 963–971.

56. D. L. Van Rooy and C. Viswesvaran, "Emotional Intelligence: A Meta-analytic Investigation of Predictive Validity and Nomological Net," *Journal of Vocational Behavior* 65, no. 1 (August 2004), pp. 71–95.

57. J. M. Conte, "A Review and Critique of Emotional Intelligence Measures," *Journal of Organizational Behavior* 26, no. 4 (June 2005), pp. 433–440; and M. Davies, L. Stankov, and R. D. Roberts, "Emotional Intelligence: In Search of an Elusive Construct," *Journal of Personality and Social Psychology* 75, no. 4 (1998), pp. 989–1015.

58. T. Decker, "Is Emotional Intelligence a Viable Concept?" *Academy of Management Review* 28, no. 2 (April 2003), pp. 433–440; and Davies, Stankov, and Roberts, "Emotional Intelligence: In Search of an Elusive Construct."

59. L. M. J. Spencer, D. C. McClelland, and S. Kelner, *Competency Assessment Methods: History and State of the Art* (Boston: Hay/McBer, 1997).

60. J. Park and M. R. Banaji, "Mood and Heuristics: The Influence of Happy and Sad States on Sensitivity and Bias in Stereotyping," *Journal of Personality and Social Psychology* 78, no. 6 (2000), pp. 1005–1023.

61. See A. M. Isen, "Positive Affect and Decision Making," in M. Lewis and J. M. Haviland-Jones (eds.), *Handbook of Emotions*, 2nd ed. (New York: Guilford, 2000), pp. 261–277.

62. L. B. Alloy and L. Y. Abramson, "Judgement of Contingency in Depressed and Nondepressed Students: Sadder but Wiser?" *Journal of Experimental Psychology: General* 108 (1979), pp. 441–485.

63. N. Ambady and H. M. Gray, "On Being Sad and Mistaken: Mood Effects on the Accuracy of Thin-Slice Judgments," *Journal of Personality and Social Psychology* 83, no. 4 (2002), pp. 947–961.

64. M. Isen, "On the Relationship Between Affect and Creative Problem Solving," in S. W. Russ (ed.), *Affect, Creative Experience and Psychological Adjustment* (Philadelphia, PA: Brunner/Mazel, 1999), pp. 3–17; and S. Lyubomirsky, L. King, and E. Diener, "The Benefits of Frequent Positive Affect: Does Happiness Lead to Success?" *Psychological Bulletin* 131, no. 6 (2005), pp. 803–855.

65. M. J. Grawitch, D. C. Munz, and E. K. Elliott, "Promoting Creativity in Temporary Problem-Solving Groups: The Effects of Positive Mood and Autonomy in Problem Definition on Idea-Generating Performance," *Group Dynamics* 7, no. 3 (September 2003), pp. 200–213.

66. S. Lyubomirsky, L. King, and E. Diener, "The Benefits of Frequent Positive Affect: Does Happiness Lead to Success?" *Psychological Bulletin* 131, no. 6 (2005), pp. 803–855.

67. N. Madjar, G. R. Oldham, and M. G. Pratt, "There's No Place Like Home? The Contributions of Work and Nonwork Creativity Support to Employees' Creative Performance," *Academy of Management Journal* 45, no. 4 (2002), pp. 757–767.

68. T. N. Hashem, "Impact of Managers' Emotional Intelligence on Marketing Creativity in Jordan Commercial Banks," *Innovative Marketing* 6, no. 3 (2010), pp. 78–86.

69. J. M. George and J. Zhou, "Understanding When Bad Moods Foster Creativity and Good Ones Don't: The Role of Context and Clarity of Feelings," *Journal of Applied Psychology* 87, no. 4 (August 2002), pp. 687–697; and J. P. Forgas and J. M. George, "Affective Influences on Judgments and Behavior in Organizations: An Information Processing Perspective," *Organizational Behavior and Human Decision Processes* 86, no. 1 (2001), pp. 3–34.

70. L. L. Martin, "Mood as Input: A Configural View of Mood Effects," in L. L. Martin and G. L. Clore (eds.), *Theories of Mood and Cognition: A User's Guidebook* (Mahwah, NJ: Lawrence Erlbaum, 2001), pp. 135–157.

71. A. Erez and A. M. Isen, "The Influence of Positive Affect on the Components of Expectancy Motivation," *Journal of Applied Psychology* 87, no. 6 (2002), pp. 1055–1067.

72. R. Ilies and T. A. Judge, "Goal Regulation Across Time: The Effect of Feedback and Affect," *Journal of Applied Psychology* 90, no. 3 (May 2005), pp. 453–467.

73. K. M. Lewis, "When Leaders Display Emotion: How Followers Respond to Negative Emotional Expression of Male and Female Leaders," *Journal of Organizational Behavior*, March 2000, pp. 221–234; and J. M. George, "Emotions and Leadership: The Role of Emotional Intelligence," *Human Relations*, August 2000, pp. 1027–1055.

74. George, "Trait and State Affect," p. 162.

75. Ashforth and Humphrey, "Emotion in the Workplace," p. 116.

76. G. A. Van Kleef, C. K. W. De Dreu, and A. S. R. Manstead, "The Interpersonal Effects of Emotions in Negotiations: A Motivated Information Processing Approach," *Journal of Personality and Social Psychology* 87, no. 4 (2004), pp. 510–528; and G. A. Van Kleef, C. K. W. De Dreu, and A. S. R. Manstead, "The Interpersonal Effects of Anger and Happiness in Negotiations," *Journal of Personality and Social Psychology* 86, no. 1 (2004), pp. 57–76.

77. W.-C. Tsai and Y.-M. Huang, "Mechanisms Linking Employee Affective Delivery and Customer Behavioral Intentions," *Journal of Applied Psychology*, October 2002, pp. 1001–1008.

78. A. A. Grandey, "When 'the Show Must Go On': Surface Acting and Deep Acting as Determinants of Emotional Exhaustion and Peer-Rated Service Delivery," *Academy of Management Journal*, February 2003, pp. 86–96.

79. See P. B. Barker and A. A. Grandey, "Service with a Smile and Encounter Satisfaction: Emotional Contagion and Appraisal Mechanisms," *Academy of Management Journal* 49, no. 6 (2006), pp. 1229–1238; and S. D. Pugh, "Service with a Smile: Emotional Contagion in the Service Encounter," *Academy of Management Journal*, October 2001, pp. 1018–1027.

80. D. E. Rupp and S. Spencer, "When Customers Lash Out: The Effects of Customer Interactional Injustice on Emotional Labor and the Mediating Role of Emotions, *Journal of Applied Psychology* 91, no. 4 (2006), pp. 971–978; and Tsai and Huang, "Mechanisms Linking Employee Affective Delivery and Customer Behavioral Intentions."

81. R. Ilies and T. A. Judge, "Understanding the Dynamic Relationships Among Personality, Mood, and Job Satisfaction: A Field Experience Sampling Study," *Organizational Behavior and Human Decision Processes* 89 (2002), pp. 1119–1139.

82. R. Rau, "Job Strain or Healthy Work: A Question of Task Design," *Journal of Occupational Health Psychology* 9, no. 4 (October 2004), pp. 322–338; and R. Rau and A. Triemer, "Overtime in Relation to Blood Pressure and Mood During Work, Leisure, and Night Time," *Social Indicators Research* 67, no. 1–2 (June 2004), pp. 51–73.

83. T. A. Judge and R. Ilies, "Affect and Job Satisfaction: A Study of Their Relationship at Work and at Home," *Journal of Applied Psychology* 89 (2004), pp. 661–673.

84. See R. J. Bennett and S. L. Robinson, "Development of a Measure of Workplace Deviance," *Journal of Applied Psychology*, June 2000, pp. 349–360. See also P. R. Sackett and C. J. DeVore, "Counterproductive Behaviors at Work," in N. Anderson, D. S. Ones, H. K. Sinangil, and C. Viswesvaran (eds.), *Handbook of Industrial, Work & Organizational Psychology*, vol. 1 (Thousand Oaks, CA: Sage, 2001), pp. 145–164.

85. A. G. Bedeian, "Workplace Envy," *Organizational Dynamics*, Spring 1995, p. 50; and Ben-Ze'ev, *The Subtlety of Emotions*, pp. 281–326.

86. Bedeian, "Workplace Envy," p. 54.

87. K. Lee and N. J. Allen, "Organizational Citizenship Behavior and Workplace Deviance: The Role of Affect and Cognition," *Journal of Applied Psychology* 87, no. 1 (2002), pp. 131–142; and T. A. Judge, B. A. Scott, and R. Ilies, "Hostility, Job Attitudes, and Workplace Deviance: Test of a Multilevel Model," *Journal of Applied Psychology* 91, no. 1 (2006) 126–138.

88. A. M. Isen, A. A. Labroo, and P. Durlach, "An Influence of Product and Brand Name on Positive Affect: Implicit and Explicit Measures," *Motivation & Emotion* 28, no. 1 (March 2004), pp. 43–63.

89. T. Sy, S. Côté, and R. Saavedra, "The Contagious Leader: Impact of the Leader's Mood on the Mood of Group Members, Group Affective Tone, and Group Processes," *Journal of Applied Psychology* 90, no. 2 (2005), pp. 295–305.

90. M. Eid and E. Diener, "Norms for Experiencing Emotions in Different Cultures: Inter- and International Differences," *Journal of Personality & Social Psychology* 81, no. 5 (2001), pp. 869–885.

91. S. Oishi, E. Diener, and C. Napa Scollon, "Cross-Situational Consistency of Affective Experiences Across Cultures," *Journal of Personality & Social Psychology* 86, no. 3 (2004), pp. 460–472.

92. Eid and Diener, "Norms for Experiencing Emotions in Different Cultures."

93. H. A. Elfenbein and N. Ambady, "When Familiarity Breeds Accuracy: Cultural Exposure and Facial Emotional Recognition," *Journal of Personality and Social Psychology* 85, no. 2 (2003), pp. 276–290.

94. D. Matsumoto, "Cross-Cultural Psychology in the 21st Century," http://teachpsych.lemoyne.edu/teachpsych/faces/script/Ch05.htm.

95. S. Nelton, "Emotions in the Workplace," *Nation's Business*, February 1996, p. 25.

96. H. Liao and A. Chuang, "A Multilevel Investigation of Factors Influencing Employee Service Performance and Customer Outcomes," *Academy of Management Journal* 47, no. 1 (2004), pp. 41–58.

97. D. J. Beal, J. P. Trougakos, H. M. Weiss, and S. G. Green, "Episodic Processes in Emotional Labor: Perceptions of Affective Delivery and Regulation Strategies," *Journal of Applied Psychology* 91, no. 5 (2006), pp. 1057–1065.

98. Press release, "BMW Group Middle East reports sustained growth in the first quarter of 2011," April 2011, www.albawaba.com/bmw-group-middle-east-reports-sustained-growth-first-quarter-2011.

99. D. Zapf and M. Holz, "On the Positive and Negative Effects of Emotion Work in Organizations," *European Journal of Work and Organizational Psychology* 15, no. 1 (2006), pp. 1–28.

Chapter 7

1. L. R. Sayles, "Work Group Behavior and the Larger Organization," in C. Arensburg, *et al.* (eds.), *Research in Industrial Relations* (New York: Harper & Row, 1957), pp. 131–145.

2. J. F. McGrew, J. G. Bilotta, and J. M. Deeney, "Software Team Formation and Decay: Extending the Standard Model for Small Groups," *Small Group Research* 30, no. 2, (1999), pp. 209–234.

3. B. W. Tuckman, "Developmental Sequences in Small Groups," *Psychological Bulletin*, June 1965, pp. 384–399; B. W. Tuckman and M. C. Jensen, "Stages of Small-Group Development Revisited," *Group and Organizational Studies*, December 1977, pp. 419–427; and M. F. Maples, "Group Development: Extending Tuckman's Theory," *Journal for Specialists in Group Work*, Fall 1988, pp. 17–23; and K. Vroman and J. Kovacich, "Computer-Mediated Interdisciplinary Teams: Theory and Reality," *Journal of Interprofessional Care* 16, no. 2 (2002), pp. 159–170.

4. J. F. George and L. M. Jessup, "Groups over Time: What Are We Really Studying?" *International Journal of Human-Computer Studies* 47, no. 3 (1997), pp. 497–511.

5. R. C. Ginnett, "The Airline Cockpit Crew," in J. R. Hackman (ed.), *Groups That Work (and Those That Don't)* (San Francisco: Jossey-Bass, 1990).

6. C. J. G. Gersick, "Time and Transition in Work Teams: Toward a New Model of Group Development," *Academy of Management Journal*, March 1988, pp. 9–41; C. J. G. Gersick, "Marking Time: Predictable Transitions in Task Groups," *Academy of Management Journal*, June 1989, pp. 274–309; M. J. Waller, J. M. Conte, C. B. Gibson, and M. A. Carpenter, "The Effect of Individual Perceptions of Deadlines on Team Performance," *Academy of Management Review*, October 2001, pp. 586–600; and A. Chang, P. Bordia, and J. Duck, "Punctuated Equilibrium and Linear Progression: Toward a New Understanding of Group Development," *Academy of Management Journal*, February 2003, pp. 106–117; see also H. Arrow, M. S. Poole, K. B. Henry, S. Wheelan, and R. Moreland, "Time, Change, and Development: The Temporal Perspective on Groups," *Small Group Research*, February 2004, pp. 73–105.

7. A. Seers and S. Woodruff, "Temporal Pacing in Task Forces: Group Development or Deadline Pressure?" *Journal of Management* 23, no. 2 (1997), pp. 169–187.

8. See D. M. Rousseau, *Psychological Contracts in Organizations: Understanding Written and Unwritten Agreements* (Thousand Oaks, CA: Sage, 1995); E. W. Morrison and S. L. Robinson, "When Employees Feel Betrayed: A Model of How Psychological Contract Violation Develops," *Academy of Management Review*, April 1997, pp. 226–256; D. Rousseau and R. Schalk (eds.), *Psychological Contracts in Employment: Cross-Cultural Perspectives* (San Francisco: Jossey-Bass, 2000); L. Sels, M. Janssens, and I. Van den Brande, "Assessing the Nature of Psychological Contracts: A Validation of Six Dimensions," *Journal of Organizational Behavior*, June 2004, pp. 461–488; and C. Hui, C. Lee, and D. M. Rousseau, "Psychological Contract and Organizational Citizenship Behavior in China: Investigating Generalizability and Instrumentality," *Journal of Applied Psychology*, April 2004, pp. 311–321.

9. See M. F. Peterson *et al.*, "Role Conflict, Ambiguity, and Overload: A 21-Nation Study," *Academy of Management Journal*, April 1995, pp. 429–452; and I. H. Settles, R. M. Sellers, and A. Damas, Jr., "One Role or Two? The Function of Psychological Separation in Role Conflict," *Journal of Applied Psychology*, June 2002, pp. 574–582.

10. P. G. Zimbardo, C. Haney, W. C. Banks, and D. Jaffe, "The Mind Is a Formidable Jailer: A Pirandellian Prison," *New York Times*, April 8, 1973, pp. 38–60; and C. Haney and P. G. Zimbardo, "Social Roles and Role-Playing: Observations from the Stanford Prison Study," *Behavioral and Social Science Teacher*, January 1973, pp. 25–45.

11. For a review of the research on group norms, see J. R. Hackman, "Group Influences on Individuals in Organizations," in M. D. Dunnette and L. M. Hough (eds.), *Handbook of Industrial & Organizational Psychology*, 2nd ed., vol. 3 (Palo Alto, CA: Consulting Psychologists Press, 1992), pp. 235–250. For a more recent discussion, see M. G. Ehrhart and S. E. Naumann, "Organizational Citizenship Behavior in Work Groups: A Group Norms Approach," *Journal of Applied Psychology*, December 2004, pp. 960–974.

12. Adapted from P. S. Goodman, E. Ravlin, and M. Schminke, "Understanding Groups in Organizations," in L. L. Cummings and B. M. Staw (eds.), *Research in Organizational Behavior*, vol. 9 (Greenwich, CT: JAI Press, 1987), p. 159.

13. C. A. Kiesler and S. B. Kiesler, *Conformity* (Reading, MA: Addison-Wesley, 1969).

14. Ibid., p. 27.

15. S. E. Asch, "Effects of Group Pressure upon the Modification and Distortion of Judgments," in H. Guetzkow (ed.), *Groups, Leadership and Men* (Pittsburgh: Carnegie Press, 1951), pp. 177–190; and S. E. Asch, "Studies of Independence and Conformity: A Minority of One Against a Unanimous Majority," *Psychological Monographs: General and Applied* 70, no. 9 (1956), pp. 1–70.

16. R. Bond and P. B. Smith, "Culture and Conformity: A Meta-analysis of Studies Using Asch's (1952, 1956) Line Judgment Task," *Psychological Bulletin*, January 1996, pp. 111–137.

17. See S. L. Robinson and R. J. Bennett, "A Typology of Deviant Workplace Behaviors: A Multidimensional Scaling Study," *Academy of Management Journal*, April 1995, pp. 555–572; S. L. Robinson and A. M. O'Leary-Kelly, "Monkey See, Monkey Do: The Influence of Work Groups on the Antisocial Behavior of Employees," *Academy of Management Journal*, December 1998, pp. 658–672; and R. J. Bennett and S. L. Robinson, "The Past, Present, and Future of Workplace Deviance," in J. Greenberg (ed.), *Organizational Behavior: The State of the Science*, 2nd ed. (Mahwah, NJ: Erlbaum, 2003), pp. 237–271.

18. C. M. Pearson, L. M. Andersson, and C. L. Porath, "Assessing and Attacking Workplace Civility," *Organizational Dynamics* 29, no. 2 (2000), p. 130; see also C. Pearson, L. M. Andersson, and C. L. Porath, "Workplace Incivility," in S. Fox and P. E. Spector (eds.), *Counterproductive Work Behavior: Investigations of Actors and Targets* (Washington, DC: American Psychological Association, 2005), pp. 177–200.

19. Robinson and O'Leary-Kelly, "Monkey See, Monkey Do."

20. See R. S. Feldman, *Social Psychology*, 3rd ed. (Upper Saddle River, NJ: Prentice Hall, 2001), pp. 464–465.

21. Cited in Hackman, "Group Influences on Individuals in Organizations," p. 236.

22. O. J. Harvey and C. Consalvi, "Status and Conformity to Pressures in Informal Groups," *Journal of Abnormal and Social Psychology*, Spring 1960, pp. 182–187.

23. See J. M. Levine and R. L. Moreland, "Progress in Small Group Research," in J. T. Spence, J. M. Darley, and D. J. Foss (eds.), *Annual Review of Psychology*, vol. 41 (Palo Alto, CA: Annual Reviews, 1990), pp. 585–634; S. D. Silver, B. P. Cohen, and J. H. Crutchfield, "Status Differentiation and Information Exchange in Face-to-Face and Computer-Mediated Idea Generation," *Social Psychology Quarterly*, 1994, pp. 108–123; and J. M. Twenge, "Changes in Women's Assertiveness in Response to Status and Roles: A Cross-Temporal Meta-analysis, 1931–1993," *Journal of Personality and Social Psychology*, July 2001, pp. 133–145.

24. J. Greenberg, "Equity and Workplace Status: A Field Experiment," *Journal of Applied Psychology*, November 1988, pp. 606–613.

25. E. J. Thomas and C. F. Fink, "Effects of Group Size," *Psychological Bulletin*, July 1963, pp. 371–384; A. P. Hare, *Handbook of Small Group Research* (New York: The Free Press, 1976); and M. E. Shaw, *Group Dynamics: The Psychology of Small Group Behavior*, 3rd ed. (New York: McGraw-Hill, 1981).

26. G. H. Seijts and G. P. Latham, "The Effects of Goal Setting and Group Size on Performance in a Social Dilemma," *Canadian Journal of Behavioural Science* 32, no. 2 (2000), pp. 104–116.

27. See, for instance, D. R. Comer, "A Model of Social Loafing in Real Work Groups," *Human Relations*, June 1995, pp. 647–667; S. M. Murphy, S. J. Wayne, R. C. Liden, and B. Erdogan, "Understanding Social Loafing: The Role of Justice Perceptions and Exchange Relationships," *Human Relations*, January 2003, pp. 61–84; and R. C. Liden, S. J. Wayne, R. A. Jaworski, and N. Bennett, "Social Loafing: A Field Investigation," *Journal of Management*, April 2004, pp. 285–304.

28. S. G. Harkins and K. Szymanski, "Social Loafing and Group Evaluation," *Journal of Personality and Social Psychology*, December 1989, pp. 934–941

29. A. Gunnthorsdottir and A. Rapoport, "Embedding Social Dilemmas in Intergroup Competition Reduces Free-Riding," *Organizational Behavior and Human Decision Processes* 101 (2006), pp. 184–199.

30. For some of the controversy surrounding the definition of cohesion, see J. Keyton and J. Springston, "Redefining Cohesiveness in Groups," *Small Group Research*, May 1990, pp. 234–254.

31. B. Mullen and C. Cooper, "The Relation Between Group Cohesiveness and Performance: An Integration," *Psychological Bulletin*, March 1994, pp. 210–227; P. M. Podsakoff, S. B. MacKenzie, and M. Ahearne, "Moderating Effects of Goal Acceptance on the Relationship Between Group Cohesiveness and Productivity," *Journal of Applied Psychology*, December 1997, pp. 974–983; and D. J. Beal, R. R. Cohen, M. J. Burke, and C. L. McLendon, "Cohesion and Performance in Groups: A Meta-analytic Clarification of Construct Relations," *Journal of Applied Psychology*, December 2003, pp. 989–1004.

32. Ibid.

33. Based on J. L. Gibson, J. M. Ivancevich, and J. H. Donnelly, Jr., *Organizations*, 8th ed. (Burr Ridge, IL: Irwin, 1994), p. 323.

34. N. Foote, E. Matson, L. Weiss, and E. Wenger, "Leveraging Group Knowledge for High-Performance Decision-Making," *Organizational Dynamics* 31, no. 2 (2002), pp. 280–295.

35. See N. R. F. Maier, "Assets and Liabilities in Group Problem Solving: The Need for an Integrative Function," *Psychological Review*, April 1967, pp. 239–249; G. W. Hill, "Group Versus Individual Performance: Are N+1 Heads Better Than One?" *Psychological Bulletin*, May 1982, pp. 517–539; A. E. Schwartz and J. Levin, "Better Group Decision Making," *Supervisory Management*, June 1990, p. 4; and R. F. Martell and M. R. Borg, "A Comparison of the Behavioral Rating Accuracy of Groups and Individuals," *Journal of Applied Psychology*, February 1993, pp. 43–50.

36. D. Gigone and R. Hastie, "Proper Analysis of the Accuracy of Group Judgments," *Psychological Bulletin*, January 1997, pp. 149–167; and B. L. Bonner, S. D. Sillito, and M. R. Baumann, "Collective Estimation: Accuracy, Expertise, and Extroversion as Sources of Intra-Group Influence," *Organizational Behavior and Human Decision Processes* 103 (2007), pp. 121–133.

37. See, for example, W. C. Swap and Associates, *Group Decision Making* (Newbury Park, CA: Sage, 1984).

38. I. L. Janis, *Groupthink* (Boston: Houghton Mifflin, 1982); W. Park, "A Review of Research on Groupthink," *Journal of Behavioral Decision Making*, July 1990, pp. 229–245; J. N. Choi and M. U. Kim, "The Organizational Application of Groupthink and Its Limits in Organizations," *Journal of Applied Psychology*, April 1999, pp. 297–306; and W. W. Park, "A Comprehensive Empirical Investigation of the Relationships Among Variables of the Groupthink Model," *Journal of Organizational Behavior*, December 2000, pp. 873–887.

39. Janis, *Groupthink*.

40. M. E. Turner and A. R. Pratkanis, "Mitigating Groupthink by Stimulating Constructive Conflict," in C. De Dreu and E. Van de Vliert (eds.), *Using Conflict in Organizations* (London: Sage, 1997), pp. 53–71.

41. See N. R. F. Maier, *Principles of Human Relations* (New York: Wiley, 1952); I. L. Janis, *Groupthink: Psychological Studies of Policy Decisions and Fiascoes*, 2nd ed. (Boston: Houghton Mifflin, 1982); C. R. Leana, "A Partial Test of Janis' Groupthink Model: Effects of Group Cohesiveness and Leader Behavior on Defective Decision Making," *Journal of Management*, Spring 1985, pp. 5–17; and N. Richardson Ahlfinger and J. K. Esser, "Testing the Groupthink Model: Effects of Promotional Leadership and Conformity Predisposition," *Social Behavior & Personality* 29, no. 1 (2001), pp. 31–41.

42. See D. J. Isenberg, "Group Polarization: A Critical Review and Meta-Analysis," *Journal of Personality and Social Psychology*, December 1986, pp. 1141–1151; J. L. Hale and F. J. Boster, "Comparing Effect Coded Models of Choice Shifts," *Communication Research Reports*, April 1988, pp. 180–186; and P. W. Paese, M. Bieser, and M. E. Tubbs, "Framing Effects and Choice Shifts in Group Decision Making," *Organizational Behavior and Human Decision Processes*, October 1993, pp. 149–165.

43. See, for example, N. Kogan and M. A. Wallach, "Risk Taking as a Function of the Situation, the Person, and the Group," in *New Directions in Psychology*, vol. 3 (New York: Holt, Rinehart and Winston, 1967); and M. A. Wallach, N. Kogan, and D. J. Bem, "Group Influence on Individual Risk Taking," *Journal of Abnormal and Social Psychology* 65 (1962), pp. 75–86.

44. A. F. Osborn, *Applied Imagination: Principles and Procedures of Creative Thinking*, 3rd ed. (New York: Scribner, 1963). See also T. Rickards, "Brainstorming Revisited: A Question of Context," *International Journal of Management Reviews*, March 1999, pp. 91–110; and R. P. McGlynn, D. McGurk, V. S. Effland, N. L. Johll, and D. J. Harding, "Brainstorming and Task Performance in Groups Constrained by Evidence," *Organizational Behavior and Human Decision Processes*, January 2004, pp. 75–87.

45. N. L. Kerr and R. S. Tindale, "Group Performance and Decision-Making," *Annual Review of Psychology* 55 (2004), pp. 623–655.

46. See A. L. Delbecq, A. H. Van de Ven, and D. H. Gustafson, *Group Techniques for Program Planning: A Guide to Nominal and Delphi Processes* (Glenview, IL: Scott, Foresman, 1975); and P. B. Paulus and H.-C. Yang, "Idea Generation in Groups: A Basis for Creativity in Organizations," *Organizational Behavior and Human Decision Processing*, May 2000, pp. 76–87.

47. See, for instance, A. B. Hollingshead and J. E. McGrath, "Computer-Assisted Groups: A Critical Review of the Empirical Research," in R. A. Guzzo and E. Salas (eds.), *Team Effectiveness and Decision Making in Organizations* (San Francisco: Jossey-Bass, 1995), pp. 46–78.

48. See G. Hofstede, *Cultures and Organizations: Software of the Mind* (New York, McGraw-Hill, 1991).

49. This section is based on P. R. Harris and R. T. Moran, *Managing Cultural Differences*, 5th ed. (Houston: Gulf Publishing, 1999).

50. D. S. Staples and L. Zhao, "The Effects of Cultural Diversity in Virtual Teams Versus Face-to-Face Teams," *Group Decision and Negotiation*, July 2006, pp. 389–406.

51. T. P. Verney, "Role Perception Congruence, Performance, and Satisfaction," in D. J. Vredenburgh and R. S. Schuler (eds.), *Effective Management: Research and Application*, Proceedings of the 20th Annual Eastern Academy of Management, Pittsburgh, PA, May 1983, pp. 24–27.

52. Ibid.

53. A. G. Bedeian and A. A. Armenakis, "A Path-Analytic Study of the Consequences of Role Conflict and Ambiguity," *Academy of Management Journal*, June 1981, pp. 417–424; and P. L. Perrewe, K. L. Zellars, G. R. Ferris, A. M. Rossi, C. J. Kacmar, and D. A. Ralston, "Neutralizing Job Stressors: Political Skill as an Antidote to the Dysfunctional Consequences of Role Conflict," *Academy of Management Journal*, February 2004, pp. 141–152.

54. Shaw, *Group Dynamics*.

55. B. Mullen, C. Symons, L. Hu, and E. Salas, "Group Size, Leadership Behavior, and Sub-ordinate Satisfaction," *Journal of General Psychology*, April 1989, pp. 155–170.

Chapter 8

1. This section is based on J. R. Katzenbach and D. K. Smith, *The Wisdom of Teams* (Cambridge, MA: Harvard University Press, 1993), pp. 21, 45, 85; and D. C. Kinlaw, *Developing Superior Work Teams* (Lexington, MA: Lexington Books, 1991), pp. 3–21.

2. See, for instance, E. Sunstrom, K. DeMeuse, and D. Futrell, "Work Teams: Applications and Effectiveness," *American Psychologist*, February 1990, pp. 120–133.

3. J. H. Shonk, *Team-Based Organizations* (Homewood, IL: Business One Irwin, 1992); and M. A. Verespej, "When Workers Get New Roles," *Industry Week*, February 3, 1992, p. 11.

4. See, for example, S. G. Cohen, G. E. Ledford, Jr., and G. M. Spreitzer, "A Predictive Model of Self-Managing Work Team Effectiveness," *Human Relations*, May 1996, pp. 643–676; C. E. Nicholls, H. W. Lane, and M. Brehm Brechu, "Taking Self-Managed Teams to Mexico," *Academy of Management Executive*, August 1999, pp. 15–27; and A. Erez, J. A. LePine, and H. Elms, "Effects of Rotated Leadership and Peer Evaluation on the Functioning and Effectiveness of Self-Managed Teams: A Quasi-experiment," *Personnel Psychology*, Winter 2002, pp. 929–948.

5. See, for instance, J. L. Cordery, W. S. Mueller, and L. M. Smith, "Attitudinal and Behavioral Effects of Autonomous Group Working: A Longitudinal Field Study," *Academy of Management Journal*, June 1991, pp. 464–476; R. A. Cook and J. L. Goff, "Coming of Age with Self-Managed Teams: Dealing with a Problem Employee," *Journal of Business and Psychology*, Spring 2002, pp. 485–496; and C. W. Langfred, "Too Much of a Good Thing? Negative Effects of High Trust and Individual Autonomy in Self-Managing Teams," *Academy of Management Journal*, June 2004, pp. 385–399.

6. G. Bodinson and R. Bunch, "AQP's National Team Excellence Award: Its Purpose, Value and Process," *The Journal for Quality and Participation*, Spring 2003, pp. 37–42.

7. M. Brunelli, "How Harley-Davidson Uses Cross-Functional Teams," *Purchasing Online*, November 4, 1999, www.purchasing.com/article/CA147865.html.

8. See, for example, J. Lipnack and J. Stamps, *Virtual Teams: People Working Across Boundaries and Technology*, 2nd ed. (New York: Wiley, 2000); C. B. Gibson and S. G. Cohen (eds.), *Virtual Teams That Work* (San Francisco: Jossey-Bass, 2003); and L. L. Martins, L. L. Gilson, and M. T. Maynard, "Virtual Teams: What Do We Know and Where Do We Go from Here?" *Journal of Management*, November 2004, pp. 805–835.

9. A. Malhotra, A. Majchrzak, and B. Rosen, "Leading Virtual Teams," *Academy of Management Perspectives*, February 2007, pp. 60–70; and J. M. Wilson, S. S. Straus, and B. McEvily, "All in Due Time: The Development of Trust in Computer-Mediated and Face-to-Face Teams," *Organizational Behavior and Human Decision Processes* 19 (2006), pp. 16–33.

10. See, for instance, J. R. Hackman, "The Design of Work Teams," in J. W. Lorsch (ed.), *Handbook of Organizational Behavior* (Upper Saddle River, NJ: Prentice Hall, 1987), pp. 315–342; and M. A. Campion, G. J. Medsker, and C. A. Higgs, "Relations Between Work Group Characteristics and Effectiveness: Implications for Designing Effective Work Groups," *Personnel Psychology*, Winter 1993, pp. 823–850.

11. D. E. Hyatt and T. M. Ruddy, "An Examination of the Relationship Between Work Group Characteristics and Performance: Once More into the Breech," *Personnel Psychology*, Autumn 1997, p. 555.

12. This model is based on M. A. Campion, E. M. Papper, and G. J. Medsker, "Relations Between Work Team Characteristics and Effectiveness: A Replication and Extension," *Personnel Psychology*, Summer 1996, pp. 429–452; D. E. Hyatt and T. M. Ruddy, "An Examination of the Relationship Between Work Group Characteristics and Performance," pp. 553–585; S. G. Cohen and D. E. Bailey, "What Makes Teams Work: Group Effectiveness Research from the Shop Floor to the Executive Suite," *Journal of Management* 23, no. 3 (1997), pp. 239–290; L. Thompson, *Making the Team* (Upper Saddle River, NJ: Prentice Hall, 2000), pp. 18–33; and J. R. Hackman, *Leading Teams: Setting the Stage for Great Performance* (Boston: Harvard Business School Press, 2002).

13. See M. Mattson, T. V. Mumford, and G. S. Sintay, "Taking Teams to Task: A Normative Model for Designing or Recalibrating Work Teams," paper presented at the National Academy of Management Conference, Chicago, August 1999; and G. L. Stewart and M. R. Barrick, "Team Structure and Performance: Assessing the Mediating Role of Intrateam Process and the Moderating Role of Task Type," *Academy of Management Journal*, April 2000, pp. 135–148.

14. Hyatt and Ruddy, "An Examination of the Relationship Between Work Group Characteristics and Performance," p. 577.

15. P. Balkundi and D. A. Harrison, "Ties, Leaders, and Time in Teams: Strong Inference About Network Structure's Effects on Team Viability and Performance," *Academy of Management Journal* 49, no. 1 (2006), pp. 49–68; G. Chen, B. L. Kirkman, R. Kanfer, D. Allen, and B. Rosen, "A Multilevel Study of Leadership, Empowerment, and Performance in Teams," *Journal of Applied Psychology* 92, no. 2 (2007), pp. 331–346; L. A. DeChurch and M. A. Marks, "Leadership in Multiteam Systems," *Journal of Applied Psychology* 91, no. 2 (2006), pp. 311–329; A. Srivastava, K. M. Bartol, and E. A. Locke, "Empowering Leadership in Management Teams: Effects on Knowledge Sharing, Efficacy, and Performance," *Academy of Management Journal* 49, no. 6 (2006), pp. 1239–1251; and J. E. Mathieu, K. K. Gilson, and T. M. Ruddy, "Empowerment and Team Effectiveness: An Empirical Test of an Integrated Model," *Journal of Applied Psychology* 91, no. 1 (2006), pp. 97–108.

16. K. T. Dirks, "Trust in Leadership and Team Performance: Evidence from NCAA Basketball," *Journal of Applied Psychology*, December 2000, pp. 1004–1012; and M. Williams, "In Whom We Trust: Group Membership as an Affective Context for Trust Development," *Academy of Management Review*, July 2001, pp. 377–396.

17. See S. T. Johnson, "Work Teams: What's Ahead in Work Design and Rewards Management," *Compensation & Benefits Review*, March–April 1993, pp. 35–41; and L. N. McClurg, "Team Rewards: How Far Have We Come?" *Human Resource Management*, Spring 2001, pp. 73–86.

18. R. R. Hirschfeld, M. H. Jordan, H. S. Feild, W. F. Giles, and A. A. Armenakis, "Becoming Team Players: Team Members' Mastery of Teamwork Knowledge as a Predictor of Team Task Proficiency and Observed Teamwork Effectiveness," *Journal of Applied Psychology* 91, no. 2 (2006), pp. 467–474.

19. For a more detailed breakdown of team skills, see M. J. Stevens and M. A. Campion, "The Knowledge, Skill, and Ability Requirements for Teamwork: Implications for Human Resource Management," *Journal of Management*, Summer 1994, pp. 503–530.

20. H. Moon, J. R. Hollenbeck, and S. E. Humphrey, "Asymmetric Adaptability: Dynamic Team Structures as One-Way Streets," *Academy of Management Journal* 47, no. 5 (October 2004), pp. 681–695; A. P. J. Ellis, J. R. Hollenbeck, and D. R. Ilgen, "Team Learning: Collectively Connecting the Dots," *Journal of Applied Psychology* 88, no. 5 (October 2003), pp. 821–835; C. L. Jackson and J. A. LePine, "Peer Responses to a Team's Weakest Link: A Test and Extension of LePine and Van Dyne's Model," *Journal of Applied Psychology* 88, no. 3 (June 2003), pp. 459–475; and J. A. LePine, "Team Adaptation and Postchange Performance: Effects of Team Composition in Terms of Members' Cognitive Ability and Personality," *Journal of Applied Psychology* 88, no. 1 (February 2003), pp. 27–39.

21. S. T. Bell, "Deep-Level Composition Variables as Predictors of Team Performance: A Meta-analysis," *Journal of Applied Psychology* 92, no. 3 (2007), pp. 595–615; and M. R. Barrick, G. L. Stewart, M. J. Neubert, and M. K. Mount, "Relating Member Ability and Personality to Work-Team Processes and Team Effectiveness," *Journal of Applied Psychology*, June 1998, pp. 377–391.

22. Ellis, Hollenbeck, and Ilgen, "Team Learning"; C. O. L. H. Porter, J. R. Hollenbeck, and D. R. Ilgen, "Backing Up Behaviors in Teams: The Role of Personality and Legitimacy of Need," *Journal of Applied Psychology* 88, no. 3 (June 2003), pp. 391–403; A. Colquitt, J. R. Hollenbeck, and D. R. Ilgen, "Computer-Assisted Communication and Team Decision-Making Performance: The Moderating Effect of Openness to Experience," *Journal of Applied Psychology* 87, no. 2 (April 2002), pp. 402–410; J. A. LePine, J. R. Hollenbeck, D. R. Ilgen, and J. Hedlund, "The Effects of Individual Differences on the Performance of Hierarchical Decision Making Teams: Much More Than G," *Journal of Applied Psychology* 82 (1997), pp. 803–811; Jackson and LePine, "Peer Responses to a Team's Weakest Link"; and LePine, "Team Adaptation and Postchange Performance."

23. Barrick, Stewart, Neubert, and Mount, "Relating Member Ability and Personality to Work-Team Processes and Team Effectiveness," p. 388; and S. E. Humphrey, J. R. Hollenbeck, C. J. Meyer, and D. R. Ilgen, "Trait Configurations in Self-Managed Teams: A Conceptual Examination of the Use of Seeding for Maximizing and Minimizing Trait Variance in Teams," *Journal of Applied Psychology* 92, no. 3 (2007), pp. 885–892.

24. C. Margerison and D. McCann, *Team Management: Practical New Approaches* (London: Mercury Books, 1990).

25. E. Mannix and M. A. Neale, "What Differences Make a Difference: The Promise and Reality of Diverse Teams in Organizations," *Psychological Science in the Public Interest*, October 2005, pp. 31–55.

26. G. S. Van der Vegt, J. S. Bunderson, and A. Oosterhof, "Expertness Diversity and Interpersonal Helping in Teams: Why Those Who Need the Most Help End Up Getting the Least," *Academy of Management Journal* 49, no. 5 (2006), pp. 877–893.

27. K. Y. Williams and C. A. O'Reilly III, "Demography and Diversity in Organizations: A Review of 40 Years of Research," in B. M. Staw and L. L. Cummings (eds.), *Research in Organizational Behavior*, vol. 20, pp. 77–140; and A. Joshi, "The Influence of Organizational Demography on the External Networking Behavior of Teams," *Academy of Management Review*, July 2006, pp. 583–595.

28. "Is Your Team Too Big? Too Small? What's the Right Number?" *Knowledge@Wharton*, June 14, 2006, pp. 1–5.

29. Hyatt and Ruddy, "An Examination of the Relationship Between Work Group Characteristics and Performance"; J. D. Shaw, M. K. Duffy, and E. M. Stark, "Interdependence and Preference for Group Work: Main and Congruence Effects on the Satisfaction and Performance of Group Members," *Journal of Management* 26, no. 2 (2000), pp. 259–279; and S. A. Kiffin-Peterson and J. L. Cordery, "Trust, Individualism, and Job Characteristics of Employee Preference for Teamwork," *International Journal of Human Resource Management*, February 2003, pp. 93–116.

30. R. Wageman, "Critical Success Factors for Creating Superb Self-Managing Teams," *Organizational Dynamics*, Summer 1997, p. 55.

31. Campion, Papper, and Medsker, "Relations Between Work Team Characteristics and Effectiveness," p. 430; B. L. Kirkman and B. Rosen, "Powering Up Teams," *Organizational Dynamics*, Winter 2000, pp. 48–66; and D. C. Man and S. S. K. Lam, "The Effects of Job Complexity and Autonomy on Cohesiveness in Collectivist and Individualist Work Groups: A Cross-Cultural Analysis," *Journal of Organizational Behavior*, December 2003, pp. 979–1001.

32. Campion, Papper, and Medsker, "Relations Between Work Team Characteristics and Effectiveness," p. 430.

33. I. D. Steiner, *Group Processes and Productivity* (New York: Academic Press, 1972).

34. K. Hess, *Creating the High-Performance Team* (New York: Wiley, 1987); J. R. Katzenbach and D. K. Smith, *The Wisdom of Teams* (Cambridge, MA: Harvard University Press, 1993), pp. 43–64; K. D. Scott and A. Townsend, "Teams: Why Some Succeed and Others Fail," *HRMagazine*, August 1994, pp. 62–67; and K. Blanchard, D. Carew, and E. Parisi-Carew, "How to Get Your Group to Perform Like a Team," *Training and Development*, September 1996, pp. 34–37.

35. J. E. Mathieu and W. Schulze, "The Influence of Team Knowledge and Formal Plans on Episodic Team Process–Performance Relationships," *Academy of Management Journal* 49, no. 3 (2006), pp. 605–619.

36. A. Gurtner *et al.*, "Getting Groups to Develop Good Strategies: Effects of Reflexivity Interventions on Team Process, Team Performance, and Shared Mental Models," *Organizational Behavior and Human Decision Processes* 102 (2007), pp. 127–142; M. C. Schippers, D. N. Den Hartog, and P. L. Koopman, "Reflexivity in Teams: A Measure and Correlates," *Applied Psychology: An International Review* 56, no. 2 (2007), pp. 189–211; and C. S. Burke, K. C. Stagl, E. Salas, L. Pierce, and D. Kendall, "Understanding Team Adaptation: A Conceptual Analysis and Model," *Journal of Applied Psychology* 91, no. 6 (2006), pp. 1189–1207.

37. E. Weldon and L. R. Weingart, "Group Goals and Group Performance," *British Journal of Social Psychology*, Spring 1993, pp. 307–334. See also R. P. DeShon, S. W. J. Kozlowski, A. M. Schmidt, K. R. Milner, and D. Wiechmann, "A Multiple-Goal, Multilevel Model of Feedback Effects on the Regulation of Individual and Team Performance," *Journal of Applied Psychology*, December 2004, pp. 1035–1056.

38. K. Tasa, S. Taggar, and G. H. Seijts, "The Development of Collective Efficacy in Teams: A Multilevel and Longitudinal Perspective," *Journal of Applied Psychology* 92, no. 1 (2007), pp. 17–27; C. B. Gibson, "The Efficacy Advantage: Factors Related to the Formation of Group Efficacy," *Journal of Applied Social Psychology*, October 2003; and D. I. Jung and J. J. Sosik, "Group Potency and Collective Efficacy: Examining Their Predictive Validity, Level of Analysis, and Effects of Performance Feedback on Future Group Performance," *Group & Organization Management*, September 2003, pp. 366–391.

39. A. P. J. Ellis, "System Breakdown: The Role of Mental Models and Transactive Memory on the Relationships Between Acute Stress and Team Performance," *Academy of Management Journal* 49, no. 3 (2006), pp. 576–589.

40. S. W. J. Kozlowski and D. R. Ilgen, "Enhancing the Effectiveness of Work Groups and Teams," *Psychological Science in the Public Interest*, December 2006, pp. 77–124; and B. D. Edwards, E. A. Day, W. Arthur, Jr., and S. T. Bell, "Relationships Among Team Ability Composition, Team Mental Models, and Team Performance," *Journal of Applied Psychology* 91, no. 3 (2006), pp. 727–736.

41. K. A. Jehn, "A Qualitative Analysis of Conflict Types and Dimensions in Organizational Groups," *Administrative Science Quarterly*, September 1997, pp. 530–557. See also R. S. Peterson and K. J. Behfar, "The Dynamic Relationship Between Performance Feedback, Trust, and Conflict in Groups: A Longitudinal Study," *Organizational Behavior and Human Decision Processes*, September–November 2003, pp. 102–112.

42. K. H. Price, D. A. Harrison, and J. H. Gavin, "Withholding Inputs in Team Contexts: Member Composition, Interaction Processes, Evaluation Structure, and Social Loafing," *Journal of Applied Psychology* 91, no. 6 (2006), pp. 1375–1384.

43. See, for instance, B. L. Kirkman and D. L. Shapiro, "The Impact of Cultural Values on Employee Resistance to Teams: Toward a Model of Globalized Self-Managing Work Team Effectiveness," *Academy of Management Review*, July 1997, pp. 730–757; and B. L. Kirkman, C. B. Gibson, and D. L. Shapiro, " 'Exporting' Teams: Enhancing the Implementation and Effectiveness of Work Teams in Global Affiliates," *Organizational Dynamics* 30, no. 1 (2001), pp. 12–29.

44. G. Hertel, U. Konradt, and K. Voss, "Competencies for Virtual Teamwork: Development and Validation of a Web-Based Selection Tool for Members of Distributed Teams," *European Journal of Work and Organizational Psychology* 15, no. 4 (2006), pp. 477–504.

45. Press Release, "HigherPro—Raising Leaders holds training workshops at the Kempinski Hotel in Amman," June 2008, www.ameinfo.com/160498.html.

46. J. S. DeMatteo, L. T. Eby, and E. Sundstrom, "Team-Based Rewards: Current Empirical Evidence and Directions for Future Research," in B. M. Staw and L. L. Cummings (eds.), *Research in Organizational Behavior*, vol. 20, pp. 141–183.

47. C. E. Naquin and R. O. Tynan, "The Team Halo Effect: Why Teams Are Not Blamed for Their Failures," *Journal of Applied Psychology*, April 2003, pp. 332–340.

48. A. B. Drexler and R. Forrester, "Teamwork—Not Necessarily the Answer," *HR Magazine*, January 1998, pp. 55–58. See also R. Saavedra, P. C. Earley, and L. Van Dyne, "Complex Interdependence in Task-Performing Groups," *Journal of Applied Psychology*, February 1993, pp. 61–72; and K. A. Jehn, G. B. Northcraft, and M. A. Neale, "Why Differences Make a Difference: A Field Study of Diversity, Conflict, and Performance in Workgroups," *Administrative Science Quarterly*, December 1999, pp. 741–763.

49. "Watson Wyatt's Global Work Studies." *WatsonWyatt.com*, www.watsonwyatt.com/research/featured/workstudy.asp.

50. C. E. Nicholls, H. W. Lane, and M. Brehm Brechu, "Taking Self-Managed Teams to Mexico," *Academy of Management Executive*, August 1999, pp. 15–27.

51. W. E. Watson, K. Kumar, and L. K. Michaelsen, "Cultural Diversity's Impact on Interaction Process and Performance: Comparing Homogeneous and Diverse Task Groups," *Academy of Management Journal*, June 1993, pp. 590–602; P. C. Earley and E. Mosakowski, "Creating Hybrid Team Cultures: An Empirical Test of Transnational Team Functioning," *Academy of Management Journal*, February 2000, pp. 26–49; and S. Mohammed and L. C. Angell, "Surface- and Deep-Level Diversity in Workgroups: Examining the Moderating Effects of Team Orientation and Team Process on Relationship Conflict," *Journal of Organizational Behavior*, December 2004, pp. 1015–1039.

52. Watson, Kumar, and Michaelsen, "Cultural Diversity's Impact on Interaction Process and Performance: Comparing Homogeneous and Diverse Task Groups."

53. "What about the Arab World?" http://geert-hofstede.com/arab-world-egiqkwlblysa.html.

Chapter 9

1. See, for example, K. W. Thomas and W. H. Schmidt, "A Survey of Managerial Interests with Respect to Conflict," *Academy of Management Journal*, June 1976, p. 317.

2. "Employers Cite Communication Skills, Honesty/Integrity as Key for Job Candidates," *IPMA HR Bulletin*, March 23, 2007, p. 1.

3. W. G. Scott and T. R. Mitchell, *Organization Theory: A Structural and Behavioral Analysis* (Homewood, IL: Irwin, 1976).

4. D. K. Berlo, *The Process of Communication* (New York: Holt, Rinehart & Winston, 1960), pp. 30–32.

5. J. Langan-Fox, "Communication in Organizations: Speed, Diversity, Networks, and Influence on Organizational Effectiveness, Human Health, and Relationships," in N. Anderson, D. S. Ones, H. K. Sinangil, and C. Viswesvaran (eds.), *Handbook of Industrial, Work and Organizational Psychology*, vol. 2 (Thousand Oaks, CA: Sage, 2001), p. 190.

6. R. L. Simpson, "Vertical and Horizontal Communication in Formal Organizations," *Administrative Science Quarterly*, September 1959, pp. 188–196; B. Harriman, "Up and Down the Communications Ladder," *Harvard Business Review*, September–October 1974, pp. 143–151; A. G. Walker and J. W. Smither, "A Five-Year Study of Upward Feedback: What Managers Do with Their Results Matter," *Personnel Psychology*, Summer 1999, pp. 393–424; and J. W. Smither and A. G. Walker, "Are the Characteristics of Narrative Comments Related to Improvement in Multirater Feedback Ratings Over Time?" *Journal of Applied Psychology* 89, no. 3 (June 2004), pp. 575–581.

7. P. Dvorak, "How Understanding the 'Why' of Decisions Matters," *Wall Street Journal*, March 19, 2007, p. B3.

8. E. Nichols, "Hyper-Speed Managers," *HR Magazine*, April 2007, pp. 107–110.

9. L. Dulye, "Get Out of Your Office," *HR Magazine*, July 2006, pp. 99–101.

10. J. Fast, *Body Language* (Philadelphia: M. Evan, 1970), p. 7.

11. A. Mehrabian, *Nonverbal Communication* (Chicago: Aldine-Atherton, 1972).

12. N. M. Henley, "Body Politics Revisited: What Do We Know Today?" in P. J. Kalbfleisch and M. J. Cody (eds.), *Gender, Power, and Communication in Human Relationships* (Hillsdale, NJ: Erlbaum, 1995), pp. 27–61.

13. See, for example, N. B. Kurland and L. H. Pelled, "Passing the Word: Toward a Model of Gossip and Power in the Workplace," *Academy of Management Review*, April 2000, pp. 428–438; and N. Nicholson, "The New Word on Gossip," *Psychology Today*, June 2001, pp. 41–45.

14. Cited in "Heard It Through the Grapevine," *Forbes*, February 10, 1997, p. 22.

15. See, for instance, J. W. Newstrom, R. E. Monczka, and W. E. Reif, "Perceptions of the Grapevine: Its Value and Influence," *Journal of Business Communication*, Spring 1974, pp. 12–20; and S. J. Modic, "Grapevine Rated Most Believable," *Industry Week*, May 15, 1989, p. 14.

16. K. Davis, "Management Communication and the Grapevine," *Harvard Business Review*, September–October 1953, pp. 43–49.

17. K. Davis, cited in R. Rowan, "Where Did That Rumor Come From?" *Fortune*, August 13, 1979, p. 134.

18. R. L. Rosnow and G. A. Fine, *Rumor and Gossip: The Social Psychology of Hearsay* (New York: Elsevier, 1976).

19. J. K. Bosson, A. B. Johnson, K. Niederhoffer, and W. B. Swann, Jr., "Interpersonal Chemistry Through Negativity: Bonding by Sharing Negative Attitudes About Others," *Personal Relationships* 13 (2006), pp. 135–150.

20. B. Gates, "How I Work," *Fortune*, April 17, 2006, http://money.cnn.com/2006/03/30/news/newsmakers/gates_howiwork_fortune/.

21. D. Brady, "*!#?@ the E-mail. Can We Talk?" *BusinessWeek*, December 4, 2006, p. 109.

22. R. Zeidner, "Keeping E-mail in Check," *HR Magazine*, June 2007, pp. 70–74; "E-mail May Be Hazardous to Your Career," *Fortune*, May 14, 2007, p. 24; "More Firms Fire Employees for E-mail Violations," *Gainesville (Florida) Sun*, June 6, 2006, p. B1.

23. K. Gurchiek, "Shoddy Writing Can Trip Up Employees, Organizations," SHRM online, April 27, 2006, pp. 1–2.

24. D. Lidsky, "It's Not Just Who You Know," *Fast Company*, May 2007, p. 56.

25. B. Fryer, "Get Smart," *INC*, September 15, 1999, p. 63.

26. E. Truch, "Managing Personal Knowledge: The Key to Tomorrow's Employability," *Journal of Change Management*, December 2001, pp. 102–105; and D. Mason and D. J. Pauleen, "Perceptions of Knowledge Management: A Qualitative Analysis," *Journal of Knowledge Management* 7, no. 4 (2003), pp. 38–48.

27. J. Gordon, "Intellectual Capital and You," *Training*, September 1999, p. 33.

28. "At Many Companies, Hunt for Leakers Expands Arsenal of Monitoring Tactics," *Wall Street Journal*, September 11, 2006, pp. B1, B3; and B. J. Alge, G. A. Ballinger, S. Tangirala,

and J. L. Oakley, "Information Privacy in Organizations: Empowering Creative and Extrarole Performance," *Journal of Applied Psychology* 91, no. 1 (2006), pp. 221–232.

29. See R. L. Daft and R. H. Lengel, "Information Richness: A New Approach to Managerial Behavior and Organization Design," in B. M. Staw and L. L. Cummings (eds.), *Research in Organizational Behavior*, vol. 6 (Greenwich, CT: JAI Press, 1984), pp. 191–233; R. L. Daft and R. H. Lengel, "Organizational Information Requirements, Media Richness, and Structural Design," *Managerial Science*, May 1986, pp. 554–572; R. E. Rice, "Task Analyzability, Use of New Media, and Effectiveness," *Organization Science*, November 1992, pp. 475–500; S. G. Straus and J. E. McGrath, "Does the Medium Matter? The Interaction of Task Type and Technology on Group Performance and Member Reaction," *Journal of Applied Psychology*, February 1994, pp. 87–97; L. K. Trevino, J. Webster, and E. W. Stein, "Making Connections: Complementary Influences on Communication Media Choices, Attitudes, and Use," *Organization Science*, March–April 2000, pp. 163–182; and N. Kock, "The Psychobiological Model: Towards a New Theory of Computer-Mediated Communication Based on Darwinian Evolution," *Organization Science* 15, no. 3 (May–June 2004), pp. 327–348.

30. R. L. Daft, R. H. Lengel, and L. K. Trevino, "Message Equivocality, Media Selection, and Manager Performance: Implications for Information Systems," *MIS Quarterly*, September 1987, pp. 355–368.

31. J. C. McCroskey, J. A. Daly, and G. Sorenson, "Personality Correlates of Communication Apprehension," *Human Communication Research*, Spring 1976, pp. 376–380.

32. See, for instance, B. H. Spitzberg and M. L. Hecht, "A Competent Model of Relational Competence," *Human Communication Research*, Summer 1984, pp. 575–599; and S. K. Opt and D. A. Loffredo, "Rethinking Communication Apprehension: A Myers-Briggs Perspective," *Journal of Psychology*, September 2000, pp. 556–570.

33. D. Tannen, *Talking from 9 to 5: Men and Women at Work* (New York: Harper, 2001), p. 15.

34. See M. Munter, "Cross-Cultural Communication for Managers," *Business Horizons*, May–June 1993, pp. 75–76.

35. See E. T. Hall, *Beyond Culture* (Garden City, NY: Anchor Press/Doubleday, 1976); E. T. Hall, "How Cultures Collide," *Psychology Today*, July 1976, pp. 67–74; E. T. Hall and M. R. Hall, *Understanding Cultural Differences* (Yarmouth, ME: Intercultural Press, 1990); R. E. Dulek, J. S. Fielden, and J. S. Hill, "International Communication: An Executive Primer," *Business Horizons*, January–February 1991, pp. 20–25; D. Kim, Y. Pan, and H. S. Park, "High- Versus Low-Context Culture: A Comparison of Chinese, Korean, and American Cultures," *Psychology and Marketing*, September 1998, pp. 507–521; M. J. Martinko and S. C. Douglas, "Culture and Expatriate Failure: An Attributional Explication," *International Journal of Organizational Analysis*, July 1999, pp. 265–293; and W. L. Adair, "Integrative Sequences and Negotiation Outcome in Same- and Mixed-Culture Negotiations," *International Journal of Conflict Management* 14, no. 3–4 (2003), pp. 1359–1392.

36. N. Adler, *International Dimensions of Organizational Behavior*, 4th ed. (Cincinnati, OH: South-Western Publishing, 2002), p. 94.

37. See, for example. R. S. Schuler, "A Role Perception Transactional Process Model for Organizational Communication-Outcome Relationships," *Organizational Behavior and Human Performance*, April 1979, pp. 268–291.

38. J. P. Walsh, S. J. Ashford, and T. E. Hill, "Feedback Obstruction: The Influence of the Information Environment on Employee Turnover Intentions," *Human Relations*, January 1985, pp. 23–46.

39. S. A. Hellweg and S. L. Phillips, "Communication and Productivity in Organizations: A State-of-the-Art Review," in *Proceedings of the 40th Annual Academy of Management Conference*, Detroit, 1980, pp. 188–192. See also B. A. Bechky, "Sharing Meaning Across Occupational Communities: The Transformation of Understanding on a Production Floor," *Organization Science* 14, no. 3 (May–June 2003), pp. 312–330.

40. Based on E. Jaffe, "The Science Behind Secrets," *HPS Observer*, July 2006, pp. 20–22.

Chapter 10

1. J. P. Kotter, "What Leaders Really Do," *Harvard Business Review*, May–June 1990, pp. 103–111; and J. P. Kotter, *A Force for Change: How Leadership Differs from Management* (New York: The Free Press, 1990).

2. See T. A. Judge, J. E. Bono, R. Ilies, and M. Werner, "Personality and Leadership: A Review," paper presented at the 15th Annual Conference of the Society for Industrial and Organizational Psychology, New Orleans, 2000; and T. A. Judge, J. E. Bono, R. Ilies, and M. W. Gerhardt, "Personality and Leadership: A Qualitative and Quantitative Review," *Journal of Applied Psychology*, August 2002, pp. 765–780.

3. J. Champy, "The Hidden Qualities of Great Leaders," *Fast Company* 76 (November 2003), p. 135.

4. Ibid 7; J. Antonakis, "Why 'Emotional Intelligence' Does Not Predict Leadership Effectiveness: A Comment on Prati, Douglas, Ferris, Ammeter, and Buckley (2003)," *International Journal of Organizational Analysis* 11 (2003), pp. 355–361; see also M. Zeidner, G. Matthews, and R. D. Roberts, "Emotional Intelligence in the Workplace: A Critical Review," *Applied Psychology: An International Review* 53 (2004), pp. 371–399; R. G. Lord, C. L. DeVader, and G. M. Alliger, "A Meta-analysis of the Relation Between Personality Traits and Leadership Perceptions: An Application of Validity Generalization Procedures," *Journal of Applied Psychology*, August 1986, pp. 402–410; and J. A. Smith and R. J. Foti, "A Pattern Approach to the Study of Leader Emergence," *Leadership Quarterly*, Summer 1998, pp. 147–160.

5. See S. Hansen, "Stings Like a Bee," *INC.*, November 2002, pp. 56–64; and J. Greenbaum, "Is Ghengis on the Hunt Again?" internetnews.com, January 14, 2005, www.internetnews.com/commentary/article.php/3459771.

6. R. M. Stogdill and A. E. Coons (eds.), *Leader Behavior: Its Description and Measurement*, Research Monograph no. 88 (Columbus: Ohio State University, Bureau of Business Research, 1951). This research is updated in C. A. Schriesheim, C. C. Cogliser, and L. L. Neider, "Is It 'Trustworthy'? A Multiple-Levels-of-Analysis Reexamination of an Ohio State Leadership Study, with Implications for Future Research," *Leadership Quarterly*, Summer 1995, pp. 111–145; and T. A. Judge, R. F. Piccolo, and R. Ilies, "The Forgotten Ones? The Validity of Consideration and Initiating Structure in Leadership Research," *Journal of Applied Psychology*, February 2004, pp. 36–51.

7. R. Kahn and D. Katz, "Leadership Practices in Relation to Productivity and Morale," in D. Cartwright and A. Zander (eds.), *Group Dynamics: Research and Theory*, 2nd ed. (Elmsford, NY: Row, Paterson, 1960).

8. R. R. Blake and J. S. Mouton, *The Managerial Grid* (Houston: Gulf, 1964).

9. See, for example, R. R. Blake and J. S. Mouton, "A Comparative Analysis of Situationalism and 9,9 Management by Principle," *Organizational Dynamics*, Spring 1982, pp. 20–43.

10. F. E. Fiedler, *A Theory of Leadership Effectiveness* (New York: McGraw-Hill, 1967).

11. F. E. Fiedler and J. E. Garcia, *New Approaches to Effective Leadership: Cognitive Resources and Organizational Performance* (New York: Wiley, 1987).

12. P. Hersey and K. H. Blanchard, "So You Want to Know Your Leadership Style?" *Training and Development Journal*, February 1974, pp. 1–15; and P. Hersey, K. H. Blanchard, and D. E. Johnson, *Management of Organizational Behavior: Leading Human Resources*, 8th ed. (Upper Saddle River, NJ: Prentice Hall, 2001).

13. Cited in C. F. Fernandez and R. P. Vecchio, "Situational Leadership Theory Revisited: A Test of an Across-Jobs Perspective," *Leadership Quarterly* 8, no. 1 (1997), p. 67.

14. R. J. House, "A Path-Goal Theory of Leader Effectiveness," *Administrative Science Quarterly*, September 1971, pp. 321–338; R. J. House and T. R. Mitchell, "Path-Goal Theory of Leadership," *Journal of Contemporary Business*, Autumn 1974, pp. 81–97; and R. J. House, "Path-Goal Theory of Leadership: Lessons, Legacy, and a Reformulated Theory," *Leadership Quarterly*, Fall 1996, pp. 323–352.

15. W. Bennis, "The Challenges of Leadership in the Modern World," *American Psychologist*, January 2007, pp. 2–5.

16. R. M. Dienesch and R. C. Liden, "Leader–Member Exchange Model of Leadership: A Critique and Further Development," *Academy of Management Review*, July 1986, pp. 618–634; G. B. Graen and M. Uhl-Bien, "Relationship-Based Approach to Leadership: Development of Leader–Member Exchange (LMX) Theory of Leadership Over 25 Years: Applying a Multi-Domain Perspective," *Leadership Quarterly*, Summer 1995, pp. 219–247; R. C. Liden, R. T. Sparrowe, and S. J. Wayne, "Leader–Member Exchange Theory: The Past and Potential for the Future," in G. R. Ferris (ed.), *Research in Personnel and Human Resource Management*, vol. 15 (Greenwich, CT: JAI Press, 1997), pp. 47–119; and C. A. Schriesheim, S. L. Castro, X. Zhou, and F. J. Yammarino, "The Folly of Theorizing 'A' but Testing 'B': A Selective Level-of-Analysis Review of the Field and a Detailed Leader–Member Exchange Illustration," *Leadership Quarterly*, Winter 2001, pp. 515–551.

17. D. Duchon, S. G. Green, and T. D. Taber, "Vertical Dyad Linkage: A Longitudinal Assessment of Antecedents, Measures, and Consequences," *Journal of Applied Psychology*, February 1986, pp. 56–60; Liden, Wayne, and Stilwell, "A Longitudinal Study on the Early Development of Leader–Member Exchanges"; and M. Uhl-Bien, "Relationship Development as a Key Ingredient for Leadership Development," in S. E. Murphy and R. E. Riggio (eds.),

Future of Leadership Development (Mahwah, NJ: Lawrence Erlbaum, 2003), pp. 129–147.

18. See V. H. Vroom and P. W. Yetton, *Leadership and Decision-Making* (Pittsburgh: University of Pittsburgh Press, 1973); and V. H. Vroom and A. G. Jago, "The Role of the Situation in Leadership," *American Psychologist*, January 2007, pp. 17–24.

19. J. A. Conger and R. N. Kanungo, "Behavioral Dimensions of Charismatic Leadership," in J. A. Conger, R. N. Kanungo and Associates (eds.), *Charismatic Leadership* (San Francisco: Jossey-Bass, 1988), p. 79.

20. J. A. Conger and R. N. Kanungo, *Charismatic Leadership in Organizations* (Thousand Oaks, CA: Sage, 1998); and R. Awamleh and W. L. Gardner, "Perceptions of Leader Charisma and Effectiveness: The Effects of Vision Content, Delivery, and Organizational Performance," *Leadership Quarterly*, Fall 1999, pp. 345–373.

21. See J. A. Conger and R. N. Kanungo, "Training Charismatic Leadership: A Risky and Critical Task," *Charismatic Leadership* (San Francisco: Jossey-Bass, 1988), pp. 309–323; A. J. Towler, "Effects of Charismatic Influence Training on Attitudes, Behavior, and Performance," *Personnel Psychology*, Summer 2003, pp. 363–381; and M. Frese, S. Beimel, and S. Schoenborn, "Action Training for Charismatic Leadership: Two Evaluations of Studies of a Commercial Training Module on Inspirational Communication of a Vision," *Personnel Psychology*, Autumn 2003, pp. 671–697.

22. R. J. Richardson and S. K. Thayer, *The Charisma Factor: How to Develop Your Natural Leadership Ability* (Upper Saddle River, NJ: Prentice Hall, 1993).

23. D. A. Waldman, B. M. Bass, and F. J. Yammarino, "Adding to Contingent-Reward Behavior: The Augmenting Effect of Charismatic Leadership," *Group & Organization Studies*, December 1990, pp. 381–394; and S. A. Kirkpatrick and E. A. Locke, "Direct and Indirect Effects of Three Core Charismatic Leadership Components on Performance and Attitudes," *Journal of Applied Psychology*, February 1996, pp. 36–51.

24. A. H. B. de Hoogh, D. N. den Hartog, P. L. Koopman, H. Thierry, P. T. van den Berg, and J. G. van der Weide, "Charismatic Leadership, Environmental Dynamism, and Performance," *European Journal of Work & Organizational Psychology*, December 2004, pp. 447–471; S. Harvey, M. Martin, and D. Stout, "Instructor's Transformational Leadership: University Student Attitudes and Ratings," *Psychological Reports*, April 2003, pp. 395–402; and D. A. Waldman, M. Javidan, and P. Varella, "Charismatic Leadership at the Strategic Level: A New Application of Upper Echelons Theory," *Leadership Quarterly*, June 2004, pp. 355–380.

25. H. L. Tosi, V. Misangyi, A. Fanelli, D. A. Waldmann, and F. J. Yammarino, "CEO Charisma, Compensation, and Firm Performance," *Leadership Quarterley*, June 2004, pp. 405–420.

26. See, for instance, R. Khurana, *Searching for a Corporate Savior: The Irrational Quest for Charismatic CEOs* (Princeton, NJ: Princeton University Press, 2002); and J. A. Raelin, "The Myth of Charismatic Leaders," *Training & Development*, March 2003, pp. 47–54.

27. See, for instance, B. M. Bass *et al.*, "Predicting Unit Performance by Assessing Transformational and Transactional Leadership," *Journal of Applied Psychology*, April 2003,

pp. 207–218; and T. A. Judge, and R. F. Piccolo, "Transformational and Transactional Leadership: A Meta-analytic Test of Their Relative Validity," *Journal of Applied Psychology*, October 2004, pp. 755–768.

28. B. M. Bass, "Leadership: Good, Better, Best," *Organizational Dynamics*, Winter 1985, pp. 26–40; and J. Seltzer and B. M. Bass, "Transformational Leadership: Beyond Initiation and Consideration," *Journal of Management*, December 1990, pp. 693–703.

29. D. I. Jung, C. Chow, and A. Wu, "The Role of Transformational Leadership in Enhancing Organizational Innovation: Hypotheses and Some Preliminary Findings," *Leadership Quarterly*, August–October 2003, pp. 525–544; D. I. Jung, "Transformational and Transactional Leadership and Their Effects on Creativity in Groups," *Creativity Research Journal* 13, no. 2 (2001), pp. 185–195; and S. J. Shin and J. Zhou, "Transformational Leadership, Conservation, and Creativity: Evidence from Korea," *Academy of Management Journal*, December 2003, pp. 703–714.

30. J. R. Baum, E. A. Locke, and S. A. Kirkpatrick, "A Longitudinal Study of the Relation of Vision and Vision Communication to Venture Growth in Entrepreneurial Firms," *Journal of Applied Psychology*, February 2000, pp. 43–54.

31. B. J. Avolio, W. Zhu, W. Koh, and P. Bhatia, "Transformational Leadership and Organizational Commitment: Mediating Role of Psychological Empowerment and Moderating Role of Structural Distance," *Journal of Organizational Behavior*, December 2004, pp. 951–968; and T. Dvir, Taly, N. Kass, and B. Shamir, "The Emotional Bond: Vision and Organizational Commitment Among High-Tech Employees," *Journal of Organizational Change Management* 17, no. 2 (2004), pp. 126–143.

32. Judge and Piccolo, "Transformational and Transactional Leadership."

33. See B. J. Avolio *et al.*, "Unlocking the Mask: A Look at the Process by which Authentic Leaders Impact Follower Attitudes and Behaviors," *Leadership Quarterly*, December 2004, pp. 801–823; W. L. Gardner and J. R. Schermerhorn, Jr., "Performance Gains Through Positive Organizational Behavior and Authentic Leadership," *Organizational Dynamics*, August 2004, pp. 270–281; and M. M. Novicevic, M. G. Harvey, M. R. Buckley, J. A. Brown-Radford, and R. Evans, "Authentic Leadership: A Historical Perspective," *Journal of Leadership and Organizational Behavior* 13, no. 1 (2006), pp. 64–76.

34. This section is based on E. P. Hollander, "Ethical Challenges in the Leader–Follower Relationship," *Business Ethics Quarterly*, January 1995, pp. 55–65; J. C. Rost, "Leadership: A Discussion About Ethics," *Business Ethics Quarterly*, January 1995, pp. 129–142; L. K. Treviño, M. Brown, and L. P. Hartman, "A Qualitative Investigation of Perceived Executive Ethical Leadership: Perceptions from Inside and Outside the Executive Suite," *Human Relations*, January 2003, pp. 5–37; and R. M. Fulmer, "The Challenge of Ethical Leadership," *Organizational Dynamics* 33, no. 3 (2004), pp. 307–317.

35. J. M. Burns, *Leadership* (New York: Harper & Row, 1978).

36. J. M. Howell and B. J. Avolio, "The Ethics of Charismatic Leadership: Submission or Liberation?" *Academy of Management Executive*, May 1992, pp. 43–55.

37. M. E. Brown and L. K. Treviño, "Socialized Charismatic Leadership, Values Congruence, and Deviance in Work Groups," *Journal of Applied Psychology* 91, no. 4 (2006), pp. 954–962.

38. See, for example, K. T. Dirks and D. L. Ferrin, "Trust in Leadership: Meta-Analytic Findings and Implications for Research and Practice," *Journal of Applied Psychology*, August 2002, pp. 611–628; the special issue on trust in an organizational context, B. McEvily, V. Perrone, and A. Zaheer, guest editors, *Organization Science*, January–February 2003; and R. Galford and A. S. Drapeau, *The Trusted Leader* (New York: The Free Press, 2003).

39. Based on S. D. Boon and J. G. Holmes, "The Dynamics of Interpersonal Trust: Resolving Uncertainty in the Face of Risk," in R. A. Hinde and J. Groebel (eds.), *Cooperation and Prosocial Behavior* (Cambridge, UK: Cambridge University Press, 1991), p. 194; D. J. McAllister, "Affect- and Cognition-Based Trust as Foundations for Interpersonal Cooperation in Organizations," *Academy of Management Journal*, February 1995, p. 25; and D. M. Rousseau, S. B. Sitkin, R. S. Burt, and C. Camerer, "Not So Different After All: A Cross-Discipline View of Trust," *Academy of Management Review*, July 1998, pp. 393–404.

40. M. Granovetter, "Economic Action and Social Structure: The Problem of Embeddedness," *American Journal of Sociology*, November 1985, p. 491.

41. R. C. Mayer, J. H. Davis, and F. D. Schoorman, "An Integrative Model of Organizational Trust," *Academy of Management Review*, July 1995, p. 712.

42. C. Johnson-George and W. Swap, "Measurement of Specific Interpersonal Trust: Construction and Validation of a Scale to Assess Trust in a Specific Other," *Journal of Personality and Social Psychology*, September 1982, p. 1306.

43. P. L. Schindler and C. C. Thomas, "The Structure of Interpersonal Trust in the Workplace," *Psychological Reports*, October 1993, pp. 563–573.

44. See, for instance, Dirks and Ferrin, "Trust in Leadership;" D. I. Jung and B. J. Avolio, "Opening the Black Box: An Experimental Investigation of the Mediating Effects of Trust and Value Congruence on Transformational and Transactional Leadership," *Journal of Organizational Behavior*, December 2000, pp. 949–964; and A. Zacharatos, J. Barling, and R. D. Iverson, "High-Performance Work Systems and Occupational Safety," *Journal of Applied Psychology*, January 2005, pp. 77–93.

45. Based on L. T. Hosmer, "Trust: The Connecting Link Between Organizational Theory and Philosophical Ethics," *Academy of Management Review*, April 1995, p. 393; and R. C. Mayer, J. H. Davis, and F. D. Schoorman, "An Integrative Model of Organizational Trust," *Academy of Management Review*, July 1995, p. 712.

46. J. M. Kouzes and B. Z. Posner, *Credibility: How Leaders Gain and Lose It, and Why People Demand It* (San Francisco: Jossey-Bass, 1993), p. 14.

47. D. Shapiro, B. H. Sheppard, and L. Cheraskin, "Business on a Handshake," *Negotiation Journal*, October 1992, pp. 365–377; R. J. Lewicki, E. C. Tomlinson, and N. Gillespie, "Models of Interpersonal Trust Development: Theoretical Approaches, Empirical Evidence, and Future Directions," *Journal of*

Management, December 2006, pp. 991–1022; and J. Child, "Trust—The Fundamental Bond in Global Collaboration," *Organizational Dynamics* 29, no. 4 (2001), pp. 274–288.

48. This section is based on Zand, *The Leadership Triad*, pp. 122–134; and A. M. Zak, J. A. Gold, R. M. Ryckman, and E. Lenney, "Assessments of Trust in Intimate Relationships and the Self-Perception Process," *Journal of Social Psychology*, April 1998, pp. 217–228.

49. M. E. Schweitzer, J. C. Hershey, and E. T. Bradlow, "Promises and Lies: Restoring Violated Trust," *Organizational Behavior and Human Decision Processes* 101 (2006), pp. 1–19.

50. M. Murray, *Beyond the Myths and Magic of Mentoring: How to Facilitate an Effective Mentoring Process*, rev. ed. (New York: Wiley, 2001); K. E. Kram, "Phases of the Mentor Relationship," *Academy of Management Journal*, December 1983, pp. 608–625; R. A. Noe, "An Investigation of the Determinants of Successful Assigned Mentoring Relationships," *Personal Psychology*, Fall 1988, pp. 559–580; and L. Eby, M. Butts, and A. Lockwood, "Protégés' Negative Mentoring Experiences: Construct Development and Nomological Validation," *Personnel Psychology*, Summer 2004, pp. 411–447.

51. T. D. Allen, E. T. Eby, and E. Lentz, "The Relationship Between Formal Mentoring Program Characteristics and Perceived Program Effectiveness," *Personnel Psychology* 59 (2006), pp. 125–153; and T. D. Allen, L. T. Eby, and E. Lentz, "Mentorship Behaviors and Mentorship Quality Associated with Formal Mentoring Programs: Closing the Gap Between Research and Practice," *Journal of Applied Psychology* 91, no. 3 (2006), pp. 567–578.

52. See C. C. Manz, "Self-Leadership: Toward an Expanded Theory of Self-Influence Processes in Organizations," *Academy of Management Review*, July 1986, pp. 585–600; C. C. Manz and H. P. Sims, Jr., *The New Superleadership: Leading Others to Lead Themselves* (San Francisco: Berrett-Koehler, 2001); C. L. Dolbier, M. Soderstrom, M. A. Steinhardt, "The Relationships Between Self-Leadership and Enhanced Psychological, Health, and Work Outcomes," *Journal of Psychology*, September 2001, pp. 469–485; and J. D. Houghton, T. W. Bonham, C. P. Neck, and K. Singh, "The Relationship Between Self-Leadership and Personality: A Comparison of Hierarchical Factor Structures," *Journal of Managerial Psychology* 19, no. 4 (2004), pp. 427–441.

53. J. Kelly and S. Nadler, "Leading from Below," *Wall Street Journal*, March 3, 2007, pp. R4, R10.

54. L. A. Hambley, T. A. O'Neill, and T. J. B. Kline, "Virtual Team Leadership: The Effects of Leadership Style and Communication Medium on Team Interaction Styles and Outcomes," *Organizational Behavior and Human Decision Processes* 103 (2007), pp. 1–20; and B. J. Avolio and S. S. Kahai, "Adding the 'E' to E-Leadership: How it May Impact Your Leadership," *Organizational Dynamics* 31, no. 4 (2003), pp. 325–338.

55. S. J. Zaccaro and P. Bader, "E-Leadership and the Challenges of Leading E-Teams: Minimizing the Bad and Maximizing the Good," *Organizational Dynamics* 31, no. 4 (2003), pp. 381–385.

56. See, for instance, J. R. Meindl, "The Romance of Leadership as a Follower-Centric Theory: A Social Constructionist Approach," *Leadership Quarterly*, Fall 1995, pp. 329–341; and

S. A. Haslam, M. J. Platow, J. C. Turner, K. J. Reynolds, C. McGarty, P. J. Oakes, S. Johnson, M. K. Ryan, and K. Veenstra, "Social Identity and the Romance of Leadership: The Importance of Being Seen to Be 'Doing It for Us,'" *Group Processes & Intergroup Relations*, July 2001, pp. 191–205.

57. R. G. Lord, C. L. DeVader, and G. M. Alliger, "A Meta-analysis of the Relation Between Personality Traits and Leadership Perceptions: An Application of Validity Generalization Procedures," *Journal of Applied Psychology*, August 1986, pp. 402–410.

58. S. Kerr and J. M. Jermier, "Substitutes for Leadership: Their Meaning and Measurement," *Organizational Behavior and Human Performance*, December 1978, pp. 375–403; J. M. Jermier and S. Kerr, "Substitutes for Leadership: Their Meaning and Measurement—Contextual Recollections and Current Observations," *Leadership Quarterly* 8, no. 2 (1997), pp. 95–101; and E. de Vries Reinout, R. A. Roe, and T. C. B. Taillieu, "Need for Leadership as a Moderator of the Relationships Between Leadership and Individual Outcomes," *Leadership Quarterly*, April 2002, pp. 121–138.

59. See, for instance, P. Dvorak, "M.B.A. Programs Hone 'Soft Skills,'" *Wall Street Journal*, February 12, 2007, p. B3.

60. See, for instance, Barling, Weber, and Kelloway, "Effects of Transformational Leadership Training on Attitudinal and Financial Outcomes"; and D. V. Day, "Leadership Development: A Review in Context," *Leadership Quarterly*, Winter 2000, pp. 581–613.

61. M. Sashkin, "The Visionary Leader," in J. A. Conger, R. N. Kanungo *et al.* (eds.), *Charismatic Leadership* (San Francisco: Jossey-Bass, 1988), p. 150.

62. D. V. Day, "Leadership Development: A Review in Context," *Leadership Quarterly*, Winter 2000, pp. 590–593.

63. M. Javidan, P. W. Dorfman, M. S. de Luque, and R. J. House, "In the Eye of the Beholder: Cross Cultural Lessons in Leadership from Project GLOBE," *Academy of Management Perspectives*, February 2006, pp. 67–90.

64. D. E. Carl and M. Javidan, "Universality of Charismatic Leadership: A Multi-Nation Study," paper presented at the National Academy of Management Conference, Washington, DC, August 2001, p. 29.

65. R. D. Arvey, Z. Zhang, and B. J. Avolio, "Developmental and Genetic Determinants of Leadership Role Occupancy Among Women," *Journal of Applied Psychology*, May 2007, pp. 693–706.

66. M. Pandya, "Warren Buffett on Investing and Leadership: I'm Wired for This Game," *Wharton Leadership Digest* 3, no. 7 (April 1999), http://leadership.wharton.upenn.edu/digest/04-99.shtml.

Chapter 11

1. R. M. Kanter, "Power Failure in Management Circuits," *Harvard Business Review*, July–August 1979, p. 65.

2. J. Pfeffer, "Understanding Power in Organizations," *California Management Review*, Winter 1992, p. 35.

3. Based on B. M. Bass, *Bass & Stogdill's Handbook of Leadership*, 3rd ed. (New York: The Free Press, 1990).

4. J. R. P. French, Jr., and B. Raven, "The Bases of Social Power," in D. Cartwright (ed.), *Studies in Social Power* (Ann Arbor, MI: University of Michigan, Institute for Social Research, 1959), pp. 150–167; B. J. Raven, "The Bases of Power: Origins and Recent Developments," *Journal of Social Issues*, Winter 1993, pp. 227–251; and G. Yukl, "Use Power Effectively," in E. A. Locke (ed.), *Handbook of Principles of Organizational Behavior* (Malden, MA: Blackwell, 2004), pp. 242–247.

5. E. A. Ward, "Social Power Bases of Managers: Emergence of a New Factor," *Journal of Social Psychology*, February 2001, pp. 144–147.

6. P. M. Podsakoff and C. A. Schriesheim, "Field Studies of French and Raven's Bases of Power: Critique, Reanalysis, and Suggestions for Future Research," *Psychological Bulletin*, May 1985, pp. 387–411; T. R. Hinkin and C. A. Schriesheim, "Development and Application of New Scales to Measure the French and Raven (1959) Bases of Social Power," *Journal of Applied Psychology*, August 1989, pp. 561–567; and P. P. Carson, K. D. Carson, and C. W. Roe, "Social Power Bases: A Meta-Analytic Examination of Interrelationships and Outcomes" *Journal of Applied Social Psychology* 23, no. 14 (1993), pp. 1150–1169.

7. H. Mintzberg, *Power In and Around Organizations* (Upper Saddle River, NJ: Prentice Hall, 1983), p. 24.

8. R. M. Cyert and J. G. March, *A Behavioral Theory of the Firm* (Upper Saddle River, NJ: Prentice Hall, 1963).

9. C. Perrow, "Departmental Power and Perspective in Industrial Firms," in M. N. Zald (ed.), *Power in Organizations* (Nashville, TN: Vanderbilt University Press, 1970).

10. See, for example, D. Kipnis and S. M. Schmidt, "Upward-Influence Styles: Relationship with Performance Evaluations, Salary, and Stress," *Administrative Science Quarterly*, December 1988, pp. 528–542; G. Yukl and J. B. Tracey, "Consequences of Influence Tactics Used with Subordinates, Peers, and the Boss," *Journal of Applied Psychology*, August 1992, pp. 525–535; G. Blickle, "Influence Tactics Used by Subordinates: An Empirical Analysis of the Kipnis and Schmidt Subscales," *Psychological Reports*, February 2000, pp. 143–154; and G. Yukl, "Use Power Effectively," pp. 249–252.

11. G. Yukl, *Leadership in Organizations*, 5th ed. (Upper Saddle River, NJ: Prentice Hall, 2002), pp. 141–174; G. R. Ferris, W. A. Hochwarter, C. Douglas, F. R. Blass, R. W. Kolodinksy, and D. C. Treadway, "Social Influence Processes in Organizations and Human Resource Systems," in G. R. Ferris and J. J. Martocchio (eds.), *Research in Personnel and Human Resources Management*, vol. 21 (Oxford, UK: JAI Press/Elsevier, 2003), pp. 65–127; and C. A. Higgins, T. A. Judge, and G. R. Ferris, "Influence Tactics and Work Outcomes: A Meta-analysis," *Journal of Organizational Behavior*, March 2003, pp. 89–106.

12. C. M. Falbe and G. Yukl, "Consequences for Managers of Using Single Influence Tactics and Combinations of Tactics," *Academy of Management Journal*, July 1992, pp. 638–653.

13. Yukl, *Leadership in Organizations*.

14. www.chicagolegalnet.com; and S. Ellison and J. S. Lublin, "Dial to Pay $10 Million to Settle a Sexual-Harassment Lawsuit," *Wall Street Journal*, April 30, 2003, p. B4.

15. L. J. Munson, C. Hulin, and F. Drasgow, "Longitudinal Analysis of Dispositional Influences and Sexual Harassment: Effects on Job and Psychological Outcomes," *Personnel Psychology*, Spring 2000, pp. 21–46; T. M. Glomb, L. J. Munson, C. L. Hulin, M. E. Bergman, and F. Drasgow,

"Structural Equation Models of Sexual Harassment: Longitudinal Explorations and Cross-Sectional Generalizations," *Journal of Applied Psychology*, February 1999, pp. 14–28; M. E. Bergman, R. D. Langhout, P. A. Palmieri, L. M. Cortina, and L. F. Fitzgerald, "The (Un)reasonableness of Reporting: Antecedents and Consequences of Reporting Sexual Harassment," *Journal of Applied Psychology*, April 2002, pp. 230–242; L. R. Offermann and A. B. Malamut, "When Leaders Harass: The Impact of Target Perceptions of Organizational Leadership and Climate on Harassment Reporting and Outcomes," *Journal of Applied Psychology*, October 2002, pp. 885–893.

16. See www.arabpsynet.com/archives/op/OP.J14Ghraibeh SexHarass.pdf.

17. R. Ilies, N. Hauserman, S. Schwochau, and J. Stibal, "Reported Incidence Rates of Work-Related Sexual Harassment in the United States: Using Meta-analysis to Explain Reported Rate Disparities," *Personnel Psychology*, Fall 2003, pp. 607–631.

18. M. Rotundo, D. Nguyen, and P. R. Sackett, "A Meta-Analytic Review of Gender Differences in Perceptions of Sexual Harassment," *Journal of Applied Psychology*, October 2001, pp. 914–922.

19. Ilies, Hauserman, Schwochau, and Stibal, "Reported Incidence Rates of Work-Related Sexual Harassment in the United States; A. B. Malamut and L. R. Offermann, "Coping with Sexual Harassment: Personal, Environmental, and Cognitive Determinants," *Journal of Applied Psychology*, December 2001, pp. 1152–1166; L. M. Cortina and S. A. Wasti, "Profiles in Coping: Responses to Sexual Harassment Across Persons, Organizations, and Cultures," *Journal of Applied Psychology*, February 2005, pp. 182–192.

20. C. R. Willness, P. Steel, and K. Lee, "A Meta-analysis of the Antecedents and Consequences of Workplace Sexual Harassment," *Personnel Psychology* 60 (2007), pp. 127–162.

21. S. A. Culbert and J. J. McDonough, *The Invisible War: Pursuing Self-Interest at Work* (New York: Wiley, 1980), p. 6.

22. Mintzberg, *Power In and Around Organizations*, p. 26. See also K. M. Kacmar and R. A. Baron, "Organizational Politics: The State of the Field, Links to Related Processes, and an Agenda for Future Research," in G. R. Ferris (ed.), *Research in Personnel and Human Resources Management*, vol. 17 (Greenwich, CT: JAI Press, 1999), pp. 1–39; and G. R. Ferris, D. C. Treadway, R. W. Kolokinsky, W. A. Hochwarter, C. J. Kacmar, and D. D. Frink, "Development and Validation of the Political Skill Inventory," *Journal of Management*, February 2005, pp. 126–152.

23. S. B. Bacharach and E. J. Lawler, "Political Alignments in Organizations," in R. M. Kramer and M. A. Neale (eds.), *Power and Influence in Organizations* (Thousand Oaks, CA: Sage, 1998), pp. 68–69.

24. D. Farrell and J. C. Petersen, "Patterns of Political Behavior in Organizations," *Academy of Management Review*, July 1982, p. 405. For analyses of the controversies underlying the definition of organizational politics, see A. Drory and T. Romm, "The Definition of Organizational Politics: A Review," *Human Relations*, November 1990, pp. 1133–1154; and R. S. Cropanzano, K. M. Kacmar, and D. P. Bozeman, "Organizational Politics, Justice, and Support: Their Differences and Similarities," in R. S. Cropanzano and

K. M. Kacmar (eds.), *Organizational Politics, Justice and Support: Managing Social Climate at Work* (Westport, CT: Quorum Books, 1995), pp. 1–18.

25. Farrell and Peterson, "Patterns of Political Behavior in Organizations," pp. 406–407; and A. Drory, "Politics in Organization and Its Perception Within the Organization," *Organization Studies* 9, no. 2 (1988), pp. 165–179.

26. J. Pfeffer, *Power in Organizations* (Marshfield, MA: Pitman, 1981).

27. Drory and Romm, "The Definition of Organizational Politics."

28. S. M. Rioux and L. A. Penner, "The Causes of Organizational Citizenship Behavior: A Motivational Analysis," *Journal of Applied Psychology*, December 2001, pp. 1306–1314; and M. A. Finkelstein and L. A. Penner, "Predicting Organizational Citizenship Behavior: Integrating the Functional and Role Identity Approaches," *Social Behavior & Personality* 32, no. 4 (2004), pp. 383–398.

29. See, for example, G. R. Ferris, G. S. Russ, and P. M. Fandt, "Politics in Organizations," in R. A. Giacalone and P. Rosenfeld (eds.), *Impression Management in the Organization* (Hillsdale, NJ: Lawrence Erlbaum, 1989), pp. 155–156; and W. E. O'Connor and T. G. Morrison, "A Comparison of Situational and Dispositional Predictors of Perceptions of Organizational Politics," *Journal of Psychology*, May 2001, pp. 301–312.

30. Farrell and Petersen, "Patterns of Political Behavior in Organizations," p. 408.

31. G. R. Ferris and K. M. Kacmar, "Perceptions of Organizational Politics," *Journal of Management*, March 1992, pp. 93–116.

32. See, for example, P. M. Fandt and G. R. Ferris, "The Management of Information and Impressions: When Employees Behave Opportunistically," *Organizational Behavior and Human Decision Processes*, February 1990, pp. 140–158; Ferris, Russ, and Fandt, "Politics in Organizations," p. 147; and J. M. L. Poon, "Situational Antecedents and Outcomes of Organizational Politics Perceptions," *Journal of Managerial Psychology* 18, no. 2 (2003), pp. 138–155.

33. Ferris, Russ, and Fandt, "Politics in Organizations"; and K. M. Kacmar, D. P. Bozeman, D. S. Carlson, and W. P. Anthony, "An Examination of the Perceptions of Organizational Politics Model: Replication and Extension," *Human Relations*, March 1999, pp. 383–416.

34. W. A. Hochwarter, C. Kiewitz, S. L. Castro, P. L. Perrewe, and G. R. Ferris, "Positive Affectivity and Collective Efficacy as Moderators of the Relationship Between Perceived Politics and Job Satisfaction," *Journal of Applied Social Psychology*, May 2003, pp. 1009–1035; C. C. Rosen, P. E. Levy, and R. J. Hall, "Placing Perceptions of Politics in the Context of Feedback Environment, Employee Attitudes, and Job Performance," *Journal of Applied Psychology* 91, no. 1 (2006), pp. 211–230.

35. G. R. Ferris, D. D. Frink, M. C. Galang, J. Zhou, K. M. Kacmar, and J. L. Howard, "Perceptions of Organizational Politics: Prediction, Stress-Related Implications, and Outcomes," *Human Relations*, February 1996, pp. 233–266; and E. Vigoda, "Stress-Related Aftermaths to Workplace Politics: The Relationships Among Politics, Job Distress, and Aggressive Behavior in Organizations," *Journal of Organizational Behavior*, August 2002, pp. 571–591.

36. Kacmar, Bozeman, Carlson, and Anthony, "An Examination of the Perceptions of Organizational Politics Model," p. 389.

37. B. E. Ashforth and R. T. Lee, "Defensive Behavior in Organizations: A Preliminary Model," *Human Relations*, July 1990, pp. 621–648.

38. M. Valle and P. L. Perrewe, "Do Politics Perceptions Relate to Political Behaviors? Tests of an Implicit Assumption and Expanded Model," *Human Relations*, March 2000, pp. 359–386.

39. See T. Romm and A. Drory, "Political Behavior in Organizations: A Cross-Cultural Comparison," *International Journal of Value Based Management* 1 (1988), pp. 97–113; and E. Vigoda, "Reactions to Organizational Politics: A Cross-Cultural Examination in Israel and Britain," *Human Relations*, November 2001, pp. 1483–1518.

40. E. Vigoda, "Reactions to Organizational Politics," p. 1510.

41. M. R. Leary and R. M. Kowalski, "Impression Management: A Literature Review and Two-Component Model," *Psychological Bulletin*, January 1990, pp. 34–47.

42. Ibid., p. 34.

43. See, for instance, B. R. Schlenker, *Impression Management: The Self-Concept, Social Identity, and Interpersonal Relations* (Monterey, CA: Brooks/Cole, 1980); W. L. Gardner and M. J. Martinko, "Impression Management in Organizations," *Journal of Management*, June 1988, pp. 321–338; D. P. Bozeman and K. M. Kacmar, "A Cybernetic Model of Impression Management Processes in Organizations," *Organizational Behavior and Human Decision Processes*, January 1997, pp. 9–30; M. C. Bolino and W. H. Turnley, "More Than One Way to Make an Impression: Exploring Profiles of Impression Management," *Journal of Management* 29, no. 2 (2003), pp. 141–160; S. Zivnuska, K. M. Kacmar, L. A. Witt, D. S. Carlson, and V. K. Bratton, "Interactive Effects of Impression Management and Organizational Politics on Job Performance," *Journal of Organizational Behavior*, August 2004, pp. 627–640; and W.-C. Tsai, C.-C. Chen, and S.-F. Chiu, "Exploring Boundaries of the Effects of Applicant Impression Management Tactics in Job Interviews," *Journal of Management*, February 2005, pp. 108–125.

44. M. Snyder and J. Copeland, "Self-monitoring Processes in Organizational Settings," in Giacalone and Rosenfeld (eds.), *Impression Management in the Organization* (Hillsdale, NJ: Lawrence Erlbaum, 1989), p. 11; A. Montagliani and R. A. Giacalone, "Impression Management and Cross-Cultural Adaptation," *Journal of Social Psychology*, October 1998, pp. 598–608; and W. H. Turnley and M. C. Bolino, "Achieved Desired Images While Avoiding Undesired Images: Exploring the Role of Self-Monitoring in Impression Management," *Journal of Applied Psychology*, April 2001, pp. 351–360.

45. Ferris, Russ, and Fandt, "Politics in Organizations."

46. Stevens and Kristof, "Making the Right Impression: A Field Study of Applicant Impression Management During Job Interviews."

47. C. A. Higgins, T. A. Judge, and G. R. Ferris, "Influence Tactics and Work Outcomes: A Meta-Analysis," *Journal of Organizational Behavior*, March 2003, pp. 89–106.

48. P. P. Fu and G. Yukl, "Perceived Effectiveness of Influence Tactics in the United States and China," *Leadership Quarterly*, Summer 2000, pp. 251–266; O. Branzei, "Cultural Explanations of Individual Preferences for Influence Tactics in Cross-Cultural Encounters," *International Journal of Cross Cultural Management*, August 2002, pp. 203–218; G. Yukl, P. P. Fu, and R. McDonald, "Cross-Cultural Differences in Perceived Effectiveness of Influence Tactics for Initiating or Resisting Change," *Applied Psychology: An International Review*, January 2003, pp. 66–82; and P. P. Fu, T. K. Peng, J. C. Kennedy, and G. Yukl, "Examining the Preferences of Influence Tactics in Chinese Societies: A Comparison of Chinese Managers in Hong Kong, Taiwan, and Mainland China," *Organizational Dynamics* 33, no. 1 (2004), pp. 32–46.

49. Fu and Yukl, "Perceived Effectiveness of Influence Tactics in the United States and China."

50. S. J. Heine, "Making Sense of East Asian Self-Enhancement," *Journal of Cross-Cultural Psychology*, September 2003, pp. 596–602.

51. J. L. T. Leong, M. H. Bond, and P. P. Fu, "Perceived Effectiveness of Influence Strategies in the United States and Three Chinese Societies," *International Journal of Cross Cultural Management*, May 2006, pp. 101–120.

52. R. M. Kanter, *Men and Women of the Corporation* (New York: Basic Books, 1977).

53. See, for instance, Falbe and Yukl, "Consequences for Managers of Using Single Influence Tactics and Combinations of Tactics."

54. See J. G. Bachman, D. G. Bowers, and P. M. Marcus, "Bases of Supervisory Power: A Comparative Study in Five Organizational Settings," in A. S. Tannenbaum (ed.), *Control in Organizations* (New York: McGraw-Hill, 1968), p. 236; M. A. Rahim, "Relationships of Leader Power to Compliance and Satisfaction with Supervision: Evidence from a National Sample of Managers," *Journal of Management*, December 1989, pp. 545–556; P. A. Wilson, "The Effects of Politics and Power on the Organizational Commitment of Federal Executives," *Journal of Management*, Spring 1995, pp. 101–118; and A. R. Elangovan and J. L. Xie, "Effects of Perceived Power of Supervisor on Subordinate Stress and Motivation: The Moderating Role of Subordinate Characteristics," *Journal of Organizational Behavior*, May 1999, pp. 359–373.

55. J. Pfeffer, *Managing with Power: Politics and Influence in Organizations* (Boston: Harvard Business School Press, 1992).

56. G. R. Ferris, P. L. Perrewé, W. P. Anthony, and D. C. Gilmore, "Political Skill at Work," *Organizational Dynamics*, Spring 2000, pp. 25–37; K. K. Ahearn, G. R. Ferris, W. A. Hochwarter, C. Douglas, and A. P. Ammeter, "Leader Political Skill and Team Performance," *Journal of Management* 30, no. 3 (2004), pp. 309–327; and S. E. Seibert, M. L. Kraimer, and J. M. Crant, "What Do Proactive People Do? A Longitudinal Model Linking Proactive Personality and Career Success," *Personnel Psychology*, Winter 2001, pp. 845–874.

57. R. W. Kolodinsky, W. A. Hochwarter, and G. R. Ferris, "Nonlinearity in the Relationship Between Political Skill and Work Outcomes: Convergent Evidence from Three Studies," *Journal of Vocational Behavior*, October 2004, pp. 294–308; W. Hochwarter, "The Interactive Effects of Pro-Political Behavior and Politics Perceptions on Job Satisfaction and Affective Commitment," *Journal of Applied Social Psychology*, July 2003, pp. 1360–1378; and P. L. Perrewé, K. L. Zellars, G. R. Ferris, A. Rossi, C. J. Kacmar, and D. A. Ralston, "Neutralizing Job Stressors: Political Skill as an Antidote to the Dysfunctional Consequences of Role Conflict," *Academy of Management Journal*, February 2004, pp. 141–152.

Chapter 12

1. See, for instance, C. F. Fink, "Some Conceptual Difficulties in the Theory of Social Conflict," *Journal of Conflict Resolution*, December 1968, pp. 412–460; and E. Infante, "On the Definition of Interpersonal Conflict: Cluster Analysis Applied to the Study of Semantics," *Revista de Psicologia Social* 13, no. 3 (1998), pp. 485–493.

2. K. W. Thomas, "Conflict and Negotiation Processes in Organizations," in M. D. Dunnette and L. M. Hough (eds.), *Handbook of Industrial and Organizational Psychology*, 2nd ed., vol. 3 (Palo Alto, CA: Consulting Psychologists Press, 1992), pp. 651–717.

3. Extract from interview between adapting author and Dr. Charbel Aoun.

4. For a comprehensive review of the interactionist approach, see C. De Dreu and E. Van de Vliert (eds.), *Using Conflict in Organizations* (London: Sage, 1997).

5. See K. A. Jehn, "A Multimethod Examination of the Benefits and Detriments of Intragroup Conflict," *Administrative Science Quarterly*, June 1995, pp. 256–282; K. A. Jehn, "A Qualitative Analysis of Conflict Types and Dimensions in Organizational Groups," *Administrative Science Quarterly*, September 1997, pp. 530–557; K. A. Jehn and E. A. Mannix, "The Dynamic Nature of Conflict: A Longitudinal Study of Intragroup Conflict and Group Performance," *Academy of Management Journal*, April 2001, pp. 238–251; and C. K. W. De Dreu and L. R. Weingart, "Task Versus Relationship Conflict, Team Performance, and Team Member Satisfaction: A Meta-Analysis," *Journal of Applied Psychology*, August 2003, pp. 741–749.

6. J. Yang and K. W. Mossholder, "Decoupling Task and Relationship Conflict: The Role of Intragroup Emotional Processing," *Journal of Organizational Behavior* 25, no. 5 (August 2004), pp. 589–605.

7. "Survey Shows Managers Have Their Hands Full Resolving Staff Personality Conflicts," *IPMA-HR Bulletin*, November 3, 2006.

8. R. S. Peterson and K. J. Behfar, "The Dynamic Relationship Between Performance Feedback, Trust, and Conflict in Groups: A Longitudinal Study," *Organizational Behavior & Human Decision Processes*, September–November 2003, pp. 102–112.

9. R. Friedman *et al.*, "The Positive and Negative Effects of Anger on Dispute Resolution: Evidence from Electronically Mediated Disputes," *Journal of Applied Psychology*, April 2004, pp. 369–376.

10. L. R. Pondy, "Organizational Conflict: Concepts and Models," *Administrative Science Quarterly*, September 1967, p. 302.

11. See, for instance, R. L. Pinkley, "Dimensions of Conflict Frame: Disputant Interpretations of Conflict," *Journal of Applied Psychology*, April 1990, pp. 117–126; and R. L. Pinkley and G. B. Northcraft, "Conflict Frames of Reference: Implications for Dispute Processes and Outcomes," *Academy of Management Journal*, February 1994, pp. 193–205.

12. A. M. Isen, A. A. Labroo, and P. Durlach, "An Influence of Product and Brand Name on Positive Affect: Implicit and Explicit Measures," *Motivation & Emotion*, March 2004, pp. 43–63.

13. Ibid.

14. P. J. D. Carnevale and A. M. Isen, "The Influence of Positive Affect and Visual Access on the Discovery of Integrative Solutions in Bilateral Negotiations," *Organizational Behavior and Human Decision Processes*, February 1986, pp. 1–13.

15. Thomas, "Conflict and Negotiation Processes in Organizations."

16. Ibid.

17. See R. A. Baron, "Personality and Organizational Conflict: Effects of the Type A Behavior Pattern and Self-monitoring," *Organizational Behavior and Human Decision Processes*, October 1989, pp. 281–296; R. J. Volkema and T. J. Bergmann, "Conflict Styles as Indicators of Behavioral Patterns in Interpersonal Conflicts," *Journal of Social Psychology*, February 1995, pp. 5–15; and J. A. Rhoades, J. Arnold, and C. Jay, "The Role of Affective Traits and Affective States in Disputants' Motivation and Behavior During Episodes of Organizational Conflict," *Journal of Organizational Behavior*, May 2001, pp. 329–345.

18. Thomas, "Conflict and Negotiation Processes in Organizations."

19. See, for instance, K. A. Jehn, "Enhancing Effectiveness: An Investigation of Advantages and Disadvantages of Value-Based Intragroup Conflict," *International Journal of Conflict Management*, July 1994, pp. 223–238; R. L. Priem, D. A. Harrison, and N. K. Muir, "Structured Conflict and Consensus Outcomes in Group Decision Making," *Journal of Management* 21, no. 4 (1995), pp. 691–710; and K. A. Jehn and E. A. Mannix, "The Dynamic Nature of Conflict: A Longitudinal Study of Intragroup Conflict and Group Performance," *Academy of Management Journal*, April 2001, pp. 238–251.

20. J. Hall and M. S. Williams, "A Comparison of Decision-Making Performances in Established and Ad-hoc Groups," *Journal of Personality and Social Psychology*, February 1966, p. 217.

21. See T. H. Cox, S. A. Lobel, and P. L. McLeod, "Effects of Ethnic Group Cultural Differences on Cooperative Behavior on a Group Task," *Academy of Management Journal*, December 1991, pp. 827–847; L. H. Pelled, K. M. Eisenhardt, and K. R. Xin, "Exploring the Black Box: An Analysis of Work Group Diversity, Conflict, and Performance," *Administrative Science Quarterly*, March 1999, pp. 1–28; and D. van Knippenberg, C. K. W. De Dreu, and A. C. Homan, "Work Group Diversity and Group Performance: An Integrative Model and Research Agenda," *Journal of Applied Psychology*, December 2004, pp. 1008–1022.

22. For example, see J. A. Wall, Jr., and R. R. Callister, "Conflict and Its Management," pp. 523–526 for evidence supporting the argument that conflict is almost uniformly dysfunctional; see also P. J. Hinds, and D. E. Bailey, "Out of Sight, Out of Sync: Understanding Conflict in Distributed Teams," *Organization Science*, November–December 2003, pp. 615–632.

23. This section is based on F. Sommerfield, "Paying the Troops to Buck the System," *Business Month*, May 1990, pp. 77–79; W. Kiechel III, "How to Escape the Echo Chamber," *Fortune*, June 18, 1990, pp. 129–130; E. Van de Vliert and C. De Dreu, "Optimizing Performance by Stimulating Conflict," *International Journal of Conflict Management*, July 1994, pp. 211–222; E. Van de Vliert, "Enhancing Performance by Conflict-Stimulating Intervention," in C. De Dreu and E. Van de Vliert (eds.), *Using Conflict in Organizations*,

pp. 208–222; K. M. Eisenhardt, J. L. Kahwajy, and L. J. Bourgeois III, "How Management Teams Can Have a Good Fight," *Harvard Business Review*, July–August 1997, pp. 77–85; S. Wetlaufer, "Common Sense and Conflict," *Harvard Business Review*, January–February 2000, pp. 114–124; and G. A. Okhuysen and K. M. Eisenhardt, "Excel Through Group Process," in E. A. Locke (ed.), *Handbook of Principles of Organizational Behavior* (Malden, MA: Blackwell, 2004), pp. 216–218.

24. J. A. Wall, Jr., *Negotiation: Theory and Practice* (Glenview, IL: Scott, Foresman, 1985).

25. R. E. Walton and R. B. McKersie, *A Behavioral Theory of Labor Negotiations: An Analysis of a Social Interaction System* (New York: McGraw-Hill, 1965).

26. J. C. Magee, A. D. Galinsky, and D. H. Gruenfeld, "Power, Propensity to Negotiate, and Moving First in Competitive Interactions," *Personality and Social Psychology Bulletin*, February 2007, pp. 200–212.

27. D. A. Moore, "Myopic Prediction, Self-Destructive Secrecy, and the Unexpected Benefits of Revealing Final Deadlines in Negotiation," *Organizational Behavior & Human Decision Processes*, July 2004, pp. 125–139.

28. Thomas, "Conflict and Negotiation Processes in Organizations."

29. P. M. Morgan and R. S. Tindale, "Group vs. Individual Performance in Mixed-Motive Situations: Exploring an Inconsistency," *Organizational Behavior & Human Decision Processes*, January 2002, pp. 44–65.

30. C. K. W. De Dreu, L. R. Weingart, and S. Kwon, "Influence of Social Motives on Integrative Negotiation: A Meta-analytic Review and Test of Two Theories," *Journal of Personality & Social Psychology*, May 2000, pp. 889–905.

31. This model is based on R. J. Lewicki, "Bargaining and Negotiation," *Exchange: The Organizational Behavior Teaching Journal* 6, no. 2 (1981), pp. 39–40.

32. J. A. Wall, Jr., and M. W. Blum, "Negotiations," *Journal of Management*, June 1991, pp. 278–282.

33. S. Kopelman, A. S. Rosette, and L. Thompson, "The Three Faces of Eve: Strategic Displays of Positive, Negative, and Neutral Emotions in Negotiations," *Organizational Behavior and Human Decision Processes* 99 (2006), pp. 81–101; and J. M. Brett, M. Olekalns, R. Friedman, N. Goates, C. Anderson, C. C. Lisco, "Sticks and Stones: Language, Face, and Online Dispute Resolution," *Academy of Management Journal* 50, no. 1 (2007), pp. 85–99.

34. C. Watson and L. R. Hoffman, "Managers as Negotiators: A Test of Power Versus Gender as Predictors of Feelings, Behavior, and Outcomes," *Leadership Quarterly*, Spring 1996, pp. 63–85.

35. A. E. Walters, A. F. Stuhlmacher, and L. L. Meyer, "Gender and Negotiator Competitiveness: A Meta-analysis," *Organizational Behavior and Human Decision Processes*, October 1998, pp. 1–29; and A. F. Stuhlmacher and A. E. Walters, "Gender Differences in Negotiation Outcome: A Meta-analysis," *Personnel Psychology*, Autumn 1999, pp. 653–677.

36. H. R. Bowles, L. Babcock, and L. Lei, "Social Incentives for Gender Differences in the Propensity to Initiate Negotiations: Sometimes It Does Hurt to Ask," *Organizational Behaviour and Human Decision Processes* 103 (2007), pp. 84–103.

37. L. J. Kray, A. D. Galinsky, and L. Thompson, "Reversing the Gender Gap in Negotiations: An Exploration of Stereotype Regeneration," *Organizational Behavior & Human Decision Processes*, March 2002, pp. 386–409.

38. C. K. Stevens, A. G. Bavetta, and M. E. Gist, "Gender Differences in the Acquisition of Salary Negotiation Skills: The Role of Goals, Self-Efficacy, and Perceived Control," *Journal of Applied Psychology* 78, no. 5 (October 1993), pp. 723–735.

39. Wall and Blum, "Negotiations," pp. 283–287.

40. M. J. Gelfand, M. Higgins, L. H. Nishii, J. L. Raver, A. Dominguez, F. Murakami, S. Yamaguchi, and M. Toyama, "Culture and Egocentric Perceptions of Fairness in Conflict and Negotiation," *Journal of Applied Psychology*, October 2002, pp. 833–845; Z. Ma, "Chinese Conflict Management Styles and Negotiation Behaviours: An Empirical Test," *International Journal of Cross Cultural Management*, April 2007, pp. 101–119.

41. "Real Estate & Development FYIs—Lebanon & the GC," *Executive Magazine*. Issue No. 140. March 2011. p. 90.

42. Gelfand *et al.*, "Culture and Egocentric Perceptions of Fairness in Conflict and Negotiation," pp. 833–845; and X. Lin and S. J. Miller, "Negotiation Approaches: Direct and Indirect Effect of National Culture," *International Marketing Review* 20, no. 3 (2003), pp. 286–303.

43. W. L. Adair, T. Okumura, and J. M. Brett, "Negotiation Behavior When Cultures Collide: The United States and Japan," *Journal of Applied Psychology*, June 2001, pp. 371–385; and W. L. Adair, L. Weingart, and J. Brett, "The Timing and Function of Offers in US and Japanese Negotiations," *Journal of Applied Psychology* 92, no. 4 (2007), pp. 1056–1068.

44. E. S. Glenn, D. Witmeyer, and K. A. Stevenson, "Cultural Styles of Persuasion," *Journal of Intercultural Relations*, Fall 1977, pp. 52–66.

45. J. Graham, "The Influence of Culture on Business Negotiations," *Journal of International Business Studies*, Spring 1985, pp. 81–96.

46. K. W. Thomas, "Toward Multidimensional Values in Teaching: The Example of Conflict Behaviors," *Academy of Management Review*, July 1977, p. 487.

47. Q. Reade, "Workplace Conflict Is Time-consuming Problem for Business," *PersonnelToday.com*, September 30, 2004, www.personneltoday.co.uk.

Chapter 13

1. See, for instance, R. L. Daft, *Organization Theory and Design*, 8th ed. (Cincinnati, OH: South-Western Publishing, 2004).

2. C. Hymowitz, "Managers Suddenly Have to Answer to a Crowd of Bosses," *Wall Street Journal*, August 12, 2003, p. B1.

3. See, for instance, L. Urwick, *The Elements of Administration* (New York: Harper & Row, 1944), pp. 52–53; and J. H. Gittell, "Supervisory Span, Relational Coordination, and Flight Departure Performance: A Reassessment of Post-bureaucracy Theory," *Organization Science*, July–August 2001, pp. 468–483.

4. J. Child and R. G. McGrath, "Organizations Unfettered: Organizational Form in an Information-Intensive Economy," *Academy of Management Journal*, December 2001, pp. 1135–1148.

5. H. Mintzberg, *Structure in Fives: Designing Effective Organizations* (Upper Saddle River, NJ: Prentice Hall, 1983), p. 157.

6. L. R. Burns and D. R. Wholey, "Adoption and Abandonment of Matrix Management Programs: Effects of Organizational Characteristics and Interorganizational Networks," *Academy of Management Journal*, February 1993, pp. 106–138.

7. See, for instance, S. M. Davis and P. R. Lawrence, "Problems of Matrix Organization," *Harvard Business Review*, May–June 1978, pp. 131–142; and T. Sy and S. Cote, "Emotional Intelligence: A Key Ability to Succeed in the Matrix Organization," *Journal of Management Development* 23, no. 5 (2004), pp. 437–455.

8. See, for instance, R. E. Miles and C. C. Snow, "The New Network Firm: A Spherical Structure Built on Human Investment Philosophy," *Organizational Dynamics*, Spring 1995, pp. 5–18; D. Pescovitz, "The Company Where Everybody's a Temp," *New York Times Magazine*, June 11, 2000, pp. 94–96; W. F. Cascio, "Managing a Virtual Workplace," *Academy of Management Executive*, August 2000, pp. 81–90; B. Hedberg, G. Dahlgren, J. Hansson, and N. Olve, *Virtual Organizations and Beyond* (New York: Wiley, 2001); J. Gertner, "Newman's Own: Two Friends and a Canoe Paddle," *New York Times*, November 16, 2003, p. 4BU; and Y. Shin, "A Person-Environment Fit Model for Virtual Organizations," *Journal of Management*, October 2004, pp. 725–743.

9. J. Bates, "Making Movies and Moving On," *Los Angeles Times*, January 19, 1998, p. A1.

10. "GE: Just Your Average Everyday $60 Billion Family Grocery Store," *IndustryWeek*, May 2, 1994, pp. 13–18.

11. GE Press Release: www.ge.com/pdf/investors/events/01212011/ge_webcast_pressrelease_01212011.pdf.

12. H. C. Lucas Jr., *The T-Form Organization: Using Technology to Design Organizations for the 21st Century* (San Francisco: Jossey-Bass, 1996).

13. T. Burns and G. M. Stalker, *The Management of Innovation* (London: Tavistock, 1961); and J. A. Courtright, G. T. Fairhurst, and L. E. Rogers, "Interaction Patterns in Organic and Mechanistic Systems," *Academy of Management Journal*, December 1989, pp. 773–802.

14. This analysis is referred to as a contingency approach to organization design. See, for instance, J. M. Pennings, "Structural Contingency Theory: A Reappraisal," in B. M. Staw and L. L. Cummings (eds.), *Research in Organizational Behavior*, vol. 14 (Greenwich, CT: JAI Press, 1992), pp. 267–309; J. R. Hollenbeck, H. Moon, A. P. J. Ellis, B. J. West, D. R. Ilgen, L. Sheppard, C. O. L. H. Porter, and J. A. Wagner III, "Structural Contingency Theory and Individual Differences: Examination of External and Internal Person-Team Fit," *Journal of Applied Psychology*, June 2002, pp. 599–606; and H. Moon, J. R. Hollenbeck, S. E. Humphrey, D. R. Ilgen, B. West, A. P. J. Ellis, and C. O. L. H. Porter, "Asymmetric Adaptability: Dynamic Team Structures as One-Way Streets," *Academy of Management Journal*, October 2004, pp. 681–695.

15. The strategy–structure thesis was originally proposed in A. D. Chandler, Jr., *Strategy and Structure: Chapters in the History of the Industrial Enterprise* (Cambridge, MA: MIT Press, 1962). For an updated analysis, see T. L. Amburgey and T. Dacin, "As the Left Foot Follows the Right? The Dynamics of Strategic and Structural Change," *Academy of Management Journal*, December 1994, pp. 1427–1452.

16. See R. E. Miles and C. C. Snow, *Organizational Strategy, Structure, and Process* (New York: McGraw-Hill, 1978); D. Miller, "The Structural and Environmental Correlates of Business Strategy," *Strategic Management Journal*, January–February 1987, pp. 55–76; D. C. Galunic and K. M. Eisenhardt, "Renewing the Strategy–Structure–Performance Paradigm," in B. M. Staw and L. L. Cummings (eds.), *Research in Organizational Behavior*, vol. 16 (Greenwich, CT: JAI Press, 1994), pp. 215–255; and I. C. Harris and T. W. Ruefli, "The Strategy/Structure Debate: An Examination of the Performance Implications," *Journal of Management Studies*, June 2000, pp. 587–603.

17. See, for instance, P. M. Blau and R. A. Schoenherr, *The Structure of Organizations* (New York: Basic Books, 1971); D. S. Pugh, "The Aston Program of Research: Retrospect and Prospect," in A. H. Van de Ven and W. F. Joyce (eds.), *Perspectives on Organization Design and Behavior* (New York: Wiley, 1981), pp. 135–166; R. Z. Gooding and J. A. Wagner III, "A Meta-Analytic Review of the Relationship Between Size and Performance: The Productivity and Efficiency of Organizations and Their Subunits," *Administrative Science Quarterly*, December 1985, pp. 462–481; and A. C. Bluedorn, "Pilgrim's Progress: Trends and Convergence in Research on Organizational Size and Environments," *Journal of Management*, Summer 1993, pp. 163–192.

18. See J. Woodward, *Industrial Organization: Theory and Practice* (London: Oxford University Press, 1965); C. Perrow, "A Framework for the Comparative Analysis of Organizations," *American Sociological Review*, April 1967, pp. 194–208; J. D. Thompson, *Organizations in Action* (New York: McGraw-Hill, 1967); J. Hage and M. Aiken, "Routine Technology, Social Structure, and Organizational Goals," *Administrative Science Quarterly*, September 1969, pp. 366–377; C. C. Miller, W. H. Glick, Y. Wang, and G. P. Huber, "Understanding Technology-Structure Relationships: Theory Development and Meta-analytic Theory Testing," *Academy of Management Journal*, June 1991, pp. 370–399; and K. H. Roberts and M. Grabowski, "Organizations, Technology, and Structuring," in S. R. Clegg, C. Hardy, and W. R. Nord (eds.), *Managing Organizations: Current Issues* (Thousand Oaks, CA: Sage, 1999), pp. 159–171.

19. See F. E. Emery and E. Trist, "The Causal Texture of Organizational Environments," *Human Relations*, February 1965, pp. 21–32; P. Lawrence and J. W. Lorsch, *Organization and Environment: Managing Differentiation and Integration* (Boston: Harvard Business School, Division of Research, 1967); M. Yasai-Ardekani, "Structural Adaptations to Environments," *Academy of Management Review*, January 1986, pp. 9–21; Bluedorn, "Pilgrim's Progress"; and M. Arndt, and B. Bigelow, "Presenting Structural Innovation in an Institutional Environment: Hospitals' Use of Impression Management," *Administrative Science Quarterly*, September 2000, pp. 494–522.

20. G. G. Dess and D. W. Beard, "Dimensions of Organizational Task Environments," *Administrative Science Quarterly*, March 1984, pp. 52–73; E. A. Gerloff, N. K. Muir, and W. D. Bodensteiner, "Three Components of Perceived Environmental Uncertainty: An Exploratory Analysis of the Effects of Aggregation," *Journal of Management*, December 1991, pp. 749–768; and O. Shenkar, N. Aranya, and T. Almor, "Construct Dimensions in the Contingency Model: An

Analysis Comparing Metric and Non-metric Multivariate Instruments," *Human Relations*, May 1995, pp. 559–580.

21. See, for instance, L. W. Porter and E. E. Lawler III, "Properties of Organization Structure in Relation to Job Attitudes and Job Behavior," *Psychological Bulletin*, July 1965, pp. 23–51; L. R. James and A. P. Jones, "Organization Structure: A Review of Structural Dimensions and Their Conceptual Relationships with Individual Attitudes and Behavior," *Organizational Behavior and Human Performance*, June 1976, pp. 74–113; D. R. Dalton, W. D. Todor, M. J. Spendolini, G. J. Fielding, and L. W. Porter, "Organization Structure and Performance: A Critical Review," *Academy of Management Review*, January 1980, pp. 49–64; and D. B. Turban and T. L. Keon, "Organizational Attractiveness: An Interactionist Perspective," *Journal of Applied Psychology*, April 1994, pp. 184–193.

22. See, for instance, B. Schneider, H. W. Goldstein, and D. B. Smith, "The ASA Framework: An Update," *Personnel Psychology* 48, no. 4 (1995), pp. 747–773.

23. P. Dvorak, "Making US Management Ideas Work Elsewhere," *Wall Street Journal*, May 22, 2006, p. B3; H. Sabri, "Knowledge Management in its context: Adapting structure to a knowledge creating culture," *International Journal of Communication and Management* 15(2), 2005, pp. 113–128.

24. See, for example, P. R. Harris and R. T. Moran, *Managing Cultural Differences*, 5th ed. (Houston: Gulf Publishing, 1999).

25. "In Focus: Lou Gerstner," *CNN World Business*, July 2, 2004, www.cnn.com.

26. W. F. Cascio, "Strategies for Responsible Restructuring," *Academy of Management Executive* 19, no. 4 (2005), pp. 39–50.

Chapter 14

1. P. Selznick, "Foundations of the Theory of Organizations," *American Sociological Review*, February 1948, pp. 25–35.

2. See L. G. Zucker, "Organizations as Institutions," in S. B. Bacharach (ed.), *Research in the Sociology of Organizations* (Greenwich, CT: JAI Press, 1983), pp. 1–47; A. J. Richardson, "The Production of Institutional Behaviour: A Constructive Comment on the Use of Institutionalization Theory in Organizational Analysis," *Canadian Journal of Administrative Sciences*, December 1986, pp. 304–316; L. G. Zucker, *Institutional Patterns and Organizations: Culture and Environment* (Cambridge, MA: Ballinger, 1988); R. L. Jepperson, "Institutions, Institutional Effects, and Institutionalism," in W. W. Powell and P. J. DiMaggio (eds.), *The New Institu—tionalism in Organizational Analysis* (Chicago: University of Chicago Press, 1991), pp. 143–163; and T. B. Lawrence, M. K. Mauws, B. Dyck, and R. F. Kleysen, "The Politics of Organizational Learning: Integrating Power into the 4I Framework," *Academy of Management Review*, January 2005, pp. 180–191.

3. See, for example, H. S. Becker, "Culture: A Sociological View," *Yale Review*, Summer 1982, pp. 513–527; and E. H. Schein, *Organizational Culture and Leadership* (San Francisco: Jossey-Bass, 1985), p. 168.

4. This seven-item description is based on C. A. O'Reilly III, J. Chatman, and D. F. Caldwell, "People and Organizational Culture: A Profile Comparison Approach to Assessing Person-Organization Fit," *Academy of Management Journal*, September 1991, pp. 487–516; and J. A. Chatman and K. A. Jehn, "Assessing the Relationship between Industry Characteristics and Organizational Culture: How Different Can You Be?" *Academy of Management Journal*, June 1994, pp. 522–553.

5. The view that there will be consistency among perceptions of organizational culture has been called the "integration" perspective. For a review of this perspective and conflicting approaches, see D. Meyerson and J. Martin, "Cultural Change: An Integration of Three Different Views," *Journal of Management Studies*, November 1987, pp. 623–647; and P. J. Frost, L. F. Moore, M. R. Louis, C. C. Lundberg, and J. Martin (eds.), *Reframing Organizational Culture* (Newbury Park, CA: Sage Publications, 1991).

6. See J. M. Jermier *et al.*, "Organizational Subcultures in a Soft Bureaucracy: Resistance Behind the Myth and Facade of an Official Culture," *Organization Science*, May 1991, pp. 170–194; and S. A. Sackmann, "Culture and Subcultures: An Analysis of Organizational Knowledge," *Administrative Science Quarterly*, March 1992, pp. 140–161; G. Hofstede, "Identifying Organizational Subcultures: An Empirical Approach," *Journal of Management Studies*, January 1998, pp. 1–12.

7. See, for example, G. G. Gordon and N. DiTomaso, "Predicting Corporate Performance from Organizational Culture," *Journal of Management Studies*, November 1992, pp. 793–798; J. B. Sorensen, "The Strength of Corporate Culture and the Reliability of Firm Performance," *Administrative Science Quarterly*, March 2002, pp. 70–91; and J. Rosenthal and M. A. Masarech, "High-Performance Cultures: How Values Can Drive Business Results," *Journal of Organizational Excellence*, Spring 2003, pp. 3–18.

8. Y. Wiener, "Forms of Value Systems: A Focus on Organizational Effectiveness and Cultural Change and Maintenance," *Academy of Management Review*, October 1988, p. 536.

9. R. T. Mowday, L. W. Porter, and R. M. Steers, *EmployeeLinkages: The Psychology of Commitment, Absenteeism, and Turnover* (New York: Academic Press, 1982); and C. Vandenberghe, "Organizational Culture, Person-Culture Fit, and Turnover: A Replication in the Health Care Industry," *Journal of Organizational Behavior*, March 1999, pp. 175–184.

10. S. L. Dolan and S. Garcia, "Managing by Values: Cultural Redesign for Strategic Organizational Change at the Dawn of the Twenty-First Century," *Journal of Management Development* 21, no. 2 (2002), pp. 101–117.

11. See C. A. O'Reilly and J. A. Chatman, "Culture as Social Control: Corporations, Cults, and Commitment," in B. M. Staw and L. L. Cummings (eds.), *Research in Organizational Behavior*, vol. 18 (Greenwich, CT: JAI Press, 1996), pp. 157–200. See also M. Pinae Cunha, "The 'Best Place to Be': Managing Control and Employee Loyalty in a Knowledge-Intensive Company," *Journal of Applied Behavioral Science*, December 2002, pp. 481–495.

12. J. Case, "Corporate Culture," *INC.*, November 1996, pp. 42–53.

13. Sorensen, "The Strength of Corporate Culture and the Reliability of Firm Performance."

14. See C. Lindsay, "Paradoxes of Organizational Diversity: Living Within the Paradoxes," in L. R. Jauch and J. L. Wall

(eds.), *Proceedings of the 50th Academy of Management Conference* (San Francisco, 1990), pp. 374–378; T. Cox, Jr., *Cultural Diversity in Organizations: Theory, Research & Practice* (San Francisco: Berrett-Koehler, 1993), pp. 162–170; and L. Grensing-Pophal, "Hiring to Fit Your Corporate Culture," *HR Magazine*, August 1999, pp. 50–54.

15. A. F. Buono and J. L. Bowditch, *The Human Side of Mergers and Acquisitions: Managing Collisions Between People, Cultures, and Organizations* (San Francisco: Jossey-Bass, 1989); S. Cartwright and C. L. Cooper, "The Role of Culture Compatibility in Successful Organizational Marriages," *Academy of Management Executive*, May 1993, pp. 57–70; E. Krell, "Merging Corporate Cultures," *Training*, May 2001, pp. 68–78; and R. A. Weber and C. F. Camerer, "Cultural Conflict and Merger Failure: An Experimental Approach," *Management Science*, April 2003, pp. 400–412.

16. "SGBL finalizes acquisition of Lebanese Canadian Bank." www.nowlebanon.com/NewsArchiveDetails.aspx?ID=309503.

17. E. H. Schein, "The Role of the Founder in Creating Organizational Culture," *Organizational Dynamics*, Summer 1983, pp. 13–28.

18. E. H. Schein, "Leadership and Organizational Culture," in F. Hesselbein, M. Goldsmith, and R. Beckhard (eds.), *The Leader of the Future* (San Francisco: Jossey-Bass, 1996), pp. 61–62.

19. See, for example, J. R. Harrison and G. R. Carroll, "Keeping the Faith: A Model of Cultural Transmission in Formal Organizations," *Administrative Science Quarterly*, December 1991, pp. 552–582; see also G. George, R. G. Sleeth, and M. A. Siders, "Organizational Culture: Leader Roles, Behaviors, and Reinforcement Mechanisms," *Journal of Business & Psychology*, Summer 1999, pp. 545–560.

20. B. Schneider, "The People Make the Place," *Personnel Psychology*, Autumn 1987, pp. 437–453; D. E. Bowen, G. E. Ledford, Jr., and B. R. Nathan, "Hiring for the Organization, Not the Job," *Academy of Management Executive*, November 1991, pp. 35–51; B. Schneider, H. W. Goldstein, and D. B. Smith, "The ASA Framework: An Update," *Personnel Psychology*, Winter 1995, pp. 747–773; A. L. Kristof, "Person–Organization Fit: An Integrative Review of Its Conceptualizations, Measurement, and Implications," *Personnel Psychology*, Spring 1996, pp. 1–49; D. M. Cable and T. A. Judge, "Interviewers' Perceptions of Person–Organization Fit and Organizational Selection Decisions," *Journal of Applied Psychology*, August 1997, pp. 546–561; and M. L. Verquer, T. A. Beehr, and S. H. Wagner, "A Meta-Analysis of Relations Between Person–Organization Fit and Work Attitudes," *Journal of Vocational Behavior*, December 2003, pp. 473–489.

21. D. C. Hambrick and P. A. Mason, "Upper Echelons: The Organization as a Reflection of Its Top Managers," *Academy of Management Review*, April 1984, pp. 193–206; B. P. Niehoff, C. A. Enz, and R. A. Grover, "The Impact of Top-Management Actions on Employee Attitudes and Perceptions," *Group & Organization Studies*, September 1990, pp. 337–352; and H. M. Trice and J. M. Beyer, "Cultural Leadership in Organizations," *Organization Science*, May 1991, pp. 149–169.

22. See, for instance, J. P. Wanous, *Organizational Entry*, 2nd ed. (New York: Addison-Wesley, 1992); G. T. Chao, A. M. O'Leary-Kelly, S. Wolf, H. J. Klein, and P. D. Gardner, "Organizational Socialization: Its Content and Consequences," *Journal of Applied Psychology*, October 1994, pp. 730–743; B. E. Ashforth, A. M. Saks, and R. T. Lee, "Socialization and Newcomer Adjustment: The Role of Organizational Context," *Human Relations*, July 1998, pp. 897–926; D. A. Major, "Effective Newcomer Socialization into High-Performance Organizational Cultures," in N. M. Ashkanasy, C. P. M. Wilderom, and M. F. Peterson (eds.), *Handbook of Organizational Culture & Climate*, pp. 355–368; D. M. Cable and C. K. Parsons, "Socialization Tactics and Person–Organization Fit," *Personnel Psychology*, Spring 2001, pp. 1–23; and K. Rollag, "The Impact of Relative Tenure on Newcomer Socialization Dynamics," *Journal of Organizational Behavior*, November 2004, pp. 853–872.

23. J. Van Maanen and E. H. Schein, "Career Development," in J. R. Hackman and J. L. Suttle (eds.), *Improving Life at Work* (Santa Monica, CA: Goodyear, 1977), pp. 58–62.

24. D. C. Feldman, "The Multiple Socialization of Organization Members," *Academy of Management Review*, April 1981, p. 310.

25. G. Chen and R. J. Klimoski, "The Impact of Expectations on Newcomer Performance in Teams as Mediated by Work Characteristics, Social Exchanges, and Empowerment," *Academy of Management Journal* 46 (2003), pp. 591–607; C. R. Wanberg and J. D. Kammeyer-Mueller, "Predictors and Outcomes of Proactivity in the Socialization Process," *Journal of Applied Psychology* 85 (2000), pp. 373–385; J. D. Kammeyer-Mueller and C. R. Wanberg, "Unwrapping the Organizational Entry Process: Disentangling Multiple Antecedents and Their Pathways to Adjustment," *Journal of Applied Psychology* 88 (2003), pp. 779–794; and E. W. Morrison, "Longitudinal Study of the Effects of Information Seeking on Newcomer Socialization," *Journal of Applied Psychology* 78 (2003), pp. 173–183.

26. E. W. Morrison, "Newcomers' Relationships: The Role of Social Network Ties During Socialization," *Academy of Management Journal* 45 (2002), pp. 1149–1160.

27. E. Ransdell, "The Nike Story? Just Tell It!" *Fast Company*, January–February 2000, pp. 44–46.

28. D. M. Boje, "The Storytelling Organization: A Study of Story Performance in an Office-Supply Firm," *Administrative Science Quarterly*, March 1991, pp. 106–126; C. H. Deutsch, "The Parables of Corporate Culture," *New York Times*, October 13, 1991, p. F25; and M. Ricketts and J. G. Seiling, "Language, Metaphors, and Stories: Catalysts for Meaning Making in Organizations," *Organization Development Journal*, Winter 2003, pp. 33–43.

29. See K. Kamoche, "Rhetoric, Ritualism, and Totemism in Human Resource Management," *Human Relations*, April 1995, pp. 367–385.

30. A. Rafaeli and M. G. Pratt, "Tailored Meanings: On the Meaning and Impact of Organizational Dress," *Academy of Management Review*, January 1993, pp. 32–55; and J. M. Higgins and C. McAllaster, "Want Innovation? Then Use Cultural Artifacts That Support It," *Organizational Dynamics*, August 2002, pp. 74–84.

31. *DCAcronyms* (Seattle: Boeing, April 1997).

32. See B. Victor and J. B. Cullen, "The Organizational Bases of Ethical Work Climates," *Administrative Science Quarterly*, March 1988, pp. 101–125; L. K. Trevino, "A Cultural

Perspective on Changing and Developing Organizational Ethics," in W. A. Pasmore and R. W. Woodman (eds.), *Research in Organizational Change and Development*, vol. 4 (Greenwich, CT: JAI Press, 1990); M. W. Dickson, D. B. Smith, M. W. Grojean, and M. Ehrhart, "An Organizational Climate Regarding Ethics: The Outcome of Leader Values and the Practices That Reflect Them," *Leadership Quarterly*, Summer 2001, pp. 197–217; and R. L. Dufresne, "An Action Learning Perspective on Effective Implementation of Academic Honor Codes," *Group & Organization Management*, April 2004, pp. 201–218.

33. J. A. Byrne, "The Environment Was Ripe for Abuse," *BusinessWeek*, February 25, 2002, pp. 118–120; and A. Raghavan, K. Kranhold, and A. Barrionuevo, "How Enron Bosses Created a Culture of Pushing Limits," *Wall Street Journal*, August 26, 2002, p. A1.

34. D. L. Nelson and C. L. Cooper (eds.), *Positive Organizational Behavior* (London: Sage, 2007); K. S. Cameron, J. E. Dutton, and R. E. Quinn (eds.), *Positive Organizational Scholarship: Foundations of a New Discipline* (San Francisco: Berrett-Koehler, 2003); and F. Luthans and C. M. Youssef, "Emerging Positive Organizational Behavior," *Journal of Management*, June 2007, pp. 321–349.

35. J. Robison, "Great Leadership Under Fire," *Gallup Leadership Journal*, March 8, 2007, pp. 1–3.

36. D. P. Ashmos and D. Duchon, "Spirituality at Work: A Conceptualization and Measure," *Journal of Management Inquiry*, June 2000, p. 139. For a comprehensive review of definitions of workplace spirituality, see R. A. Giacalone and C. L. Jurkiewicz, "Toward a Science of Workplace Spirituality," in R. A. Giacalone and C. L. Jurkiewicz (eds.), *Handbook of Workplace Spirituality and Organizational Performance* (Armonk, NY: M. E. Sharpe, 2003), pp. 6–13.

37. This section is based on C. Ichniowski, D. L. Kochan, C. Olson, and G. Strauss, "What Works at Work: Overview and Assessment," *Industrial Relations*, 1996, pp. 299–333; I. A. Mitroff and E. A. Denton, *A Spiritual Audit of Corporate America: A Hard Look at Spirituality, Religion, and Values in the Workplace* (San Francisco: Jossey-Bass, 1999); J. Milliman, J. Ferguson, D. Trickett, and B. Condemi, "Spirit and Community at Southwest Airlines: An Investigation of a Spiritual Values-Based Model," *Journal of Organizational Change Management* 12, no. 3 (1999), pp. 221–233; and E. H. Burack, "Spirituality in the Workplace," *Journal of Organizational Change Management* 12, no. 3 (1999), pp. 280–291.

38. M. Conlin, "Religion in the Workplace: The Growing Presence of Spirituality in Corporate America," *BusinessWeek*, November 1, 1999, pp. 151–158; and P. Paul, "A Holier Holiday Season," *American Demographics*, December 2001, pp. 41–45.

39. Cited in Conlin, "Religion in the Workplace," p. 153.

40. C. P. Neck and J. F. Milliman, "Thought Self-Leadership: Finding Spiritual Fulfillment in Organizational Life," *Journal of Managerial Psychology* 9, no. 8 (1994), p. 9; for a recent review, see J.-C. Garcia-Zamor, "Workplace Spirituality and Organizational Performance," *Public Administration Review*, May–June 2003, pp. 355–363.

41. D. W. McCormick, "Spirituality and Management," *Journal of Managerial Psychology* 9, no. 6 (1994), p. 5; E. Brandt,

"Corporate Pioneers Explore Spiritual Peace," *HR Magazine* 41, no. 4 (1996), p. 82; P. Leigh, "The New Spirit at Work," *Training and Development* 51, no. 3 (1997), p. 26; P. H. Mirvis, "Soul Work in Organizations," *Organization Science* 8, no. 2 (1997), p. 193; and J. Milliman, A. Czaplewski, and J. Ferguson, "An Exploratory Empirical Assessment of the Relationship Between Spirituality and Employee Work Attitudes," paper presented at the National Academy of Management Meeting, Washington, DC, August 2001.

42. J. A. Chatman, "Matching People and Organizations: Selection and Socialization in Public Accounting Firms," *Administrative Science Quarterly*, September 1991, pp. 159–184; and A. E. M. Van Vianen, "Person–Organization Fit: The Match Between Newcomers' and Recruiters Preferences for Organizational Cultures," *Personnel Psychology*, Spring 2000, pp. 113–149.

43. J. E. Sheridan, "Organizational Culture and Employee Retention," *Academy of Management Journal*, December 1992, pp. 1036–1056; and Ibid., p. 68.

Chapter 15

1. See B. Becker and B. Gerhart, "The Impact of Human Resource Management on Organizational Performance: Progress and Prospects," *Academy of Management Journal*, August 1996, pp. 779–801; J. T. Delaney and M. A. Huselid, "The Impact of Human Resource Management Practices on the Perceptions of Organizational Performance," *Academy of Management Journal*, August 1996, pp. 949–969; M. A. Huselid, S. E. Jackson, and R. S. Schuler, "Technical and Strategic Human Resource Management Effectiveness as Determinants of Firm Performance," *Academy of Management Journal*, February 1997, pp. 171–188; and G. A. Gelade and M. Ivery, "The Impact of Human Resource Management and Work Climate on Organizational Performance," *Personnel Psychology*, Summer 2003, pp. 383–404; C. J. Collins, and K. D. Clark, "Strategic Human Resource Practices, Top Management Team Social Networks, and Firm Performance: The Role of Human Resource Practices in Creating Organizational Competitive Advantage," *Academy of Management Journal*, December 2003, pp. 740–751; and D. E. Bowen and C. Ostroff, "Understanding HRM–Firm Performance Linkages: The Role of the 'Strength' of the HRM System," *Academy of Management Review*, April 2004, pp. 203–221.

2. www.shrm.org.

3. "Arab world insurance sector poised for growth.", *Booze & Company*, June 2007, www.booz.com/me/home/what_we_think/40007409/40007869/42004865.

4. See, for instance, C. T. Dortch, "Job–Person Match," *Personnel Journal*, June 1989, pp. 49–57; and S. Rynes and B. Gerhart, "Interviewer Assessments of Applicant 'Fit': An Exploratory Investigation," *Personnel Psychology*, Spring 1990, pp. 13–34.

5. E. E. Ghiselli, "The Validity of Aptitude Tests in Personnel Selection," *Personnel Psychology*, Winter 1973, p. 475.

6. R. J. Herrnstein and C. Murray, *The Bell Curve: Intelligence and Class Structure in American Life* (New York: The Free Press, 1994); and M. J. Ree, J. A. Earles, and M. S. Teachout, "Predicting Job Performance: Not Much More

Than g," *Journal of Applied Psychology*, August 1994, pp. 518–524.

7. M. R. Barrick, M. K. Mount, and T. A. Judge, "Personality and Performance at the Beginning of the New Millennium: What Do We Know and Where Do We Go Next?" *International Journal of Selection & Assessment*, March–June 2001, pp. 9–30; M. R. Barrick, G. L. Stewart, and M. Piotrowski, "Personality and Job Performance: Test of the Mediating Effects of Motivation Among Sales Representatives," *Journal of Applied Psychology*, February 2002, pp. 43–51; and C. J. Thoresen, J. C. Bradley, P. D. Bliese, and J. D. Thoresen, "The Big Five Personality Traits and Individual Job Performance and Growth Trajectories in Maintenance and Transitional Job Stages," *Journal of Applied Psychology*, October 2004, pp. 835–853.

8. P. Carbonara, "Hire for Attitude, Train for Skill," *Fast Company*, Greatest Hits, vol. 1, 1997, p. 68.

9. See, for instance, A. C. Spychalski, M. A. Quinones, B. B. Gaugler, and K. Pohley, "A Survey of Assessment Center Practices in Organizations in the United States, *Personnel Psychology*, Spring 1997, pp. 71–90; C. Woodruffe, *Development and Assessment Centres: Identifying and Assessing Competence* (London: Institute of Personnel and Development, 2000); and J. Schettler, "Building Bench Strength," *Training*, June 2002, pp. 55–58.

10. R. A. Posthuma, F. P. Moregeson, and M. A. Campion, "Beyond Employment Interview Validity: A Comprehensive Narrative Review of Recent Research and Trend Over Time," *Personnel Psychology*, Spring 2002, p. 1; and S. L. Wilk and P. Cappelli, "Understanding the Determinants of Employer Use of Selection Methods," *Personnel Psychology*, Spring 2003, p. 111.

11. N. R. Bardack and F. T. McAndrew, "The Influence of Physical Attractiveness and Manner of Dress on Success in a Simulated Personnel Decision," *Journal of Social Psychology*, August 1985, pp. 777–778; R. Bull and N. Rumsey, *The Social Psychology of Facial Appearance* (London: Springer-Verlag, 1988); and L. M. Watkins, and L. Johnston, "Screening Job Applicants: The Impact of Physical Attractiveness and Application Quality," *International Journal of Selection & Assessment*, June 2000, pp. 76–84.

12. "Basic Skills Training Pays Off for Employers," *HR Magazine*, October 1999, p. 32.

13. A. Bernstein, "The Time Bomb in the Workforce: Illiteracy," *BusinessWeek*, February 25, 2002, p. 122.

14. See H. R. Hammoud, "Illiteracy in the Arab world," paper commissioned for the *EFA Global Monitoring Report 2006: Literacy for life*, 2005, http://unesdoc.unesco.org/images/0014/001462/146282e.pdf; and "Universalization of education and improvement of its quality and relevance to prepare for the twenty-first century," Fifth Conference of Ministers of Education and Those Responsible for Economic Planning in the Arab States, Cairo, Egypt, 1994, MINEDARAB 3, p. 12.

15. C. Ansberry, "A New Blue-Collar World," *Wall Street Journal*, June 30, 2003, p. B1.

16. See, for example, D. Seligman, "Oxymoron 101," *Forbes*, October 28, 2002, pp. 160–164; and R. B. Schmitt, "Companies Add Ethics Training; Will It Work?" *Wall Street Journal*, November 4, 2002, p. B1.

17. Press Release, Saudi Arabia, "Middle Eastern Bank Deploys Ethics Training from Edcomm Group Banker's Academy," July 11, 2009, www.ameinfo.com/203302.html.

18. S. J. Wells, "Forget the Formal Training. Try Chatting at the Water Cooler," *New York Times*, May 10, 1998, p. BU-11.

19. D. A. Kolb, "Management and the Learning Process," *California Management Review*, Spring 1976, pp. 21–31; and B. Filipczak, "Different Strokes: Learning Styles in the Classroom," *Training*, March 1995, pp. 43–48.

20. J. A. Colquitt, J. A. LePine, and R. A. Noe, "Toward an Integrative Theory of Training Motivation: A Meta-Analytic Path Analysis of 20 Years of Research," *Journal of Applied Psychology*, October 2000, pp. 678–707.

21. "Should Performance Reviews Be Fired?" *Knowledge@ Wharton*, April 2011, http://knowledge.wharton.upenn.edu/article.cfm?articleid=2760.

22. "Performance appraisals don't serve any purpose, say 43% of job seekers, latest Bayt.com online poll series finds" *Bayt.com*, January 27, 2009, www.arabianbusiness.com/press-release/?pressReleaseId=36866.

23. W. F. Cascio, *Applied Psychology in Human Resource Management*, 5th ed. (Upper Saddle River, NJ: Prentice Hall, 1998), p. 59.

24. See C. Mabey and G. Salaman, *Strategic Human Resource Management* (London: Blackwell, 1995).

25. A. H. Locher and K. S. Teel, "Appraisal Trends," *Personnel Journal*, September 1988, pp. 139–145.

26. See Abubakr Mohyeldin Tahir Suliman, "Self and Supervisor Ratings of Performance: Evidence from an Individualistic Culture," *Employee Relations* 25, no. 4 (2003), pp. 371–388; A. Suliman, "The Relationships Between Perceived Work Environment, Commitment and Performance in Jordanian Industries," Unpublished PhD thesis, Liverpool Business School, Liverpool John Moores University, Liverpool, UK, 2000; M. Al-Faleh, "Cultural Influences on Arab Management Development: A Case Study of Jordan," *Journal of Management Development* 6, no. 3 (1989), pp. 19–33; and F. A. Muna, *The Arab Executive* (New York: St. Martins Press, 1980).

27. See, for instance, J. D. Facteau and S. B. Craig, "Are Performance Appraisal Ratings from Different Rating Sources Compatible?" *Journal of Applied Psychology*, April 2001, pp. 215–227; J. F. Brett and L. E. Atwater, "360-Degree Feedback: Accuracy, Reactions, and Perceptions of Usefulness," *Journal of Applied Psychology*, October 2001, pp. 930–942; F. Luthans and S. J. Peterson, "360 Degree Feedback with Systematic Coaching: Empirical Analysis Suggests a Winning Combination," *Human Resource Management*, Fall 2003, pp. 243–256; and B. I. J. M. van der Heijden, and A. H. J. Nijhof, "The Value of Subjectivity: Problems and Prospects for 360-Degree Appraisal Systems," *International Journal of Human Resource Management*, May 2004, pp. 493–511.

28. J. S. Lublin, "It's Shape-up Time for Performance Reviews," *Wall Street Journal*, October 3, 1994, p. B1.

29. Much of this section is based on H. H. Meyer, "A Solution to the Performance Appraisal Feedback Enigma," *Academy of Management Executive*, February 1991, pp. 68–76.

30. R. J. Burke, "Why Performance Appraisal Systems Fail," *Personnel Administration*, June 1972, pp. 32–40.

31. A. Suliman, "The Relationships Between Perceived Work Environment, Commitment and Performance in Jordanian Industries," Unpublished PhD thesis, Liverpool Business

School, Liverpool John Moores University, Liverpool, UK, 2000; M. Al-Faleh, "Cultural Influences on Arab Management Development: A Case Study of Jordan," *Journal of Management Development* 6, no. 3 (1989), pp. 19–33; and F. A. Muna, *The Arab Executive* (St. Martins Press, New York, NY, 1980).

32. See, for instance, J. W. Hedge and W. C. Borman, "Changing Conceptions and Practices in Performance Appraisal," in A. Howard (ed.), *The Changing Nature of Work* (San Francisco, CA: Jossey-Bass, 1995), pp. 453–459.

33. See, for instance, T. R. Athey and R. M. McIntyre, "Effect of Rater Training on Rater Accuracy: Levels-of-Processing Theory and Social Facilitation Theory Perspectives," *Journal of Applied Psychology*, November 1987, pp. 567–572; and D. J. Woehr, "Understanding Frame-of-Reference Training: The Impact of Training on the Recall of Performance Information," *Journal of Applied Psychology*, August 1994, pp. 525–534.

34. M. S. Taylor, K. B. Tracy, M. K. Renard, J. K. Harrison, and S. J. Carroll, "Due Process in Performance Appraisal: A Quasi-Experiment in Procedural Justice," *Administrative Science Quarterly*, September 1995, pp. 495–523.

35. N. B. Henderson, "An Enabling Work Force," *Nation's Business*, June 1998, p. 93.

36. See J. Hickman, "50 Best Companies for Minorities," *Fortune*, June 28, 2004, pp. 136–142.

37. For more, see J. Shen, A. Chanda, B. D'Netto, and M. Monga, "Managing diversity through human resource management: an international perspective and conceptual framework," *International Journal of HRM* 20, no. 2 (2009), pp. 235–251.

38. See, for instance, *Harvard Business Review on Work and Life Balance* (Boston: Harvard Business School Press, 2000); and R. Rapoport, L. Bailyn, J. K. Fletcher, and B. H. Pruitt, *Beyond Work–Family Balance* (San Francisco: Jossey-Bass, 2002).

39. Press Release, UAE, "Dubai Customs Celebrates the Opening of First Nursery in a Government Department," April 2009, www.ameinfo.com/191619-large.html.

40. "On the Daddy Track," *Wall Street Journal*, May 11, 2000, p. A1.

41. Jon R. Katzenbach. *Peak Performance: Aligning the Hearts and Minds of Your Employees* (Boston: Harvard Business School Press, 2000), pp. 51–158.

42. S. D. Friedman and J. H. Greenhaus, *Work and Family—Allies or Enemies?* (New York: Oxford University Press, 2000)

43. Cited in "Survey Shows 75 percent of Large Corporations Support Diversity Programs," *Fortune*, July 6, 1998, p. S14.

44. See, for example, J. K. Ford and S. Fisher, "The Role of Training in a Changing Workplace and Workforce: New Perspectives and Approaches," in E. E. Kossek and S. A. Lobel (eds.), *Managing Diversity* (Cambridge, MA: Blackwell Publishers, 1996), pp. 164–193; and J. Barbian, "Moving Toward Diversity," *Training*, February 2003, pp. 44–48.

45. See M. Neal, "When Arab-expatriate Relations Work Well: Diversity and Discourse in the Gulf Arab Workplace," *Team Performance Management* 16, no. 5/6 (2010), pp. 242–266.

46. See, for instance, C. Fletcher and E. L. Perry, "Performance Appraisal and Feedback: A Consideration of National Culture and a Review of Contemporary Research and Future Trends," in N. Anderson, D. S. Ones, H. K. Sinangil, and C. Viswesvaran (eds.), *Handbook of Industrial, Work, & Organizational Psychology*, vol. 1 (Thousand Oaks, CA: Sage, 2001), pp. 127–144.

47. A. M. Ryan *et al.*, "An International Look at Selection Practices: Nation and Culture as Explanations for Variability in Practice," *Personnel Psychology*, 1999, pp. 359–392.

48. Press release, UAE, "Telecommuting Good for Both Employees and Employers Say 72 Percent of Region's Professionals, Reveals Bayt.com poll," 2009, www.ameinfo.com/217861.html.

49. C. Soltis, "Eagle-Eyed Employers Scour Résumés for Little White Lies," *Wall Street Journal*, March 21, 2006, p. B7.

Chapter 16

1. See, for instance, K. H. Hammonds, "Practical Radicals," *Fast Company*, September 2000, pp. 162–174; and P. C. Judge, "Change Agents," *Fast Company*, November 2000, pp. 216–226.

2. J. Taub, "Harvard Radical," *New York Times Magazine*, August 24, 2003, pp. 28–45+.

3. A. Finder, P. D. Healy, and K. Zernike, "President of Harvard Resigns, Ending Stormy 5-Year Tenure," *New York Times*, February 22, 2006, pp. A1, A19.

4. P. G. Audia and S. Brion, "Reluctant to Change: Self-Enhancing Responses to Diverging Performance Measures," *Organizational Behavior and Human Decision Processes* 102 (2007), pp. 255–269.

5. J. P. Kotter and L. A. Schlesinger, "Choosing Strategies for Change," *Harvard Business Review*, March–April 1979, pp. 106–114.

6. Q. N. Huy, "Emotional Balancing of Organizational Continuity and Radical Change: The Contribution of Middle Managers," *Administrative Science Quarterly*, March 2002, pp. 31–69; D. M. Herold, D. B. Fedor, and S. D. Caldwell, "Beyond Change Management: A Multilevel Investigation of Contextual and Personal Influences on Employees' Commitment to Change," *Journal of Applied Psychology* 92, no. 4 (2007), pp. 942–951; and G. B. Cunningham, "The Relationships Among Commitment to Change, Coping with Change, and Turnover Intentions," *European Journal of Work and Organizational Psychology* 15, no. 1 (2006), pp. 29–45.

7. D. B. Fedor, S. Caldwell, and D. M. Herold, "The Effects of Organizational Changes on Employee Commitment: A Multilevel Investigation," *Personnel Psychology* 59 (2006), pp. 1–29.

8. S. Oreg, "Personality, Context, and Resistance to Organizational Change," *European Journal of Work and Organizational Psychology* 15, no. 1 (2006), pp. 73–101.

9. See J. Pfeffer, *Managing with Power: Politics and Influence in Organizations* (Boston: Harvard Business School Press, 1992), pp. 7, and 318–320.

10. See, for instance, W. Ocasio, "Political Dynamics and the Circulation of Power: CEO Succession in US Industrial Corporations, 1960–1990," *Administrative Science Quarterly*, June 1994, pp. 285–312.

11. K. Lewin, *Field Theory in Social Science* (New York: Harper & Row, 1951).

12. P. G. Audia, E. A. Locke, and K. G. Smith, "The Paradox of Success: An Archival and a Laboratory Study of Strategic Persistence Following Radical Environmental Change," *Academy of Management Journal*, October 2000, pp. 837–853.

13. J. P. Kotter, "Leading Changes: Why Transformation Efforts Fail," *Harvard Business Review*, March–April 1995, pp. 59–67; and J. P. Kotter, *Leading Change* (Harvard Business School Press, 1996).

14. See, for example, C. Eden and C. Huxham, "Action Research for the Study of Organizations," in S. R. Clegg, C. Hardy, and W. R. Nord (eds.), *Handbook of Organization Studies* (London: Sage, 1996).

15. For a sampling of various OD definitions, see N. Nicholson (ed.), *Encyclopedic Dictionary of Organizational Behavior* (Malden, MA: Blackwell, 1998), pp. 359–361; H. K. Sinangil and F. Avallone, "Organizational Development and Change," in N. Anderson, D. S. Ones, H. K. Sinangil, and C. Viswesvaran (eds.), *Handbook of Industrial, Work and Organizational Psychology*, vol. 2 (Thousand Oaks, CA: Sage, 2001), pp. 332–335.

16. See, for instance, R. Lines, "Influence of Participation in Strategic Change: Resistance, Organizational Commitment and Change Goal Achievement," *Journal of Change Management*, September 2004, pp. 193–215.

17. S. Highhouse, "A History of the T-Group and Its Early Application in Management Development," *Group Dynamics: Theory, Research, & Practice*, December 2002, pp. 277–290.

18. J. E. Edwards and M. D. Thomas, "The Organizational Survey Process: General Steps and Practical Considerations," in P. Rosenfeld, J. E. Edwards, and M. D. Thomas (eds.), *Improving Organizational Surveys: New Directions, Methods, and Applications* (Newbury Park, CA: Sage, 1993), pp. 3–28.

19. E. H. Schein, *Process Consultation: Its Role in Organizational Development*, 2nd ed. (Reading, MA: Addison-Wesley, 1988), p. 9. See also E. H. Schein, *Process Consultation Revisited: Building Helpful Relationships* (Reading, MA: Addison-Wesley, 1999).

20. W. Dyer, *Team Building: Issues and Alternatives* (Reading, MA: Addison-Wesley, 1994).

21. See, for example, R. Fry, F. Barrett, J. Seiling, and D. Whitney (eds.), *Appreciative Inquiry & Organizational Transformation: Reports From the Field* (Westport, CT: Quorum, 2002); J. K. Barge and C. Oliver, "Working with Appreciation in Managerial Practice," *Academy of Management Review*, January 2003, pp. 124–142; and D. van der Haar and D. M. Hosking, "Evaluating Appreciative Inquiry: A Relational Constructionist Perspective," *Human Relations*, August 2004, pp. 1017–1036.

22. See, for instance, R. M. Kanter, "When a Thousand Flowers Bloom: Structural, Collective and Social Conditions for Innovation in Organizations," in B. M. Staw and L. L. Cummings (eds.), *Research in Organizational Behavior*, vol. 10 (Greenwich, CT: JAI Press, 1988), pp. 169–211.

23. F. Damanpour, "Organizational Innovation: A Meta-Analysis of Effects of Determinants and Moderators," *Academy of Management Journal*, September 1991, p. 557.

24. See P. R. Monge, M. D. Cozzens, and N. S. Contractor, "Communication and Motivational Predictors of the Dynamics of Organizational Innovation," *Organization Science*, May 1992, pp. 250–274.

25. J. M. Howell and C. A. Higgins, "Champions of Change," *Business Quarterly*, Spring 1990, pp. 31–32; and D. L. Day, "Raising Radicals: Different Processes for Championing Innovative Corporate Ventures," *Organization Science*, May 1994, pp. 148–172.

26. Howell and Higgins, "Champions of Change."

27. See, for example, T. B. Lawrence, M. K. Mauws, B. Dyck, and R. F. Kleysen, "The Politics of Organizational Learning: Integrating Power into the 4I Framework," *Academy of Management Review*, January 2005, pp. 180–191.

28. D. H. Kim, "The Link Between Individual and Organizational Learning," *Sloan Management Review*, Fall 1993, p. 37.

29. C. Argyris and D. A. Schon, *Organizational Learning* (Reading, MA: Addison-Wesley, 1978).

30. B. Dumaine, "Mr. Learning Organization," *Fortune*, October 17, 1994, p. 148.

31. See, for instance, K. Slobogin, "Many US Employees Feel Overworked, Stressed, Study Says," *CNN.com*, May 16, 2001, www.cnn.com; and S. Armour, "Rising Job Stress Could Affect Bottom Line," *USA Today*, July 29, 2003, p. 1B.

32. A. R. Elangovan, 2001, "Causal Ordering of Stress, Satisfaction and Commitment, and Intention to Quit: A Structural Equations Analysis," *Leadership & Organization Development Journal* 22, no. 4, pp. 159–165.

33. Darwish A. Yousef, 2002, "Job Satisfaction as a Mediator of the Relationship Between Role Stressor and Organizational Commitment: A Study from an Arabic Cultural Perspective," *Journal of Managerial Psychology* 1, no. 4, pp. 250–266.

34. N. P. Podsakoff, J. A. LePine, and M. A. LePine, "Differential Challenge–Hindrance Stressor Relationships with Job Attitudes, Turnover Intentions, Turnover, and Withdrawal Behavior: A Meta-analysis," *Journal of Applied Psychology* 92, no. 2 (2007), pp. 438–454; J. A. LePine, M. A. LePine, and C. L. Jackson, "Challenge and Hindrance Stress: Relationships with Exhaustion, Motivation to Learn, and Learning Performance," *Journal of Applied Psychology*, October 2004, pp. 883–891.

35. N. W. Van Yperen and O. Janssen, "Fatigued and Dissatisfied or Fatigued but Satisfied? Goal Orientations and Responses to High Job Demands," *Academy of Management Journal*, December 2002, pp. 1161–1171; and N. W. Van Yperen and M. Hagedoorn, "Do High Job Demands Increase Intrinsic Motivation or Fatigue or Both? The Role of Job Control and Job Social Support," *Academy of Management Journal*, June 2003, pp. 339–348.

36. For example, L. N. Dyrbye, *et al.*, "The Learning Environ—ment and Medical Student Burnout: A Multicentre Study," *Medical Education*, 43, no. 3 (2009), pp. 274–282; and Supe A. N., "A study of Stress in Medical Students at Seth GS Medical College, *Journal of Postgraduate Medicine* 44 (1998), pp. 1–6.

37. M. A. Elzubeir, K. E. Elzubeir, and M. E. Magzoub, "Stress and Coping Strategies among Arab Medical Students: Towards a Research Agenda," *Education for Health* 23, no. 1 (2010).

38. A. O. Carter *et al.*, "Health and Lifestyle Needs Assessment of Medical Students in the United Arab Emirates," *Medical Teacher* 25, no. 5 (2003), pp. 492–496.

39. H. M. Abdulghani, "Stress and Depression Among Medical Students: A Cross Sectional Study at a College in Saudi

Arabia," *Pakistan Journal of Medical Sciences Quarterly* 24, no. 1 (2008), pp. 12–17.

40. A. H. El-Gilany, M. Amr, and S. Hammad, "Perceived Stress Among Male Medical Students in Egypt and Saudi Arabia: Effects of Sociodemographic Factors," *Annals of Saudi Medicine* 28, no. 6 (2008), pp. 442–448.

41. This section is adapted from C. L. Cooper and R. Payne, *Stress at Work* (London: Wiley, 1978); S. Parasuraman and J. A. Alutto, "Sources and Outcomes of Stress in Organizational Settings: Toward the Development of a Structural Model," *Academy of Management Journal* 27, no. 2 (June 1984), pp. 330–350; and P. M. Hart and C. L. Cooper, "Occupational Stress: Toward a More Integrated Framework," in N. Anderson, D. S. Ones, H. K. Sinangil, and C. Viswesvaran (eds.), *Handbook of Industrial, Work and Organizational Psychology*, vol. 2 (London: Sage, 2001), pp. 93–114.

42. A. E. Rafferty and M. A. Griffin, "Perceptions of Organizational Change: A Stress and Coping Perspective," *Journal of Applied Psychology* 71, no. 5 (2007), pp. 1154–1162.

43. H. Garst, M. Frese, and P. C. M. Molenaar, "The Temporal Factor of Change in Stressor-Strain Relationships: A Growth Curve Model on a Longitudinal Study in East Germany," *Journal of Applied Psychology*, June 2000, pp. 417–438.

44. See, for example, M. L. Fox, D. J. Dwyer, and D. C. Ganster, "Effects of Stressful Job Demands and Control of Physiological and Attitudinal Outcomes in a Hospital Setting," *Academy of Management Journal*, April 1993, pp. 289–318.

45. G. W. Evans and D. Johnson, "Stress and Open-Office Noise," *Journal of Applied Psychology*, October 2000, pp. 779–783.

46. V. S. Major, K. J. Klein, and M. G. Ehrhart, "Work Time, Work Interference with Family, and Psychological Distress," *Journal of Applied Psychology*, June 2002, pp. 427–436; see also P. E. Spector, C. L. Cooper, S. Poelmans, T. D. Allen, M. O'Driscoll, J. I. Sanchez, O. L. Siu, P. Dewe, P. Hart, L. Lu, L. F. R. De Moreas, G. M. Ostrognay, K. Sparks, P. Wong, and S. Yu, "A Cross-National Comparative Study of Work-Family Stressors, Working Hours, and Well-Being: China and Latin America Versus the Anglo World," *Personnel Psychology*, Spring 2004, pp. 119–142.

47. H. Selye, *The Stress of Life*, rev. ed. (New York: McGraw-Hill, 1956).

48. S. J. Motowidlo, J. S. Packard, and M. R. Manning, "Occupational Stress: Its Causes and Consequences for Job Performance," *Journal of Applied Psychology*, November 1987, pp. 619–620.

49. Melissa Karnaze, "Salovey & Mayer on Emotional Intelligence, 1990," http://mindfulconstruct.com/2009/03/31/salovey-mayer-on-emotional-intelligence-1990.

50. R. S. Schuler, "Definition and Conceptualization of Stress," *Organizational Behavior and Human Performance*, April 1980, pp. 200–205; and R. L. Kahn and M. Byosiere, "Stress in Organizations," in M. D. Dunnette and L. M. Hough (eds.), *Handbook of Industrial and Organizational Psychology*, 2nd ed., vol. 3 (Palo Alto, CA: Consulting Psychologists Press, 1992), pp. 604–610.

51. B. D. Steffy and J. W. Jones, "Workplace Stress and Indicators of Coronary-Disease Risk," *Academy of Management Journal*, September 1988, p. 687.

52. M. de Croon, J. K. Sluiter, R. W. B. Blonk, J. P. J. Broersen, and M. H. W. Frings-Dresen, "Stressful Work, Psychological Job Strain, and Turnover: A 2-Year Prospective Cohort Study of Truck Drivers," *Journal of Applied Psychology*, June 2004, pp. 442–454; and R. Cropanzano, D. E. Rupp, and Z. S. Byrne, "The Relationship of Emotional Exhaustion to Work Attitudes, Job Performance, and Organizational Citizenship Behaviors," *Journal of Applied Psychology*, February 2003, pp. 160–169.

53. The following discussion has been influenced by J. E. Newman and T. A. Beehr, "Personal and Organizational Strategies for Handling Job Stress," *Personnel Psychology*, Spring 1979, pp. 1–38; J. M. Ivancevich and M. T. Matteson, "Organizational Level Stress Management Interventions: A Review and Recommendations," *Journal of Organizational Behavior Management*, Fall–Winter 1986, pp. 229–248; M. T. Matteson and J. M. Ivancevich, "Individual Stress Management Interventions: Evaluation of Techniques," *Journal of Management Psychology*, January 1987, pp. 24–30; J. M. Ivancevich, M. T. Matteson, S. M. Freedman, and J. S. Phillips, "Worksite Stress Management Interventions," *American Psychologist*, February 1990, pp. 252–261; and R. Schwarzer, "Manage Stress at Work Through Preventive and Proactive Coping," in E. A. Locke (ed.), *Handbook of Principles of Organizational Behavior* (Malden, MA: Blackwell, 2004), pp. 342–355.

54. T. H. Macan, "Time Management: Test of a Process Model," *Journal of Applied Psychology*, June 1994, pp. 381–391; and B. J. C. Claessens, W. Van Eerde, C. G. Rutte, and R. A. Roe, "Planning Behavior and Perceived Control of Time at Work," *Journal of Organizational Behavior*, December 2004, pp. 937–950.

55. J. Kiely and G. Hodgson, "Stress in the Prison Service: The Benefits of Exercise Programs," *Human Relations*, June 1990, pp. 551–572.

56. See, for instance, B. Leonard, "Health Care Costs Increase Interest in Wellness Programs," *HR Magazine*, September 2001, pp. 35–36; and "Healthy, Happy and Productive," *Training*, February 2003, p. 16.

57. See S. Shane, S. Venkataraman, and I. MacMillan, "Cultural Differences in Innovation Championing Strategies," *Journal of Management* 21, no. 5 (1995), pp. 931–952.

58. See "Lack of recognition biggest barrier to productivity, say 41% of job seekers," March 9, 2009, www.ameinfo.com/187790.html.

59. H. M. Addae and X. Wang, "Stress at Work: Linear and Curvilinear Effects of Psychological-, Job-, and Organization-Related Factors: An Exploratory Study of Trinidad and Tobago," *International Journal of Stress Management*, November 2006, pp. 476–493.

60. P. S. Goodman and L. B. Kurke, "Studies of Change in Organizations: A Status Report," in P. S. Goodman (ed.), *Change in Organizations* (San Francisco: Jossey-Bass, 1982), p. 1.

61. Kahn and Byosiere, "Stress in Organizations," pp. 605–608.

62. For contrasting views on episodic and continuous change, see K. E. Weick and R. E. Quinn, "Organizational Change and Development," in J. T. Spence, J. M. Darlcy, and D. J. Foss (eds.), *Annual Review of Psychology*, vol. 50 (Palo Alto, CA: Annual Reviews, 1999), pp. 361–386.

63. This perspective is based on P. B. Vaill, *Managing as a Performing Art: New Ideas for a World of Chaotic Change* (San Francisco: Jossey-Bass, 1989).

64. J. D. Breul, "Setting Stretch Goals Helps Agencies Exceed Their Reach," *Government Leader* 1, no. 9 (September/October 2006), www.governmentleader.com/issues/1_9/commentary/205-1.html); G. Stoller, "Frequent Business Travelers Pack Guilt, *USA Today*, June 22, 2006, www.usatoday.com/money/biztravel/2006-06-21-road-warriors-usat_x.htm.

Chapter 17

1. See C. E. Aronoff and J. L. Ward, *Family Business Governance: Maximizing Family and Business Potential*, 2nd ed. (Marietta, GA: Business Owner Resources, 1996).

2. T. G. Habbershon, M. Williams, and I. C. MacMillan, "A Unified Systems Perspective of Family Firm Performance," *Journal of Business Venturing* 18 (2003), pp. 451–465.

3. See P. Sharma and J. Chrisman, "Toward a Reconciliation of the Definitional Issues in the Field of Corporate Entrepreneurship," *Entrepreneurship Theory and Practice* 23, no. 3 (1999), pp. 11–27; J. H. Chua, J. J. Chrisman, and P. Sharma, 2003, "Succession and Non-Succession Concerns of Family Firms and Agency Relationship with Non-Family Managers," *Family Business Review* 16 (2003), pp. 89–107.

4. R. Tagiuri and J. A. Davis, "On the Goals of Successful Family Companies," *Family Business Review* 5, no. 1 (1992), pp. 43–62.

5. J. Chrisman, J. Chua, and P. Sharma, *A Review and Annotated Bibliography of Family Business Studies* (Boston: Kluwer, 1996).

6. M. C. Shanker and J. H. Astrachan, "Myths and Realities: Family Businesses' Contribution to the US Economy—A Framework for Assessing Family Business Statistics," *Family Business Review* 9, no. 2 (1996).

7. The definitions are based on two sources: N. B. Upton and D. L. Sexton, "Family Business Succession: The Female Perspective," paper presented at the 32nd Annual Conference of the International Center of Small Business (ICSB), 1987; and J. L. Ward, *Keeping the Family Business Healthy: How to Plan for Continuing Growth, Profitability, and Family Leadership* (San Francisco, CA: Jossey-Bass, 1987).

8. B. Bigliardi and A. I. Dormio, "Successful Generational Change in Family Business," *Measuring Business Excellence* 13, no. 2 (2009).

9. Statistics in this section taken from S. Perman, "Taking the Pulse of Family Business," *Bloomberg Business Week*, March 2010; E. J. Poza, *Family Business* (Mason, OH: South-Western Cengage Learning, 2010); "Family Business Statistics," *Gaebler Ventures*, May 5, 2010, www.gaebler.com/Family-Business-Statistics.htm; "Middle Eastern Family Businesses Have Unique Challenges," November 2009, www.familybusinesswiki.ning.com/profiles/blogs/middle-eastern-family; and J. Fahed-Sreih, *Facts and Figures Concerning Family Businesses in Lebanon* (Texas: Franklin Publishing Company, 2005).

10. E. J. Poza, *Family Business* (South Western College, 2009).

11. M. Carney, "Corporate Governance and Competitive Advantage in Family Controlled Firms," *Entrepreneurship Theory and Practice* 29 (2005), pp. 249–265.

12. S. E. Johnston, *The Family Business: Statistics, Profiles and Peculiarities*, 2004.

13. For more information, visit http://geert-hofstede.com/website/national-culture.html.

14. J. Hartley, "Family Business Key to Surviving Economic Storm," *ArabianBusiness.com*, ITP Publishing Group, March 2, 2009.

15. Arab Human Development Report 2005: Towards the Rise of Women in the Arab World, *United Nations Development Programme*.

16. Fahed-Sreih, "Middle Eastern Family Businesses Have Unique Challenges," http://familybusinesswiki.ning.com/profiles/blogs/middle-eastern-family.

17. W. G. Dyer, *Cultural Change in Family Firms: Anticipating and Managing Business and Family Transitions*, (San Francisco: Jossey-Bass, 1986).

18. G. W. Rimler and D. Ingersol, "How to Professionalize the Family Firm," *Air Conditioning, Heating & Refrigeration News*, June 2001, p. 1.

19. Habbershon, Williams, and MacMillan, "A Unified Systems Perspective of Family Firm Performance", pp. 451–465.

20. Ibid.

21. M. E. Shehadi, "How to Ensure Continuity in Lebanese Family Businesses," MBA Research Project, Notre Dame University, Lebanon, 2011.

22. W. S. White, T. D. Krinke, D. L. Geller, "Family Business Succession Planning: Devising an Overall Strategy," *Journal of Financial Services Professionals* 67 (May 2004).

23. K. O'Brien, "How to Succeed in Business," *American Printer* 60 (April 1998).

24. "Family business owners optimistic about growth, but many aren't making adequate provisions for the future, says PwC," *Price Waterhouse Coopers (PwC) Belgium* website, November 3, 2010, www.pwc.be/en/press/2010-11-03-family-business-owners-optimistic-about-growth.jhtml.

25. S. Nelton, "Timeless Insights through Oral Histories," *Nation's Business* 72, March 1998.

26. "The Five Crises Facing GCC Family Businesses", *Booz & Company*, November 8, 2009, www.booz.com/me/home/thought_leadership_strategy/40007409/40007869/46570190?pg=0.

27. Ibid.

28. Z. BitaStaff, "Keeping it All in the Family," *Gulf News*, June 14, 2010, http://gulfnews.com/business/features/keeping-it-all-in-the-family-1.640715.

29. N. Drozdow, "What Is Continuity?" *Family Business Review* 11 (April 2004), pp. 337–347.

30. "Family business owners optimistic, but many aren't making provisions for the future," *Business Intelligence Middle East*, November 4, 2010.

31. For sources relating to this section, see Barclays Wealth and *The Economist* Intelligence Unit, "Family Business: In Safe Hands?" *Barclays Wealth Insights* 8 (2009); S. A. Zahra, "Entrepreneurial Risk Taking in Family Firms," *Family Business Review*, March 2005; Z. Fernández and M. J. Nieto, "Internationalization Strategy of Small and Medium-Sized Family Businesses: Some Influential Factors," *Family Business Review*, March 2005; M. Carney, "Minority Family Business in Emerging Markets: Organization Forms and Competitive Advantage," *Family Business Review*, December 2007.

32. See *Tharawat Magazine*, www.tharawat-magazine.com; Barclays Wealth & *The Economist* Intelligence Unit, "Family Business: In Safe Hands?"; P. Raven and D. H. B. Welsh, "Family Business in the Middle East: An Exploratory Study of Retail Management in Kuwait and Lebanon," *Family Business Review*, March 2006.

Chapter 18

1. S. Green quoted in R. T. Moran, P. R. Harris, and S. V. Moran, *Managing Cultural Differences: Global Leadership Strategies for Cross Cultural Business Success*, (Routledge 2010), p. 1.

2. G. Hofstede, *Cultures and Organizations: Software of the Mind* (London: McGraw-Hill, 1991).

3. See C. Rosado, "What Do We Mean By 'Managing Diversity'?" in Sumati Reddy (ed.), *Workforce Diversity* 3 (Hyderabad, India: ICAFAI University, 2008).

4. Harris *et al.*, *Managing Cultural Differences: Global Leadership Strategies for the 21st Century*, pp. 41–42.

5. H. Bedi, as quoted in Moran *et al. Managing Cultural Differences: Global Leadership Strategies for Cross Cultural Business Success*, p. 107.

6. G. P. Ferraro, *The Cultural Dimension of International Business*. 3rd ed. (Prentice-Hall, 1998), p. 115. Reprinted and electronically reproduced by permission of Pearson Education, Inc., Upper Saddle River, New Jersey.

7. Ibid., p. 127

8. See J. W. Salacuse, *Making Global Deals: Negotiating in the International Marketplace* (Boston: Houghton Mifflin, 1991), p. 164.

9. D. W. Klopf, *Intercultural Encounters* (Englewood, CO: Morton Publishing, 1991); G. F. Simons, C. Vaszquez, and P. R. Harris, *Transcultural Leadership* (Houston, TX: Gulf Publishing, 1993).

10. Harris *et al.*, *Managing Cultural Differences: Global Leadership Strategies for the 21st Century*, p. 21.

11. M. J. Bennett (ed.), *Basic Concepts of Intercultural Communication* (Yarmouth, ME: Intercultural Press, 1998). Reproduced with permission of Nicholas Brearley Publishing.

12. R. Kassab and R. G. Najjar, "Those Who Lead and Those Who Follow," *Executive Magazine* 122, 2009, pp. 32–34.

13. B. Ruben, *Handbook of Intercultural Skills*, vol. 1 (New York: Pergamon Press, 1983).

14. S. H. Rhinesmith (1996), as quoted in Harris *et al.*, *Managing Cultural Differences: Global Leadership Strategies for the 21st Century*, p. 24.

15. C. A. Bartlett and S. Ghoshal (1992), as quoted in Harris *et al.*, *Managing Cultural Differences: Global Leadership Strategies for the 21st Century*, pp. 24–25.

16. See A. Kapiszewski, *Nationals and Expatriates: Population and Labor Dilemmas of the Gulf Cooperation Council States* (New York: Ithaca Press, 2001),

17. For the original data in this and the following paragraph, see A. J. Fish and J. Wood, "A Review of Expatriate Staffing Practices in Australian Business Enterprises," *The International Journal of Human Resource Management* 7, no. 4 (1996), pp. 846–865. R. L. Tung, "A Contingency Framework of Selection and Training of Expatriates Revisited," *Human Resource Management Review* 8, no. 1 (1998), pp. 23–37; Z. Aycan, "Acculturation of Expatriate Managers: A Process Model of Adjustment and Performance," in Z. Aycan (ed.), *New Approaches to Employee Management* vol. 4 (Montreal, Canada: JAI Press, 1997); P. M. Caliguiri, "The Big Five Personality Characteristics As Predictors of Expatriate Success," *Personnel Psychology*, 2000, pp. 53, 67–88; R. J. Stone, "Expatriate Selection and Failure," *Human Resource Planning* 14, no. 1 (1991); M. Mendenhall, E. Dunbar, and G. Oddou,

"Expatriate Selection, Training and Career Pathing: A Review Critique," *Human Resource Management* 26, no. 3 (1987), pp. 331–345; J. S. Black, and H. B. Gregersen, "The Right Way to Manage Expats," *Harvard Business Review* 77, no. 2 (1997), pp. 52–63.

18. Harris *et al.*, *Managing Cultural Differences: Global Leadership Strategies for the 21st Century*, p. 192.

19. Ferraro, *The Cultural Dimension of International Business*, p. 149.

20. Ibid. pp. 159–161.

21. See R. R. Gesteland, *Cross-Cultural Business Behavior-Marketing: Negotiating, and Managing Across Cultures* (Copenhagen, Denmark: The Copenhagen Business School Press, 1999).

22. See E. T. Hall and M. R. Hall, *Hidden Differences: Doing Business with the Japanese* (New York: Anchor/Doubleday, 1987).

23. See V. Terpstra and K. David, *The Cultural Environment of International Business* (Cincinnati, OH: South-Western Publishing, 1958); F. Trompenaars, *Riding the Waves of Culture* (London: Economist Books, 1997), p. 3.

24. I. Asherman, J. W. Bing, and L. Laroche, "Building Trust Across Cultural Boundaries," *Regulatory Affairs Focus*, May 2000. Available at: http://asherman.com/downloads/article-btacb.pdf.

Chapter 19

1. For a discussion of possible characteristics, see M. Firestone, "Personal Characteristics of Successful Women Entrepreneurs," *Woman Presidents' Organization*, accessible at http://us.smetoolkit.org/us/en/content/en/2252/Personal-Characteristics-of-Successful-Women-Entreprenuers.

2. C. Prifti *et al.*, *Middle East Local and Regional Women Entrepreneurship* (Institute of International Relations, 2009).

3. An Interview with Kenneth Morse, *Executive Magazine*, no. 131, June 2010, pp. 42–44.

4. E. A. Nassim, "Excelling Despite Challenges", *Oman Economic Review*, July 2007.

5. T. Neese, "Women Play Increasing Roles in the Business World," *Journal Record*, May 1999.

6. American Express OPEN "State of Women–Owned Businesses" Report, March 2011.

7. "Women at work," *OECD Observer*, no. 275 (November 2009).

8. *Women Entrepreneurs in the Middle East and North Africa: Characteristics, Contributions and Challenges* (The International Finance Corporation and the Center of Arab Women for Training and Research, 2007).

9. "First Arab Women's Leadership Forum announced," *GulfNews.com*, August 31, 2008.

10. Figures taken from US Bureau of Labor Statistics.

11. Figures based on USA National Center for Education Statistics.

12. "Earnings and Incomes of Canadians Over the Past Quarter Century, 2006 Census: Earnings," *Statistics Canada* , October 2009, www12.statcan.ca/census-recensement/2006/as-sa/97-563/p4-eng.cfm.

13. Ibid.

14. The discussion of nepotism is based largely on C. Young, "Employee Favoritism and Nepotism—Employee Morale Cancer," *Rain Maker Group* website blog, September 2008, www.therainmakergroupinc.com/blog/bid/91330/Employee-Favoritism-and-Nepotism-Employee-Morale-Cancer.

15. Oxford Dictionaries, *Oxford University Press (OUP)*, (UK) (English), http://oxforddictionaries.com/definition/nepotism?region=us.

16. *Women Entrepreneurs in the Middle East and North Africa: Characteristics, Contributions and Challenges* (The International Finance Corporation and the Center of Arab Women for Training and Research 2007).

17. "Female Entrepreneurs in Middle East and North Africa Defy Expectations," *WorldBank.org*, December 18, 2007, http://web.worldbank.org/WBSITE/EXTERNAL/NEWS/0,,contentMDK:21589991~pagePK:64257043~piPK:437376~theSitePK:4607,00.html.

18. "6 reasons successful women intimidate men", *Femeo website*, August 3, 2011, http://femeo.bayt.com/en/articles/career-development/6-reasons-successful-women-intimidate-men. Reproduced with permission of Bayt.com.

19. M. Scott Bortot, "Qatari Entrepreneur Leads Effort to Empower Businesswomen: Buthaina Al-Ansari's Qatariat Company Trains and Inspires Qatari Women," Embassy of the United States of America, April 21, 2010, www.uspolicy.be/headline/qatari-entrepreneur-leads-effort-empower-businesswomen.

20. N. Jackson, "Break Your Own Glass Ceiling," *Glassdoor Blog*, June 22, 2010, www.glassdoor.com/blog/break-glass-ceiling.

21. Data in this section is from D. Tucker, "Arab Women Beginning to Crack the Glass Ceiling," *Huffington Post*, March 18, 2009, www.huffingtonpost.com/diane-tucker/arab-women-beginning-to-c_b_176137.html; and "Women Increasing Economic Power in Global Market", *MS Magazine*, July 29, 1998, www.msmagazine.com/news/uswirestory.asp?id=2470.

22. Irene Natividad, quoted in S. E. Jalbert *Women Entrepreneurs in the Global Economy*, March 17, 2000, p. 9, available at www.cipe.org/programs/women/pdf/jalbert.pdf.

23. As reported by the Economic and Social Commission for Western Asia (ESCWA), www.escwa.un.org/divisions/events/ecwsession/mainE.asp.

24. "Women Matter: Gender Diversity, a Corporate Performance Driver", A McKinsey and Company publication, 2007. Available at www.mckinsey.com/locations/swiss/news_publications/pdf/women_matter_english.pdf.

25. N. Wilson, "Women in the Boardroom Help Business Succeed", *The Times*, March 19, 2009.

26. Condoleezza Rice, 2005 speaking in Cairo. Reported on http://www.arabist.net/blog/2005/6/20/condoleezza-rices-remarks-from-her-cairo-speech-at-auc.html.

Appendix A

1. J. A. Byrne, "Executive Sweat," *Forbes*, May 20, 1985, pp. 198–200.

2. See D. P. Schwab, *Research Methods for Organizational Behavior* (Mahwah, NJ: Lawrence Erlbaum Associates, 1999); and S. G. Rogelberg (ed.), *Blackwell Handbook of Research Methods in Industrial and Organizational Psychology* (Malden, MA: Blackwell, 2002).

3. B. M. Staw and G. R. Oldham, "Reconsidering Our Dependent Variables: A Critique and Empirical Study," *Academy of Management Journal*, December 1978, pp. 539–559; and B. M. Staw, "Organizational Behavior: A Review and Reformulation of the Field's Outcome Variables," in M. R. Rosenzweig and L. W. Porter (eds.), *Annual Review of Psychology*, vol. 35 (Palo Alto, CA: Annual Reviews, 1984), pp. 627–666.

4. R. S. Blackburn, "Experimental Design in Organizational Settings," in J. W. Lorsch (ed.), *Handbook of Organizational Behavior* (Upper Saddle River, NJ: Prentice Hall, 1987), pp. 127–128; and F. L. Schmidt, C. Viswesvaran, and D. S. Ones, "Reliability Is Not Validity and Validity Is Not Reliability," *Personnel Psychology*, Winter 2000, pp. 901–912.

5. G. R. Weaver, L. K. Trevino, and P. L. Cochran, "Corporate Ethics Practices in the Mid-1990's: An Empirical Study of the Fortune 1000," *Journal of Business Ethics*, February 1999, pp. 283–294.

6. S. Milgram, *Obedience to Authority* (New York: Harper & Row, 1974). For a critique of this research, see T. Blass, "Understanding Behavior in the Milgram Obedience Experiment: The Role of Personality, Situations, and Their Interactions," *Journal of Personality and Social Psychology*, March 1991, pp. 398–413.

7. See, for example, W. N. Kaghan, A. L. Strauss, S. R. Barley, M. Y. Brannen, and R. J. Thomas, "The Practice and Uses of Field Research in the 21st Century Organization," *Journal of Management Inquiry*, March 1999, pp. 67–81.

8. A. D. Stajkovic and F. Luthans, "A Meta-Analysis of the Effects of Organizational Behavior Modification on Task Performance, 1975–1995," *Academy of Management Journal*, October 1997, pp. 1122–1149.

9. See, for example, K. Zakzanis, "The Reliability of Meta Analytic Review," *Psychological Reports*, August 1998, pp. 215–222; C. Ostroff and D. A. Harrison, "Meta-Analysis, Level of Analysis, and Best Estimates of Population Correlations: Cautions for Interpreting Meta-Analytic Results in Organizational Behavior," *Journal of Applied Psychology*, April 1999, pp. 260–270; R. Rosenthal and M. R. DiMatteo, "Meta-Analysis: Recent Developments in Quantitative Methods for Literature Reviews," in S. T. Fiske, D. L. Schacter, and C. Zahn-Wacher (eds.), *Annual Review of Psychology*, vol. 52 (Palo Alto, CA: Annual Reviews, 2001), pp. 59–82; and F. L. Schmidt and J. E. Hunter, "Meta-Analysis," in N. Anderson, D. S. Ones, H. K. Sinangil, and C. Viswesvaran (eds.), *Handbook of Industrial, Work & Organizational Psychology*, vol. 1 (Thousand Oaks, CA: Sage, 2001), pp. 51–70.

10. For more on ethical issues in research, see T. L. Beauchamp, R. R. Faden, R. J. Wallace, Jr., and L. Walters (eds.), *Ethical Issues in Social Science Research* (Baltimore, MD: Johns Hopkins University Press, 1982); and J. G. Adair, "Ethics of Psychological Research: New Policies, Continuing Issues, New Concerns," *Canadian Psychology*, February 2001, pp. 25–37.

11. J. Kifner, "Scholar Sets Off Gastronomic False Alarm," *New York Times*, September 8, 2001, p. A1.

Comprehensive Cases

1. "Nightmare on Wall Street," *The Economist*, September 15, 2008.

2. "Bahrain Hotel Occupancy Rates Fall" *Arabian Business*, November 27, 2008.

3. "Hotel Occupancy Rates Down," *Dubai Online*, January 20, 2009.

4. "Atlantis Cuts 70 jobs, Jumeirah to Reduce Staff," *Arabian Business*, February 17, 2009.

5. "But Have We Learned Enough?" *New York Times*, October 25, 2008.

Glossary

Ability | القدرة
An individual's capacity to perform the various tasks in a job.

Absenteeism | ظاهرة الغياب
The failure to report to work.

Accommodating | الملاءمة / التلاؤم / التراضي المتبادل
The willingness of one party in a conflict to place the opponent's interests above his or her own.

Acculturation | التبادل الثقافي / الامتزاج الثقافي
Adaptation and integration into another culture.

Action research | البحث المقترن بالإصلاح
A change process based on systematic collection of data and then selection of a change action based on what the analyzed data indicate.

Adjourning stage | مرحلة الإرجاء
The final stage in group development for temporary groups, characterized by concern with wrapping up activities rather than task performance.

Affect | وجدان
A broad range of feelings that people experience.

Affect intensity | الشدة الوجدانية / العاطفية
Individual differences in the strength with which individuals experience their emotions.

Affective commitment | الالتزام الوجداني / العاطفي
An emotional attachment to an organization and a belief in its values.

Affective component | المكون الوجداني / العاطفي
The emotional or feeling segment of an attitude.

Affective events theory (AET) | نظرية الأحداث الوجدانية
A model that suggests that workplace events cause emotional reactions on the part of employees, which then influence workplace attitudes and behaviors.

Agreeableness | المقبولية
A personality dimension that describes someone who is good natured, cooperative, and trusting.

Anchoring bias | التحيز الراسخ
A tendency to fixate on initial information, from which one then fails to adequately adjust for subsequent information.

Anthropology | الأنثروبولوجيا / علم الإنسان
The study of societies to learn about human beings and their activities.

Appreciative inquiry (AI) | التقصي الإيجابي
An approach that seeks to identify the unique qualities and special strengths of an organization, which can then be built on to improve performance.

Arbitrator | المحكّم / الوسيط
A third party to a negotiation who has the authority to dictate an agreement.

Assessment centers | مراكز التقييم
Places where job candidates are evaluated as they go through one to several days of exercises that simulate real problems they would confront on the job.

Attitudes | الاتجاهات
Evaluative statements or judgments concerning objects, people, or events.

Attribution theory | نظرية النسبية / العزو
An attempt to determine whether an individual's behavior is internally or externally caused.

Attribution theory of leadership | نظرية النسبية / العزو للقيادة
A leadership theory that says that leadership is merely an attribution that people make about other individuals.

Authentic leaders | قادة يتميزون بالأصالة
Leaders who know who they are, know what they believe in and value, and act on those values and beliefs openly and candidly. Their followers would consider them to be ethical people.

Authority | السلطة
The rights inherent in a managerial position to give orders and to expect the orders to be obeyed.

Autonomy | الاستقلالية
The degree to which a job provides substantial freedom, independence, and discretion to the individual in scheduling the work and in determining the procedures to be used in carrying it out.

Availability bias | التحيز للموجود
The tendency for people to base their judgments on information that is readily available to them.

Avoiding | التحاشي
The desire to withdraw from or suppress a conflict.

Behavioral component | المكون السلوكي
An intention to behave in a certain way toward someone or something.

Behavioral theories of leadership | النظريات السلوكية للقيادة
Theories proposing that specific behaviors differentiate leaders from nonleaders.

Behaviorally anchored rating scales (BARS) | مقياس التدرج البياني السلوكي
Scales that combine major elements from the critical incident and graphic rating scale approaches: the appraiser rates the employees based on items along a continuum, but the points are examples of actual behavior on the given job rather than general descriptions or traits.

Behaviorism | المذهب السلوكي
A theory that argues that behavior follows stimuli in a relatively unthinking manner.

Big Five model | نموذج العوامل الخمسة الكبرى
A personality assessment model that taps five basic dimensions.

Biographical characteristics | السمات الشخصية
Personal characteristics—such as age, gender, race, and length of tenure—that are objective and easily obtained from personnel records.

Bonus | المنحة / المكافأة
A pay plan that rewards employees for recent performance rather than historical performance.

Boundaryless organization | مؤسسة بلا حدود
An organization that seeks to eliminate the chain of command, have limitless spans of control, and replace departments with empowered teams.

Bounded rationality | الرشد المحدود
A process of making decisions by constructing simplified models that extract the essential features from problems without capturing all their complexity.

Brainstorming | العصف الذهني
An idea-generation process that specifically encourages any and all alternatives while withholding any criticism of those alternatives.

Bureaucracy | البيروقراطية
A structure with highly routine operating tasks achieved through specialization, very formalized rules and regulations, tasks that are grouped into functional departments, centralized authority, narrow spans of control, and decision making that follows the chain of command.

Business continuity | استمرارية الأعمال
The ability of a business to continue during and after a setback.

Centralization | المركزية
The degree to which decision making is concentrated at a single point in an organization.

Chain of command | تسلسل الأوامر
The unbroken line of authority that extends from the top of the organization to the lowest echelon and clarifies who reports to whom.

Challenge stressors | ضغوط المهام
Stressors associated with workload, pressure to complete tasks, and time urgency.

Change | التغيير
Making things different.

Change agents | عوامل التغيير
People who act as catalysts and assume the responsibility for managing change activities.

Channel richness | وفرة القناة
The amount of information that can be transmitted during a communication episode.

Charismatic leadership theory | نظرية القيادة الكاريزماتية
A leadership theory that states that followers make attributions of heroic or extraordinary leadership abilities when they observe certain behaviors.

Classical conditioning | الإشراط الكلاسيكي
A type of conditioning in which an individual responds to some stimulus that would not ordinarily produce such a response.

Coercive power | قوة الإكراه
A power base that is dependent on fear.

Cognitive component | المكون المعرفي / الإدراكي
The opinion or belief segment of an attitude.

Cognitive dissonance | التنافر المعرفي
Any incompatibility between two or more attitudes or between behavior and attitudes.

Cognitive evaluation theory | نظرية التقييم المعرفي
A theory that states that allocating extrinsic rewards for behavior that had been previously intrinsically rewarding tends to decrease the overall level of motivation.

Cognitive resource theory | نظرية الموارد المعرفية
A theory of leadership that states that stress unfavorably affects a situation and that intelligence and experience can reduce the influence of stress on the leader.

Cohesiveness | التماسك
The degree to which group members are attracted to each other and are motivated to stay in the group.

Collaborating | متعاون / مشترك
A situation in which the parties to a conflict each desire to satisfy fully the concerns of all parties.

Collectivism | الجماعية
A national culture attribute that describes a tight social framework in which people expect others in groups of which they are a part to look after them and protect them.

Command group | مجموعة الأوامر
A group composed of the individuals who report directly to a given manager.

Communication | الاتصال
The transfer and understanding of meaning through verbal and nonverbal messages.

Communication apprehension | مخاوف الاتصالات
Undue tension and anxiety about oral communication, written communication, or both.

Communication process | عملية الاتصال
The steps between a source and a receiver that result in the transfer and understanding of meaning.

Competing | متنافس / منافس
A desire to satisfy one's interests, regardless of the impact on the other party to the conflict.

Compromising | وسيطي
A situation in which each party to a conflict is willing to give up something.

Conceptual skills | المهارات الفكرية
The mental ability to analyze and diagnose complex situations.

Conciliator | موفق / مُصالِح / وسيط
A trusted third party who provides an informal communication link between the negotiator and the opponent.

Confirmation bias | الميل للتأكد
The tendency to seek out information that reaffirms past choices and to discount information that contradicts past judgments.

Conflict | النزاع
A process that begins when one party perceives that another party has negatively affected, or is about to negatively affect, something that the first party cares about.

Conflict management | إدارة النزاعات
The use of resolution and stimulation techniques to achieve the desired level of conflict.

Conflict process | عملية النزاع
A process that has five stages: potential opposition or incompatibility, cognition and personalization, intentions, behavior, and outcomes.

Conformity | المطابقة / التماثل
The adjustment of one's behavior to align with the norms of the group.

Conscientiousness | الضميرية
A personality dimension that describes someone who is responsible, dependable, persistent, and organized.

Consideration | المراعاة
The extent to which a leader is likely to have job relationships characterized by mutual trust, respect for subordinates' ideas, and regard for their feelings.

Consultant | مستشار
An impartial third party, skilled in conflict management, who attempts to facilitate creative problem solving through communication and analysis.

Contingency variables | متغيرات التصادف
Situational factors: variables that moderate the relationship between two or more other variables.

Continuance commitment | الانتماء الاستمراري
The perceived economic value of remaining with an organization compared with leaving it.

Continuous reinforcement | التعزيز المستمر
Reinforcing a desired behavior each time it is demonstrated.

Contrast effects | تأثيرات المغايرة
Evaluation of a person's characteristics that is affected by comparisons with other people recently encountered who rank higher or lower on the same characteristics.

Controlling | مراقب
Monitoring activities to ensure that they are being accomplished as planned and correcting any significant deviations.

Core self-evaluation | التقييم الجوهري للذات
The degree to which an individual likes or dislikes himself or herself, whether the person sees himself or herself as capable and effective, and whether the person feels in control of his or her environment or powerless over the environment.

Core values | القيم الجوهرية / الأساسية
The primary or dominant values that are accepted throughout the organization.

Corporate culture | الثقافة المشتركة
The internal culture that determines the atmosphere and work environment of an organization.

Cost-minimization strategy | استراتيجية تقليص التكاليف
A strategy that emphasizes tight cost controls, avoidance of unnecessary innovation or marketing expenses, and price cutting.

Creativity | الإبداع
The ability to produce novel and useful ideas.

Critical incidents | الأحداث الحرجة / الخطرة
A way of evaluating the behaviors that are key in making the difference between executing a job effectively and executing it ineffectively.

Cross-cultural training (CCT) | تدريب التواصل بين الثقافات
Training given so that employees can communicate and interact more successfully with different cultures.

Cross-functional teams | الفرق متعددة الوظائف
Employees from about the same hierarchical level, but from different work areas, who come together to accomplish a task.

Cultural synergy | التآزر الثقافي
Increased effectiveness within an organization or environment as a result of combining the perceptions, knowledge, and practices of people from different cultures.

Culture | الثقافة
The values, beliefs, behavior and customs of a particular group of people.

Decisions | قرارات
Choices made from among two or more alternatives.

Deep acting | التصرف الوجداني / العميق
Trying to modify one's true inner feelings based on display rules.

Defensive behaviors | التصرفات / السلوكيات الدفاعية
Reactive and protective behaviors to avoid action, blame, or change.

Demands | المطالب / الاحتياجات
Responsibilities, pressures, obligations, and even uncertainties that individuals face in the workplace.

Departmentalization | التقسيم الإداري
The basis by which jobs in an organization are grouped together.

Dependency | الاعتماد / التبعية
B's relationship to A when A possesses something that B requires.

Dependent variable | متغير تابع
A response that is affected by an independent variable.

Deterrence-based trust | الثقة القائمة على الردع
Trust based on fear of reprisal if the trust is violated.

Deviant workplace behavior | السلوك المنحرف بمكان العمل
Voluntary behavior that violates significant organizational norms and, in so doing, threatens the wellbeing of the organization or its members. Also called antisocial behavior or workplace incivility.

Displayed emotions | الانفعالات البادية / الظاهرة
Emotions that are organizationally required and considered appropriate in a given job.

Distributive bargaining | مساومة التوزيع
Negotiation that seeks to divide up a fixed amount of resources; a win–lose situation.

Distributive justice | عدالة التوزيع
Perceived fairness of the amount and allocation of rewards among individuals.

Diversity | التنوع
The differences that people bring to an organization or group.

Dominant culture | الثقافة المسيطرة
A culture that expresses the core values that are shared by a majority of the organization's members.

Double-loop learning | التعلم ثنائي الحلقة
A process of correcting errors by modifying the organization's objectives, policies, and standard routines.

Driving forces | القوى الدافعة
Forces that direct behavior away from the status quo.

Dysfunctional conflict | الصراع الغير وظيفي
Conflict that hinders group performance.

Effectiveness | التأثير / الفاعلية
Achievement of goals.

Efficiency | الكفاية / القدرة
The ratio of effective output to the input required to achieve it.

Electronic meeting | اجتماع إلكتروني
A meeting in which members interact on computers, allowing for anonymity of comments and aggregation of votes.

Emotional contagion | العدوى العاطفية
The process by which people's emotions are caused by the emotions of others.

Emotional dissonance | التنافر العاطفي
Inconsistencies between the emotions people feel and the emotions they project.

Emotional intelligence (EI) | الذكاء العاطفي
The ability to detect and to manage emotional cues and information.

Emotional labor | الجهد العاطفي
A situation in which an employee expresses organizationally desired emotions during interpersonal transactions at work.

Emotional stability | الاتزان الانفعالي
A personality dimension that characterizes someone as calm, self-confident, secure (positive) versus nervous, depressed, and insecure (negative).

Emotions | الانفعالات
Intense feelings that are directed at someone or something.

Employee engagement | إدماج الموظفين
An individual's involvement with, satisfaction with, and enthusiasm for the work he or she does.

Employee involvement | إشراك الموظفين
A participative process that uses the input of employees and is intended to increase employee commitment to an organization's success.

Employee stock ownership plan (ESOP) | برنامج مشاركة الموظفين في ملكية الشركة
A company-established benefits plan in which employees acquire stock, often at below-market prices, as part of their benefits.

Employee-oriented leader | القائد المتعاطف مع الموظفين
A leader who emphasizes interpersonal relations, takes a personal interest in the needs of employees, and accepts individual differences among members.

Encounter stage | مرحلة المواجهة
The stage in the socialization process in which a new employee sees what the organization is really like and confronts the possibility that expectations and reality may diverge.

Entrepreneurial stage | مرحلة المبادرة والتأسيس
The first stage in the evolution of the family business, whereby development is driven by personal and family goals.

Environment | البيئة
Institutions or forces outside an organization that potentially affect the organization's performance.

Equity theory | نظرية العدالة
A theory that says that individuals compare their job inputs and outcomes with those of others and then respond to eliminate any inequities.

ERG theory | نظرية إي أر جي (الوجود – الارتباط – النمو)
A theory that posits three groups of core needs: existence, relatedness, and growth.

Escalation of commitment | تصعيد الانتماء
An increased commitment to a previous decision in spite of negative information.

Esprit de corps | التضامن / روح الجماعة
Teamspirit among colleagues or coworkers.

Ethical dilemmas | المعضلات الأخلاقية
Situations in which individuals are required to define right and wrong conduct.

Evidence-based management (EBM) | الإدارة المبنية على البراهين
Basing managerial decisions on the best available scientific evidence.

Evolutionary psychology | علم النفس التطوري / الارتقائي
An area of inquiry which argues that we must experience the emotions we do because they serve a purpose.

Exit | المغادرة / الرحيل / الخروج
Dissatisfaction expressed through behavior directed toward leaving the organization.

Expatriates | المغتربون
People who live outside of their native country.

Expectancy theory | نظرية التوقع
A theory that says that the strength of a tendency to act in a certain way depends on the strength of an expectation that the act will be followed by a given outcome and on the attractiveness of that outcome to the individual.

Expert power | تأثير قائم على الخبرة
Influence based on special skills or knowledge.

Extraversion | الانبساط النفسي
A personality dimension describing someone who is sociable, gregarious, and assertive.

Family business | الشركات العائلية
A complex dual system that is made up of the family and the business.

Feedback | التغذية الراجعة
The degree to which carrying out the work activities required by a job results in the individual obtaining direct and clear information about the effectiveness of his or her performance.

Felt conflict | صراع محسوس / مُدرك
Emotional involvement in a conflict that creates anxiety, tenseness, frustration, or hostility.

Felt emotions | انفعالات محسوسة / مدركة
An individual's actual emotions.

Femininity | الأنوثة
A national culture attribute that has little differentiation between male and female roles, where women are treated as the equals of men in all aspects of the society.

Fiedler contingency model | نموذج فيدلر للظرفية / الموقفية / الاحتمالية
The theory that effective groups depend on a proper match between a leader's style of interacting with subordinates and the degree to which the situation gives control and influence to the leader.

Filtering | تصفية / ترشيح
A sender's manipulation of information so that it will be seen more favorably by the receiver.

Five-stage group-development model | نموذج المراحل الخمس لتطوير الجماعة
The five distinct stages groups go through: forming, storming, norming, performing, and adjourning.

Fixed pie | الكمية الثابتة
The belief that there is only a set amount of goods or services to be divided up between the parties.

Fixed-interval schedule | جدول الفترة الثابتة
Spacing rewards at uniform time intervals.

Fixed-ratio schedule | جدول النسبة المتغيرة
Initiating rewards after a fixed or constant number of responses.

Flexible benefits | مزايا مرنة
A benefits plan that allows each employee to put together a benefits package individually tailored to his or her own needs and situation.

Flextime | ساعات العمل المرنة
Flexible work hours.

Foreign labor | العمالة الأجنبية
Work carried out by people who are nationals of a foreign country.

Formal channels | قنوات رسمية
Communication channels established by an organization to transmit messages related to the professional activities of members.

Formal group | جماعة رسمية
A designated work group defined by an organization's structure.

Formalization | إضفاء الطابع الرسمي
The degree to which jobs within an organization are standardized.

Forming stage | مرحلة التكوين
The first stage in group development, characterized by much uncertainty.

Framing | تأطير
A way of using language to manage meaning.

Friendship group | جماعة الصداقة
People brought together because they share one or more common characteristics.

Functional conflict | صراع وظيفي
Conflict that supports the goals of the group and improves its performance.

Fundamental attribution error | خطأ العزو الأساسي
The tendency to underestimate the influence of external factors and overestimate the influence of internal factors when making judgments about the behavior of others.

Gainsharing | المشاركة في الأرباح
A formula-based group incentive plan.

Glass ceiling | حاجز الترقي
An unacknowledged barrier that prevents women and minorities from advancing to higher levels in their profession.

Goal-setting theory | نظرية وضع الأهداف
A theory that says that specific and difficult goals, with feedback, lead to higher performance.

Grapevine | شبكة اتصال المنظمة
An organization's informal communication network.

Graphic rating scales | طريقة التدرج البياني
An evaluation method in which the evaluator rates performance factors on an incremental scale.

Gross Domestic Profit (GDP) | إجمالي الناتج المحلي
The market value of all the goods and services produced within a country's borders within a given period of time.

Group | الجماعة
Two or more individuals, interacting and interdependent, who have come together to achieve particular objectives.

Group order ranking | تصنيف ترتيب الجماعة
An evaluation method that places employees into a particular classification, such as quartiles.

Groupshift | انجراف المجموعة
A change in decision risk between a group's decision and an individual decision that a member within the group would make; the shift can be toward either conservatism or greater risk.

Groupthink | التفكير الجماعي
A phenomenon in which the norm for consensus overrides the realistic appraisal of alternative courses of action.

Halo effect | خطأ الهالة / حالة الابتهار
The tendency to draw a general impression about an individual on the basis of a single characteristic.

Heredity | الوراثة
Factors determined at conception; one's biological, physiological, and inherent psychological makeup.

Hierarchy of needs theory | نظرية هرم الاحتياجات الإنسانية
A hierarchy of five needs—physiological, safety, social, esteem, and self-actualization—in which, as each need is substantially satisfied, the next need becomes dominant.

High-context cultures | الثقافات عالية السياق
Cultures that rely heavily on nonverbal and subtle situational cues in communication.

Higher-order needs | الحاجات العليا
Needs that are satisfied internally, such as social, esteem, and self-actualization needs.

Hindrance stressors | الضغوط المعوقة
Stressors that keep you from reaching your goals (red tape, office politics, confusion over job responsibilities).

Hindsight bias | تحيز الإدراك المتأخر
The tendency to believe falsely, after an outcome of an event is actually known, that one would have accurately predicted that outcome.

Human relations view of conflict | وجهة نظر العلاقات التقليدية للصراع
The belief that conflict is a natural and inevitable outcome in any group.

Human skills | المهارات البشرية
The ability to work with, understand, and motivate other people, both individually and in groups.

Hygiene factors | عوامل الصحة
Factors—such as company policy and administration, supervision, and salary—that, when adequate in a job, placate workers. When these factors are adequate, people will not be dissatisfied.

Idea champions | أبطال الأفكار
Individuals who take an innovation and actively and enthusiastically promote the idea, build support, overcome resistance, and ensure that the idea is implemented.

Identification-based trust | الثقة القائمة على المطابقة / التماثل
Trust based on a mutual understanding of each other's intentions and appreciation of each other's wants and desires.

Illegitimate political behavior | السلوك السياسي غير الشرعي
Extreme political behavior that violates the implied rules of the game.

Imitation strategy | استراتيجية التقليد / المحاكاة
A strategy that seeks to move into new products or new markets only after their viability has already been proven.

Impression management (IM) | إدارة الانطباعات
The process by which individuals attempt to control the impression others form of them.

Independent variable | متغير مستقل
The presumed cause of some change in a dependent variable.

Individual ranking | التصنيف الفردي
An evaluation method that rank-orders employees from best to worst.

Individualism | الفردية
A national culture attribute that describes the degree to which people prefer to act as individuals rather than as members of groups.

Informal channels | قنوات غير رسمية
Communication channels that are created spontaneously and that emerge as responses to individual choices.

Informal group | جماعة غير رسمية
A group that is neither formally structured nor organizationally determined; such a group appears in response to the need for social contact.

Information overload | الإغراق المعلوماتي
A condition in which information inflow exceeds an individual's processing capacity.

Initiating structure | هيكلية العمل
The extent to which a leader is likely to define and structure his or her role and those of subordinates in the search for goal attainment.

Innovation | الابتكار / الاستحداث
A new idea applied to initiating or improving a product, process, or service.

Innovation strategy | استراتيجية الابتكار / الاستحداث
A strategy that emphasizes the introduction of major new products and services.

Institutionalization | وضع الأنظمة / التكوين النظامي
A condition that occurs when an organization takes on a life of its own, apart from any of its members, and acquires immortality.

Instrumental values | القيم الأدائية
Preferable modes of behavior or means of achieving one's terminal values.

Integration | التكامل
The process of uniting different groups or parts of an organization to form a larger group or whole, in order to create better workplaces, products and services.

Integrative bargaining | المساومة التكاملية
Negotiation that seeks one or more settlements that can create a win–win solution.

Intellectual abilities | القدرات العقلية
The capacity to do mental activities—thinking, reasoning, and problem solving.

Intentions | النوايا
Decisions to act in a given way.

Interacting groups | جماعات متفاعلة
Typical groups in which members interact with each other face-to-face.

Interactional justice | عدالة تفاعلية
The perceived degree to which an individual is treated with dignity, concern, and respect.

Interactionist view of conflict | وجهة النظر التفاعلية للصراع
The belief that conflict is not only a positive force in a group but that it is also an absolute necessity for a group to perform effectively.

Interest group | جماعة أصحاب المصلحة
People working together to attain a specific objective with which each is concerned.

Intergroup development | التطور بين الجماعات
OD efforts to change the attitudes, stereotypes, and perceptions that groups have of each other.

Intermittent reinforcement | التعزيز المتقطع
Reinforcing a desired behavior often enough to make the behavior worth repeating, but not every time it is demonstrated.

Intuition | الحدس
A gut feeling not necessarily supported by research.

Intuitive decision making | اتخاذ القرار الحدسي
An unconscious process created out of distilled experience.

Job characteristics model (JCM) | نموذج خصائص العمل
A model that proposes that any job can be described in terms of five core job dimensions: skill variety, task identity, task significance, autonomy, and feedback.

Job design | تصميم العمل
The way the elements in a job are organized.

Job enlargement | التوسع الوظيفي
Increasing the number and variety of tasks that an individual performs. Job enlargement results in jobs with more diversity.

Job enrichment | إثراء العمل
The vertical expansion of jobs, which increases the degree to which the worker controls the planning, execution, and evaluation of the work.

Job involvement | الانغماس الوظيفي
The degree to which a person identifies with a job, actively participates in it, and considers performance important to self-worth.

Job rotation | التنقلات الوظيفية
The periodic shifting of an employee from one task to another.

Job satisfaction | الرضا و الاشباع الوظيفي
A positive feeling about one's job resulting from an evaluation of its characteristics.

Job sharing | مشاركة العمل
An arrangement that allows two or more individuals to split a traditional 40-hour-a-week job.

Knowledge management (KM)
The process of organizing and distributing an organization's collective wisdom so the right information gets to the right people in the right time.

Knowledge-based trust | الثقة القائمة على المعرفة
Trust based on behavioral predictability that comes from a history of interaction.

Leader–member exchange (LMX) theory | نظرية علاقة الفرد – برئيسه
A theory that supports leaders' creation of in-groups and out-groups; subordinates with in-group status will have higher performance ratings, less turnover, and greater job satisfaction.

Leader–member relations | العلاقات بين الفرد – ورئيسه
The degree of confidence, trust, and respect subordinates have in their leader.

Leader-participation model | نموذج القيادة المشاركة
A leadership theory that provides a set of rules to determine the form and amount of participative decision making in different situations.

Leadership | القيادة
The ability to influence a group toward the achievement of a vision or set of goals.

Leading | قيادي
A function that includes motivating employees, directing others, selecting the most effective communication channels, and resolving conflicts.

Learning | التعلم
A relatively permanent change in behavior that occurs as a result of experience.

Learning organization | المنظمة المتعلمة / التعلمية
An organization that has developed the continuous capacity to adapt and change.

Least preferred coworker (LPC) questionnaire | استبيان زمالة العمل الأقل تفضيلا
An instrument that purports to measure whether a person is task or relationship oriented.

Legitimate political behavior | السلوك السياسي الشرعي
Normal everyday politics.

Legitimate power | القوة المشروعة / الشرعية

The power a person receives as a result of his or her position in the formal hierarchy of an organization.

Level-5 leaders | قادة المستوى الخامس

Leaders who are fiercely ambitious and driven but whose ambition is directed toward their company rather than themselves.

Long-term orientation | التوجيه طويل المدى

A national culture attribute that emphasizes the future, thrift, and persistence.

Low-context cultures | ثقافات السياق المنخفض

Cultures that rely heavily on words to convey meaning in communication.

Lower-order needs | الحاجات الدنيا

Needs that are satisfied externally, such as physiological and safety needs.

Loyalty | الولاء

Dissatisfaction expressed by passively waiting for conditions to improve.

Machiavellianism | مذهب المكيافيلية

The degree to which an individual is pragmatic, maintains emotional distance, and believes that ends can justify means.

Major characteristic | ميزة / صفة / سمة رئيسية

The significant overlap between the family and the business that is considered to be a major characteristic of a family business.

Management by objectives (MBO) | الإدارة بالأهداف

A program that encompasses specific goals, participatively set, for an explicit time period, with feedback on goal progress.

Manager | مدير

An individual who achieves goals through other people.

Managerial grid | الشبكة الإدارية

A nine-by-nine matrix outlining 81 different leadership styles.

Managerial stage | المرحلة الإدارية

The second stage in the evolution of the family business, whereby development requires expertise, financial discipline, structure, and accountability.

Masculinity | الرجولة

A national culture attribute that describes the extent to which the culture favours traditional masculine work roles of achievement, power, and control. Societal values are characterized by assertiveness and materialism.

Matrix structure | الهيكل المصفوفي

A structure that creates dual lines of authority and combines functional and product departmentalization.

McClelland's theory of needs | نظرية ماكليلاند للحاجات

A theory which states that achievement, power, and affiliation are three important needs that help explain motivation.

Mechanistic model | النموذج الآلي

A structure characterized by extensive departmentalization, high formalization, a limited information network, and centralization.

Mediator | الوسيط

A neutral third party who facilitates a negotiated solution by using reasoning, persuasion, and suggestions for alternatives.

Mental models | النماذج العقلية

Team members' knowledge and beliefs about how the work gets done by the team.

Mentor | مرشد

A senior employee who sponsors and supports a less-experienced employee, called a protégé.

Merit-based pay plan | برنامج الأجور على أساس الاستحقاق / الجدارة

A pay plan based on performance appraisal ratings.

Metamorphosis stage | مرحلة التحول الشكلي / البنيوي

The stage in the socialization process in which a new employee changes and adjusts to the job, work group, and organization.

Model | نموذج

A simplified representation of some real-world phenomenon.

Moods | الأمزجة

Feelings that tend to be less intense than emotions and that lack a contextual stimulus.

Motivating potential score (MPS) | درجة الدافعية الكامنة

A predictive index that suggests the motivating potential in a job.

Motivation | الحفز

The processes that account for an individual's intensity, direction, and persistence of effort toward attaining a goal.

Movement | حركة

A change process that transforms the organization from the status quo to a desired end state.

Multi-team systems | نظم الفرق المتعددة

Systems in which different teams need to coordinate their efforts to produce a desired outcome.

Myers-Briggs Type Indicator (MBTI) | مؤشر مايرز بريدج للأنماط

A personality test that taps four characteristics and classifies people into 1 of 16 personality types.

Narcissism | النرجسية

The tendency to be arrogant, have a grandiose sense of self-importance, require excessive admiration, and have a sense of entitlement.

Need for achievement (nAch) | الحاجة للإنجاز

The drive to excel, to achieve in relation to a set of standards, and to strive to succeed.

Need for affiliation (nAff) | الحاجة للانتماء

The desire for friendly and close interpersonal relationships.

Need for power (nPow) | الحاجة للسلطة

The need to make others behave in a way in which they would not have behaved otherwise.

Negative affect | عاطفة سلبية

A mood dimension that consists of emotions such as nervousness, stress, and anxiety at the high end, and relaxation, tranquility, and poise at the low end.

Neglect | إهمال

Dissatisfaction expressed through allowing conditions to worsen.

Negotiation | المفاوضة

Interaction between two or more parties for the purpose of reaching a mutually beneficial agreement.

Nepotism | محاباة الأقارب

The showing of favoritism in business toward relatives and friends, based upon that relationship, rather than on an objective evaluation of ability, merit or suitability.

Nominal group technique | أسلوب الجماعات الأسمية

A group decision-making method in which individual members meet face-to-face to pool their judgments in a systematic but independent fashion.

Non-family business | الشركات اللاعائلية
A business system that is usually governed by contract.

Normative commitment | الانتماء المعياري
An obligation to remain with an organization for moral or ethical reasons.

Norming stage | مرحلة وضع القواعد / المعايير
The third stage in group development, characterized by close relationships and cohesiveness.

Norms | قواعد / معايير
Acceptable standards of behavior within a group that are shared by the group's members.

OB Mod (oganizational behavior modification) | (تعديل السلوك التنظيمي) OB Mod
The application of reinforcement concepts to individuals in the work setting.

Openness to experience | الانفتاح على الخبرة
A personality dimension that characterizes someone in terms of imagination, sensitivity, and curiosity.

Operant conditioning | الإشراط الإجرائي / الكلاسيكي
A type of conditioning in which desired voluntary behavior leads to a reward or prevents a punishment.

Organic model | نموذج التنظيم العضوي
A structure that is flat, uses cross-hierarchical and cross-functional teams, has low formalization, possesses a comprehensive information network, and relies on participative decision making.

Organization | التنظيم / المنظمة
A consciously coordinated social unit, composed of two or more people, that functions on a relatively continuous basis to achieve a common goal or set of goals.

Organizational behavior (OB) | السلوك التنظيمي
A field of study that investigates the impact that individuals, groups, and structure have on behavior within organizations, for the purpose of applying such knowledge toward improving an organization's effectiveness.

Organizational citizenship behavior (OCB) | سلوك المواطنة التنظيمي
Discretionary behavior that is not part of an employee's formal job requirements but that nevertheless promotes the effective functioning of the organization.

Organizational commitment | الانتماء التنظيمي
The degree to which an employee identifies with a particular organization and its goals and wishes to maintain membership in the organization.

Organizational culture | الثقافة التنظيمية
A system of shared meaning held by members that distinguishes the organization from other organizations.

Organizational demography | الديموغرافيا التنظيمية
The degree to which members of a work unit share a common demographic attribute, such as age, sex, race, educational level, or length of service in an organization, and the impact of this attribute on turnover.

Organizational development (OD) | التطوير التنظيمي
A collection of planned change interventions, built on humanistic-democratic values, that seeks to improve organizational effectiveness and employee wellbeing.

Organizational justice | العدالة التنظيمية
An overall perception of what is fair in the workplace, composed of distributive, procedural, and interactional justice.

Organizational structure | الهيكل التنظيمي
The way in which job tasks are formally divided, grouped, and coordinated within an organization.

Organizing | تنظيم
Determining what tasks are to be done, who is to do them, how the tasks are to be grouped, who reports to whom, and where decisions are to be made.

Parsimony | البخل / القصد
The unwillingness of a business to use its financial resources.

Participative management | الإدارة المشارِكة
A process in which subordinates share a significant degree of decision-making power with their immediate superiors.

Particularism | الانصرافية
Exclusive commitment to the interests of one's own group or family.

Path-goal theory | نظرية مسار الوصول إلى الهدف
A theory that states that it is the leader's job to assist followers in attaining their goals and to provide the necessary direction and/or support to ensure that their goals are compatible with the overall objectives of the group or organization.

Perceived conflict | الصراع المُدرك
Awareness by one or more parties of the existence of conditions that create opportunities for conflict to arise.

Perceived organizational support | الدعم التنظيمي المُدرك
The degree to which employees believe an organization values their contribution and cares about their wellbeing.

Perception | الإدراك
A process by which individuals organize and interpret their sensory impressions in order to give meaning to their environment.

Performing stage | مرحلة الأداء
The fourth stage in group development, during which the group is fully functional.

Personalism | الشخصانية
A doctrine that emphasizes the value of the individual person within his or her social, political or familial environment.

Personality | الشخصية
The sum total of ways in which an individual reacts to and interacts with others.

Personality traits | صفات الشخصية
Enduring characteristics that describe an individual's behavior.

Personality–job fit theory | نظرية توافق الوظيفة حسب الشخصية
A theory that identifies six personality types and proposes that the fit between personality type and occupational environment determines satisfaction and turnover.

Physical abilities | القدرات البدنية
The capacity to do tasks that demand stamina, dexterity, strength, and similar characteristics.

Piece-rate pay plan | برنامج دفع الأجر حسب القطعة
A pay plan in which workers are paid a fixed sum for each unit of production completed.

Planned change | التغيير المخطط
Change activities that are intentional and goal oriented.

Planning | التخطيط
A process that includes defining goals, establishing strategy, and developing plans to coordinate activities.

Political behavior | السلوك السياسي

Activities that are not required as part of a person's formal role in the organization but that influence, or attempt to influence, the distribution of advantages and disadvantages within the organization.

Political skill | المهارة السياسية

The ability to influence others in such a way as to enhance one's objectives.

Position power | سلطة المنصب

Influence derived from one's formal structural position in the organization; includes power to hire, fire, discipline, promote, and give salary increases.

Positive affect | عاطفة إيجابية

A mood dimension that consists of specific positive emotions such as excitement, self-assurance, and cheerfulness at the high end, and boredom, sluggishness, and tiredness at the low end.

Positive organizational culture | الثقافة التنظيمية الإيجابية

A culture that emphasizes building on employee strengths, rewards more than punishes, and emphasizes individual vitality and growth.

Positive organizational scholarship | المنح التنظيمية الإيجابية

An area of OB research that concerns how organizations develop human strength, foster vitality and resilience, and unlock potential.

Positivity offset | بدل الإيجابية

The tendency of most individuals to experience a mildly positive mood at zero input (when nothing in particular is going on).

Power | سلطة / قوة / تأثير

A capacity that A has to influence the behavior of B so that B acts in accordance with A's wishes.

Power distance | مسافة السلطة / القوة

A national culture attribute that describes the extent to which a society accepts that power in institutions and organizations is distributed unequally.

Power tactics | طرق القوة

Ways in which individuals translate power bases into specific actions.

Prearrival stage | مرحلة ما قبل الوصول

The period of learning in the socialization process that occurs before a new employee joins the organization.

Proactive personality | الشخصية الاستباقية / الفاعلة

People who identify opportunities, show initiative, take action, and persevere until meaningful change occurs.

Problem | مشكلة

A discrepancy between the current state of affairs and some desired state.

Problem-solving teams | فرق حل المشكلات

Groups of 5 to 12 employees from the same department who meet for a few hours each week to discuss ways of improving quality, efficiency, and the work environment.

Procedural justice | عدالة الإجراءات

The perceived fairness of the process used to determine the distribution of rewards.

Process conflict | صراع العمليات

Conflict over how work gets done.

Process consultation (PC) | مؤتمر / اجتماع العمليات

A meeting in which a consultant assists a client in understanding process events with which he or she must deal and identifying processes that need improvement.

Production-oriented leader | القائد ذو التوجه الإنتاجي

A leader who emphasizes technical or task aspects of the job.

Productivity | الإنتاجية

A performance measure that includes effectiveness and efficiency.

Professional stage | المرحلة المهنية / الاحترافية

The third stage in the evolution of the family business, whereby development is driven by what is best for the business.

Profiling | تنميط

A form of stereotyping in which a group of individuals is singled out—typically on the basis of race or ethnicity—for intensive inquiry, scrutiny, or investigation.

Profit-sharing plan | برنامج المشاركة في الأرباح

An organization-wide program that distributes compensation based on some established formula designed around a company's profitability.

Psychological contract | العقد النفسي

An unwritten agreement that sets out what management expects from an employee and vice versa.

Psychological empowerment | التمكين النفسي

Employees' belief in the degree to which they affect their work environment, their competence, the meaningfulness of their job, and their perceived autonomy in their work.

Psychology | علم النفس

The science that seeks to measure, explain, and sometimes change the behavior of humans and other animals.

Punctuated-equilibrium model | نموذج التوازن المتقطع

A set of phases that temporary groups go through that involves transitions between inertia and activity.

Quality circle | لجنة دائرة النوعية

A work group of 8–10 employees and supervisors who have a shared area of responsibility and who meet once a week to discuss quality problems.

Randomness error | خطأ العشوائية

The tendency of individuals to believe that they can predict the outcome of random events.

Rational | منطقي / عقلاني

Characterized by making consistent, value-maximizing choices within specified constraints.

Rational decision-making model | نموذج اتخاذ القرار المنطقي

A decision-making model that describes how individuals should behave in order to maximize some outcome.

Recruitment | الاستقطاب

Locating, identifying, and attracting capable applicants.

Reference groups | الجماعات المرجعية

Important groups to which individuals belong or hope to belong and with whose norms individuals are likely to conform.

Referent power | قوة الاعجاب

Influence based on possession by an individual of desirable resources or personal traits.

Reflexivity | الانعكاسية

A team characteristic of reflecting on and adjusting the master plan when necessary.

Refreezing | عدم التجدد
Stabilizing a change intervention by balancing driving and restraining forces.

Reinforcement theory | نظرية التعزيز
A theory that says that behavior is a function of its consequences.

Relationship conflict | صراع العلاقات
Conflict based on interpersonal relationships.

Representative participation | المشاركة التمثيلية
A system in which workers participate in organizational decision making through a small group of representative employees.

Resources | الموارد
Things within an individual's control that can be used to resolve demands.

Restraining forces | القوى المعيقة
Forces that hinder movement from the existing equilibrium.

Reward power | التأثير بالمكافأة
Compliance achieved based on the ability to distribute rewards that others view as valuable.

Rituals | الطقوس
Repetitive sequences of activities that express and reinforce the key values of the organization, which goals are most important, which people are important, and which are expendable.

Role | الدور
A set of expected behavior patterns attributed to someone occupying a given position in a social unit.

Role conflict | صراع الأدوار
A situation in which an individual is confronted by divergent role expectations.

Role expectations | توقعات أداء الأدوار
How others believe a person should act in a given situation.

Role identity | هوية الأدوار
Certain attitudes and behaviors consistent with a role.

Role perception | إدراك الأدوار
An individual's view of how he or she is supposed to act in a given situation.

Selective perception | الإدراك الإنتقائي
The tendency to selectively interpret what one sees on the basis of one's interests, background, experience, and attitudes.

Self-actualization | تحقيق الذات
The drive to become what a person is capable of becoming.

Self-efficacy | الكفاءة الذاتية
An individual's belief that he or she is capable of performing a task.

Self-fulfilling prophecy | التوجه نحو إشباع الذات
A situation in which a person inaccurately perceives a second person, and the resulting expectations cause the second person to behave in ways consistent with the original perception.

Self-leadership | القيادة الذاتية
A set of processes through which individuals control their own behavior.

Self-managed work teams | فرق العمل ذاتية الإدارة
Groups of 10 to 15 people who take on responsibilities of their former supervisors.

Self-monitoring | مراقبة الذات
A personality trait that measures an individual's ability to adjust his or her behavior to external, situational factors.

Self-serving bias | التحيز للذات
The tendency for individuals to attribute their own successes to internal factors and put the blame for failures on external factors.

Sensitivity training | تدريب الحساسية
Training groups that seek to change behavior through unstructured group interaction.

Sexual harassment | التحرش الجنسي
Any unwanted activity of a sexual nature that affects an individual's employment and creates a hostile work environment.

Shaping behavior | تشكيل السلوك
Systematically reinforcing each successive step that moves an individual closer to the desired response.

Short-term orientation | التوجيه قصير المدى
A national culture attribute that emphasizes the past and present, respect for tradition, and fulfillment of social obligations.

Simple structure | الهيكل البسيط
A structure characterized by a low degree of departmentalization, wide spans of control, authority centralized in a single person, and little formalization.

Single-loop learning | التعلم أحادي الحلقة
A process of correcting errors using past routines and present policies.

Situational leadership theory (SLT) | نظرية القيادة الموقفية
A contingency theory that focuses on followers' readiness.

Skill variety | تنوع المهارات
The degree to which a job requires a variety of different activities.

Skill-based pay | الأجر حسب المهارة
A pay plan that sets pay levels on the basis of how many skills employees have or how many jobs they can do.

Social loafing | التبطل الاجتماعي
The tendency for individuals to expend less effort when working collectively than when working individually.

Social psychology | علم النفس الاجتماعي
An area of psychology that blends concepts from psychology and sociology and that focuses on the influence of people on one another.

Socialization | الاندماج في المجتمع
A process that adapts employees to the organization's culture.

Socialized charismatic leadership | القيادة الكاريزماتية الاجتماعية
A leadership concept that states that leaders convey values that are other-centered versus self-centered and who role model ethical conduct.

Social-learning theory | نظرية التعلم الاجتماعي
The view that people can learn through observation and direct experience.

Sociology | علم الاجتماع
The study of people in relation to their social environment or culture.

Span of control | نطاق السيطرة والتحكم
The number of subordinates a manager can efficiently and effectively direct.

Status | مكانة / حالة / وضع
A socially defined position or rank given to groups or group members by others.

Status characteristics theory | نظرية خصائص المكانة
A theory that states that differences in status characteristics create status hierarchies within groups.

Stereotyping | التنميط / الصورة النمطية
Judging someone on the basis of one's perception of the group to which that person belongs.

Storming stage | مرحلة العصف / الصراع
The second stage in group development, characterized by intragroup conflict.

Stress | الإجهاد
A dynamic condition in which an individual is confronted with an opportunity, a demand, or a resource related to what the individual desires and for which the outcome is perceived to be both uncertain and important.

Strong culture | الثقافة القوية
A culture in which the core values are intensely held and widely shared.

Subcultures | الثقافات الفرعية
Minicultures within an organization, typically defined by department designations and geographical separation.

Succession | التعاقب / الخلافة
The process of transferring leadership to the next generation.

Surface acting | التصرف السطحي
Hiding one's inner feelings and forgoing emotional expressions in response to display rules.

Survey feedback | التغذية الراجعة للاستبيان
The use of questionnaires to identify discrepancies among member perceptions; discussion follows, and remedies are suggested.

Systematic study | دراسة منهجية
Looking at relationships, attempting to attribute causes and effects, and drawing conclusions based on scientific evidence.

Task conflict | صراع المهام
Conflict over content and goals of the work.

Task group | جماعة المهام
People working together to complete a job task.

Task identity | هوية المهام
The degree to which a job requires completion of a whole and identifiable piece of work.

Task significance | مغزى المهام
The degree to which a job has a substantial impact on the lives or work of other people.

Task structure | هيكل المهام
The degree to which job assignments are procedurized.

Team building | بناء الفريق / المجموعة
High interaction among team members to increase trust and openness.

Technical skills | مهارات تقنية / فنية
The ability to apply specialized knowledge or expertise.

Technology | التقنية
The way in which an organization transfers its inputs into outputs.

Telecommuting | العمل عن بعد
Working from home at least two days a week on a computer that is linked to the employee's office.

Terminal values | القيم النهائية
Desirable end-states of existence; the goals a person would like to achieve during his or her lifetime.

Theory X | نظرية إكس
The assumption that employees dislike work, are lazy, dislike responsibility, and must be coerced to perform.

Theory Y | نظرية واي
The assumption that employees like work, are creative, seek responsibility, and can exercise self-direction.

Three-component model of creativity | نموذج المكونات الثلاثة للإبداع
The proposition that individual creativity requires expertise, creative-thinking skills, and intrinsic task motivation.

Traditional view of conflict | وجهة النظر التقليدية للصراع
The belief that all conflict is harmful and must be avoided.

Trait theories of leadership | نظريات السمات للقيادة
Theories that consider personal qualities and characteristics that differentiate leaders from nonleaders.

Transactional leaders | القادة الإجرائيون
Leaders who guide or motivate their followers in the direction of established goals by clarifying role and task requirements.

Transformational leaders | القادة التحويليون
Leaders who inspire followers to transcend their own self-interests and who are capable of having a profound and extraordinary effect on followers.

Trust | الثقة
A positive expectation that another will not act opportunistically.

Turnover | معدل دوران العمل
Voluntary and involuntary permanent withdrawal from an organization.

Two-factor theory | نظرية العاملين / العامل الثنائي
A theory that relates intrinsic factors to job satisfaction and associates extrinsic factors with dissatisfaction. Also called motivation-hygiene theory.

Type A personality | شخصية من النوع (أ)
Aggressive involvement in a chronic, incessant struggle to achieve more and more in less and less time and, if necessary, against the opposing efforts of other things or other people.

Type B personality | الشخصية نوع (ب)
Rarely harried by the desire to obtain a wildly increasing number of things or participate in an endless growing series of events in an ever decreasing amount of time.

Uncertainty avoidance | تحاشي المجهول
A national culture attribute that describes the extent to which a society feels threatened by uncertain and ambiguous situations and tries to avoid them.

Unfreezing | عدم التوقف / التجدد
Changing to overcome the pressures of both individual resistance and group conformity.

Unity of command | وحدة الأمر
The idea that a subordinate should have only one superior to whom he or she is directly responsible.

Utilitarianism | مذهب المنفعة
A system in which decisions are made to provide the greatest good for the greatest number.

Value system | نظام القيمة
A hierarchy based on a ranking of an individual's values in terms of their intensity.

Values | القيم
Basic convictions that a specific mode of conduct or end-state of existence is personally or socially preferable to an opposite or converse mode of conduct or end-state of existence.

Variable-interval schedule | جدول الفترة الزمنية المتغيرة
Distributing rewards in time so that reinforcements are unpredictable.

Variable-pay program | برنامج الأجور المتغيرة
A pay plan that bases a portion of an employee's pay on some individual and/or organizational measure of performance.

Variable-ratio schedule | جدول النسبة المتغيرة
Varying the reward relative to the behavior of the individual.

Virtual organization | المنظمة الافتراضية
A small, core organization that outsources major business functions.

Virtual teams | الفرق الافتراضية
Teams that use computer technology to tie together physically dispersed members in order to achieve a common goal.

Vision | رؤية
A long-term strategy for attaining a goal or goals.

Vision statement | بيان الرؤية
A formal articulation of an organization's vision or mission.

Voice | حق التعبير
Dissatisfaction expressed through active and constructive attempts to improve conditions.

Web log (blog) | سجل على شبكة الانترنت (مدونة)
A website where entries are written, generally displayed in reverse chronological order, about news, events, and personal diary entries.

Wellness programs | برامج الرعاية
Organizationally supported programs that focus on the employee's total physical and mental condition.

Whistle-blowers | الواشون
Individuals who report unethical practices by their employer to outsiders.

Work group | جماعة العمل
A group that interacts primarily to share information and to make decisions to help each group member perform within his or her area of responsibility.

Work sample test | نموذج اختبار للعمل
A test that is a miniature replica of a job that is used to evaluate the performance abilities of job candidates.

Work specialization | التخصص في العمل
The degree to which tasks in an organization are subdivided into separate jobs.

Work team | فريق العمل
A group whose individual efforts result in performance that is greater than the sum of the individual inputs.

Workforce diversity | تنوع القوى العاملة
The concept that organizations are becoming more diverse in terms of gender, age, race, ethnicity, sexual orientation, and inclusion of other groups.

Workplace spirituality | الروحانية في مكان العمل
The recognition that people have an inner life that nourishes and is nourished by meaningful work that takes place in the context of community.

Index

Figures, boxes, and tables are denoted by page number followed by f, b, or t respectively.